Korea

a Lonely Planet travel survival kit

한국

Robert Storey
Geoff Crowther

Korea

3rd edition

Published by
Lonely Planet Publications
Head Office: PO Box 617, Hawthorn, Vic 3122, Australia
Branches: 155 Filbert St, Suite 251, Oakland, CA 94607, USA ì
                10 Barley Mow Passage, Chiswick, London W4 4PH, UK
                71 bis rue du Cardinal Lemoine, 75005 Paris, France

Printed by
Pac-Rim Kwartanusa Printing
Printed in Indonesia

Photographs by
John Banagan (JB), Adrian Buzo (AB), Geoff Crowther (GC), Choe Hyung Pun (CHP), Richard
I'Anson (RI'A), Martin Moos (MM), Robert Storey (RS), Deanna Swaney (DS), Chris Taylor (CT)

Front cover: Haeinsa Temple, South Korea (JB, The Image Bank)
Back cover: Tightrope Dance, Korean Folk Village (CT)

First Published
1988

This Edition
May 1995
Reprinted with June 1996 Update supplement

National Library of Australia Cataloguing in Publication Data

Storey, Robert
    Korea– a travel survival kit.

    3rd ed.
    Includes index.
    ISBN 0 86442

    1. Korea – Guidebooks. I. Crowther, Geoff 1944-
    I.Korea. II. Title. (Series : Lonely Planet travel survival kit).

915.190443

text & maps © Lonely Planet 1995
photos © photographers as indicated 1995
climate charts compiled from information supplied by Patrick J Tyson, © Patrick J Tyson, 1995

Robert Storey

Robert has had a colourful and chequered past, starting with his first job (a monkeykeeper at a zoo) and continuing with a stint as a slot machine repairman in a Las Vegas casino. After graduating from the University of Nevada in Las Vegas with a worthless liberal arts degree, he then went on-the-road. However, the degree proved to be worth something in Taiwan, where he started a new and distinguished career as an English teacher. Robert then diligently learned Chinese, wrote a textbook for teaching English (*Creative Conversation*), went to work for Lonely Planet and became a respectable citizen and a pillar of his community. However, no one is quite sure which community that is – he was last seen in Taiwan. Anyone with information on his whereabouts should contact his employer.

Geoff Crowther

Geoff was born in Yorkshire, England and started his travelling days as a teenage hitchhiker. Later, after many short trips around Europe, two years in Asia and Africa and short spells in the overgrown fishing village of Hull and on the bleak and beautiful Cumberland fells, Geoff got involved with the London underground information centre BIT. He helped put together their first tatty, duplicated overland guides and was with them from their late 1960s heyday right through to the end. Since his first Lonely Planet guide (to Africa), Geoff has written or collaborated on guides to South America, Malaysia, East and North Africa, and India. Geoff lives with Hyung Pun, who he met in Korea, and their son Ashley, in the rainforests near the New South Wales/Queensland border. In between travel he spends his time pursuing noxious weeds, cultivating tropical fruit and brewing mango wine.

mee, An Su-young, Kim Sung-hee, Shin Yong-jeoung (Tarzan), Kwon O Duke, Kwon Young-joung and Yoon Kil-sup. We are also indebted to a number of expats who have made Korea their home – at least temporarily – including David A Mason, Gary Rector, Shane Nunn, Trish Conville, Scott Foster, Kim Sung-hee and Craig Soucie.

From the Authors

We'd like to thank a number of Korean nationals who contributed valuable information, advice and hospitality, not to mention a few bottles of *soju*. The list includes, but is not limited to, Yook Kyong-lan, Hong Eun-

This book

This book has had a long and twisted history, having originally started out as *Korea-Taiwan A Travel Survival Kit*. The first edition was written by Geoff Crowther following two trips to Korea in 1982 and 1983. While on the road conducting his research, Geoff met Choe Hyung Pun of Taejŏn, who became his friend, travelling companion and then his wife.

When it came time to produce a 2nd edition, it had become increasingly obvious that Korea and Taiwan had little in common other than both being in Asia, so the Taiwan chapter was spun off into a separate book and *Korea – a travel survival kit* was born. Its production was very much a team effort between Geoff and Hyung Pun, who by then were living in Australia. A subsequent update was another joint venture involving Geoff, Hyung Pun, Choe Hyung Soon (Hyung Pun's sister) and Helga Vogel.

This edition is a major update by Robert Storey, who spent many months on the road exploring the backwaters of South Korea. Robert also had the good fortune of being allowed a quick visit to North Korea just before that country shut its door (again) to the outside world.

From the Publisher

Back at Lonely Planet, Melbourne, this edition of Korea was edited by Katie Cody. Marcel Gaston was responsible for design, layout, mapping and script. Thanks to Stephen Townshend for proofreading; Adrienne Costanzo and Jane Fitzpatrick for the artwork check; Rachel Black and Jacqui Saunders for pasting in script; Tamsin Wilson for illustrations; Glenn Beanland, Sandra Smythe and Chris Lee Ack for additional mapping; and Valerie Tellini for cover design.

Last, but certainly not least, we'd like to thank the many travellers out there on the road who took the time to write. Travellers to whom we are indebted for their informative and, on occasion, abrasive comments include:

Blair Anderson, Robert Aronoff (USA), Alan Arthur (Aus), Pete Atkins (UK),Willard Bannister (USA), Amanda Barnes (USA), Alfred Belluche (USA), Douglas Bergman, Jan Boonstra, Inge Brandt (Aus), Kari Brooks (USA), Arthur Brothers (USA), Stephen Canner (USA), Michael Connor (C), Del Corneli (USA), H Dammerboer (D), Hans Damon (Nl), Ron Dean (UK), Lindsay Dick (UK), Marg Dillon, P C Dodge (UK), George Dolan, Timothy Donaldson (USA), Gian Carlo Dozio (CH), Mark Elliott, David Evans, Hok-Cheong Felix, Scott Frost, Bruce Glass (NZ), Elizabeth & Eric Grove (UK), Alison Gunn (Aus), Sam Hawley, Carin Holroyd (C), Jake Hooker (Aus), Cheryl Hyland, Ian W Johnston (Aus), Mark Jung (C), Klaus Kautzor-Schrode (CH), David Kennedy (USA), Gene Krell (USA), Fritz & Joanna Lebenaun (C), Glen Lorentzen (Aus), Dr Juergen Lucas (D), Goran Lukic, Michael Majors (USA), Jeff Martin, Chris Mead (UK), Sung Hi Moon (Kor), M Moos (CH), Meena Mylvaganam-Tay, A B Outwin (UK), Dr Paul Radmore (UK), Michael Ratcliff, Barbara Reissland (D), Warren Keith Russell (USA), Oleta Seckler, Mrs Selin (USA), Colin Sellar, Amar Shahi, Alison Sizer (UK), Alex Smith, A G Smith (UK), Julia Song, J David Spencer, Karen Steffen Chung, Tom Sumne, Kevin Thomas, Ron Thompson, David Thornton (USA), Eric Thurston (C), Steve Till (UK), Lorraine Tuckey (UK), Margaret Vannan (Aus), Monty Vierra, Matthew Walsh (UK), Lori Warchow, Scott Wilson (C), Randall & Rose Witt (USA), Robert Wivchar, Susan Wolcott (USA), Tim Woodward, Alistair Wright (Aus), Leslie G Zalewski

Warning & Request

A travel writer's job is never done. Before the ink is dry on a new book, things change. At Lonely Planet we get a steady stream of mail from travellers and it all helps – whether it's a few lines scribbled on the back of a used paper plate or a stack of neat typewritten pages spewing forth from our fax machine. Prices go up, new hotels open, old ones degenerate, some burn down, others get renovated and renamed, bus routes change, bridges collapse and recommended travel agents get indicted for fraud. Remember, this book is meant to be a guide, not the oracle – since things go on changing we can't tell you exactly what to expect all the time. Hopefully this book will point you in the right direction and save you some time and money. If you find that Korea is not identical to the way it's described herein, don't get upset but get out your pen or word processor and write to Lonely Planet. Your input will help make the next edition better. As usual, the writers of useful letters will score a free copy of the next edition, or another Lonely Planet guide if you prefer.

Contents

Map Legend

BOUNDARIES

.... International Boundary
.... Regional Boundary
.... Suburb Boundary

ROUTES

.... Freeway
.... Highway
.... Major Road
.... Unsealed Road or Track
.... City Road
.... City Street
.... Railway
.... Underground Railway
.... Tram
.... Walking Track
.... Ferry Route
.... Cable Car or Chairlift

AREA FEATURES

.... Park, Gardens
.... National Park
.... Built-Up Area
.... Pedestrian Mall
.... Market
.... Cemetery
.... Reef
.... Beach or Desert
.... Rocks

HYDROGRAPHIC FEATURES

.... Coastline
.... River, Creek
.... Intermittent River or Creek
.... Lake, Intermittent Lake
.... Canal
.... Swamp

SYMBOLS

✪ CAPITAL		.... National Capital	
◉ Capital		.... Regional Capital	
◍ CITY		.... Major City	
● City		.... City	
● Town		.... Town	
● Village		.... Village	
■		.... Place to Stay	
▼		.... Place to Eat	
▼		.... Pub, Bar	
✉	☎	.... Post Office, Telephone	
❶	❾	.... Tourist Information, Bank	
❒	℗	.... Transport, Parking	
🏛	⌂	.... Museum, Youth Hostel	
⊞	⚐	Caravan Park, Camping Ground	
†	❏	†	.... Church, Cathedral
⚲	✿	.... Mosque, Synagogue	
⊞	⚌	Buddhist Temple, Hindu Temple	

⊕	★	.... Hospital, Police Station	
✈	✝	.... Airport, Airfield	
▱	✿	.... Swimming Pool, Gardens	
❖	🐘	.... Shopping Centre, Zoo	
←	A25	One Way Street, Route Number	
	∴	...... Archaeological Site or Ruins	
⚑	▲	.... Ski Field, Monument	
⛩	▣	.... Castle, Tomb	
⌒	⌂	.... Cave, Hut or Chalet	
▲	※	.... Mountain or Hill, Lookout	
🏮	⚓	.... Lighthouse, Shipwreck	
)(	⚯	.... Pass, Spring	
		.... Ancient or City Wall	
		.... Rapids, Waterfalls	
		.... Cliff or Escarpment, Tunnel	
		.... Railway Station	
		Underground Railway Station	

Note: not all symbols displayed above appear in this book

Introduction

South Korea is still very much off the beaten track. Quite a few travellers get to the capital, Seoul, usually en route to somewhere else, and a few intrepid individuals make it to Kyŏngju and the island province of Chejudo, but hardly anyone seems to take the time to explore the other attractions of the country.

Undoubtedly the magnets of Japan and China serve to distract most people's attention, yet Korea is one of the most fascinating enigmas of the Far East. Its history is one of the world's most turbulent sagas of a small nation's struggle for survival against almost insurmountable odds. Sandwiched between vastly more powerful neighbours who, for at least two millennia, have sought to absorb it, South Korea has nevertheless preserved its own unique character and cultural identity.

You might be forgiven for thinking that the most coveted gems of oriental culture are to be found either in Japan or China and that Korea merely offers a pale reflection of these. But you would be wrong. Korea has some of the world's most enchanting countryside: beautiful, forested mountains, offering endless trekking possibilities, are at their most colourful in spring or autumn and misty and romantic during the wet season. In the forests you will find sublimely crafted temple complexes whose origins stretch back 1500 years. A visit to any one of these hauntingly beautiful places will leave an indelible impression. Many of them are still functioning monasteries, and the monks are friendly and hospitable. Then there are Korea's innumerable islands scattered like confetti off its southern and eastern shores; many of them with intriguing variations of the mainland culture and some have yet to see a visitor from abroad.

And what of the people? Koreans are a proud, romantic, spontaneous and friendly people. You will not encounter that feeling of disinterest which Westerners often experience in China. Even in cosmopolitan Seoul

you'll be regarded with curiosity. Wherever you go, but especially in the smaller places, you'll constantly be approached by people who want to strike up a conversation, whether they be soldiers, hotel proprietors, students or businesspeople. They will try their best, regardless of language or cultural differences, to establish some rapport with you, yet always with humour and never in an overbearing manner. If you respond with friendship and a little imagination you will often find yourself the recipient of the most unexpected and often disarming hospitality. It's not that Koreans don't have fairly rigidly defined rules of social conduct and public behaviour in common with other Oriental people – they do, and you will often be aware of this – but for a foreigner they'll bend the rules to make you feel at home.

Not surprisingly, history holds sway over these people. The cost of their survival as a nation has, at times, been devastating. The most recent example of this was the Korean War in the early 1950s. Continually on the alert and prepared for invasion, the armed forces have always been an important element of Korean society. It would be fatuous to ignore the ubiquitous presence of the army (and its American allies) in South Korea – conscription is a three-year stint – but it would also be a grave mistake to allow these realities to prejudice your view of this country and its people. These people have felt the pressure of superpower rivalry for centuries. Perhaps that's why they're so keen to establish friendships and exchange views with foreign visitors, but then again maybe it's just their natural disposition. Whatever the reasons, the line drawn between guest and lifelong friend is very much a question of your own attitude.

There's one last plus which ought to put Korea firmly on the traveller's route and that is its safety and cleanliness. Public transport is well organised and all but the most rural of roads are paved. True, you can find similar conditions in Japan, but at two to three times the price.

Korea is one of the unexplored gems of Asia. It once acquired the nickname of the 'Hermit Kingdom', after it closed its borders to all foreigners in the late 19th century as a result of what seemed like insuperable pressures from the outside. That name perhaps still fits North Korea, but South Korea is certainly one of the most open and rapidly changing societies in Asia.

Facts about the Country

HISTORY

Korean folk legends fix the date of the nation's birth from a semi-deity named Tan'gun at around 2333 BC, but according to the latest research its origins go back even further to 30,000 BC when migrating tribes from Central and Northern Asia first arrived in the peninsula. They brought with them their own folk myths and animistic religion as well as their own language, the latter a branch of the Ural-Altaic group which also includes Finnish, Hungarian and Turkish. This distinct language, although it borrowed Chinese script (until *han'gŭl* was invented in the 15th century) and some of its vocabulary, has been of the utmost importance in maintaining Korean cultural identity through the centuries.

The earliest influences assimilated by these nomadic tribes came from the Chinese, who had established an outpost near present-day P'yŏngyang during the Han dynasty. Constant wars with the Chinese necessitated an early alliance between the tribes of the north which eventually led to the formation of the first Korean kingdom – Koguryo – around the 1st century AD, and the uniting of the northern half of the peninsula four centuries later following the demise of Han. Not being subject to the same immediate pressures, the related tribes of the south were slower to coalesce, but by the 3rd century two powerful kingdoms – Shilla and Paekche – had emerged to dominate the southern half of the peninsula. Sandwiched between them in the south was the loose confederacy of Kaya, but this had a relatively brief existence since the leaders of its constituent tribes were rarely able to present a common front when threatened with invasion.

Three Kingdoms Period

The next four centuries – known as the Three Kingdoms period (Koguryo, Paekche and Shilla) – witnessed a remarkable flowering of the arts, architecture, literature and state-craft as Chinese influences continued to be absorbed, reinterpreted and alloyed with traditional Korean ideas and practices. Probably the single most formative influence was Buddhism which, in time, became the state religion of all three kingdoms. Buddhism has immeasurably enriched Korean culture, and even though it was suppressed in favour of Confucianism when the Koryŏ dynasty was overthrown at the end of the 14th century, it remains an integral part of modern Korea. It has left an indelible mark on the language, manners, customs, art and folklore of the people.

The Three Kingdoms period was also the time when the developments which were taking place in Korea began to be exported to Japan. Architects and builders from Paekche, for instance, were primarily responsible for the great burst of temple construction which occurred in Japan during the 6th century. This transmission of cultural developments naturally accelerated during periods of conflict and there were times in Japan's early history when there were more Koreans involved in influential secular and religious positions than Japanese.

There was, of course, much rivalry between the three kingdoms and wars were fought constantly in attempts to gain supremacy, but it was not until the 7th century that a major shift of power occurred.

Shilla Dominance

The rise of the Tang dynasty in China during the 7th century provided Shilla with the opportunity to expand its dominion over the whole peninsula. An alliance of the two was formed, and the combined armies first attacked Paekche, which fell shortly afterwards, followed by Koguryo in 668 AD.

The alliance, however, was short-lived since it turned out to have been a convenient ruse by the Tang ruler to establish hegemony over Korea. The Shilla aristocracy had no

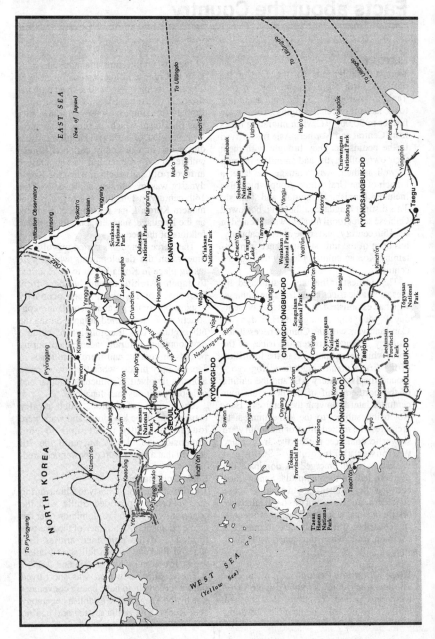

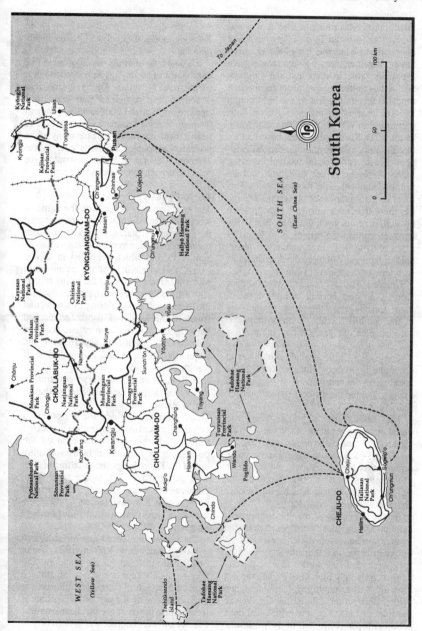

intention of subscribing to such a plan and so, in order to thwart Tang designs, switched allegiance to what was left of the Koguryo forces. Together, the two Korean forces were eventually able to drive out the Chinese. Shilla thus united the peninsula for the first time and this unification was to last through various changes of regime right up until partition after WW II. Yet Shilla was to learn, as all other Korean dynasties have had to, that the price of this often precarious independence depended on the recognition of the vastly superior forces of China and its acknowledgment in the form of tribute. This traditional tributary relationship with China has more than once thrown Korea, through no action of its own, into the lion's den between contending armies from China at times of dynastic change, and left it vulnerable to Japanese military adventurism on its own territory and that of China's.

Unified Shilla presided over one of Korea's greatest eras of cultural development, and nowhere is this more apparent than in the countless tombs, temples, pagodas, palaces, pleasure gardens and other relics which dot the countryside in and around Kyŏngju, the Shilla capital. Buddhism in particular flourished, with state funds being lavished on the construction of temples and images, and monks dispatched to China and India for study.

The cohesiveness of Shilla society was based on the twin pillars of *kolpum* – a rigid hierarchy of rank based on ancestry – and the *hwarang* – a kind of paramilitary youth organisation for the training and education of the sons of the Shilla elite. Yet it was the rigidity of this system which also brought about its eventual downfall.

By the beginning of the 9th century, discontent among those who were excluded from power had reached such a pitch that the kingdom began to fall apart. Threatened by rival warlords to the north and west, the end came surprisingly bloodlessly when the last king of Shilla, unwilling to contemplate further destruction, offered his kingdom to the ruler of Later Koguryo which had been set up in the northern half of the peninsula.

As a result, the capital was moved to Kaesŏng, north of Seoul, and the peninsula reunited.

The last king of Shilla was allowed to live out the rest of his days as an honoured guest in his rival's capital. Kyŏngju sank into obscurity and remained that way until 'rediscovered' in the 20th century. This was in many ways a fortunate event: had there been a major conflict at the time many of the priceless archaeological finds now in the National Museum at Kyŏngju would have been destroyed, looted or lost forever.

Koryŏ Dynasty

The new dynasty, which took the name of Koryŏ, abolished kolpum and restructured the government, placing emphasis on a Confucian examination system for state officials similar to that which prevailed in China, except that eligibility for the examination was limited to the sons of the ruling oligarchy. With stability restored, the new dynasty prospered and it was during this time that Buddhism, through royal patronage, reached the height of its development and acquired considerable secular power through the acquisition of land and accumulation of wealth.

In time, however, the Koryŏ government became as despotic and arrogant as that of Shilla, except that in this case it was the literati who monopolised the top positions rather than warrior-aristocrats. Disaffected military officers eventually reduced the power of these bureaucrats by assassinating one of the Koryŏ kings and installing his son as a puppet ruler. Yet, at the same time, events were taking place on Korea's northern borders which would radically affect the nation's survival as an independent kingdom.

Throughout the later years of the Koryŏ dynasty, marauding Khitan tribes began making life difficult for the kingdom, and they were only kept in check by an alliance with the Mongols of China. The alliance was a reluctant one on the part of Koryŏ since it involved the payment of considerable annual tribute, and eventually it was broken off.

The reckoning didn't come until 1231 since the Mongols were preoccupied with their own internal problems, but when it did the decision to rescind the treaty proved to be a disastrous one. The Mongols invaded with vastly superior forces, quickly taking Kaesŏng and forcing the king to take refuge on Kanghwa Island where he remained relatively safe but totally powerless while the Mongols laid waste to the peninsula for the next 25 years. A truce was finally arranged in 1259, despite opposition from a die-hard Koryŏ faction. The Koryŏ monarch was restored to his kingdom (minus Chejudo Island which the Mongols used for rearing horses) on condition that Koryŏ crown princes would be held hostage at Beijing until the deaths of their fathers, that they would be forced to marry Mongol princesses and that the tribute would be restored.

The tribute demanded by the settlement was a heavy one for Korea to shoulder. It included gold, silver, horses, ginseng, hawks, artisans, women and eunuchs; but that was not all that Koryŏ was compelled to provide. There were also demands to provide soldiers and ships for the ill-fated Mongol attempt to invade Japan between 1274 and 1281. These various exactions plus the powerful influence which the Mongol princesses wielded at the Koryŏ court led to intolerable strains being placed on the fabric of Korean society and were the root cause of the eventual downfall of Koryŏ.

Still, Koryŏ survived for a little while longer and reasserted its independence when rebellions in China led to the ousting of the Mongols and their replacement by the Ming dynasty. There were reforms and wholesale purges of pro-Mongol aristocrats, but the rot had spread too far, and rebellions broke out which climaxed in the overthrow of the Koryŏ monarch and the foundation of a new dynasty by one of the king's former generals, Yi Song-Gye.

Yi (Chosŏn) Dynasty

The new regime staked its future on the ideals and practices of Neo-Confucianism which combined the sage's original ethical and political ideas with a quasi-religious practice of ancestor worship and the idea of the eldest male as spiritual head of the family. At the same time, Buddhism, regarded as an enemy and rival, was suppressed. The monasteries' estates were confiscated, their wealth sequestered and the building of monasteries limited to rural areas. Buddhism has never recovered its former dominance as a result of these events, but it still wields considerable influence and its economic clout is definitely on the rise. Nevertheless, Neo-Confucianism remains the moral foundation of the nation although few Koreans would actually acknowledge it as their 'religion'.

The next 150 years were a time of relative peace and prosperity during which great strides were made under a succession of enlightened kings, the greatest of whom was probably Sejong (1418-50). It was he who presided over the invention of a phonetic script – han'gŭl – for the Korean language. The new script was an outstanding achievement and, since it was infinitely simpler than Chinese, it led to a vast increase in literacy. However, it was not introduced without considerable opposition among the intelligentsia, many of whom regarded it as subversive and worried about the reaction of the Ming court.

Japanese Invasion of 1592

The period of peace came to a dramatic end in 1592 when the country was invaded by a newly-united Japan under Toyotomi Hideyoshi, following Korea's refusal to join with them in an invasion of China. Exploiting their superior weaponry – muskets supplied by the Portuguese – the Japanese overran the peninsula in just one month. At sea, however, they were soundly defeated by Korea's most famous admiral, Yi Sun-Sin, the inventor of the world's first ironclad ships (known as turtle ships or *gobugson*). In their naval encounters with Admiral Yi Sun-Sin, the Japanese lost more than 500 ships in less than six months. Unfortunately the admiral fell foul of the Yi court and was dismissed, only to be recalled at a later date when his successor failed to match up.

Admiral Yi Sun-Sin

in China. The Manchus were in the process of overthrowing the Ming court with whom the Koreans had treaty obligations. Initially unsure as to which side to declare for, the Korean court eventually settled with the Ming, thus incurring the wrath of the Manchus who, as soon as they had consolidated their hold over China, turned to invade Korea. The Korean forces were routed and severe restrictions were placed on the country's sovereignty.

Korea – the Hermit Kingdom

Shocked and exhausted by this series of events, Korea looked inward over the next century while the pace of international change continued to accelerate – largely due to the spread of Western ideas and contacts. Nowhere was this more apparent than in the number of converts to Catholicism and, later, to various sects of Protestantism. Frightened by the growing influence of these groups, the Yi court panicked and in the repression which followed, hundreds of people were executed. But the major event which most shook their confidence was the occupation of Beijing by the French and British in 1860. Korea was closed to all foreigners including the Japanese: as a result of this period the country was called the 'Hermit Kingdom'.

The policy of exclusion was doomed to failure. The late 19th century was no time to turn a blind eye to the increasing industrial and military might of the European maritime nations, the USA and Japan. Sooner or later, one or more of these nations would force Koreans to open its doors. This eventuated some 25 years later as a result of independent occupations of Kanghwa Island by the French and Americans and a naval skirmish engineered by the Japanese which led to a so-called treaty of 'friendship'. The treaty was naturally biased in favour of the Japanese. Korean ports were opened to Japanese traders and the policy of excluding foreigners was abandoned. Suddenly, very ill prepared, Korea found herself subject to imperial rivalry. Although she made a valiant effort to modernise and meet the challenge it was too late.

The war dragged on for four years until Korean guerrilla resistance and Chinese intervention forced its end. Nevertheless, the Japanese invaded again the following year, although this time the war was confined to the southern provinces and came to a speedier end when Hideyoshi died and the invaders withdrew.

The Japanese invasion was an unprecedented disaster for Korea. Many craftspeople and intellectuals were taken prisoner and transported to Japan and almost all Korea's temples and palaces were burnt to the ground during this period. Yet there was to be no early respite.

The Manchu Invasion

The early 17th century was a time of conflict

Japanese Control

The Tonghak Uprising in 1894 – by follow- ers of a new religious sect founded in 1860 by Choe Che-U which combined elements of Confucianism, Buddhism, Taoism and Sha- manism – set off a chain of events which led to the Sino-Japanese War, the defeat of China and the installation of a Japanese-controlled government in Seoul. With China elimi- nated, Russia quickly jumped into the political arena and the Koreans became pawns in yet another struggle between giants. During this time, pro-Japanese and pro-Russian governments followed each other in rapid succession in Seoul. Queen Min – the real power behind the Yi throne – was assassinated by Japanese agents, and for a year and a half King Kojong took refuge inside the Russian legation. In the end the struggle for supremacy was settled by the Russo-Japanese War of 1904 and Korea was occupied by the Japanese. Shortly after, in 1910, following public riots and serious guerrilla activity by elements of the dis- banded Korean army, the Japanese annexed the country, abolished the monarchy and began to mould the country's economy along lines which would best exploit its resources and maximise returns for its colonial master.

With a long tradition of resistance to foreign domination, however, the Koreans did not simply lie down and accept annexa- tion by Japan. After the failure of a Korean delegation to gain the right of self-determi- nation at the Versailles Conference following WW I, an independence move- ment was formed by a group of patriots. They leafleted Seoul and provoked public demonstrations against the Japanese occupa- tion. The unrest quickly spread to the rest of the country. The Japanese troops and police panicked, and in the brutal repression which followed over 7000 Koreans were shot and many thousands seriously injured. Cosmetic reforms were brought in to try and contain the uprising, but at the same time the ranks of the secret police were rapidly expanded and censorship tightened.

As WW II drew near, Japan's grip over Korea was tightened even further. The Jap- anese language was made mandatory as the medium of instruction in schools, all public signs had to be in Japanese, the teaching of Korean history was banned and hundreds of thousands of Korean labourers were con- scripted to assist the Japanese army both in Korea and in China. The Koreans characterised this period as one of attempted cultural genocide and the effect continue to be felt today. Despite political shifts of power since WW II, Koreans still despise Japan for what it did to their country and rows between Seoul and Tokyo are not infre- quent.

Post WW II

When the Americans dropped the atomic bombs on Japan in 1945, most Koreans thought two bombs weren't enough. As much as the Koreans rejoiced at being freed of Japanese rule, the country's hopes for a new era of peace were soon dashed. A deal had been struck between the USSR, USA and Britain over the fate of postwar Korea in which the USSR was to occupy the peninsula north of the 38th parallel and the USA the south. Though never intended as a perma- nent division, it soon turned out that way once the occupying troops were in position. Negotiations for a provisional government floundered when neither side was willing to make concessions which would result in the loss of its influence over the proposed new government. A United Nations (UN) com- mission was set up to try and resolve the problem and to oversee elections for a united government, but it was denied entry to the north and was forced to confine its activities to the south. The new government which was elected in the south declared its indepen- dence and provoked the Communists in the north to do likewise. The stage was set for the Korean War.

The Korean War

By 1948, Soviet and American troops had been withdrawn, but while the Americans supplied only arms considered necessary for self-defence to the regime in the south the USSR provided the North with a vast array of weaponry with which to create a powerful army. On 25 June 1950, the North Korean army invaded. The Americans responded by sending in troops who were soon joined by contingents from 16 other countries following a UN resolution supporting the American action. The USSR absented itself from the Security Council deliberations.

The war went badly for the UN at first and its troops were soon pushed into a small pocket around Pusan but, following a daring landing at Inch'ŏn under the command of General MacArthur, its fortunes changed and within a month the North Korean army had been thrown back to the borders of Manchuria. Such a development was anathema to the new Communist regime in China. In November of the same year, Mao Zedong decided to intervene on behalf of North Korea. The Chinese poured troops into the war and the UN forces were pushed back below the 38th parallel. The conflict continued for the next six months with both sides alternately advancing and retreating until a stalemate was reached just north of the 38th parallel.

Negotiations for a truce began but dragged on for two years, eventually leading to the creation of the De-Militarised Zone (DMZ) and the truce village of P'anmunjŏm where both sides have met periodically ever since to exchange rhetoric and deny provocations.

At the end of the war, Korea lay in ruins. Seoul had changed hands no less than four times and was flattened. Millions of people were left homeless, industry was destroyed and the countryside devastated. In the south, 47,000 Koreans had lost their lives and around 200,000 were wounded. Of the UN troops, 37,000 had been killed (most of them Americans) and 120,000 wounded. Combined military and civilian casualties in the North were estimated at $1\frac{1}{2}$ to two million.

Post Korean War

North Korea North Korea went on to become one of the most closed countries in the world, ruled by the eccentric and uncompromising Kim Il-sung whose position as

head of state was maintained by a constant barrage of propaganda about his boundless wisdom, doctrinal purity, superhuman feats and godlike qualities. If anyone deserves an accolade for having outdone Mao Zedong in the business of personality cults then it's Kim Il-sung.

A similar barrage of self-congratulatory rhetoric is now being churned out for the benefit of his son, Kim Jong-il, who succeeded his father after his death. It is doubtful, however, that he will ever be able to match his father's grip on power. See the North Korea chapter for more details.

South Korea In the South, economic recovery was slow and the civilian government of President Syngman Rhee proved weak and corrupt. In 1961, following blatantly fraudulent elections, massive student demonstrations and the resignation of Rhee, a military dictatorship was established with General Park Chung-hee emerging as its strongman. Pressures soon mounted for the return of a civilian government and in 1963 Park retired from the army and stood as a candidate for the Democratic Republican Party. The party won the elections and Park was named president. Park was re-elected as president in 1967 and again in 1971 (only narrowly missing defeat at the hands of his rival, Kim Dae-jung).

On the positive side, Park created an efficient administration and was the architect of South Korea's economic 'miracle' which he modelled on Japan. But in October 1972, in an attempt to secure his position, he declared martial law, clamped down on political opponents and instituted an era of intensely personal rule. Like Kim Il-sung, he created his own personality cult but his record on human rights grew progressively worse. A botched assassination attempt in 1975 killed his wife. A rigged poll in 1978 resulted in Park's 're-election', but this only further fuelled discontent. Finally, on 26 October 1979, he was assassinated by Kim Chae-kyu, the chief of the Korean Central Intelligence Agency.

The 1980s

After 18 years of Park's tyrannical rule, Koreans were ready for change. The brief period of political freedom which followed Park's death aroused popular sentiment for free elections and the dawning of Korean democracy. Unfortunately, such hopes were soon dashed. On 17 May 1980, a group of army officers headed by General Chun Doo-Hwan re-established martial law and arrested leading opposition politicians, including Kim Dae-jung. Student protests erupted the next day in Kim's home town of Kwangju and were brutally put down: about 200 civilians were killed, over 1000 injured and thousands more arrested. The 'Kwangju Massacre' has haunted the nation's conscience ever since (see the Kwangju section of the Chŏllanam-do chapter for details).

In the rigged elections which soon followed, Chun secured his position as president (since over 500 former politicians were banned from political activity during the campaign the result was a foregone conclusion). Kim Dae-jung was tried for treason and sentenced to death, but so transparent were the charges against him that Chun was reluctantly forced to commute the sentence to life imprisonment following worldwide protests. Probably the single most important factor which saved Kim was Chun's need for a continued and substantial US military presence in South Korea (every main city has one or more American base). Although President Reagan had just come to power in the USA and was intent on keeping US forces in South Korea, Chun's insistence on going through with Kim's execution was placing in jeopardy Congressional approval for Reagan's wishes. Kim Dae-jung was released some time later in order to allow him to go to the USA for medical treatment. He stayed on there as a lecturer at Harvard University until his return to Korea in 1987.

Having consolidated his power base, Chun, on the other hand, lifted martial law, granted amnesty to a number of detainees, and allowed the National Assembly to debate issues somewhat more freely than was ever possible during Park's presidency. Press censorship, nevertheless, remained tight under a 'voluntary restraint' system and the authorities steadfastly refused to allow any substantive discussion to emerge on the question of reunification. It was evident, too, that corruption and cronyism still existed within the government following the breaking of a scandal involving the embezzlement of millions of dollars of government funds by one of Chun's immediate family members.

While Chun survived the scandal, many high-ranking government ministers and army officers were forced to resign. He also miraculously escaped assassination by North Korean agents in late 1983 while on an official visit to Burma.

The killings returned relations between North and South Korea to subzero level despite an apparent slight thaw the previous year. In 1987, two North Koreans posing as Japanese tourists bombed a Korean Air flight causing 115 deaths. South Korean authorities believe that the bombing was done to sabotage the upcoming Olympic Games.

Despite frosty relations, South Korea did attempt to make substantial concessions to the North over a sharing of events for the 1988 Olympics in order to head off another boycott by Communist countries (the USSR boycotted the 1984 Olympics in Los Angeles in retaliation for a US boycott of the 1980 Olympics in Moscow). In the event, North Korea refused the South's offers and became one of only two nations to boycott the Olympics.

While negotiations for the Olympics were going on, Chun announced his intention to step down from the presidency in February 1988. Shortly afterwards, Roh Tae-Woo, a classmate and confidant of Chun's, was nominated by the ruling party to succeed him. For a while it seemed that real democracy was still just a distant dream.

What happened next took the world by storm. Overnight, thousands of students in every city across the nation took to the streets to demonstrate. They were met by riot police, tear gas and mass arrests and within a matter of days the country was at flash point. The students were quickly joined by tens of thousands of industrial and office workers and even Buddhist monks. The subways and streets of Seoul reeked of tear gas and gas masks became an essential item of equipment. Something had to give. Although threatening draconian measures to quell the disturbances, Chun largely took a back seat and left Roh to negotiate.

Under intense American pressure to compromise, and well aware of the obvious fact that the government wasn't just confronted with a bunch of radical students, Roh invited the leaders of the opposition Reunification Democratic Party to talks. The two figureheads of the opposition were Kim Young-sam and Kim Dae-jung.

Kim Dae-jung had returned from exile in the USA the year before but had since been kept under virtual house arrest. The two opposition leaders suddenly found themselves centre stage, but a deal with the government proved elusive. What was being demanded were free, direct, popular presidential elections, the release of political prisoners, freedom of the press and a number of other reforms. Roh felt he could not concede these demands and so negotiations were broken off. But not for long. While massive demonstrations continued on the streets, the country was convulsed by a wave of strikes by industrial workers. Civil war and a military coup were getting dangerously close. Realising this, Chun gave Roh the go-ahead to concede all of the opposition's demands. The country reeled with a mixture of disbelief and ecstasy and the demonstrations stopped. Although strikes continued at various industrial plants over the next few weeks, they were mainly about wage increases and better conditions. At last it seemed that years of iron-fisted military rule, oppression, arrests, torture and censorship had come to an end.

The deal set in motion campaigns for the coming presidential elections by both the ruling Democratic Justice Party and the opposition Reunification Democratic Party. At first, it seemed that the two Kims of the opposition party would form an alliance and agree to one of them running for president in order not to split the opposition vote. A lot of pledges were made in this respect early on in the campaign but, in the end, they both announced their candidacy after touring the major cities and testing the depth of their respective support. In terms of gaining the presidency, this proved to be a fatal decision.

In the elections which followed (judged to have been the fairest ever held), neither of the Kims were able to match Roh's share of the vote (37%) although their combined total (55%) was considerably more than Roh's. Roh therefore became the next president and his party the government. There was a good deal of sabre-rattling during the election campaign with various army officers threatening a coup should Kim Dae-jung win the election, but the one thing which probably restrained them most was the thought that the 1988 Olympics scheduled for Seoul might have been cancelled if such an event occurred. As a matter of national pride, few people in South Korea wanted to see that happen.

Following the elections there were the inevitable accusations of vote-rigging and electoral fraud but much of this was simply sour grapes on behalf of the opposition. And there were the inevitable clashes between extremist student demonstrators and police. The failure of the opposition to win the presidency, however, was far more prosaic than sinister and was largely a question of egos getting in the way of practicalities. By failing to compromise and running against one another, the opposition was doomed from the start. Even Kim Young-sam admitted as much when, after the result was announced, he publicly apologised to the country for having failed to reach an agreement with Kim Dae-jung and field a single opposition candidate.

With Roh in power but restrained by two quite powerful opposition parties, some of the heat went out of South Korean politics. The students continued violent demonstrations every spring (coinciding with mid-term exams which were cancelled as a result), but the radicals began to look increasingly out of touch. Roh's government brought forward numerous democratic reforms, giving South Koreans an unprecedented level of freedom to voice their opinions without fear of imprisonment. Restrictions of South Koreans travelling abroad were also lifted.

Throughout 1989, trips to P'yŏngyang by various activists became almost daily news. Even Catholic priests who had connections with farmers' and other labour organisations were discovered to have gone. In some cases it seems that P'yŏngyang was not only funding the trips but providing money to dissident organisations in the south. The whole sad affair – sad in the sense of a people's legitimate longing – came to a head with the well-publicised visit of Lim Soo-Kyong to the 1989 P'yŏngyang Youth Festival. Lim, a Seoul University student, had gone there via Europe, made impassioned speeches in favour of reunification and then attempted, with the encouragement of the North Korean authorities, to return to South Korea via P'anmunjŏm. No-one is allowed to do this without the approval of both the North Koreans and the UN and she was, at first, refused. Two weeks later, after a flurry of diplomatic activity, she was finally allowed through only to be promptly arrested and taken to Seoul. She spent four years in prison for her efforts, but has remained unrepentant and continues to make radical speeches on campuses. It was a measure of the degree of press and television freedom now allowed in South Korea that her trip was widely reported and included footage of her speeches in P'yŏngyang on the government-controlled KBS TV network.

While the students achieved widespread support for their courageous opposition to the repressive Chun regime, renewed violent protests quickly squandered this goodwill and even produced a strange nostalgia for Chun's military dictatorship. Public disgust with the students sharply increased in 1989 after students set a fire trap which killed seven policemen and injured 30 others at Tongui University in Pusan. The police were on campus at the time to rescue another policeman who had been kidnapped by the students.

The 1990s

Seoul made considerable progress on the diplomatic front by establishing relations with the Soviet Union in September 1990. Another milestone was the establishment of diplomatic relations with China in 1992, an act which greatly angered North Korea. It also greatly angered Taiwan (the Republic of China), with no advance warning, the Taiwanese were given just a couple of hours to vacate their embassy, which was then handed over to the People's Republic of China. Taiwan responded to the insult by abruptly severing its considerable economic ties to South Korea.

On 18 December 1992, the DLP candidate Kim Young-sam (who had merged his opposition party with the DLP in 1990) won the general election, soundly defeating his old opposition rival, Kim Dae-jung, and the billionaire head of the Hyundai company, Chung Ju-yung. In 1993, Kim Dae-jung retired from politics.

Immediately after the election, President Kim embarked on his promised anti-corruption campaign. He publicly stated his own net worth at US$2.1 million (almost poverty level for a South Korean president), and then pushed through legislation to force other government officials to reveal their assets. Revelations of ill-gotten gains forced a number of politicians to resign, and senior prosecutor Lee Kun-kae was given an 18-month prison term for accepting bribes. A widely-used loophole for hiding wealth was closed by the passing of a real-name financial transaction act – previously, politicians could hide their income simply by using a fictitious name.

Since the advent of democracy, South Korea's violent student movement has shrunk considerably to a small hardcore faction which is thoroughly and unabashedly pro-North Korea. Student protests aside, the big unresolved issue which continues to obsess the country is reunification of the two Koreas. Although the election of President

Kim set off a flurry of predictions that reunification was just around the corner, such hopes were quickly dashed by continued reports of North Korea's rapidly developing nuclear weapons programme (see the North Korea chapter for details).

GEOGRAPHY

The Korean peninsula borders China and Russia in the north, faces China in the west across the Yellow Sea (which the Koreans call the West Sea) and Japan to the east and south across the Sea of Japan (which

Koreans label the East Sea). Its overall length from north to south is approximately 1000 km while its narrowest point is 216 km wide. In terms of land area it is about the same size as the UK. The peninsula is divided roughly in half just north of the 38th parallel between the two countries, North and South Korea. The great bulk of the country is mountainous, and the highest peak in South Korea is Hallasan (1950 metres) in the island province of Cheju-do. North Korea can claim the highest peak in the whole peninsula, Paekdusan (2744 metres).

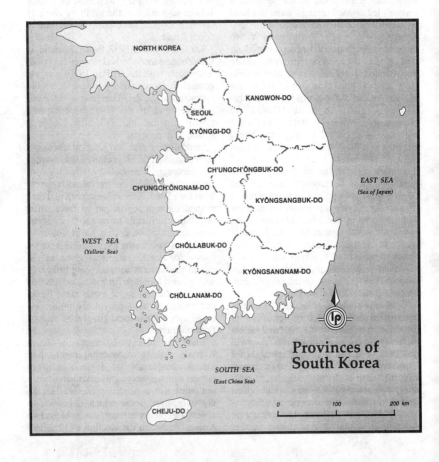

Provinces of
South Korea

CLIMATE

Korea has four distinct seasons. Autumn is the best time to visit – the forests are riotously colourful – and at its best in late October and early November. April, May and June are generally good months, before the summer monsoon rains. Winter, from November to March, sees temperatures hovering around both sides of 0°C, but it can be bitter in the mountains with temperatures down to minus 15°C. The snow, however, is picturesque.

Chejudo, off the south coast, is the warmest place in South Korea and also the wettest. Winter is particularly dreary and will leave you wondering why the whole island doesn't wash away.

FLORA & FAUNA

Various wars and the Japanese occupation took a serious toll on Korea's environment. The Japanese were not the least bit squeamish about exploiting Korea's resources for the war effort, and this meant chopping down trees and digging up whatever minerals could be useful. However, South Korea is one of the world's leading nations in reafforestation and this effort has paid off.

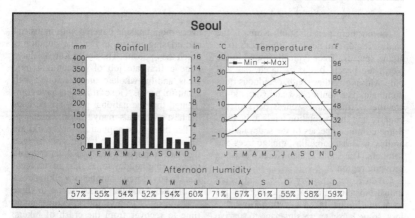

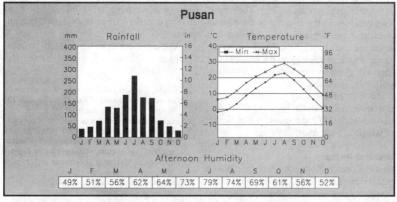

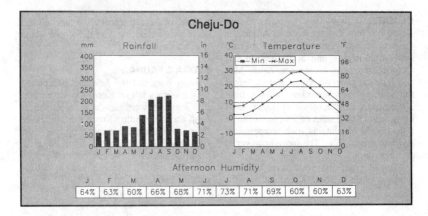

The northern part of South Korea is the coldest region and here the flora tends to be alpine species. Trees typically found in the North are beech, birch, fir, larch, oak and pine. Moving further south, deciduous trees dominate. The south coast and Chejudo-do are the warmest and wettest parts of the country and the vegetation tends to be lush. Some common species of the south include aralias, azaleas, camellias, ginkgo trees and heathers. The south is also Korea's ginseng growing region.

Given Korea's history of war and recent industrialisation, it's not surprising that the local wildlife has taken a beating. Nevertheless, some hardy species manage to survive in the remote mountain regions. The largest wild creature in the country is the Korean black bear, and deer are reasonably common in the national parks. Siberian tigers are no longer found in Korea, and it's possible that they will even become extinct in Siberia as well.

Birds do a reasonably good job of surviving alongside human society. Biologists have identified 379 species of birds in Korea, of which 266 are migratory.

National Parks

Given Korea's small size, high population and booming economy, one would expect to find every tree and every beach polluted and every mountainside covered with industrial and housing estates. In fact, the situation is much the opposite. The South Koreans have done a first-rate job of protecting scenic areas, and the whole country is dotted with beautiful parks. A lot of travellers have commented that the national parks are perhaps the best of Korea's many fine attractions.

The three most popular national parks are Sŏraksan, Hallasan and Chirisan. In fact, they are so popular that you'd better avoid them during holiday times. The government has already closed a number of walking trails in the most popular parks for up to three years in order to give the wilderness some time to recover from the crush of hikers. Fires and cooking are prohibited in most national parks except in designated campsites.

At the present time, there are 20 national parks:

Ch'iaksan: This park is in Kangwon-do Province, east of Wŏnju, and the site of Kuryongsa Temple. The summit of Ch'iaksan reaches 1288 metres.

Chirisan: The park straddles the border of three provinces: Chŏllanam-do, Chŏllabuk-do and Kyŏngsangnam-do. The summit of Chirisan reaches 1751 metres, making it South Korea's second highest peak. Hwaŏmsa is the most important temple found in this park.

Chuwangsan: This park is in Kyŏngsangbuk-do Province near Ch'ŏngsong.

Hallasan: This park on Chejudo Island is dominated by an extinct volcano, South Korea's highest peak.

Kayasan: This park is in Kyŏngsangbuk-do and Kyŏngsangnam-do provinces, 64 km west of Taegu. The highest peak in the park is 1430 metres and the temple of Haeinsa is located here.

Kyeryongsan: This park is in Ch'ungch'ongnam-do Province, just west of Taejŏn.

Naejangsan: This park is just north of Kwangju straddling the border of Chŏllanam-do and Chŏllabuk-do provinces.

Odaesan: This park is in Kangnam-do Province south of Sŏraksan.

Puk'ansan: This park is in the northern suburbs of Seoul and is therefore very accessible.

Sobaeksan: This park straddles the border between Kyŏngsangbuk-do and Ch'ungch'ŏngbuk-do to the north of Yŏngju.

Songnisan: This park is 15 km east of Poŭn in Ch'ungch'ŏngbuk-do Province. Within the park is Pŏpchusa, a famous temple.

Sŏraksan: Located in Kangwon-do, near the city of Sokch'o, this is perhaps South Korea's most beautiful and popular park.

Tŏgyusan: This park is in Chŏllabuk-do, south-east of Taejŏn.

Wolch'ulsan: This park in the south-west corner of Chŏllanam-do is known for its rugged rock formations.

Woraksan: This park, in Ch'ungch'ŏngbuk-do, is near the very popular Suanbo Ski Resort and Suanbo Hot Springs.

Kyŏngju: This park is near Kyŏngju city in Kyŏngsangbuk-do Province. Unlike the previously mentioned parks, the attractions here are mainly cultural. Kyŏngju was the capital of the ancient Shilla kingdom and there are many historical relics and temples.

Hallyŏ Haesang: Off the southern coast near Pusan, there are approximately 400 small islands within the park's boundaries.

Pyŏnsanbando: This park, on a peninsula in the western part of Chŏllabuk-do, is dotted with temples such as Naesŏsa and Kaeamsa.

T'aean Haean: This coastal park is at the western end of Ch'ungch'ŏngnam-do Province.

Tadohae Haesang: This huge marine park consists of hundreds of islands along the south-western tip of Korea. The westernmost part of the park is spectacular Hondo Island.

Provincial Parks

There are 19 provincial parks in South Korea and some of them are easily as spectacular as the national parks. Furthermore, provincial parks tend to be relatively uncrowded simply because they are less well known.

Chŏllabuk-do The following provincial parks are in this province:

Taedunsan (878 metres) is a very small and compact place and spectacularly beautiful. It's notable for granite spires, cliffs, great views and hiking trails.

Maisan (685 metres) means 'horse ears mountain', which roughly describes the shape of the two rocky outcrops which make up the peaks. T'apsa Temple is stuck right between the two 'horse ears'.

Moaksan (794 metres), south-west of Chŏnju, is where you'll find Kŭmsansa, a temple famous for shamanism.

Sŏnunsan is a beautiful place with Sŏnunsa Temple and small sub-temples perched all around a gorge near the sea.

Chŏllanam-do The following provincial parks are in this province:

Mudŭngsan (1187 metres) is just east of Kwangju. There are numerous hiking trails and it's a popular walking area for residents of Kwangju. However, it's not otherwise spectacular.

Chogyesan (884 metres) is the home of Songgwangsa, the main temple of the Chogye sect of Korean Buddhism.

Turyunsan (703 metres) is the most south-western peak in Korea and the location of Taehŭngsa, a major Zen meditation temple.

Ch'ungch'ongnam-do The following provincial parks are in this province:

Tŏksan is known for its waterfalls, valleys and hot springs. The largest temple here is Sudoksa. The park is to the west of Ch'ŏnan.

Ch'ilgapsan (561 metres) is a small but very steep mountain. Temples in this thickly-forested park include Changgoksa and Chonghyesa.

Kangwon-do The following provincial parks are in this province:

Tonghae is also known as Naksan Provincial Park, this beachside park has fine facilities for swimming. Other major sights in the park include Naksansa and Uisangdae Pavilion.

Kyŏngp'o is another beachside park, but it's very developed and touristy. It's six km north of Kangnŭng.

T'aebaeksan (1568 metres) is the sixth highest peak in South Korea and one of the country's three sacred mountains.

Kyŏnggi-do The following provincial parks are in this province:

Namhansansong is an old mountain fortress is about 26 km south-east of central Seoul and makes a good day trip from the city.

Kyŏngsangbuk-do The following provincial parks are in this province:

Ch'ŏngnyangsan (870 metres) has 11 other scenic peaks, eight caves and a small temple, Ch'ongnyangsa.

Mun-gyŏng Saejae straddles the mountain pass connecting Ch'ungch'ŏngbuk-do and Kyŏngsangbuk-do. It's not spectacular but does offer pleasant scenery.

P'algongsan is north of Taegu and has a big temple called Tonghwasa. There is also a big standing Buddha on the peak of a mountain.

Kŭmosan is just outside the city of Kumi, a major industrial area, and the park is mostly a recreational area for the local workers.

Kyŏngsangnam-do The following provincial parks are in this province:

Kajisan has a collection of major temples including Sŏngnamsa (right at the mountain), Unmunsa (to the north of the mountain), P'yoch'ungsa (south of the mountain and just outside the park boundary). Nearby (but outside the park) is T'ongdosa, one of the five big temples of Korea.

Yŏnhwasan: (477 metres) is home to one moderate-sized temple, Okch'onsa, and several hermitages.

GOVERNMENT

Power emanates from the Blue House (the president's residence and office), which is behind Kyŏngbokkung in Seoul. In theory, the president shares power with the legislative and judicial branches, but in practice the president is far stronger than the entire 299-member National Assembly. The president is democratically elected. There has been no vice-president since the 1960s. The president and members of the National Assembly serve five-year terms.

The prime minister – the head of the cabinet – in theory wields considerable power, but in practice is mostly a figurehead. In the National Assembly, there is one

---

The Korean Flag

The South Koreans may well have the most philosophical flag in the world. The white background represents Confucian 'purity' or the Buddhist concept of 'emptiness'. In the centre lies a T'aegŭk, the Taoist symbol of the balance of or harmony between opposites. It was adapted from the Chinese, who usually depicted it in black & white, and divided vertically. The Korean version is more colourful and divided horizontally, with the red top half representing Yang (Heaven, day, male, heat, active, construction etc.). The blue lower half represents Yin (Earth, night, female, cold, passive, destruction etc). These twin cosmic forces are cycled perpetually, in perfectly balanced harmony, despite their superficial opposition; wisdom doesn't see them as fighting each other, but rather as two sides of the same coin.

The three lines at each corner, known as trigrams, were borrowed from the most important ancient book of Chinese thought, the *Classic of Changes* (Korean: the Chu Yŏk; Chinese: the I Ching). The three unbroken bars symbolise Heaven-Creative, while the opposite three broken bars symbolise Earth-Receptive. The trigram in the upper right corner is Water-Treacherous Danger, and in the opposite corner lies Fire-Loyal Love.

Something similar to this flag was created in 1882 by a team of reformist envoys to Japan, as they realised they had no modern standard to represent Korea as an equal among nations. The current design was adopted by the Shanghai-based government-in-exile, and became standardised as the national flag of the Republic of Korea in 1948. It is called the T'aegŭkki. One may well wonder whether the top half of the horizontally-divided T'aegŭk, being red, was some sort of omen of the north half of Korea becoming communist.

David A Mason

South Korean Flag

elected member from each constituency and up to 10 non-elected members 'at large' for each party. All the parties have been known to sell the 'at large' seats to the highest bidder as a means of raising money, but this practice is being increasingly criticised.

Federal judges are appointed by the executive branch and confirmed by the National Assembly. As time goes on, South Korea's judiciary has become increasingly independent of politicians.

In early 1990, several parties merged to form the ruling Democratic Liberal Party (DLP) (whose name was unabashedly cloned from Japan's ruling Liberal Democratic Party). The party has been riven by factions, which has made governing the country a delicate balancing act. The Democratic Party is the main opposition party, and has also been riven by factions.

ECONOMY

South Korea is one of Asia's 'little tigers' (also called 'little dragons'). In the 1950s, Korea began an industrial revolution based on low-wage but labour-intensive manufacturing of cheap goods for export. But now these industries are dying as the country moves upmarket into high-technology and service industries.

South Korea now enjoys a standard of living approaching that of Hong Kong, Singapore and Taiwan, but there are significant differences. Unlike the other tigers, South Korea's economy is dominated by huge, corporate conglomerates *(chaebol)* whose charitable contributions to the government have raised more than a few eyebrows. These companies are concentrated around Seoul, but there are some manufacturing plants in Taegu and Pusan. In more or less descending order the 'big 10' companies are: Hyundai, Daewoo, Samsung, Lucky-Goldstar, Sunkyong, Hanjin, Ssangyong, Kia, Hanhaw and Lotte.

The South Koreans often decry the centralisation of wealth into so few channels, and newspaper editorials frequently mention that perhaps Korea should follow the model of Taiwan (where small business leads the way). Interestingly, newspaper editorials in Taiwan often suggest that perhaps Taiwan should follow the big-business model of Korea.

However, it is Japan – not Taiwan – which has been Korea's mentor. Former president Park Chung-hee laid down the formula for Korea's economic development, which borrowed heavily from the Japanese model. Indeed, the notion of 'Korea Inc' seems even more valid than the familiar 'Japan Inc'. In other words, South Korea is *not* a true free-wheeling capitalist country. Rather, the government is heavily involved in all sectors of the economy and has built up a formidable bureaucracy to regulate everything from the price of automobiles to what types of snacks restaurants can serve.

The bureaucratic controls extend through the chaebol and the banking system down to the smallest enterprises. The regulations are often used to keep imports out – one importer of foreign ice cream was told he could only import flavours that were already being produced by Korean manufacturers because 'foreign flavours might hurt Korean stomachs'.

Not surprisingly, giving bureaucrats enormous power provides fertile ground for corruption – many large companies admit paying bribes in order to avoid tax audits, price controls and other problems. Those companies which have offended the government (as happened in 1992 when Hyundai chief Chung Ju-yung ran for president) have suddenly seen their access to cheap credit cut off.

The bureaucracy plus high labour costs have forced most large Korean companies to move manufacturing facilities abroad. Many foreign firms have also found Korea's investment climate too harsh, and are pulling out. This has alarmed the Korean government and there are now serious calls for reform. Kim Young-sam's government has committed itself to follow the more liberal trading policies required by the General Agreement on Tariffs & Trade (GATT). There are Korean economists who argue that the government should ease up regulation of land use, the banking system, interest rates, foreign exchange controls, price controls, import barriers and other forms of bureaucratic meddling. There are many special interests which vehemently resist change.

As in Japan, France and elsewhere, farmers can be very vocal about defending their interests and can generate a good deal of political heat. In 1994, when Korea opened 1% of its rice market to imports, the farmers protested and students quickly took up their cause, leading to full-scale riots. But despite the fact that the government has bent over backwards to protect domestic farmers from cheap imports, agriculture is clearly declining and import barriers are not likely to save it. If you travel through the countryside at times other than school holidays, you will notice that the countryside seems to be populated almost entirely by the elderly. Indeed, most Korean farmers are over the age of 60 – the young people flock to the cities in search of a better life. Korea will almost certainly have to import food in ever larger quantities in the years ahead.

Despite the paternalistic approach taken to the economy, the government goes light when it comes to social welfare programmes. Given the large amounts that South Korea must, by necessity, spend on defence, there is little cash left over to shovel into free medical care, unemployment benefits and retirement schemes.

POPULATION
The population of South Korea stands at 43.7 million. Population density is 444 sq km – in other words, it's crowded. However, the population is very unevenly distributed – over 70% live in urban areas while some mountainous regions remain largely unpopulated. About 25% of South Koreans live in the capital city, Seoul, but the figure rises to 35% when you include Seoul and its suburbs. The breakdown in population for Korea's six largest cities is as follows:

Seoul	10.8 million
Pusan	3.6 million
Taegu	2.1 million
Inch'ŏn	1.4 million
Kwangju	1 million
Taejŏn	900,000

The population is increasing 0.8% annually – one of the lowest rates of population growth in Asia.

PEOPLE
The Koreans are a group who show remarkably few cultural or physical differences. Korean origins probably lie in the assimilation of local aboriginal tribes with newcomers of central Asian origin who migrated into the peninsula from around 5000 to 1000 BC. The Koreans claim to be 'of the Mongolian race', something you are likely to doubt if you ever visit Mongolia.

Korean creation myths suggest that the Koreans are of divine origin: the offspring of a heavenly king and a woman who started life as a bear. The bear became human by living on 20 cloves of garlic in a cave for 100 days. (The Korean obsession with the pungent garlic clove apparently started early.) The bear element in the myth is shared by Siberian creation myths, supporting the hypothesis of the central Asian origins of the Koreans.

The only ethnic minority are approximately 50,000 people of Chinese ancestry who fled the Communist takeover of China in 1949. Most are from China's Shandong Province, which explains the abundance of Shandong dishes served in Seoul's Chinese restaurants. Although most of the ethnic Chinese speak perfect Korean, most do *not* have Korean nationality. When they travel abroad, they carry a passport issued by Taiwan.

EDUCATION
Korean Education
Needless to say, the han'gŭl alphabet (as opposed to the old system of writing in Chinese characters) has been a boon to literacy in Korea. The literacy rate in South Korea has now reached 96%. For most Koreans, 12 years of education is the norm (from age 6 to 18 years).

As in Japan, gaining entrance to a university is a formidable task and students are pushed, pulled and badgered for years by their parents to prepare for the much-feared entrance exams. Preparation begins at an early age, so getting into a good elementary school is important. One reason why virtually all Koreans want to live in Seoul is because the best schools are there.

The 'examination hell' has profound effects on Korean society and some students commit suicide in desparation. Pity the poor middle-school students who must spend all evening, weekends and holidays studying. The final irony is that those students who successfully pass the entrance exams, can then look forward to a four-year study-free holiday – university students are practically guaranteed to graduate no matter how poor their academic performance.

In the past, academically unqualified children from well-to-do families simply bribed their way into universities, but this practice is now highly illegal and parents who indulge in it can be imprisoned. However, wealthy families can still hire private tutors, in the process creating lucrative jobs for foreign English teachers.

Schools for Foreigners
There are several schools in Seoul catering to the children of expat workers. If this interests you, try contacting one of the following:

Seoul International School
San 32-16, Pokchong-dong, Chung-gu (☎ 233-4551/2)

Seoul Academy, 988-5, Taech'i-dong, Kangnam-gu (☎ 554-1690)
Seoul Foreigners' Academy
55, Yonhui-dong, Sodaemun-gu (☎ 335-5101/5)
French School
San 85-24, Panp'o-dong, Soch'o-gu (☎ 535-1158)
Samyuk Foreigners' School
San 6-2, Hwigyong-dong, Tongdaemun-gu (☎ 248-8682)
Seoul German School
4-13, Hannam-dong, Yongsan-gu (☎ 792-0797)
Centennial Christian School
2-22, Namsan-dong, Chung-gu (☎ 773-8460)
Seoul Liberty Foreigners' School
260-7, Pogwang-dong, Yongsan-gu (☎ 792-4116/7)
Hanyong School of Foreign Language
166, Sang-il-dong, Kangdong-gu (☎ 429-0360)

ARTS
Traditional Korean folk dances take a wide variety of forms. The most popular ones include drum dances *(sungmu)*, mask dances *(t'alchum)* and solo improvisational dances *(salpuri)*.

Many foreign visitors are fond of the musical performances done with traditional stringed instruments. Not surprisingly, there are many different types of such instruments, but the most popular one seems to be the *Stringed Instruments;Kayagum.*

Traditional operas also take different forms. A solo storyteller singing to the beat of a drum while telling a story (and sometimes waving a paper fan) is called *p'ansori.* Somewhat more similar to Western opera is *ch'ang*, which can involve a large caste of characters.

Performances of traditional arts can be seen at the Sejong Cultural Centre in Seoul and the Korean Folk Village near Suwon.

Calligraphy – writing with brush pens and ink – is an ancient art from China which the Koreans have perfected for their own needs. Calligraphy can be done in both traditional Chinese (*hanja*) characters or in the Korean phonetic alphabet (han'gŭl).

CULTURE
Traditional Lifestyle
Meeting the Koreans Koreans don't have the Japanese obsession with bowing, but a

short nod or bow is considered respectful when greeting somebody or departing.

Korea is probably the most Confucian nation in Asia, even more so than China where Confucianism originated. This makes for some behaviour that many Westerners take time getting used to. At the heart of Confucian doctrine are the so-called Five Relationships. These prescribe behaviour between ruler and subject, father and son, husband and wife, old and young, and between friends. This structuring of relationships is very important in making sense of Korean society, as well as the nearby cultures of China and Japan.

Newly arrived visitors to Seoul may remark on the jostling of the crowds, the queue jumpers, inconsiderate driving and the tendency of Koreans to be late for appointments (although Koreans are not alone in this). However, to put it down to plain rudeness would be somewhat wide of the mark. All relationships require a placement of some kind in order for one party to determine how to behave with respect towards the other. The middle-aged male office worker thrusting ahead of you to pay for a Coke at the 7-Eleven store may not even register your presence. You, as a foreigner, have not been introduced and he has nowhere to place you on the scale of relationships. An introduction and an exchange of business cards would immediately place you into a category that would demand certain behaviour from him.

Once contact has been established everything changes. Most Koreans are extremely courteous and will go out of their way to accommodate you. Korean rules of etiquette are fairly complex, but allowances will be made for foreigners.

As for being late for appointments, this is also complicated by one's status – the person with higher status is allowed to be later than the person of lower status. High status is governed by many factors. For example, who is the older of the two? Who has the more prestigious job? Who attended the better university or primary school?

Koreans are a proud people who enjoy boasting of their 5000-year-old cultural heritage and ethnic uniqueness. This pride is complicated by what many Koreans feel to be the indignity of their turbulent recent history: the occupation by the Japanese, the carving up of the country by foreign powers and the presence of American armed forces personnel. This means you should be aware in your dealings with Koreans that they are very sensitive to any perceived slights of their culture. It is a good idea to behave pleasantly when bargaining over prices, and to avoid contentious remarks regarding Korea and its culture when chatting with Koreans.

You are likely to encounter peculiar kinds of strongly held opinions from Koreans themselves. Examples might be that the han'gŭl script is the most perfect writing system in the world or that there is no such thing as homosexuality in Korea. There is probably not much point arguing about these kinds of issues.

The Family The ideal of the Confucian household is 'five generations under one roof'. In times past the mortality rate rarely allowed this to happen, but when the old people hung on, it was common for grandparents, parents and their children to live together. Even in modern Korea this is still often the case, in part because of the outrageous cost of housing. Koreans find the idea of packing off their parents to an old people's home abhorrent. Usually it is the responsibility of the eldest son to live with the parents, even after marriage. Today, despite the increasing prevalence of the nuclear family, this is still a tradition that exerts a lot of pressure on young Korean men.

In the past marriages were always arranged. Traditionally, the young couple had no contact until the night of the wedding. In modern Korea, couples generally marry for romantic reasons, but family approval remains of paramount importance. Parental choice is based on more 'practical' considerations (such as background, education, job prospects and, in the case of women, ability to fulfil the domestic duties of marriage).

Men & Women Korea is still very much a

male-oriented society, and women's rights have been slow in making an impression. There is traditionally a clear delineation in the respective responsibilities of men and women. In general terms it can be said that the male preserve is public, while women cater to the private, personal world of the home. These values have lingered into the 1990s with Korean public life very much dominated by men. Even the traditional separation of male-female education lingers in some of the women's universities in Seoul.

Nevertheless, compared to the Yi dynasty era, things have improved considerably. There is virtual equality in access to education for men and women, and women have entered politics, although admittedly in very small numbers. As in other parts of the world the corporate world is almost strictly a male domain. Furthermore, young Koreans often participate in nonsegregated activities such as evenings out and hikes, something that was extremely rare even 10 years ago.

Still, old habits die hard, and although two-worker families are becoming more common in South Korea, and particularly in Seoul, women usually accept lower-paid, more menial positions. Many working women are also expected to retain their traditional household responsibilities, putting an additional strain on them. Korean male office workers are expected to make frequent appearances in after-hours' drinking bouts, and spend much of their free time in the company of male colleagues. Such situations exclude women. When guests visit, the men will often sit and eat together separately from the women, who will grab a bite together in between preparing food. The younger generation is starting to challenge these customs.

The one area where Korean women have some authority is in controlling the family finances. The husband is expected to hand over his salary (at least most of it) to the wife, and she is then supposed to pay all the bills.

Women are expected to be virgins when they marry and many Korean girls will go so far as to have their virginity 'restored' surgically. The idea that women should enjoy sex is also a somewhat new and radical idea in Korea. Not so long ago wives were regarded as little more than domestic help, and men were just as likely as not to seek female companionship elsewhere.

Geomancy Derived from the Chinese characters meaning 'wind and water', geomancy *(pungsu)* is the art of remaining in proper physical harmony with the universe. If Korean people find that their business is failing, a geomancer might be consulted. Sometimes the solution will be to move the door of the business establishment, at other times the solution may be to relocate an ancestor's grave.

Korea's former and present rulers have all understood the importance of geomancy. When one empress died, 16 hours were spend arranging the feet of her corpse to get them into the auspicious position before the funeral could commence. The palaces and temples of Seoul have all been correctly arranged according to the laws of geomancy. When the Japanese came to conquer Korea, they deliberately constructed their Capitol building to obstruct the geomantic 'axis of power' on which the nation's fate was hinged.

In this day of modern high-rises and housing estates, most Koreans have had to push aside concerns about which direction their home or business is oriented. However, the position of an ancestor's grave is still taken very seriously.

The Zodiac The Korean zodiac *(shipijikan)* is the same as that used by the Chinese. As in the Western system of astrology, there are 12 signs of the Korean zodiac. Unlike the Western system, your sign is based on which year rather than which month you were born, although the exact day and time of your birth are also carefully considered in charting your astrological path.

Fortune tellers are common in Korea. Making use of astrology, palm reading and face reading, fortune tellers claim they can accurately predict the future. If you are so inclined, you can try out this service, though you are almost certain to need an interpreter since few fortune tellers in Korea can speak English.

If you want to know your sign in the Korean zodiac, look up your year of birth in the following chart (future years are given so you know what's coming). However, it's a little more complicated than this because Korean astrology goes by the lunar calendar. The lunar New Year usually falls in late January or early February, so the first month will be included in the year before.

It's said that the animal year chart originated when Buddha commanded all the beasts of the earth to assemble before him. Only 12 animals came and they were rewarded by having their names given to a specific year. Buddha also decided to name each year in the order in which the animals arrived – the first was the rat, then the ox, tiger, rabbit and so on.

Lunar Calendar Westerners are familiar with the Gregorian (solar) calendar. The Korean lunar calender is another borrowing from China, and it's also used by other countries in the region including Japan, Taiwan, Vietnam and Mongolia.

Lunar dates do not correspond exactly with solar dates because a lunar month is slightly shorter than a solar month. The Koreans add an extra month every 30 months to the lunar calendar, essentially creating a lunar leap year. Thus, the lunar New Year can fall anywhere between 21 January and 28 February on the Gregorian calendar. Were it not for the lunar leap year, the solar and lunar seasons would get totally out of synchronisation.

The Koreans believe that their race was born precisely in the year 2333 BC. Therefore, the year 1995 is 4328 in the traditional calendar, and you'll find this date printed on Korean-made calendars even now.

Taboos
Losing Face The one thing to bear in mind is the Korean concept of *kibun*, a sense of well-being or harmony between people. In actual practice this is very similar to the idea of 'face'. Efforts are made to smooth over potential problems, such as remarks that could lead to political disagreements. If you say something silly, there will be, at the most, an embarrassed laugh before someone steers the topic on to safer ground. Arguments, or any situation that is going to lead to one party having to back down, will involve a loss of face, and this is a big no-no in East-Asian cultures. Be sure not to accidentally put yourself in a situation where you cause someone else to lose face.

Unlucky Numbers When the Koreans borrowed the Chinese counting system, they also borrowed the 'unlucky' number four. It's unlucky because it also sounds just like the Korean word for death *(sa)* which was

Lunar Calendar							
Rat	1924	1936	1948	1960	1972	1984	1996
Ox/Cow	1925	1937	1949	1961	1973	1985	1997
Tiger	1926	1938	1950	1962	1974	1986	1998
Rabbit	1927	1939	1951	1963	1975	1987	1999
Dragon	1928	1940	1952	1964	1976	1988	2000
Snake	1929	1941	1953	1965	1977	1989	2001
Horse	1930	1942	1954	1966	1978	1990	2002
Goat	1931	1943	1955	1967	1979	1991	2003
Monkey	1932	1944	1956	1968	1980	1992	2004
Rooster	1933	1945	1957	1969	1981	1993	2005
Dog	1934	1946	1958	1970	1982	1994	2006
Pig	1935	1947	1959	1971	1983	1995	2007

A | Resting from study, Hahoe near Andong (CHP)
B | Traditional wedding, Korean Folk Village (CT)
C | 75 year-old man at Sŏkkuram Grotto (MM)
D | Picture time, Kyŏngbokkung Palace (CT)

Top: Namdaemun Gate (CT)
Middle: Lotte World ice-skating rink (CT)
Bottom: Seoul traffic, Chong-no (CT)

also borrowed from Chinese. If you have any Korean friends coming to visit you in your own country, you probably should not check them into a 4th floor hotel room. This will not be a problem in Korea itself, because most hotels have no fourth floor and hospitals *never* do.

Avoiding Offence
Body Language Beckoning someone is done with the palm down and fluttering fingers – avoid pointing or gesturing with one finger at somebody as this is considered impolite.

Deadly Chopsticks Sticking your chopsticks upright into the rice is a definite no-no. This resembles burning sticks of incense in an incense bowl, a sure death sign. Like other peoples in this part of the world, the Koreans are extremely superstitious when it comes to anything relating to death and a faux pas like this one would create extreme embarrassment with your hosts or fellow diners.

Don't Touch One thing worth bearing in mind is that a foreign man with a Korean woman (or a woman who looks Korean) runs a particularly high risk of being the recipent of Korean male belligerence. The woman will also be given a hard time. If you are male accompanying a Korean female friend, it's certainly advisable that you do not get intimate (like holding hands) in public.

Red Ink Don't write a note in red ink. If you want to give someone your address or telephone number, write in any colour but red. Red ink conveys a message of unfriendliness. If you're teaching in Korea it's OK to use red ink to correct students' papers but if you write extensive comments or suggestions on the back of the paper, use some other colour besides red.

RELIGION
There are four broad streams of influence in the Korean spiritual and ethical outlook: shamanism, which originated in central Asia;

Buddhism, which entered Korea from China around the 4th century AD; Confucianism, a system of ethics of Chinese origin; and Christianity, which first made inroads into Korea in the 18th century. To a certain extent, shamanism has been stigmatised by modern education as a form of superstition, and about half of all Koreans nowadays profess to be religious sceptics. But shamanism continues to be an active cultural force, and official records claim that there are 40,000 registered shaman priests *(mudang)* in South Korea. Anthropologists maintain that as many mudang do not register, the actual figure is perhaps closer to 100,000.

Shamanism is also thought to have had a significant influence on other religions entering Korea. Buddhism certainly made itself more accessible to the common people by incorporating shamanistic rites and identifying Buddhist saints with shamanistic gods. Others point to the similarities between Pentecostal Christian services and certain elements of shamanistic ritual, which could be a factor in the popularity of Christianity in Korea.

Shamanism
Shamanism is not an organised religion. It has no temples, no body of scriptures or written texts. Nonetheless, it is an important part of Korean religious experience. Central to shamanism is the mudang or priest, whose role is to serve as an intermediary between the living and the spirit worlds. The mediating is carried out through a *kut*, a ceremony that includes dance, song and even dramatic narrative. Mudang are almost always female, and find their calling in one of two ways. The most common is through inheritance of the skill from ancestors. But mudang may also acquire their spiritual connections after being possessed by a spirit themselves. After the spirit has been 'enshrined' in the body of the mudang she can then go on to study kut rituals with an experienced mudang. This period of study can take anywhere from two to 10 years.

Shamanist ceremonies are held for a variety of reasons. At a most basic level they might be held on the occasion of a minor illness or before setting out on a journey. In this case the arrangements will be a simple affair of some food offerings and a prayer offered by a mudang. While praying the mudang simply rubs her hands together. Strictly speaking, a ceremony of this kind is known as a *pison*. More serious matters, such as deep financial problems, will require a more elaborate ceremony known as a *kosa*. Ceremonies of this kind will require the mudang to communicate human wishes to the spirit world by dance and song accompanied by drums and cymbals. Finally, the kut itself is a more elaborate affair with many participants. It might be held to send a deceased family member safely into the spirit world, or it might be held by a village on a regular basis to ensure the safety and harmony of its members.

It is remarkable that shamanism has survived as long as it has. It has been subject to persecution since early in the Yi dynasty. Its practitioners are female and usually uneducated and for this reason it is scorned most by educated urban males. Yet many Koreans continue to turn to mudang for solace and assistance.

Buddhism

The founder of Buddhism was Siddhartha Gautama. He was born around 563 BC at Lumbini, on the border of present-day Nepal and India. Born of a noble family, he questioned the comforts of his existence and for many years led the life of an ascetic. He was to turn his back on this life too. After a period of intense meditation he achieved 'enlightenment', which is the essence of Buddhahood.

Buddhism has been greatly complicated by the fact that it has fractured into a vast number of schools of thought. Basically these can be divided into the Hinayana (Lesser Vehicle) and the Mahayana (Greater Vehicle) schools, the former emphasising personal enlightenment and the latter seeking the salvation of all beings. Nevertheless, at the heart of all Buddhism is the teachings of Gautama, the founder of Buddhism.

Buddhism in Korea, like Japan and China, belongs to the Mahayana school, and since its arrival, has split into a great number of smaller schools of thought. The most famous is Sŏn, better known to the outside world by its Japanese name Zen.

There are 18 Buddhist sects in Korea, but the largest by far is the Chogye sect with its headquarters in Seoul's Chogyesa (Chogye Temple). It is an amalgamation of two Korean schools of Buddhism: the Sŏn sect, which relies on meditation and the contemplation of riddles among other things to achieve sudden enlightenment; and the *Kyo* school, which relies more heavily on extensive scriptural study. The major temples of the Chogye sect are located as follows (by province):

Seoul: Chogyesa, Hwagyesa, Pongŭnsa, Tosŏnsa

Ch'ungch'ŏngbuk-do: Tukjusa, Kosansa, Miruksa-ji, Pŏpchusa, Toduksa

Ch'ungch'ŏngnam-do: Kapsa, Kwanch'oksa, Magoksa, Shinwonsa, Sudŏksa, Tonghaksa

Cheju-do: Kimnyongsa, Kwanumsa

Chŏllabuk-do: Anguksa, Kŭmsansa, Miruksa-ji, Naejangsa, Naesosa, Shilsangsa, Songkwangsa, Sŏnunsa, T'apsa (Unsusa)

Chŏllanam-do: Chungshimsa, Hwaomsa, Mihwangsa, Paekyangsa, Sŏnamsa, Songkwangsa, T'aeamsa, Taehŭngsa, Unjusa

Kangwon-do: Ch'ŏngp'yŏngsa, Kukhyangsa, Kuryongsa, Naksansa, Pobhungsa, Sangwonsa, Shinhŭngsa, Sut'asa, Wolchŏngsa

Kyŏnggi-do: Chŏndŭngsa, Pongsonsa, Shillŭksa, Yongjusa

Kyŏngsangbuk-do: Chikchisa, Huibangsa, Hungyungsa, Kounsa, Namsan Mountain (five temples), Paekyunsa, Pulguksa, Punhwangsa, Pusŏksa, Shinsonsa, Tonghwasa, Ŭnhaesa, Unmunsa

Kyŏngsangnam-do: Haeinsa, Kuwolsa, Pŏmŏsa, P'yoch'ungsa, Sŏknamsa, Ssanggyesa, T'ongdosa

The Chogye sect represents around 90% of Korean Buddhists. Next in size is the T'aego sect representing about 7% of the total. The T'aego sect distinguishes itself by permitting its monks to marry. The Japanese installed this system of married monks during their occupation of Korea. Apparently, married monks were easier to control than other-worldly meditative monks. Headquarters for the T'aego sect is in Seoul at Pongwonsa, a temple close to Ehwa Women's University. This magnificent temple is noted for its paintings.

Buddhism, a remarkably adaptive faith, has co-existed closely with shamanism in Korea. Almost all Buddhist temples have a *samsŏng-gak* (three spirit hall) on their grounds which houses shamanistic deities. Buddhist priests often carry out activities associated with shamanism, such as fortune telling and the sale of good-luck charms.

Buddhism suffered a sharp decline after WW II. Part of the reason had to do with the Japanese colonisation of Korea – Buddhist monks were coerced to support unity with Japan. Those monks who proved uncooperative simply disappeared. Furthermore, as South Korea's postwar economic boom got underway, Buddhism seemed to have little to offer – Koreans were not about to cast off their pursuit of worldly desires to become a nation of fasting monks and nuns.

Ironically, South Korea's recent status as a developed nation has caused Buddhism to suddenly revive. Westernisation has gone so far in South Korea that the country is suffering from an identity crisis – the last thing Koreans want to be called is Westernised Asians. As national pride reasserts itself, more and more South Koreans are seeking to rediscover their cultural roots and this includes Buddhism. Pilgrimages to temples have increased enormously and a huge amount of money is now flowing into temple reconstruction. It is estimated that approximately 25% of South Koreans now call themselves Buddhists, about equal to the number of practicing Christians.

Maps produced in Korea mark temple sites with what appears to be a swastika. You will also see this symbol on the temples themselves. But if you look more closely,

Budhhist Symbol

you'll see that it's actually the reverse image of a swastika. This is, in fact, an old Buddhist religious symbol with which you should become familiar.

Confucianism

Confucianism is a system of ethics rather than a religion. Confucius (551 BC to 479 BC) lived in China during a time of great chaos and feudal rivalry known as the Warring States Period. He emphasised devotion to parents and family, loyalty to friends, justice, peace, education, reform and humanitarianism. He also emphasised respect and deference to those in positions of authority, a philosophy which was to be heavily exploited by emperors and warlords. However, not everything said by Confucius has been universally praised – it seems that he was a male chauvinist who firmly believed that men are superior to women.

Confucius preached the virtues of good government, but his philosophy was used to justify China's horrifying bureaucracy which exists to this day. On a more positive note, his ideas led to the system of civil service and university entrance examinations, where one gained position through ability and merit rather than from noble birth and connections. Confucius preached against practices such as corruption, war, torture and excessive taxation. He was the first teacher to open his school to all students on the basis of their eagerness to learn rather than their noble birth and ability to pay for tuition.

The evolution of Confucianism in Korea produced Neo-Confucianism. This combined the sage's original ethical and political ideas with a quasi-religious practice of ancestor worship and the idea of the eldest male as spiritual head of the family.

Confucianism was viewed as being enlightened and radical when it first gained popularity. However, over the years it has become very paternalistic and conservative. It's even fair to say that many younger Koreans regard Confucianism as something of an embarrassment, which explains why many have defected to Christianity. Yet ironically, Confucianism lives on as a kind of ethical bedrock (at least subconsciously) in the minds of most Koreans. South Korea is frequently described as the most Confucian society in the world, and most of Korean social behaviour confirms this.

Christianity

Korea's first exposure to Christianity was via the Jesuits from the Chinese imperial court of the late 18th century. A Korean aristocrat was baptised in Beijing in 1784. When it was introduced to Korea the Catholic faith took hold and spread quickly, so quickly in fact that it was perceived as a threat by the royal family and vigorously suppressed, creating Korea's first Christian martyrs. (During the Pope's visit to South Korea in 1985 to celebrate the bicentennial of Catholicism on the peninsula, 103 martyred Christians were canonised.)

Christianity got a second chance in the 1880s with the arrival of American Protestant missionaries. The founding of schools and hospitals won them many followers.

Nowhere else in Asia, with the exception of the Philippines, have the efforts of proselytising missionaries been so successful. About 25% of all Koreans consider themselves Christians.

Young people have been particularly eager to make the jump to Christianity. Perhaps unfortunately, those with political ambitions have used the church to catapult themselves into prominence, and a number of church leaders have assumed major roles in anti-government protests. It's only fair to point out that most of these self-proclaimed leaders adopt the label 'reverend' even though they have no official church backing: The enthusiasm that Koreans have shown for Christianity probably has much to do with the spiritual aridness of Confucianism. When the missionaries first arrived, Buddhism had been banished to the mountains and the Yi royalty had put a great deal of pressure on shamanism. If Korea needed anything, it needed change. Christianity must have seemed both a dynamic and consoling faith that held the promise of ushering in a new age for the old Korea.

Church Services For those who are interested in attending English-language church services, there is a listing every week in the Saturday edition of the newspaper *Korea Times*.

LANGUAGE

Korean is a knotty problem for linguists. Various theories have been proposed to explain its origins, but the most widely accepted is that it is a member of the Ural-Altaic family of languages, specifically belonging to the Tungusic branch. This is not particularly enlightening in itself, although it helps to know that other members of the same linguistic branch are Turkish and Mongolian. In reality, Korean shares much more with Japanese and Chinese than it does with

---

Reverend Moon

'Reverend' Moon Ik-kwan was never a practising minister, and few doubt that he was exploiting the church to lend respectability to his own political campaign. He made no secret of the fact that he intended to run for president. He ran afoul of South Korean law when he travelled to North Korea and appeared on public TV hugging Kim Il-sung. When he returned to South Korea, he was arrested and spent two years in prison before being let out on an amnesty. Unrepentant, he continued to travel around South Korea blatantly encouraging students to violence. In one of his famous speeches he proclaimed: We will smash the skulls of dictatorship with the iron bars of democracy'. The Reverend promised that if he became president, he would reunify Korea and jointly govern with Kim Il-sung. However, these plans were cut short when Reverend Moon unexpectedly died in 1993. Although the church wants nothing to do with him, he has been unofficially 'canonised' by both leftists in South Korea and the North Korean leadership. ∎

either Turkish or Mongolian. This should come as no surprise given all the contact (not always happy) between these three countries.

Korean suffixes indicating time, place and relationship are piled on the end of verbs, much the same as in Japanese. Basic sentence order is subject-object-verb, unlike the English subject-verb-object ordering. In the past, Korean was written using Chinese characters. Given the fact that the average Korean had neither the time to study nor the money for tuition, most remained illiterate. Reading and writing was the pursuit of the elite and monks, and conservative Confucianists wanted to keep it that way. This all changed when the Koreans introduced han'gŭl, a cursive alphabet developed under King Sejong in the 15th century.

Han'gŭl originally consisted of 28 characters, but has since been reduced to only 24. Not surprisingly, it's very easy to learn. However, the formation of words using han'gŭl is very different from the way that Western alphabets form words. The emphasis is on the formation of a syllable in such a way that it resembles a Chinese character. Thus the first syllable of the word 'han'gŭl' is formed by an 'h' in the top left corner, an 'a' in the top right corner and an 'n' at the bottom, with the whole syllabic grouping forming what looks like a Chinese character. These syllabic characters are strung together to form words. Spaces should appear between written words, but these are often randomly deleted, causing great confusion for foreign students of Korean. Traditionally the language was written top to bottom and right to left as in Chinese, but now the Western practice of writing horizontally from left to right is the standard.

Despite the best efforts of a conservative educational system, all languages change over time. The pronunciation of Korean words has changed in the 500-plus years since han'gŭl was first introduced, with the result that you will often encounter words which are not pronounced as they are spelled.

Like most non-European languages, the romanisation of Korean has been applied in fits and starts with all sorts of irregularities. Officially, the McCune-Reischauer system is supported by the Korean government as the standard romanisation system, and it is used in this book. However, most Koreans have never studied the McCune-Reischauer system and therefore use all kinds of mismatched transliterations. Many Koreans write their names in romanised spellings of their own fancy, so Mr Chae and Miss Choi might be brother and sister. There are also wide divergences in the spelling of place names. You might, for example, see Pusan spelled as Busan, or Poshingak as Bosingag. The thing to do is to stay on your toes and try to anticipate these discrepancies. Best of all, learn enough han'gŭl to be able to double check place names.

Features of the McCune-Reischauer system are the use of apostrophes (') to indicate aspirated (accompanied by a puff of air) consonants, as in P'yŏngyang. The apostrophe is also used to differentiate between 'n' and 'ng'. Thus 'han'gŭl' is written with an apostrophe (although a hyphen will do) to be sure it is not pronounced 'hang-ŭl'. A final feature of the McCune-Reishauer system is the use of diacritics on the 'o' and 'u' vowel sounds to fully represent the values of Korean vowels. Under this system, the capital city should be spelled 'Sŏul' rather than 'Seoul', but it's difficult to change an already accepted standard so 'Seoul' remains the official spelling.

Korean is a language that is much complicated by the degrees of status codified into the grammar. Those of higher status need to be spoken to in a more polite manner than those of lower status. You can easily offend someone by using the wrong level of politeness, especially when you are talking to an older person. Young Koreans tend to use the very polite forms a lot less than the generations before them, but for safety's sake the sentences in this section all employ polite forms.

It's advisable to learn han'gŭl in its correct alphabetical order since this will enable you to use a Korean-English dictionary.

Consonants

Korean Letters	Initial Position	Medial Position	Final Position
ㄱ	k	g	k
ㄴ	n	n	n
ㄷ	t	d	t
ㄹ	r	r/n	l
ㅁ	m	m	m
ㅂ	p	b	p
ㅅ	s/sh	s	t
ㅇ	silent	ng	ng
ㅈ	ch	j	t
ㅊ	ch'	ch'	t
ㅋ	k'	k'	k
ㅌ	t'	t'	t
ㅍ	p'	p'	p
ㅎ	h	h	ng

ㅅ is pronounced (*sh*) if followed by the vowel ㅣ (*i*).

Medial ㄹ is pronounced *n* when it follows ㅁ (*m*), ㄴ (*n*) or ㅇ (*ng*).

Vowels

ㅏ	a	like the 'a' in 'car'
ㅑ	ya	like the 'ya' in 'yard'
ㅓ	ŏ	like the 'o' in 'of'
ㅕ	yŏ	like the 'yo' in 'young'
ㅗ	o	like the 'o' in 'home'
ㅛ	yo	like the 'yo' in 'yoke'
ㅜ	u	like the 'u' in 'flute'
ㅠ	yu	like the word 'you'
ㅡ	ŭ	like the 'oo' in 'look'
ㅣ	i	like the 'ee' in 'beet'

Double Consonants

Double consonants are said with more stress than single consonants.

Korean Letters	Initial Position	Medial Position	Final Position
ㄲ	kk	gg	k
ㄸ	tt	dd	–
ㅃ	pp	bb	–
ㅆ	ss	ss	t
ㅉ	tch	tch	–

Complex Consonants

These occur only in a medial or final position in a word.

Korean Letters	Initial Position	Medial Position	Final Position
ㄱㅅ	–	ks	k
ㄴㅈ	–	nj	n
ㄴㅎ	–	nh	n
ㄹㄱ	–	lg	k
ㄹㅁ	–	lm	m
ㄹㅂ	–	lb	p
ㄹㅅ	–	ls	l
ㄹㅌ	–	lt'	l
ㄹㅍ	–	lp'	p
ㄹㅎ	–	lh	l
ㅂㅅ	–	ps	p

Combination Vowels

ㅐ	ae	like the 'a' in 'hat'
ㅒ	yae	like the 'ya' in 'yam'
ㅔ	e	like the 'e' in 'ten'
ㅖ	ye	like the 'ye' in 'yes'
ㅘ	wa	like the 'wa' in 'waffle'
ㅙ	wae	like the 'wa' in 'wax'
ㅚ	oe	like the 'wa' in 'way'
ㅝ	wo	like the 'wo' in 'won'
ㅞ	we	like the 'we' in 'wet'
ㅟ	wi	like the word 'we'
ㅢ	ŭi	'u' plus 'i'

Greeting & Civilities

Hello
annyŏng hashimnika (formal)
안녕하십니까
annyŏng haseyo (less formal)
안녕하세요
Goodbye. (to person leaving)
annyŏnghi kaseyo
안녕히가세요
Goodbye. (to person staying)
annyŏnghi kyeseyo
안녕히계세요
Please.
put'ak hamnida
부탁합니다
Thank you.
kamsa hamnida
감사합니다
Yes.
ye/ne
예 / 네

No.
anyo
아니오

Excuse me.
shillye hamnida
실례합니다

Getting Around

I want to go to...
...e kago shipsŭmnida
...에 가고싶습니다

What time does it leave?
myŏtshi e ch'ulbal hamnigga?
몇시에 출발합니까?

What time does it arrive?
myŏtshi e toch'ak hamnigga?
몇시에 도착합니까?

Does this train stop at...?
i yŏlchanŭn...e sŏmnigga?
이 열차는 ... 에 섭니까?

Where can I catch the bus to...?
...haeng bŏsŭnŭn ŏti e sŏ tapnigga?
...행 버스는 어디에서 탑니까?

airport
konghang
공항

Asiana Airlines ticket office
ashiana hangkong mepyoso
아시아나항공 매표소

Korean Air ticket office
taehan hangkong mepyoso
대한항공 매표소

bus
bŏsŭ
버스

airport bus
konghang bŏsŭ
공항버스

bus stop
bŏsŭ chŏngnyujang
버스 정류장

express bus terminal
kosok bŏsŭ t'ŏminŏl
고속버스터미널

inter-city bus terminal
shi'oe bŏsŭ t'ŏminŏl
시외버스터미널

taxi
t'aekshi
택시

long-distance (bullet) taxi
ch'ong'al t'aekshi
총알택시

I want to get off here.
yŏgiyae naeryŏ chuseyo
여기에 내려 주세요

train
kich'a
기차

1st class train
saemaul ho
새마을호

2nd class train
mugunghwa ho
무궁화호

3rd class train
t'ongil ho
통일호

4th class train
pidulgi ho
비둘기호

railway station
kich'a yok
기차역

boat
pae
배

ferry pier
pudutga
부둣가

ticket
p'yo
표

ticket office
maep'yoso
매표소

one-way (ticket)
p'yŏndo
편도

return (ticket)
wangbok
왕복

refund a ticket
hwanbul
환불

subway station
chihach'ŏl yŏk
지하철역

open/closed
yŏngŏpchung/hyuil
영업중 / 휴일

lost & found office
punshilmulpo kwansaenta
분실물보관센타

left-luggage room
mulpumbo gwanch'anggo
물품보관창고

lockers
lakk'a
락카

car park
chuch'ajang
주차장

Necessities

toilet
hwajangshil
화장실

toilet paper
hwajangji
화장지

tampons
tempo
템포

sanitary pads
saengnidae
생리대

condoms
kondom
콘돔

pharmacy (medicine)
yak
약

anti-diarrhoeal drug
sŭlsa yak
설사약

laxative
pyunbi yak
변비약

pain killer/Tylenol
chintongche/tailenol
진통제 / 타이레놀

electric mosquito incense
chŏnja mugihyang
전자 모기향

Communication

post office
uch'eguk
우체국

stamp
u'pyo
우표

aerogramme
hanggong sŏ gan
항공서간

International Express Mail (EMS)
kŏkje t'ŭkgŭ pop'yŏn
국제특급우편

telephone office
chŏnhwa kuk
전화국

telephone card
chŏnhwa kadŭ
전화카드

Around Town

Where is the...?
ŭn ŏdi'imnigga?
...은 어디입니까?

bank
ŭnhaeng
은행

Bank of Korea
hanguk ŭnhaeng
한국은행

Hanil Bank
hanil ŭnhaeng
한일은행

Chohung Bank
chohŭng ŭnhaeng
조흥은행

Korea Exchange Bank
oehwan ŭnhaeng
외환은행

Korea First Bank
cheil ŭnhaeng
제일은행

tourist information office
kwangwang annaeso
관광안내소

migration office
chul'ibkuk kwali so
출입국관리소

private language school
hagwon
학원

Money

May I have change please?
chandonŭro pakkwo chuseyo?
잔돈으로 바꿔 주세요

How much does it cost?
ŏlmayeyo?
얼마예요?

Too expensive.
nŏmu pissayo
너무 비싸요

Can I have a discount?
chom ssage hae juseyo?
좀 싸게 해 주세요?

Accommodation

Camping ground
yayŏngji
야영지

youth hostel
yusu hosutel
유스호스텔

hotel
hot'el
호텔

cheap hotel
yŏgwan
여관

cheapest hotel
yŏinsuk
여인숙

home stay
minbak
민박

What is the address?
chuso ga ŏdi imnigga
주소가 어디입니까?

Please write it down.
ssŏ chuseyo
써주세요

single room
singgul lum
싱글룸

double room
tobul lum
더블룸

with shared bath
yokshil omnun pang chuseyo
욕실 없는 방 주세요

with private bath
yokshil innun pang chuseyo
욕실 있는 방 주세요

May I see the room?
pang'ŭl polsu issŏyo?
방을 볼 수 있어요?

Do you have anything cheaper?
tŏ ssan kot sun ŏpsŭmnigga
더 싼 것은 없습니까?

Can you have my clothes washed?
setak ssobisŭ taemnikka
세탁 써비스 됩니까?

towel
sugŏn
수건

hotel namecard
myongham
명함

bathhouse
mok yok t'ang
목욕탕

Time

When?
ŏnje imnigga?
언제 입니까?

today
onŭl
오늘

tomorrow
naeil
내일

in the morning
ochŏne
오전에

in the afternoon
ohu'e
오후에

Emergencies

Help!
saram sallyŏ
사람살려!

Thief!
todduk iya
도둑이야!

Fire!
pul'iya
불이야!

Call a doctor!
ŭisarul pulŏ chuseyo
의사를 불러 주세요!

Call the police!
kyŏngch'alŭl pulŏ chuseyo
경찰을 불러주세요!

hospital
  pyŏngwon
  병원
I'm allergic to penicillin.
  penishillin allerugiga issŏyo
  페니실린 알레르기가 있어요
I'm allergic to antibiotics.
  hangsaengche allerugiga issŏyo
  항생제 알레르기가 있어요
I'm diabetic.
  tangnyopyŏngi issŏyo
  당뇨병이 있어요

Map Reading

beach
  hesuyokjang
  해수욕장
big (great)
  dae
  대
cave
  donggul
  동굴
city
  shi
  시
east
  tong
  동
fortress
  sŏng
  성
gate
  mun
  문
hermitage
  am
  암
hot springs
  wonch'ŏn
  온천
island
  do
  도
lake
  ho
  호
mountain
  san
  산

north
  puk
  북
park
  kongwon
  공원
pavilion
  gak
  각
province
  do
  도
river
  gang
  강
road
  no, ro
  로
sea
  hae
  해
section
  ga
  가
shrine
  myo, tae
  묘, 대
south
  nam
  남
street
  gil
  길
temple
  sa
  사
tomb
  nŭng, rŭng
  릉
valley
  kyŏgok
  계곡
city
  shi
  시
county
  gun
  군
town
  ŭp
  읍

township
myŏn
면
village
ri or *ni*
리
west
sŏ
서
hall
jŏng
정
waterfall
p'okp'o
폭포

Numbers

Korean has two counting systems. One is of Chinese origin and the other is a native Korean system. Korean numbers only go up to 99 and are used to count days, minutes and mileage (as long as the total doesn't exceed 99). The Chinese system is used to count money, not surprising since the smallest Korean banknote is W1000.

Number	Chinese		Korean	
0			*yŏng*	영
1	*il*	일	*hana*	하나
2	*i*	이	*tul*	둘
3	*sam*	삼	*set*	셋
4	*sa*	사	*net*	넷
5	*o*	오	*tasŏt*	다섯
6	*yuk*	육	*yŏsŏt*	여섯
7	*ch'il*	칠	*ilgop*	일곱
8	*p'al*	팔	*yŏdŏl*	여덟
9	*ku*	구	*ahop*	아홉
10	*ship*	십	*yŏl*	열

Hanja

Around 70% of all Korean dictionary entries are of Chinese origin, although the two languages are completely unrelated. The loan words from Chinese are apparent to anyone who has studied both languages. For example, 'mountain' is *shan* in Chinese and *san* in Korean; 'south' is *nan* in Chinese and *nam* in Korean. Before the invention of the hangul alphabet, Korean was written exclusively in Chinese characters known as *hanja*.

In 1970, President Park Chung-hee banned hanja because hangul is so much easier to learn and was seen as the key to increasing literacy. Furthermore, the hangul alphabet is Korea's own invention, while Chinese characters are an exotic import and thus an insult to national pride. The Koreans were further infuriated by the fact that the Japanese (who also use Chinese characters) tried to force Korea to abandon hangul and adopt hanja during the Japanese occupation.

The South Koreans had a sudden change of heart in 1975. Hanja was restored to high school textbooks, but placed in parentheses after the hangul words. The Ministry of Education drew up an official list of 1800 hanja characters which Korean students had to learn. Korean dictionaries identify 4888 characters, but very few Koreans know even half of these. Ironically, the ban on hanja remains in elementary schools, though it is not enforced and private elementary schools often teach hanja.

Interest in learning Chinese characters was given a big boost in 1993 when Korea established diplomatic relations with China. Unfortunately, the issue has been complicated by the fact that communist China simplified 2238 characters in the 1950s, thus making them look very different from hanja (which is based on traditional Chinese). However, the traditional characters are used in Hong Kong and Taiwan, and now there is a serious movement afoot in mainland China to return the characters to their original complex form.

Nowadays, very few South Koreans could be described as being functionally literate in hanja. In Korea, Chinese characters are usually restricted to maps, limited use in newspapers, restaurant signs and occasionally for writing names (as in name cards).

From its founding, North Korea banned the use of Chinese characters. However, this was rescinded in 1964. Officially, North Korean students are expected to learn around 2000 Chinese characters, though it's questionable how many of them really do. Certainly the shortage of reading material in the North would mean that few have the opportunity to practice hanja. ■

Number	Combination				
			300	*sampaek*	삼백
11	*ship'il*	십일	846	*p'alpaek*	
20	*i'ship*	이십		*saship'yuk*	팔백사십육
30	*sam'ip*	삼십	1000	*ch'ŏn*	천
40	*sa'ip*	사십	2000	*i'ch'ŏn*	이천
48	*sa'shippal*	사십팔	5729	*o'ch'ŏn ch'ilpaek*	
50	*o'ship*	오십		*i'shipku*	오천칠백이십구
100	*paek*	백	10,000	*man*	만
200	*i'paek*	이백			

Facts for the Visitor

VISAS & EMBASSIES

With an onward ticket, visitors from almost anywhere – excepting the Philippines, eastern Europe and countries with governments not recognised by South Korea (Cuba, Laos and Cambodia) – will be granted a stay of up to 15 days without a visa. But be warned, this is not extendible and there are steep fines of between W50,000 and W200,000 for overstaying your visa. In addition, South Korea grants visa exemptions to nationals of any west European nation except Ireland. If you fall into this category you'll be given a 90-day or three-month permit; 60 days in the cases of Italy and Portugal.

Nationals of all other countries – including Australia, Canada, New Zealand and the USA – require visas for stays over 15 days. If your nationality does not permit a visa exemption and you need more than 15 days, apply for a visa before you go to South Korea. It's worth bearing in mind that South Korean embassies and consulates are notoriously slow in issuing visas, so allow for a few days no matter what they tell you. Tourist visas are usually issued for a stay of 90 days. Onward tickets and/or proof of 'adequate funds' are not normally required. If you apply for a visa in your own country you might get a multiple-entry visa – you usually *cannot* get this if you apply at a South Korean embassy in a nearby Asian country.

Applying for a work visa in South Korea requires a letter of invitation from your prospective employer and a signed contract. You will also need to supply your passport, academic records and other documentation as the job requires. Applications must be made outside the country and they take a month to process. This is probably not such a problem if you are applying from your home country. It is more of a problem, however, if you arrive in South Korea looking for teaching work. After you find a school willing to provide sponsorship it will be necessary to leave the country and wait a month for the processing to be completed. For more details see the Work section in this chapter.

South Korean Embassies

There are South Korean embassies and consulates in the following countries:

Australia
    113 Empire Circuit, Yarralumla, Canberra ACT 2600 (☎ (06) 273-3044)
    Sydney Consulate, 8th Floor, Challenge Bank, 32-36 Martin Place, Sydney, NSW 2000 (☎ (02) 221-3866)
Austria
    Prater Str 31, 1020 Vienna (☎ (0222) 216-3441)
Belgium
    Avenue Hamoir 3, 1180 Bruxelles (☎ (02) 375.39.80)
Canada
    151 Slater St, 5th Floor, Ottawa, Ontario K1P 5H3 (☎ (613) 232-1715)
    Toronto Consulate, 555 Avenue Rd, Toronto, Ontario, M4V 2J7 (☎ (416) 920-3809)
    Vancouver Consulate, 830-1066 West Hastings St, Vancouver, BC V6E 3X1 (☎ (604) 681-9581/2)
China
    China World Trade Centre, 1 Jianguomenwai Dajie, Beijing (☎ 505-2608)
    Shanghai Consulate, 4th Floor, Shanghai International Trade Centre, 2200 Yan'an Xilu, Shanghai (☎ (021) 219-6917)
Denmark
    Svanemollevej 104, 2900 Hellerup (☎ (45) 39-401233)
France
    125 Rue De Grenelle, 75007 Paris (☎ (01) 47.75.01.01)
Germany
    Adenauerallee 124, 5300 Bonn 1 (☎ (0228) 267960)
    Berlin Consulate, Kurfuerstendamm 180, 1000 Berlin 33 (☎ (30) 885-9550)
    Frankfurt Consulate, Eschersheimer-Landstrasse 327, 6000 Frankfurt (☎ (069) 563051/3)
Greece
    1 Eratosthenous Str, 6th Floor, GR-116 35, Athens (☎ (01) 701-2122)
Hong Kong
    5th Floor, Far East Finance Centre, 16 Harcourt Rd, Central (☎ 529-4141)
Indonesia
    57 Jalan Gatot Subroto, Jakarta (☎ 520-1915)

Ireland
>   20 Clyde Rd, Ballsbridge, Dublin 4 (☎ (01) 608800)

Japan
>   205 Minami-Azabu, 1-chome, Minato-Ku, Tokyo 106 (☎ (03) 3452-7611/8)
>   Fukuoka Consulate (☎ (092) 771-0461)
>   Kobe Consulate (☎ (078) 221-4853/5)
>   Nagoya Consulate (☎ (052) 935-4221)
>   Naha, Okinawa Consulate (☎ (0988) 676940/1)
>   Niigata Consulate (☎ (025) 230-3400)
>   Osaka Consulate (☎ (06) 213-1401)
>   Sapporo Consulate (☎ (011) 621-0288/9)
>   Sendai Consulate (☎ (022) 221-2751)
>   Shimonoseki Consulate (☎ (0832) 665341/4)
>   Yokohama Consulate (☎ (045) 621-4531)

Malaysia
>   22nd Floor, Wisma Mca No 163, Jalan Ampang 50450, Kuala Lumpur (☎ (03) 262-2377)

Mongolia
>   Baga Toyruu St 37, Ulaanbaatar (☎ 23541)

New Zealand
>   Level 6, Digital House, 86 Victoria St, 6th Elders, Wellington (☎ (04) 473-9073/4)

Netherlands
>   Verlengde Tolweg 8, 2517 JV, The Hague, Netherlands (☎ (070) 352-0621)

Norway
>   Inkognitogaten 3, 0224, Oslo 2 (☎ (02) 2255-2018/9)

Philippines
>   Alpap 1 Floor, 140 Alfaro St, Salcedo Village, Makati, Manila (☎ (02) 817-5827)

Poland
>   I Krasickiego 25, 02-611, Warsaw (☎ (483337)

Portugal
>   Avenida Miguel Bombarda, 36-7 1000, Lisbon (☎ (01) 793-7200/3)

Russia
>   Ul Alexeya, Tolstova 14, Moscow (☎ 203-3850)
>   Vladivostok Consulate, Room 512-529, 45A October 25th St, Vladivostok 690009 (☎ (4332) 227729)

Singapore
>   101 Thomson Rd, United Square, 10-02/04, 13-05, Singapore 1130 (☎ 256-1188)

Spain
>   Miguel Angel 23, 28010, Madrid (☎ 310-0053)

Sri Lanka
>   98 Dharmapala Mawatha, Colombo 7 (☎ (01) 699036)

Sweden
>   Sveavagen 90, Stockholm (☎ (08) 160-480)

Switzerland
>   Kacheggweg 38, 3006 Bern (☎ (031) 431-081)

Thailand
>   23 Thirmruammit Rd, Ratchadpisek, Huay Kwang, Bangkok 10310 (☎ (02) 247-7537)

UK
>   4 Palace Gate, London W8 5NF (☎ (071) 581-0247)

USA
>   2450 Massachusetts Ave, NW, Washington DC (☎ (202) 939-5600)
>   Agana Consulate, 305 GCIC Bldg, Agana, Guam 96910 (☎ (671) 472-6488)
>   Anchorage Consulate, 101 Benson Blvd, Suite 304, Anchorage, AL 99503 (☎ (907) 561-5488)
>   Atlanta Consulate, 229 Peachtree St, Cain Tower, Suite 500, Atlanta, GA 30303 (☎ (404) 522-1611/3)
>   Boston Consulate, 15th Floor, Financial Center 1, Boston, MA 02111 (☎ (617) 348-3660)
>   Chicago Consulate, 455 North Cityfront Plaza Drive NBC Tower, 27th Floor, Chicago, IL 60611 (☎ (312) 822-9485/8)
>   Honolulu Consulate, 2756 Pali Hwy, Honolulu, HI 96817 (☎ (808) 595-6109)
>   Houston Consulate, 1990 Post Oak Blvd, Suite 1250, Houston, TX 77056 (☎ (713) 961-0186)
>   Los Angeles Consulate, 3243 Wilshire Blvd, Los Angeles, CA 90010 (☎ (213) 385-9300)
>   Miami Consulate, Suite 800, Miami Center 201, South Biscayne Blvd, Miami, FL 33131 (☎ (305) 372-1555)
>   New York Consulate, 460 Park Ave at 57th St, 5th Floor, New York, NY 10022 (☎ (212) 752-1700)
>   San Francisco Consulate, 3500 Clay St, CA 94118 (☎ (415) 921-2251)
>   Seattle Consulate, Suite 1125, United Airline Bldg, 2033 6th Ave, Seattle, WA 98121 (☎ (206) 441-1011)

Vietnam
>   3rd Floor, Boss Hotel, 60-62 Nguyen Du St, Hanoi (☎ (04) 269160)

Visa Extensions

As a general rule, tourist visas cannot be extended. The only exceptions are for emergencies such as accidents or illness, cancelled flights, loss of a passport etc. You are supposed to apply for this extension at least one day before the visa expires and overstaying your visa can result in a stiff fine.

Working visas are valid for one year and are extendible for a further year. For a second extension you will need to leave the country for about two weeks.

Re-Entry Permits

If you don't want to forfeit your working visa you should apply for a multiple re-entry visa before making any trips out of the country. This must be done at the immigration office in the province where you live.

DOCUMENTS
Resident Certificate
If you are working or studying in South Korea on a long-term visa it is necessary to apply for a residence certificate within 90 days of arrival. This must be done at the immigration office for your province of residence, which is not necessarily the closest immigration to where you live.

Passport
A passport is essential, and if yours is within a few months of expiration, get a new one now – Korea and many other countries will not issue a visa if your passport has less than six months of validity remaining. Also, be sure it has plenty of space for visas and entry and exit stamps.

Losing your passport is very bad news – getting a new one means a trip to your embassy or consulate and usually a long wait while they send faxes or telexes (at your expense) to confirm that you exist. If you're going to be in Korea for a long time, it might be wise to register your passport at your country's consulate, which will expedite matters should you need a replacement.

Driver's Licence
If you plan to be driving abroad, get an International Driving Permit from your local automobile association. These are normally valid for one year only so there's no sense getting one far in advance of departure. Make sure that your permit states that it is valid for motorbikes if you plan to drive one.

Health Certificate
An International Health Certificate to record any vaccinations you've had may be useful. These can also be issued in Korea.

Student ID Card
Full-time students in the USA, Australia and Europe can often get good discounts on tickets with the help of an International

Student Identity Card (ISIC). This card entitles the holder to a number of discounts on airfares, trains, museums etc. To get this card, enquire at the education institution you attend. These can be issued in Korea at the Korean International Student Exchange Society (KISES) (☎ 733-9494; fax 732-9568) in room 505 of the YMCA building on Chongno 2-ga (next to Chonggak subway station) in Seoul. A student ID card or a university letter of acceptance is required.

STA Travel issues STA Youth Cards to people aged 13 to 26 years.

Miscellaneous
If you're travelling with your spouse a photocopy of your marriage licence might come in handy if you need to deal with the law, hospitals or other bureaucratic authorities.

If you're planning on working or studying in Korea it could be helpful to have copies of transcripts, diplomas, letters of reference and other professional qualifications.

A collection of small photos for visas (about 10 should be sufficient) will be useful if you're planning on visiting several countries but will also come in handy if you apply for work. Of course, these can be obtained in South Korea and elsewhere. Visa photos must have a neutral background.

CUSTOMS
Because of high duties on many imported goods, customs is very thorough with returning Koreans. For visiting foreigners, customs is very easy. Although it's not mandatory, Korean customs advises travellers to declare any items worth more than W300,000 (US$375) so that you won't get taxed when you try to depart with these goods. In reality, you may be wiser to not make a declaration since they will stamp your passport and you'll have to pay duty if you do not depart with the goods. You must declare foreign currency worth over US$10,000 (and this includes travellers' cheques). By not doing so you could risk having the balance confiscated when you try to leave with it.

There is a duty-free allowance of 200

cigarettes (or 50 cigars), two ounces of perfume and one bottle of spirits (not exceeding a total of one litre). It's prohibited to bring in two-way radios or any literature, cassette tapes or motion pictures that are deemed 'subversive to national security or harmful to public interests'. You can leave any prohibited items in bonded luggage for about US$2 per day.

If you have any further queries there is a Customs Information Service (☎ 665-3100) at Kimp'o International Airport.

For those leaving the country with antiques purchased in South Korea, take note of the Cultural Properties Preservation Law. The law forbids the export of items deemed as 'important cultural properties'. If there is any doubt as to whether one of your purchases might fall into this category, you should contact the Art & Antiques Assessment Office (☎ 662-0106).

Needless to say, Customs will not be amused if you try to import explosives, guns or narcotics. While most budget travellers leave their dynamite and AK-47s at home, more than a few foreigners have run into trouble with drugs. Unless you wish to research the living conditions of Korean prisons, it would be wise to leave any recreational chemicals at home.

MONEY
Currency
The US dollar is the most acceptable foreign currency, but you won't have trouble exchanging other major currencies. The South Korean unit of currency is the won (W) with coins of W1, W5, W10, W50, W100 and W500. The W1 coins are rarely seen outside of banks. Notes come in denominations of W1000, W5000 and W10,000.

Exchange Rates
At the time of writing exchange rates were:

Australia	A$1	=	W599
Canada	C$1	=	W603
China	Y1	=	W95
France	Ffr1	=	W144
Germany	DM1	=	W495
Hong Kong	HK$1	=	W107
Japan	¥1	=	W7.98
New Zealand	NZ$1	=	W483
Singapore	S$1	=	W533
Switzerland	Sfr1	=	W600
Taiwan	NT$1	=	W31
UK	£1	=	W1236
USA	US$1	=	W830

Changing Money
There are numerous banks around the country which cash travellers' cheques or exchange US dollars cash for Korean won. However, finding a place to change money in rural areas can be problematic, so take care of this in large cities. Also be sure you have enough Korean cash on hand during weekends and holidays when banks are closed. If you run out of won at such times, your only recourse will be to head for one of the three international airports where moneychangers work extended hours.

The Korean won is *not* a freely traded currency, and you'll have a hard time unloading it once you're outside the country. Foreigners working illegally quickly learn, to their grief, that South Korean banks will not exchange won for foreign currency without proper authorisation. Ditto for transferring Korean won abroad by telegraphic transfer. Foreigners who wish to open up won-denominated bank accounts in South Korea must have a residency permit.

On the other hand, up to US$500 can be reconverted into hard currency on departure without exchange receipts. If you save your receipts you can reconvert the amount you originally converted within 90 days.

Credit Cards
You will have no problem finding opportunities to put any of your credit cards to use in Korea, especially in Seoul. International credit cards such as American Express, Diners Club, Visa, MasterCard and JCB are widely accepted at large department stores and hotels. Of course, don't expect to use a credit card in small shops. The main offices are:

American Express
   181-1 Buam-dong, Chongno-gu, Seoul (☎ (02) 398-0114)
Diners Club
   59-4 Banpo-dong, Sŏcho-gu, Seoul (☎ (02) 596-0411)
Visa
   50 Sogong-dong, Chung-gu (☎ 752-6523)

Costs

Korea is steadily shouldering its way into the big league when it comes to costs. In many respects it is already on a par with Australia, Europe and the USA. On the other hand, it offers far more value for money than Japan.

So how much can you reckon on spending a day in Korea? Of course this depends on where you stay and how you spend your time. Budget travellers could get by on US$20 per day, but this means going for the cheapest accommodation and doing a fair bit of self-catering when it comes to food. Transport costs can be reduced by not doing much travelling beyond hitchhiking.

Korea is much kinder to the visitor with a few more dollars to throw around. Spending a few extra dollars allows you to eat well, sleep well, move around a fair bit, enjoy some simple nightlife and buy some souvenirs. It is possible to do all this quite comfortably on US$30 to US$40 a day.

To save money on haircuts, men should go to a women's beauty shop – barbershops do manicures and massage, and some are fronts for prostitution. A haircut costs around W3000 in a beauty shop while a barbershop charges about W10,000.

Tipping

Tipping is generally not necessary or expected in Korea. A 10% service charge is added to the bill at tourist hotels which is a mandatory 'tip'. Like elsewhere, porters at international hotels also expect tips.

Bargaining

There is some latitude for bargaining in cheaper hotels, in street markets and with taxi drivers where they quote you a price before you set off. Politeness is the key word to remember when dealing with Koreans. Nastiness when bargaining will backfire on you in a big way and you'll come out the loser.

Consumer Taxes

Most items purchased in South Korea are subject to a 10% value-added tax (VAT) which is included in the selling price. At upmarket hotels there is also a 10% VAT, but you escape this at the budget hotels.

WHEN TO GO

The best time of year for a visit is autumn (from September to November). The sight of leaves turning red and yellow in autumn is considered one of Korea's great splendours. Even though there is always a possibility that a late typhoon could interfere with some of your sightseeing plans in September, the autumn period is generally a time of sunny skies and little rain.

Winter is dry and cold, but some travellers enjoy this season. There is no question that this is a very picturesque time in Korea, with brilliant skies and snow draping the roofs of temples. There are also opportunities to enjoy skiing. Except during the Christmas and Lunar New Year holidays, you can look forward to a scarcity of crowds almost everywhere you go. However, you need to deal with subzero temperatures.

April and May are beautiful with flowers blooming everywhere and mild temperatures. However, it's important to note that Japan has a holiday during the first week of May called 'golden week', and Japanese tourists flood into Korea at this time. The Japanese tend to book out all the top-end and mid-range accommodation, but the bottom-end hotels don't seem to be very heavily affected.

Summer is not a particularly good time to be in Korea. While it's the only time for the beach, you will have to deal with hot and muggy weather plus jumbo crowds of people in all scenic areas. Hotels even raise their prices at this time. This is also the wet season, in which Korea gets 70% of its annual rainfall. Occasional typhoons during summer can also hole you up in your hotel room for a couple of days and play havoc with a tight travel itinerary.

WHAT TO BRING

In most cases anything you forget to bring along can be purchased inexpensively in Seoul. If you plan on doing any camping or hiking – popular activities among the Koreans – the markets in Seoul are excellent places to pick up anything you need, and prices will generally be lower than you would pay at home.

Mosquito repellent and sunblock (UV) lotion are hard to come by. Shaving cream, vitamins and medicines also tend to be expensive, although not prohibitively so. Deodorant is only available from big tourist hotels, such as the Lotte Hotel pharmacy in Seoul. Tampons (tempo) are available from some pharmacies and supermarkets.

Luggage Storage

International airports have left-luggage facilities, but once you've passed through customs you will not be able to gain access to any luggage you leave until you depart the country. Needless to say, it will also be necessary to depart from the same airport.

Left-luggage rooms are exceedingly rare in Korea, although a few national parks have luggage rooms where you can store things while you go hiking. However, there are lockers at most major railway, subway and bus stations. These can be used for a maximum of three days – don't go over the limit or your goods could be confiscated and you'll have to pay a fine to get them back. The price for renting a locker varies from W300 to W700 and the machines accept W100 coins only. You feed money into the coin slot for the first day, but if you leave things overnight you must put in more coins to get them out again.

TOURIST OFFICES
Local Tourist Offices

The Korean National Tourism Corporation (KNTC) deserves a plug for being one of the most helpful and best organised tourist offices in Asia, if not the world. KNTC pro-

duces an extensive range of well-illustrated booklets and maps, and you can pick some of these up at the three international airports: Kimp'o (☎ 665-0088), Cheju (☎ (064) 42-0032) and Kimhae (☎ (051) 973-1100). KNTC has an excellent tourist information centre (☎ (02) 757-0086) in Seoul – see the Seoul chapter for details.

Almost every city has a tourist information centre in the city hall which exists to assist visitors. In large cities these offices are well equipped with English-speakers and maps, but in remote places the staff might only speak Korean and have scant literature to offer you. Not surprisingly, Seoul has the biggest and best tourist office, but you'll also find a decent one in Pusan city hall.

In some large cities, there are also information booths with English speakers located in crucial spots such as tourist attractions and some railway or bus stations. Again, these information booths are most numerous in Seoul, but they can be found elsewhere – the one in Kyŏngju may be particularly useful. See the relevant chapters for directions on where to find these booths.

KNTC Overseas Tourist Offices

Overseas, KNTC has offices in the following countries:

Australia
    17th Floor, Tower Bldg, Australia Square, George St, Sydney 2000 (☎ (02) 252-4147; fax 251-2104)
Canada
    Suite 406, 480 University Ave, Toronto, Ontario M5G 1V2 (☎ (416) 348-9056; fax 348-9058)
France
    Tour Maine Montparnesse, 33 Avenue de Maine, Paris (☎ (01) 45-38-71-23; fax 45-38-74-71)
Germany
    Mainzer Land Strasse 71, 60329 Frankfurt am Main 1 (☎ (069) 233226; fax 253519)
Hong Kong
    Suite 3203, 32nd Floor, Citibank Tower, 3 Garden Rd, Central (☎ 523-8065; fax 845-0765)
Japan
    Room 124, Sanshin Bldg, 4-1 1-chome, Yuraku-cho, Chiyoda-ku, Tokyo (☎ (03) 3580-3941; fax 3591-4601)
    Fukuoka (☎ (092) 471-7174)

Osaka (☎ (06) 266-0847)
Sapporo (☎ (011) 210-8081)
Singapore
24 Raffles Place, 20-03 Clifford Centre, Singapore 0104 (☎ 533-0441; fax 845-0765)
Switzerland
PO Box 343, CH-8126, Zumikon (☎ (01) 918-0882)
Taiwan
Room 1813, International Trade Centre Bldg, 333 Keelung Rd, Section 1, Taipei (☎ (02) 720-8049; fax 757-6514)
Thailand
15th Floor, Silom Complex, 191 Silom Rd, Bangkok 10500 (☎ 231-3895; fax 231-3897)
UK
2nd Floor, Vogue House, 1 Hanover Square, London W1R 9RD (☎ (071) 409-2100; fax 491-2302)
USA
3435 Wilshire Blvd, Suite 350, Los Angeles, CA 90010 (☎ (213) 382-3435; fax 480-0483)
205 North Michigan Ave, Suite 2212, Chicago, IL 60601 (☎ (312) 819-2560; fax 819-2563)
2 Executive Drive, 7th Floor, Fort Lee, NJ 07024 (☎ (201) 585-0909; fax 585-9041)

USEFUL ORGANISATIONS
Travellers' Complaints
If you have trouble with transport, food, shopping or accommodation, there is a KNTC Tourist Complaint Centre (☎ (02) 735-0101), 10 Ta-dong, Chung-gu, Seoul 100-180. For complaints about taxis and other transport, you can also try the Transportation Complaint Centre (☎ (02) 392-4745), 122 Pongnae-dong 2-ga, Chung-gu, Seoul 100-162.

Travellers' Assistance
Outside of Seoul, the provincial governments have offices to assist travellers experiencing difficulties: Taegu (☎ (053) 422-5611); Ch'ŏngju (☎ (0431) 52-0202); in all other cities, dial the area code followed by 0101.

Business Travellers
Business travellers might find it useful to contact one of the following organisations:

Federation of Korean Industries (FKI)
28-1 Yŏŭido-dong, Yŏngdŭngp'o-gu, Seoul (☎ (02) 780-0821; fax 782-6425)

Korea Chamber of Commerce & Industry (KCCI)
45 Namdaemunno 4-ga, Chung-gu, Seoul (☎ (02) 757-0757; fax 757-9475)
Korea Foreign Trade Association (KFTA)
159-1 Samsŏng-dong, Kangnam-gu, Seoul (☎ (02) 551-5114; 551-5100)
Korea World Trade Centre (KWTC)
159-1 Samsŏng-dong, Kangnam-gu, Seoul (☎ (02) 551-5114; fax 551-5100)
Korea Exhibition Centre (KOEX)
159-1 Samsŏng-dong, Kangnam-gu, Seoul (☎ (02) 551-0114; fax 555-7414)
Korea Trade Promotion Corporation (KOTRA)
159-1 Samsŏng-dong, Kangnam-gu, Seoul (☎ (02) 551-4181; fax 551-4477)

BUSINESS HOURS & HOLIDAYS
For most government offices, business hours are from 9 am to 6 pm Monday to Friday and from 9 am to 1 pm on Saturday. From November to February government offices close at 5 pm.

Private businesses normally operate from 8.30 am until 7 pm on weekdays, and from 8.30 am to 2 pm on Saturdays. Department stores are open from 10.30 am to 7.30 pm daily, while small shops may stay open from dawn until late at night.

There are two types of public holidays – those from the solar calendar and those from the lunar calendar. Solar holidays include:

1 & 2 January
New Year's Day
1 March
Independence Movement Day Anniversary of the 1919 Independence Movement against the Japanese.
5 April
Arbour Day Trees are planted across the nation as part of South Korea's ongoing reafforestation programme.
5 May
Children's Day
6 June
Memorial Day
17 July
Constitution Day
15 August
Liberation Day In memory of the Japanese acceptance of the Allied terms of surrender in 1945.
3 October
National Foundation Day
25 December
Christmas Day

Lunar holidays fall on different dates in different years. There are three lunar festivals which are designated public holidays:

Lunar New Year
Also called (sŏlnal), this holiday falls on the first day of the first moon. You can expect Korea (and the rest of North-East Asia) to grind to a halt. Future dates are: 31 January 1995, 19 February 1996, 7 February 1997, 28 January 1998, 16 February 1999, 5 February 2000.

Buddha's Birthday
Also called Feast of the Lanterns or (puch'ŏnim oshilnal), the holiday falls on the eighth day of the fourth moon. Future dates are: 7 May 1995, 24 May 1996, 14 May 1997, 3 May 1998, 22 May 1999, 11 May 2000.

Harvest Moon Festival
Korean Thanksgiving or (chusŏk) falls on the fifteenth day of the eighth moon and is the most important of South Korea's lunar holidays. Seoul is almost deserted as most city dwellers return to their family homes and prepare offerings for their ancestral tombs. As in other North-East Asian countries, moon viewing is another feature of the festival. Future dates are: 9 September 1995, 27 September 1996, 16 September 1997, 5 October 1998, 24 September 1999, 12 September 2000.

CULTURAL EVENTS
Festivals
There are a large number of festivals held annually throughout South Korea, as well as smaller festivals held only in particular locations. Some of the more important festivals include:

Sŏkchŏnje
This fascinating ceremony is held twice a year according to the lunar calendar (first day of the second moon, and first day of the eighth moon). In the solar calendar, it's roughly March and August. The ceremony is only staged in the courtyard of the Confucius Shrine at Sungkyunkwan University in the north of Seoul. Performances are done by a traditional court orchestra and full-costume rituals are enacted. To get to the university, take the subway to Hyehwa subway station.

Buddha's Birthday
This is held on the eighth day of the fourth moon (see the lunar holidays list). It's celebrated in Seoul with an evening lantern parade from Yŏŭido Plaza to the temple of Chogyesa, starting around 6.30 pm. On the same evening, there is a

similar lantern parade at Pŏpchusa, a temple in Songnisan National Park.

Chyongmyo T'aeje
Called the 'Royal Shrine Rites' in English, this is a homage to the kings and queens of the Chosŏn kingdom. Full costume parades are held along with court music. It takes place in Seoul's Chongmyo Shrine on the first Sunday of May.

Tano Festival
This is held throughout South Korea on the fifth day of the fifth lunar month (around June). The festival features processions of shamans and mask dance dramas.

National Folk Arts Festival
The date and the venue for the National Folk Arts Festival changes from year to year, but falls around September. It is an excellent opportunity to see traditional Korean festival activities, and includes real crowd-pullers like the wagon battle and torch-hurling events. Check with KNTC to find out when it's scheduled.

Cherry Blossom Festival
This week-long event is held in the southern city of Chinhae, usually occurring in the first half of April. An exact date is hard to give because the weather (and thus the cherry blossoms) won't always cooperate.

Paper Lantern hung to commemorate
Buddha's Birthday

POST & TELECOMMUNICATIONS
Postal Rates

Domestic rates are W110 for up to 50 grams and postcards cost W80. International rates vary according to region. The Korean postal service divides the world into four zones: Zone 1 is Japan, Taiwan, Hong Kong and Macau; Zone 2 is China and South-East Asia; Zone 3 is Australia, New Zealand, the USA, Middle East and Western Europe; Zone 4 is Latin America, Africa, Eastern Europe and the Pacific Islands. The rates are as follows:

	Zone 1	Zone 2	Zone 3	Zone 4
aerogrammes	W350	W350	W350	W350
postcards	W300	W300	W300	W300
letters (10 grams)	W370	W400	W440	W470
letters (20 grams)	W400	W460	W540	W600
registered letter (10 grams)	W1170	W1200	W1240	W1270
printed matter (20 grams)	W200	W220	W250	W300

Sending Mail

Post offices are open from 9 am to 6 pm Monday to Friday (9 am to 5 pm during winter) and from 9 am to noon on Saturday. Public mail boxes are always coloured red. Domestic mail can be delivered in about two days if it bears an address in Korean characters – if written in English, figure on a week.

If you're sending parcels or printed matter, don't worry about chasing around for cardboard boxes and the like. Major post offices like the Seoul CPO have excellent, inexpensive packing services.

Sending printed matter is about 40% cheaper than letters, but to get this discount you must seal the envelope with string rather than with tape or glue. The postal packing services know just how to prepare printed matter so that you can get this discount, so it's worth your while to let them do it.

If speed is of the utmost importance, you can send documents and small packets by Express Mail Service (EMS) Speedpost (*kokje t'ŭkgŭ pop'yŏn*).

Private Carriers

If you need to send things too large or valuable to trust to the post office, or simply need it done straight away, there are a number of foreign private carriers and courier services available. Most operate exclusively from Seoul. Some private carriers include Federal Express (☎ (02) 754-5011/9) and United Parcel Service (☎ (02) 323-0011/6).

Receiving Mail

Poste restante is available at all central city post offices, but only in Seoul and Pusan will you find a counter dealing exclusively with poste restante. Elsewhere, such letters may go astray because few postal workers speak English.

At poste restante counters, all incoming mail is entered into a logbook which you have to sign when you pick up mail – check carefully for your name as letters are often misfiled. Hotels will hold mail for a limited period, and perhaps a longer period if you let them know you are expecting mail.

The Inn Daewon – a favourite of travellers on a budget – has a box for letters that have come in. Some of them seem to have been there for many months, so it's probably safe to say that this one would serve well as a long-term poste restante.

Telephone

There is a 30% discount on calls made between 9 pm and 8 am Monday to Saturday and all day on Sundays and public holidays.

Pay phones accept three types of coins, W10, W50 and W100 (but *not* W500). Pay phones can be used for local and long distance calls, and there is no time limit as long as you keep feeding money into the machine. The cost for local calls is W30 for three minutes.

When using local-call phones you will often find that the phone is off the hook and there is still a credit on the phone. The reason for this is that it is not possible to get change from a W50 or W100 coin, but you can use the credit from a W30 call to make further calls as long as you don't hang up. To make another call, simply press the green button on the phone (but it doesn't always work).

Korea abounds with card phones and these can be used for local, long-distance and international calls. The magnetic telephone cards come in denominations of W3000, W5000 and W10,000 but these are discounted to W2900, W4800 and W9500 respectively. The phone cards (*chŏnhwa kadŭ*) can be bought from banks, shops near the card telephones and 24-hour convenience stores. The cards are notoriously poor quality – the charge on the cards will often disappear a week or two after you've broken the seal on the plastic packet! If this happens, try flexing the card (not too vigorously) and it *might* reappear again. If not, take the card to any phone company office and it will be exchanged for free. Needless to say, this is a hassle best avoided, so try to purchase the minimum denomination (W3000) cards and use them up quickly before they go bad.

Of course, you will need to know the area codes when dialling outside your local calling area. It's worth noting that the first two digits of an area code gives a hint as to what part of the country you're calling: 03 is the northern region, 04 is west-central, 05 is south-east and 06 is south-west. The following area codes are for major cities:

Seoul 02, Inch'ŏn 032, Kwangju 062, Pusan 051, Taegu 053, Taejŏn 042

The area codes for major towns by province are:

Kyŏnggi-do Ansan 0345, Ansŏng 0334, Hwasong 0339, Ich'ŏn 0336, Kanghwa 0349, Kapyong 0356, Kimp'o 0341, Koyang 0344, Kuri 0346, Kwangju 0347, P'aju 0348, P'och'ŏn 0357, P'yŏngt'aek 0333, Sanjŏng Lake 0357, Sŏngnam 0342, Suwon 0331, Uijŏngbu 0351, Yangp'yŏng 0338, Yonchon 0355, Yong-in 0335, Yŏju 0337

Kangwon-do Ch'unch'ŏn 0361, Cholwon 0353, Chŏngson 0398, Hoengsŏng 0372, Hongch'ŏn 0366, Hwach'ŏn 0363, Inje 0365, Kangnŭng 0391, Naksan 0396, Osaek Hot Springs 0396, P'yŏngch'ang 0374, Samch'ŏk 0397, Sokch'o 0392, Sŏrak-dong 0392, T'aebaek 0395, Tonghae 0394, Wŏnju 0371, Yangyang 0396, Yanggu 0364, Yŏngwol 0373

Ch'ungch'ŏngbuk-do Ch'ŏngju 0431, Ch'ungju 0441, Chech'ŏn 0443, Chinch'ŏn 0434, Koesan 0445, Okch'ŏn 0475, Poŭn 0433, Songnisan 0433, Suanbo 0441, Tanyang 0444, Umsong 0446, Yongdong 0414

Ch'ungch'ŏngnam-do Ch'ŏnan 0417, Choch'iwan 0415, Chongyang 0454, Hongsŏng 0451, Kongju 0416, Kŭmsan 0412, Nonsan 0461, Onyang 0418, Puyŏ 0463, Sosan 0455, Sŏch'on 0459, Taech'ŏn 0452, Tangjin 0457, Yesan 0458

Kyŏngsangbuk-do Andong 0571, Ch'ŏngdo 0542, Ch'ŏngsong 0575, Chŏmch'on 0581, Chuwangsan 0575, Hayang 0541, Kimch'ŏn 0547, Koryŏng 0543, Kumi 0546, Kunwi 0578, Kyŏngju 0561, P'ohang 0562, Ponghwa 0573, Sangju 0582, Sŏngju 0544, Uljin 0565, Ullŭngdo 0566, Ŭisŏng 0576, Waegwan 0545, Yŏngch'ŏn 0563, Yŏngdŏk 0564, Yŏngju 0572, Yŏngyang 0574

Kyŏngsangnam-do Ch'angnyŏng 0559, Ch'angwon 0551, Ch'ungmu 0557, Chinhae 0553, Chinju 0591, Hadong 0595, Haman 0552, Hamyang 0597, Hapch'ŏn 0599, Kimhae 0525, Koje 0558, Kosŏng 0556, Kŏch'ang 0598, Miryang 0527, Namhae 0594, Samch'ŏnp'o 0593, Sanch'ŏng 0596, Taewonsa 0596, Ulsan 0522, Ŭiryŏng 0555, Yangsan 0523

Chŏllabuk-do Changsu 0656, Chinan 0655, Chŏngju 0681, Chŏnju 0652, Imshil 0673, Iri 0653, Kimje 0658, Koch'ang 0677, Kunsan 0654, Moaksan 0658, Muju 0657, Namwon 0671, Puan 0683, Sunch'ang 0674, Sŏnunsan 0677

Chŏllanam-do Changhŭng 0665, Changsŏng 0685, Chindo 0632, Haenam 0634, Hamp'yŏng 0615, Hongdo 0631, Hŭksando 0631, Hwasun 0612, Kangjin 0638, Kohŭng 0666, Koksŏng 0688, Mokp'o 0631, Wando 0633, Yŏng-am 0693, Yŏnggwang 0686, Yŏsu 0662

Cheju-do Cheju 064

International Calls International Direct Dialling (IDD) calls can be placed through Korea Telecom (dial 001) or Dacom (dial 002). Calls placed through Dacom are 5% cheaper, but you can only do this from a private phone – Korea Telecom owns the public phones and their phones will not connect to Dacom. To make an IDD call, first dial 001 (or 002), then the country code, area code (minus the initial zero if it has one) and then the number you want to reach. You receive a 30% discount on calls made between 9 pm and 8 am (Monday to Saturday) and all day on Sundays and holidays.

To place an international call through an English-speaking operator, dial 0077. For information about international dialling (country codes, rates, time differences etc, dial 0074). Placing a call through an international operator means that you must pay for a three-minute minimum call. There are four types of operator-assisted calls: station to station, person to person, reverse charges and credit card calls.

The following are the daytime IDD rates when dialling the 001 prefix:

Region	First Minute	Additional Minutes
South-East Asia	W1210	W900
North America & Oceania	W1580	W1180
Europe, West Asia		
Latin America & Africa	W1860	W1400
UK	W1510	W1130

Another dialling option is called 'home country direct', which allows you to talk directly to an operator in the country which you are calling. This system is useful only for collect calls or if you want to charge to a credit card, and it's not available for every country. There are two ways to make a call from a public card phone using home country direct: 1) using a phone card; 2) *without* using a phone card. For option No 1, insert the card, dial 0090 (or 0091 for the USA) plus the country direct number (see the following list). For option No 2, press the red button on the card phone, dial the special code (see following list) and then the asterisk. The codes you need for home country direct dialling are as follows:

Country	With Card	Without Card
Australia	0090+610	Red+17+*
Brazil	0090+055	–
Canada	0090+015	Red+10+*
Chile	0090+560	–
Denmark	0090+450	–
Finland	0090+358	–
France	0090+330	–
Germany	0090+049	–
Guam	0090+671	Red+07+*
Hawaii	0090+012	Red+14+*
Hong Kong	0090+852	Red+13+*
Hungary	0090+036	Red+01+*
Indonesia	0090+620	Red+08+*
Italy	0090+390	Red+20+*

Japan	0090+081	Red+12+*
Macau	0090+853	–
Malaysia	0090+060	Red+05+*
Netherlands	0090+310	Red+16+*
New Zealand	0090+640	–
Philippines (Philcom)	0090+631	–
(PLDT)	0090+630	–
Portugal	0090+351	Red+19+*
Singapore	0090+650	Red+09+*
Spain	0090+034	–
Taiwan	0090+886	Red+04+*
Thailand	0090+660	Red+18+*
UK (BT)	0090+440	Red+15+*
(Mercury)	0090+441	–
USA, AT&T	0091+1	Red+11+*
IDB	0091+8	–
MCI	0091+4	Red+03+*
Sprint	0091+6	Red+02+*

Useful Phone Numbers The *Korea Yellow Pages* is published annually in English, and is available from major bookshops in Seoul. There are no white pages available in English, so you'll have to manage with han'gŭl. A few useful telephone numbers and prefixes could include the following:

IDD, Korea Telecom	☎ 001
IDD, Dacom	☎ 002
Korea's Country Code	– 82
Phone Repairs	☎ 110
Police	☎ 112
Report A Spy	☎ 113
Directory Assistance	☎ 114
International Operator	☎ 0077
International Dialling Assistance	☎ 0074
Telegram (domestic)	☎ 115
Telegram (international)	☎ 005
Time	☎ 116
Ambulance	☎ 119
Fire	☎ 119
Weather (Seoul)	☎ 131
Immigration (Seoul)	☎ 653-3041

Fax, Telex & Telegraph
If you want to send a telegram, it's probably easiest to go to the telephone office and write it out on paper. However, you can call one in on a private phone by dialling 115 (domestic) or 005 (international). Domestic telegrams are of two types: ordinary and express. Domestic telegrams in English cost W80 per word and express costs W160 per

word. For international telegrams the cost per word is as follows:

Australia W660, Canada W430, France W450, Germany W430, Hong Kong W270, Japan W240, Taiwan W240, UK W610 and USA W280

In big cities like Seoul, you can always find business centres at upmarket hotels which have fax and telex machines. This will be easier than handling it at a post office, as hotel staff will generally speak better English and be more accustomed to dealing with foreigners.

Electronic Mail

If you're daunted by bits, bytes and keyboards, don't bother reading this section – it's for computer buffs only. Electronic mail (E-mail or *chonja meil*) offers a number of advantages over fax machines, but you need a computer, modem, a bit of spare cash and enough free time to learn the in-and-outs of telecomputing.

There are a number of Korean companies that offer domestic E-mail, with gateways to international services. Korea's only E-mail operator that caters to English speakers is POS-Serve and they are also CompuServe's representative.

Short-term visitors with a credit card can get connected by subscribing to POS-Serve. If you already belong to CompuServe, simply plug a phone line into your modem and dial ☎ (02) 561-7611. When you reach the @ prompt, type CNS, hit the enter key and you will be connected to CompuServe. The connect time charges (W200 per minute) will automatically be billed to your CompuServe account. If you need assistance, enquire at POS-Serve's representative in Korea, ATEL (☎ (02) 528-0467; fax 528-0597), 942-1 Taechi-dong, Kangnam-gu, Seoul.

Korea's two phone companies, Dacom and Korea Telecom, operate several E-mail and database services for people who read Korean. Dacom's Chollian (☎ 220-7077, 220-7057) seems to be the most popular service, but Dacom also runs Hitel which is geared more towards business users and researchers. Korea Telecom operates Ketel which is also geared towards technical and business users.

The information superhighway has not gone unnoticed by Korea's Ministry of Information and its special branch dealing with foreigners, the Korean Overseas Information Service (KOIS). In co-operation with POS-Serve and Chollian, KOIS has launched KOISnet, an online information network covering a wide range of Korean topics. The ever-enterprising KNTC has gotten into the act, and is developing a special section of KOISnet dealing with tourism. This will be in English, and foreigners with access to the Internet or CompuServe may wish to participate. This is a new service and details are sketchy – contact KNTC in Seoul (☎ (02) 757-0086) for more details.

TIME

The time in South Korea is Greenwich Mean Time plus nine hours. When it is noon in South Korea it is 2 pm in Sydney, 3 am in London, 10 pm the previous day in New York and 7 pm the previous day in Los Angeles or San Francisco. Daylight savings time is *not* observed.

ELECTRICITY

Both 110 V and 220 V are in common use. The way to tell the difference is from the design of the electrical outlets – two flat pins is 110 V and two round pins is 220 V. There is no third wire for ground (earth).

LAUNDRY

Most hotels, including cheap *yŏgwan*, can do laundry if you prefer not to do it yourself. Charges for this service are usually reasonable, but ask first.

Laundromats do exist in large cities (especially Seoul) and are most common around university areas. Charges are typically W4000 for a large load.

WEIGHTS & MEASURES

In former times, Korea used the traditional Chinese system of weights and measures.

Nowadays, the international metric system is used for everything except the measurement of real estate. In the case of buying or renting a flat, area is measured in *p'yŏng* with one p'yŏng being equal to 3.3 sq metres.

BOOKS & MAPS

There is good news and bad news. The good news is that there are some excellent books in print about Korea, covering the country's history, religion and culture. The bad news is that these books are hard to obtain outside Korea. Furthermore, Seoul is really the only place in Korea to go hunting for books printed in English, although you might stumble across something in Pusan. Outside of Korea, you will probably have to obtain books by special order.

History

One of the most up-to-date histories is *Korean Old & New – A History* (Korea Institute, Harvard University). Also very current is *Korea, Tradition & Transformation* by Andrew C Nahm (Hollym Publications, Seoul).

The entire Chosŏn dynasty is well-covered by *The Confucian Transformation of Korea* by Martina Deuchler. The same author also did a fine earlier work, *Confucian Gentlemen & Barbarian Envoys* which covers the opening of Korea between 1875 and 1885.

Culture & Society

A good primer is *Korea's Cultural Roots* by Joan Carter Covell which covers shamanism, Confucianism and Buddhism. Sequels by the same author include *Korea's Colorful Heritage* and *The World of Korean Ceramics*. Teaming up with her son Alan, the Covell's produced *Korean Impact on Japanese Culture – Japan's Hidden History*. Alan Covell went on to write *Folk Art & Magic – Shamanism in Korea*. All these books are published by Hollym Publications in Seoul.

Those interested in South Korea's economy should pick up a copy of *The Chaebol* by Steers, Shin & Ungson (Harper & Row, New York, 1989).

Religion

Korea, A Religious History by James Huntley Grayson (Oxford University Press) is a fine scholarly work.

To understand the heart and soul of Korean Confucianism, the book to read is *To Become A Sage – The Ten Diagrams on Sage Learning* by Yi T'oegye (Columbia University, New York).

Two intellectual works from the Asian Humanities Press in Berkeley, California, are *Introduction of Buddhism to Korea* and *Assimilation of Buddhism in Korea* by Lancaster & Yu.

Guidebooks

Korea, A Sensory Journey (Woojin Publications, Seoul) by Marc Verin, David A Mason & Ji Eun Park, is the best coffee table guidebook on the country.

Korea Guide – A Glimpse of Korea's Cultural Legacy by Edward B Adams (Seoul International Publishing House) is highly informative and colourful. If you want to appreciate the splendour of Kyŏngju, the same author has done a magnificent job in *Korea's Golden Age*.

Discovering Seoul: An Historical Guide (RAS Publications 1986) by James Grayson & Donald Clark is strong on historical Seoul, and is useful for those who want to identify every nook and cranny of the palaces. *Seoul* (Times Editions 1988) by Rose E Lee is a good introduction to the city.

For illuminating background reading and good photographs, turn to the Insight Guide *Korea* (APA Publications 1991). Lonely Planet publishes a *Seoul City Guide* and *North East Asia on a shoestring*.

Language

Unlike Chinese and Japanese, Korean has not caught on as a popular language for Westerners to learn, and consequently much of the Korean language teaching and self-study material available seems dated and badly organised. Lonely Planet's *Korean Phrasebook*, is a basic guide to phrases that you might need while travelling around. The Berlitz *Korean for Travellers* is a more complex phrasebook. To delve further into the language, *An Introductory Course in Korean* by Fred Lukoff (Yonsei University Press) is a popular textbook available within Korea.

Bookshops

In Seoul, the three best places to pick up books about Korea are the English-language sections of the Kyobo Book Centre, the Ŭlchi Book Centre and the Royal Asiatic Society. The latter, with its specialist collection of titles on Korea is probably the best, and they will even provide a stool for browsing in comfort. Another drawcard of the Royal Asiatic Society is that they put out a publications list. This provides information on virtually every book available relevant to Korea.

Maps

The KNTC has a number of giveaway maps, and these are certainly worth picking up. Do this in Seoul because these maps are not readily available elsewhere.

Korea's largest retail outlet for maps is Chung'ang Atlas Map Service (☎ (02) 720-9191), 125-1 Gongpyeong Dong, Chongno-gu, Seoul. Maps here come in two sizes – big and enormous. If you are planning on doing any serious hiking this is certainly the place to come and stock up.

If you plan on driving or cycling in South Korea, take a look at the *Korea Road Atlas* (Chung'ang Atlas Company). This contains detailed road maps with all major points of interest, plus many reasonably detailed city maps. Unfortunately, it's partially in English and the rest in Chinese characters (rather than han'gŭl script). You'll do better to get an atlas which has han'gŭl script – a good one is *Road Maps to Tourist Attractions in Korea*. These atlases and fold-out maps can be bought at major bookshops.

In every large town, the tourist office at the city hall has excellent and detailed maps. These usually are in han'gŭl and English and often they are given away for free. Unfortunately, the staff generally can't speak English and they often run out of maps. Still,

it could be worth a try if you want something more detailed than what is available in atlases.

Very few maps produced in Korea (both North and South) show the heavily-fortified DMZ. The idea is to maintain the illusion that Korea is an undivided nation. Unaware of Korea's politics, a few travellers have been misled by the maps to such an extent that they thought they could travel north all the way to China. You can rest assured that this is impossible – despite the creative map-making, the border between the two Koreas does indeed exist and you cannot cross it.

MEDIA

Newspapers & Magazines

There are two locally produced English-language newspapers available: the *Korea Times* and the *Korea Herald*. These papers are printed daily except Monday and public holidays. Apart from the titles, it's rather difficult to tell the two newspapers apart, and many local residents maintain that they are identical newspapers.

Korea Economic Report is a worthwhile monthly publication costing W4000 per issue. Annual subscriptions cost as follows: Korea (US$50); the rest of Asia (US$78); Africa & South America (US$85); Europe, Oceania and North America (US$82). To subscribe, contact Korea Economic Report (☎ (02) 783-5283/7; fax 780-1717), Yŏido PO Box 963, Seoul 150-609.

Some other local monthly magazines in English include the *Korea Post* and *Business Korea*.

Large bookshops in Seoul and most of the large hotels sell imported publications. The best coverage of Korea in foreign publications seems to be in the *Asian Wall Street Journal* and the *Economist*.

In the not too distant past, the Korean-language news media was little more than a mouthpiece for the government. However, things have changed considerably, and the news media has become increasingly critical and outspoken.

Perhaps most interesting are the leftist publications circulated by students on university campuses. This includes *Rodong Shinmun*, a North Korean hardline communist mouthpiece. There are also taped radio broadcasts from P'yŏngyang's *Voice of National Salvation*. It's here where you'll find xenophobic diatribes against foreigners committing heinous crimes against the Korean people, like trying to force open South Korea's closed markets.

Radio & TV

There are four Korean-language TV networks: KBS, MBC, SBS and EBS. A few programmes are bilingual, but a special TV is needed to switch between Korean and English. Korean TV broadcasts on weekdays from 6 am to 10 am and from 5.30 pm until midnight; on Saturdays from 6 am to 10 am and from 1 pm until midnight; and on Sundays from 6 am until midnight.

AFKN is an English-language station run by the US military and features typical US shows, but with judicious censorship of the sex scenes so as to not offend Korean sensibilities. The commercial advertising is replaced with military advice and safety tips like 'wear your uniform proudly' and 'driving and alcohol don't mix'. Broadcasting is 24 hours a day, although it's mostly trash between midnight and 6 am. An odd coalition of extreme Korean leftists and right-wingers has for years been trying to get AFKN banned from the airwaves, but so far it hasn't happened. However, AFKN's signal is weak outside of Seoul except near US military bases.

AFKN radio broadcasts in English 24 hours a day on AM (549 kHz) and FM (102.7 mHz). A complete schedule of TV and radio programmes is listed in the daily English-language newspapers. Unlike AFKN TV, you should have no problem picking up the signal outside of Seoul.

Video

For those with the right equipment there are video rental shops in abundance and satellite TV hookups. Video tapes from abroad will only work in South Korean video tape players if they are NTSC standard. This is the same standard used in the USA, Canada and Japan, but is incompatible with the PAL standard (Australia, UK etc) and SECAM (France).

FILM & PHOTOGRAPHY

Unless you're a professional, there's no need to worry about your film needs. All the big-name brands of print film are readily available in Korea and at reasonable prices. Photoprocessing facilities are of an international standard and also not expensive.

Slide film is a little more difficult to come by, and is most readily available in Seoul. See the Seoul section for details.

For processing slide film, prices seem to vary depending on where you ask. Professional photoprocessing shops are often cheapest and fastest, usually offering one-day service. Ordinary camera shops can take three days and charge double.

Korea is not a particularly good place to buy photographic equipment due to prohibitive import taxes. If you're going further afield to Hong Kong, Singapore, Taipei or even Tokyo, you should wait. There are, however, a couple of areas in major cities with hole-in-the-wall second-hand camera shops.

A related point is that the traditional Korean ondol or underfloor heating system can do nasty things to your film if you leave it or your camera on the floor.

Be careful about taking liberties photographing monks. South Korea is a country still technically at war, and photographing military installations or anything of a military nature is prohibited. Student rioters are not particularly fond of being photographed.

HEALTH

Travel health depends on your predeparture preparations, your day-to-day health care while travelling and how you handle any medical problem or emergency that does develop. While the list of potential dangers can seem quite frightening, with a little luck, some basic precautions and adequate information, few travellers experience more than upset stomachs.

Predeparture Preparations

Health Insurance A travel insurance policy to cover theft, loss and medical problems is a wise idea. There are a wide variety of policies and your travel agent will have recommendations. The international student travel policies handled by STA Travel or other student travel organisations are usually good value. Some policies offer lower and higher medical expenses options but the higher one is chiefly for countries like the USA which have extremely high medical costs. Check the small print:

- Some policies specifically exclude 'dangerous activities' which can include scuba diving, motorbiking, even trekking. If such activities are on your agenda you don't want that sort of policy. A locally acquired motor cycle licence may not be valid under your policy.
- You may prefer a policy which pays doctors or hospitals direct rather than you having to pay on the spot and claim later. If you have to claim later make sure you keep all documentation. Some policies ask you to call back (reverse charges) to a centre in your home country where an immediate assessment of your problem is made.
- Check if the policy covers ambulances or an emergency flight home. If you have to stretch out you will need two seats and somebody has to pay for them!

Medical Kit A small, straightforward medical kit is a wise thing to carry. A possible kit list includes:

- Aspirin or Panadol – for pain or fever.
- Antihistamine (such as Benadryl) – useful as a decongestant for colds, allergies, to ease the itch from insect bites or stings or to help prevent motion sickness. Antihistamines may cause sedation and interact with alcohol so care should be taken when using them.
- Antibiotics – useful if you're travelling well off the beaten track, but they must be prescribed and you should carry the prescription with you. Some individuals are allergic to commonly prescribed antibiotics such as penicillin or sulfa drugs. It would be sensible to always carry this information when travelling.
- Kaolin preparation (Pepto-Bismol), Imodium or Lomotil – for stomach upsets.
- Rehydration mixture – for treatment of severe diarrhoea. This is particularly important if travelling with children, but is recommended for everyone.
- Antiseptic such as Betadine, which comes as impregnated swabs or ointment, and an antibiotic powder or similar 'dry' spray – for cuts and grazes.
- Calamine lotion – to ease irritation from bites or stings.
- Bandages and Band-aids – for minor injuries.
- Scissors, tweezers and a thermometer (note that mercury thermometers are prohibited by airlines).
- Insect repellent, sunscreen, suntan lotion, chap stick and water purification tablets.

Ideally, antibiotics should be administered only under medical supervision and should never be taken indiscriminately. Take only the recommended dose at the prescribed intervals and continue using the antibiotic for the prescribed period, even if the illness seems to be cured earlier. Antibiotics are quite specific to the infections they can treat. Stop immediately if there are any serious reactions and don't use the antibiotic at all if you are unsure that you have the correct one.

Health Preparations Make sure you're healthy before you start travelling. If you are embarking on a long trip make sure your teeth are OK. If you wear glasses take a spare pair and your prescription. If you require a particular medication take an adequate supply, as it may not be available in South Korea. Take the prescription or, better still, part of the packaging showing the generic rather than the brand name (which may not be locally available), as it will make getting replacements easier. It's a wise idea to have a legible prescription with you to show you legally use the medication.

Immunisation

No vaccinations are required to enter South Korea, although this doesn't mean you shouldn't get any. Especially if you'll be travelling to neighbouring Asian countries (such as China), it certainly isn't a bad idea to get a few prophylactic jabs. Shots recommended by vaccination enthusiasts include cholera, rabies, hepatitis B, BCG (tuberculosis), polio, and TABT (protects against typhoid, paratyphoid A and B, and tetanus) and diphtheria.

That having been said, South Korea is a very healthy country – you are unlikely to encounter any of the things that might have you running for the nearest pharmacy in India, the Philippines or Indonesia.

Basic Rules

Food & Water Care in what you eat and drink is the most important health rule; stomach upsets are the most likely travel health problem (between 30% and 50% of travellers in a two-week stay experience this) but the majority of these upsets will be relatively minor. Don't become paranoid; trying the local food is part of the experience of travel, after all.

Water The number one rule is *don't drink the water* and that includes ice. If you don't know for certain that the water is safe always assume the worst. If you do drink unboiled water there is little chance of contracting serious intestinal infections and it's unlikely you'll suffer anything more serious than diarrhoea. Reputable brands of bottled water or soft drinks are generally fine, although in some places bottles refilled with tap water are not unknown. Only use water from containers with a serrated seal – not tops or corks. Take care with fruit juice, particularly if water may have been added. Milk should be treated with suspicion, as it is often unpasteurised. Boiled milk is fine if it is kept hygienically and yoghurt is always good. Tea or coffee should also be OK, since the water should have been boiled.

Food There is an old colonial adage which says: 'If you can cook it, boil it or peel it you can eat it...otherwise forget it'. Salads and fruit should be washed with purified water or peeled where possible. Ice cream is usually OK if it is a reputable brand name, but beware of Third World street vendors and of ice cream that has melted and been refrozen. Thoroughly cooked food is safest but not if it has been left to cool or if it has been reheated. Shellfish such as mussels, oysters and clams should be avoided as well as undercooked meat, particu-larly in the form of mince. Steaming does not make shellfish safe for eating.

If a place looks clean and well run and if the vendor also looks clean and healthy, then the food is probably safe. In general, places that are packed with travellers or locals will be fine, while empty restaurants are questionable. Busy restaurants mean the food is being cooked and eaten quite quickly and is probably not being reheated.

Nutrition If your food is poor or limited in availability, if you're travelling hard and fast and therefore missing meals, or if you simply lose your appetite, you can soon start to lose weight and place your health at risk.

Make sure your diet is well balanced. Eggs, tofu, beans, lentils and nuts are all safe ways to get protein. Fruit you can peel (bananas, oranges or mandarins for example) is always safe and a good source of vitamins. Try to eat plenty of grains (rice) and bread. Remember that although food is generally safer if it is cooked well, over-cooked food loses much of its nutritional value. If your diet isn't well balanced or if your food intake is insufficient, it's a good idea to take vitamin and iron pills.

Everyday Health A normal body temperature is $98.6°F$ or $37°C$; more than $2°C$ higher is a 'high' fever. A normal adult pulse rate is 60 to 80 per minute (children 80 to 100, babies 100 to 140). You should know how to take a temperature and a pulse rate. As a general rule, the pulse increases about 20 beats per minute for each $°C$ rise in fever.

Respiration (breathing) rate is also an indicator of illness. Count the number of breaths per minute: between 12 and 20 is normal for adults and older children (up to 30 for younger children, 40 for babies). People with a high fever or serious respiratory illness (like pneumonia) breathe more quickly than normal. More than 40 shallow breaths a minute usually mean pneumonia.

Medical Problems & Treatment

Potential medical problems can be broken down into several areas. First there are the climatic and geographical considerations – problems caused by extremes of temperature, altitude or motion. Then there are diseases and illnesses caused through poor environmental sanitation, insect bites or stings, and animal or human contact. Simple cuts, bites or scratches can also cause problems.

Self-treatment poses some risks, but Korean pharmacists are willing to sell you all sorts of dangerous drugs over the counter without a prescription. Korean pharmacists know the English names of most drugs but can't pronounce them. However, they can generally read English well, so try writing down what you want to avoid misunderstandings. Pharmacies seem to be everywhere, and can be found in most bus terminals. To find a Korean pharmacy, simply look for the character:

약

Although we do give treatment dosages in this section, they are for emergency use only. Medical advice should be sought where possible before administering any drugs. An embassy or consulate can usually recommend a good place to go for such advice. So can five-star hotels, although they often recommend doctors with five-star prices. (This is when that medical insurance really comes in useful!)

Diseases of Poor Sanitation

Diarrhoea A change of water, food or climate can all cause the runs; diarrhoea caused by contaminated food or water is more serious. Despite all your precautions you may still have a bout of mild travellers' diarrhoea but a few rushed toilet trips with no other symptoms is not indicative of a serious problem. Moderate diarrhoea, involving half-a-dozen loose movements in a day, is more of a nuisance. Dehydration is the main danger with any diarrhoea, particularly for children where dehydration can occur quite quickly. Fluid replacement remains the mainstay of management. Weak black tea with a little sugar, soda water, or soft drinks allowed to go flat and diluted 50% with water are all good. With severe diarrhoea a rehydrating solution is necessary

to replace minerals and salts. Commercially available oral rehydration salts (ORS) is very useful; add the contents of one sachet to a litre of boiled or bottled water. In an emergency you can make up a solution of eight teaspoons of sugar to a litre of boiled water and provide salted cracker biscuits at the same time. You should stick to a bland diet as you recover.

Lomotil or Imodium can be used to bring relief from the symptoms, although they do not actually cure the problem. Only use these drugs if absolutely necessary: if you *must* travel. For children, Imodium is preferable, but under all circumstances fluid replacement is the main message. Do not use these drugs if the person has a high fever or is severely dehydrated.

In certain situations, antbiotics may be indicated:

Watery diarrhoea with blood and mucus. (Gut-paralysing drugs like Imodium or Lomotil should be avoided in this situation.)
Watery diarrhoea with fever and lethargy.
Persistent diarrhoea for more than five days.
Severe diarrhoea, if it is logistically difficult to stay in one place.

Giardiasis The parasite causing this intestinal disorder is present in contaminated water. The symptoms are stomach cramps, nausea, a bloated stomach, watery, foul-smelling diarrhoea and frequent gas. Giardiasis can appear several weeks after you have been exposed to the parasite. The symptoms may disappear for a few days and then return; this can go on for several weeks. Tinidazole, known as Fasigyn, or metronidazole Flagyl are the recommended drugs for treatment. Either can be used in a single treatment dose. Antbiotics are of no use.

Viral Gastroenteritis This is caused not by bacteria but, as the name suggests, by a virus. It is characterised by stomach cramps, diarrhoea, and sometimes by vomiting and/or a slight fever. All you can do is rest and drink lots of fluids.

Hepatitis Hepatitis A is a very common

problem among travellers to areas with poor sanitation. With good water and adequate sewage disposal in most industrialised countries since the 1940s, very few young adults now have any natural immunity and must be protected. Protection is through the new vaccine Havrix or the antibody gammaglobulin. The antibody is short-lasting.

The disease is spread by contaminated food or water. The symptoms are fever, chills, headache, fatigue, feelings of weakness and aches and pains, followed by loss of appetite, nausea, vomiting, abdominal pain, dark urine, light-coloured faeces, jaundiced skin and the whites of the eyes may turn yellow. In some cases you may feel unwell, tired, have no appetite, experience aches and pains and be jaundiced. You should seek medical advice, but in general

there is not much you can do apart from rest, drink lots of fluids, eat lightly and avoid fatty foods. People who have had hepatitis must forego alcohol for six months after the illness, as hepatitis attacks the liver and it needs that amount of time to recover.

Hepatitis B, which used to be called serum hepatitis, is spread through contact with infected blood, blood products or bodily fluids: sexual contact, unsterilised needles and blood transfusions. Other risk situations include having a shave or tattoo in a local shop, or having your ears pierced. The symptoms of type B are much the same as type A except that they are more severe and may lead to irreparable liver damage or even liver cancer. Although there is no treatment for hepatitis B, an effective prophylactic vaccine is readily available in most countries. The

Acupuncture

Can you cure people by sticking needles into them? The Chinese think so, and the Koreans borrowed the concept along with other aspects of Chinese culture. Acupuncture is still widely available in Korea, and some of the young acupuncturists even speak English. Many of the traditional herbal doctors also perform acupuncture. Now the technique of acupuncture is gaining adherents in the West.

Getting stuck with needles might not sound pleasant, but if done properly it doesn't hurt. Knowing just where to insert the needle is crucial. Acupuncturists have identified more than 2000 insertion points, but only about 150 are commonly used.

The exact mechanism by which acupuncture works is not fully understood. Practitioners talk of energy channels or meridians which connect the needle insertion point to the particular organ, gland or joint being treated. The acupuncture point is sometimes quite far from the area of the body being treated. Acupuncture is even used to treat impotency, but it might be better not to ask just where the needle is inserted.

As with herbal medicine, the fundamental question asked by potential acupuncture patients is: 'Does it work?' The answer has to be: 'That depends.' It depends on the skill of the acupuncturist and the condition being treated. Like herbal medicine, acupuncture tends to be more useful for those who suffer from long-term conditions (like chronic headaches) rather than sudden emergencies (like an acute appendicitis).

However, there are times when acupuncture can be used for an immediate condition. For example, some major surgical operations have been performed using acupuncture as the only aneesthetic (this works best on the head). In this case, a small electric current (from batteries) is passed through the needles. This is a good example of how Western medicine and traditional medicine can be usefully combined.

Suction is a related technique. This employs suction cups made of bamboo placed on the patient's skin. A burning piece of alcohol-soaked cotton is briefly put inside the cup to drive out the air before it is applied. As the cup cools, a partial vacuum is produced, leaving a nasty-looking but harmless red circular mark on the skin. The mark goes away in a few days.

Moxibustion is another variation on the theme. Various types of herbs, rolled into what looks like a ball of fluffy cotton, are held near the skin and ignited. A slight variation of this method is to place the herb on a slice of ginger and then ignite it. The idea is to apply the maximum amount of heat possible without burning the patient. This heat treatment is supposed to be good for such diseases as arthritis. ■

immunisation schedule requires two injections at least a month apart followed by a third dose five months after the second. Persons who should receive a hepatitis B vaccination include anyone who anticipates contact with blood or other bodily secretions, either as a health care worker or through sexual contact with the local population, particularly those who intend to stay in the country for a long period of time.

Hepatitis Non-A Non-B is a blanket term formerly used for several different strains of hepatitis, which have now been separately identified. Hepatitis C is similar to B but is less common. Hepatitis D (the 'delta particle') is also similar to B and always occurs in concert with it; its occurrence is currently limited to intravenous drug users. Hepatitis E, however, is similar to A and is spread in the same manner, by water or food contamination.

Tests are available for these strands, but are very expensive. Travellers shouldn't be too paranoid about this apparent proliferation of hepatitis strains; they are fairly rare (so far) and following the same precautions as for A and B should be all that's necessary to avoid them.

Sexually Transmitted Diseases
Sexual contact with an infected partner spreads these diseases. While abstinence is the only 100% preventative, using condoms is also effective. Gonorrhoea and syphilis are the most common of these diseases; sores, blisters or rashes around the genitals, discharges or pain when urinating are common symptoms. Symptoms may be less marked or not observed at all in women. Syphilis symptoms eventually disappear completely but the disease continues and can cause severe problems in later years. The treatment of gonorrhoea and syphilis is by antibiotics.

There are numerous other sexually transmitted diseases; most can be treated effectively. However, there is no cure for herpes and there is also no cure for AIDS.

HIV/AIDS The Human Immunodeficiency Virus (HIV), may develop into Acquired Immune Deficiency Syndrome (AIDS). HIV is a major problem in many countries. Any exposure to blood, blood products or bodily fluids may put the individual at risk. In many developing countries transmission is predominantly through heterosexual sexual activity. This is quite different from industrialised countries where transmission is mostly through contact between homosexual or bisexual males or contaminated needles used by intravenous drug takers. Apart from abstinence, the most effective preventative is always to practise safe sex using condoms. It is impossible to detect the HIV-positive status of an otherwise healthy-looking person without a blood test.

HIV/AIDS can also be spread through infected blood transfusions; most developing countries cannot afford to screen blood for transfusions. It can also be spread by dirty needles – vaccinations, acupuncture, tattooing and ear or nose piercing can potentially be as dangerous as intravenous drug use if the equipment is not clean. If you do need an injection, ask to see the syringe unwrapped in front of you, or better still, take a needle and syringe pack with you overseas – it is a cheap insurance package against infection with HIV.

Fear of HIV infection should never preclude treatment for serious medical conditions. Although there may be a risk of infection, it is very small indeed.

Bites & Stings
Thanks to Korea's cold climate, insects are not a major threat to your health as they can be in tropical countries. Nevertheless, insect bites can be a nuisance if you do much summer hiking. For those with allergies, certain types of insect bites can even be life-threatening.

Mosquitos are an annoyance during summer, especially in the far south. Electric mosquito zappers are useful, but are too heavy for travelling. Mosquito incense coils are also effective, but these put out a large amount of nasty smoke and the incense coils break easily when travelling. The Korean solution to these problems is 'electric mos-

Top Left: Paper window, Tŏksugung Palace (CT)
Top Right: Handicrafts shop, Insadong (CT)
Bottom: Highrise apartments, central Seoul (CT)

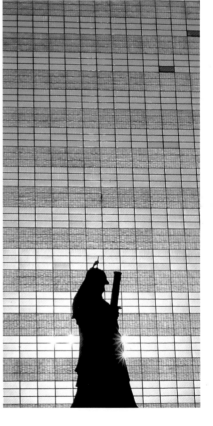

A Traditional painting (AB)
B Poetry carving, Kyŏngbokkung Palace (CT)
C Wall design, Tŏksugung Palace (CT)
D Statue of Admiral Yi Sun-shin (CT)

quito incense' *(chŏnja mugihyang)*, which consists of a small plastic bottle of insecticide which is slowly vapourised by an electric heater. The entire unit (bottle and electric heater) only weighs a few grams and is easy to travel with. You can purchase both the heater and bottles of insecticide in Korean pharmacies. A variation on the theme is a cardboard pad (soaked in insecticide) and an electric heater – this design is perhaps superior since there is no possibility of a leaky bottle making a mess out of your backpack. Breathing the vapourised insecticide over the long-term may have unknown health effects – at the very least, it seems to irritate the nasal passages, but all the manufacturers of this stuff insist that it's safe. However, if you're going to resort to such chemical weapons, it might be prudent to keep a window partially open.

If you are allergic to red-ant bites or bee and wasp stings, it might be prudent to carry some epinephrine in your first-aid kit.

Women's Health

Gynaecological Problems Poor diet, lowered resistance due to the use of antibiotics for stomach upsets and even contraceptive pills can lead to vaginal infections when travelling in hot climates. Keeping the genital area clean, and wearing skirts or loose-fitting trousers and cotton underwear will help to prevent infections.

Yeast infections, characterised by a rash, itch and discharge, can be treated with a vinegar or even lemon-juice douche or with yoghurt. Nystatin suppositories are the usual medical prescription. Trichomonas is a more serious infection; symptoms are a discharge and a burning sensation when urinating. Male sexual partners must also be treated, and if a vinegar-water douche is not effective medical attention should be sought. Metronidazole (Flagyl) is the prescribed drug.

Pregnancy Most miscarriages occur during the first three months of pregnancy, so this is the most risky time to travel as far as your own health is concerned. Miscarriage is not uncommon, and can occasionally lead to severe bleeding. The last three months should also be spent within reasonable distance of good medical care. A baby born as early as 24 weeks stands a chance of survival, but only in a good modern hospital. Pregnant women should avoid all unnecessary medication, but vaccinations and malarial prophylactics should still be taken where possible. Additional care should be taken to prevent illness and particular attention should be paid to diet and nutrition. Alcohol and nicotine, for example, should be avoided.

Women travellers often find that their periods become irregular or even cease while they're on the road. Remember that a missed period in these circumstances doesn't necessarily indicate pregnancy. There are health posts or Family Planning clinics in many small and large urban centres in developing countries, where you can seek advice and have a urine test to determine whether you are pregnant or not.

Herbal Medicine

Korea has two systems of medicine – Western and traditional or herbal *(hanyak)*. Korea's traditional medicine has largely been influenced by the Chinese variety, although the Korean's have added their own ingredients to the herbal brew. If any herb is associated with Korea, it's ginseng *(insam)*. There are two kinds of ginseng: red ginseng, which is sold under a government monopoly with strict-quality controls; and white ginseng, which is privately cultivated and treated. Not surprisingly, the red ginseng is the most expensive. It is possible to buy ginseng in a number of forms: in its raw state in the markets, in capsules, in tea, as a powder, and as a liquid extract.

The second most popular herb in Korea is a mushroom called *yonji pŏsŏt*, known to Westerners as *ganoderma lucidium karst*. It's expensive stuff, but claimed to be effective against everything from stomach ulcers to aging. Considerably less expensive is another mushroom called *unji pŏsŏt*, which could be translated into English as 'cloud fungus'. This one has recently been touted as a possible cure for cancer.

There are many other types of herbs. Possible ingredients – to name a few – include ginger, cinnamon, anise, nutmeg, the dried skins of fruits, powdered deer antlers, rhinoceros horn, cockroach droppings, dead bees and snake bile.

Adherents of herbal medicine claim that you don't use a single herb but rather a combination of herbs to produce the desired result. The herbs, when properly mixed, are believed to have a synergistic effect. That is, the whole is greater than the sum of its parts.

Another important property of herbal medicine is that the effects are supposed to be gradual, not sudden or dramatic. That is, you start taking herbs at the first sign of illness, such as a scratchy throat, or even before you get sick as a preventive measure. So in the cold and flu season you might start taking herbs before you even have your first cough or sniffle, so that you can build up resistance.

When reading about the theory behind herbal medicine, the word 'holistic' appears often. Basically, this means that herbal medicine seeks to treat the whole body rather than focusing on a particular organ or disease. Using appendicitis as an example, a

Korean Ginseng

doctor may try to fight the infection using the body's whole defences, whereas a Western doctor would simply cut out the appendix. In the case of appendicitis, the Western method might be more effective, but herbal medicine has sometimes proven better in treating chronic illnesses such as migraine headaches and asthma.

WOMEN TRAVELLERS

On the whole, Korea is a safe place for women travellers. However, there is no revolution in sexual roles looming on the horizon and Korea remains very much a male-dominated society. The men also tend to have firm ideas of how women should dress and behave. Some Western women in Korea have complained that they sometimes get shouted at if they are seen smoking, wearing sunglasses or flip-flops (thongs) in the street. All three of these things are considered extremely unladylike; all three in combination may get a few local zealots hopping mad.

Walking alone late at night is probably not a good idea anywhere, and you shouldn't make an exception for Korean cities. Koreans tend to be big drinkers, and you may meet some fairly aggressive drunks. It's quite common from 10 pm onwards for the streets to be crowded with swaying packs of drunken office workers. Consensus is that foreign women are fairly safe, but rapes do occur and as a foreigner you are by no means immune to trouble.

Korean women complain of furtive groping on crowded trains and buses. It is said that some carry pins and umbrellas expressly for the purpose of deterring this kind of behaviour.

DANGERS & ANNOYANCES

Korea is one of the safest countries in Asia with very strict gun control laws and almost no drug addicts. Unfortunately, Korea is no longer the crime-free country it once was. In Seoul, burglaries have become common while muggings and rapes are on the rise. It's still much safer than Manila or New York, but you should keep your valuables secure.

The back alleys of any large city are best avoided late at night, but you can walk major streets after dark without fear. However, pickpockets work in all crowded areas.

Student rioting is most common in late spring or early summer. Although fatalities are rare, injuries are common. It's best to avoid riots unless your idea of a good time is getting clubbed or tear-gassed (by police), firebombed or stoned (by students). Riots seem to be less frequent, largely because the government has made some major political concessions and the students are having a difficult time finding issues.

Males who head out for a late night on the town should watch out for aggressive locals. In particular, gangs of young toughs have given foreigners trouble in the back alleys of the It'aewon neighbourhood of Seoul (where there is a US military base). However, there is very little problem elsewhere.

In winter, Koreans use a form of heating known as ondol in which the floor is heated, turning it into a giant radiator. In traditionally constructed houses charcoal is burned in an oven under the floor and there is a danger of carbon monoxide poisoning if the floor develops cracks. Concrete floors are usually safe, but older buildings usually have a floor made of stone or clay with a wooden surface which are prone to leaking carbon monoxide. Modern houses use a safer system – hot water is pumped through pipes in the floor. In the older buildings it would be prudent to leave a window partially open at night.

Air-raid drills are held occasionally, but never more than once a month. When you hear the sirens you must get off the streets and keep away from doors and windows. If you're on a bus during an air raid, the bus will stop and you'll have to get off and seek shelter. After the all-clear signal is given, you are permitted to get back on the bus again without paying an additional fare – some people take advantage of this to get a free ride.

WORK

One unusual method of fund-raising is to turn in a North Korean spy – the government pays from W1,000,000 to W5,000,000 for each one you report. Phone the spy hotline on ☎ 113.

Failing that, you just might need to get a job. Korea in general, and Seoul in particular, is becoming a popular place to look for work – mainly teaching English at private language schools (hagwon). Although it is illegal to work on a tourist visa, many people still do. This brings with it certain risks: you might get caught in one of the government's periodic sweeps of the English-language schools and deported. But this is not enough to deter a steady trickle of travellers who look to Korea as a place to rest up and collect together a bit of money before moving on again.

Of course, if you are suitably qualified (with a degree in something) and are prepared to spend a bit of time in Korea, there is no need to run the risks of working illegally. Many schools in Korea are willing to sponsor English teachers on one-year contracts, but don't sign any contracts until after you receive the work visa. Remuneration for English teaching on this basis can be quite lucrative, but there are several drawbacks. The first is that many contracts include ways to keep you to the end of your contract (a fine of two month's wages for early resignation is common and because schools pay monthly this is easily enforced). The second is that applying for a work visa requires a trip out of the country and a wait of one month while the application is being processed. The third problem is that some schools simply cheat on wages. If you are being paid less than your contract stipulates, there isn't a whole lot you can do other than quit. Unfortunately, you will lose your work visa within just a few days of quitting, which means you must leave the country. A work visa is valid for one job only – if you quit and want to seek other employment, you must apply for a new work visa. In theory, if you've been cheated by an employer, you can take the case to court – in practice this seldom works.

Despite these drawbacks, it can all pay off. If you feel that you can guarantee your employer a year of your time, can afford the expense of waiting in another country for a month, and are willing to run the risk of working for someone who might cheat you, then it would be worth your while scouting around for a school in Korea that is willing to offer you sponsorship.

So how do you find teaching work in Korea? The obvious place to look is the classifieds section of the daily English-language newspapers. Some people maintain that the best jobs are never advertised here, and that it is only the schools that consistently lose staff that need to advertise. Nevertheless, it is possible to meet teachers who have found jobs through the newspaper and are happy with their work – it would not be a good idea to write the newspapers off entirely. Another method is to pop down to the British Council Library next to the Tŏksugung Palace in Seoul and ask at the counter for their list of English-language schools. Be warned, it's a *long* list, and a little out of date. But it's by phoning schools that many foreign teachers land a job.

You can also simply walk door to door and talk to the schools – many are located in the Chonggak area near the YMCA. The other way to find work is to book yourself in to the Inn Daewon in Seoul (see the Places to Stay section in the Seoul chapter). This is where most destitute backpackers end up, and it's a standby for English-language schools that need to find a substitute teacher in a hurry.

Even if you're not staying at the Inn Daewon, it might be worth turning up there occasionally and checking for notices posted by English-language schools looking for teachers.

ACTIVITIES
Sporting Association
Traditional Korean sports have a heavy tendency to be based on martial arts and hunting. One of the best places to contact for information about traditional and modern sports is the Korean Amateur Sport Association (☎ (02) 420-3333; fax 414-5583), Oryun-dong, Songp'a-gu, Seoul.

Archery
Both traditional Korean-style archery *(kungdo)* and the Western form are practised in South Korea. The traditional Korean

---

Desperately Seeking Kim

There are only a few hundred surnames in Korea. However, over 20% of the population uses the surname 'Kim' and 15% are named 'Lee', though there are some variations in the romanised spellings. In traditional Confucian culture, it is considered incest to marry someone with the same surname (thus, the same clan), which certainly limited marriage prospects among Koreans! It was only in 1988 that the law was amended to permit marriage within the same clan – Confucianists were very much opposed to this legal change.

Korean surnames are invariably one syllable in length, while the given name is usually (but not always) a two-syllable word separated by a hyphen in romanised form. Thus, a name like Kim Chung-hi would be typical. However, for the 'benefit of foreigners', some Koreans will reverse the order on their name cards so the preceding example becomes Chung-hi Kim. Just look for the hyphen to figure out which is the given name. However, most Koreans will insist that you call them by their family name until you get to know them very well, so it's just 'Kim' or 'Lee'. This means that if you stay in the country for any length of time, you will soon have dozens of friends with the same name – it's quite a drag when your roommate leaves a written message saying 'Kim called at 4 pm and wants you to call back'.

With scant few exceptions, Koreans will *not* assume English nicknames even for the purpose of taking an English class. This means that if you teach English in Korea and say, ' Kim, please answer the question', you can expect about a dozen answers at once. In general, students will not appreciate any attempts by you to give them English names, so don't even try. This is in sharp contrast to China where every English student wants an English nickname.

The Koreans are also fond of titles. If you're teaching English, you might find yourself addressed as 'Teacher John', 'Teacher Mary' etc. ■

wooden bow has gradually given way to more modern fibreglass models.

Competitions are most common during festivals, and this is one of the few traditional sports in which women can participate. Archery ranges are usually out of town.

For further information, contact the Korean Amateur Sport Association.

T'aekwondo

An effective form of self-defence, *t'aekwondo* was developed in Korea. The original form of t'aekwondo is called *t'aekkyŏn* and is still practiced by enthusiasts. If you're interested in either observing or studying, call the Korea T'aekwondo Association (☎ (02) 420-4271).

International competitions are hosted by the World T'aekwondo Federation (☎ (02) 566-2505; fax 553-4728), 635 Yŏksam-dong, Kangnam-gu, Seoul.

Canoeing & Rafting

Korea doesn't have a large number of wild rivers to support the activities of whitewater enthusiasts, but there are a few good spots in the Sŏraksan area for canoeing (*k'anu*) and rafting (*kŭmnyut'agi*). The organisation to contact is the Pine River Canoe School (☎ (02) 722-6805), 55 Kong Pyong-Dong, Chongno-gu, Seoul. The secretary, Ms Jeong Mi-Kyung, speaks English and can fill you in on the details.

Cycling

Riding a bike (*ssaik'ŭlling*) is almost suicidal in cities, but is a reasonable form of recreation in the countryside. Bikes are usually only available for rent in tourist areas.

The Korean Mountain Biking Association (KMTBA) (☎ (02) 967-9287) is a friendly organisation based in Seoul that arranges outings. If you don't already have a mountain bike, the KMTBA can direct you to a shop that rents bikes. This organisation is very 'foreigner friendly', although you might want to have a Korean phone for you to avoid any language problems.

Golf

Japanese golfers are enthralled with South Korea because green fees are so much cheaper than at home. But for many Western visitors, prices won't seem like such a bargain. You can expect to pay W50,000 to W65,000 for a game of golf (*golpŭ*), and club rental will also set you back somewhere in the vicinity of W20,000. Golf clubs should be declared at customs when you enter the country.

There are over 60 golf courses in Korea and the number continues to grow, with some serious consequences for the natural environment. To see the current complete list of golf courses, visit the KNTC (☎ (02) 757-6030) in Seoul.

Hang Gliding

This sport is just starting to catch on. The most popular hang gliding (*haeng gŭllaiding*) venue seems to be around the base of Hallasan on the island of Chejudo.

Hiking

Every province of Korea offers outstanding opportunities for hiking (*tŭngsan*). Indeed, you'll find many challenging walking and climbing areas in the suburban heart of Seoul.

Perhaps the biggest problem with hiking in Korea is escaping the crowds. Some areas are so popular that you sometimes have to stand in line to reach the summit of a peak. The problem with crowds can be formidable – at times it feels as if you're riding the Seoul subway rather than visiting the wilderness. Fortunately, this predicament can be bypassed if you simply avoid the most popular spots during weekends and holidays.

If you want to travel with a group, Korean friends can help you join a mountaineering club (*san ak hoi*). Don't expect hikers at the Korean clubs to be able to speak much English.

The United Service Organization (USO) in Seoul operates an English-speaking hiking club. Although geared towards US military personnel, civilians are welcome to participate. You can ring up the club (☎ (02) 795-0392) for information.

Koreans are serious about the great outdoors; any excursion away from the concrete of Seoul is prepared for with a thoroughness worthy of an expedition primed to assault Everest. This includes ice axes (in summer) and ropes (for walking up a gentle slope). Koreans must also be the best-dressed hikers in the world – check out the red vests, yellow caps and multi-coloured knee-high socks. All the equipment and fancy clothing makes for heroic photos – a camera is *de rigueur*.

While the Koreans no doubt overdo it, there are a few things which you should bring. Useful if not fashionable items include sun protection (sunglasses, sunscreen lotion and sunhat), rain gear, food, water, maps, compass, mosquito repellent and warm clothing. Mountain areas have notoriously fickle weather, and this problem should not be taken lightly – at high altitudes, it can go from sunny and mild to dangerously cold and wet in remarkably little time. It's best to dress in layers – shirts, sweaters and nylon windjackets can be peeled off and put on as needed.

As for purchasing mountaineering equipment, you'll find everything you need in Korea so it's not imperative to bring anything from abroad.

Hot Springs

On paper, Korea seems like an ideal place for relaxing in natural hot springs *(wonch'ŏn)*. At least the tourist maps of Korea indicate that many hot-spring resorts exist all around the peninsula. And indeed, the spas do exist. The drawback is that every single useable hot spring has been overdeveloped.

You can forget about frolicking nude in a large outdoor pool surrounded by trees, and then jumping into a snow-drift while your body is still steaming hot – Koreans wanting to do that head for Canada or Europe. In Korea, the hot water is simply piped into hotels and guests are expected to do their frolicking in the privacy of their own rooms. The Koreans just don't have the idea of

outdoor spas, although a few do have large indoor pools (swimsuits required).

Admittedly, soaking in a hotel bathtub isn't the worst way to spend a cold winter evening, but you could do the same thing in your own home (assuming you live in a place that has cold winter evenings). All sorts of health benefits are claimed for the natural hot baths due to the mineral content of the water. The Japanese are most enthusiastic about pursuing this hobby, and large tour groups from Japan often spend a full-week holiday going from one spa to another to sample the mineral water of each. Each spa tries to outdo the others, advertising that only its mineral water can cure arthritis, asthma, constipation, impotency or whatever. Certainly there is no harm in trying it, but staying at a hot-springs resort in Korea is not the cheapest of pastimes.

Perhaps the most enjoyable hot springs are the ones found in ski resorts. The Suanbo Hot Springs in the central part of South Korea is such a place. You can get in a full day of skiing and soak those tired muscles in the evening.

Korean Chess

This game is virtually identical to the Japanese *go*, although it originated in China. Flat black and white stones are moved around on a playing board. As with Western chess, the rules are simple but the techniques can be very complex.

It's easy to find partners who can teach you the art of Korean chess *(paduk)* – try the local pubs. Frequently, a fair bit of alcohol is consumed during these games and wagers often change hands. As with Western chess, major championships are followed in the news media.

Skating

Skating *(sŭk'eit'ŭ)* – both roller skating and ice skating – is a popular pastime. A few large cities have good indoor ice-skating rinks, but in most other areas it's outdoors and therefore strictly a winter sport.

Skiing

Although Korea's mountains don't compare with the Swiss Alps, there are some good places where you can practise the art of sliding downhill *(sŭk'i)*. The ski season is from about early December to mid-March. Facilities include hotels, artificial snow and equipment hire. These places can be crowded at weekends – get there early if you need to hire equipment. Since ski resorts are on remote mountaintops, some of them don't have a regular bus service, but numerous travel agencies run tour buses up to these places as part of a package tour. Otherwise, hire a taxi for the last leg of the journey, or hitchhike.

For half a day of skiing at the Alps resort, prices for equipment hire are W11,800 and lift tickets are W9900. For a full day, equipment hire costs W16,000 and lift tickets are W16,700.

The USO runs inexpensive weekend ski trips to Bear's Town, Alps and Yongpyeong resorts. They also sell tickets for the daily shuttle bus to Bear's Town and Yongpyeong. Korea Travel Bureau (☎ (02) 778-0150) organises full-day trips to the Bear's Town resort for W27,000 which includes transport from Seoul, equipment, lift tickets and lunch – KTB is on the 3rd floor of the Lotte Hotel.

All ski resorts have a representative office in Seoul that you can call for information. The seven resorts are as follows:

Yongpyŏng (Dragon Valley): South Korea's premier resort is about 3½ hours from Seoul, just south of Odaesan National Park on the east coast. It has 16 slopes and night skiing (☎ (02) 548-2251)

Alps Ski Resort: This resort, about 45 minutes north-west of Sokch'o and just north of Sŏraksan National Park, gets the most snow and has the longest season. It has eight slopes (☎ (02) 756-5481).

Bear's Town: This resort is about 40 minutes north-east of Seoul and has seven slopes (☎ (02) 546-7210).

Chonmasan: This resort, about 50 minutes north-east of Seoul, has six slopes (☎ (02) 744-6019).

Yangji: This resort is near the Korean Folk Village in Suwon, about one hour from Seoul. It has seven slopes (☎ (02) 511-3033).

Suanbo Aurora Valley: This resort is by Suanbo Hot Springs about three hours south-east of Seoul, near Woraksan National Park. There are seven slopes. (☎ (02) 546-5171)

Muju: This resort is 3½ hours from Seoul in Tŏgyusan National Park, south-east of Taejŏn. There are three slopes (more planned). (☎ (02) 515-5500).

Swimming

In crowded South Korea, most urban residents do their swimming *(suyŏng)* in shallow pools in which there is no chance of drowning. The short warm season also makes indoor pools more practical than the outdoor variety. There are a number of inexpensive public pools which get very crowded, and private ones which cost quite a bit more. Five-star hotels usually have pools, and even non-guests can generally use these facilities *if they pay*. If you live in Korea long-term, it may be worthwhile joining a health club (also at major hotels) where you can use the pool and exercise equipment.

Most of South Korea's lakes are in fact reservoirs. Swimming is not permitted at such places since this is drinking water. Also, the lake levels drop during dry weather, leaving a rather ugly 'bathtub ring' around the reservoirs which makes swimming unaesthetic.

It's a different story at the seashore. The season is basically July and August, and during the rest of the year most beaches are not even open to the public. As you will soon discover, South Korea's beaches are lined with barbed-wire fences. These are partially removed during the summer months to give the public access, but all coastal areas are heavily guarded and that particularly applies to areas close to North Korea. You are not supposed to be on the beach at night, and soldiers enforce this rule strictly. The situation is similar in North Korea, except that the fences are electrified and seem mainly designed to keep people in rather than out.

The well-known beaches near urban areas can be extremely crowded. The best all-around beaches are found on the island of Chejudo, which also has the warmest weather.

A feature of South Korea's beaches is that

the water tends to be calm and shallow on the west coast, while the eastern seaboard has deep water and rough surf.

Tennis

Public tennis courts exist in city parks. These tend to be very crowded, but if you want to play tennis *(t'enisŭ)* you can sometimes get on if you go during normal working hours. Forget it on weekends and holidays.

Not surprisingly, large tourist hotels offer even better facilities but expect to pay five-star prices.

Windsurfing

The art of windsurfing *(windŭsŏping)* is just starting to take off in southern areas such as Pusan and Cheju-do. Haeundae Beach in Pusan is where windsurfing championships are sometimes held. For more information, you can contact the Korean Windsurfing Association (☎ (02) 511-7522; fax 511-7523), Room 402, Songhŏn Bldg, 55-3 Nonhyŏn-dong, Kangnam-gu, Seoul

Courses

It is very important that you obtain a student visa *before* enrolling in any kind of course – the schools will not tell you this! Even if you already have a work visa, you cannot legally enrol in a school without first getting permission stamped into your residence permit by immigration. The fine for breaking this rule is at least W100,000.

The most popular courses for foreigners are of course language courses. Most foreigners study in Seoul, although you can certainly study at schools elsewhere. There are several large government-run language schools in Seoul such as the Yonsei University Foreign Language Institute (FLI), Sogang University and Ehwa Women's University. The Language Research Teaching Centre (LRTC) in Seoul is a well-known private language school. Other language schools advertise in the *Korea Times* and *Korea Herald* – the *Korea Herald* itself operates a language school at its branch off of Myŏng-dong. Just remember that the school

must be government-approved in order to sponsor you for a student visa.

HIGHLIGHTS

In terms of culture and history, one of South Korea's top attractions is Kyŏngbokkung Palace in Seoul. Kyŏngju in south-east Korea has an overwhelming collection of cultural sights.

Perhaps the most outstanding natural beauty spot is Sŏraksan National Park on the east coast. Songnisan National Park boasts both outstanding scenery and one of Korea's finest temples. The island of Chejudo, off the south coast, is well worthwhile for the chance to climb South Korea's highest peak, Hallasan.

The southern coast of Korea is dramatic and much of it can be explored by boat and on foot. The same goes for the rugged island of Ullŭngdo off the east coast.

ACCOMMODATION

Camping

At least when the weather cooperates, Korea is a paradise for campers. Every national park has camping grounds and most are free. When a fee is charged, it's usually no more than W2000 and this buys you access to fine facilities like hot showers and flushing toilets. There are a few private camping grounds, but most are government-run.

Seoul is a good place to stock up on camping equipment such as tents, sleeping bags and stoves (see the Things to Buy section in the Seoul chapter).

Because Korea is a crowded place, the wilderness really takes a beating. Therefore, campers should be extra diligent in the matter of protecting the environment. If you intend to cook you should carry a portable gas stove. Building wood fires in the forest is not recommended – it's environmentally ruinous, not to mention hazardous when the weather is dry. Human waste and used toilet paper should be buried at least 50 metres from surface water. However, other paper and plastic rubbish should not be buried – if you carried it in, you can carry it out. Remember the old wilderness explorers' slogan: take nothing but pictures, leave nothing but footprints.

The national park service has closed a number of back-country areas to camping and cooking in order to give the wilderness a badly needed rest. If you have any questions about where camping is prohibited, make enquiries locally.

Mountain Huts & Shelters

Along the hiking trails in many national parks are strategically-located shelters *(taepiso)* or huts *(sanjang)*. Don't expect five-star facilities – basically, you only get a wooden floor on which to roll out a sleeping bag. Toilets tend to be smelly latrine style. Drinking water is almost always available, and some huts have basic items for sale like food and drinks, although don't count on this.

The huts and shelters are almost certain to be open during the busy summer hiking season, and often in autumn when Koreans head for the hills to watch the leaves turn colours. A few huts and shelters are open in the springtime, but you can forget it in winter.

The better-appointed places charge a basic fee of W1000 to W2000 for use of the facilities.

Hostels

There are 10 youth hostels scattered around the country. Unlike their counterparts in Europe, America and Australia, South Korean hostels are generally huge, luxurious places with incredible facilities and some private rooms. The problem is that there simply aren't very many hostels, and none at all in places where you'd expect to find them (ie Cheju-do and Kyŏngju). Dorm beds vary between W5000 and W9000 but the private rooms cost as much as W30,000. All the hostels have their own restaurants with meals at very reasonable prices.

There are three offices in Korea where you can join the Korean Youth Hostel association (KYHA) and book rooms. The main one is in Seoul, and there is a branch in Chŏnju and

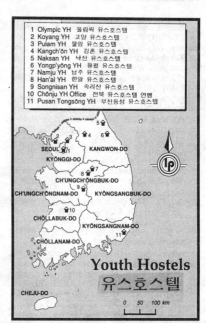

1 Olympic YH 올림픽 유스호스텔
2 Koyang YH 고양 유스호스텔
3 Pulam YH 불암 유스호스텔
4 Kangch'ŏn YH 강촌 유스호스텔
5 Naksan YH 낙산 유스호스텔
6 Yongp'yŏng YH 용평 유스호스텔
7 Namju YH 남주 유스호스텔
8 Han'al YH 한알 유스호스텔
9 Songnisan YH 속리산 유스호스텔
10 Chŏnju YH Office 전북 유스호스텔 연맹
11 Pusan Tongsŏng YH 부산동성 유스호스텔

SEOUL KANGWON-DO
KYŎNGGI-DO
CH'UNGCH'ŎNGBUK-DO
CH'UNGCH'ŎNGNAM-DO KYŎNGSANGBUK-DO
CHŎLLABUK-DO
KYŎNGSANGNAM-DO
CHŎLLANAM-DO
CHEJU-DO

Youth Hostels
유스호스텔

0   50   100 km

Pusan. Alternatively, you can call the hostels themselves, and some hostels even have a phone number in Seoul.

For more information and reservations contact the KYHA (☎ (02) 725-3031; fax 725-3113), Room 409, Chŏksŏn Hyŏndae Bldg, Chŏksŏn-dong, Chongno-gu, Seoul, 110-052.

Olympic YH, 88 Bangyi-dong, Songpa-gu, Seoul (take subway line No 2 to Songnae station and walk ½ km), 1234 beds, W9900 per bed (☎ (02) 410-2114; fax 410-2100)

Koyang YH, 278-3 Koyang-dong, Koyang City, Kyŏnggi-do (700 metres from Koyang Market), 200 beds, W5000 per bed (☎ (0344) 62-9049; fax 62-9579)

Pulam YH, 99 Hwajup-ri, Byulne-myŏn, Namyangju-gun, Kyŏnggi-do (take Seoul subway line No 1 to Ch'ŏngnyangni, then the train to Sŏkkye and walk for 15 minutes towards Mt Bulam) 200 beds, W5000 per bed (☎ (0346) 65-8081, (02) 212-0291; fax (02) 212-9050)

Kangch'ŏn YH, 366 Kangch'on-ni, Namsan-myŏn, Ch'unch'ŏn-gun, Kangwon-do (from

Kangch'on walk one km towards Kugok Falls)
(☎ (0361) 262-1201; fax 262-1204).

Naksan YH, 30-1 Chŏnjin-ni, Yangyang-gun,
Kanghyŏn-myŏn (200 metres from Nakansa),
300 beds, W5000 per bed (☎ (0396) 672-3416,
(02) 540-0382; fax (0396) 672-3418, (02) 549-
0563)

Yongp'yŏng YH, 130 Yongsan-ni, Toam-myŏn,
P'yŏngch'ang-gun (in Yongpyŏng Ski Resort),
600 beds, W5500 per bed, W66, 000 for doubles
(☎ (0374) 32-5757, (02) 561-6255; fax (0374)
32-5769, (02) 561-6272)

Namju YH, 52 Onch'ŏn-ni, Sangmo-myŏn,
Chungwon-gun, Ch'ungch'ŏngbuk-do (1½ km
from Suanbo towards skiing grounds), 300 beds,
W6600 per bed (☎ (0441) 846-0397/8; fax 846-
0396)

Han'al YH, 730 Onch'ŏn-ni, Sangmo-myŏn,
Chungwon-gun, Ch'ungch'ŏngbuk-do (one km
from Suanbo), 724 beds but *always* full
(☎ (0441) 846-3151, (02) 752-0803; fax (0441)
846-3159, (02) 752-0804)

Songnisan YH, 3-8 Sangp'an-ni, Naesokri-myŏn,
Ch'ungch'ŏngbuk-do (½ km from the bus stop
at Songni-dong near Pŏpchusa), 1200 beds,
W6600 per bed (☎ (0433) 42-5211, (02) 555-
8458; fax (0433) 42-5215, (02) 556-5185)

Chŏnju YH Office, 92-9 Taga-dong 2-ga, Hansan-gu,
Chŏnju City (☎ (0652) 86-6534; fax 231-6641)

Pusan Tongsŏng YH, 206-11 Songjŏng-dong,
Haewudae-gu, Pusan City (east of town, take the
train to Songjŏng station and walk 10 minutes),
141 beds, W5000 per bed (☎ (051) 743-8466; fax
743-7564)

Guesthouses

Yŏinsuk & Yŏgwan Western-style accommodation in the major centres is generally very expensive so budget travellers usually head for the traditional Korean inns known as *yŏinsuk* or *yŏgwan*. The more upmarket yŏgwan are called *jang yŏgwan* (sometimes just abbreviated to *jang*).

The name gives an indication of what facilities you can expect and the price you'll pay. Yŏgwan usually have at least some rooms with private bath, while yŏinsuk almost never do. Rooms in the jang yŏgwan all have private bath. Basic yŏinsuk rooms generally cost no more than W10,000 and sometimes as low as W7000. Prices in yŏgwan start around W15,000, but W18,000 or more isn't unusual in jang yŏgwan. Prices in Seoul are slightly higher than elsewhere.

The yŏinsuk and cheaper yŏgwan are becoming an endangered species, while relatively pricey jang yŏgwan are rapidly multiplying. To judge from some of the sounds coming through the paper-thin walls, many of the cheaper yŏinsuk are surviving primarily as short-time love hotels or else Koreans are afflicted with severe breathing problems.

Probably the easiest way to save money on accommodation is to double up. Doubles and singles are usually the same price, although a third person might be charged extra.

The proprietors are highly unlikely to speak English but they'll expect you to want to see the room and bathroom facilities before you decide to stay. If they don't offer to show you the room, then ask to see it (*pang'ŭl polsu issŏyo*).

Yŏinsuk and yŏgwan are usually clustered around bus and railway stations. If you can't read Korean, at least learn the symbol for bath, which is as follows:

You'll find this symbol on the signs of all jang yŏgwan, which indicates that all rooms have private bath. But be forewarned that the same symbol is used on public bathhouses (*mok yok t'ang*).

Since yŏinsuk have such primitive bathing facilities, you might indeed want to visit a bathhouse. This can be a very pleasant experience and a great way to get the winter chill out of your bones. Men and women have separate facilities, and most bathhouses close during summer. You can rent towels and soap and bathe for as long as you like for around W1500. Many bathhouses employ staff to give massages, but enquire about the price first.

Never wear your shoes into the yŏgwan – take them off and leave them outside or place them on a sheet of paper so they don't touch the floor.

Most yŏgwan are run by married women, and you should refer to them by the title *ajimah*.

The KNTC tourist information booth at Seoul's Kimp'o Airport has information on yŏgwan in the form of hand-outs and individual business cards (usually including an abstract map for finding the place).

Many older yŏgwan and yŏinsuk seem to have been designed for midgets, and the low doorways constitute a real hazard to travellers over 150 cm tall. Some swear that these are a leftover booby-trap from the Korean War. One Lonely Planet writer (we won't mention any names) suffered a mild concussion after cracking his skull on one of these doorways when searching for the toilet in the middle of the night.

Minbak Another form of traditional accommodation is *minbak*, which could be translated as 'home stay'. Essentially, it's a room in a private house. Bathing and cooking facilities are shared with the family, although occasionally you may find separate facilities for guests. Some of these places will be signposted but many are not. Souvenir shops, teashops and small restaurants can usually point you in the right direction and may actually be minbak themselves. In many rural areas, minbak may be the only form of accommodation available. Prices are always on a 'per room' basis and should cost roughly W10,000, except in Seoul where they charge around W12,000. Meals can generally be provided on request. Minbak offer considerable discounts if you plan to stay for a month or more.

Hotels

If you've got more cash to burn, Korea can accommodate you in style. Hotels start at the W20,000 level and easily accelerate to over W150,000 for deluxe rooms in Seoul. For the purposes of this book, we'll consider anything up to W25,000 to be 'bottom-end', while 'mid-range' is defined as W26,000 to W75,000. Anything above W75,000 qualifies as 'top-end'.

In addition to this, many mid-range places and all top-end ones will charge an extra 10% tax plus another 10% service charge.

Rentals

An increasing number of foreigners (especially English teachers) are basing themselves in Korea for long periods. In many cases they come to an agreement with the owners of a yŏgwan for a better monthly deal on a room. This, however, has drawbacks, like not being able to cook for yourself and not having your own telephone. An alternative solution is to find an apartment or alternatively to rent a room in a boarding house, known locally as *haksulchip* – this costs around US$200 a month in Seoul.

The Korean government copied its land use policy from Japan, with the same result – there is a housing shortage. Building permits are difficult to obtain and bank loans for aspiring home owners simply do not exist. For tenants, this translates into high rents, outrageous deposits and long-term leases that heavily favour the landlord. Needless to say, the housing shortage has become a hot political issue and there have been calls for reform. Recent amendments to the land use law are making it easier to build apartments, and this should eventually result in cheaper housing. The government has also embarked on a programme of building public housing estates. You can see these all around Korea now – row after row of ugly identical buildings which are auctioned off to hopeful buyers via a lottery system.

All of which means that apartment hunting is quite an expedition, and the help of a Korean friend is practically mandatory. The biggest problem is the requirement of astronomical deposits (known as 'key money') – another obnoxious custom borrowed from Japan. A figure of 20 times the monthly rent is not uncommon, and in choice neighbourhoods of Seoul this can add up to over US$40,000! Most Koreans do not have this kind of money, and many are forced to borrow it and pay interest. Basically, the higher the deposit the lower your rent will be. In some cases, a sky-high deposit will yield you one-year's rent-free accommodation, and at the end of the year your deposit will be refunded. As locals point out, however, this is a dangerous system. In some cases your money will be channelled into dodgy investments, and there is always the risk that you will never see it again.

Boarding houses are probably a better alternative to the expense of renting an apartment. But conditions in these houses are not always ideal. It's wise to look around for a while before committing yourself to anything. Check to see that there are cooking facilities and whether there is a curfew in effect. Best of all, if you're working in Korea, enquire as to whether a provision of accommodation can be built into your contract. Many jobs provide accommodation for their foreign staff, and there's no reason why *your* employer shouldn't make some effort towards helping you to get set up in Korea as well.

Fed up with high rents and outrageous deposits, some long-term foreign residents have wondered if they could simply buy a house in Korea. In most cases, the answer is a resounding 'no'. The only foreigners who are permitted to buy real estate in Korea are veterans of the Korean War.

FOOD

The four generic cuisines available in South Korea are Korean, Chinese, Japanese and Western. Western food needs little introduc-

tion, and most Japanese restaurants in Seoul offer similar fare to other Japanese restaurants around the world (but spicier). Chinese cuisine is much like it is elsewhere in the world (excellent), but a few spicy Korean side dishes are usually thrown in. And then, of course, there is Korean cuisine itself.

Main Dishes

Korean *Kimbap* is the Korean version of Japanese sushi. Thanks to the liberal use of spices, the Korean version is usually tastier. This is an inexpensive dish which you can find at hole-in-the-wall restaurants everywhere.

An omelette with rice (*omǔ raisǔ*) is another cheapie dish which has sustained many a backpacker.

Moving upmarket, the standard Korean meal is known as *pekpan* and consists of rice, soup and vegetable dishes that vary in type and number from restaurant to restaurant. They can number a dozen or more but will always include *kimch'i* – a fiery hot fermented cabbage which makes a reasonable substitute for tear gas. A basic pekpan meal will cost around W2500, but you can pay a lot more as the number of dishes increases.

Korean cuisine is outstanding and many

Eating Etiquette

If you're invited out for a meal or even just a drinking session with Korean friends, you'll find it difficult to pay for the bill yourself or even contribute to it. The same applies even if it's you that's doing the inviting. All manner of ruses will be used to beat you to the cashier even if it means that the person who pays is going to have to live on bread and water for the next week. The bill for a group is always paid by one person and one only. If you want to contribute, then make these arrangements before you go out and square up after you leave. Never attempt to do it in front of the cashier or you will seriously embarrass your host. Indeed, by doing anything like this, you may embarrass them to such a degree that they'll never be able to return to that particular restaurant or club.

If you're a man taking a woman out for dinner, you pay. Furthermore, a man is expected to escort his date home to make sure she arrives safely, unless she insists otherwise.

Another aspect of eating etiquette is the use of a toothpick. You should use two hands, one to operate the pick and one to block the view of this process. Many foreigners think that using the second hand makes the whole thing far more conspicuous, but local custom demands you do it this way. Just watch how the Koreans do it.

If you haven't already mastered the use of chopsticks, you'd better start practising now. Korea is exceptional in that the chopsticks are usually made of metal, which makes them even more difficult to operate than the wooden Chinese variety. ■

Westerners find it very appealing, but there is one qualifier – you must like spicy food. If you can't eat fiery hot food then that eliminates about 80% of what's on the menu. Of course, you can inform the Korean waiter or cook that you don't want spicy dishes, but that's rather like walking into KFC and saying you don't eat meat. Remember, it's the spices that makes Korean cuisine so unique.

Garlic also figures prominently in the Korean diet. Many restaurants hand out complimentary sticks of chewing gum after the meal. The breath freshening effects probably last about two minutes before being overpowered by the odorous combination of garlic and fermented vegetables.

Many Westerners take to kimch'i like naturals, but others can't abide it. If you fall into the latter category, you can still survive but it will require effort. One alternative that most foreigners have little difficulty in taking to – unless you're vegetarian – is *pulgogi*. Pulgogi literally means 'fire beef', but is usually translated as Korean barbecue.

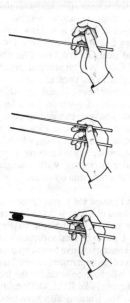

Using Chopsticks

Strips of beef marinated in soy sauce, sesame oil, garlic and chilli are grilled on a hot plate in front of the diner. Typical prices for pulgogi hover around W10,000 per person.

Along similar lines is *kalbi*, which uses short ribs instead of strips of beef. Most pulgogi restaurants also specialise in kalbi, and it is also featured in another popular local dish *kalbi t'ang* (*t'ang* means soup). The soup is served with rice and kimch'i.

A dish that uses kimch'i as an ingredient is *pibimpap*. Even if you don't particularly like kimch'i as a rule, it's worth trying pibimpap. It often includes meat which, along with the vegetables, is placed on a bed of rice. Usually it is served in a thick, heated iron bowl, so that the dish is still cooking when it is placed in front of you. The whole thing should be stirred with a spoon before eating.

Similar to the Japanese *shabu shabu* is *shinsŏllo*. Meat, fish, vegetables and bean curd are simmered together in a broth in front of the diner. This is another dish that most foreigners enjoy. The Koreans also enjoy noodle soup dishes. A particular Korean speciality is *naeng myŏn* or 'cold buckwheat noodles' which is served with a broth. It doesn't sound particularly appetising but it is surprisingly good, especially in hot summer weather.

Korean *haute cuisine* is best represented by *hanjŏngshik*, a banquet meal with a vast array of side dishes served together with pulgogi. At the other end of the spectrum are cheap but filling dishes like *mandu-guk*, a Korean equivalent of the Chinese *wonton* soup. It's a lot more filling than the Chinese variety, and is a cheap way of filling yourself up.

As for devoted vegetarians, the situation doesn't look too good. There are a couple of odd restaurants which don't serve meat – these places cater to strict Buddhists or trendy Koreans looking for something different. But overall, Korea is hell for vegetarians. If you really can't eat meat, then you'll probably have to do a fair bit of self-catering.

Korean stews (*tchigae*) are very tasty and inexpensive. There seems to be an almost endless variety of stews, but one of the most popular is *tobu tchigae* or 'bean curd stew'. The broth is made with a bean paste mixture that is very similar to Japanese *miso*. Another popular, though more expensive, stew is *kalbitchim*, in which the main ingredient is kalbi short ribs. There are also kimch'i stews for those who can't get enough of the stuff in the side dishes provided. Rice is always served with Korean stews.

Korea's cold winter climate has given rise to a number of interesting soup dishes. Probably the most famous of these is *samgye t'ang* or 'ginseng chicken soup'. A small whole chicken, stuffed with ginseng and sticky rice, comes in a clay pot. The chicken and the soup are said to have great powers as health supplements. Kalbi-t'ang is another famous soup that has already been mentioned. *Sŏlnong t'ang* is a beef stock soup that is also worth sampling.

A visit to at least one Korean noodle shop should be on anyone's itinerary, even if you don't like noodles. Apart from naeng-myŏn there are noodle dishes that you won't find elsewhere in Asia. *Kong kuksu*, for example, is a noodle dish made in a soy milk broth. A more accessible noodle dish is *mak kuksu*, a combination of vegetables and meat slices with noodles in chicken broth.

The back streets of Korean cities and towns abound in small roadside stalls selling snacks. Some of the more popular varieties are *oksusu*, corn on the cob, and *p'ajŏn*, green onion pancakes. For the adventurous, *ppŏndaegi* is a side dish of boiled silkworms. Japanese tempura *(twigim* in Korean) is also a popular street-stall dish.

Chinese Chinese food is very common in Korea and it seems to be increasing in popularity. Just to remind you that you are not in China, some Korean side dishes like kimch'i and raw onions are thrown in.

Most Chinese restaurants in Korea cater to the lower end of the dining market, which means you can count on fairly reasonable prices. If there are Chinese characters on the doorway, chances are good that the owner is an ethnic Chinese and will be able to speak

Chinese. However, many Koreans also run Chinese restaurants, although they don't put Chinese characters on the door or menu.

One of the most popular Chinese dishes is *tchajang myŏn*, a northern Chinese speciality that is a little similar to spaghetti bolognese. You can safely go into any Korean Chinese restaurant and request this one – they are bound to have it on the menu. For the more cautious, most Chinese restaurants also have fried rice, which is *poggŭm bap* in Korean. Another popular item is *t'angsu yuk*, probably more familiarly known to Westerners as sweet & sour pork.

Japanese Japanese restaurants have become almost as common as Chinese restaurants and can be found all over the country, but they invariably belong in the outrageous price range so treat them as a splurge. The cheaper hot dishes at these restaurants include tempura (twigim) – battered, deep-fried cuisine. The most usual are shrimp tempura with vegetables *(sae'o twigim)*, fish tempura *(saengsŏn twigim)* and vegetable tempura *(yach'ae twigim)*.

The main cold dish is sashimi *(saengsŏn hoe)* – raw fish with either soy or hot chilli sauce and rice. Cooked fish is far cheaper than raw fish – you get charged much extra for having them *not* cook it!

The Koreans have adopted sushi *(kimbap)* as their own, but if you order it in a Japanese restaurant you get charged double what you'd pay in a Korean restaurant. A variation on the theme is *yubu ch'obap*, which is prepared in a similar way to kimbap except bean curd and rice mixed with vinegar are wrapped in a very thin omelette.

Western Perhaps the biggest problem with Western food in Korea is that it isn't readily available unless you have a fat expense account. Upmarket Western restaurants are found in either exclusive tourist hotels or the top floors of big department stores. Those on a budget will have to settle for the familiar fast food chains like KFC, McDonald's and Wendy's. The Koreans also have produced some home-grown Western-style fast food chains. *Lotteria* is a joint Japanese-Korean attempt to combine McDonald's and KFC, but the food doesn't quite come up to Big Mac standards.

Salt is a hard thing to come by in Western restaurants in Korea. It's almost never put out on the tables, and even fast-food restaurants don't have it for their French fries. But you can usually get it on request (the Korean word is *sogǔm*) – someone will have to go back into the kitchen and bring it to you on a paper plate or napkin. If you want to avoid this hassle, you can carry around your own little stash of salt (empty film containers are good for this).

Desserts

While the Koreans produce all sorts of scrumptious pastries and chocolates, eating dessert after a meal is not the usual custom. However, Western influence is creeping in – more and more Koreans are acquiring the habit of munching junk food after a meal.

Of course, there's all the usual stuff like ice cream and pie, but you might want to try something distinctly Korean. A popular dessert which seems to be a Korean-Chinese-Western hybrid is known as red bean parfait *(p'atbingsa)*. It's made with sweetened red beans mixed with crushed ice, fruit cocktail, milk and ice cream. It can be bought in numerous places, but is probably most accessible at Hardees fast-food restaurant (a foreign-owned chain with branches all over Seoul).

Fruit

Korea's climate is ideal for cold weather fruits such as apples and pears. Korean pears are particularly delicious and are an important export item. Bananas, pineapples and other tropical fruits are grown in green houses and are very expensive.

Self-Catering

Given the expense of eating out, self-catering is not a bad idea at all. One great feature of Korea is the existence of little hole-in-the-wall grocery stores open from early morning

to late at night. These are found everywhere, so you'll never have to walk far to pick up that package of noodles, ham, bread, biscuits or coffee.

By contrast, large Western-style supermarkets are a rarity because urban land prices are so prohibitive. In cities, look for supermarkets in the basements of large department stores. They can also be found in some suburban areas, but these are places that travellers rarely get to.

The biggest problem with self-catering is simply finding cooking facilites. Some yŏgwan will allow you access to the kitchen or at least have hot water available, but you can seldom count on this.

In large cities such as Seoul, your salvation may be convenience stores. You can find 24-hour chains such as 7-Eleven, Family Mart, Lawson's, Circle K, LG-25 (Lucky-Goldstar) etc, and these stores always have microwave ovens, hot water and even a table where you can stand (but not sit) while eating. Everything you need is included: a styrofoam bowl, plastic spoon and chopsticks.

An alternative is to carry a small electric heating coil or electric teapot for boiling water. One complication is the existence of two voltages (see the Electricity section in this chapter). Of course, you can try living on foods that don't need to be cooked (peanut butter and bread, for example), but most travellers grow tired of this *very* quickly.

Useful Phrases

I am vegetarian.
 ch'aeshik juwi imnida
 채식주의 입니다.

I can't eat spicy food.
 meiwun umshigun mukji motamnida
 매운 음식은 먹지 못합니다.

restaurant
 shikdang
 식당

Korean Food 한국음식

omelette with rice
 omǔ raisǔ
 오므라이스

barbecued beef & vegetables grill
  pulgogi
  불고기

barbecued marinated beef/pork ribs
  pulgalbi
  불갈비

barbecued beef ribs
  kalbi
  갈비

barbecued beef ribs soup
  kalbi t'ang
  갈비탕

barbecued beef ribs stew
  kalbitchim
  갈비찜

chicken stew
  talgtchim
  닭찜

roasted chicken
  t'ongdalggui
  통닭구이

mixed vegetables & beef with soybean noodles
  chapch'ae
  잡채

rice, egg, meat & vegetables with hot sauce
  bibimpap
  비빔밥

meat, fish, vegetables & bean curd broth (cooked at table)
  shinsŏllo
  신선로

noodles
  myŏn or *kuksu*
  면, 국수

cold buckwheat noodles & broth
  naeng myŏn
  냉면

noodles & soy milk broth
  kong kuksu
  콩국수

vegetables, meat, noodles & chicken broth
  mak kuksu
  막국수

soup
  kuk or *t'ang*
  국 / 탕

beef stock & rice soup
  sŏlnong t'ang
  설렁탕

ginseng chicken soup
  samgye t'ang
  삼계탕

boiled silkworm snack
  ppŏndaegi
  뻔데기

dumplings
  mandu
  만두

soup with meat-filled dumplings
  mandu guk
  만두국

stew
  tchigae
  찌개

bean curd stew
  tobu tchigae
  두부찌개

seafood & vegetables fried in batter
  t'oekim
  튀김

pickled vegetables, garlic & chilli
  kimch'i
  김치

Korean sushi
  kimbap
  김밥

corn on the cob (street-stall food)
  oksusu
  옥수수

green onion pancakes (street stall food)
  p'ajŏn
  파전

pickled daikon radish (with every meal)
  tongchimi
  동치미

dogmeat
  poshint'ang
  보신탕

Chinese Food 중국음식
Chinese Restaurant
  chungkuk chip
  중국집

noodles with hot beef sauce
  tchajang myŏn
  짜장면

thick noodles with sauce
  udong
  우동

spicy seafood noodle soup
tchambbong
짬뽕

vegetables with noodles & hot beef sauce
kan tchajang myŏn
간짜장면

soupy noodles
ul myŏn
울면

noodles & spicy sauce
samsŏn tchajang
삼선짜장

noodles & flavoured sauces
samsŏn ganjajang
삼선간짜장

spicy noodles with vegetables
samsŏn tchambbong
삼선짬뽕

seafood noodles
samsŏn udong
삼선우동

seafood soupy noodles
samsŏn ul myŏn
삼선울면

fried rice
poggŭm bap
볶음밥

fried rice with noodles
chapch'ae bap
잡채밥

assorted seafood, meat, vegetables & rice
chapt'ang bap
잡탕밥

rice with mushroom sauce
song'idŏp bap
송이덮밥

shrimp fried rice
sae'u poggŭm bap
새우볶음밥

fried dumplings
kun mandu
군만두

Chinese Side Dishes

egg soup
kyeran t'ang
계란탕

fried vermicelli, meat & vegetables
chapch'ae
잡채

sweet & sour pork
t'angsu yuk
탕수육

pork & green pepper rice
koch'u chapch'ae
고추잡채

pork & scallions rice
puch'u chapch'ae
부추잡채

seafood & vegetables
p'albo ch'ae
팔보채

chicken dish
kkanp'unggi
깐풍기

spicy chicken dish
rajogi
라조기

spicy pork & beef dish
rajouk
라조육

assorted soup
chap t'ang
잡탕

minced pork or beef balls
nanjawansŭ
난자완스

shrimp dish
sae ut'wikim
새우튀김

prawns
k'ŭnsae ut'wikim
큰새우튀김

Sichuan dish
sach'ŏn t'angyuk
사천탕육

cold Chinese salad
samp'um naengch'ae
삼품냉채

sliced meats
ohyang jangyuk
오향장육

Japanese Food 일식

Japanese Restaurant
ilshikchib
일식집

shrimp tempura with vegetables
sae'o twigim
새우튀김

fish tempura
saengsŏn twigim
생선튀김

vegetable tempura
yach'ae twigim
야채튀김

sashimi (raw fish)
saengsŏn hoe
생선회

sushi
kimbap
김밥

egg-wrapped sushi
yubu ch'obap
유부초밥

Western Food 양식

cheeseburger
ch'ijŭ bŏgŏ
치즈버거

hamburger
haem bŏgŏ
햄버거

hot dog
hatdogŭ
핫도그

fried chicken
takt'ikim
닭튀김

French fries
kamjat'ikim
감자튀김

steak
sŭt'eik'ŭ
스테이크

salad
saellŏdŭ
샐러드

bread
ppang
빵

roll
roulpang
로울빵

toast
t'osŭt'ŭ
토스트

ham
haem
햄

sandwich
saendŭwich'i
샌드위치

boiled egg
salmŭn kyeran
삶은계란

fried egg
keranhufurai
계란후라이

Seafood 생선요리

clam
taehap
대합

crab
ke
게

fish
saengsŏn
생선

oyster
kul
굴

shrimp
saeu
새우

eel
paemjangŏ
뱀장어

Meat 육류

beef
sogogi
소고기

chicken
takkogi
닭고기

mutton
yanggogi
양고기

pork
taejigogi
돼지고기

Vegetables 야채요리

cucumber
oi
오이

garlic
  manŭl
  마늘
onion
  yangp'a
  양파
potato
  kamja
  감자
mushroom
  pŏsŏt
  버섯
radishes
  muu
  무우
green or red pepper
  koch'u
  고추
spinach
  shigumchi
  시금치
dried seaweed
  kim
  김
soybean sprouts
  k'ongnamul
  콩나물
beans
  k'ong
  콩
lotus root
  yŏn'gŭn
  연근
rice
  pap
  밥

Desserts 디저트
ice cream
  aisŭk'ŭrim
  아이스크림
cake
  k'eik'ŭ
  케이크
pie
  p'ai
  파이
pastry
  kwaja
  과자

waffles
  wap'ŭl, p'ulbbang
  와플, 풀빵
red bean parfait
  p'atbingsu
  팥빙수

Condiments 양념
salt
  sogŭm
  소금
butter
  pŏt'ŏ
  버터
jam
  chaem
  잼
black pepper
  huch'u
  후추
sugar
  sŏltang
  설탕
hot chilli pepper
  koch'u karu
  고추가루
hot sauce
  koch'ujang
  고추장
ketchup
  k'ech'ŏp
  케찹
mayonnaise
  mayonejŭ
  마요네즈
mustard
  kyŏja
  겨자
soy sauce
  kanjang
  간장
soybean paste
  toenjang
  된장
vinegar
  shikch'o
  식초

DRINKS
Nonalcoholic Drinks
Tea or coffee rooms *(tabang)* are great social

centres. No food is served (by government edict), but it is possible to take sandwiches in. Most tabang employ a girl to take coffee to yŏgwan and shops in the area, and if you live or work nearby you can get free delivery. There are at least 20 coffee-shop chains in Seoul alone. The cheaper ones have self-service – you go up to the counter and get your own. Fancier places have plush surroundings and waiters, but you pay about double for the luxury. You can grab breakfast at some of these places since they usually have cakes and sandwiches at reasonable prices. Prices for a coffee in a self-service coffee-shop chain like Doutor or Caravan are around W1000. Slightly more upmarket is the Waltz chain (70 coffee shops in Seoul alone!).

Korea produces some fine herb teas. Ginseng tea *(insam ch'a)* is the most famous, but also check out spicy herbal tea *(ssanghwa ch'a)* made from three different roots and often served with an egg yolk or pine nuts floating in it. Ginger tea *(saengkang ch'a)* is also excellent. But the thumbs-down award goes to mugwort tea *(ssuk ch'a)* – definitely an acquired taste. There are lots of instant herbal teas available from supermarkets.

Western soft drinks are sold in Japanese-sized (read 'small') tins. You might find that you need to buy two of them to quench your thirst.

Alcoholic

Koreans love their booze and there is no shortage of drinking establishments. Drinking habits, however, are a bit on the rough side. Drinking is primarily a male activity and most Korean men usually drink to get drunk (as the number of passed-out and vomiting drunks in the evening will attest to). Korean men do pay a price for all this – along with eating kimch'i, the drinking contributes heavily to a very high incidence of stomach and intestinal problems. Of course, you are not obligated to drink yourself into a coma.

A popular traditional drink is *makkŏli*, a kind of milky-white rice brew which is cheap but, like kimch'i, an acquired taste. It's sold in raucous beverage halls known as *makkŏli jip*. 'Potato vodka' (if you want to call it that) is the local firewater, known in Korean as *soju*. Lemon soju tastes nice but will knock you across the room! Makkoli and soju are often consumed along with various snacks known as *anju*. They include fresh oysters, dried squid, salted peanuts and *kim* (seaweed).

Korea's best wine is *Kyŏngju Beobjoo* – a rice wine made with herbs. There are two domestic brands of beer *(maekju)* – OB and Crown. Both companies also produce a premium beer – Crown markets Hite and OB sells Ice. Budweiser and Carlsberg have joint-venture factories in Korea and are widely available. If you drink in a beer hall, the management expects you to buy some snacks along with it. All of these drinks can also be bought in the 24-hour convenience stores at a fraction of the price you'd pay in a club. Korean beers are generally around W1000 a bottle in a store, while soju can be bought for as little as W300 for a small waxed carton.

Drinks

hot water
toun mul
더운물

cold water
ch'an mul
찬물

mineral water
sengsu, kwangch'ŏnsu
생수, 광천수

tea
ch'a
차

arrowroot tea
ch'ik ch'a
칡차

barley tea
bori ch'a
보리차

black tea
hong ch'a
홍차

Chinese matrimony vine tea
  kugija ch'a
  구기자차
citron tea
  yuja ch'a
  유자차
ginger tea
  saengkang ch'a
  생강차
ginseng tea
  insam ch'a
  인삼차
green tea
  nok ch'a
  녹차
honey tea
  kkul ch'a
  꿀차
honey-ginseng tea
  kkul sam ch'a
  꿀삼차
Job's Tears tea
  yulmu ch'a
  율무차
jujube tea
  taech'u ch'a
  대추차
lemon tea
  remon ch'a
  레몬차
mugwort tea
  ssuk ch'a
  쑥차
pine nuts, walnuts & adlay tea
  yulmu ch'a
  율무차
spicy herbal tea
  ssanghwa ch'a
  쌍화차
coffee
  kŏpi
  커피
hot cocoa
  k'ok'oa
  코코아
juice
  chyusŭ
  쥬스
orange juice
  orenji chyusŭ
  오렌지쥬스

milk
  oyu
  우유
Coca-Cola
  k'ok'a k'olra
  코카콜라
beer
  maekju
  맥주
wine
  p'odoju
  포도주
Kyŏngju Beobjoo (wine)
  Kyŏngju pŏbju
  경주법주
milky white rice brew
  makkŏli
  막걸리
potato vodka
  soju
  소주

ENTERTAINMENT
Pubs & Bars
Korea's nightlife is significantly dampened by government-imposed midnight closing hours. This restriction has its roots in a curfew which was enforced back in the days when Korea was a military dictatorship. The dictatorship is gone, but the government feels the need to shut down bars at midnight to protect the morals of the nation. In some pubs, you will be allowed to remain after midnight if you are already inside when they lock their doors, but the door will not be opened to admit new customers.

Pubs are also known as hofs *(hop'ŭ)* or soju parlours *(soju bang)*, but these places can be expensive. Sometimes they have karaoke, and you can think of these places as classy cocktail lounges.

One Korean innovation with a long history are soju tents *(taep'otjip)*. These are usually set up in the evening alongside the bank of a river, and feature inexpensive drinks and snacks. Although they are extremely popular the government frowns on these places, believing that they are a relic from the poverty-stricken past and have no place in modern Korea. However, soju tents are now banned in Seoul, although they can still be found in most other cities and towns. If the government ever gets really serious about cracking down, soju tents will become a thing of the past.

Billiards & Bowling

The Koreans are keen on bowling (polling). and even keener on billiards (tanggu). Billiard halls are everywhere with an unmistakable sign. Koreans can advise you on the location of bowling alleys, although they are not difficult to find. Operating hours are from about 10 am until midnight.

Cinemas

Young Koreans are certainly fond of movies, and the cinemas (yŏnghwa gwan, kukjang) tend to pack out on weekends and holidays. Indeed, you might even have to buy a ticket from scalpers who hang around the cinemas on Sundays. However, there are seldom problems on weekdays.

Foreign movies (English dialogue, Korean subtitles) are popular. So popular that the government has felt the need to 'encourage' the production of Korean films by forcing cinemas to limit foreign movies to 60% of the total shown. The problem is that the Korean movies have not proved very popular. Indeed, the cinemas have had no choice but to subsidise the Korean film industry with box office revenues gained from showing foreign films – otherwise, there would simply not be enough Korean films to fill the 40% quota.

One reason why Korean-produced films have not done well is that they are carefully censored. Political content is a particularly thorny issue, but there are also supposedly controls on sex and violence. Of course, foreign movies also have to get past the censors, but political content is less of a problem since they are rarely about Korea.

Theatres

Most of Korea's theatres (sokŭk jang) are concentrated in Seoul, especially in the Taehangno entertainment district (see Entertainment in the Seoul chapter).

Unfortunately, performances are almost entirely in Korean.

Gambling

The only forms of legal gambling (norŭm) available to the average Korean is the national lottery (tickets can be bought everywhere) and horse racing (see the Seoul Horse Race Track section in the Kyŏnggi-do chapter). It's a different story for foreigners. If you're a compulsive gambler and can't wait to get to Las Vegas, you can lose your fortune in South Korea at one of the special casinos (k'ajino) designed to milk foreign tourists only (no Koreans allowed). Japanese and Arabs are the most favoured customers, but all non-Koreans with excess cash are welcome.

The casinos are in major tourist hotels including the following:

Sheraton Walker Hill Hotel, Seoul (☎ (02) 453-0121); Olympos Hotel, Inch'ŏn (☎ (032) 762-5181); KAL Hotel, Cheju City (☎ (064) 53-6151); Grand Hotel, Cheju City (☎ (064) 47-5000); Oriental Hotel, Cheju City (☎ (064) 52-8222); Nam Seoul, Cheju City (☎ (064) 42-4111); Hyatt Regency, Sŏgwip'o, Cheju-do (☎ (064) 33-1234); Shilla Hotel, Sŏgwip'o (☎ (064) 33-4466); KAL Hotel, Sŏgwip'o (☎ (064) 32-9851); Sŏrak Park Hotel, Sŏraksan (☎ (0392) 34-7711); Riviera Yousung Hotel, Taejŏn (☎ (042) 823-2111); Paradise Beach Hotel, Pusan (☎ (051) 742-2121); Kolon Hotel, Kyŏngju (☎ (0651) 746-9001); and the Songnisan Hotel, Songnisan (☎ (0433) 42-5281/8).

Karaoke

Karaoke (empty music; norae bang, KTV)) is a Japanese invention. For the uninitiated it's basically a big amateur singing contest to the accompaniment of a video tape (or laser disk). The idea is to give you the chance to be a star, even if nobody but you gets to hear the performance.

There are variations on the theme. One type of karaoke is a bar or lounge in which you sing in front of others. In this type of place there will usually be no cover charge, though you are expected to buy drinks and snacks. Another type is a little booth (around W12,000 per hour) in which you sit by yourself (or with a friend) and sing along with a video tape and record your performance. You can take home your recorded tape to enjoy at your leisure.

Korea is unusual in that the karaoke business is somewhat organised. Songs (some of which are in English) are numbered and all the clubs use the same numbering system – if you ask for song No 112, it will be the same at every karaoke place in Korea.

In general, karaoke gets the thumbs down from Westerners while most Koreans (along with most other Asians) love it. There appears to be a clear cultural difference here. Whether you like it or not, there is no denying its popularity – karaoke parlours are spreading around the world.

Discos

Discos *(tisŭk'o chang)* certainly exist in Korea, but they have declined somewhat. Apparently, the karaoke business has offered formidable competition.

A pretty steep 'table charge' gets you your first few beers and anju at the Korean-style places. The system may differ in places that cater to foreigners, such as in Seoul's It'aewon neighbourhood.

The discos at the big tourist hotels are flashy and very good for meeting people, but these places cost big money. If it helps any, they accept credit cards.

Video Parlours

These are supposedly illegal, which explains why they try to maintain a low profile. Video parlours *(pidio bang)* are no different from video rental shops except that you watch the movies on their equipment. There is no reason why they should be illegal, except that Hollywood fears that these places compete against box office cinemas. The dispute over video parlours has boiled over into trade negotiations between South Korea and the USA, thus the need for the Koreans to at least maintain the appearance of illegality. Legal or not, you can find these places easily enough if you ask a local to assist you.

Spectator Sports

Ssirŭm is a traditional form of Korean wrestling. Two opponents face off against each other, and one loses if any part of the body other than the feet touch the ground. Ssirŭm bears some resemblance to the better-known Japanese sumo style. Indeed, some of Japan's best sumo wrestlers are in fact ethnic Koreans, though the Japanese are loathe to admit this. For their part, the Koreans say the Japanese borrowed the idea of sumo wrestling from Korea. The Korean Amateur Sport Association can give you information about competitions and classes.

These days, Korea's mass media focuses on Western-style sports. Baseball is a long-time favourite, but soccer is starting to catch on. Basketball appeals to the affluent Westernised class in Seoul.

THINGS TO BUY

Although the Koreans like to deny it, Korea is one of the most protectionist countries in Asia. The significance of this to visitors is that Korean-made goods will be far cheaper than anything imported. That means you can forget about finding bargains on such things as imported Japanese cameras or Taiwanese portable computers.

On the positive side, Korea does produce some excellent products and there are bargains on good-quality merchandise.

One of Korea's main exports is sporting equipment. There are good deals on tents, sleeping bags, hiking boots, backpacks, rock climbing equipment, tennis rackets and other such items. Indoor sports enthusiasts will find various sorts of springs, weights, trampolines and other contortionist devices.

Korea is the ginseng capital of the world, and for many Asians it is a magical cure-all. Japanese and Chinese tourists buy as much of the stuff as they can get their hands on, and as a result, the government has restricted the amount an individual can take out of the country to three kg in its raw state.

Name Chops

When the Koreans adopted the Chinese writing system, they also took the concept of a name chop *(tojang)* or seal. The traditional name chop has been in use in China for thousands of years. It's likely that people began using name chops because Chinese characters are so complex and few people in ancient times were able to read and write. In addition, chops date back to a time when there was no other form of identification such as fingerprinting, picture ID cards and computer files.

A chop served both as a form of identification and as a valid signature. All official documents in both Korea and China needed to be stamped with a chop to be valid. Naturally, this made a chop quite valuable because with another person's chop it was possible to sign contracts and other legal documents in their name.

Today, most Koreans have abandoned the use of Chinese characters, preferring the much simpler han'gŭl system. Furthermore, chops are no longer recognised as a valid signature on legal documents in Korea, although they are still used this way in China. Nevertheless, traditions die hard and you will still find plenty of shops in Korea which carve name chops. Normally, highly-decorative Chinese characters are still used to produce a name chop, although you can have one carved in han'gŭl. When stamping your 'signature' with a name chop, only red ink is used. On traditional Korean watercolour paintings and decorative scrolls, you will always find the telltale red chop mark which identifies the artist.

Many foreigners enjoy having a chop made as a souvenir. These can be carved quickly, sometimes while you wait. Of course, you'll first need to have your name translated into Chinese characters or han'gŭl.

There are many different sizes and styles of chops. Inexpensive small chops can be carved from wood or plastic for about W2000 or so. Chops can be carved from ivory, jade, marble or steel and cost W50,000 and up.

Arts & Crafts

Lacquerware is one of Korea's ancient arts and lacquer boxes are just one example of this tradition. It also encompasses furniture from tables and chairs to wardrobes and storage chests. The latter can be particularly stunning and a great deal of attention is also given to the brass fittings. Naturally, these larger items are bulky – and more expensive – so, if you were to buy them, you'd have to arrange for them to be shipped to your home country. Most retailers can make these arrangements for you.

In most of the shops which sell lacquerware there is a wide selection of brassware as well. Hand-hammered and moulded brassware is made into everything including paperweights, plates, goblets, lamps, vases and even beds. There's also much which draws its inspiration from Buddhist statuary. Prices are reasonable.

Ceramics are another Korean craft with a long pedigree going back to the days of the Koryŏ dynasty when the pale blue-green, crackle-glazed celadon pottery was regarded as perfection itself. It was much sought after, even in China which had its own highly developed ceramics. The tradition of excellence has been maintained and there are many beautiful pieces to be found in specialist shops. It is, however, generally expensive so don't expect to pick up pieces for a song. Ceramics definitely fall into the realm of art rather than craftwork.

Much cheaper, are the carved wooden masks you'll come across in many a souvenir shop in country areas. Only rarely do these resemble the shamanistic spirit posts

Hand-Carved Wooden Mask

found at the entrance to rural villages. Instead they concentrate on exaggerated facial expressions and range from the grotesque to the humorous. They're easily carried in the average backpack and usually cost between W10,000 and W20,000, although the detail determines the price.

Visit any Korean home and you'll see scores of examples of embroidery. It's a national hobby among the women and highly regarded as a decorative art. Many fabric shops specialise in embroidery along with incredibly ornate brocades and you can pick up everything from handkerchiefs and pillow cases to room-sized screens. Many such shops do personalised embroidery either to their own or to the customer's designs. Another similar national hobby is

macrame. Common items are colourful wall hangings and the long *norigae* tassles which adorn the front of every Korean woman's traditional costume. The latter always hang from a painted brass headpiece which itself is often very colourful.

Korea produces a wide range of precious and semiprecious stones including amethyst, smoky topaz, rubies, sapphires, emeralds and, of course, jade. Korean jade is paler than Chinese green jade and is often almost white, but it's a lot cheaper. You will find jewellery shops everywhere and at most of them you have a choice of mounted and unmounted stones. As with buying stones anywhere else in the world, you will need to have a good knowledge of current prices and know what to look for in order to find bargains.

Getting There & Away

AIR

Most major international airlines fly into South Korea. The Koreans also operate two airlines of their own, Asiana Airlines (*ashiana hangkong*) and Korean Air (KAL) (*tashan hangkong*).

Seoul's Kimp'o Airport is the principal gateway to South Korea, but there are international airports at Pusan and Chejudo mostly serving the Japanese market. Direct flights connect Seoul with most of the capital cities of South and North-East Asia, the major exception being P'yŏngyang in North Korea. If you're flying from a country which does not have direct air service to Seoul, you can almost always get there by making a quick change of planes at Japan's Narita Airport.

Flights can be heavily booked during peak times, mainly the Lunar New Year, Chusŏk and Christmas. It can also be difficult to get economy trans-Pacific tickets on short notice during the summer school holidays, though you can always get a seat if you're willing to pay for a business or first-class ticket.

Tickets

Ironically, both Asiana and KAL are relatively expensive if you buy tickets in Korea, but cheap when you purchase the ticket abroad. In Korea you'll often get a better deal from a major foreign carrier such as British Airways, Garuda, Northwest Airlines, Singapore Airlines, THAI Airways, United Airlines etc.

The same discrepancy in airfares is found when you are purchasing a ticket with a stopover in Korea. For example, a Los Angeles to Hong Kong ticket with a stopover in Seoul is cheaper on Northwest Airlines than on KAL. However, a direct Los Angeles-Seoul return ticket is cheaper on KAL!

While Korea is not the cheapest place in Asia to purchase air tickets, it's by no means the worst. Buying tickets from a travel agent is almost always cheaper than buying directly from the airline because airlines don't give discounts. It's a good idea to call the airline first and see what their cheapest ticket costs. Use that as your starting point when talking to travel agents. There are tremendous variations between the prices quoted by travel agencies, so it pays to shop around. Many travel agents charge the full fare, but other agents will knock off up to 40%. The cheapest air tickets can be bought in Seoul rather than in small cities or rural areas. (See the Seoul chapter for some recommended discount travel agencies.)

Use common sense before handing over the cash and always get a receipt. Whenever possible, try to avoid handing over the cash until they hand over the ticket, or else pay only a deposit and be sure your receipt clearly states the total amount due.

It's important to understand that when you buy an air ticket from a travel agent, you must go back to that agent if you want a refund – the airlines will only make a direct refund if you purchased the ticket from the airline yourself. While this is no problem if you don't change your travel plans, it can be quite a hassle if you decide to change the route halfway through your trip. In that case, you'd have to return to the place where you bought the ticket to refund the unused portion of the journey. Of course, if you had a reliable friend whom you could mail the ticket to, that person could possibly obtain the refund for you, but don't count on it. It's also true that some travel agents (and airlines) are extremely slow to issue refunds – some travellers have had to wait up to a year!

APEX Tickets Apex (Advance Purchase Excursion) tickets are sold at a discount but will lock you into a rigid schedule. Such tickets must be purchased two or three weeks ahead of departure, do not permit stopovers and may have minimum and maximum stays as well as fixed departure and return dates. Unless you definitely must return at a certain time, it's best to purchase APEX tickets on a one-way basis only. There are stiff cancellation fees if you decide not to use your ticket.

Round-the-World Tickets 'Round-the-world' tickets (RTW) are usually offered by an airline or combination of airlines, and let you take your time (six months to a year) moving from point to point on their routes for the price of one ticket. The main restriction is that you have to keep moving in the same direction; a drawback is that because you are usually booking individual flights as you go, and can't switch carriers, you can get caught out by flight availabilities, and have to spend more or less time in a place than you want.

Group Tickets 'Group' tickets are well worth considering. You usually do *not* need to travel with a group. However, once the departure date is booked it may be impossible to change – you can only depart when the 'group' departs, even if you never meet or see another group member. It's possible that you will need to book the group ticket far in advance, but that isn't always the case. The good news is that the return date can usually be left open, but there could be other restrictions – you might have to complete the trip in 60 days, or perhaps can only fly off-season or during weekdays. It's important to ask the travel agent what conditions and restrictions apply to any tickets you intend to buy.

Back-to-Front Ticket One thing to avoid is a 'back-to-front' ticket. These are best explained by example – if you want to fly from Korea (where tickets are relatively expensive) to Hong Kong (where tickets are up to 20% cheaper), you can pay by cheque or credit card and have a friend or travel agent in Hong Kong mail the ticket to you. The problem is that the airline computer will show that the ticket was issued in Hong Kong rather than Korea, and they will refuse to honour it. Consumer groups have filed lawsuits over this practice with mixed results, but in most countries the law protects the airlines, not consumers. In short, the ticket is only valid starting from the country where it was issued. The only exception is if you pay the full fare, thus foregoing any possible discounts that Hong Kong travel agents can offer.

Frequent Flyer 'Frequent-flyer' plans are offered by most airlines, even some budget ones. Basically, these allow you a free ticket if you chalk up so many km with the same airline. US-based airlines tend to offer the most generous frequent-flyer programmes. However, the plans aren't always as good as they sound – some airlines require you to use all your frequent-flyer credits within one year or you lose the lot. Sometimes you find yourself flying on a particular airline just to get frequent-flyer credits, but the ticket is considerably more expensive than a ticket from a discount airline without a frequent-flyer bonus. Many airlines have 'blackout' periods – peak times when you cannot use the free tickets you obtained under the frequent-flyer programme.

Whenever you purchase a ticket, be sure to give the ticket agent your frequent-flyer membership number, and again when you check in for your flight. A common complaint seems to be that airlines forget to record your frequent-flyer credits when you fly with them – save all your boarding passes and ticket receipts and be prepared to push if no bonus is forthcoming. Some airlines have cooperative arrangements where you can combine the credits earned on two or more different airlines to get a free ticket. These arrangements are worth looking into – for example, Korea's Asiana Airlines has a working agreement with America's Northwest.

Student Tickets Some airlines offer discounts of up to 25% to student-card holders. In some countries, an official-looking letter from the school is also needed. You also must be age 26 or younger. These discounts are generally only available on advertised

Air Travel Glossary

Apex Apex, or 'advance purchase excursion' is a discounted ticket which must be paid for in advance. There are penalties if you wish to change it.

Baggage Allowance This will be written on your ticket: usually one 20 kg item to go in the hold, plus one item of hand luggage.

Bucket Shop An unbonded travel agency specialising in discounted airline tickets.

Bumped Just because you have a confirmed seat doesn't mean you're going to get on the plane – see Overbooking.

Cancellation Penalties If you have to cancel or change an Apex ticket there are often heavy penalties involved; insurance can sometimes be taken out against these penalties. Some airlines impose penalties on regular tickets as well, particularly against 'no show' passengers.

Check In Airlines ask you to check in a certain time ahead of the flight departure (usually 1½ hours on international flights). If you fail to check in on time and the flight is overbooked the airline can cancel your booking and give your seat to somebody else.

Confirmation Having a ticket written out with the flight and date you want doesn't mean you have a seat until the agent has checked with the airline that your status is 'OK' or confirmed. Meanwhile you could just be 'on request'.

Discounted Tickets There are two types of discounted fares – officially discounted (see Promotional Fares) and unofficially discounted. The lowest prices often impose drawbacks like flying with unpopular airlines, inconvenient schedules, or unpleasant routes and connections. A discounted ticket can save you other things than money – you may be able to pay Apex prices without the associated Apex advance booking and other requirements. Discounted tickets only exist where there is fierce competition.

Full Fares Airlines traditionally offer first class (coded F), business class (coded J) and economy class (coded Y) tickets. These days there are so many promotional and discounted fares available from the regular economy class that few passengers pay full economy fare.

Lost Tickets If you lose your airline ticket an airline will usually treat it like a travellers' cheque and, after enquiries, issue you with another one. Legally, however, an airline is entitled to treat it like cash and if you lose it then it's gone forever. Take good care of your tickets.

No Shows No shows are passengers who fail to show up for their flight, sometimes due to unexpected delays or disasters, sometimes due to simply forgetting, sometimes because they made more than one booking and didn't bother to cancel the one they didn't want. Full-fare passengers who fail to turn up are sometimes entitled to travel on a later flight. The rest of us are penalised (see Cancellation Penalties).

On Request An unconfirmed booking for a flight; see Confirmation.

Open Jaws A return ticket where you fly to one place but return from another. If available, this can save you backtracking to your arrival point.

economy-class fares. You wouldn't get one, for instance, on an APEX or RTW ticket since these are already discounted.

Courier Tickets Courier flights can be a bargain if you're fortunate enough to find one. The way it works is that an air freight company takes over your entire checked baggage allowance. You are permitted to bring along a carry-on bag, but that's all. In return, you get a steeply discounted ticket. These arrangements usually have to be made a month or more in advance and are only available on certain routes. Also, such tickets are sold for a fixed date and schedule

changes can be difficult or impossible to make. Courier flights are occasionally advertised in the newspapers, or contact air freight companies listed in the phone book.

Children's Tickets Airlines usually carry babies up to two years of age at 10% of the relevant adult fare; a few may carry them free of charge. Reputable international airlines usually provide nappies (diapers), tissues, talcum and all the other paraphernalia needed to keep babies clean, dry and half-happy. For children between the ages of two (on some airlines four) and 12, the fare on

Overbooking Airlines hate to fly empty seats and since every flight has some passengers who fail to show up (see No Shows), airlines often book more passengers than they have seats. Usually the excess passengers balance those who fail to show up, but occasionally somebody gets bumped. If this happens guess who it is most likely to be? The passengers who check in late.

Promotional Fares Officially discounted fares like Apex fares which are available from travel agents or direct from the airline.

Reconfirmation At least 72 hours prior to departure time of an onward or return flight, you must contact the airline and 'reconfirm' that you intend to be on the flight. If you don't do this the airline can delete your name from the passenger list and you could lose your seat. You don't have to reconfirm the first flight on your itinerary or if your stopover is less than 72 hours. It doesn't hurt to reconfirm more than once.

Restrictions Discounted tickets often have various restrictions on them – advance purchase is the most usual one (see Apex). Others are restrictions on the minimum and maximum period you must be away, such as a minimum of 14 days or a maximum of one year. See Cancellation Penalties.

Standby A discounted ticket where you only fly if there is a seat free at the last moment. Standby fares are usually only available on domestic routes.

Tickets Out An entry requirement for many countries is that you have an onward or return ticket, in other words, a ticket out of the country. If you're not sure what you intend to do next, the easiest solution is to buy the cheapest onward ticket to a neighbouring country or a ticket from a reliable airline which can later be refunded if you do not use it.

Transferred Tickets Airline tickets cannot be transferred from one person to another. Travellers sometimes try to sell the return half of their ticket, but officials can ask you to prove that you are the person named on the ticket. This is unlikely to happen on domestic flights; on an international flight, tickets may be compared with passports.

Travel Agencies Travel agencies vary widely and you should ensure you use one that suits your needs. Some simply handle tours while full-service agencies handle everything from tours and tickets to car rental and hotel bookings. A good one will do all these things and can save you a lot of money but if all you want is a ticket at the lowest possible price, then you really need an agency specialising in discounted tickets. A discounted ticket agency, however, may not be useful for other things, like hotel bookings.

Travel Periods Some officially discounted fares, Apex fares in particular, vary with the time of year. There is often a low (off-peak) season and a high (peak) season. Sometimes there's an intermediate or shoulder season as well. At peak times, when everyone wants to fly, not only will the officially discounted fares be higher, so will the unofficially discounted fares or there may simply be no discounted tickets available. Usually the fare depends on your outward flight – if you depart in the high season and return in the low season, you pay the high-season fare. ■

international flights is usually 50% of the regular fare or 67% of a discounted fare.

To/From Australia

Australia is not a cheap place to fly out of, and air fares between Australia and Asia are absurdly expensive considering the distances flown. However, there are a few ways of cutting the costs.

Among the cheapest regular tickets available in Australia are APEX tickets. The cost depends on your departure date from Australia. The year is divided into 'peak' (expensive), 'shoulder' (less expensive) and 'low' (relatively inexpensive) seasons; peak season is December to January.

It's possible to get reductions on the cost of APEX and other fares by going to the student travel offices and/or some of the travel agents in Australia that specialise in discounting.

The weekend travel sections of papers like *The Age* (Melbourne) or the *Sydney Morning Herald* are good sources of travel information. Also look at *Student Traveller*, a free newspaper published by STA Travel, the travel organisation which now has offices worldwide. STA Travel has offices all around Australia (check your phone directory) and you do not have to be a student to use them.

Also well worth trying is the Flight Shop (☎ (03) 670-0477), 386 Little Bourke St, Melbourne. They also have branches under the name of the Flight Centre in Sydney (☎ (02) 233-2296) and Brisbane (☎ (07) 229-9958).

Discount one-way/return tickets between Sydney and Seoul cost about US$700/950.

To/From Canada

Getting discount tickets in Canada is much the same as in the USA – go to the travel agents and shop around until you find a good deal.

CUTS is Canada's national student bureau and has offices in a number of Canadian cities including Vancouver, Edmonton, Toronto and Ottawa – you don't necessarily have to be a student. There are a number of good agents in Vancouver for cheap tickets. Budget one-way/return fares between Vancouver and Seoul are US$870/1100.

To/From China

China has always regarded Korea as an inferior vassal state which must pay tribute, and nowhere is this more evident than in the matter of aviation rights. The Chinese government claims the entire West Sea (Yellow Sea) as its own, right up to the Korean coastline. While the Koreans rightly dispute this claim, there is little that they can do about it short of going to war with China. As a result of the ongoing war-of-words, flights between Seoul and Beijing are currently prohibited from flying over the Yellow Sea – the planes have to fly all the way down to Shanghai and make a sharp turn to the north! This doubles the flight time and increases the expense of the tickets. However, this seems set to change as negotiations between the two sides have been proceeding.

At the time of writing, KAL flies to Shanghai and Asiana flies to Tianjin. However, this seems set to change soon – Asiana has announced that flights to Beijing will begin 'soon', whenever that is. In Shanghai, you can book tickets at KAL (☎ 258-8450),

Rooms 104 & 105, Hotel Equatorial, 65 Yan'an Xilu. In Beijing, you can book tickets at Asiana Airlines (☎ 500-2233 ext 134), Room 134, Jianguo Hotel, 5 Jianguomenwai. However, the Chinese government prohibits the Korean airlines to actually *sell* tickets in China – for this, you must go to the Chinese airline, CAAC. The KAL or Asiana offices will tell you where to pick up the tickets after you've booked them.

The Bank of China at Tianjin Airport appears to be dysfunctional (at least during departure times), so arrive at the airport with just enough money to pay the departure tax and perhaps buy a drink. Many have suggested that this situation is no accident, the motive being to force you to spend your excess Chinese currency in the airport's duty-free shop.

Travel agents cannot give discounts on China-Korea tickets, and return tickets cost exactly double the one-way fare. The one-way fare between Seoul and Shanghai is US$250. Seoul-Tianjin one way costs US$330, but this may drop considerably if China and Korea ever sort out their dispute over aviation rights.

Definitely avoid getting a visa for China while you're in Korea. China's visa office in Seoul (which is *not* in the Chinese embassy) is notoriously arrogant and inefficient. It's open from just 9 am to 11.30 am but hundreds of people show up and you have to start queuing by 7 am or you won't get inside.

To/From Europe

The Netherlands, Brussels and Antwerp are good places for buying discount air tickets. In Antwerp, WATS has been recommended. In Zurich, try SOF Travel and Sindbad. In Geneva, try Stohl Travel. In the Netherlands, NBBS is a reputable agency.

To/From Guam & Saipan

For the Koreans, Guam and the nearby island of Saipan have emerged as popular honeymoon and vacation spots. Guam is just 4½ hours from Seoul by air. KAL flies into Guam and Asiana flies into Saipan. One-way/return fares begin at US$300/360.

To/From Hong Kong

Hong Kong travel agents dish out some of the cheapest tickets to be found anyplace on earth. Many of the airlines offer special promotional fares for a short time only, and not all of the travel agents are aware of these cut-rate fares, so ask around at a couple of places before buying. Also note that some of these super-cheap tickets have restrictions, such as flying only on Tuesdays and Thursdays or having to complete your round-trip itinerary within 60 days, and so on. Be sure you understand these restrictions when buying rock-bottom priced tickets.

In Hong Kong, buying tickets requires some caution because there are quite a few tricky travel agents. The most common trick is a request for a non-refundable deposit on an air ticket. So you pay a deposit for the booking, but when you go to pick up the tickets they say that the flight is no longer available, but that there is another flight at a higher price, sometimes 50% more!

It is best not to pay a deposit, but to rather pay for the ticket in full and get a receipt clearly showing that there is no balance due, and that the full amount is refundable if no ticket is issued. Tickets are normally issued the next day after booking, but for the really cheapie tickets (actually group tickets) you must pick these up yourself at the airport from the 'tour leader' (who you will never see again once you've got the ticket). One caution: when you get the ticket from the tour leader, check it carefully. Occasionally, there are errors, such as you're issued a ticket with the return portion valid for only 60 days when you paid for a ticket valid for one year etc.

Some agents we've found to be cheap and reliable in Hong Kong include the following:

Phoenix Services, Room B, 6th Floor, Milton Mansion, 96 Nathan Rd, Tsimshatsui, is scrupulously honest and gets good reviews from travellers (☎ 722-7378; fax 369-8884).

Shoestring Travel, Flat A, 4th Floor, Alpha House, 27-33 Nathan Rd, Tsimshatsui (☎ 723-2306; fax 721-2085).

Traveller Services, Room 1012, Silvercord Tower 1, 30 Canton Rd, Tsimshatsui (☎ 375-2222; fax 375-2233).

Victoria Travel is connected to Victoria Hostel on the 1st Floor at 33 Hankow Rd, Tsimshatsui (☎ 376-0621; fax 376-2609).

The lowest one-way/return prices on the Hong Kong-Seoul route are US$201/272.

To/From Indonesia

Garuda Airlines has direct flights from Jakarta to Seoul, and from Denpasar to Seoul via Jakarta. KAL flies Jakarta-Seoul direct. Cheap discount air tickets out of Indonesia can be bought from travel agents in Kuta Beach, Bali and in Jakarta. There are numerous discount travel agents around Kuta Beach – several on the main strip, Jalan Legian. You can also buy discount tickets in Kuta for departure from Jakarta. In Jakarta, there are a few discounters on Jalan Jaksa. Discount one-way/return prices for Jakarta-Seoul are currently US$544/720.

To/From Japan

Japan is not a good place to buy cheap air tickets. In fact, there is hardly anything you can buy cheaply in Japan, not even rice. The cheapest way to get out of Japan is by ferry to Korea.

Airfares are definitely cheaper if you purchase your ticket in Korea. The following are the cheapest prices you can expect on tickets booked in Seoul:

Route	One Way	Return
Fukuoka-Chejudo	US$112	US$224
Fukuoka-Pusan	US$76	US$192
Fukuoka-Seoul	US$105	US$210
Hiroshima-Seoul	US$146	US$292
Nagoya-Seoul	US$170	US$240
Okinawa-Seoul	US$153	US$306
Sendai-Chejudo	US$269	US$538
Sendai-Pusan	US$231	US$462
Sendai-Seoul	US$257	US$514
Takamatsu-Seoul	US$158	US$316
Tokyo-Seoul	US$176	US$352
Toyama-Seoul	US$199	US$398

If you must buy an air ticket in Japan, Tokyo is the best place to shop around for discounts. You should start your search by checking the travel ad section of the *Tokyo Journal*. Three long-standing travel agencies which usually sell discount tickets and have English-speaking staff are:

Across Traveller's Bureau (☎ (03) 3374-8721 Shinjuku; ☎ (03) 5391-2871) Ikebukuro); STA (☎ (03) 5269-0751 Yotsuya; ☎ (03) 5485-8380 Shibuya; ☎ (03) 5391-2922 Ikebukuro); Just Travel (☎ (03) 3207-8311 Takadanobaba).

To/From New Zealand

Both KAL and Air New Zealand can shuttle you between Auckland and Seoul. Tickets are not especially cheap. Discount one-way/return fares begin at US$850/1350.

To/From the Philippines

Bottom-end one-way/return fares between Seoul and Manila are US$215/369.

To/From Singapore

A good place for buying cheap air tickets in Singapore is Airmaster Travel Centre. Also try STA Travel. Other agents advertise in the *Straits Times* classified columns.

One-way/return Singapore Seoul tickets start at US$407/680.

To/From Taiwan

Discount travel agents advertise in Taiwan's two English-language newspapers, the *China News* and *China Post*. Don't believe the advertised rock-bottom fares – many are elusive 'group fares' which are not accessible to the individual traveller. Another thing to be cautious of is sending money through the mail – this never seems to work as well as visiting the travel agent with cash in hand.

A long-running discount travel agent with a good reputation is Jenny Su Travel (☎ 594-7733, 596-2263; fax 592-0068), 10th Floor, 27 Chungshan N Rd, Section 3, Taipei. Wing On Travel and South-East Travel have branches all over the island, and both have good reputations and offer reasonable prices.

Discount tickets on the Taipei-Seoul route start at US$150/320.

To/From Thailand

Check out the travel agents on Khao San Rd in Bangkok, and shop around a little for the best price. The Bangkok-Seoul run is served by numerous carriers, and it's often possible to get a stopover in Hong Kong for little extra. Bangkok-Seoul one-way/return fares start at US$400/550.

To/From the UK

Both British Airways and KAL offer London-Seoul service at competitive prices.

Air-ticket discounting is a long-running business in the UK and it's wide open. The various agents advertise their fares and there is nothing under-the-counter about it at all. To find out what's going, there are a number of magazines in Britain which have good information about flights and agents. These include: *Trailfinder*, free from the Trailfinders Travel Centre in Earls Court; and *Time Out* or *City Limits*, London weekly entertainment guides widely available in the UK.

Discount tickets are almost exclusively available in London. You may find discounters in various smaller cities, but forget it in the countryside. The danger with discounted tickets in Britain is that some of the 'bucket shops' (as ticket discounters are known) are unsound. Sometimes the backstairs over-the-shop travel agents fold up and disappear after you've handed over the money and before you've received the tickets. Get the tickets before you hand over the cash.

Two reliable London bucket shops are Trailfinders in Earls Court, and STA Travel with several offices. Another place to try is Regent Holidays (UK) Ltd (☎ (0117) 9211711; telex 444606; fax 254866), 15 John St, Bristol BS1 2HR.

The discount end of the market for London-Seoul tickets is US$1000/1300.

To/From the USA

There are some very good open tickets which remain valid for six months or one year (opt for the latter), but don't lock you into any fixed dates of departure and allow multiple stopovers. For example, there are cheap tickets between the US west coast and Hong Kong with a stopover in Korea for very little extra money – the departure dates can be changed and you have one year to complete the journey. However, be careful during the peak season (Christmas, Lunar New Year and summer holidays) because seats will be hard to come by on short notice.

Usually, and not surprisingly, the cheapest fare to whatever country is offered by a discount travel agency owned by someone of that particular ethnic origin. San Francisco is the air ticket discounters' capital of America, although some good deals can be found in Los Angeles, New York and other cities. Travel agents can be found through the Yellow Pages or the major daily newspapers. Those listed in both Roman and Oriental scripts are invariably discounters. A more direct way is to wander around San Francisco's Chinatown where most of the shops are – especially in the Clay St and Waverly Place area. Many of these are staffed by recent arrivals from Asia who speak little English. Enquiries are best made in person. One place popular with budget travellers is Wahlock Travel in the Bank of America Building on Stockton St.

It's not advisable to send money (even cheques) through the post unless the agent is very well established – some travellers have reported being ripped off by fly-by-night mail-order ticket agents. Nor is it wise to hand over the full amount to Shady Deal Travel Services unless they can give you the ticket straight away – most US travel agencies have computers that can spit out the ticket on the spot.

Council Travel is the largest student travel organisation, and, though you don't have to be a student to use them, they do have specially discounted student tickets. Council Travel has an extensive network in all major US cities and is listed in the telephone book. There are also Student Travel Network offices which are associated with STA Travel.

One of the cheapest and most reliable travel agents on the west coast is Overseas Tours (☎ (800) 222-5292), 475 El Camino Real, Room 206, Millbrae, CA 94030. Another good agent is Gateway Travel (☎ (214) 960-2000, (800) 441-1183), 4201

Spring Valley Rd, Suite 104, Dallas, TX 75244. Both of these places seem to be trustworthy for mail-order tickets.

Some quotations for one-way/return tickets are: Honolulu-Seoul US$450/700; Los Angeles-Seoul US$500/750; New York-Seoul US$870/1050.

To/From Vietnam
Air service between Ho Chi Minh City and Seoul is offered by Asiana, KAL and Vietnam Airlines. Budget one-way/return fares are US$665/725.

LAND
Despite the fact that digging invasion tunnels under the so-called 'Demilitarised Zone' is a favourite preoccupation of North Koreans, you can forget about entering South Korea by land.

SEA
To/From China
International ferries connect the South Korean port of Inch'ŏn with three cities in China: Weihai, Qingdao and Tianjin. Weihai and Qingdao are in China's Shandong Province (the closest province to South Korea) and boats are operated by the Weidong Ferry Co. Tianjin is near Beijing and boats are run by the Tianjin Ferry Company.

The phone numbers for Weidong Ferry Company are: Seoul (☎ (02) 711-9111); Inch'ŏn (☎ (032) 886-6171); Weihai (☎ (0896) 232634); Qingdao (☎ (0532) 221152). Phone numbers for Tianjin Ferry Company are: Seoul (☎ (02) 517-8671); Inch'ŏn (☎ (032) 887-3963); Tianjin (☎ (022) 359000). In Seoul, tickets for any boats to China can be bought from the Universal Travel Service, otherwise known as UTS (☎ (02) 722-1057; fax 737-2764) behind City Hall. In China, tickets can be bought cheaply at the pier, or from China International Travel Service (for a very *steep* premium).

The Inch'ŏn International Ferry Terminal is the next to last stop on the Inch'ŏn-Seoul commuter train (red subway line from downtown) – the train takes one hour and from the station it's either a long walk or short taxi ride to the terminal. You must arrive at the terminal at least one hour before departure or you won't be allowed to board.

Inch'ŏn-Weihai The trip takes a minimum of 17 hours. Departures from Weihai are Monday and Friday at 5 pm. Departures from Inch'ŏn are on Wednesday and Saturday at 4 pm. The cost is US$90 in economy class and up to US$250 in deluxe class. There are also several classes in between.

Inch'ŏn-Qingdao This trip takes a minimum of 24 hours. Departures from Qingdao are only once a month on the second Saturday. The boat leaves Qingdao at 11 am, and departures from Inch'ŏn are at 2 pm. The fare varies from US$100 in economy to US$300 for deluxe service.

Inch'ŏn-Tianjin This popular ferry runs once every five days and the journey takes a minimum of 28 hours. Departures from Tianjin are at 10 am. The boat departs Inch'ŏn at 2 pm. The fare is US$100 to US$250.

The boat doesn't dock at Tianjin proper, but rather at the nearby port of Tanggu. Accommodation in Tianjin is outrageously expensive, but Tanggu has at least one economical accommodation, the Seamen's Hotel. Tanggu has trains directly to Beijing.

To/From Japan

There are several ferries linking Japan to South Korea. Purchasing a round-trip ticket gains you a 10% discount on the return half, but fares from Japan are higher and there is a Y600 departure tax in Japan. Korea-Japan-Korea tickets work out to be the same or less than a straight one-way Japan-Korea ticket. So for the numerous travellers who work in Japan and need to make visa runs, consider taking a one-way ticket to Korea the first time if you intend to cross the waters more than once a year.

Pusan-Shimonoseki This is the most popular boat, and is run by the Pukwan Ferry Company. The one-way journey takes 14½

hours. Daily departures from Pusan (South Korea) or Shimonoseki (Japan) are both at 6 pm and arrival is at 8.30 am. Fares on tickets bought in Korea for 1st class are US$80 to $90; 2nd class costs US$55 to $65. Students can receive a 20% discount and bicycles are carried free. Tickets are available in Shimonoseki (☎ (0832) 243000), Pusan (☎ (051) 463-3161/4) or Seoul (☎ (02) 738-0055/9).

The same company also runs hydrofoils daily between Pusan and Shimonoseki (3½ hours, US$62 to US$88, Korean prices). These depart Shimonoseki at 9.30 am, while departures from Pusan are at 1.40 pm.

In addition, there are combination discount ferry-train tickets allowing you to make the Tokyo-Seoul run without taking to the air. Other ticket combinations are possible (for example, Osaka-Taegu by train and hydrofoil). Several travel agents can book these tickets, including Nippon Travel Agency (☎ (06) 312-0451), Osaka; or Aju Travel Service (Pusan (051) 462-6661, Seoul ☎ (02) 753-5051).

Pusan-Hakata Korea Ferry (Pusan ☎ (051) 466-7799, Hakata ☎ (092) 262-2323) plies thrice weekly between Pusan and Hakata in 16 hours. This costs US$55 to $US110, and students can enjoy a 20% discount. Departure from Kakata is at 5 pm on Tuesday, Thursday and Saturday. Departures from Pusan are at 5.40 pm on Monday, Wednesday and Friday.

Note that in Hakata, the name of the wharf for Pusan (and for boats to Okinawa) is Chuo Futoh and it is across the bay, a long walk from Hakata Futoh (bayside place) which has other domestic boats.

Hydrofoils also connect Pusan with Hakata (three hours, US$62). Hydrofoils depart from Hakata at 9.30 am and from Pusan at 2 pm. These hydrofoils are operated by Korea Marine Express (Hakata ☎ (092) 281-2315, Pusan (051) 465-6111, Seoul (02) 753-1661).

Pusan-Kobe/Osaka The Kuk Jae Ferry Company connects both Kobe and Osaka with Pusan. The trip takes 22 hours and tickets cost from US$100 to US$250. A 20% student discount is available in 2nd class. Departures from Osaka (☎ (06) 348-9807) are on Wednesday and Saturday at noon; and from Pusan (☎ (051) 463-7000) to Osaka on Monday and Thursday at 5 pm. Departures from Kobe (☎ (078) 322-1117) are on Monday and Friday at noon; and from Pusan to Kobe on Wednesday and Saturday at 5 pm. Tickets can be also purchased in Seoul (☎ (02) 754-7786), 8th Floor, Centre Building, 118 Namdaemunno 2-ga, Chung-gu.

TOURS

Apart from the Japanese, most of the tour groups heading for Korea are geared towards returning veterans of the Korean War and their families. Given the fact that the war ended in 1953, it should come as no surprise that most of the tour participants are elderly.

To book an organised tour from outside Korea, it's probably best to contact an over-

seas branch of the KNTC (see the Organised Tours section in the Facts for the Visitor chapter for addresses). It's much easier to join an organised tour after you've already arrived in Korea (for details see the Getting Around chapter).

LEAVING KOREA
Reconfirmations

As in most Asian cities, it's essential to reconfirm all onward tickets if you're stopping in Seoul for more than 72 hours. Even if you're stopping for less than 72 hours, reconfirm your flight as soon as you arrive. Otherwise, it's entirely possible that your reserved seat will be given to someone else.

Departure Tax

If you are leaving Korea by air, there's a departure tax of W8000 which should be paid in local currency. If you are leaving Korea by boat, departure tax is W2000.

Getting Around

Koreans are very helpful to lost-looking foreigners, so if you stand around looking bewildered with a map in your hands, someone will probably offer to assist you. However, if you hand a Korean your map and ask directions, be sure that they don't have a pen in their hands – they will draw and write directions all over the map until it becomes illegible.

One thing you will come to appreciate is the public toilet facilities found in all stations (bus, train, subway etc) and adjacent shopping arcades. Even in busy Seoul, toilets are invariably located just where you need them and are kept spotlessly clean. It's a sharp contrast to other cities in the region (shame on you, Hong Kong).

Although transport around the country and within cities is excellent, finding an address can be a real chore.

'I know it's here somewhere...'

In Korea, an 'address' exists in name only. In the entire country, there are almost no signs labelling street names. Indeed, most streets do not have names at all. Nor do houses have numbers attached to the outside, though every house does in fact have an official number. Unfortunately, even these 'secret numbers' mean little – numbers are assigned to houses when they are built, so house No 27 could be next to house No 324, and so on.

Even Koreans find it close to impossible to locate an address. In fact, the only useful purpose served by knowing an address is simply to receive mail. Pity the poor postal workers who must actually track down these buildings! On the other hand, the system (or lack of a system) provides a form of job security for letter carriers – no one dares to fire them since only they can interpret the otherwise meaningless addresses which appear on envelopes.

All that having been said, there is a skeletal system of sorts and it helps if you learn it. A province is a *do*. Thus we have Kangwon-do, Kyonggi-do etc. *Buk* means 'north' and *nam* means 'south', and there are a few provinces where knowing this is useful – Chŏllabuk-do is 'Chŏlla North Province' and Chŏllanam-do is 'Chŏlla South Province'. Provinces are subdivided into counties, or *gun*, for example: Ch'unch'ŏn-gun. A *ri* is a small village. Thus, we can have an address like this: 366 Kangch'on-ri, Namsan-myŏn, Ch'unch'ŏn-gun, Kangwon-do.

It gets a lot more complicated in cities. A *gu* is an urban district only found in large cities like Seoul and Pusan. A *dong* is a neighbourhood smaller than a gu. Seoul presently has 22 gu and 494 dong. Thus, an address like 104 Itaewon-dong, Yongsan-gu, means building No 104 in the Itaewon neighbourhood of the Yongsan district. However, you could wander around Itaewon for hours in search of this building with no hope of finding it, even with the help of a Korean friend. This is the time to make a phone call to the place you are looking for and get instructions or find a local police box or tourist information booth and ask them. Larger buildings have names, and these can be crucial landmarks for finding your goal.

The word for a large street or boulevard is *no* or *ro*. So Chongno means Chong St, Ulchiro is Ulchi St etc. Also worth knowing is that large boulevards are divided into sections called *ga*. Thus, you'll see on the Seoul subway map that there is a station for Ulchiro 3-ga, Ulchiro 4-ga – these are just different sections of a street named Ulchi St. A *gil* is a smaller street than a *nŏro* – Sambonggil is one such example.

You might speculate as to how or why the Koreans ever came up with such a chaotic system for addressing houses. The simple answer is that the Koreans borrowed the system from Japan during the colonial era. Given the fact that the Koreans are not generally fond of the Japanese, one has to wonder why they would want to borrow such a dysfunctional system from their former colonial masters. Posing this question to Koreans, we've received the surprising answer that it was the Japanese who borrowed the system from Korea. If true, then the Koreans have got their revenge against Japan after all. ∎

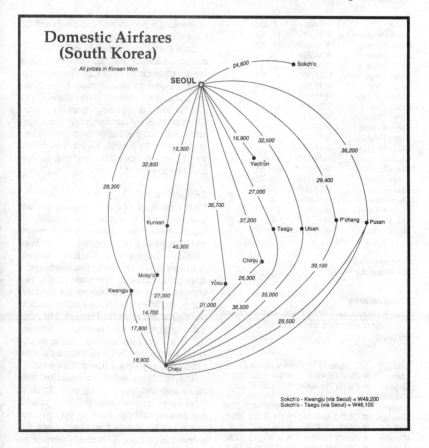

Domestic Airfares
(South Korea)

All prices in Korean Won

SEOUL

24,600 — Sokch'o

16,900   32,500

36,200

19,300

Yech'ŏn

32,800

29,400

28,300

27,000

36,700

P'ohang   Pusan

Kunsan

37,200

Taegu   Ulsan

46,300

Chinju

Mokp'o

39,100

Yŏsu

Kwangju

26,300

27,000

35,000

14,700

21,000   36,500

17,800

29,500

18,900

Cheju

Sokch'o - Kwangju (via Seoul) = W49,200
Sokch'o - Taegu (via Seoul) = W46,100

AIR

There are two domestic carriers – Korean Air
(KAL) and Asiana Airlines. Both have a
good network of flights connecting all the
main cities and the principal tourist sites.

Fares are the same on either airline, and
both offer 10% discounts to students. Children under two years old travel free and those
aged two to 12 years old travel at 50% of the
adult fare. Military personnel get a 30% discount. There is no financial penalty for
cancellation if you do so at least three hours
before departure time.

You must have your passport handy

before boarding a domestic flight – you
won't be allowed on the plane unless you
have it. You are not allowed to take photographs from a plane.

The Sokch'o-Kwangju and Sokch'o-
Taegu flights are via Seoul. The following
are the routes and airfares available, and you
must add a domestic departure tax of W2000:

Route	Fare	Airline
Seoul-Cheju	W46,300	(A, K)
Seoul-Chinju	W37,200	(A, K)
Seoul-Kunsan	W19,300	(K)
Seoul-Kwangju	W28,300	(A, K)

Route	Fare	Airline
Seoul-Mokp'o	W32,800	(A, K)
Seoul-P'ohang	W29,400	(A, K)
Seoul-Pusan	W36,200	(A, K)
Seoul-Sokch'o	W24,600	(K)
Seoul-Taegu	W27,000	(A, K)
Seoul-Ulsan	W32,500	(A, K)
Seoul-Yech'ŏn	W16,900	(A)
Seoul-Yŏsu	W36,700	(A, K)
Cheju-Chinju	W26,300	(K)
Cheju-Kunsan	W27,000	(K)
Cheju-Kwangju	W17,800	(A, K)
Cheju-Mokp'o	W14,700	(K)
Cheju-P'ohang	W39,100	(A)
Cheju-Pusan	W29,500	(A, K)
Cheju-Taegu	W36,500	(A, K)
Cheju-Ulsan	W35,000	(A, K)
Cheju-Yŏsu	W21,000	(K)
Pusan-Kwangju	W18,900	(A)
Sokch'o-Kwangju	W49,200	(K)
Sokch'o-Taegu	W46,100	(K)

A = Asiana Airlines
K = Korean Air (KAL)

Reservations

The location and telephone numbers for domestic reservation and ticket offices are as follows:

City	Asiana	Korean Air
Cheju	☎ (064) 43-4000	☎ (064) 52-2000
Chinju	☎ (0591) 758-4000	☎ (0591) 57-2000
Kangnŭng	–	☎ (0391) 43-2000
Kunsan	–	☎ (0654) 471-2000
Kwangju	☎ (062) 226-4000	☎ (062) 222-2000
Mokp'o	☎ (0631) 78-4000	☎ (0631) 73-2000
P'ohang	☎ (0562) 77-4000	☎ (0562) 72-2000
Pusan	☎ (051) 465-4000	☎ (051) 463-2000
Seoul	☎ (02) 774-4000	☎ (02) 756-2000
Sokch'o	–	☎ (0392) 32-2000
Taegu	☎ (053) 421-4000	☎ (053) 423-2000
Ulsan	☎ (0522) 61-4000	☎ (0522) 71-2000
Yech'ŏn	☎ (0584) 54-4000	–
Yŏsu	☎ (0662) 652-4000	☎ (0662) 41-2000

BUS

South Korean bus travel is a dream come true – fast, frequent and on time. It's even safe – quite a luxury after China.

Hang on to your tickets even after you board a bus. Most bus companies want you to give the ticket to the driver when you alight, although not all will require this.

Smoking is prohibited on all buses and the rules are generally enforced.

Sitting in the rear of the bus might help you escape the infernal karaoke music that some bus drivers like to play on their beloved cassette players. However, modern buses have speakers, and in that case there is no escape. If you find the music unappealing (most Westerners do), you might try carrying a few music cassettes and see if you can persuade your driver to play them. In general, Korean bus drivers won't play hard rock but something mellow might go down well.

Classes

Most Korean cities and even some obscure towns have at least two bus stations, an express bus terminal (kosok bŏsŭ t'ŏminŏl) and an inter-city bus terminal (shi'oe bŏsŭ t'ŏminŏl). Logically, you might conclude that express buses are faster and more expensive, while inter-city buses are slower and cheaper. However, this is often not the case. The so-called express buses can be 1st class (udŭng) or 2nd class (chikhaeng). The price differential between the two can be substantial. Buses from the inter-city bus terminals are almost always 2nd class but they are not necessarily any slower than the 'express'.

The 1st class coaches are luxurious, with cushy seats and plenty of legroom. Some of these buses are even equipped with cellular pay-phones, although none as yet have on-board toilets. Standing passengers are not accepted in 1st class, but normally there are no assigned seat numbers so sit where you like.

Local (wanheng) long-distance constitute the 3rd class. These buses operate on set routes and will pick up and drop off anywhere. There are no reserved seats, often as many standing as sitting passengers, and all but the bulkiest of freight may also be squeezed on. You will probably not be using these for long-distance travel, but you might occasionally need to take one to a remote spot.

Reservations

You can buy an advance ticket for buses that reserves you a particular time and date. Seat numbers are not assigned, so you can sit wherever there is space. If you miss your bus you can board the next on a space-available basis.

In most cases you won't need an advance ticket, but seats are hard to come by on weekends and holidays. At such peak times, you might have to queue for hours to buy a ticket in Seoul. Things are easier in smaller cities and towns, but travel during holidays is synonymous with packed-out buses.

Costs

Given the high standard of service, bus fares are certainly reasonable in Korea. The 1st-class coaches cost about 50% more than regular inter-city buses – you pay a lot for those comfortable seats. Just about the longest bus ride you can take in the entire country is Seoul-Pusan (453 km), which costs W10,600 for 2nd class and W15,800 for 1st class.

TRAIN

South Korea has an excellent railway network connecting all major cities and the ticketing system is computerised. Smoking is prohibited on trains, but there is usually a smoking car.

Few ticket clerks speak any English. Some of the larger stations have English signs indicating special ticket windows for foreigners. They were installed for the 1988 Olympics and subsequently went to pot, but were revived once again for the 1993 Taejŏn Expo. At the moment, it seems that these places do function at least part-time, so they're worth trying. The stations which have these special ticket windows are as follows:

Seoul (☎ (02) 392-7811) and Ch'ŏngnyangni (Seoul ☎ (02) 966-0018); Tongdaegu (east Taegu ☎ (053) 955-8877); Pusan (☎ (051) 463-5782); Taejŏn (☎ (042) 253-7451); Iri (☎ (0653) 52-7788); Mokp'o (☎ (0631) 42-7788); Kyŏngju (☎ 0561) 43-8052); Yŏsu (☎ (0662) 62-6491)

With advance notice you can buy train tickets from the KNTC office in the basement of the KNTC building in Seoul.

There's a monthly timetable available from bookshops – this contains schedules for all forms of transport throughout the country, but only the rail section is in English. The Korean name for the timetable is *shigakp'yo* 시각표 .

Classes

There are four classes of trains. The fastest are called *saemaul-ho*. Then come the limited stop *mugunghwa-ho*. Similar, but not air-con, are the *t'ongil-ho* trains – the best deal (reserve a seat). Finally there are the incredibly slow 4th-class (local) trains known as *pidulgi-ho* – avoid these! Seats on the 4th-class trains cannot be booked; on the middle-range trains there are 1st class and economy seats and standing tickets.

Reservations

There are no reservations as such, but you can purchase train tickets up to three months in advance. As long as you don't need to travel during weekends or holidays there should be no need to buy a ticket in advance. However, the situation is much the opposite during non-working days. Departing Seoul on a Friday night or Saturday is almost impossible if you haven't bought a ticket in advance. Indeed, even the standing-room tickets sell out on holidays! The moral of the story is either get a train ticket well in advance or don't plan to move around at all during holidays. If you really get stuck, your only alternative will be to queue for the buses.

Costs

Just about the longest trip you can do by train is Seoul-Pusan, a distance of 453 km. The schedule and price breakdown is as follows:

Class	Hours	Price
Saemaul-ho	4 hrs 10 min	W21,500
Mugunghwa-ho	5 hrs	W11,000
T'ongil-ho	5 hrs 20 min	W7,600

As a basis for comparison, flying costs W36,200 plus W2000 departure tax. Flying time is only 50 minutes, but you'll have to allow an hour each end for getting to/from the airport.

BULLET TAXI

Long-distance share taxis are affectionately known as 'bullet taxis' *(ch'ong'al t'aekshi)* because the drivers tend to drive like maniacs. These taxis can be found at two places – at some major tourist attractions and at bus or train stations. For example, they often meet incoming ferries such as the boat on Lake Soyangho near Ch'unch'ŏn. You can also find taxis around the Seoul Express Bus Terminal at night when the regular buses stop running.

Meters are not used, so you must negotiate the fare in advance. Try to find a group of Koreans and let them do the bargaining.

CAR & MOTORBIKE

It makes little sense to rent a car in South Korea – the cost will burn a hole in all but the deepest pockets, while public transport is cheap and excellent. Driving in the larger cities is particularly not recommended, but driving in rural areas can be a relaxing way to explore the backwaters. Rural roads are generally excellent and have little traffic, except during holiday times when Koreans head for the hills.

Korean drivers seem to be totally oblivious to the presence of motorbikes – ride one at your peril! Your chances of getting squashed by a car or taxi are reduced if you keep your headlights on even during the daytime – at least this makes you more visible. Rural roads are certainly safer and more enjoyable than the mean streets of Seoul. Motorbikes are seldom available for hire, so if you need one you'll probably have to buy your own.

Signposting inside cities and large towns is inadequate especially if you're trying to find your way out. Most of the signposting is for the various *dong* (suburbs) and such things as 'Railway Station', 'City Hall' or 'Express Bus Terminal'.

A detailed road atlas is essential, and these are readily available from major bookshops.

Road Rules

The speed limits vary considerably and there are not many signs indicating what they are. In general, the limits are 100 km/h on expressways, 80 km/h on main highways, 60 km/h on provincial roads, and 50/60 km/h in urban areas. Speed cops are out in force at weekends and holidays. This doesn't stop drivers exceeding the limits by considerable margins. Drivers coming in the opposite direction will often indicate the presence of a speed trap ahead by flashing their lights. Foreigners should not consider themselves above the law in Korea, but sometimes you can talk your way out of a fine if you are friendly, apologetic and humble.

The police do spot checks for drunk drivers. If there's evidence that you've been drinking they'll breathalise you, and the fines are heavy. When sober, driving is on the right side of the road.

Accidents and traffic jams are disturbingly frequent and it is wise not to expect any consideration from other road users. In major cities except Seoul, there is virtually no legal parking other than in private garages. However, you would never know that to look around – there appear to be no *enforced* rules for parking, and if there's a space then someone will park there. Drivers *do* respect traffic lights, and they are supposed to respect pedestrian crossings even when these are not controlled by lights.

It is required by law that the driver and front seat passengers wear seatbelts. Safety helmets are mandatory for cyclists, and life insurance (not required) wouldn't be a bad idea either.

Driving Licence If you intend to drive in Korea you must be at least 21 years old, have one year's driving experience, a passport and an international driving permit. A driving licence from your own country is not acceptable. It is possible to obtain a temporary Korean driving licence valid for three months against your driving licence in Seoul but you'll waste a day doing so and it's not exactly cheap.

There are three places in Seoul where you

can get this licence but you must make sure that your temporary address is covered by the office you apply to. Seoul's three offices are:

Kangnam, near the Samsŏng subway station on line No 2 (☎ 555-0855)
Kangso, near Kimp'o Airport (☎ 664-3610)
Tobong, near the Nowon subway station on line No 4 (☎ 975-4710)

All the licensing centres have a counter which deals exclusively with the temporary licences for foreigners so you won't have to join the endless queues at the other counters.

You will need your passport plus photocopies of the relevant front pages and your Korean visa page; your national driving licence plus a copy of both sides; six photographs of a size suitable for the Korean licence (about half the size of a normal passport photograph); money to pay for the licence (approximately W8000 depending on nationality and visitor status).

Photographs, photocopies and fiscal stamps can all be obtained at the licensing centres. The forms you will be given are entirely in Korean but the staff can usually help you fill them in. You must also take a compulsory eye test (the chart has numbers on it, not Korean letters of the alphabet). Assuming you pass it, you can pick up your licence 24 hours later.

The procedure for getting a permanent driving licence (valid for five years) is much the same, but you'll need a Korean residence permit to qualify. Furthermore, you must surrender your own country's driving licence to the Korean authorities in order to obtain the Korean licence.

Rental

You can forget about imported cars since they are virtually banned in Korea. Only Korean cars are available for hire but that doesn't mean they're cheap – prices start at W32,000 for a 10-hour period with unlimited km. Most vehicles are hired out for 24-hour periods, with prices starting at W44,000. Discounts are available for longer-term rentals.

Cars are available for hire in Seoul, Cheju, Inch'ŏn, Kwangju, Pusan, Taegu and Taejŏn. See those sections for details.

BICYCLE

While riding a bicycle in Seoul is almost certain death, it's not a bad way to move around in rural areas if you're experienced in this kind of travel. Apart from urban traffic, there are a few other obstacles to consider – remember that Korea has four seasons and the summer can sometimes be very wet. Korea is also fairly hilly, so you'll need to be athletically inclined.

Long-term rentals are impossible to find, but good 10-speed bikes can easily be purchased in Korea.

HITCHING

Hitching is never entirely safe in any country in the world, and we don't recommend it. Travellers who decide to hitch should understand that they are taking a small but potentially serious risk. People who do choose to hitch will be safer if they travel in pairs and let someone know where they are planning to go.

Hitchhiking is not customary among the Koreans, and indeed, there is no particular signal for it. If you stand by the side of the road with your thumb out, many Koreans will just think you're weird. Nevertheless, hitching is a possibility and probably safer in Korea than in many Western countries. Koreans are generally kindly disposed to foreigners, and if you are standing by the roadside waving and looking like you need assistance, Korean drivers will usually stop to help. However, they may not be amused if they think you're just hitching to save money – after all, bus transport is not that expensive in Korea. On the other hand, there are parts of Korea where public transport is poor, especially during the off-season when rural backwaters (including the national parks) may be devoid of visitors. In such a situation, hitching may be your only option.

BOAT

Korea has an extensive network of ferries that service the offshore islands as well as several lakes.

You can travel by boat to numerous islands off the west and south coasts, and to Ullŭngdo off the east coast. Chejudo, Korea's largest island, can be reached by both car and passenger ferry from Mokp'o, Wando and Pusan. There are daily departures and a wide choice of ferries from each of these towns. If you want to explore the smaller islands of the south-west then Mokp'o and Wando are the main departure points. All of these ferries are dealt with in detail in the Getting There & Away sections of each town.

For all those seafaring souls who prefer the rolling of the waves to the bumping of a bus, there is a ferry connecting the mainland towns of Wando and Mokp'o (seven hours), and the *Angel* hydrofoil plies between Pusan and Yŏsu. The latter is a popular trip as it goes through the beautiful Hallyŏ Haesang National Park and stops at the islands and main towns along the way. The journey takes only about three hours, although some trips only go between Pusan and Ch'ungmu.

You can get ferries to Ullŭngdo from P'ohang, Hup'o and Tonghae, but those from Hup'o and Tonghae only operate on a daily basis during the summer months. During rough weather the ferries can be cancelled, and it is wise to book in advance during the summer months.

As well as the sea ferries, there are boats on several large lakes. These can be found on P'aroho and Soyangho lakes in the province of Kangwon-do, and further south on Ch'ungjuho Lake in Ch'ungch'ong-do.

LOCAL TRANSPORT
City Bus

Inside cities and their outlying suburbs, buses are classified as ordinary *(ipsŏk)* and seat *(chwasŏk)*. The former generally cost W300 regardless of distance (or W290 if you buy tokens from a booth beforehand) but they get incredibly crowded at rush hours. A chwasŏk bus over the same route will cost W600. All city buses carry a route number and a destination on the front and the sides. Bus stops, likewise, carry panels on the post indicating the route served. None of these will be in English so you need to be able to recognise the name of your destination in Korean.

Subway

Seoul and Pusan have subway systems, which are a very convenient and cheap way of getting around. All signs for both the trains and the subway stations are in Korean and English. Tickets are bought at vending machines or at ticket windows. For more details, see the Getting Around sections for those two cities.

Taegu is also building a subway system which might be open (don't count on it though) by the time you read this.

Taxi

There are two types of taxis: 'ordinary' and 'deluxe'. 'Deluxe' not only means that the taxi is very pleasant inside (some have cellular pay phones!), but also that it functions the way you expect a taxi to work. That is, you flag down a taxi, get inside and say where you want to go. A deluxe taxi *(mobŏm t'aekshi)* is black with a yellow sign on the roof and the words 'Deluxe Taxi' written on the sides. Deluxe taxis are only supposed to pick up passengers at designated stands at hotels, bus terminals, train stations and certain major streets.

It is a very different situation with the ordinary taxis, which are (unfortunately) the vast majority of taxis on the road. The way it works is that you stand by the roadside and shout out your destination. Usually the taxi will slow down long enough to hear your call, and in nine cases out of 10 will then shoot off again. There is a simple rule to this one for non-Korean speakers: memorise a few commonly known landmarks around town that taxi drivers are likely to understand in English (major hotels will suffice).

If you find that empty taxis are not stopping to pick you up or refuse to take you after you've told them your destination, you might be standing on the wrong side of the street. At least in larger cities, taxi drivers are not willing to change their direction.

The other factor in these unique arrangements is that the ordinary taxis basically operate as minibuses. Once the driver is on a certain route he will continue to slow down to listen out for the calls of other hopefuls as long as there is spare seating in the taxi. This won't make your fare any cheaper, although it does make sorting out exactly how much it should be a bit more complicated. To protect yourself, you must look at the meter when you get into the taxi, note the fare, and subtract it from what the meter says when you get out. Some drivers will try to cheat foreigners this way. If two or more of you get in the taxi at the same time for the same destination, you should pay a single fare, not the same fare multiplied two or more times.

Single women travelling late at night should be especially wary about getting into a taxi with other passengers – rapes have occurred when the driver and other 'passengers' turn on the unsuspecting victim.

City taxis have meters, but there are times (especially rush hour) when drivers will refuse to use them and insist on a flat fee. The Koreans get this too, it's not just foreigners. If the driver isn't going to use the meter, be sure you agree on the fare in advance. In some ways a flat fare is better, because when the meter is running, some drivers may take you for a long ride.

The basic charges for ordinary taxis is W1000 for the first two km and an additional W100 for every 381 metres. From midnight there is a 20% surcharge. When caught in traffic and going slower than 15 km/h, there is a surcharge of W100 for every 92 seconds. Fares are 20% higher from midnight to 4 am.

The deluxe taxis cost considerably more, and a receipt will be issued. Flagfall is W3000 which takes you three km, then W200 for each additional 250 metres or each 60 seconds when the speed drops below 15 km per hour. On the other hand, there is *no* late-night surcharge for the deluxe taxis.

In the countryside, many taxis are not metered so you'll have to negotiate the fare before you set off. On the positive side, taxi drivers in rural areas and small towns are generally more cooperative than their urban counterparts. That is, they are willing to stop when you try to flag them down, rather than thumbing their nose at you while driving away.

You'll occasionally come across private cars which stop and announce that they're a private taxi. It's up to you whether you take them but Koreans strongly advise against it (there have been occasional horror stories). You'd naturally have to negotiate a fare if you did decide to take one of these.

If you take a metered taxi to a place where the driver won't necessarily get a return fare (to a temple outside of a town, for instance), he will usually demand you pay 1½ times what the meter says at the end of the journey. This can work in your favour if you didn't take a taxi out but want to take one for the return journey.

TOURS

The Royal Asiatic Society (RAS)(☎ (02) 763-9483; fax 766-3796) in Seoul operates tours every weekend. The day tours are reasonably priced, but overnight trips are somewhat expensive because they stay in good hotels rather than cheap yŏgwan. The RAS is in Room 611 of the Korean Christian Building (also called the CBS Building) on Taehangno. Office hours are from 10 am to 5 pm, Monday to Friday. Take the subway to Chongno 5-ga station (line No 1).

The United Service Organization (USO) (☎ (02) 795-3063/3028) runs tours at bargain prices and you don't have to be a member of the US military to join. The Seoul office is opposite Gate 21 of the Yongsan military compound. There is also a USO in Pusan (☎ (051) 462-3732).

There are, of course, plenty of commercial travel agents which can arrange tours to almost anywhere for a fee. While some of these tours are not horribly expensive, few could be regarded as cheap. Large groups can bargain for a reduced price. If any of this interests you, the following are some of the Seoul travel agencies recommended by the KNTC:

Global Tour, Global Building, 186-43, Tongkyodong, Map'o-gu, Seoul (☎ (02) 335-0011; fax 333-0066)

Korea Travel Bureau, 1465-11 Sŏch'o-dong, Sŏcho-gu, Seoul (☎ (02) 585-1191; fax 585-1187)

Seojin Travel Service, Seojin Building, 149-1 P'yŏng-dong, Chongno-gu, Seoul (☎ (02) 732-4400; fax 732-1285)

Seoul Travel Service, Room 508, Kumjung Building, 192-11 Ŭlchiro 1-ga, Chung-gu, Seoul (☎ (02) 754-6831; fax 753-9076)

Prices are not cheap, but groups may have some latitude for bargaining. Just to give an idea of what's available, Seoul Travel Service charges US$1530 for a 'Korea in Depth' tour which includes Seoul, Korean Folk Village, Sŏraksan, Songnisan, Pŏpchusa, Haeinsa, Kyŏngju, T'ongdosa, Pusan, Chejudo, returning to Seoul by air.

Seoul 서울

The capital of South Korea, Seoul is a city of incredible contrasts. It was flattened during the Korean War but has risen from the ashes to become a modern metropolis with a population of 10.8 million. By some estimates, Seoul rates as the fifth largest city in the world. Although Korea's capital now boasts high-rise buildings, 12-lane boulevards and urban problems to match, the centuries-old royal palaces, temples, pagodas and imposing stone gateways set in huge traditional gardens remain timeless and elegant.

Seoul dates from the establishment in 1392 of the Yi dynasty, which ruled Korea until 1910. During this time, when Korea was largely closed to the outside world, the shrines, palaces and fortresses that still stand today were built. Government funding for the repair and restoration of historic sites is outstanding in South Korea and is the reason the very new and the ancient continue to exist side by side.

Seoul is the political, economic and educational hub of the country to a dangerous degree. So much of the country's wealth, industry and technology is concentrated here that it's a prime target for attack by North Korea. Even the Defence Ministry is headquartered in Seoul. With this in mind, former president Chun Doo-Hwan made an attempt to move some government ministries out of the capital. However, Chun met with fierce opposition and had to drop the plan. As far as Koreans are concerned, Seoul is *the* place to live because of its educational and economic opportunities. Another factor is prestige – in the face game, you gain a lot of points by having a Seoul address.

Seoul is also a magnet for foreigners, most of whom are more interested in the economic opportunities than prestige. If the motive for your visit is sightseeing rather than job-hunting, Seoul is still certainly worth a week of your time. However, once you've taken in the major sights, you'd be well advised to get down to a bus or railway station and get out of town.

Orientation

The Han River (Han-gang) flows from east to west and bisects the city. There are 12 urban districts on the north side of the river and 10 districts on the south side. The city is further subdivided into 494 dongs or neighbourhoods.

Chung-gu is the central district around the city hall area south to Namsan Park. Chongno-gu is from Chongno (Chong Rd) northwards to the Kyŏngbok-kung Palace area. This district has most of the budget hotels and the city's best sights. It'aewon-dong is a neighbourhood in Yongsan-gu on the south side of Namsan Park, and is famous for its shopping, bars and nightlife.

Kangnam-gu is the district on the south side of the Han River and includes two of Seoul's most modern neighbourhoods – Yong-dong and Chamshil-dong. For Koreans this is the most prestigious area to live, but foreigners usually prefer the north side of the river.

If you can't find a certain address, try the police boxes which are in every neighbourhood. A surprisingly large number of police speak English, although it still helps considerably if you have your destination written in Korean script.

Information

Tourist Office The best source of information about Seoul itself is the Seoul City Tourist Information Centre (☎ (02) 731-6337, 735-8688) inside City Hall. It's open every day from 9 am to 6 pm, but closed from noon to 1 pm.

The municipal Seoul Tourist Information kiosks around town are as follows:

Chongno 5-ga: in front of the Cheil Bank (☎ 272-0348)
It'aewon: in front of Wendy's (☎ 794-2490)
Kwanghwamun: in front of the Kyobo building (☎ 735-0088)
Myŏng-dong: in front of the Hanil Bank (☎ 757-0088)

Nandaemun: in front of the Shinsegae Department Store (☎ 779-3644)
T'apkol (Pagoda) Park: in front of the park near entrance of Insadong-gil (☎ 739-4331)
Seoul express bus terminal, in front of the terminal (☎ 537-9198)
Seoul station (☎ 392-7811)
Tŏksugung: in front of the palace (☎ 756-0045)

You can get information about Seoul and the rest of Korea by visiting the KNTC Tourist Information Centre (☎ (02) 757-0086) in the basement of the KNTC Bldg, 10 Ta-dong, Chung-gu. There are computers here where you can choose a destination and get a print-out of bus routes, accommodation, things to see, etc. KNTC is open daily from 9 am until 6 pm (9 am to 5 pm from November to February).

The KNTC also operates the tourist information counter at the international terminal of Kimp'o Airport (☎ 665-0086). The Seoul City government operates an information

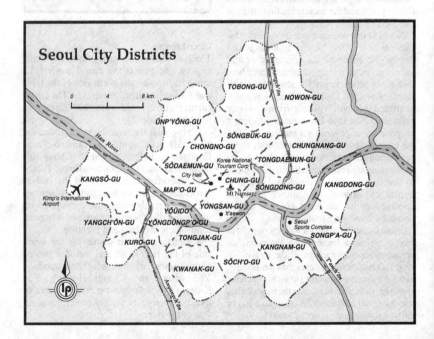

Seoul City Districts

counter (☎ 664-5197) in the domestic terminal.

There is also a Subway Information Centre (☎ 583-8923), but most visitors will find little reason to ring them up.

The Royal Asiatic Society (☎ (02) 763-9483; fax 766-3796) is in room 611 of the Korean Christian building on Taehangno. The RAS is a gold mine of information for people who want to dig deep into Korea's culture, history, economy and geography. The society sells books, sponsors free lectures and runs weekend trips. Take the subway to Chongno 5-ga subway station (line No 1). Office hours are from 10 am to 5 pm, Monday to Friday. The mailing address is CPO Box 255, Seoul.

It's also worth trying the USO (☎ (02) 792-3028/3063), 104 Galwol-dong, Yongsan-gu, just opposite Gate 21 of the Yongsan US army base down the road past Seoul railway station. The USO is an information, entertainment and cultural centre that serves the US army base here, although you don't have to be with the military to get in. Take the subway to Namyong subway station (line No 1, one stop south of Seoul station) and walk south for five minutes. Office hours are from 8 am to 8 pm daily.

Money The branch of Korea Exchange Bank (☎ 729-0114) is at 181 Ŭlchiro 2-ga, and you'll also find Cho Hung Bank (☎ 733-2000) nearby. However, foreign exchange banks are so ubiquitous in Seoul that it's hardly worth commenting on where to find them.

The one place that *does* deserve special note is the tiny black market. You *won't* get a better exchange rate than the bank's, but black marketeers will reconvert Korean won back to US dollars without requiring bank receipts. For foreigners working illegally in Seoul, this has some obvious advantages. The black market is illegal, but it's no secret and everyone (including the police) knows about it. It can be found on the east side of Nandaemun Gate as you emerge from the pedestrian underpass. Look for the old women hanging around by the underpass.

Post & Telecommunications Poste Restante is on the 3rd floor of the Central Post Office (CPO). All incoming letters are entered into a logbook which you have to sign when you pick up a letter or package – look over this logbook carefully for your name because they often misfile letters.

The telecommunications building is just behind the CPO – fax, telephone and telex service is available.

Foreign Embassies Embassies in Seoul include the following:

Argentina
    135-53, It'aewon-dong, Yongsan-gu (☎ 793-4062)
Australia
    11th Floor, Kyobo Bldg, 1-1 Chongno 1-ga, Chongno-gu (☎ 730-6490/5)
Austria
    1, Chongno 1-ga, Chongno-gu (☎ 732-9071/2)
Bangladesh
    33-5, Hannam-dong, Yongsan-gu (☎ 796-4056/7)
Belgium
    1-65, Tongbinggo-dong, Yongsan-gu (☎ 749-0381/6)
Brazil
    192-11, Ŭlchiro 1-ga, Chung-gu (☎ 755-6379)
Canada
    10th Floor, Kolon Bldg, 45 Mugyo-dong, Chung-gu (☎ 753-2605/8)
Chile
    142, Nonhyon-dong, Kangnam-gu (☎ 549-1654/6)
China (PRC)
    83 Myŏng-dong 2-ga, Chung-gu (☎ 773-0214)
Colombia
    San 1-139, It'aewon-dong, Yongsan-gu (☎ 793-1369)
Czech
    657-42, Hannam-dong, Yongsan-gu (☎ 796-6453/4)
Denmark
    Suite 701, Namsong Bldg, 260-199, It'aewon-dong, Yongsan-gu (☎ 795-4187/9)
Finland
    1, Chongno 1-ga, Chongno-gu (☎ 732-6737)
France
    30 Hap-dong, Sŏdaemun-gu (☎ 312-3272)
Germany
    4th Floor, Daehan Fire & Marine Insurance Bldg, 51-1 Namch'ang-dong, Chung-gu (☎ 726-7114)
Greece
    1, Changgyo-dong, Chung-gu (☎ 752-9662)

Hungary
1-104, Tongbinggo-dong, Yongsan-gu (☎ 792-2105)
India
37-3 Hannam-dong, Yongsan-gu (☎ 798-4257)
Indonesia
Yŏŭido-dong, Yŏngdŭngp'o-gu (☎ 783-5675/7)
Ireland
Daehan Fire & Marine Insurance Bldg, 51-1 Namch'ang-dong, Chung-gu (☎ 774-6455)
Israel
823-21 Yŏksam-dong, Kangnam-gu (☎ 564-3448)
Italy
1-398 Hannam-dong, Yongsan-gu (☎ 796-0491)
Japan
18-11 Chunghak-dong, Chongno-gu (☎ 733-5626)
Malaysia
4-1 Hannam-dong, Yongsan-gu (☎ 794-7205)
Mexico
118, Changch'ung-dong 1-ga, Chung-gu (☎ 269-4011/2)
Myanmar (Burma)
723-1, Hannam-dong, Yongsan-gu (☎ 792-3341)
Netherlands
14th Floor, Kyobo Bldg, 1-1 Chongno 1-ga, Chongno-gu (☎ 737-9514/6)
New Zealand
18th Floor, Kyobo Bldg, Chongno 1-ga, Chongno-gu (☎ 730-7794)
Norway
124-12, It'aewon-dong, Yongsan-gu (☎ 795-6850/1)
Pakistan
58-1, Shinmunno 1-ga, Chongno-gu (☎ 739-4422)
Philippines
559-510 Yŏksam-dong, Kangnam-gu (☎ 568-9434)
Poland
448-144, Huam-dong, Yongsan-gu (☎ 779-0163/5)
Portugal
89-29, Shinmunno 2-ga, Chongno-gu (☎ 738-2078/9)
Russia
1001-13, Taech'i-dong, Kangnam-gu (☎ 552-7094/8)
Singapore
89-29, Shinmunno 2-ga, Chongno-gu (☎ 722-0442/5)
South Africa
Office 230, Hotel Westin Chosŭn (☎ 317-0466)
Spain
726-52, Hannam-dong, Yongsan-gu (☎ 794-3581/2)

Sri Lanka
1, Chongno 1-ga, Chongno-gu (☎ 735-2966)
Sweden
8th Floor, Boyung Bldg, 108-2 P'yŏng-dong, Chongno-gu (☎ 738-1149, 738-0846)
Switzerland
32-10, Songwol-dong, Chongno-gu (☎ 739-9511/4)
Taiwan
6th Floor, Kwanghwamun Bldg, Chung-gu (☎ 399-2767)
Thailand
653-7 Hannam-dong, Yongsan-gu (☎ 795-3098)
Turkey
726-116, Hannam-dong, Yongsan-gu (☎ 794-0255)
UK
4 Chŏng-dong, Chung-gu (☎ 735-7341/3)
USA
82 Sejongno, Chongno-gu (☎ 738-7118, 393-4114)
Vietnam
33-1 Hannam-dong, Yongsan-gu (☎ 741-0036)

Immigration The main headquarters of the Seoul Immigration Office (☎ (02) 653-3041/8) covers both Seoul and the province of Kyŏnggi-do. It's inconveniently located in Yangcho'ŏn-gu out near the airport. You can get there by taking the subway to Shindorim subway station (line No 2), and then transferring to a spur subway line to the Yangch'ŏn-gu Office subway station. From there you have to walk two blocks to the north.

Fortunately, there is also a much more convenient branch in the city centre (☎ 732-6214) on the 5th floor of the Chŏksŏn Hyŏndae building. Take the subway to Kyŏngbokkung subway station (line No 2) and leave the station by exit No 7 (sign says 'Seoul Metropolitan Police Administration').

Cultural Centres The Seoul Arts Centre (☎ (02) 585-3151), 700 Socho-dong, Socho-gu, is the best place to go to see folk dances, court dances and other traditional performances. Admission costs only W3000 and there are performances every Saturday. Take the subway to the Cargo Truck Terminal subway station (line No 3) at the south end of town.

Korea House (☎ (02) 266-9101) has similar performances to those of the Seoul Arts Centre, but they are performed every evening at 7.20 and 8.40 pm. Unfortunately, these shows are expensive at W14,300. This place is also a restaurant (not cheap) at night – you can eat and watch a performance. It's on the north side of Namsan Park – take the subway to Ch'ungmuro subway station (line No 3 or 4).

Nanjang is a privately run music house near Shinch'on subway station which features various programmes of traditional Korean music and dance performances.

The National Theatre on the slopes of Namsan Park (just behind Dongguk University and right across from the Shilla Hotel) has various performances (opera, dance, etc). Check with one of the tourist information centres for the current programme.

Sejong Cultural Centre does modern performances and exhibits – classical music, art exhibitions, piano recitals, etc. During the warm weather amateur troupes give free outdoor performances almost daily at noon for the benefit of office workers.

The Seoul Nori Madang (☎ (02) 414-1985) is an open-air theatre for traditional dance performances. It's just behind the Lotte World Shopping Complex near Chamshil subway station (line No 2).

Travel Agencies There are hundreds of travel agencies in Seoul, but English is not spoken in many of them and they are unlikely to be accustomed to Westerners' preoccupation with getting the cheapest price. Highest recommendations go to Joy Travel Service (☎ (02) 776-9871; fax 756-5342), 10th Floor, 24-2 Mukyo-dong, Chung-gu, Seoul, which is directly behind City Hall. You'll also find two good discounters on the 5th floor of the YMCA building on Chongno 2-ga (next to Chonggak subway station): Korean International Student Exchange Society (KISES) (☎ 733-9494; fax 732-9568) in room 505, and Top Travel (☎ 739-5231; fax 736-9078) in room 506.

Bookshops The best all-round bookshop is Ŭlchi Book Centre (☎ 757-8991) in the north-east section of the underground arcade at the Ŭlchiro 1-ga subway station (intersection of Namdaemunno and Ŭlchiro). This is *not* Seoul's largest bookshop, but it's got a great selection, prices are lower than elsewhere, the manager speaks English and you can even special order books here (the other bookshops will never do that for you).

Seoul's largest bookshop is the Kyobo Book Centre in the basement of the Kyobo building on the north-east corner of Sejongno and Chongno – you can enter through the pedestrian subway.

Youngpoong Bookstore is a rather poor third choice. It's a huge place with a great stationery section (in the second basement), but most of the books are in Korean. There is a good selection of textbooks here which may be of interest to foreigners teaching English in Seoul. The bookshop is down in the Chonggak subway station, exactly across the street from the KNTC building.

Chongno Book Centre – just across the street from the YMCA – is a huge bookshop but most books are in Korean only. Still, it's worth a browse. There is a small English section up on the 5th and 6th floors and we've stumbled across the odd rare gem here such as the *Whole Earth Catalog*.

There are some obscure used bookshops in It'aewon which take some effort to track down. One worth looking for is It'aewon Foreign Books (☎ 793-8249), 533 It'aewon-dong.

Libraries There are two excellent libraries with English-language books. The largest is at USIS, just east of City Hall. The other is the British Council, just north of Tŏksugung and east of the British Embassy.

For those with more specialised interests, it might be worth dropping by the National Central Library. This is in the southern part of Seoul not far from the Seoul express bus terminal. Take the subway and get off at the Seoul National Teachers' College subway station (line Nos 2 or 3).

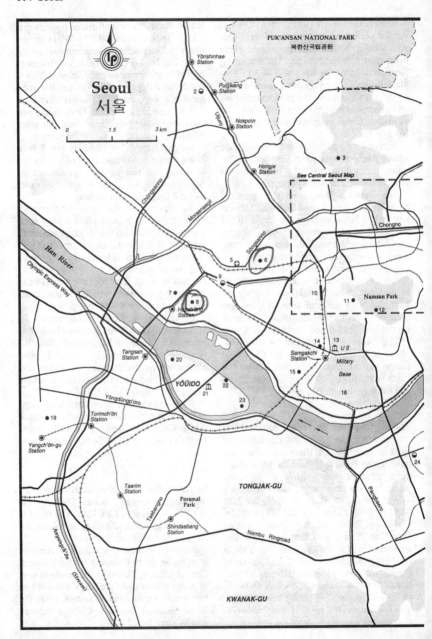

Seoul
서울

PUK'ANSAN NATIONAL PARK
북한산국립공원

Yŏn'shinhae Station

Pulgwang Station

Nokpo\n Station

Uijuro

2

Ch'ŏngsanno

Moraenaegil

Hongje Station

See Central Seoul Map

3

Chongno

Sŏngsanno

5

6

9

7

8
Hapchŏng Station

10

Namsan Park

11

12

Han River

Olympic Express Way

Tangsan Station

20

YŎŬIDO

22
21

14   13
US
Samgakchi Station

15

Military Base

16

23

Yŏngdŭngp'oro

Torimch'ŏn Station

19

Yangch'ŏn-gu Station

Taerim Station

TONGJAK-GU

24

Taebangno

Poramal Park

Shindaebang Station

Nambu Ringroad

Panghwaro

Anyangch'ŏn (Stream)

KWANAK-GU

0   1.5   3 km

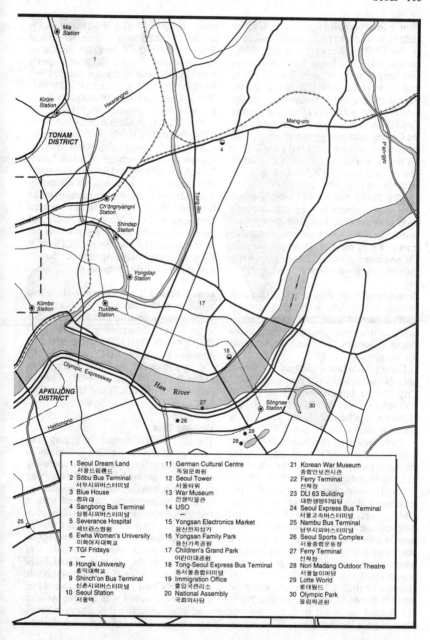

1 Seoul Dream Land 서울드림랜드	**11** German Cultural Centre 독일문화원	**21** Korean War Museum 종합안보전시관
2 Sŏbu Bus Terminal 서부시외버스터미널	**12** Seoul Tower 서울타워	**22** Ferry Terminal 선착장
3 Blue House 청와대	**13** War Museum 전쟁박물관	**23** DLI 63 Building 대한생명63빌딩
4 Sangbong Bus Terminal 상봉시외버스터미널	**14** USO —	**24** Seoul Express Bus Terminal 서울고속버스터미널
5 Severance Hospital 세브란스병원	**15** Yongsan Electronics Market 용산전자상가	**25** Nambu Bus Terminal 남부시외버스터미널
6 Ewha Women's University 이화여자대학교	**16** Yongsan Family Park 용산가족공원	**26** Seoul Sports Complex 서울종합운동장
7 TGI Fridays —	**17** Children's Grand Park 어린이대공원	**27** Ferry Terminal 선착장
8 Hongik University 홍익대학교	**18** Tong-Seoul Express Bus Terminal 동서울종합터미널	**28** Nori Madang Outdoor Theatre 서울놀이마당
9 Shinch'on Bus Terminal 신촌시외버스터미널	**19** Immigration Office 출입국관리소	**29** Lotte World 롯데월드
10 Seoul Station 서울역	**20** National Assembly 국회의사당	**30** Olympic Park 올림픽공원

Film & Photography If you're looking for slide or professional film, one place to check is the Ŭlchiro Arcade near the Korea Exchange Bank in Seoul. Large bookshops also keep a stock of slide film. If you're looking for professional slide film, check out Fujicolor Plaza which has several branches – there is one just north of City Hall (see the City Hall Area map) and a larger one west of the Ch'ungmuro subway station (see Central Seoul map). Just one block to the north of the Ch'ungmuro Fujicolor Plaza is the Kodak Photo Shop (☎ 269-8582) which also has professional slide film.

QSS Photo Shop (☎ 273-3552) offers good same-day service for processing both slide and print film. This place does professional developing and charges reasonable prices. It's in the Kuk Dong Arcade near Ch'ungmuro subway station, opposite Fujicolor Plaza (see Central Seoul map).

Emergency Asia Emergency Assistance (☎ (02) 353-6475/6) has English-speaking staff on duty 24 hours daily. This organisation will relay your request for help to the proper authorities. However, a fee is charged for this service.

During office hours, you might be able to get a call for help relayed through the Seoul City Tourist Information Centre (☎ (02) 735-8688) or KNTC (☎ 757-0086). However, don't count on it if your life (or someone else's) is in danger.

If you want to try your luck with someone who probably won't speak English, the emergency telephone number for police is ☎ 112; for an ambulance or fire it's ☎ 119.

Seoul has a number of good hospitals with English-speaking doctors, but most are horribly overcrowded. All of the useful hospitals seem to be at least one km from the nearest subway station, which means you'll have to get a taxi, walk or crawl the last 1000 metres. For emergencies, the biggest, best and jam-packed is Seoul National University Hospital (☎ (02) 762-5171) – it's about one km from Hyehwa subway station (line No 4). For normal outpatient treatment, the best place to go is the Foreigners' Clinic at Sev-

erance Hospital (☎ (02) 392-0161) which is attached to the Yonsei University Medical School – take the subway to Shinch'on subway station (line No 2). Other hospitals with English-speaking doctors include Cheil (☎ (02) 269-2151), Ewha (☎ (02) 762-5061), Soonchunhyang (☎ (02) 794-7191) and Saint Mary's (☎ (02) 789-1114).

The Foreign Community Service (FOCUS) (☎ (02) 798-7529, 797-8212) provides referrals to hospitals, doctors, lawyers, schools and other services in South Korea. This place could be good for advice on activities, renting apartments etc, but it's mostly oriented to long-term foreign residents rather than short-term travellers. The office is open from 9 am to 5 pm, Monday to Friday and there's a 24-hour answering machine for emergencies. The address is 5th Floor, B Bldg, Namsan Village Apartments, San 1-139, It'aewon-dong, Yongsan-gu.

Lost & Found If you leave something in a taxi or on public transport, there is a chance of recovering it from the Lost & Found office at the Korean Broadcasting System (KBS) Bldg (☎ (02) 781-1325) on the island of Yŏŭido. However, first try calling the Citizen's Room of the Seoul Metropolitan Police Bureau (☎ (02) 725-4401). There is also a subway Lost & Found office (☎ 753-2408).

Walking Tour

The logical starting place for getting your bearings in Seoul is the City Hall Plaza. In actual fact it is less a plaza than a confusing swirl of intersecting roads, and the only way to get across it on foot is to take the underpass – for newcomers not equipped with a compass, it is unlikely that you'll come up at the exit you were aiming for once you've made your descent. The major buildings on the plaza form a triangle: the palace of Tŏksugung to the west; the Seoul Plaza Hotel to the south; and City Hall to the north.

The **City Hall** building is a four-storey granite affair topped with a dome. As with most other neo-classical structures in Seoul, it is a legacy of the Japanese colonial years.

Striking north from here along T'aepyŏngno, you pass the Press Centre on the right and the Koreana Hotel on the left. Ahead is the important Kwanghwamun intersection. It is the only intersection in Seoul from which each of the four radiating roads have different names. Slightly to the north of the intersection, in the middle of Sejongno, is a bronze statue of **Admiral Yi Sun-shin** (1545-98), possibly the most revered figure in Korean history. Yi Sun-shin was a masterful military strategist, and was the inventor of the *kŏbuksŏn*, the so-called 'turtle ship'. By cladding the wooden ships of the time in sheets of armour, he was able to achieve stunning victories over Hideyoshi's numerically and militarily stronger Japanese navy.

To the right of the statue is the Kyobo building. The building is not particularly interesting in itself, but the basement is home to the vast Kyobo Book Centre. Huddled in the shadow of the Kyobo building is tiny **Pigak**, a pavilion built in 1903 to commemorate the enthronement of King Kojong.

Continue north up Sejongno in the direction of the Kwanghwamun Gate. The street you are walking on is named after King Sejong, who is held in reverence by Koreans as the father of the han'gŭl Korean writing system. Sejongno, of great symbolic significance as the road that led from the gate of the royal palace into Seoul during the Chosŏn dynasty, now buzzes with 14 lanes of traffic.

Turn right at the end of Sejongno. Opposite is the gate of Kwanghwamun and the National Museum. Behind them is the Kyŏngbokkung Palace. To the east is a road called Ujŏnggukno, and a little way down this road is **Chogyesa**, the main temple of Korea's huge Chogye sect. The temple area is not particularly extensive and it doesn't take long to look around it. In the vicinity of Chogyesa, out on the main road, are a number of Buddhist supply shops selling everything from alms bowls to tapes of Buddhist meditation chants.

Walk back up to the intersection, turn right and then right again into **Insadonggil**. This busy little street is the focus of Seoul's antiques district. Most of the shops sell antiques, folk crafts and calligraphy supplies, with the odd private art gallery thrown in for good measure. Some of the alleys running off the north eastern end of Insadonggil are worth poking around in – there are some beautiful traditional-style houses built around courtyards here.

Walk down Insadonggil until you reach Chongno. You can head back westwards along Chongno to **Poshingak**, the city's belfry. Chongno, which means 'Bell St', derives its name from its city bell. The old city bell, dating from the mid-15th century, is in the National Museum, and a new city bell is now hung in Poshingak. In the past, the bell was struck daily at dawn and dusk to signal the opening and closing of the city gates. Nowadays, it's only sounded to usher in the new year and mark Independence Movement Day and National Liberation Day. The pavilion area is fenced off and, while there's not a lot to see, it is worth a look if you are passing by. The most exciting time to visit is New Year's Eve at midnight, when thousands converge here to witness the ringing of the bell – this event is also shown live on TV.

On the corner of Insadonggil and Chongno is **T'apkol Park**, also known as Pagoda Park. The park is named after the 10-tier marble pagoda inside, and it was founded as a memorial to the anti-Japanese independence movement. The statue in the park is Sun Pyong-hui, the leader of the independence movement. The Declaration of Independence was read here in 1919, and its entire contents are reproduced on a brass plaque alongside the statue. Look also for the murals along the wall of the park depicting the activities of the independence movement.

If you are up for another 10 to 15 minutes of walking, eastwards along Chongno is Tongdaemun (Great East Gate). It dates from 1869 but had to be renovated after it was damaged during the Korean War. Nearby is the Tongdaemun Market. This stretch of Chongno is a bustling shopping district, and

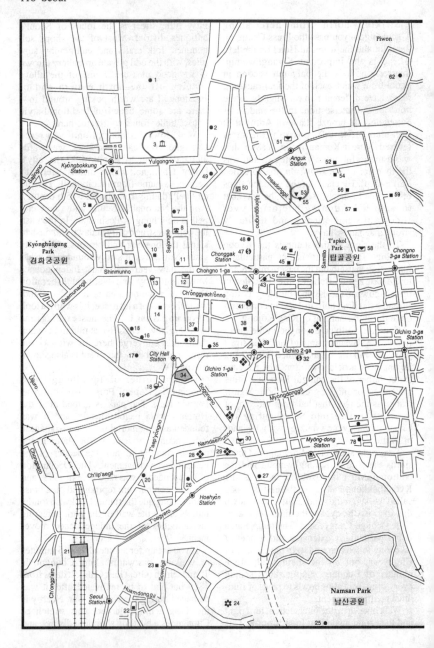

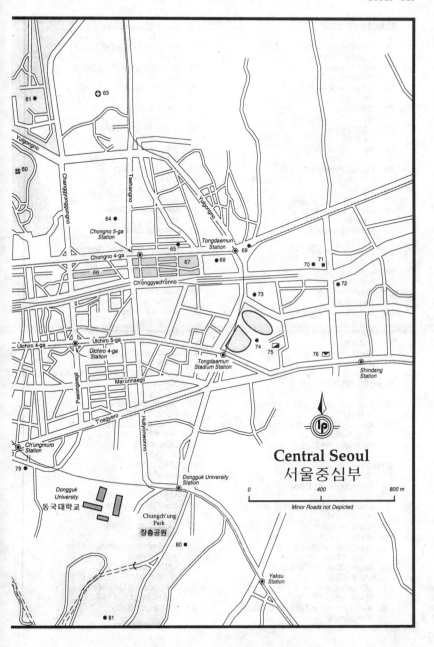

Central Seoul
서울중심부

0   400   800 m

Minor Roads not Depicted

PLACES TO STAY

5 Inn Sung Do & Inn Sam Sung
성도여관, 삼성여관

10 Inn Daewon
대원여관

14 Koreana Hotel
코리아나호텔

22 Yŏinsuk
여인숙

23 Hilton Hotel
힐튼호텔

34 Seoul Plaza Hotel
—

38 Kwang Pyung Yŏgwan
광평여관

45 YMCA
—

46 Taewon Yŏgwan
대원여관

52 Munhwa Yŏgwan
문화여관

54 Motel Jongrowon
종로원여관

56 Hotel Sangwon
상원호텔

57 Hotel Emerald
애머랄드호텔

59 Sun Ch'ang Yŏgwan
순창여관

71 Samho Hotel
삼호호텔

80 Shilla Hotel
호텔신라

PLACES TO EAT

53 Sanch'on Vegetarian Restaurant
산촌식당

55 Airirang Restaurant & Yet Ch'at
Chip Teashop
아리랑식당, 옛찻집다실

OTHER

1 Kyŏngbokkung Palace
경복궁

2 French Cultural Centre
불란서문화원

3 National Museum
국립중앙박물관

4 Immigration Office & KYHA
적선현대빌딩

6 Sejong Cultural Centre
세종문화회관

7 US Embassy
미국대사관

8 Kwanghwamun Telephone Office
광화문전화국

9 Koryŏ Supermarket
고려쇼핑

11 Kyobo Book Centre
교보문고

12 Kwanghwamun Post Office
광화문우체국

13 Airport Bus Stop
정류장 (공항)

15 British Embassy
영국대사관

16 British Council Library
영국문화원

17 Tŏksugung Palace
덕수궁

18 Airport Bus Stop
정류장 (공항)

19 Korean Air
대한항공

20 Namdaemun Gate
남대문

21 Seoul Station
서울역

24 Namsan Botanical Garden
남산식물원

25 Seoul Tower
서울타워

26 Namdaemun Market
남대문시장

27 Asiana Airlines
아시아나항공

28 Saerona Department Store
새로나 백화점

29 Shinsegae Department Store
신세계 백화점

30 Central Post & Telephone Office
(CPO)
중앙우체국, 중앙전화국

31 Midopa Department Store
미도파 백화점

32 Korea Exchange Bank
외환은행

33 Lotte World
롯데백화점

35 USIS Library
미국문화원

36 City Hall
시청

37 Joy Travel Service
죠이항공

39 Ŭlchi Book Centre
을지서적

40 Printemps Department Store
쁘렝땅 백화점

41 KNTC Building
한국관광공사

42 Youngpoong Bookshop
영풍문고

43 Poshingak Belfry
보신각

44	Chongno Book Centre 종로서적	67	Tongdaemun Market 동대문시장
47	Korea First Bank 제일은행	68	Tongdaemun Chain Store 동대문종합시장
48	Chung'ang Map & Atlas 중앙지도	69	Tongdaemun Gate 동대문
49	Japan Embassy 일본대사관	70	Shoe Shops 신발류도매시장
50	Chogye Temple 조계사	72	Hwanghak-dong Flea Market 황학동시장
51	Anguk Post Office 안국우체국	73	Hŭng'in Market 흥인시장
58	T'apkol Post Office 탑골우체국	74	Tongdaemun Stadium 동대문운동장
60	Chongmyo (Royal Shrine) 종묘	75	Swimming Pool 수영장
61	Ch'anggyŏnggung Palace 창경궁	76	Hŭng'in-dong Post Office 흥인동우체국
62	Ch'angdŏkkung Palace 창덕궁	77	Kodak Photo Shop 코닥양행
63	Seoul National University Hospital 서울대학교병원	78	Fujicolor Plaza 후지칼라 프라자
64	Royal Asiatic Society (RAS) 로얄아시아협회	79	Korea House 한국의집
65	Herbal Medicine Arcade 한약상가	81	National Theatre 국립극장
66	Kwangjang Market 광장시장		

there are roadside stalls everywhere specialising in dried squid, silkworm soup and bootleg cassettes.

Tŏksugung 덕수궁

This palace was built in the mid-15th century by King Sejo for his grandson, Prince Wolson. Even though it is the smallest of Seoul's palaces, it has twice served temporarily as the royal residence: once for 15 years after Hideyoshi's 1592 sacking of Seoul; and on a second occasion from 1897 to 1907 when King Kojong made it his residence following a year-long asylum in the Russian legation. After his son King Sunjong took power in 1907, Kojong remained in Tŏksugung until his death in 1919.

The entrance to Tŏksugung is opposite the Seoul Plaza Hotel. Immediately through the entrance is an extensive lawn. At the end of it is a statue of King Sejong, the most legendary of Korean kings and the man who set a team of scholars working to devise han'gŭl, the Korean written script. The most interesting of the palace buildings is Chunghwajŏn (Hall of Central Harmony) which was the throne hall and audience chamber of the king.

Tŏksugung's grounds also contain a Western-style garden and a curious neo-classical Western building fronted with columns and fountains. It has had a varied history, and is now an annexe to the National Museum of Modern Art.

Tŏksugung is open from 9 am to 6 pm March to October, and from 9 am to 5 pm November to February. The entrance fee is W550. It's closed on Mondays.

Kyŏngbokkung 경복궁

This palace at the far north end of Sejongno has long been Korea's seat of power, although today it's only a pale shadow of its former glory. Built by the first Yi dynasty king when he relocated the capital to Seoul, this palace was the focus of royal power and the royal residence for around 200 years. Before the Japanese Hideyoshi invasion the grounds housed some 500 buildings. The Japanese onslaught of 1592 saw most of these destroyed. The palace was then neglected until an ambitious reconstruction scheme commenced during the reign of King Kojong (1864-1907). By 1872 some 200 buildings had been completed. Today, another Japanese occupation having occurred in the interim, only 10 remain.

Entrance to the Kyŏngbokkung is via Kwanghwamun (Gate of Radiant Transformation). The gate is flanked by two *haet'ae* statues. Like the fierce gods that can be seen guarding Chinese and Japanese temples and imperial residences, they hold evil forces at bay, although in the case of haet'ae there is a particular insurance against the risks of fire. To the right of the gate, set in the middle of the road, is the Tongshipjagak (Eastern Crossroads Pavilion). It was once part of the palace walls before the road was widened to ease congestion.

Probably the most impressive palace structure on the grounds is the first that you come to: the Kunjongjon. It was the royal throne hall, and is the largest surviving wooden structure in South Korea. There are usually young women here in *hanbok* (the bulging but colourful traditional Korean dress) charging ridiculous amounts of money for a photograph – they seem to be raking it in with the Japanese tour groups.

Not far away to the north is the Kyŏnghoeru, the largest pavilion in South Korea. The pavilion is set in the middle of a lotus pond, its roof supported by 48 enormous stone pillars. This was one of the buildings rebuilt during the reign of King Kojong.

At the northern end of the palace grounds are the Hwangwon-jong, an attractive hexagonal pavilion set in the centre of a lotus pond. If you were permitted to wander just a little further north, you would discover that Kyŏngbokkung is actually still the seat of power in South Korea. Just beyond the area open to the public is the Blue House where South Korea's president lives. It's walled off and heavily guarded, so don't expect to leisurely stroll in there.

Kyŏngbokkung is open from 9 am to 6 pm March to October and from 9 am to 5 pm November to February. The entrance fee is W550. It is closed on Tuesdays.

Ch'angdŏkkung 창덕궁

East of Kyŏngbokkung is Ch'angdŏkkung, yet another of Seoul's famous palaces. There are still members of the royal family living here, and this means you have to join a guided tour to see the palace buildings and the attached Piwon (Secret Garden). Despite this minor drawback, it is still the best pre-

---

National Museum

The National Museum building, directly through Kwanghwamun, is the former Capitol building, built by the Japanese in 1926. However, there is a 50% chance that by the time you read this, it will be gone. In violation of all the laws of geomancy, the Japanese deliberately constructed it to symbolically intersect the line of power that flowed from the throne hall through Kwanghwamun, and the building was constructed in the shape of the Japanese character for Japan. Although the Koreans located their national collection here, it has long been argued that the building is an insult to national pride. In 1994, it was finally decided that the museum will be moved and the building demolished.

The new National Museum is slated to be opened by 1998 in the Yongsan area on the site of a former golf course built by the US military. Logically, the old museum should be preserved until the new one opens, but the Koreans are very keen to tear the building down before national pride gets wounded any further. This will pose a significant problem since no one has yet answered the question of where to house the ancient relics while the new museum is being constructed. For this reason, it's possible the old building will have to remain standing for a few more years. ■

served of the palaces and definitely worth visiting. Tours take around 90 minutes, and although English tours are only available at 11.30 am, 12.30 and 3.30 pm, there are Korean-language tours on the hour from 9 am to 5 pm. Joining a Korean language tour is no problem as all the sights have English explanations posted.

Unlike Kyŏngbokkung, which was left neglected after the ravages of the Hideyoshi invasion, Ch'angdŏkkung was rebuilt in 1611. It was originally constructed in 1405 as an annexe to the former Kyŏngbokkung, but from 1611 to 1872 served as the royal residence for Yi kings and queens. The royal family moved back to Ch'angdŏkkung in 1907.

Entry to the palace is via the Tonhwamun, a gate which is believed to be Seoul's most ancient. Inside, the grounds contain three major groupings of buildings and Piwon. The Naksonjae, in the far south-east corner of the grounds, is the residence of surviving members of the royal family and not open to the public. The nearest buildings to the gate are the Injongdon (Palace of Benevolent Government), the Throne Hall, and next door the Sonjongjon (Hall of Illustrious Government), which was used for administrative affairs. The buildings are exquisite, and it would be better to have more time to poke around rather than being shepherded through by the tour leader. To the right of the Sonjongjon is the entrance to Piwon.

Piwon makes for a very pleasant stroll. The 32-hectare grounds contain ponds and pavilions and some interesting gates such as Pullomun – passing under it is said to guarantee permanent youthfulness. Perhaps most attractive are the gnarled ancient trees – it's reassuring to see some real trees in sprawling Seoul.

Tours of Ch'angdŏkkung are W1800. It's closed on Mondays.

Chongmyo 종묘

Chongmyo (Royal Shrine) was originally built concurrently with Kyŏngbokkung to enshrine the ancestral tablets of the first Yi king, Yi T'ae-jo. Today, with the exception of two kings of some disrepute, the ancestral tablets of all 27 Yi kings are enshrined here. There are two shrine buildings on the grounds: the Chŏngjon and the Yŏngnyŏngjon.

During the Chosŏn dynasty, Confucian rituals held in reverence to royal ancestors were observed in the shrine with great pomp and ceremony five times a year. This tradition has been kept, although it is now only observed once a year on the first Sunday of May. For anyone in Seoul at this time, it is an opportunity that should not be missed. The proceedings are carried out in full court regalia. Traditional court music is performed by the Royal Court Orchestra, and the ceremony is overseen by the royal family.

Chongmyo is connected by a footbridge to Ch'anggyŏnggung, and it makes sense to continue on into the grounds of the latter. Yulgongno, the road that separates the shrine from the palace is yet another work of the Japanese during their occupation of Korea from 1910 to 1945. Again, as in the construction of the Capitol building on the grounds of Kyŏngbokkung, the separation of the royal palace from the shrine of its royal ancestors was designed to have a symbolic value, and was part of a systematic onslaught on traditional Korean culture. However, the Koreans have not yet proposed to rip out Yulgongno as they are doing to the old Capitol building. Chongmyo is open daily, except Tuesday, and from 9 am to 6 pm March to October, 9 am to 5 pm November to February. The entrance fee is W550.

Ch'anggyŏnggung 창경궁

Ch'anggyŏnggung was originally a Koryŏ summer palace built in 1104. In the early 1390s the first Yi king, T'ae-jo, lived here while Kyŏngbokkung was being completed. During the Japanese occupation, the palace was demoted to a park, a colonial-style red building was constructed, and a botanical garden and zoo moved here. The zoo has since been relocated to Seoul Grand Park.

The main gate for Ch'anggyŏnggung is Honghwamun on the east wall. Unlike north-south orientation of the Yi dynasty palaces in

Seoul, Ch'anggyŏnggung has an east-west orientation, a Koryŏ dynasty feature. The most notable structure on the palace grounds is the throne room, which survived the 1592 Japanese invasion and dates back to the 15th century.

Ch'anggyŏnggung is open daily, except Tuesday, from 9 am to 6 pm March to October, and from 9 am to 5 pm November to February. The entrance fee is W550.

Kyŏnghŭigung 경희궁

West of the Sejong Cultural Centre is the site of another palace, Kyŏnghŭigung. The original palace was erected in 1616. For the time being this area is a park, the palace structures having been relocated to other parts of Seoul. However, there are plans afoot to restore it. The mulberry trees planted in the park have given it the alternative name of the Mulberry Palace.

Namdaemun 남대문

South of the City Hall down T'aepyŏngno, Namdaemun (South Great Gate) was once Seoul's chief city gate, in keeping with the geomantic principles that determined the layout of the Yi palaces. It makes an impressive sight, surrounded by tall office buildings and knots of jostling traffic. It was originally built in the late 14th century. The latest reconstruction work was completed in the 1960s for damage sustained in the Korean War.

Namsan Park 남산공원

Namsan (South Mountain) once marked the southern extent of old royal Seoul, and remains of the city walls can still be seen in the park's wooded grounds. The peak was also once crowned with defensive fortifications, although these have now been replaced by Seoul Tower.

In the western section, not far from Nandaemun Market, there is the **Namsan Botanical Gardens**, a library and the odd statue. The botanical gardens are not very extensive, but they make for a pleasant stroll.

At the top of Namsan is **Seoul Tower**, which reaches the grand height of 483 metres. Seoul Tower is Korea's answer to Tokyo Tower, and you can be certain that this type of tourist adventure will cost significantly more in Japan. There's an observation deck, which provides excellent views of the city in clear weather (an increasingly rare phenomenon in Seoul). The tower features a booth where you and your significant-other can have a photograph printed onto a T-shirt inscribed with the words 'for the precious love' for only W30,000. Also look out for the display of towers of the world on the ground floor. The aim seems to be to make as clear as possible that Seoul's Tower is the tallest – the cynics might remark that putting it on top of a small mountain played no small part in this particular achievement. Other attractions in the tower include the Oceanarium, Ocean Life Museum, Funny World and Natural Stone Exhibits. If this kind of tourist action appeals, the B ticket for the tower includes all the attractions including the observation deck for W3500. For those content with the view and a T-shirt, the A ticket at W1300 will suffice.

You can get up to the tower either by walking from the botanical gardens or via the cable car. The latter runs at 10-minute intervals throughout the day and into the evening. The nearest subway station is Myŏng-dong.

Yongsan Family Park 용산가족공원

Gazing southwards from Seoul Tower, you can clearly see (smog permitting) the Yongsan Military Base which is run by the US military. Possibly within the lifespan of this book, the Yongsan base will be moved out of Seoul. There have been plans to do this for years, but the big obstacle is that the Korean government and US government continue to wrangle over who will pay for the move. Another factor is that Korea's leftist students have already staged riots at the proposed site for the new base, and more are promised if the base is actually moved.

At the moment, Yongsan Family Park consists of only the former US-military golf course. If and when the base moves, the park will expand enormously. Korea's new

National Museum is also slated to be built on this site.

Yŏŭido 여의도

Touted as Seoul's answer to Manhattan, Yŏŭido is an island in the Han River. It's certainly got Seoul's largest collections of skyscrapers, one of which is a hotel called the Manhattan. Yŏŭido is basically an administrative and business centre, and not really what most people regard as a tourist attraction. During office hours the streets are eerily deserted, but the atmosphere changes on Sundays when the enormous Yŏŭido Plaza fills up with Seoulites on an afternoon outing. Stalls are often set up, and many people zip around on the bicycles that are available for hire. In October the plaza hosts a major ceramics market in which potters set up stalls selling their products at prices much cheaper than elsewhere around town.

Up the road and around the corner from the Lucky Goldstar building is the **Korean War Museum**. It is an outdoor museum with tanks and aircraft scattered across the lawns. If you are not particularly interested in military hardware there's also an interesting historical remains section with lots of memorabilia from the Korean War. The museum is open daily from 9 am to 6.30 pm and the entrance fee is W200. Children and US military personnel are free.

Continuing along the same road that the Korean War Museum is on brings you to the **Korean Stock Exchange** on the second street to the right. There's a free observation room on the 4th floor with English explanations of the stock exchange activities provided by phones. Don't expect to see the kind of frantic trading one sees on Wall St.

From the stock exchange it's a 10 to 15-minute walk eastwards to the 63-storey **Daehan Life Insurance (DLI 63) building**. Actually, the '63' figure is misleading – there are 60 storeys above ground and three more in the basement. At 264 metres, it's the nation's tallest building. The 60th floor has an observation deck with an entrance fee of W3500, but you can see the same view for free by eating at the reasonably priced Sky

Pizza on the 59th floor. The building also contains an aquarium (adults W5200, children W4000) and the IMAX Theatre (adults W4500, children W3200). The latter offers a viewing screen 10 times larger than the average cinema and foreigners get earplugs to hear the dialogue in English – stunning sound and visuals that will blow you away! The shows are typically travelogue-type productions with features on the Korean cultural heritage, all filmed with the special Imax camera. The ground level has a good selection of restaurants, a shopping centre, bowling alley, health club and sauna. You can purchase an all-round ticket for the aquarium, observatory and IMAX theatre for W10,000. The building is open from 9.30 am until 9 pm daily.

Close to the DLI 63 building is the **Riverside Park**. It no doubt holds great promise, but for the moment it is a vast barren expanse interrupted by the occasional forlorn patch of grass. If you cross the road from the DLI 63 building and wander into the park, you can find a ferry terminal next to the Han River. This is the starting point for the riverboat cruises. (See the Riverboat Cruises section in this chapter.)

Lotte World 롯데월드

If you are a fan of mall culture you'll love Lotte World. It is a city within a building, of the kind much beloved by the Japanese. All within the one complex, are Lotte World Adventure, Lotte World Folk Village, Hotel Lotte World, Lotte Department Store, Lotte Super Store, Lotte World Shopping Mall, Lotte World Sports, Lotte World Swimming and Lotte World Plaza. If this is not enough, there's a Disneyland look-a-like next door at Magic Island. It would easily be possible to spend an entire rainy day exploring the place, and it would be ideal for children – you could probably leave them there for good and they'd never miss you.

Getting to Lotte World is no problem. Chamshil subway station has clearly marked signs leading the way and you don't even need to poke your head above ground.

Postal Museum 우체국박물관

Strictly for the keen philatelist, the Postal Museum is on the 4th floor of the CPO. It has a reasonably extensive collection of 19th-century stamps and items related to the postal industry.

Sajik Park 사직공원

Sajik Park is not far to the west of the Kyŏngbokkung Palace. It was originally the site of two ceremonial altars established by the first Yi king, T'aejo. Agricultural rites and sacrifices were held here twice yearly until 1897. The remains of the altars are still here, although today they are two visually unimpressive mounds. The park itself is a pleasant retreat, and worth strolling down to from the Kyŏngbokkung Palace.

Children's Grand Park 어린이대공원

Out near the Sheraton Walker Hill Hotel in eastern Seoul, Children's Grand Park has plenty to keep the kids amused. There are rides, play areas, fountains and ponds, and even a small zoo. The park is open daily from 9 am to 7 pm and the entrance fee is W600 for adults, W300 for children over 12, free for under-12-year-olds. It is a 10-minute walk north of Konkuk University subway station.

Seoul Dream Land 서울드림랜드

This is the largest amusement park within Seoul's city limits (there are larger ones in suburbia). It's mostly for children, but the swimming pool might interest adults. There are also some thrilling rides which adult-children might enjoy – the Jet Coaster is said to be good. Admission for adults is W700, but you pay extra for each ride – the Astrojet is most expensive at W1800.

Seoul Dream Land (☎ 982-6800) is a two-km bus ride from the Miasamgŏri subway station (line No 4).

Subterranean City 지하상가

One sight often overlooked by visitors is the Subterranean City – the underground shopping arcades and interconnecting passages. There is a maze of these arcades twisting and winding under the city – the tourist bureau maps show only part. Longest is the Ŭlchiro Underground Arcade running from City Hall to the Ŭlchiro 7-ga subway station – about 2.8 km. More interesting is the Sogong Arcade (near the Seoul Plaza Hotel) which connects to the Myŏng-dong Arcade (near the CPO) and connects to the basement of the Lotte Department Store – a good walk with plenty to see.

Olympic Stadium 올림픽스타디움

The enormous Olympic Stadium on the south bank of the Han River was the venue for the 1988 summer olympics. The stadium accommodates around 100,000 spectators and the surrounding sports complex (Olympic Park) covers almost three sq km. The stadium and sports complex are open to the public.

Riverboat Cruises

During the summer months there are six different cruises on the Han River. There are less frequent cruises in spring and autumn, but you can forget it in winter unless you want to hire an icebreaker.

There are several routes, the longest being 15 km (Yŏŭido-Chamshil). The cruises are operated by Semo Corporation, which you can contact for reservations and information (☎ 499-6262/3 Main Office; ☎ 785-5522 Yŏŭido; ☎ 416-8615 Chamshil; ☎ 469-4459 Ttuksŏm). In summer boats run from 10 am until 9.10 pm. The routes are as follows:

Route	Duration	Fare
Yŏŭido-Chamshil	70 min	W4000
Chamshil-Yŏŭido	70 min	W4000
Ttuksŏm-Yŏŭido	60 min	W3400
Yŏŭido-Ttuksŏm	60 min	W3400
Yŏŭido-Tongjak Bridge -Yŏŭido	60 min	W3400
Chamshil-Tongho Bridge -Chamshil	60 min	W3400
Ttuksŏm-Tongho Bridge -Ttuksŏm	60 min	W3400
Ttuksŏm-Chamshil	10 min	W650
Chamshil-Ttuksŏm	10 min	W650

Activities

Computer Club The Seoul Computer Club is an English-speaking organisation inside the US military base in Yongsan. You don't have to be a member of the military to participate in club activities. If you have a computer and modem, you might want to ring up the club's electronic bulletin board service (BBS, ☎ 7913-6821, 7913-3264).

Swimming Thanks to the 1988 Olympics, there are several indoor Olympic-sized swimming pools. One is in the Seoul Sports Complex and another is in Olympic Park. There are many others inside five-star hotels, and it is possible to use these facilities without being a hotel guest if you pay a monthly fee. You will have to call to make enquiries. A selection of swimming pools in Seoul follows:

Chamshil YMCA, 27-11, Chamshil 5-dong, Songp'a-gu (☎ 424-7513)

Changch'ung Outdoor, San 7-22, Changch'ung-dong 2-ga, Chung-gu (☎ 296-4107)

Cheil Sports Centre, Karak-dong, Songp'a-gu (☎ 402-9436)

Children's Centre, Nung-dong, Songdong-gu (☎ 446-6061)

Children's Grand Park, 18, Nung-dong, Songdong-gu (☎ 447-9371)

Chosŭn Hotel, Sogong-dong, Chung-gu (☎ 753-3141)

Chung'ang Culture Centre, Unni-dong, Chongno-gu (☎ 751-5681)

Grand Sports Centre, Taech'i-dong, Kangnam-gu (☎ 553-0101)

Hanshin Sports Centre, Togok-dong, Kangnam-gu (☎ 574-3600)

Hilton Hotel, Namdaemunno 5-ga, Chung-gu (☎ 759-7788)

Hyatt Regency Hotel, Hannam-dong, Yongsan-gu (☎ 797-1234)

Kangnam YMCA, 225-6 Nonhyon-dong, Kangnam-gu (☎ 548-9419)

Lotte Hotel, Sogong-dong, Chung-gu (☎ 411-7114)

Lotte World, 40-1, Chamshil-dong, Songp'a-gu (☎ 411-4503/6)

Mugunghwa Sports Centre, Taech'i-dong, Kangnam-gu (☎ 555-5746)

Nam Seoul, Hwagok-dong, Kangso-gu (☎ 691-9981)

Namsan Sports Club, It'aewon-dong, Yongsan-gu (☎ 795-0131)

New World Hotel, Samsong-dong, Kangnam-gu (☎ 557-0111)

Olympia Hotel, P'yongch'ang-dong, Chongno-gu (☎ 353-5121)

Olympia Indoor, 468-3, Kalhyon-dong, Unp'yong-gu (☎ 386-6055)

Olympic, Oryun-dong, Songp'a-gu (☎ 410-1696)

Pangbae Sports Plaza, Pangbae-dong, Soch'o-gu (☎ 532-6921)

Piwon Hyondae Sports Club, Wonso-dong, Chongno-gu (☎ 741-2111)

Renaissance Hotel, Yoksam-dong, Kangnam-gu (☎ 555-0501)

The Big 'I Do'

The Seoul Olympic Stadium, despite all the type and cries of 'keep the Olympic torch burning', is more than a little forlorn and generally deserted except for the occasional tourist or two. But it may be that the stadium has found a new lease on life...in the mass wedding industry.

On 25 August 1992, the Seoul Olympic Stadium was host to the largest mass wedding in history. A total of 41,650 members of the Unification Church, whose followers are better known as 'Moonies' after their spiritual leader and self-styled Son of God, the Reverend Sun Myung-moon, collectively said 'I do' in the stadium. The participants were by no means all Korean. The Unification Church is not even particularly popular in the Reverend Moon's homeland. In fact, the brides and grooms were as international as the Olympic competitors for which the stadium was originally built, hailing from over 130 nations the world over.

If this all seems a little curious, the pairing up procedures prior to the wedding were even more bizarre. The Reverend Moon and his confidants match spouses by means of photographs according to the compatibility of facial features. Naturally such a specialised service is not without its costs: participants were billed on a sliding scale according to nationality, with Japanese heading the list at US$2000.

And what about the mass honeymoon? Well, it was put on hold. Moonie weddings are followed by 40 days of celibate comtemplation before knuckling down to the less contemplative business of creating blessed families. ∎

Samwon Sports, Suyu 2-dong, Tobong-gu (☎ 904-4232)

Samyong Indoor, Shillim-dong, Kwanak-gu (☎ 886-3304)

Seoul Health Sports Club (☎ 759-3999)

Shilla Hotel, Changch'ung-dong 2-ga, Chung-gu (☎ 233-3131)

Skyway, Songbuk-dong, Songbuk-gu (☎ 762-1447)

Sogyo Hotel, Sogyo-dong, Map'o-gu (☎ 333-7771)

Swiss Grand Hotel, Hong-un-dong, Sodaemun-gu (☎ 356-5656)

Tower Hotel, Changch'ung-dong 2-ga, Chung-gu (☎ 236-2121)

Ujong Sports Centre, Ilwon-dong, Kangnam-gu (☎ 577-3476)

Ujong Sports Leisure, 194-28, Yonhui-dong, Sodaemun-gu (☎ 332-0222)

Yongwon Sports Centre, Shinwol-dong, Yangch'on-gu (☎ 693-3365)

Yŏŭido, 42-1, Yŏŭido-dong, Yongdungp'o-gu (☎ 782-4584)

Places to Stay – bottom end

Hostels Yŏinsuk and yŏgwan are generally a better deal – the hostels operated by the Korea Youth Hostels Association (KYHA) are not particularly cheap and tend to be inconveniently located. However, they are very clean and comfortable.

The only hostel within the city itself is the *Olympic Youth Hostel* (☎ (02) 410-2114; fax 410-2100) where dorm beds cost a heart-stopping W9900. Take subway line No 2 and exit at Songnae subway station, and from there walk ½ km.

There are hostels out in the suburban areas of Koyang and Bulam. These are cheaper at W5000 per bed, but are so inconveniently located that most travellers will not bother. For directions on how to get there, see the Accommodation section in the Facts for the Visitor chapter.

Yŏinsuk & Yŏgwan The cheapest place where you can have your own private room is just to the south-east of Seoul station (see the Central Seoul map). There are three alleys here harbouring eight yŏinsuk, although every one of them is a grim, windowless hovel. Don't even bother asking the *ajimah* to change the sheets, and look at the closet-sized rooms first before you dish out the W7000. On the north alley you'll find

Hanwon Yŏinsuk and *Sŏjŏng Yŏinsuk*. The tiny east alley has just one place, the *Kwangshil Yŏinsuk*. The south alley has five yŏinsuk; the *Kyŏnggi, Songning, Myŏngshil, Sŏngnam* and *Hyŏndae*.

If you're feeling lonely you may want to stay at the *Inn Daewon* (☎ (02) 735-7891), 26 Tangju-dong, Chongno-gu. Many budget travellers wind up here largely because of its central location, because it's cheap and because nearby competing yŏgwan have sold out to high-rise developers. A dormitory bed in this firetrap costs W6000 and double rooms cost W10,000. All share one grotty bathroom with barely functional plumbing. There have been rumours for years that this place will also be sold and demolished (it should be), but so far the building has managed to survive. If it isn't torn down soon, it might just fall down by itself.

The second most popular place with budget travellers is the *Inn Sung Do* (☎ (02) 737-1056, 738-8226), 120 Naesu-dong, Chongno-gu. This place belongs to the same family that owns Inn Daewon, but there is a difference – it's livable. In fact, rooms are pretty decent and it's often full with long-termers. Doubles with shared bath cost W10,000, and a double with private bath costs W15,000. This yŏgwan has a sign in English.

Just next door to the Inn Sung Do is the *Inn Sam Sung* (☎ 737-2177). Rates are exactly the same as its neighbour.

Highly recommended is the *Munhwa Yŏgwan* (☎ (02) 765-4659), 69 Unni-dong, Chongno-gu, where beautiful double rooms with shared bath cost W8000. With private bath it's W12,000. This place is very close to Duksung Women's University, a few blocks north of T'apkol Park. The English sign is yellow with blue letters and says 'hotel'.

Just a few doors south of the Munhwa Yŏgwan is the *Motel Jongrowon* (☎ 745-6876). This is a fancy yŏgwan with beautiful rooms for W18,000.

A little north of the Chongno 3-ga subway station and just west of Chongmyo (Royal Shrine) is an alley where you'll find *Sun Ch'ang Yŏgwan* (☎ 765-0701). At W10,000

Namdaemun Gate at night (MM)

Top: Pulguksa Temple, Kyŏngju (DS)
Bottom: Chongmyo Shrine (CT)

Kwanghwamun Area
광화문

0   100   200 m

PLACES TO STAY

3 Inn Sung Do
   성도여관
4 Inn Sam Sung
   삼성여관
9 Inn Daewon
   대원여관
17 Koreana Hotel
   코리아나호텔
18 Hwangsil-jang Yŏgwan
   황실장여관
29 New Seoul Hotel
   뉴서울관광호텔
30 New Kukje Hotel
   뉴국제호텔

PLACES TO EAT

6 Pizza Inn
   피자인
7 Paris Baguete
   부산회집
8 Sapporo Pub & Restaurant
   삿뽀로우동
10 Koryŏ Supermarket
   고려쇼핑
11 Hardee's
   하디스
12 Wendy's
   웬디스
16 Kentucky Fried Chicken
   캔터키 프라이 치킨
26 Uncle Joe's Hamburgers
   조아저씨
27 Chinese Restaurant
   중국집

OTHER

1 Kyŏngbokkung Subway Station
   경복궁 지하철역
2 Immigration Office & KYHA
   적선현대빌딩
5 Sejong Cultural Centre
   세종문화회관
13 Yi Sun-shin Statue
   이순신장군동상
14 Airport Bus Stop
   정류장 (공항)
15 Donghwa Duty-Free Shop &
   Kwanghwamun Building
   동화면세백화점, 광화문 빌딩
19 Japanese Embassy
   일본 대사관
20 US Embassy
   미국대사관
21 Kwanghwamun Telephone Office
   광화문전화국
22 Kyobo Building
   교보빌딩
23 Kyobo Book Centre
   교보문고
24 Tourist Information Kiosk
   관광안내소
25 Pigak Pavilion
   비각
28 Kwanghwamun Post Office
   광화문무제국

Naejadonggil

Sejongno

Uhjungno

Shinmunno 1-Ga

Chongno 1-Ga

Ch'ŏnggyech'ŏnno

T'aepyŏngno

Sŏsomunno

Sogong
Underground
Arcade

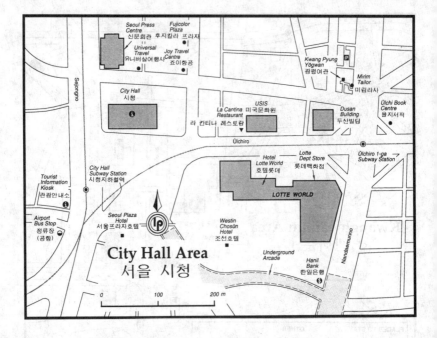

Seoul Press Centre
신문회관
Fujicolor Plaza
후지칼라 프라자
Universal Travel
유니버살여행사
Joy Travel Centre
조이항공
Kwang Pyung Yŏgwan
광평여관
Mirim Tailor
미림라사
City Hall
시청
USIS
미국문화원
La Cantina Restaurant
라 칸티나 레스토랑
Dusan Building
두산빌딩
Ülchi Book Centre
을지서적
Sejongno
Ülchiro
City Hall Subway Station
시청지하철역
Hotel Lotte World
호텔롯데
Lotte Dept Store
롯데백화점
Ülchiro 1-ga Subway Station
Tourist Information Kiosk
관광안내소
LOTTE WORLD
Airport Bus Stop
정류장
(공항)
Seoul Plaza Hotel
서울프라자호텔
Westin Chosŭn Hotel
조선호텔
Underground Arcade
Hanil Bank
한일은행
Nandaemunno

City Hall Area
서울 시청

0   100   200 m

it's reasonable although the rooms are small. There is a small courtyard and the ajimah is very nice.

As you face the YMCA, on the right side of the building you'll find an alley. If you head up this alley, you'll find a sign in English saying 'Hotel' – this is the *Taewon Yŏgwan* (☎ (02) 735-1588) where doubles with shared bath cost W8000.

Another popular yŏgwan in the same price bracket is over near the Lotte Hotel in the City Hall area. The *Kwang Pyung Yŏgwan* (☎ 778-0104), 123-1, Ta-dong, has rooms arranged around a traditional courtyard for W15,000. To find it, look for the lane with the Mirim Tailor shop and then look out for the sign advertising the yŏgwan.

If you're prepared to spend a little more for your creature comforts check out Insadonggil, the antiques street. As you walk up the road you will see bathhouse symbols on almost every one of the side alleys. Most of these places are of a similar standard and

charge similar prices. Most travellers head for the Anguk subway station end of Insadonggil because that's easiest for transport. One of the many offerings in this area is the *Hanhung-jang Yŏgwan* (☎ 734-4265), 99, Kwanhun-dong, where a double room with private bath costs W20,000. Further down the alley is the *Kwanhun-jang Yŏgwan* with the same deal – no English is spoken but the staff are very friendly. At the end of this alley is the *Shingung-jang Yŏgwan* (☎ 732-1682), which offers the same deal as its neighbours.

Some budget travellers head over to It'aewon, although this is a much less popular area than Insadong. The *Sungji Hotel* (☎ 795-1691), 211-30, It'aewon 2-dong, is a popular option, with rooms with a private bath going for W18,000. Right in the heart of the action, at the top of that infamous stretch of alleyway known by locals as 'hooker hill', is the *Hilltop Motel* with singles/doubles with private bath, colour TV and air-con at W18,000. The sign is in English and the staff speak some English too. This place probably gets pretty rowdy at night. Back down the hill on the left-hand side is a sign simply saying 'motel'. Rooms here are also W18,000. Finally, back on the main drag is the *Mido Hotel* where a single room with private bath costs W18,000.

Perhaps worth mentioning as a place to avoid are the numerous yŏgwan near Ch'ŏngnyangni railway station (the eastern terminus of subway line No 1). Most of these yŏgwan are brothels, but in this neighbourhood foreigners are *not* welcome.

Places to Stay – middle

Hotels There are no shortage of places to stay in this category, it just depends where you want to base yourself. All of the places listed here are in the central area since that's where most foreigners want to stay. In many respects, the lower end of the mid-range accommodation represents less of a bargain than Seoul's yŏgwan. But there are benefits like English-speaking staff and (sometimes) business facilities like fax and international phone call service.

An old reliable standby is the *YMCA* (☎ (02) 732-8261) on Chongno 2-ga. It's on the north side of the street just west of T'apkol Park. Singles/doubles cost W26,400/34,100.

In an alley just to the north of T'apkol Park by the Nagwan elevated arcade is the *Hotel Emerald* (☎ (02) 743-2001), 75 Nagwondong, Chongno-gu. A comfortable double with private bath goes for W23,000. In another alley just slightly to the north is the relatively upmarket *Hotel Sangwon* (☎ (02) 765-0441) 33 Nagwon-dong, Chongno-gu, where singles/twins are W30,300/38,100.

In an alley right by the south-east corner of Ŭlchiro and Tonhwamunno is the *Eulji Hotel* (☎ (02) 278-5000), 291-45 Ŭlchiro 3-ga, Chung-gu. Korean and Western-style doubles are W22,000/25,000.

Transport is so good that there's little need to stay out by Kimp'o Airport. But if you're catching a very early flight and you're paranoid about traffic, consider the *Airport Hotel* (☎ 662-1113; fax 663-3355) which is a five-minute bus ride from the airport. Singles/doubles are reasonable at W23,000/28,600 plus 20% tax and surcharge.

The following places will add a 20% tax and surcharge to the prices listed here:

Astoria: 13-2, Namhak-dong, Chung-gu (a five-minute walk from Ch'ungmuro subway station on line No 3 or 4); doubles/twins cost W34,686/36,668 (☎ 268-7111; fax 274-3187)

Chonji: 133-1, Ŭlchiro 5-ga, Chung-gu (a five-minute walk from Tongdaemun Stadium subway station on line No 2); doubles/twins cost W24,200/30,000 (☎ 265-6131; fax 279-1184)

City Palace Tourist: 497-23, Tapshimni 5-dong, Tongdaemun-gu (a five-minute walk from Shindang subway station on line No 2); twins cost W38,000 (☎ 244-2222; fax 246-6542)

Daehwa: 18-21, Ŭlchiro 6-ga, Chung-gu (a five-minute walk from Tongdaemun Stadium subway station on line No 2 or 4); singles & twins cost W30,000, suites cost W35,000 (☎ 265-9181/9; fax 277-9820)

Eastern Tourist: 444-14, Ch'angshin-dong, Chongno-gu (a three-minute walk from Tongdaemun subway station on line No 1 or 4); singles/twins cost W37,000/42,000(☎ 741-7811; fax 744-1274)

Hamilton: 119-25 It'aewon-dong, Yongsan-gu (connected to Ashoka Indian Restaurant); singles/doubles cost W51,000/75,000 (☎ 794-0171, fax 795-0457)

Kaya Tourist: 98-11, Kalwol-dong, Yongsan-gu (a one-minute walk from Namyŏng subway station, one stop south of Seoul station on line No 1); singles/doubles/twins cost W28,925/31,405/37,190 (☎ 798-5101; fax 798-5900)

Metro: 199-33, Ŭlchiro 2-ga, Chung-gu (a two-minute walk from Ŭlchi 1-ga subway station on line No 2); singles/doubles cost W33,000/36,300, twins/suites cost W41,800/90,000 (☎ 752-1112; fax 757-4411)

New Oriental: 10, Hoehyon-dong 3-ga, Chung-gu (a three-minute walk from Myŏngdong subway station on line No 4); singles/doubles cost W30,580/36,300, twins/suites cost W41,800/62,700 (☎ 753-0701; fax 755-9346)

Poongjun: 73-1, Inhyon-dong 2-ga, Chung-gu (a two-minute walk from Ŭlchiro 4-ga subway station on line No 2); singles/doubles cost W47,900/60,000, twins/suites cost W68,500/120,000 (☎ 266-2151; fax 274-5732)

Rio Tourist: 72-7, Kwanghui-dong 1-ga, Chung-gu (a five-minute walk from Tongdaemun Stadium subway station on line Nos 2 and 4); singles/doubles/twins cost W25,000/35,000/38,000 (☎ 278-5700; fax 275-7207)

Savoy: 23-1, Ch'unmuro 1-ga, Chung-gu (a two-minute walk from Myŏngdong subway station on line No 4); singles/doubles cost W33,000/38,500, twins/suites W41,800/66,300 to W101,200 (☎ 776-2641; fax 755-7669)

Seoul Prince: 1-1, Namsan-dong 2-ga, Chung-gu (a two-minute walk from Myŏngdong subway station on line No 4); singles/doubles cost W27,000/33,000, twins/suites cost W38,000/65,000 (☎ 752-7111; fax 752-7119)

Seoul Tourist: 92, Ch'ongjin-dong, Chongno-gu (a three-minute walk from Chonggak subway station on line No 1); doubles/twins cost W43,000/49,000 (☎ 735-9001; fax 733-0101)

Tongseoul Tourist: 595, Kuui-dong, Songdong-gu (a one-minute walk from Tong-Seoul bus terminal); singles cost W49,500, doubles/twins cost W75,350/75,350 (☎ 455-1100; fax 455-6311)

Yŏŭido Tourist: 10-3, Yŏŭido-dong, Yongdungp'o-gu (on Yŏŭido Island right on Yŏŭido Plaza); twins cost W39,670 (☎ 782-0121; fax 785-2510)

Places to Stay – top end

The following places charge a 20% tax and surcharge on top of the listed rates:

Capital: 22-76, It'aewon-dong, Yongsan-gu (It'aewon); twins cost W110,000 (☎ 792-1122; fax 796-0918)

Crown Tourist: 34-69, It'aewon-dong, Yongsan-gu (It'aewon); twins cost W60,000 (☎ 797-4111; fax 796-1010)

Grand Hyatt Seoul: 747-7, Hannam-dong, Yongsan-gu (a short walk east of It'aewon); twins cost W150,000 (☎ 797-1234; fax 798-6953)

Holiday It'aewon: 737-32, Hannam-dong, Yongsan-gu (It'aewon); singles/twins cost W52,600/75,300 (☎ 792-3111; fax 798-8256)

Intercontinental Seoul: 159-8, Samsong-dong, Kangnam-gu (a three-minute walk from Samsong subway station on line No 2); singles/twins cost W108,000/153,300 (☎ 555-5656; fax 559-7990)

Koreana: 61-1, T'aep'yongno 1-ga, Chung-gu (a five-minute walk north of City Hall); doubles/twins/suites cost W105,000/111,000/350,000 (☎ 730-9911; fax 734-0665)

Lotte World: 40-1, Chamshil-dong, Songp'a-gu (a two-minute walk from Chamshil subway station on line No 2); twins cost W153,300 (☎ 419-7000; 417-3655)

Lotte: 1, Sogong-dong, Chung-gu (a two-minute walk from Ŭlchi 1-ga subway station on line No 2); twins/suites cost W153,300/W210,000 to W3,400,000 (☎ 771-1000; fax 756-8049)

Manhattan: 13-3, Yŏŭido-dong, Yongdungp'o-gu (on Yŏŭido Island); twins cost W90,000 (☎ 780-8001; fax 784-2332)

New Hilltop Tourist: 152, Nonhyon-dong, Kangnam-gu (one km north of Yŏksam subway station on line No 2); doubles/twins cost W57,850/66,115, suites cost W99,170 to W115,700 (☎ 540-1121; fax 542-9491)

New Kukje: 29-2, T'aep'yongno 1-ga, Chung-gu (a five-minute walk from City Hall subway station); singles/twins cost W50,200/71,900 (☎ 732-0161; fax 732-1774)

New Seoul: 29-1, T'aep'yongno 1-ga, Chung-gu (two-minute walk from City Hall subway station); singles/doubles/twins cost from W60,000/70,000/80,000 (☎ 735-9071; fax 735-6212)

New World: 112-5, Samsong-dong, Kangnam-gu (a 10-minute walk from Sŏllŭng subway station on line No 2); twins cost W123,700 to W140,000 (☎ 557-0111; fax 557-0141)

Pacific: 31-1, Namsan-dong 2-ga, Chung-gu (a two-minute walk from Myŏng-dong subway station on line No 4); doubles/twins cost W64,600/68,200 (☎ 777-7811; fax 755-5582)

President: 188-3, Ŭlchiro 1-ga, Chung-gu (a five-minute walk from City Hall subway station); singles/doubles cost W70,300/106,500 (☎ 753-3131; fax 752-7417)

Riverside: 6-1, Chamwon-dong, Soch'o-gu (a two-minute walk from Shinsa subway station on line No 3); twins cost W97,000 (☎ 543-1001; fax 543-5310)

Sejong: 61-3, Ch'unmuro 2-ga, Chung-gu (just in front of Myŏng-dong subway station on line No 4); singles cost W83,100 to W109,700, doubles cost W109,700 to W118,100 (☎ 776-1811; fax 755-4906)

Seoul Hilton International: 395, Namdaemunno 5-ga, Chung-gu (a 10-minute walk from Seoul station); singles/doubles cost W153,300/153,300 (☎ 753-7788; fax 754-2510)

Seoul Palace: 63-1, Panp'o-dong, Soch'o-gu (a five-minute walk from Seoul express bus terminal); singles/doubles/ cost W68,000/106,000 twins cost W111,000 to W112,500 (☎ 532-5000; fax 532-0399)

Seoul Plaza: 23, T'aep'yongno 2-ga, Chung-gu (a two-minute walk from City Hall subway station on line Nos 1 or 2); singles/doubles cost W130,000/140,000 (☎ 771-2200; fax 755-8897)

Seoul Renaissance: 676, Yoksam-dong, Kangnam-gu (a five-minute walk from Yŏksam subway station on line No 2); doubles/twins cost W153,000/173,300 (☎ 555-0501; fax 553-8118)

Seoul Royal 6, Myŏng-dong 1-ga, Chung-gu (a five-minute walk from Myŏng-dong subway station on line No 4); singles/doubles cost W83,100/108,500 to W118,100 (☎ 756-1112; fax 756-1119)

Sheraton Walker Hill: San 21, Kwangjang-dong, Songdong-gu (two km east of Children's Grand Park); doubles/suites cost W145,000/180,000 to W300,000. This place boasts Seoul's only casino.(☎ 453-0131; fax 452-6867)

Shilla: 202, Changch'ung-dong 2-ga, Chung-gu (a five-minute walk from Dongguk University subway station on line No 3) twins cost W153,000 to W280,000(☎ 233-3131; fax 233-5073)

Sofitel Ambassador: 186-54, Changch'ung-dong, Chung-gu (a three-minute walk from Tongguk University subway station on line No 3); twins cost W112,500 (☎ 275-1101; fax 272-0773)

Tower: San 5-5, Changch'ung-dong 2-ga, Chung-gu (a five-minute walk from Dongguk University subway station on line No 3); singles/doubles cost W75,000/113,000 (☎ 236-2121; fax 235-0276)

Westin Chosŭn: 87, Sogong-dong, Chung-gu (a two-minute walk from City Hall subway station on line Nos 1 and 2); superior/deluxe/executive cost W150,000/168,000/195,000 suites cost W350,000 to W400,000 (☎ 771-0500, fax 752-1443)

Places to Eat

The only problem finding food is deciding where to start – the supply is limitless. If you're on a tight budget the best bargains are found in the basements of large department stores where you can often find supermarkets and lunch counters. The Saerona Department Store is a personal favourite, mainly because it's relatively uncrowded. The Shinsegae Department Store has some cheap lunch counters in the basement, although the selection is limited. The Printemps Department Store has excellent restaurants in the basement and on the 7th floor. The Lotte Department Store is the largest but is very crowded.

If you're in the area of the Inn Daewon or the Kyobo Book Centre, a place you should definitely check out is *Koryŏ Supermarket* (no English sign). The lunch counters are hidden in the back and to your right – you can eat well for around W1500. The supermarket itself is one of the cheapest and has sustained many a budget traveller.

One place to get a broad overview of what Korean food is all about, is the Lotte Department Store. The 9th floor is restaurant city, and for the most part it is given over to Korean food. The restaurants have no English names, but as they each specialise in a few dishes there's no problem sorting out which is which. Best of all, most of the restaurants have plastic imitations of the meals they serve on display with English labelling.

Yet another place to look is in the large subway stations and underground shopping malls – sushi with soup and pickled vegetables should go for around W2000.

Uncle Joe's Hamburgers not only has good hamburgers, but also the best ice cream in Korea. There are 45 branches around Seoul, mostly *not* in the centre because of sky-high rents. The one branch in the centre is very tiny, but popular with foreigners – it's just east of Kyobo Book Centre. There is another (much larger) branch in the trendy Taehangno entertainment district near the Hyehwa subway station (line No 4).

Coco Fried Rice is another chain store, with about 30 branches in Seoul. The speciality is a sort of Korean-Chinese fast food, which isn't bad at all. One of the more accessible branches is in the Taehangno district near the Hyehwa subway station on subway line No 4.

Sapporo Pub & Restaurant is opposite Sejong Cultural Centre on the south side of the street. The Japanese food here is very reasonably priced (a rare find). You can have dessert and coffee just next door at *Paris Baguete*, or walk just one door to the west to sample the delights at *Pizza Inn*.

The area around the Chinese Embassy in Myŏng-dong is the place to look for Chinese restaurants. This small collection of restaurants and one or two bookshops is about as close as Seoul gets to a Chinatown. On the north side of the CPO is a restaurant with a sign in English that simply says *Chinese Restaurant*. Most of the others bear the same name.

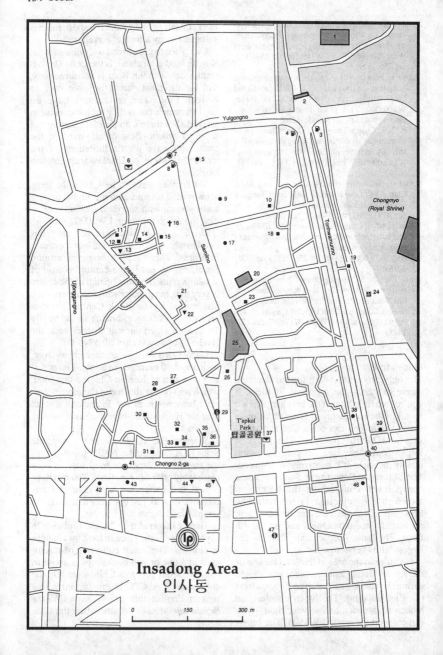

Chongmyo
(Royal Shrine)

Yulgongno

Tonhwamuno

Samilno

Insadongjil

Uljongudngno

T'apkol
Park
탑골공원

Chongno 2-ga

Insadong Area
인사동

0   150   300 m

PLACES TO STAY

10 Munhwa Yŏgwan
문화여관
11 Pochŏvn-jang Yŏgwan
보천장여관
12 Hanhung-jang Yŏgwan
한흥장여관
14 Kwanhun-jang Yŏgwan
관훈장여관
15 Shingung-jang Yŏgwan
신궁장여관
18 Motel Jongrowon
종로원여관
19 Sun Ch'ang Yŏgwan
순창여관
20 Hotel Sangwon
상원호텔
23 Hotel Emerald
애머랄드호텔
26 Tongsan Yŏgwan
동산여관
27 Kŭmjwa-jang Yŏgwan
금좌장여관
30 Taewon Yŏgwan
대원여관
31 YMCA
─
32 Wonkap Yŏgwan
원갑여관
33 Chongno Yŏgwan
종로여관
34 Sobok Yŏgwan
소복여관
35 Unjong-jang Yŏgwan
운종장여관
36 Insŏng Yŏgwan
인성여관

PLACES TO EAT

13 Youngbin Garden Restaurant
영빈식당
21 Sanch'on Vegetarian Restaurant
산촌식당
22 Airirang Restaurant &
Yet Ch'at Chip Teashop
아리랑식당, 옛찻집다실
44 Hardee's
하디스
45 McDonald's
맥도날드

OTHER

1 Ch'angdŏkkung Palace
창덕궁
2 Tonhwamun Gate
돈화문
3 Petrol Station
주유소
4 Petrol Station
주유소
5 Japanese Cultural Centre
일본문화원
6 Anguk Post Office
안국우체국
7 Anguk Subway Station
안국 지하철역
8 Petrol Station
주유소
9 Duksung Women's University
덕성여자대학교
16 Church
교회
17 Kyodong Primary School
교동국민학교
24 T'aegaksa Temple
태각사
25 Nakwon Multi-Storey Arcade
낙원상가
28 Hollywood Cinema
허리우드극장
29 Tourist Information Kiosk
관광안내소
37 T'apkol Post Office
탑골우체국
38 Picadilly Cinema
피카디리극장
39 Danseongsa Cinema
단성사극장
40 Chongno 3-ga Subway Station
종로3가 지하철역
41 Chonggak Subway Station
종각 지하철역
42 Poshingak Belfry
보신각
43 Chongno Book Centre
종로서적
46 Seoul Cinema Town
서울시네마타운
47 Chohung Bank
조흥은행
48 Cine Plaza Cinema
시네프라자극장

The Insadong area is good for upmarket, traditional-style Korean restaurants. The most well known of these restaurants is

Sanch'on (☎ 735-0312). It specialises in Buddhist temple cuisine (vegetarian) – the W17,000 special full course allows you to

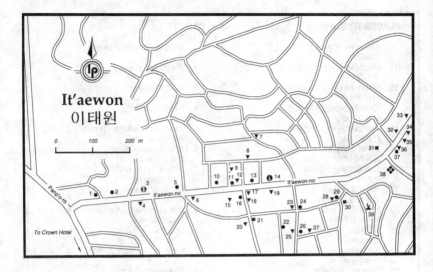

It'aewon
이태원

0   100   200 m

Panp'o-ro

To Crown Hotel

---

sample 15 courses that include such oddities as acorn jelly and wild sesame gruel. Seating is by way of cushions on the floor, and there are traditional dance performances every evening from 8 to 9 pm to the twingings and twangings of Korean stringed instruments. Sanch'on is down a small alley off Insadonggil, but it's easy to find because of the English sign out on the street.

Almost next door is the *Airirang Restaurant* which does traditional Korean food. Just upstairs is the *Yet Ch'at Chip Teashop* which is well worth stopping into – live birds flutter around the shop as you drink your tea.

Pizza Gillio is a popular and inexpensive Italian restaurant dishing up pizza, salad and spaghetti. Particularly recommended is the salad bar – for W4000 you can stack the salad as high as possible in your bowl. This restaurant is right inside the Anguk subway station, just next to the equally fine *Boutique Bakery*.

La Cantina (☎ 777-2579) is a good but definitely upmarket Italian restaurant right opposite the Hotel Lotte on the west side of the USIS building.

Not surprisingly, It'aewon has a number of restaurants offering non-Korean food and English speaking waiters. Some places catering to foreign tastes include:

Ashoka (☎ 794-1171) Indian; *Chalet Swiss* (☎ 795-1723) Swiss; *La Cucina* (☎ 798-1631) Italian; *Moghul* (☎ 796-5501/2) Pakistani; *Shakey's Pizza* (☎ 793-3122/3) fast food; *Sebastian* (☎ 796-2384) Western

Self Catering Down the hill from the Hyatt Hotel is *Jiel Deli*, an important landmark for self-caterers. This place features fantastic bread, imported jams, cheeses and other rare delights that you won't find in Korean markets.

Entertainment

Taehangno 대학로 Taehangno literally means 'University St' because it was the former campus of Seoul National University. The university has long since moved, but the area near to Hyehwa subway station (line No 4) has evolved into Seoul's trendiest café, pub, video parlour, karaoke and theatre district. Street theatre is frequently held here, although only Korean is spoken. Your best

PLACES TO STAY

11	Hamilton Hotel
21	Yŏgwan/Motel
30	Hilltop Motel
31	Holiday It'aewon Hotel
37	Mido Hotel

PLACES TO EAT

4	Pizza Pair
6	Popeye House
7	Chalet Swiss Restaurant
8	Itaewon Garden Restaurant
9	Moghul Restaurant
12	Paris Croissant
15	Nashville
17	Burger King
18	Sebastian Restaurant
19	Subway Sandwiches
20	Peiliciana Chicken
23	Outdoor Tempura Stalls
25	Guest Restaurant
27	Samrat Restaurant
28	Kettle House & Popay House

32	Shakey's Pizza
33	Pizza Hut
34	Old Germany
35	New York Pizza
36	Deutches Haus

OTHER

1	NL Eel Skin Shop
2	Reebok Store
3	Korea Exchange Bank
4	Reebok Store
5	All That Jazz Club
10	Kabbu Leather
13	Hamilton Store
14	Tourist Information
16	Adidas Store
22	Soul Train
24	Heavy Metal Club
26	King Club
29	Stomper Bar
38	Viva Department Store
39	Korean Islam Mosque

chances of seeing street theatre are on Saturday or Sunday afternoons, especially if the weather is fine. Taehangno is usually closed to traffic from 6 pm to 10 pm on Saturdays and from noon to 10 pm on Sundays.

Tonam 도남동 From Taehangno, continue north on subway line No 4 for two stops to reach Sungshin Women's University subway station. It's here that you'll find the Tonam district, a smaller but lively entertainment area. Of course, there is plenty of Korean food on offer, not to mention pubs, video parlours and karaoke joints. When the weather is warm, there is also a street market of sorts here.

It'aewon 이태원 Officially called It'aewon-dong, it's on the south side of Namsan Park near the US military base. It's an area of bars, music and dancing clubs, restaurants, brothels and more. The area used to cater solely to US soldiers, but it's becoming more and more Koreanised. One place which has become a legend in It'aewon is the King Club, which features disco music, a dance floor and no cover charge, although you're expected to buy drinks. Just across the street is another lively place, Heavy Metal. Also in the neighbourhood is All That Jazz. Nashville is reputed to have good hamburgers, and boasts big screen movies and dart games along with the drinks.

To get there catch bus No 23 from directly in front of the YMCA or from in front of the Samsung building.

Myŏng-dong 명동 Myŏng-dong is east of the CPO. It's a very exclusive neighbourhood and prices aren't cheap, but there are some discos charging reasonable rates that include a beer and a snack for the price. Quite a few movie theatres and restaurants can be found here too.

Shinch'on 신촌 Shinch'on is a conglomeration of several neighbourhoods. Besides It'aewon and Myŏng-dong, Shinch'on is the only other area where discos seem to welcome foreigners.

Taking the subway westwards from the centre to Ehwa Women's University subway station (line No 2) to find Taehyŏn. This neighbourhood is a lively shopping and entertainment district with many businesses that cater to women.

The entertainment gets a little more raucous as you move west. Next stop down the subway line is Shinch'on in the Ch'angch'ŏn district. It's here that you'll find Woodstock (☎ 334-1310), Ch'angch'ŏn-dong 52-69, Sŏdaemun-gu, which attracts a foreign clientele with its 1960s rock music. There are two universities within easy walking distance of here (Sogang and Yonsei), so the student crowd is much in evidence.

At the entrance of Sogang University is a health club with sauna and exercise room, but it's for men only (pumping iron is not considered a female activity in Korea). The cost is W60,000 for the first month, with discounts thereafter.

Hongik 홍익 If you take the subway to Hongik University subway station (line No 2) you will find yourself in the hangout of the rich kids, known to Koreans as the 'Orange Gang'. Most Koreans profess to hate the Orange Gang, but they all love to hang out with them. Being a member of the Orange Gang requires that you spend at least US$200 a night on entertainment, and there are plenty of trendy clubs in the Hongik area catering to this market. If you stop in any of these pubs, discos and coffee shops, enquire about the price first! Just a sample of clubs in this neighbourhood is: Fellini, Club Ivy League, Lust, Taboo and NASA. The street where most of the clubs are found is unofficially called 'Picasso Rd'. It's worth taking a look even if you can't afford to drink here – the proprietors at least deserve a lot of credit for their artistic design.

One place in this neighbourhood which is attractive to foreigners is TGI Fridays (☎ 322-6321). This is an American chain with branches in several Asian countries – there are three in Seoul but the Hongik branch is most accessible.

It's just to the south-west of the Hongik University subway station.

Chonggak 종각 The area south of the YMCA (around Chonggak subway station on line No 1) is a good nightlife area. A little further east near the Chongno 3-ga subway station is the big movie district, but it's best avoided on weekends when the cinemas pack out. Movies are sometimes advertised in the English newspapers, but you'll need to get a Korean paper to find out screening times. Tickets cost around W4000 unless you buy them from scalpers.

Things to Buy
Namdaemun Market 남대문시장 The open-air markets are said to have the best

deals. Close to the CPO is Namdaemun (south gate) Market. In Namdaemun, look for camping gear on the south side of the market (facing the Hoehyŏn subway station on line No 4). Also within Namdaemun is Namraemun, two floors (underground) where black-market goods (smuggled off US military bases) are sold. It's one of the few places in Seoul where you can buy deodorant, but prices are not cheap. Namdaemun is closed on Sundays.

Tongdaemun Market 동대문시장 The market is right near the Chongno 5-ga subway station on line No 1. Of special note are the camping stores which are *the* place to hunt for very cheap rucksacks, tents, etc. Tongdaemun Market is also a good place to pick up more fancy travel bags and suitcases. The market is closed on the first and third Sunday of each month.

Herbal Medicine Arcade 한약상가 On the north side of Chongno, opposite Tongdaemun Market, is the Herbal Medicine Arcade *(yakryŏng shijang)*. Everything from ginseng to dried sea horses are for sale, not to mention mundane Western medicines.

Hwanghak-dong Flea Market 황학동시장 This is perhaps the most important shopping area for newly-arrived shoestring travellers looking to get set up in Seoul. Everything from second-hand furniture to used refrigerators can be bought here. The market is east of Tongdaemun. Take the subway to Shindang subway station (line No 2) and walk north. You will first encounter the Chung'ang Market, which basically sells food (even live chickens and dogs). Continue north for another block and you'll find the flea market – if you've passed the elevated roadway then you've gone too far.

It'aewon 이태원 The nearby US military base has made It'aewon a shopping district second to none. In all of Korea, it's the cheapest and best shopping district for clothing, shoes and leathercraft.

Insadonggil 인사동길 This traditional shopping street is north of the YMCA. It's a popular place for buying antiques, arts and crafts.

Yongsan Electronics Market 용산전자상가 This area just to the west of It'aewon is a good place to look for all manner of electric appliances – computers (including software), tape players, Nintendo games, etc. You can reach the market by taking the Suwon train on subway line No 1 and getting off at Yongsan subway station – from there follow the elevated walkway over the tracks. Part of the electronics market is in one enormous building (a former bus terminal), but the market now spills out into many side streets as well.

Department Stores 백화점 Although not the cheapest place to buy things, the large department stores near the CPO are worth exploring, at least to see what's available. Popular stores in this area include Lotte (closed Tuesday), Midopa (closed Wednesday) and Shinsegae (closed first and third Monday). East of the CPO is a shopping district called Myŏng-dong. It's expensive, but you can try bargaining. Lotte World, at the Chamshil subway station (line No 2), is a long way from the city centre but is one of the largest shopping malls in the world.

Other Stores In the centre, north of the Koreana Hotel, is the multi-storey Donghwa Duty-Free Shop. It's questionable just what great bargains you can find here as 'duty-free' shops tend to be more expensive than the department stores. Nevertheless, it's worth a peek for the chocolate-coated macadamia nuts if nothing else. You might also want to check out the running shoes – at least you can find large sizes here. In most cases, you must pick up duty-free goods at the airport on departure. If you need booze and cigarettes, you might be better off purchasing this stuff right in the airport itself or on board the aircraft.

Few foreigners bother, but if you want to see the latest trends in Korean fashions then the place to go is the Kangnam area (south of the Han River). It's here where you'll find a place nicknamed 'Trendy St'. To get there, take the subway to Apkujŏng subway station (line No 3) and walk east along Apkujŏngno.

Getting There & Away
It's said that about two million Seoulites depart their city every Saturday for various destinations around the country, only to return on Sunday. It's like an immense tidal wave that rolls out and rolls in again. If you don't want to be caught in riptide, avoid weekend travel unless absolutely necessary.

Air Not surprisingly, Seoul has extensive domestic air connections to the rest of the country. There are direct flights from Seoul to 12 other cities in Korea. (For a complete list and air fares see the Getting Around chapter.)

If you've arrived in Korea with an onward ticket you need to reconfirm your reservation at least 72 hours before departure. The current list of airline offices in Seoul includes:

Airline	Code	Telephone
Aeroflot Soviet Airline	SU	☎ 551-0321/4
Air China	CA	☎ 518-0330
Air France	AF	☎ 773-3151
Air New Zealand	NZ	☎ 777-6626
Alitalia Airlines	AZ	☎ 779-1676
All Nippon Airways	NH	☎ 752-5500
Asiana Airlines	OZ	☎ 774-4000
British Airways	BA	☎ 774-5511
Cathay Pacific Airways	CX	☎ 773-0321
China Eastern Airlines	MU	☎ 518-0330
Continental Airlines	CO	☎ 773-0100
Delta Airlines	DL	☎ 754-1921/3
Garuda Indonesia Airways	GA	☎ 773-2092/3
Japan Airlines	JL	☎ 757-1720
Japan Air System	JD	☎ 752-9090/1
KLM Royal Dutch Airlines	KL	☎ 753-1093
Korean Air	KE	☎ 756-2000
Lufthansa German Airlines	LH	☎ 538-8141
Malaysia Airlines	MH	☎ 777-7761/2
Northwest Airlines	NW	☎ 734-7800
Philippine Airlines	PR	☎ 774-3581

Buses from the Kyŏngbusŏng Building, Seoul Express Bus Terminal

Destination	First	Last	Frequency	Fare	Travel Time in Hours
Ansŏng	6.30 am	9.30 pm	15 min	W1900	1 hr
Ch'angwon	6 am	6 pm	1 hr	W9500	5½ hrs
Ch'ŏnan	6.30 am	9 pm	15 min	W2200	1 hr
Ch'ŏngju	5.50 am	10 pm	10 min	W3300	1¾ hrs
Chinju	6.30 am	6 pm	25 min	W10,300	5½ hrs
Kimch'ŏn	7 am	6 pm	1¼ hrs	W5800	3 hrs
Kongju	7 am	7 pm	40 min	W3900	2½ hrs
Kumi	6 am	7.40 pm	1¼ hrs	W6500	3¼ hrs
Kŭmsan	7 am	5.50 pm	50 min	W5100	2¾ hrs
Kyŏngju	7 am	6.10 pm	35 min	W9000	4¼ hrs
Masan	6 am	6.30 pm	10 min	W9400	5 hrs
Onyang	6.30 am	9 pm	20 min	W2600	1¾ hrs
P'ohang	6.30 am	6.30 pm	20 min	W9900	5 hrs
P'yŏngt'aek	6 am	9.35 pm	15 min	W1800	1 hr
Poŭn	7.30 am	6.40 pm	1½ hrs	W5300	2½ hrs
Pugok	8 am	6 pm	2 hrs	W8800	4¾ hrs
Pusan	6 am	6.40 pm	5-10 min	W10,600	5¼ hrs
Sangju	7 am	6.30 pm	1¼ hrs	W6700	3¾ hrs
Taegu	6 am	8 pm	5-10 min	W7500	4 hrs
Taejŏn	6 am	9.40 pm	5-10 min	W4000	2 hrs
Ulsan	6.30 am	6.30 pm	15 min	W10,00	5 hrs
Yŏngdong	7.10 am	6.40 pm	1½ hrs	W5300	2¾ hrs

Qantas Airways	QF	☎ 777-6871/3
Singapore Airlines	SQ	☎ 755-1226
Swiss Air	SR	☎ 757-8901/8
Thai Airways Int'l	TG	☎ 754-9960/5
United Airlines	UA	☎ 757-1691
Vietnam Airlines	VN	☎ 775-5477/8

Bus The main bus station is the Seoul express bus terminal (*Seoul kosok t'ŏminŏl*) which is also called the Kangnam express bus terminal. It's on the south side of the Han River – take subway line No 3 and get off at the Express Bus Terminal subway station. The terminal is very well organised, with signs in English and Korean over all the ticket offices and bus bays. This huge terminal actually consists of two buildings: Kyŏngbusŏn and Honam-Yŏngdongsŏn. Kyŏngbusŏn is a ten-storey building with everything useful on the 1st floor, while the Honam-Yŏngdongsŏn building is a two-storey

structure with ticket offices and platforms on the 1st floor and a cafeteria on the 2nd floor. See the bus timetables for details of which buses depart from each building.

In addition to these buses, there are some night buses from Seoul to major cities like Pusan, Taegu and Kwangju. For definition purposes, a 'night bus' is one which departs between 10 pm and midnight. There are no night buses departing between midnight and 5.30 am, but that could change. All night buses depart from the Seoul express bus terminal.

The Tong-Seoul (east Seoul) bus terminal is also useful, especially for getting to places on the east coast and some tourist spots such as Yong-in Farmland, Ch'ungju, Suanbo Hot Springs, Onyang, Andong, and Songnisan and Chuwangsan national parks.

You can reach Tong-Seoul bus terminal by taking the subway to Kangbyŏn subway

Buses from the Honam-Yŏngdongsŏn Building, Seoul Express Bus Terminal

Destination	First	Last	Frequency	Fare	Travel Time in Hours
Ch'ungju	6 am	8.30 pm	30 min	W3180	2 hrs
Chech'ŏn	6.30 am	8 pm	40-50 min	W4300	2¾ hrs
Chŏngju	6 am	8 pm	20-30 min	W6700	3¼ hrs
Chŏnju	6 am	8.30 pm	5-15 min	W5900	2¾ hrs
Ich'ŏn	6.30 am	9.20 pm	20-30 min	W1900	1 hr
Iri	6 am	8.40 pm	20 min	W5800	2¾ hrs
Kangjin	6.30 am	6.30 pm	1 hr	W9600	5¼ hrs
Kangnŭng	6 am	7.40 pm	10-20 min	W6200	3¾ hrs
Kimje	6.40 am	7.30 pm	40 min	W6200	3¼ hrs
Kunsan	6 am	7 pm	20-30 min	W6300	3¼ hrs
Kwangju	5.30 am	8 pm	5-10 min	W8000	4 hrs
Mokp'o	6 am	6.30 pm	35 min	W9500	5½ hrs
Naju	7.40 am	4.10 pm	2 hrs	W8300	4½ hrs
Namwon	6.30 am	6 pm	50 min	W7400	4¼ hrs
Nonsan	6.30 am	7.50 pm	1¼ hrs	W5300	2¾ hrs
Sokch'o	6.30 am	6.40 pm	40 min	W7900	5¼ hrs
Sunch'ŏn	6.30 am	6 pm	30-40 min	W10,000	5¼ hrs
Tonghae	6.30 am	6.50 pm	40 min	W7200	4¾ hrs
Wŏnju	6 am	9 pm	10-15 min	W3100	1¾ hrs
Yong-in	6.30 am	9.30 pm	10-15 min	W1100	40 min
Yŏju	6.30 am	9.20 pm	30-40 min	W2300	1¼ hrs
Yŏnggwang	7 am	7 pm	50 min	W8000	4¼ hrs
Yŏngsanp'o	8.40 am	5.40 pm	2 hrs	W8500	4¾ hrs
Yŏnmudae	7 am	7.30 pm	1 hr	W5100	2½ hrs
Yŏsu	6.40 am	5.40 pm	55 min	W10,800	5½ hrs
Yusŏng	6 am	8.30 pm	30 min	W4000	2 hrs

Buses from the Tong Seoul Bus Terminal, Seoul

Destination	First	Last	Frequency	Fare	Travel Time in Hours
Ch'ŏngju	6 am	9 pm	30 min	W3500	1¾ hrs
Ch'ungju	6.20 am	8.40 pm	20 min	W3180	3¾ hrs
Chŏngju	6.30 am	6.40 pm	1½ hrs	W7000	3¼ hrs
Chŏnju	6 am	8.20 pm	40 min	W6200	2¾ hrs
Kangnŭng	6.30 am	7.40 pm	45 min	W6200	3½ hrs
Kwangju	6 am	7.30 pm	30 min	W8300	4 hrs
Kwangyang	7 am	5.40 pm	80 min	W10,400	5¼ hrs
Pusan	6 am	6.40 pm	30 min	W10,900	5¼ hrs
Samch'ŏk	7.30 am	6.40 pm	2½ hrs	W7600	4½ hrs
Sokch'o	6.30 am	6.40 pm	1½ hrs	W7900	5 hrs
Taegu	6 am	8 pm	30 min	W7800	3¾ hrs
Taejŏn	6 am	8.30 pm	30 min	W4300	1¾ hrs
Tonghae	7.30 am	6.40 pm	2½ hrs	W7200	4¼ hrs

station (line No 2). Buses leave according to the schedule in the Tong-Seoul table.

Sangbong bus terminal, in the eastern suburbs, is useful to people heading east. It's the terminal for buses to and from Ch'unch'on, Sokch'o, Kangnŭng, Wŏnju, Tongduch'on, Soyosan, Ŭijŏngbu and Yŏju. Sangbong bus terminal is connected by bus with Ch'ŏngnyangni railway station (the terminus of subway line No 1). From Ch'ŏngnyangni it takes 15 minutes to reach Sangbong on bus Nos 38-2, 165, 165-2, 166 and 522-1; or 50 minutes by bus from Chongno 1-ga on bus Nos 131 and 131-1.

Other bus terminals in descending order of usefulness include:

Shinch'on bus terminal: offers non-stop bus services to Kanghwa Island every 10 minutes.

Nambu (south) bus terminal: operates buses to destinations in Kyŏnggi-do, such as Kanghwa Island, Yong-in Farmland and Ansung; to destinations in Ch'ungch'ong-do, and parts of Chŏllabuk-do and Kyongsang-do.

Sŏbu (west) bus terminal: is easily accessible from subway line No 3, and runs buses bound for the north-western part of Kyŏnggi-do including Freedom Bridge, Imjingak, Kwangt'an, Pogwangsa, Munsan, Munbong, Pobwonni, Choksong, Pyokche, Songch'u and Ŭijŏngbu.

Train Most long-distance trains departing from Seoul leave from Seoul station. The one important exception is the train heading east towards Ch'unch'ŏn. For this, go to Ch'ŏngnyangni railway station, which you reach by taking subway line No 1 to its terminus.

Getting Around

To/From the Airport Kimp'o Airport is 18 km west of the centre, and handles both domestic and international flights. Construction is proceeding apace on the subway connection between the airport and central Seoul. This will undoubtedly be the most convenient transport option when it goes into operation – completion is scheduled for late 1995.

When the subway gets running, it will no doubt cause major changes in the bus routes. At present, there are five kinds of buses going to Kimp'o Airport charging different prices. Some buses are express and some are not, but it makes little difference – traffic jams are the key factor in determining how long the journey takes. However, the fancier buses do offer better facilites and extra room to store luggage.

The best deal is bus No 600 or No 601, both of which are express buses and guarantee a seat for all passengers. The No 601 bus goes into central Seoul, stopping at Shinch'on subway station, the Koreana

Hotel, Tŏksugung, Seoul station, Nandaemun, Chongno 3-ga, Chongno 6-ga, Tongdaemun Gate and on to the Sheraton Walker Hill Hotel. The No 600 bus goes from Kimp'o into the areas south of the Han River, stopping at the National Cemetery, Palace Hotel, Seoul express bus terminal, Yŏngdong Market, Nam Seoul Hotel, KOEX, the Seoul Sports Complex and Chamshil subway station. There is also a bus No 600-602, which follows the same route as the 600 but terminates at the Seoul express bus terminal. These buses leave every seven minutes from 5.40 am to 10 pm. The cost is W700.

Alternatively, there are local buses. These are more frequent than express buses and cost W600. The No 63 bus stops next to Tŏksugung and just north of the Koreana Hotel at the Donghwa Duty-Free Shop. The No 68 bus also stops close to City Hall and Midopa Department Store. The disadvantage of both these buses is that they will allow standing passengers and there is very little room for luggage.

Noticeably more upmarket is bus No 1002, which costs W1300. It follows much the same route as the No 63 and stops at the same spots in the centre.

Special airport express buses also travel between Kimp'o International Airport and the Korea City Air Terminal (KCAT) in the Korea World Trade Centre south of the Han River. This service is more expensive than the express buses at W2500 and it is also less frequent, running every 10 to 15 minutes from 7.20 am to 9.40 pm. It is probably only useful to visitors staying at the Inter-Continental, Lotte World and Ramada Renaissance Hotels, all of which are in the near vicinity. A note about Korea City Air Terminal – you can actually complete your entire check-in procedure here (as opposed to checking in at the airport), provided that you are flying with Aeroflot, Asiana, Cathay Pacific or Northwest.

The *crème de la crème* of Seoul's airport transport is the KAL limousine bus. There is no saving in time, but you get cushy seats, air-con, videos, cellular phones and cellular fax machines – just the thing for the executive on the go. All that's missing is the sauna. The price tag for this luxury is W3500. These buses run from 7 am to 10 pm, once every 20 to 30 minutes. There are five routes covering 19 luxury hotels – ask at the airport information desk (or your hotel service desk) if interested.

Taxis are convenient if you don't mind paying for one. There are often traffic police handing out official complaint forms at the taxi ramp outside the airport to discourage bad behaviour from the drivers, and most now seem resigned to using their meters. The trip into town should take around 30 minutes and cost around W10,000.

One of the confusing things about Kimp'o Airport is that there are three terminals – two for international and one for domestic. The terminals are too far apart to walk from one to the other, but a free shuttle bus zips around the airport every few minutes. It's useful to know that buses heading into the airport first stop at international terminal No 2, then the domestic terminal and finally international terminal No 1 – tell the bus driver which one you want to get off at. It could change, but at the time of writing you'll find the airlines distributed as follows:

International Terminal No 1: Aeroflot, Air France, All Nippon Airways, Brazilian Airlines, British Airways, Cathay Pacific, Delta, Japan Air System, Japan Airlines, KLM, Northwest, Philippine Airlines, Singapore Airlines, THAI Airways, United

International Terminal No 2: Alitalia, Asiana, Continental, Garuda Indonesia, Korean Air, Lufthansa, Malaysia (MAS), Qantas, Swiss Air, Vietnam Airlines

Bus City buses run from approximately 5.30 am until midnight. The ordinary buses are colour-coded purple and white or blue and white, and cost W300 (exact change please) or W290 with a token (same word in Korean) bought from one of the bus token booths found at most major bus stops. The green and white chwasŏk buses (the ones with seats) cost W600 and no tokens are available. The

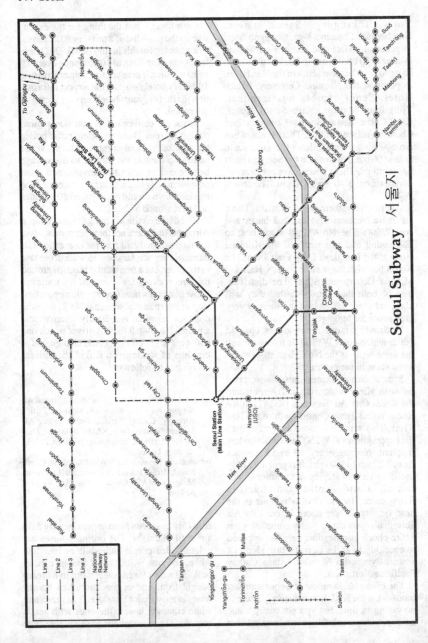

Seoul Subway 서울지

Line 1
Line 2
Line 3
Line 4
National Railway Network

token booths sell a *Bus Route Guide (bŏsŭ nosŏn onnae)* 버스노선안내 for W700, but it's written entirely in Korean even though some editions have had an English title on the cover.

Minibuses are privately owned and operate illegally, but are tolerated by the government because they provide services to isolated areas not reached by public transport. The fare depends on the distance travelled.

Subway The Seoul subway system is modern, fast and cheap, but can be so crowded that if you drop dead, you'll never hit the ground. There are four lines in total, all of them colour-coded. The system is very user friendly, and finding your way around should be no trouble. Trains run at least every six minutes from 5 am until midnight.

The basic charge is W350 for Zone 1 which includes most of the city. The fare rises to W400 if you cross into Zone 2 – the machines where you buy tickets have a self-explanatory fare map, but you'll rarely need to go outside Zone 1. There are additional charges for suburban lines like the one to Suwon – buy these tickets from the ticket windows.

If you do much commuting, you might want to buy a multiple-use ticket which gains you a 10% bonanza. A W10,000 ticket actually costs W9000, and a W20,000 ticket can be purchased for W18,000.

The subway system is still expanding. By 1997, the city hopes to have completed four new lines, thus doubling capacity. Most useful will be line No 5 which will extend all the way out to Kimp'o International Airport via Yŏŭido.

Taxi Demand is so much greater than supply that you practically have to throw yourself in front of a cab to get the driver's attention. However, drivers of the deluxe (expensive) taxis are often on the prowl for foreigners. If you don't mind paying for this luxury, you'll have some tactical advantage over the locals.

As for the ordinary taxis, you'll have to fight it out (literally) with the Koreans. Remember as the taxi goes sailing past that you must look confident and shout loudly. There is no room for the meek when it comes to trying to catch a taxi in Seoul.

Multiplying complaints have finally spurred the government into a campaign to

Traditional Tomb Site Guard

clean up the sordid reputation of Seoul taxi drivers. There are complaint forms available from the Ministry of Transport, and the public have been encouraged to record details of taxi drivers who drive dangerously or attempt to charge more than the amount on the meter. However, the authorities won't entertain any complaint about taxis not stopping for you.

Car While driving your own vehicle in Seoul is not recommended, some are determined to do it. If this interests you, cars can be rented from any of the following companies:

Donghwa (☎ 790-1750); 88 (☎ 699-3885); Hanyang (☎ 553-5812); Jangwon (☎ 951-5001); Korea (☎ 585-0801); Korea Express (☎ 719-7295); Kumho (☎ 758-1561); Saehan (☎ 896-0031); Sambo (☎ 797-5711); Seoul (☎ 474-0011); Sungsan (☎ 552-1566); VIP (☎ 737-7878)

If you want to travel in style, chauffeur-driven cars can be rented (W50,000 for 10 hours) by calling Korea Car Rental Union (☎ 533-2503).

Kyŏnggi-do 경기도

The province of Kyŏnggi-do surrounds Seoul, and part of the province even pokes into North Korea. You have about as much chance of visiting the moon as you do of crossing the DMZ, but all other parts of Kyŏnggi-do can be reached from Seoul as a day trip.

PUK'ANSAN NATIONAL PARK
북한산국립공원

This magnificent mountain park is to the north of Seoul and boasts many massive white granite peaks, forests, temples, rock-cut Buddhist statues and tremendous views from various points.

Puk'ansan (837 metres) is the highest peak in the area, but there are at least 20 others within the park boundary. Other notable peaks near Puk'ansan (and connected to it by ridges) include Insubong, Paekundae, Nojŏkbong, Pohyŏnbong, Pibong and Wonhyobong. Insubong (812 metres), Mangyŏngdae (800 metres) and Paekundae (836 metres) form a triangle which is named Samgaksan (Triangle Mountain). The rugged granite face of Insubong is a challenge to rock climbers, who turn out in force whenever weather permits.

At the northern end of the park is Tobongsan (740 metres), which is joined by ridges to Chaunbong, Manjangbong, Soninbong and Obong.

At the southern part of the park is Puk'ansansŏng (North Mountain Fortress). The fortress was originally built during the Paekche dynasty but the present walls date from the time of the Yi king, Sukchong, who rebuilt the battlements in the 16th century following invasions from China. Sections of the wall were destroyed during the Korean War but have since been restored.

As national parks go, it's fairly small (about 78 sq km) but still large enough to get lost in. There are a variety of well-marked trails into the park and along the ridges, and seven huts with simple accommodation (bring bedding) as well as a limited selection

of canned and packaged food. There are 32 officially recognised campsites. Water is available at the huts as well as at many other points along the trails. It's advisable to buy a map from the Chung'ang Atlas Map Service in Seoul. Entry to the national park costs W700.

South Area

Recommended hiking routes include:

North-South Route 1
Ui-dong, U-i Hut, Paekundae Peak, Taedongmun Gate, Kugi-dong (9.1 km)
North-South Route 2
Chŏngnŭng Resort, Pogukmun Gate, Yŏngammun Gate, Nojŏkbong Peak, Paekundae Peak (8.5 km, 3½ hours)
East-West Route 1
Ui-dong, Paekun Hut, Taesomun Gate (6.5 km)
East-West Route 5
Puk'ansansŏng Fortress Entrance, Taesŏmun Gate, Paekundae Peak, U-i Hut (11 km, 4½ hours)
Circular Route 1
Ui-dong – Paekundae Peak, Puk'ansan Hut – Chŏngnŭng Resort (7.1 km)

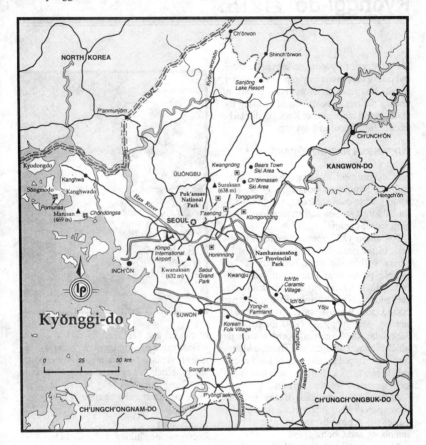

Kyŏnggi-do

Hiking Routes cont:
Circular Route 2
    Ui-dong, Puk'ansan Hut, Paekundae Peak, Ui-dong (8.1 km)
Circular Route 3
    Ui-dong, Tosŏnsa Temple, Paekun Hut, Paekundae Peak, Nojŏkbong Peak, Yŏngammun Gate, Ui-dong Resort (6.3 km, 3½ hours)
Circular Route 4
    Kugi-dong, Taesŏngmun Gate, Taedongmun Gate, 4.19 Memorial Tower (5 km)
Circular Route 5
    Segŏmjŏng Resort, Munsusa Hermitage, Taenammun Gate, Pogukmun Gate, Chŏngnŭng Resort (7.5 km, 4 hours)

North Area (Tobongsan)
Recommended hiking routes include:

East-West Route 2
    Tobong-dong, Podae Ridge, Obong Peak, Ui-dong (8.5 km)
East-West Route 3
    Tobong-dong, Tobong Hut, Kwanumam Hermitage, Ui-dong (7.9 km)
East-West Route 4
    Tobong-dong, Kwanumam Hermitage, Obong Peak, Ui-dong (8.3 km)
Circular Route 6
    Tobong-dong – Ch'onch'uksaTemple – Mangwolsa Temple, Changsuwon (6.7 km)

Getting There & Away

Getting to Puk'ansan by public transport is easy, although there are a number of entrances to the park. Some of the possibilities include:

City Hall to Ui-dong: bus Nos 6, 8 and 23 (50 minutes)
Chongno 1-ga to Chŏngnŭng Resort: bus No 5 (40 minutes)
Chongno 1-ga to Segŏmjŏng Resort: bus No 59 (20 minutes)
Sejong Cultural Centre to Puk'ansansŏng: bus No 156 (40 minutes)
Sejong Cultural Centre to Ui-dong, bus No 8 (50 minutes)

Alternatively, you could take the subway to the Kup'abal station (line No 3), then travel the last three km north-east towards the park by bus, taxi or on foot.

SURAKSAN 수락산

To the east of Puk'ansan National Park is Suraksan (638 metres) which is another attractive climbing area. It's not a national park, but it's still popular (too popular!) with weekend Seoulites trying to get away from it all.

Suraksan is just north of the Seoul city limits, but is connected by a ridge to Puramsan (508 metres) which is in Seoul. Hiking along the ridge between the two peaks is recommended.

Access to Suraksan is possible from several different points, and it's not a bad idea to ascend and descend the mountain by different routes. An easy way to begin would be to take the subway to Sanggye station (line No 4) – Puramsan is two km to the east of this station. From Puramsan you can follow the ridge north about seven km to Suraksan. Along the way you must cross a small highway, and off to the east is the interesting temple of Hungguksa, which is worth the small detour. From here there are several obvious trails down – one leads north-west to Ŭijŏngbu from where there are trains back to Seoul. Be forewarned that this is a long walk and will take a full day, so start early.

KWANAKSAN 관악산

Straddling the southern boundary of metropolitan Seoul and Kyŏnggi-do, Kwanaksan is a popular hiking spot. The summit is a moderate 632 metres above sea level.

You reach the peak starting from the campus of Seoul National University. To get there, take the subway to the Seoul National University station (line No 2), and from there a bus southwards about another two km to the campus. From the campus, Kwanaksan is the large and obvious peak towards the south-east. There are a number of hiking trails and students can easily point out the way.

SEOUL GRAND PARK 서울대공원

In the suburbs south of the megalopolis is Seoul Grand Park, a huge sprawling affair with a number of attractions. Although it's largely geared towards kids, there are also some sights for adults too. The park contains the National Museum of Modern Art, a major zoo with a botanical garden and Seoul Land, a hi-tech amusement park in the Disney tradition. If you don't want to be fighting with crowds all day, it is best to choose a weekday to visit.

The zoo has a good collection of animals, many of them in attractive roomy enclosures. There is even an ant ground. Dolphin shows take place three times daily at 11.30 am, 1.30 and 3.30 pm. There is an extra charge of W300 for adults and W100 for children for the latter. Admission to the zoo is W1000 for adults and W500 for children. Under-six-year-olds are admitted free. The zoo is open daily from 9 am to 7 pm from April to October, and from 9 am to 6 pm from November to March.

Seoul Land is an afternoon out in itself. It has plenty of rides of the white-knuckle variety, as well as theme concepts like Tomorrow World and Dream World. Admission to Seoul Land is W2500 for adults and W800 for children. It has the same opening hours as the zoo.

The nearest subway station to Seoul Grand Park is Sadang subway station (line

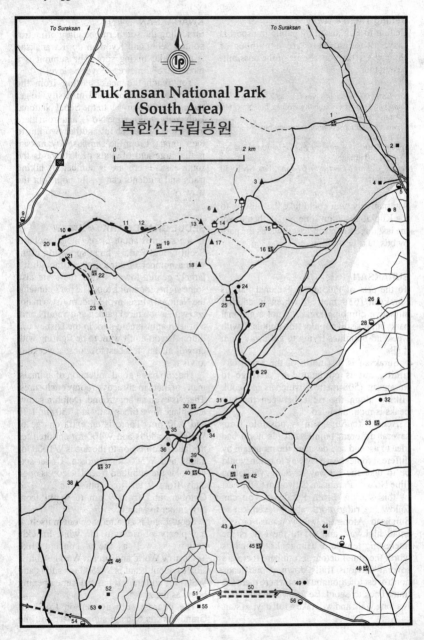

To Suraksan

To Suraksan

Puk'ansan National Park
(South Area)
북한산국립공원

0   1   2 km

PLACES TO STAY

2 Ui-dong Resort
우이동유원지

4 Green Park Hotel
그린파크호텔

7 Insu Hut
인수산장

14 Paekun Hut
백운산장

15 Ui Hut
우이산장

20 Puk'ansan Resort
북한산유원지

25 Puk'ansan Hut
북한산장

44 Chŏngnŭng Resort
정릉유원지

51 Pugak Park Hotel
북악파크호텔

52 Segŏmjŏng Resort
세검정유원지

55 Ramada Olympia
Hotel
(라마다) 올림피아호텔

OTHER

1 Yongdŏksa Temple
용덕사

3 Yŏngbong (604 m)
영봉

5 Bus Stop
정류장

6 Insubong (812 m)
인수봉

8 Ui-dong
우이동

9 Bus Stop
정류장

10 Sŏammun Gate
서암문

11 Wonhyobong
원효봉

12 Pukmun Gate
북문

13 Paekundae (836 m)
백운대

16 Tosŏnsa Temple
도선사

17 Mangyŏngdae
(800 m)
만경대

18 Nojŏkbong (716 m)
노적봉

19 Taedongsa Temple
대동사

21 Taesŏmun Gate
대서문

22 Sŏmunam
Hermitage
서문암

23 Iksŏngbong
익성봉

24 Yŏngammun Gate
용암문

26 4.19 Memorial
Tower
4.19기념탑

27 Puk'ansansŏng
(North Mountain
Fortress)
북한산성

28 Bus Stop
정류장

29 Taedongmun Gate
대동문

30 Taesŏngam
Hermitage
대성암

31 Pogukmun Gate
보국문

32 Suyu-dong
수유동

33 Hwagyesa Temple
화계사

34 Taesŏngmun Gate
대성문

35 Taenammun Gate
대남문

36 Munsusa
Hermitage
문수사

37 Sŭnggasa Temple
승가사

38 Pibong (560 m)
비봉

39 Pohyŏnbong
보현봉

40 Ilsŏnsa Temple
일선사

41 Yŏngch'usa Temple
영추사

42 Sambongsa Temple
삼봉사

43 Hyŏngjebong
(462 m)
형제봉

45 Yŏngbulsa Temple
영불사

46 Kwanŭmsa Temple
관음사

47 Bus Stop
정류장

48 Kyŏngguksa
Temple
경국사

49 Kookmin University
국민대학교

50 Pugak Tunnel
북악터널

53 Kugi-dong
구기동

54 Bus Stop
정류장

56 Bus Stop
정류장

No 4). From this point there are buses out to the park. Take a No 6 if there are no shuttle buses operating. There are serious plans to extend the subway all the way to the park and perhaps that will be accomplished by the time you read this.

SEOUL HORSE RACE TRACK
서울승마공원

In order to project a family image, the race track is officially called the Seoul Equestrian Park (☎ 500-1273). Horse racing is one of the very few legal gambling activities open to Koreans but the race season is deliberately kept short. The track is open to the public during December and January on Saturdays and Sundays only from 11 am to 6 pm. Admission costs W200 and bets range from a minimum of W100 to a maximum of W200,000. To give even more of a family

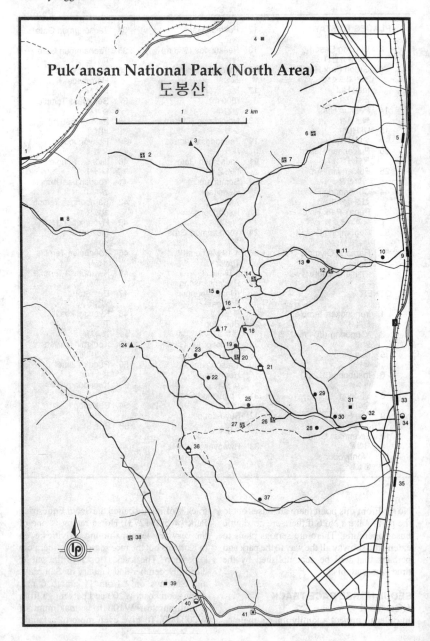

Puk'ansan National Park (North Area)
도봉산

PLACES TO STAY

4 Angol Resort
안골유원지

8 Songch'u Resort
송추유원지

11 Wondobong Resort
원도봉유원지

21 Tobong Hut
도봉산장

31 Tobong Resort
도봉유원지

36 Pomun Hut
보문산장

39 Ui-dong Resort
우이동유원지

OTHER

1 Songch'u Railway Station
송추역

2 Wongaksa Temple
원각사

3 Sap'aesan (552 m)
사패산

5 Hoeryong Railway Station
회룡역

6 Sŏkch'ŏnsa Temple
석천사

7 Hoeryongsa Temple
호룡사

9 Mangwolsa Railway Station
망월사역

10 Changsuwon
장수원

12 Ssangryongsa Temple
쌍룡사

13 Chijangam Hermitage
지장암

14 Mangwolsa Temple
망월사

15 P'odae Ridge
포대능선

16 Tobongsan (717 m)
도봉산

17 Chaunbong (740 m)
자운봉

18 Manwolam Hermitage
석월암

19 Sŏkgulam
석굴암

20 Ch'ŏnch'uksa Temple
천축사

22 Kŏbukam Hermitage
거북암

23 Kwanŭmam Hermitage
관음암

24 Obong Peak
오봉

25 Sŏngdowon
성도원

26 Kubongsa Temple
구봉사

27 Ch'ŏnjinsa Temple
천지사

28 Nŭngwonsa
능원사

29 Nokyawon Hermitage
녹아원

30 Manjangsa Temple
만장사

32 Bus Stop
정류장

33 Tobongsan Railway Station
도봉산역

34 Bus Stop
정류장

35 Tobong Railway Station
도봉역

37 Chahyŏnam Hermitage
자현암

38 Yongdŏksa Temple
용덕사

40 Bus Stop
정류장

41 Tomb
연산군묘

image to this activity, baby carriages and children's bicycles are available for hire at the track (but cannot be ridden on the track). The races can also be viewed on large-screen TVs located at betting offices in downtown Seoul.

The race track is next door to Seoul Grand Park. Take the subway to Sadang station (line No 4) and then a bus. The subway will

eventually be extended all the way to the Seoul Grand Park and the race track.

NAMHANSANSŎNG PROVINCIAL PARK 남한산도립공원

About 26 km south-east of Seoul is the peak of Namhansan. Like Puk'ansan, it's topped by a fortress (Namhansansŏng) originally built during the Paekche dynasty about 2000 years ago. However, the present walls are of more recent vintage (about 1626) and were constructed by the Yi rulers as protection against the Manchus. It was here, in 1637, that King Injo, along with 14,000 of his troops, was forced to surrender to an overwhelming Manchu invasion force which eventually led to Korea being forced to accept the suzerainty of China. It's probably the nearest thing you'll find in Korea to the Great Wall of China. The stone walls – up to seven metres high – and massive gates of this fortress snake for some eight km around the mountains above Sŏngnam City, south-east of Seoul, and are very popular as a picnic spot at weekends and public holidays (so if you like to take in your ruins in peace, avoid times like these). The views from the top are stupendous.

Getting There & Away

There are buses from the Kwanghwamun bus stop, which is just north of the Koreana Hotel. Another option is bus No 66 from Ŭlchiro 5-ga. Between 8.20 am and 7 pm, there are buses to the park once hourly from the Tong-Seoul bus terminal (take subway line No 2 to Kangbyŏn station). Except for the last option, buses do not take you into the park but rather to Sŏngnam City (it takes almost forever to get there from Seoul). Just before entering Sŏngnam City, the bus will have to climb up a steep slope – get off at the next stop. From there, cross the street and hop on bus No 88 which will take you to the bottom of the hill on which the fortress is located – from there it's a 20-minute walk up the hill. Admission to the park costs W300.

THE YI DYNASTY ROYAL TOMBS
이조왕릉

Of the 115 Yi dynasty tombs (105 of them in South Korea and the rest in North Korea), most are within easy reach of the centre of Seoul. All of these consist of the traditional earthen burial mound (similar to those of the Shilla kings in Kyŏngju) but most of them are guarded by beautifully carved granite sentries and real or mythical animals. The similarities with the Ming tombs outside of

Beijing are unmistakable although here they are on a somewhat smaller scale. All the Yi kings have been buried at one or other of these sites (from the first, King Taejo in 1408, to the last crown prince, Yongchinwang, in 1970).

The five most interesting sites are T'aenŭng, Tonggurŭng, Kumgongnŭng and Kwangnŭng (east and north-east of Seoul) and Honinnŭng (south of Seoul). T'aenŭng and Honinnŭng are perhaps the most well known and the easiest to get to although Tonggunŭng is the largest site with nine tombs in all, including that of Taejo and Honjong (the last Yi dynasty king). All the tombs are open to the public between 9 am and 6.30 pm. Entry costs W340 (W170 for children).

Some of the burial sites may be closed to the public from time to time (to allow archaeological excavations, for instance) so it might be a good idea to check with the tourist office in Seoul before you set off.

Getting There & Away

The national tourist organisation, USO, RAS and private touring companies generally offer organised trips to one or other of these burial sites but you can also get there individually by local buses (with some hassle).

The following local buses will take you to the various sites:

T'aenŭng: bus No 10 or 215 from Tongdaemun or bus No 45 from Seoul railway station.
Kumgoknŭng: bus No 165 or 765 from Ch'ŏngnyangni.
Tonggunnŭng: bus No 55-1 from Ch'ŏngnyangni or bus No 755 from Seoul railway station.
Kwangnŭng: bus No 7 from Ch'ŏngnyangni or No 21 from Ŭijŏngbu.
Honinnŭng: bus No 36 from in front of Seoul express bus terminal.

SUWON 수원

Suwon is an ancient fortress city 48 km south of Seoul and the provincial capital of Kyonggi Province. The walls were constructed in the later part of the 18th century by King Kongjo in an unsuccessful attempt to make Suwon the nation's capital. They

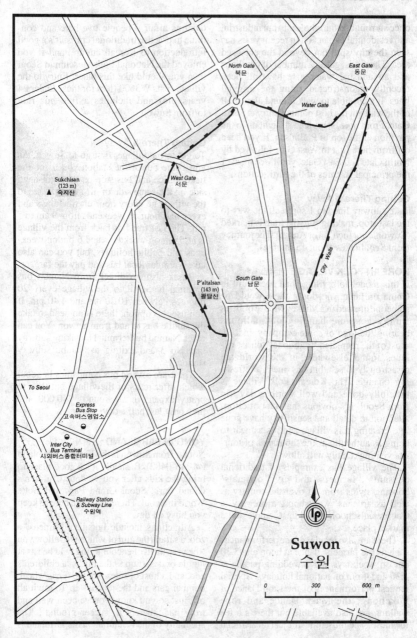

North Gate
북문

East Gate
동문

Water Gate

Sukchisan
(123 m)
숙지산

West Gate
서문

City Walls

P'altalsan
(143 m)
팔달산

South Gate
남문

To Seoul

Express
Bus Stop
고속버스영업소

Inter City
Bus Terminal
시외버스종합터미널

Railway Station
& Subway Line
수원역

Suwon
수원

0   300   600 m

once surrounded the whole city but industrial and residential expansion in recent years has seen the city spill out beyond the enclosed area. The walls, gates, a number of pavilions and an unusual water gate have all been recently reconstructed along the original lines. It's possible to walk around almost all of the wall but the best point of entry is South Gate. From here, steps lead straight up to the pavilion at the top of P'altalsan. If you head off from here first to West Gate followed by North Gate and East Gate, you'll see most of the principal features of the fortifications.

Getting There & Away

Take subway line No 1 south all the way to the last stop, making sure the train is marked 'Suwon' (not Inch'ŏn or Ansan). The journey from Seoul takes about 45 minutes.

KOREAN FOLK VILLAGE 한국민속촌

If this model folk village had been built in China or Japan, no doubt there would be someone dressed in a Mickey Mouse or Bugs Bunny costume handing out balloons bearing the logo of some company. Indeed, most of the recreated 'traditional' tourist villages found elsewhere in the world are disastrously kitsch, but this one is a refreshing change. The Korean Folk Village is tastefully done and well worth a day trip from Seoul. It's obvious that a lot of effort, attention to detail and sensitivity have gone into creating this village and it's as near to being as authentic as the thousands of tourists visiting it daily will allow.

The village has examples of traditional peasants', farmers' and civil officials' housing styles from all over the country as well as artisans' workshops, a brewery, a Confucian school, a Buddhist temple and a market place.

There are also regular dance performances such as the farmers' dance at noon and 3.30 pm on weekdays and a wedding parade at 1.30 and 4 pm on national holidays. Special request performances of the Lion Dance of Pukchong, the Mask Dance and rope walking are also available but there's a fee for these. The museum isn't just an artificial

daytime affair – people live here and continue to practise traditional crafts. It's a good introduction to Korean culture, and if you enjoyed the National Folk Museum in Seoul then you should like this place. Entry to the village costs W3600 (less for those under 24 years old) and includes a free bus ride to/from Suwon.

Getting There & Away

To get to the village, first go to Suwon. As you come out of the station you'll see the ticket office and bus stop on the right-hand side on the same side of the street. Buses to the village go every hour on weekdays and every half hour on weekends from 9 am to 5 pm. The last free bus back from the village is at 5 pm on weekdays and 6 pm on weekends and public holidays, but you can also take a regular local bus and pay the fare.

Buses also go direct from Nambu bus terminal in Seoul to the village every 20 minutes between 10.20 am and 4.40 pm. If you use this option, there is no need to take the shuttle bus to and from Suwon. You can reach Nambu bus terminal by taking subway line No 3 and exiting at Nambu subway station.

There are several bus companies in Seoul which offer tours of the village but they're pretty expensive at around W40,000 and they only last half a day.

YONG'IN FARMLAND 용인자연농원

Not far from Suwon is the Yong'in Farmland (☎ 745-0482). Basically it's a good place to bring the kids after you've done Children's Grand Park, Seoul Grand Park and Lotte World in Seoul. There's enough here to keep you busy all day.

Attractions include botanical gardens, a zoo, a safari (the aim of which is to allow you 'the very thrill of encountering wild beasts at jungle or desert up to the hilt'!), a children's zoo, and a host of rides like the ferris wheel, bumper cars and the jet coaster. To top it all off, just so you know you've been well and truly had, there's a 'succer ground'. The speciality of the restaurant at the farmland is barbecued whole wild boar, which, it is claimed, is a 'traditional health food'.

On a more dignified note, you might want to visit the **Hoam Art Museum**. This is a private collection of Korean art that is owned by the founder and chairman of the Samsung group. Sixty of the items on display here have been designated as National Treasures. The collection is very eclectic, featuring painting, sculpture, pottery, folk crafts and even prehistoric relics.

The Yong'in Farmland is open daily from 9 am to 6 pm (10 pm in the summer) and an all-inclusive ticket costs W8000; W6000 for children. There are buses running out to Yong'in Farmland from Suwon subway station.

ICH'ŎN CERAMIC VILLAGE 이천도예촌

This is perhaps a specialised interest, but the Ich'ŏn Ceramic Village does attract a small but loyal following of pottery buffs. The Ich'on region – and nearby Kwangju – has been the centre of the Korean ceramics industry, going back at least to the Chosŏn dynasty (1392-1910). White porcelain is still an export item of Korea, although these days there is heavy competition from low-wage sweatshops in China. Nonetheless, the ceramic kilns of Ich'ŏn are still of great historical importance to Korea.

Ich'ŏn is also the home of the Haegang Ceramics Museum (☎ 34-2226) – admission is W1000.

Getting There & Away

There are at least two options for getting to Ich'ŏn. Perhaps easiest is from the Seoul express bus terminal – buses run once every 20 minutes from 6.30 am until 9.20 pm, taking just over an hour to make the journey. Buses leave every 15 minutes from the Tong-Seoul (east Seoul) express bus terminal and the journey takes 50 minutes.

You must tell the driver that you want to get off at the Ich'ŏn Ceramic Village rather than in Ich'ŏn itself which is about 10 km further down the highway. The Ceramics Village is actually about halfway between

Ich'ŏn and Kwangju. Some tours (not many) take in both the Yong'in Farmland and the Ich'ŏn Ceramic Village in one trip.

YŎJU 여주

About two km to the east of Yŏju is Shilŭksa, a magnificent temple built around 580 AD. The temple is open from 8 am to 4 pm.

A short bus ride to the west of Yŏju is Yŏngnŭng, where you can find the Tomb of King Sejong. The tomb site is open from 8.30 am to 6 pm, and there is a small museum on the grounds.

Yŏju is to the south-east of Seoul. You can get there by bus from Seoul's Sangbong bus terminal.

SUWON-INCH'ŎN NARROW-GAUGE RAILWAY 수인선

This is an interesting alternative route back to Seoul after, perhaps, spending a morning exploring the Suwonsŏng Fortress walls. The miniature train chugs its way across some 50 km of rural Korea, taking around 1½ hours to reach Inch'ŏn. From Inch'ŏn you can catch the subway back to Seoul (line No 1). The narrow-gauge railway between Suwon and Inch'ŏn is one of South Korea's earliest rail routes and was established to help farmers get their produce to the market place. Even today, for the most part, the scenes from the window remain picturesque. Trains run three times a day: in the morning, around 1 pm and in the afternoon. The narrow-gauge railway is known as the *suinsŏn* in Korean.

INCH'ŎN 인천

Along with Pusan, Inch'ŏn is one of Korea's two foremost seaports. As might be expected, it's not a port with quaint wooden sailing ships and fishing piers. Rather, it's a world of container ships and high-rise housing developments to house the population of 2.2 million. Inch'ŏn's importance to Korea is likely to grow – it's been selected as the site of Korea's next international airport, which is expected to open in the year 2020.

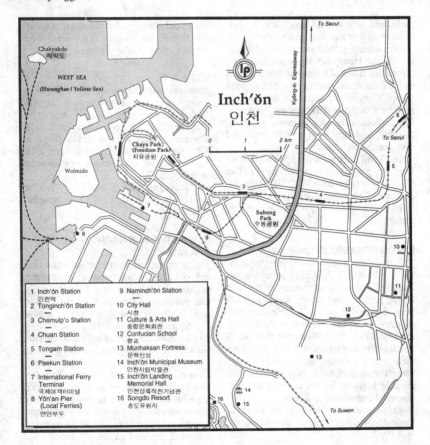

Inch'ŏn
인천

1 Inch'ŏn Station
인천역
2 Tonginch'ŏn Station
3 Chemulp'o Station
4 Chuan Station
5 Tongam Station
6 Paekun Station
7 International Ferry Terminal
국제여객터미널
8 Yŏn'an Pier (Local Ferries)
연안부두

9 Naminch'ŏn Station
10 City Hall
시청
11 Culture & Arts Hall
종합문화회관
12 Confucian School
향교
13 Munhaksan Fortress
문학산성
14 Inch'ŏn Municipal Museum
인천시립박물관
15 Inch'ŏn Landing Memorial Hall
인천상륙작전기념관
16 Songdo Resort
송도유원지

Inch'ŏn became well known to the rest of the world in 1950 when US General Douglas MacArthur led UN forces in a daring landing here behind enemy lines. Military experts doubted such a tactic could succeed, but it did and within a month the North Koreans were all but defeated. Unfortunately for the allies, in November of the same year Chinese troops stormed across the border into Korea.

Most foreigners who come to Inch'ŏn only do so to catch a ferry to China, and it's unlikely you'll want to come here just to see the town; it does have, however, a few charms.

Information

Tourist Information The Inch'ŏn Tourist Association (☎ 883-3068) operates a tourist information kiosk inside the International ferry terminal.

Chayu Park 자유공원

At the centre of Chayu (Freedom) Park is a statue of General MacArthur who led the famous Inch'ŏn landing during the Korean War. The park is next to Inch'ŏn Harbour.

Munhaksan Fortress 문학산성

This was the seat of government of the old

Peikje kingdom. Within the perimeters of the fort is a small lighthouse only three metres high. The surrounding park has an outdoor swimming pool.

The park is in the south side of the city in an area called Nam-gu.

Confucian School 향교

The school first opened in the Koryŏ dynasty. It reached its height of glory during the Chosŏn dynasty (1392-1910) and was later annexed to a Confucian temple. These days the school now serves as a shrine and no classes are held.

The Confucian School is just to the north of Munhaksan Fortress.

Inch'ŏn Municipal Museum
인천시립박물관

There are about 1200 ancient artefacts on display, including some large temple bells from China. Next to the museum is the Landing Commemoration Hall, another reminder of MacArthur's landing at Inch'ŏn.

The Municipal Museum is at the south end of town just east of Songdo Amusement Park.

Culture & Arts Hall 종합문화회관

This brand new cultural centre has both indoor and outdoor performance halls for Korean dancing, drama, drum shows etc. Art exhibits are also regularly presented here. The Culture & Arts Hall is one km north-east of the Inch'ŏn Confucian School.

Wolmido 월미도

This place was once an island, but land reclamation has turned it into a peninsula on the north-west side of Inch'ŏn Harbour. Wolmido is a very trendy spot, boasting everything from raw fish restaurants to art galleries and street opera on summer weekends. Along the waterfront is the Wolmido Cultural St where various cultural performances are scheduled during summer weekends and holidays. There is also a small tourist information booth here.

A large sightseeing cruise ship – the

Cosmos – docks at Wolmido and offers dinner cruises with a view. The Inch'ŏn city government has plans to construct an Inch'ŏn Tower in this area to rival the one in Seoul.

Yŏn'an Pier 연안부두

About 300 fishing boats dock here (not all at one time though), and this is where you'll find some of the best fish markets and seafood restaurants in Korea. Yŏn'an Pier is also where you catch ferries to several of the small islands off the coast of Inch'ŏn.

Chakyakdo 작약도

This island is three km north of Wolmido. In summer the island is known for peonies (*chakyak*, hence the island's name). You can reach the island easily by taking a boat from Yonan Pier.

Songdo Resort 송도유원지

The resort has an amusement park atmosphere and is mainly geared towards locals rather than tourists – when you see it, you'll understand why. Features include two artificial lakes and even an artificial beach. Think of it as a place for rowboats, paddleboats, drown-proof swimming and cotton candy. Overlooking the southern lake is the Hotel Songdo Beach.

Subong Park 수봉공원

The park is a good place for exercise with walking tracks and recreation facilities. The park is dressed up with a war memorial, and a ferris wheel and other amusements for the kiddies. Subong Park is about three km east of Inch'ŏn Harbour.

Organised Tours Besides the baffling city bus system, there are also special tourist buses offering budget tours. These run twice daily at 11 am and 1 pm, and cost W4000. You catch these buses at the Wolmido Cultural St Tourist Information Booth.

Getting There & Away

Subway line No 1 in Seoul connects to the trains heading to Inch'ŏn. The Inch'ŏn-Seoul journey takes about one hour. More interesting is to travel between Inch'ŏn and Suwon on the Suwon-Inch'ŏn narrow-gauge railway (see preceding section).

Getting Around

Subway Inch'ŏn is building a subway, but there is no word yet on when it will be finished.

Boat Wolmido is also where you can take a cruise on the good ship *Cosmos*. This costs W4500 for a one-hour cruise, and the official departure times are as follows: 11 am, 12.30, 2, 3.30, 5, 6.30 and 8 pm. It's entirely possible that this schedule is reduced somewhat during winter.

Car Although self-drive transport is not especially recommended around the urban confines of Inch'ŏn, vehicles can be hired from the following companies:

Kyong-In (☎ 52-5444); New Inch'ŏn (☎ 882-0106); Paldo (☎ 864-8688)

P'ANMUNJŎM 판문점

This is a good place to visit for a sobering dose of reality. Situated 56 km north of Seoul, P'anmunjŏm is the truce village on the ceasefire line established at the end of the Korean War in 1953. It's in a building here that the interminable 'peace' discussions continue.

There's nowhere else in South Korea where you can get quite so close to North Korea without being arrested or shot and the tension is palpable. In 1968, the crew of the American warship USS *Pueblo* (kidnapped at sea by the North Koreans 11 months earlier) were allowed to cross to the South here. In 1976, two American servicemen were hacked to death with axes by the North Koreans at P'anmunjŏm. It was also here that an American soldier peacefully defected to

North Korea in 1983. Just a year later, a Russian tourist defected to the South at P'anmunjŏm, setting off a gun battle that killed three North Koreans and one South Korean soldier.

P'anmunjŏm was also in the news in mid-1989. It was here that Lim Soo-kyong, a Seoul university student, and the Reverend Moon Gyu-hyon, a Catholic priest, were finally allowed to return to South Korea after protracted negotiations following Lim's visit to the Youth Festival in Pyongyang earlier in the year. Both were promptly arrested, whisked off to Seoul by helicopter and charged with violating the national security laws. Lim, a radical fervently committed to the reunification of Korea, had previously attempted to make the crossing several weeks before with the encouragement of the North Korean authorities but had been refused. The event made front-page news at the time both in Korea and elsewhere.

P'anmunjŏm is perhaps overrated as a 'tourist attraction' but that doesn't seem to stop the hordes flocking here to gawk at this tense 'truce village', learn the history of the DMZ and come face to face with the stern-looking North Korean soldiers.

Commercial tours usually take in a visit to the 'Third Tunnel of Aggression' (see the boxed aside on the following page). The discovery of a fourth tunnel was announced in 1990 – this one large enough to accommodate trucks and tanks.

Part of the ongoing Cold War between North and South is the existence of two civilian villages at P'anmunjŏm. On the southern side is Taesŏng-dong (Great Success Village), but the Americans call it 'Freedom Village'. It isn't terribly free for the villagers, who must be out of the fields after dark and in their homes with doors locked by 11 pm. By way of compensation, it's a very prosperous agricultural community by South Korean standards – the villagers have plentiful land and large homes. On the north side is Kijong-dong, which the Americans call 'Propaganda Village'. It differs from its southern counterpart in that it's uninhabited. However, it

Haeinsa Temple, near Taegu (GC)

Left: Temple eaves, Pulguksa Temple, Kyŏngju (GC)
Top: Command Post, Sŭwonsŏng Fortress, Suwŏn (CT)
Middle: Colourful guardians of Kirimsa Temple, Kyŏngju (MM)
Bottom: Doors and woodwork at Pŏmŏsa Temple, near Pusan (RI'A)

would be fair to say that both villages exist for no other purpose than propaganda.

While you are permitted to take photos and use binoculars, there are a number of restrictions that visitors must adhere to: you must bring your passport; children under 10 years of age are not allowed and Korean nationals are not allowed unless special permission is obtained (a formidable bureaucratic procedure which takes over a month). Furthermore, there is strict dress code which civilians must follow, and many travellers run afoul of this rule! Shaggy or 'unkempt' hair (especially on men) also disqualifies some travellers. The military lists the following as examples of inappropriate clothing for this formal occasion:

* Shirts (top) without sleeves, T-shirts, tank tops and shirts of similar design.
* Dungarees or blue jeans of any kind, including 'designer jeans'.
* Shorts of any style, including hiking, bermuda, cut-offs, or 'short-shorts'.
* Miniskirts, halter tops, backless dresses and other abbreviated items of similar design.
* Any item of outer clothing of the sheer variety.
* Shower shoes, thongs or 'flip-flops'.
* Items of military clothing not worn as an integral part of a prescribed uniform.
* Any form-fitting clothing including tight-knit tops, tight-knit pants and stretch pants.

In addition, you are warned:

* Visitors must remain in a group from the beginning to the end of the tour and will follow all instructions issued by their tour guide.
* Any equipment, microphones or flags belonging to the communist side in the Military Armistice Commission (MAC) conference room are not to be touched.
* Do not speak with, make any gesture toward or in any way approach or respond to personnel from the other side.
* Firearms, knives or weapons of any type cannot be taken into the Joint Security Area.

Getting There & Away

Access to P'anmunjŏm is permitted for tour groups only – this is not a do-it-yourself trip. Your Korean tour guide will accompany you to Camp Bonifas on the southern side of the DMZ where the group eats lunch and you'll have an opportunity to play slot machines (the military must really need the money). You are then given a slide show and briefing by an American soldier, who will then accompany your group on a military bus into the Joint Security Area of .

Commercial tours are available but they're expensive. The market seems to have been sewn up by Korea Travel Bureau (☎ 585-1191), which has an office on the 3rd floor of the Hotel Lotte in Seoul. Tours cost

---

Brass Plaque

A brass plaque in P'anmunjŏm gives this account of the Third Tunnel of Aggression:

On 15 November 1974, members of a Republic of Korea Army (ROKA) patrol, inside the southern sector of the DMZ, spotted vapour rising from the ground. When they began to dig into the ground to investigate, they were fired upon by North Korean snipers. ROKA units secured the site and subsequently uncovered a tunnel dug by the North Koreans which extended 1.2 km into the Republic of Korea. On 20 November, two members of a United Nations Command (UNC) investigation team were killed inside the tunnel when dynamite planted by the North Koreans exploded. The briefing hall at Camp Kitty Hawk is named after one of the officers killed, Lieutenant Commander Robert N Ballinger. In March 1975, a second North Korean tunnel was discovered by a UNC tunnel detection team. In September 1975, a North Korean engineer escaped and provided valuable intelligence concerning the communist tunnelling activities. Acting on the information, a tunnel detection team successfully intercepted a third tunnel in October 1978, less than two km from here. Today, the North Koreans continue to dig tunnels beneath the DMZ. The UNC and ROKA have fielded tunnel detection teams which drill around the clock in the hope of intercepting these tunnels of aggression which threaten the security of the Republic of Korea. ■

W45,000 – if it helps any, lunch is thrown in free. The tour cost is reduced to W25,400 if 'military or other official considerations prevent entry into the Joint Security Area'. The tour includes a visit to the Third Tunnel of Aggression. Tours run daily except Saturday and Sunday. The tour takes seven hours and you must have your passport with you. Departure is from the Lotte Hotel on Ŭlchiro, and you're expected to arrive 20 minutes before departure time. Bookings can be made through the tourist offices in Seoul but you need to reserve a spot well in advance as the tours are frequently booked out.

If you go through any other tour company, make sure that they are going to take you all the way to P'anmunjŏm and not just to the Military Checkpoint on the southern side of the Imjin River. This can cost almost the same but it's essentially a ripoff.

The cheapest tours to P'anmunjŏm are offered by the USO (☎ 795-3028), the US Army's cultural and social centre opposite Gate 21 of the Yongsan Army Base in Seoul. They have at least one tour (usually two) weekly and it costs US$21 or the equivalent in won, but doesn't include lunch or a visit to the Third Tunnel of Aggression. However, there are separate USO tours to the tunnels which are worthwhile, and Korean nationals may go on these. Because USO tours are cheap, they tend to be very heavily subscribed and you have to book weeks in advance.

KANGHWADO 강화도
Kanghwado (Kanghwa Island), west of Seoul and north of Inch'ŏn, played its part in Korean history. It's where the Koryŏ court took refuge during the Mongol invasions of the 13th century, and where the Koreans resisted American and French troops in the late 19th century. It is also where the second set of the 80,000 wood blocks of the Tripitaka Koreana were carved in the 14th century. The wood blocks were later moved to Haeinsa Temple, outside Taegu, during the early years of the Yi dynasty.

Being an island fortress, Kanghwado has seen its fair share of fortifications, palaces

and the like, but it's overrated as a tourist attraction. The tourist literature and some guide books to Korea rave on about Kanghwado's attractions giving you the impression that the island is littered with fascinating relics and ruins. To a degree it is, but you'd have to be a real relic enthusiast to want to make the effort. One of the few redeeming features of a trip here is the temple of Pomunsa, but this is actually on a smaller island off the west coast of Kanghwado.

At the south-west tip of the island is Manisan (468 metres), which has on its summit a five-metre-high altar called Chamsongdan. This is dedicated to Tan'gun, the mythical first Korean born in 2333 BC. Koreans like to make the pilgrimage to the summit by foot from Chŏndŭngsa, a temple at the base of the mountain. This involves a five-km walk each way.

Kanghwa City 강화시
Despite all the hype, this city is a profound disappointment. True, the city gates still stand but the enclosing wall has disappeared. Likewise, the site of the Koryŏ court has a couple of traditional buildings of slight interest, but that's all and you'll have to pay W500 to see it. If your time is limited, you can skip all this without feeling a deep sense of loss.

Pomunsa 보문사
This important temple sits high up in the mountains on the island of Sŏngmodo off the western coast of Kanghwado. The compound is relatively small but there is some superb and very ornate painting on the eaves of the various buildings and especially those of the bell pavilion. The famous grotto here is quite plain and uninteresting, although it is cool in there on a hot summer's day. One of the most interesting sights is the 10-metre-high rock carving of Kwansŭm Posal, the Goddess of Mercy, which stands below a granite overhang high above the temple compound. The carving was completed about 60 years ago and is quite unlike any

statues of the goddess to be seen elsewhere in Korea.

It's a steep walk up to the temple from where the bus drops you and there's a small tourist village with souvenir shops and restaurants at the bottom of the hill.

Getting There & Away

Buses to Kanghwado leave from the Shinchon bus terminal in the western part of Seoul. Take the subway to Shinch'on station (line No 2) and ask directions from there. It's a five-minute walk.

Buses leave every 10 minutes from 5.40 am to 9.30 pm, take one hour and cost W1900. The buses drop you at Kanghwa City bus terminal.

To get to Pomunsa from Kanghwa City, take a bus from the same bus station to Oep'ori. These depart every 20 minutes from 7.40 am to 6.40 pm, cost W400 and the ride takes 20 minutes. The bus will drop you in front of the main ferry terminal, but this caters only for long-distance ferries and is not the one you want. Walk through to the front of the terminal, turn right and continue down the waterfront for about 100 metres. You'll see a concrete ramp going down to the water and another ferry terminal on the right. From here ferries, run daily to Sŏkmo-ri on Songmodo approximately every hour from 7 am to 7 pm and they take both people and vehicles. It takes 10 minutes to cross the straits. Before buying a ticket you have to fill in a form (available in the ticket hall) stating your name, address and passport number (Kanghwado is very close to North Korea). The form is collected before you board the ferry.

On the opposite side there are buses to Pomunsa which take about half an hour.

SANJŎNG LAKE RESORT 산정호수

This small but lovely alpine lake is adjacent to the border with Kangwon-do Province and also not far from North Korea. Indeed, North Korea's former dictator Kim Il-sung is said to have briefly used the resort for some relaxation during the Korean War when the North controlled this area.

Nowadays, it's getting a bit commercialised and should be avoided on weekends and holidays. However, it can be most enjoyable when the masses are busy working or in school. You can expect a wide range of facilites, including a marina and mini-amusement park.

Nearby sights include Chainsa, a small temple. Also close by are three waterfalls: Tungnyong, Pison and Sanjŏng. Climbers may wish to challenge nearby Myŏngsŏng-san (924 metres), which is four km to the north and just across the border in Kangwon-do.

Places to Stay

Budget travellers can make use of the *Sanjŏng Camping Ground*. Alternatively, there are a number of yŏgwan, all charging around W16,000 for a double, although expect to pay more on holidays (if you can find a room at all!). The selection of yŏgwan include:

Cheil-jang (☎ 32-6118); *Sanho Pake* (☎ 34-0081); *Sŏul-jang* (☎ 34-4590); *Shilla-jang* (☎ 32-5604); *Sopyongyang* (☎ 32-5064); and *Yŏnghwa-jang* (☎ 32-5616)

Those requiring cushy facilities might want to check out the *Sanjŏnghosu Hotel* (☎ 34-4061) which has double rooms ranging from W25,000 to W47,000.

Getting There & Away

The nearest town is Unch'on. Buses between Unch'on and Sanjŏng Lake run every 30 minutes from 7 am to 7.50 pm, and the journey takes 15 minutes and costs W300.

To reach Unch'on from Seoul, you can take a bus from Sangbong bus terminal. These run every 15 minutes between 5.20 am and 8.35 pm. The ride takes 1½ hours and costs W2440.

Kangwon-do 강원도

The north-east province of Kangwon-do is one of the least populated, most mountainous and scenic in South Korea. It's here that you'll find numerous opportunities for hiking and winter skiing.

CH'UNCH'ŎN 춘천

Ch'unch'ŏn is the provincial capital of Kangwon-do and the urban centre of Korea's northern lake district, which includes lakes Soyangho and P'aroho. It's a very beautiful mountainous area and one of its principal attractions is boat trips on the lakes. The town is fairly pleasant and is a major educational centre with two universities plus a teachers' college.

It's unlikely you'd come to Ch'unch'ŏn just for the sake of the city itself, but it makes a good stopover en route to Sŏraksan National Park if you'd prefer the bus and boat combination rather than taking a bus all the way. The express buses from Seoul to Sŏraksan do not take the scenic route through the park from Inje to Yangyang. Instead, they use the Seoul to Kangnŭng (Yŏngdong) Expressway.

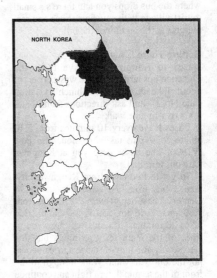

Orientation

An American military base, Camp Page, takes up a large slice of the town. This would be of no particular interest to travellers except that Ch'unch'ŏn railway station is directly opposite the base. This means you step out of the railway station and find yourself one km from the nearest yŏgwan, restaurants and bus station. Buses to the railway station are infrequent and you may have to opt for a taxi or a long walk.

On the southern end of town is Nam Ch'unch'ŏn railway station which is better situated, but it's still a long way from the centre and the bus station.

Information

There is a small (and not always open) information booth at the Folk Museum between Ch'unch'ŏn Stadium and the express bus terminal.

Confucian School 향교

Like virtually everywhere in Korea, Ch'unch'ŏn has a Confucian School which taught the Chinese classics until the government examination system was abolished in 1894.

The school was originally built during the Chosŏn dynasty, but the Japanese burned it and much of Korea down in 1592 during an invasion. It was rebuilt in 1594 and is now used as a shrine.

The Confucian School is just east of City Hall.

Ŭiam Lake 의암호

For some rest and relaxation you could do worse than spend a lazy afternoon rowing around Ŭiam Lake. Boats can be hired by Ethiopia House which is under the railway

Kangwon-do 강원도

bridge from the bus terminal. They cost W2000 to W3000 per hour.

Kugok Waterfall 구곡폭포

This is also a popular place to visit from Ch'unch'ŏn. The waterfall is about 20 km south-west of the city, and although it's at its best during and just after the monsoon, it's worth visiting at any time of year. Entry costs W300. There are cafes and snack bars at the waterfall.

The best way to get there is to take the chaesok bus No 50 from the bus stop on the main street near the post office. They go every 40 minutes from 6.45 am to 6.15 pm and take about 20 minutes. The fare is W300. The last bus back from the waterfall is at 6.50 pm. After that you will have to take a taxi. The waterfall is the last stop for the No 50 bus so you can't go wrong. From where it drops you, it's a 10 to 15-minute walk to the waterfall.

West of Ch'unch'ŏn, on the other side of the lake is another waterfall, Tungson Pokpo, which is said to be even more beautiful.

Samaksan 삼악산

For a panoramic view of Ch'unch'ŏn and the

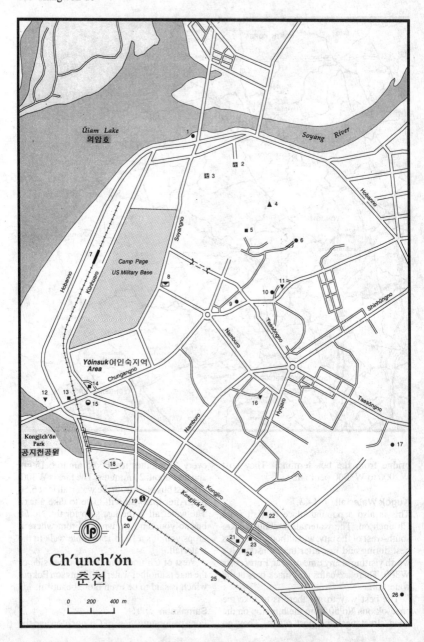

Ŭiam Lake
의암호

Soyang River

Hobanno

Soyangno

Korinuaro

7

Camp Page
US Military Base

8

9

5

6

11

10

Taesŏngno

Shinhŭngno

Namburo

Yŏinsuk 여인숙지역
Area

Chungangno

14

12   13

15

16

Hyojaro

Taesŏngno

Kongjich'ŏn
Park
공지천공원

17

18

Namburo

19

20

Kongjiro

Kongjich'ŏn

22

21   23
      24

25

26

Ch'unch'ŏn
춘천

0   200   400 m

PLACES TO STAY

5 Sejong Hotel
세종호텔
13 Ch'ŏnghwa-jang Yŏgwan
청화장여관
14 Yŏŭn-jang Yŏgwan
여은장여관
21 P'yŏngnam Yŏinsuk
평남여인숙
22 Yunil-jang Yŏgwan
윤일장여관
23 Kangnam-jang Yŏgwan
강남장여관
24 Kŭmsu-jang Yŏgwan
금수장여관

PLACES TO EAT

11 Puil Shikdang
부일식당
12 Ethiopa House
이디오피아의집
16 Pyŏldang Makguksu Restaurant
별당막국수

OTHER

1 Local Ferry Terminal
서면배터

2 Chŏngt'osa
정토사
3 Sŏgwangsa
석왕사
4 Pongŭisan (302 m)
봉의산
6 Hallim University
한림대학교
7 Ch'unch'ŏn Railway Station
춘천역
8 Central Post & Telephone Office
우체국, 전화국
9 City Hall
시청
10 Confucian School
향교
15 Inter-City Bus Terminal
시외버스터미널
17 Kangwon University
강원대학교
18 Ch'unch'ŏn Stadium
춘천공설운동장
19 Folk Museum & Tourist Information
향토박물관
20 Express Bus Terminal
고속버스터미널
25 Nam Ch'unch'ŏn Railway Station
남춘천역
26 Ch'unch'ŏn National Teachers' College
국립춘천교육대학

lake, you can make the steep climb up Samaksan. Take bus No 81 from near Ethiopia House in the direction of Seoul. After 15 minutes the bus crosses a bridge and turns right – the entrance to Samak is 50 metres down the road. It's a steep climb past a small temple but well worth it for the views. Down the other side you pass another temple and enter a beautiful narrow gorge. Follow it down to the road and catch a local bus (any will do) upstream to Ch'unch'ŏn.

If you stay on the No 81 bus past Samak and get off at the last stop you'll find the huge grave site of General Shin off to the right. About a thousand years ago, the general disguised himself as the king and as a consequence was killed by the enemy. The king had the tomb built out of gratitude for his act of sacrifice and loyalty.

Chŏngt'osa 정토사
Slightly to the north-east of Camp Page is Chŏngt'osa, on the lower slopes of Pongŭisan. The temple is nestled between some trees and houses, and offers a good view of Ŭiam Lake. The temple's caretakers live in the house just below and you have to go through their gateway to get to the temple.

Places to Stay – bottom end
The main places for cheap yŏinsuk (about W8000) is to the north-east of the bus terminal on the way towards the post office. There are plenty of more expensive yŏgwan (W18,000) near the bus terminal. Some good places near the bus terminal include the *Ch'ŏnghwa-jang Yŏgwan* and *Yŏŭn-jang Yŏgwan*.

The other option is near Nam Ch'unch'ŏn

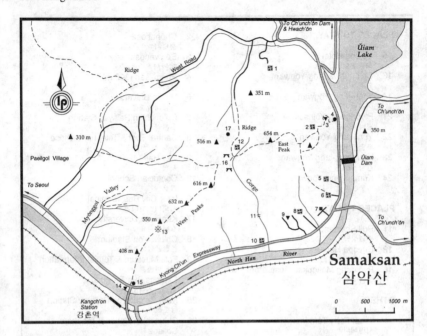

railway station, but most travellers will find this location inconvenient.

Places to Stay – top end

Upmarket accommodation is offered at the *Rio Tourist Hotel* (☎ 56-2525; fax 55-8400), 300-3, Samch'on-dong, which has 60 Western-style and 18 Korean-style rooms. Korean-style rooms are W60,000 for two people. In the Western-style rooms, doubles are W55,000, twins W57,000 and suites W120,000. Add 20% tax and surcharge to these prices.

The *Ch'unch'ŏn Tourist Hotel* (☎ 55-3300; fax 55-3372), 30-1 Nakwon-dong, is a recently remodelled three-star hotel. Room rates for doubles/twins are W36,300/48,400 plus 20%.

The *Sejong Hotel* (☎ 52-1191; fax 54-3347), San 1, Pongui-dong, is also three-star. Doubles cost W37,200 while twins go for W41,300 to W49,600, plus the requisite 20%.

Places to Eat

Pyŏldang Makguksu (☎ 54-9603) is famous in Ch'unch'ŏn as the place to get the best buckwheat noodles. There are also many other fine dishes on the menu, and the atmosphere is very pleasant.

Puil Shikdang also boasts a quaint environment and marvellous Korean food. For some odd reason this place is always empty, but it's been around for years despite the lack of clientele.

Ethiopia House is more memorable for its fine lakeside atmosphere than it's food, but it's worth a try.

Entertainment

There are a number of bars and (fairly tame) nightclubs along the street leading to the main entrance of Camp Page if you're in search of a place for a few beers in the evening. Most of them are largely patronised by personnel from the US base.

PLACES TO STAY

7 Wiam Mountain Hotel
위암산장

PLACES TO EAT

3 Rest House (coffee, snack)
휴게소

9 Valley of Restaurants
레스토랑

14 Kangchon House Restaurant
강촌의집

OTHER

1 Pongdŏksa Temple
봉덕사

2 Sangwonsa Temple
상원사

4 East Gate (Ticket Booth)
동문

5 Chŏngyangsa Temple
정양사

6 Tongch'ŏnsa Temple
동천사

8 Shinhŭngsa Temple
신흥사

10 Kŭmsŏnsa Temple & South Gate
금선사. 남문

11 Tŭngsŏn Waterfall
등선폭포

12 Hŭnggunsa Temple
흥국사

13 Scenic Overlook
전망대

15 West Gate (no tickets)
서문

16 Picnic Areas
야영장

17 Rock Wall
산성

Getting There & Away

Bus There are two bus terminals at Ch'unch'ŏn: one for express and the other for inter-city buses. Only a few buses depart from the express bus terminal:

Taegu: buses depart three times daily between 6 am and 5 pm. The fare is W14,000 (1st class) or W9400 (2nd class) and the journey takes 5½ hours.

Pusan: buses depart three times daily between 7 am and 5 pm. The fare is W18,500 (1st class) or W12,300 (2nd class) and the journey takes 6½ hours.

Kwangju: buses depart three times daily between 7 am and 5 pm. The fare is W14,900 (1st class) or W9900 (2nd class) and the journey takes 5½ hours.

The majority of departures and arrivals use the inter-city bus terminal. From this terminal, some of the places you can get to include:

Ch'ŏngju: buses depart twice daily at 7.30 am and 3.55 pm. The fare is W7800 and the journey takes 3¾ hours.

Kangnŭng: buses depart every hour from 7 am to 6.20 pm. The fare is W7000 and the journey takes just over four hours.

Pusan: buses depart six times daily between 7 am and 3.10 pm. The fare is W16,500 and the journey takes seven hours.

Seoul: depart every 10 minutes from 5.15 am to 9.30 pm. The fare is W3300 and the journey takes 1¾ hours. These buses depart Seoul at Sangbong bus terminal near Ch'ŏngnyangni subway station.

Sokch'o: buses depart 17 times daily between 6 am and 6.50 pm. The fare is W7200 and the journey takes four hours. The buses follow a beautiful route via Inje and Wontong (a few km past Inje) and takes the Hangyeryong road which passes through the southern part of Sŏraksan National Park.

Taegu: buses depart eight times daily between 7.10 am and 5.10 pm. The fare is W12,700 and the journey takes 5¾ hours.

Taejŏn: buses depart four times daily between 7.17 am and 2.25 pm. The fare is W8700 and the journey takes 5¾ hours.

Wonju: buses depart every 15 minutes from 6.05 am to 9 pm. The fare is W3500 and the journey takes 1¾ hours.

Train Trains to Ch'unch'ŏn depart from Seoul's Ch'ŏngnyangni station at the terminus of subway line No 1. Unfortuntely, Ch'unch'ŏn's two railway stations in town are both equally far from the bus terminal, so you'll need to deal with the city buses, take a taxi or walk about 1½ km. The schedule from Seoul is in the train timetable section at the end of this chapter.

Boat East and north-east of Ch'unch'ŏn are the two huge artificial lakes of Soyangho and P'aroho. Soyangho is Korea's largest lake, and Soyang Dam (123 metres) is claimed to be the largest in Asia. The lake is a favourite recreation spot for Koreans. There are ferries to Shinnam (throughout the year) and to Inje (37 km away) when the water level allows it. The level of water in Soyangho is lowered before the summer monsoon to accommodate the extra water which flows into it, so for part of the year the ferries only run from Ch'unch'ŏn to Shinnam. The boat/bus combination from Ch'unch'ŏn to Inje and the east coast (via Shinnam) is a popular way of travelling this part of Korea.

It's also possible to take these ferries if you're heading for Yanggu, but they will drop you at the Yanggu wharf and from there you take a bus the remaining 13 km into Yanggu.

Ferries leave from Soyang Dam wall. To get there from Ch'unch'ŏn, you take bus No 11 or 12 from the city centre which run every 10 minutes and does the journey in 25 minutes. The buses will drop you at the top of the dam wall and from there it's a short walk to the ferry piers. Only buses are allowed up to the top of the dam wall, so if you have your own transport you have to leave it in the car park at the checkpoint and take a bus from there.

There are also speed boats for hire at the dam wall to take you to Ch'ongpyongsa, a Buddhist temple in the hills north of the lake. These are six-seaters and the cost is shared by the number of people in the boat. Larger boats leave every 40 minutes from 9.30 am until 5.30 pm and take 20 minutes to make the journey. From where the boat drops you it's a four-km hike to the temple, so make sure you're wearing suitable footwear.

To Yanggu, there are slow ferries to Yanggu Wharf at 9 and 11 am and 4 pm in the low season and every hour from 8 am to 6 pm in the high season. In the opposite direction, they leave Yanggu Wharf at 10.20

am, 12.20 and 5.20 pm in the low season and every hour from 8 am to 6.20 pm in the high season.

There are also fast boats to Yanggu wharf which leave at 9 and 11 am, 1 and 4 pm. In the opposite direction they leave at 10.20 am, 12.20, 2.20 and 5.20 pm.

Ferries to Shinnam leave at 11 am, 1 and 3 pm and return from Shinnam at 1.20, 2.30 and 4.30 pm.

SŎRAKSAN NATIONAL PARK
설악산국립공원

This is one of the most beautiful areas in Korea with high craggy peaks, pine and mixed hardwood forests, tremendous waterfalls, boulder-strewn rivers with crystal-clear water, old temples and hermitages whose roots go back to the Shilla era. It's at its colourful best from mid to late autumn, when the leaves begin to change hue and the mountainsides are transformed into a riot of colour, but a visit is rewarding at any time of the year. The nearby coast has some of Korea's best beaches.

Unfortunately, Sŏraksan's attractiveness is its biggest problem. It's easily Korea's most popular national park, and on holidays you could be forgiven for thinking that they should have named this place Sŏraksan National Car Park. Even beyond the highways, the crunch of hikers can be oppressive. At times you will literally have to queue to get on the various trails leading to the waterfalls and peaks. Under the impact of so many feet, the park service has had no choice but to build concrete paths and steps – it's wilderness with handrails and public toilets.

The peak season (July to mid-August) is summer, although autumn leaf-changing show also attracts a flood of weekend trippers. If you prefer to take in nature in more tranquil conditions, then you have little choice but to visit during non-holiday times when the students are still in school. You can also escape some of the crowds by heading for remote trails far from the entrance roads. For some idea of what to expect during the holiday season, the newspapers reported over one million tourists visiting the

Sŏraksan/Sokch'o area during one weekend in July. Traffic jams along the coast road and at Sŏrak-dong and buses packed like sardine cans are all part of this massive annual influx.

The other drawback to visiting Sŏraksan during the peak season is that the cost of accommodation skyrockets and you'll find yourself having to pay up to three times the normal rates. Even a simple room in a minbak can cost you W30,000. Officially this is illegal since room rates are government-controlled, but it happens every year. Only in Sokch'o will you be able to find a room at a reasonable price and even then rates are still higher in summer.

Entry to Sŏraksan National Park costs W1600 (less for students and anyone under 24 years old).

Orientation

The park is divided into three sections: Outer Sŏrak, Inner Sŏrak and South Sŏrak. Inner Sŏrak is furtherest inland, while Outer Sŏrak is closest to the sea. The main tourist village and entry point is Sŏrak-dong in Outer Sŏrak. Although the entire park is beautiful, Outer Sŏrak is regarded as the most scenic area because of its many craggy peaks.

The goal of many hikers is the highest peak in the park, Taech'ŏnbong (1708 metres).

Serious hikers should pick up a good map of the area in Seoul from Chung'ang Map & Atlas Service or from various bookshops in Seoul (see the Seoul chapter for details) before you come here. No maps seem to be available for sale at the park, although there is a free tourist pamphlet which includes a basic hiking map.

What the maps don't show is that many of the trails are periodically closed. This usually occurs in the springtime when the danger of forest fires is highest. However, there is also a campaign to close Sŏraksan's most popular trails on a rotating basis for a full three years. This is to allow the wilderness to recover from being trampled by the hordes of summer hikers.

Kwonkŭmsŏng 권금성산장

Almost everyone takes the 1100-metre cable car to Kwonkŭmsŏng. It's good value at W1350 (one way) and W2700 (return) and you'll be rewarded with absolutely spectacular views. Cars go every 20 to 30 minutes. It's a 10-minute walk to the summit from the cable car. Unless the weather is clear, expect mist to shroud the summit for much of the day.

This cable car gives immediate access to the trails which lead to Inner Sŏrak, but only if the trail is open. In fact, the trail has been closed for the past couple of years due to landslides and there is no word yet on when it will reopen. You'll easily discover if the trail is open or not; when it's closed, you will only be sold a return ticket on the cable car even if you request a one-way fare.

Tottering Rock 흔들바위

Known in Korean as Hŭndŭlbawi, this is another of those 'must-see' spots for domestic tourists. You'll see photographs of this large rock in just about all the tourist literature for this region. It's famous because it can be rocked to and fro by just one person. In fact, it's surprising it hasn't been completely rocked off its base by now since half the population of Korea must have had a go! There can't be a single family in the whole of Korea that has visited this place and not had their photograph taken pushing this rock. The adjacent temple, Sinhŭngsa, was first constructed in 653 AD but later burnt to the ground and was only rebuilt in 1645.

The hike to the rock from Sŏrak-dong takes 45 to 60 minutes.

Yukdam, Piryong & T'owangsŏng Falls
육담폭포, 비룡폭포, 토왕성폭포

Another short trip in the immediate vicinity is to the waterfalls. These are all along the same trail and the Towangsong Falls are particularly impressive. The trail is well marked and involves crossing many suspension bridges and climbing flights of steel

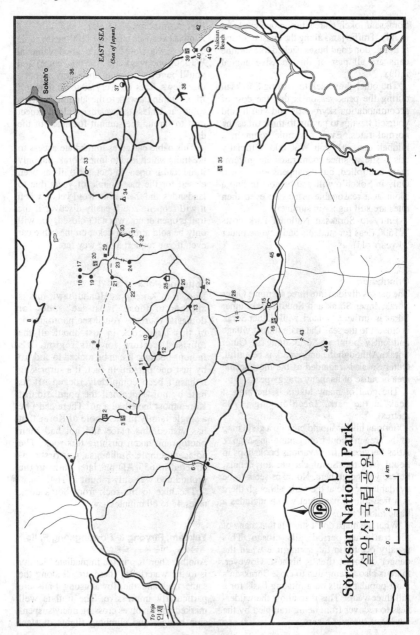

EAST SEA
(Sea of Japan)

Sokch'o

Naksan
Beach

To Inje
인제

Sŏraksan National Park
설악산국립공원

0   2   4 km

PLACES TO STAY

25 Yangpuk Hut
양푹산장
29 Sŏrak Tourist Hotel
설악관광호텔
34 Camping ground
야영지
40 Naksan Youth Hostel
낙산 유스호스텔

OTHER

1 Yongdae-ri
용대리
2 Parking Lot
주차장
3 Paekdamsa Temple
백담사
4 Shelter
대피소
5 Taesŭngryŏng Pass
대승령
6 Taesŭng Waterfall
대승폭포
7 Changsudae Rest Area
장수대휴게소
8 Mishinyŏng Pass
미시령
9 Chohangnyŏng Pass
저항령
10 Ose'am Hermitage
오세암
11 Yŏngshi'am Hermitage
영시암
12 Surŏmdong Shelter
수렴동대피소
13 Pongjŏng'am Hermitage
봉정암
14 Tokju Waterfall
독주폭포
15 Osaek Hot Springs
오색약수
16 Sŏngguksa Temple
성국사
17 Tottering Rock
흔들바위
18 Kyejo'am Hermitage
계조암

19 Naewon'am Hermitage
내원암
20 Shinhŭngsa Temple
신흥사
21 Pisŏndae (Slick Rock)
비선대
22 Kamganggul Cave
김강굴
23 Cable Car
케이블카
24 Kwonkŭmsŏng
권금성산장
26 Hŭiungak Shelter
회운각 대피소
27 Taech'ŏngbong (1708 m)
대청봉
28 Sŏrak Waterfall
설악폭포
30 Yukdam Waterfall
육담폭포
31 Piryong Waterfall
피룡폭포
32 T'owangsŏng Waterfall
토왕성폭포
33 Ch'ŏksan Hot Spring
직산온천
35 Yŏnghyŏlsa Temple
영혈사
36 Sokch'o Beach
속초 해수욕장
37 Mulch'i Bus Stop
물치정류장
38 Sokch'o Airport
속초공항
39 Naksansa Temple
낙산사
41 Bus Stop
정류장
42 Naksan Beach
낙산 해수욕장
43 Ongnyŏ Waterfall
옥녀폭포
44 Chŏmbongsan
점봉산
45 Mullebanga Rest Area
물레방아 휴게소

stairs. There are various soft drink and snack stalls along the way. The most convenient entrance to this trail is across the bridge which spans the river a few hundred metres before you get to the cable car station.

Treks

It's nearly impossible to describe all the various treks into Inner and South Sŏrak, but the accompanying map should give you a good idea of the scope. However, you shouldn't take the map as anything other than a rough guide since there are detailed large-sized colour topographic maps available. The park service can tell you which trails are closed.

There are several shelters at various points along the hiking trails where you can stay overnight but most are closed in winter. Accommodation is on bare boards at W2000 per night and you must have your own sleeping bag and do your own cooking. A limited range of canned, bottled and packeted goods are for sale but at higher than normal prices. Plenty of water is available at all the huts – either pump-fed or spring-fed. The shelters are marked on the tourist maps of the area.

Places to Stay – bottom end

Minbak is the cheapest alternative, but prices can be high. Expect to pay around W15,000 per room on average out of season but three times that amount during July and August. A gaggle of ajimahs plugging minbak tend to meet buses stopping in Sŏrak-dong, but if they don't find you, just look for the signs which are everywhere.

For those with camping equipment, there's a huge camping ground on the south side of the river in Sŏrak-dong. It has good facilities and costs W1000 per site but, in the high season, it's like a rock festival site with about a metre between tents.

Instead of staying at Sŏrak-dong you can use the Youth Hostel or beach houses at Naksan nearby on the coast, or a yŏgwan or yŏinsuk in Sokch'o. Frequent local buses connect Naksan and Sokch'o with Sŏrak-dong.

Places to Stay – middle

There's plenty of mid-range accommodation in Sŏrak-dong because of the large number of visitors, but it's a hotelier's market so prices are high. Expect to pay W15,000 minimum in the low season though possibly less if you can find an empty hotel among the scores available and haggle them down. You would expect your own bathroom, hot water and a colour TV for that price.

Most of these hotels are clustered together

on the opposite side of the river from the main road and are adjacent to the camping ground. There's not a lot to choose between them – all are of much the same standard – but they're often booked out in advance during the high season. Get there early in the day if you want to have a sporting chance of finding a room at that time of year.

Some mid-range yŏgwan to consider include the following: *Haedong* (☎ 34-7791), *Ihwasan-jang* (☎ 34-7113), *Kinyang* (☎ 34-7178), *Korea* (☎ 34-7282), *Sansu-jang* (☎ 34-7167), *Sorim* (☎ 34-7171) and *Tongsan-jang* (☎ 34-7339).

Places to Stay – top end

Except for one hotel located next to the Osaek hot springs, all Sŏraksan's top end hotels are at Sŏrak-dong. Add 20% tax and surcharge to the room rates of the following hotels:

New Sŏrak Hotel, Sŏrak-dong, doubles cost W61,000, twins W68,000 to W90,000, and suites W132,232 (☎ 34-7131; fax 34-7150)

Sŏrak Park Hotel, Sŏrak-dong, twins cost W100,000 to W120,000, and suites W180,000 to W1,200,000 (☎ 34-7711; fax 34-7732)

Korea Condominium (☎ 34-7661; fax 34-8274), Sŏrak-dong, rates are W71,080 for non-members with 30% discount on weekdays

Sŏraksan Tourist Hotel (☎ 34-7101; fax 34-7106), Sŏrak-dong, Korean-style/twins/suites cost W32,550/42,000/100,000

Osaek Greenyard Family Hotel (☎ 672-8500; fax 672-0480), Osaek Hot Springs, rates are W65,289 to W338,843 depending on room size

Places to Eat

There are all manner of restaurants in Sŏrak-dong but prices are significantly higher than what you would pay for the same thing elsewhere. Make sure you know what the prices are before you order. There are heaps of grocery stores scattered around if you want to put your own food together.

Getting There & Away

The main entry to Sŏraksan is via the tourist village of Sŏrak-dong, which is at the end of the road which branches off from the coast road about halfway between Naksan and

Sokch'o. There are frequent buses both from Yangyang, a few km south of Naksan, and from Sokch'o every five to 10 minutes from around dawn to 9.30 pm. From Sokch'o, catch bus No 7 which starts from the 2nd-class bus terminal and passes by the Korean Air ticket office and the express bus terminal. The fare is W300 from Sokch'o to Sŏrak-dong.

If you're not planning on staying in Sŏrak-dong but only visiting for the day, get off the bus at the very last stop which is about three km beyond the main part of the tourist village. This will save you a fair bit of walking.

You can enter Inner Sŏrak via a road that terminates at the temple of Paekdamsa, but buses only go as far as Yongdae-ri (8½ km from Paekdamsa). Buses between Sokch'o and Ch'unch'ŏn stop at Yongdae-ri.

For South Sŏrak, take a bus from Yangyang to Oga-ri near Osaek Hot Springs.

NAKSAN 낙산

Naksan is a pleasant summer resort east of Sŏraksan, by the sea.

Naksan Provincial Park 낙산도립공원

Naksan's major attractions are in Naksan Provincial Park just outside of town. This park is also known as Tonghae (East Sea) Provincial Park. Whatever you call it, the park is famous for its temple, Naksansa, and its huge white statue of Kwanum, the Goddess of Mercy, which faces out to sea from atop a small, pine-covered rocky outcrop. The temple was built originally in 671 AD, rebuilt in 858 AD and burned to the ground during the Korean War. It was reconstructed in 1953 along the original lines. The 15-metre-high statue of Kwanum is more recent and was completed only in 1977. At the entrance to the temple, the stone arch with a pavilion on top dates from 1465. Entry to the temple costs W1660 (less for students and those under 24 years old). It's a beautiful spot and very peaceful in the early mornings before the tour groups arrive. It's also one of the very few Korean temples which over-

looks the sea. Don't forget to visit the Uisang Pavilion which sits right on top of a cliff next to the ocean shaded by an old (and ailing) pine tree. It's an excellent spot to watch the sunrise.

Below the temple is Naksan Beach, one of the best in the area, but unbelievably crowded during July and August.

Places to Stay

There's plenty of accommodation at Naksan, ranging from simple minbak to more expensive yŏgwan and you should expect to pay W7000 for the cheapest rooms in the low season. As elsewhere around Sŏraksan, however, prices triple in the high season and you can expect to pay W15,000 minimum at that time.

An excellent alternative is the *Naksan Youth Hostel* (☎ 3416/8 on the same hillock as Naksansa. There's a large sign at the turn-off on the coast road written in English and Korean. Like other youth hostels in Korea this is a huge, plush place with its own restaurant, coffee shop, etc. There are five dormitory rooms with varying numbers of beds which cost W5000 per bed. They also have more expensive private rooms for US$18 to US$24 a single and US$29 to US$41 a double. It's a beautifully furnished place, spotless and well maintained. The bathrooms have hot and cold running water. This place is excellent value and the cheapest place to use as a base for Sŏraksan, but you need to book in advance in the high season. English is spoken and cheap meals are available.

There's also the five-star *Naksan Tourist Hotel* (☎ 672-4000; fax 742-9900), 3-2 Chonjin-ni, Kanghyon-myon, Yangyang-gun, which has rooms for W54,000 up to a breathtaking W223,141, plus 20% tax and surcharge.

Getting There & Away

All the local buses plying between Sokch'o and Yangyang pass by Naksan and since there's one every 10 to 15 minutes you'll have no problems getting to Naksan. Bus No

9 runs between Sokch'o and Yangyang and costs W300.

SOKCH'O 속초

Sokch'o is a sprawling fishing town, north of Sŏraksan, almost enclosing a lagoon which is connected to the sea. It is the last major centre of population before the border with North Korea. There's not much of interest here for the traveller but it does have a lot of seafood restaurants and yŏgwan and it can be used as a base for exploring Sŏraksan.

There are two bus terminals in Sokch'o.

The inter-city bus terminal is in the centre of town but the express bus terminal is a long way from the centre on the south side of the lagoon. Local bus No 2 connects the two terminals. Buses to Sŏrak-dong and Naksan start from the local bus terminal but can also be caught outside the express terminal.

Places to Stay – bottom end

Most of the cheap yŏinsuk are clustered around the inter-city bus terminal in the centre of town. The *Hyŏndae Yŏinsuk* and *Ŭngwang Yŏinsuk* are found here and you

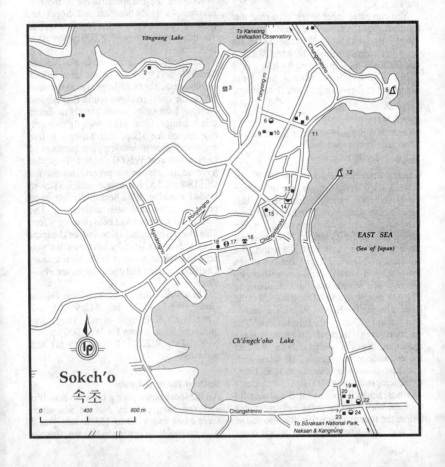

Yŏngnang Lake

To Kansong
Unification Observatory

Ponyong-ro

Chungshinmno

Ponyongno

Kyodongno

Ponyongno

Chungshinmno

EAST SEA
(Sea of Japan)

Ch'ŏngch'oho Lake

Chungshimno

To Sŏraksan National Park,
Naksan & Kangnŭng

Sokch'o
속초

0   400   800 m

PLACES TO STAY

2 Sŏrak Plaza Resortel
–
4 Sŏrak Beach Hotel
설악비치리조트호텔
7 Yugwang-jang Yŏgwan
유관장여관
8 Petel-jang Yŏgwan
벧엘장여관
9 Yŏngho-jang Yŏgwan
영호장여관
10 Hyŏndae & Ŭngwang Yŏinsuk
현대여인숙. 은광여인숙
19 Usŏng-jang Yŏgwan
우성장여관
20 Royal-jang Yŏgwan
로얄장여관
21 Myŏshi Yŏinsuk
머시여인숙
23 Tongsŏ-jang Yŏgwan
동서장여관

OTHER

1 Sokch'o Country Club
속초컨트리클럽
3 Pogwangsa Temple
보광사
5 Lighthouse
등대
6 Inter-City Bus Terminal
시외버스터미널
11 Pagoda Park
탑공원
12 Lighthouse
등대
13 City Hall
시청
14 Post Office
우체국
15 Chung'ang Market
중앙시장
16 Telephone Company
전화국
17 Chohŭng Bank
조흥은행
18 Korean Air
대한항공 매표소
22 Express Bus Terminal
고속버스터미널
24 Bus Stop (To Sŏraksan & Naksan)
정류장 (설악산. 낙산)

can expect to find doubles for around W10,000. Also around this bus terminal are the *Yŏngho-jang Yŏgwan* and the *Yugwang-jang Yŏgwan* where doubles go for W18,000.

The express bus terminal is five km further south, and you may actually find it more convenient to stay in this area as it's closer to Sŏraksan and the beaches. Here you'll find the *Myŏshi Yŏinsuk* where rooms are just W10,000. There is also a woman who hangs around here offering minbak.

More expensive yŏgwan can be found around the express bus terminal. Cheapest of the lot in this neighbourhood is *Usŏng-jang Yŏgwan* which cost W18,000, but the rooms are grotty and hardly worth it. Conditions are somewhat better at the nearby *Royal-jang Yŏgwan* which costs W20,000. Across the street is the very plush *Tongsŏ-jang Yŏgwan* which is also very friendly, but at W25,000 it stretches the definition of 'budget accommodation'.

Places to Stay – middle & top end

About one km north of the inter-city bus terminal is the *Sokch'o Beach Hotel* (☎ 31-8700; fax 31-6758). Doubles are W49,700 to W68,000 and suites go for W150,000, plus 20%.

The area in the north-west part of town along Yŏngnang Lake is dotted with condominiums and a golf course. These places are open to non-members, although you can expect to pay a hefty fee. A good example of this genre is the *Sŏrak Plaza Resortel* (☎ 635-7711; fax 635-8011) where 'family' rooms cost W71,500 and 'royal' rooms are W104,500, plus 20% tax and surcharge.

Places to Eat

With a fishing fleet stationed at Sokch'o you would expect an excellent range of seafood restaurants. There are indeed a lot of them, most tucked into the short streets between the main road and the lagoon off to the right between the post office and the Chung'ang Market. You can't miss them as they all have huge aquariums as well as a plethora of maroon plastic buckets full of live fish and various crustaceans. The only problem is the price of a meal. The majority only offer raw

town and the express bus terminal far from the centre on the south-eastern side of the lagoon.

From the express bus terminal there are buses departing to the following locations:

Seoul: buses depart every 30 minutes from 6.30 am to 6.40 pm. The fare is W11,800 (1st class) or W7900 (2nd class) and the journey takes 5¼ hours.

Tong-Seoul: (east Seoul) buses depart every 2½ hours from 7 am to 6.30 pm. The fare is W11,800 (1st class) or W7900 (2nd class) and the journey takes 4¾ hours.

The inter-city bus terminal has extensive departures, including the following:

Ch'unch'ŏn: buses depart 17 times daily from 6.40 am to 6.15 pm. The fare is W6220 and the journey takes 3½ to four hours depending on route.

Kangnŭng: buses depart every 25 minutes between 6.10 am and 8.30 pm. The fare is W2540 and the journey takes 1¼ hours.

Pusan: buses depart 10 times daily between 6.40 am and 1.40 pm. The fare is W14,400 and the journey takes 7½ hours.

Seoul: buses depart 47 times daily between 6.10 am and 6.05 pm. The fare is W8590 and the journey takes 4½ to 5½ hours depending on route.

T'aebaek: buses depart eight times daily between 8.08 am and 6.12 pm. The fare is W6200 and the journey takes six hours.

Taegu: buses depart 13 times daily between 6.10 am and 2.45 pm. The fare is W14,090 and the journey takes 8½ hours.

Wonju: buses depart four times daily between 7.45 am and 6.30 pm. The fare is W6580 and the journey takes four hours.

All the buses which depart from the inter-city bus terminal can also be picked up at Yangyang south of Naksan.

Local buses to Sŏrak-dong and Naksan also start from the inter-city bus terminal but you can easily pick them up anywhere along their route, including outside the express bus terminal.

seafood and the average price of a meal is an incredible W30,000 – spread between however many people eat at the same table. How Koreans afford this sort of meal given current wage levels is a mystery but the restaurants don't seem to suffer from a lack of custom.

The only way round this is to eat standard (non-seafood) meals or to find a restaurant which offers cooked seafood.

Getting There & Away

Air Korean Air is the only carrier flying to Sokch'o. There are several flights daily between Sokch'o and Seoul. There are also Sokch'o-Kwangju and Sokch'o-Taegu flights via Seoul.

Bus There are two bus stations in Sokch'o: the inter-city bus terminal in the centre of

Boat Sokch'o is one of the places where you can catch a boat to the islands of Ullŭngdo off the east coast. A timetable and other relevant details are provided in the Ullŭngdo section of the Kyŏngsangbuk-do chapter.

Getting Around

To/From the Airport The airport is just south of town, about 15 to 20 minutes by bus. Buses to the airport run from both bus terminals and cost W300 if standing is permitted, or W600 for a seat bus. Taxis charge W6000 from the inter-city bus terminal, or W5000 from the express bus terminal.

NORTH OF SOKCH'O
Beaches 해수욕장

There are a number of sheltered sandy coves and beaches north of Sokch'o and they're far less crowded than those to the south, although you're only allowed onto them at certain points and only at certain times of year. In the low season that endless razorwire fence which stretches along the whole of the eastern coast of Korea is firmly sealed and you'll be arrested (or, worse, shot at) if you venture onto the beaches.

The best of the coves are to be found at Taejin, north of Kansong. Taejin is a small fishing village which also doubles as a small, laid-back resort during the summer months. You can rent a room at a minbak, plus there are a few relatively cheap yŏgwan with the usual facilities. The nearest sandy beach to Taejin is called Kŏjin Beach, and it can be reached by bus from Sokch'o via Kansong. These leave every half hour from 6.30 am to 7.20 pm and take 70 minutes.

The most touristy beach north of Sokch'o is Songjiho.

Unification Observatory 통일전망대

The ironically-named Demilitarised Zone (DMZ) is four km wide and 248 km long, and a visit to the Unification Observatory (T'ongil Chŏnmangdae) is as close as most civilian Koreans can get to the DMZ. P'anmunjŏm, north of Seoul, is more interesting and can be visited by foreigners, but Koreans are not normally allowed there.

Since the Unification Observatory does offer South Koreans a rare peak at the forbidden north, tourists by the bus load turn up daily throughout the summer months. However, you don't have to book weeks in advance like you often do for P'anmunjŏm. It isn't quite the same as going to P'anmunjŏm, however. There's little of the palpable tension evident at P'anmunjŏm since the Unification Observatory isn't actually in the DMZ but a few km away, so if you want to see anything at all (such as the UN post, the North Korean post in the distance and the North's propaganda signs) then you have to use the telescopes – at W500 a pop for two minutes' viewing. It's essentially a non-event but it's a pleasant day out, there are no dress or age regulations, it's much cheaper than going to P'anmunjŏm and the government lays on a free slide show.

Information There is an information kiosk (☎ 681-0088) at the observatory with the usual collection of freebie brochures.

Getting There & Away Local buses run between Sokch'o and the Unification Security Centre every five minutes between 6.30 am and 8.40 pm. The journey takes 1½ hour and costs W1200. From the Unification Security Centre, you have to take another bus for the 15-minute ride to the observatory. This is a tour of sorts costing W2000, and there are normally only five of these buses running daily between 9.40 am and 3 pm.

Another option is to take an organised bus tour. A number of commercial tour companies in Sokch'o and Sŏrak-dong put on coaches to the observatory including Sŏrak Tourist Company (☎ 32-8989). The round trip costs W10,000 and takes about five hours.

The final option is to have your own set of wheels. With your own transport you head first for Taejin. About one km north of Taejin you'll find the Unification Hall to your left surrounded by a sort of tourist village (souvenir shops, restaurants and the like) and vast car parks. This is where you complete the necessary formalities. First you have to fill in a form which is entirely in Korean stating name, address, passport number, nationality and the vehicle registration number. One

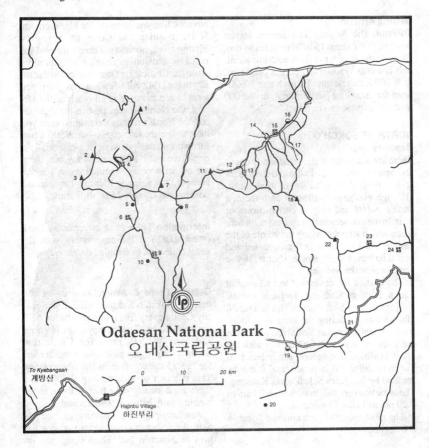

Odaesan National Park
오대산국립공원

To Kyebangsan
계방산

0   10   20 km

Hajinbu Village
하진부리

form is sufficient for everyone in the vehicle. When you hand this in, you'll be given a numbered identification card. Next you line up for the slide show which takes place every half hour or so and lasts about 20 minutes.

The numbered identification card has to be surrendered at the first checkpoint and then you'll be allowed to drive to the next checkpoint where you have to leave one passport per car. After that you can drive to the Observatory without further ado. On the way back you collect your passport at the same checkpoint. It's all very efficient and there's no charge for anything. The roads are excellent

and the various obstacles – designed to bring to a rapid halt any attempt at an invasion by North Korea – are formidable. Not only that, but the guards will salute you as you pass through the last checkpoint!

ODAESAN NATIONAL PARK
오대산국립공원

Like Sŏraksan, Odaesan is another mountain massif where nature reigns supreme. There are excellent hiking possibilities and superb views. It also hosts one of Korea's foremost winter skiing resorts at Yongpyong, south of

1	Turobong (1422 m) 두로봉	13	Iryŏn Waterfall 이련폭포
2	Pirobong (1563 m) 비로봉	14	Ch'ŏngshimdae Waterfall 청심대폭포
3	Horyŏngbong (1560 m) 호령봉	15	Kŭmgangsa Temple 금강사
4	Sangwonsa Temple 상원사	16	Bus Stop 정류장
5	Shelter 대피소	17	Ch'ungmu Waterfall 중무폭포
6	Yŏnggamsa Temple 영감사	18	Maebong (1173 m) 매봉
7	Tongdaesan (1434 m) 동대산	19	Hoenggyŏ Bus Stop 횡거정류장
8	Sanak Ski Resort 산악스키장	20	Yongpyŏng Ski Resort 용평스키장
9	Wolchŏngsa Temple 월정사	21	Taegwanryŏng Rest Area 대관령휴게소
10	Chijang'am Hermitage 지장암	22	Koshinbong (1131 m) 곤신봉
11	Noinbong (1338 m) 노인봉	23	Pohyŏngsa Temple 보형사
12	Nagyŏng Waterfall 낙영폭포	24	Pogwangsa Temple 보광사

the park. Deep inside the western section of the park are two prominent Buddhist temples: Wolchŏngsa and Sangwonsa.

Pirobong (1563 metres) is the highest peak in the park. It's part of a ridge, which means you can walk along the ridge and climb neighbouring peaks such as Horyŏngbong (1560 metres) and Sangwangbong (1493 metres)

As with Sŏraksan, the best times to visit are early spring and late autumn when the colours of the landscape are at their best. Entry to Odaesan National Park costs W1600.

Backcountry cooking and camping is currently prohibited.

Wolchŏngsa 월정사

Although there are numerous hiking possibilities from various points around the perimeter of the park, most visitors begin their tour of Odaesan with a visit to Wolchŏngsa.

This temple was founded in 654 AD by the Zen Master Chajangyulsa during the reign of Queen Sondok of the Shilla dynasty in order to enshrine relics of Sakyamuni (the historical Buddha). Over the next 1300 years or so, it went through various trials and tribulations and was destroyed by fire on at least three occasions, notably in 1307 during the Koryŏ dynasty and again during the Korean War in 1950.

Yet today you would hardly suspect these disasters had ever happened. The 1969 reconstruction is simply magnificent and the internal painting of the main hall containing the Buddha image is a masterpiece of religious art. Not even in Tibet will you find anything quite as intricate, well-balanced and spellbinding as this.

Luckily, not everything was destroyed in the various disasters which have befallen this temple over the centuries. Prominent remains from the Koryŏ era include a kneeling – and smiling! – stone Bodhisattva and a number of interesting stone stupas. There's also a unique, octagonal nine-storied pagoda dating from the same period which is classified as a national treasure. There's no entry charge as such for

Wolchŏngsa – it's included in the national park entry fee.

Sangwonsa 상원사

Much deeper into Odaesan, some nine km beyond Wolchŏngsa at the end of a relatively well-maintained gravel road which hugs the side of the mountain stream, is this famous temple constructed by the Zen master after whom it was named. Like Wolchŏngsa, it has seen its share of hard times and was last burned to the ground in 1949, but reconstructed the following year. If you're familiar with Tibetan Buddhist temples, the external painting of the buildings may well remind you of them. There are a number of superbly executed gold images here, including Mansuri and her son, but the temple's most famous possession is its bronze bell, one of the oldest and the second largest in Korea (after the Emille Bell in the Kyŏngju National Museum). It was cast in 663, one year after the construction of the temple commenced.

Kyebangsan 계방산

Odaesan has some of the highest peaks in the nation, although they tend to be rounded rather than sharply spectacular as in Sŏraksan. Just west of the park is Kyebangsan (1577 metres), one of South Korea's highest peaks. It was originally left out of the park because the military placed it off-limits to civilians, but this rule has now been relaxed and it is possible to walk to the summit. A trail follows the ridge between Kyebangsan and Pirobong. The walk is spectacular but isn't popular, so the trail is blessedly uncrowded. You can approach Kyebangsan from highway 31.

Getting There & Away

A trip to Odaesan starts in Kangnŭng and there's a choice of direct buses or local buses which involve a change at Chinbu, just off the expressway.

There are direct buses from Kangnŭng to Wolchŏngsa every hour from 6.10 am to 6.45

pm for most of the year (less in winter). The fare is W1040 and the journey takes about 1½ hours. These buses will have Wolchŏngsa on their destination indicator.

Alternatively, take a bus from in Kangnŭng to Chinbu (this is what they will have on the destination indicator). These buses leave every five minutes from the inter-city bus terminal. At Chinbu, change to a local bus which will have Sangwonsa on the destination indicator. There are seven of these buses per day (less in winter) with the last bus back from Sangwonsa to Chinbu at 5.30 pm. The journey takes about half an hour, and the ride between Wolchŏngsa and Sangwonsa takes a further 20 to 25 minutes. As their direction indicates, they terminate at Sangwonsa. There's no need to get off the bus at the entrance to the national park to pay the entrance fee – an official will get on the bus to sell you a ticket.

KANGNŬNG 강릉

Kangnŭng is the largest city on the north-east coast of Korea. It is worth staying overnight

Traditional Korean Musician

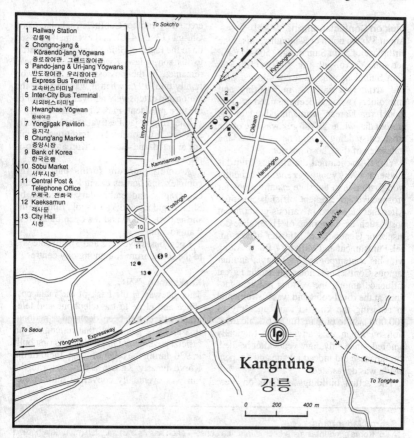

1 Railway Station
  강릉역
2 Chongno-jang &
  Kŭraendŭ-jang Yŏgwans
  종로장여관·그랜드장여관
3 Pando-jang & Uri-jang Yŏgwans
  반도장여관·우리장여관
4 Express Bus Terminal
  고속버스터미널
5 Inter-City Bus Terminal
  시외버스터미널
6 Hwanghae Yŏgwan
  황해여관
7 Yongjigak Pavilion
  용지각
8 Chung'ang Market
  중앙시장
9 Bank of Korea
  한국은행
10 Sŏbu Market
   서부시장
11 Central Post &
   Telephone Office
   우체국·전화국
12 Kaeksamun
   객사문
13 City Hall
   시청

To Sokch'o

Kyodongno

To Seoul

Yŏngdong Expressway

To Tonghae

Kangnŭng
강릉

0   200   400 m

here if you have an interest in Confucianism, but the city is otherwise unremarkable. Most travellers simply pass through en route to Sŏraksan, Odaesan or points further south.

Information

The Kangnŭng City Tourism Bureau (☎ 43-6487) has a branch in the Kangnŭng bus terminal.

Tano Festival 단오제

Probably the only time you would come to Kangnŭng is to see the shamanist festival of Tano which takes the city by storm for a whole week on the 5th day of the 5th lunar month (early June on the solar calendar). People flock into the city from all over the surrounding area for this festival and a tent city rises to accommodate them. There are circus and carnival acts, folk operas, farmers' bands and all manner of stalls and hawkers which create an atmosphere redolent of a medieval fair. It's also the nearest you'll get to seeing aspects of Korea's original religion unless you have contacts who can put you in touch with its practitioners. Don't miss it if you're in the area at the time.

Ojuk'ŏn Confucian Shrine 오죽헌

About 3½ km north of Kangnŭng, this is the birthplace of Shin Saimdang (1504-51) and her son, Yi Yul-gok (or Yi-yi) (1536-84). Shin Saimdang was an accomplished poet and artist (specialising in painting and embroidery) who has been regarded as a role model for Korean womanhood up to the present day while Yi Yul-gok was one of the most outstanding Confucian scholars and statesmen of the Chosŏn period.

Yi Yul-gok learned the classics from his mother at a very young age and subsequently won first prize in the state examinations for prospective government officials in 1564. After that he served in various government posts such as Governor of Hwanghae-do, Inspector General, and Minister of Personnel, Punishment and Military Affairs. Along with his contemporary, Yi Toegye, another famous Confucian scholar, he wielded great influence among the various political factions at the royal court and was instrumental in advising the king to raise an army of 100,000 men to prepare for a possible invasion by Japan. His advice was tragically ignored, since only eight years after he died, the Japanese did indeed invade and the peninsula was devastated.

The actual buildings at Ojuk'ŏn were erected by another Confucian scholar, Choe Chi-un (1390-1440), and eventually passed on to the father of Shin Saimdang who left it to his son-in-law, Kwon Hwa. The house remained in the possession of the Kwon family until 1975 when it was given to the nation and extensively renovated by order of the then president, Park Chung-hee.

The Yulgok-jae Festival is held annually here on 26 October when traditional rituals are enacted and classical Korean music is played.

A small museum forms part of the complex and houses examples of painting, calligraphy and embroidery executed by Shin Saimdang and Yi Yul-gok. Entry to the shrine costs W500 and it's open daily from 9 am to 5 pm.

Local buses (Nos 1, 2 and 3) will take you to the shrine from Kangnŭng city centre.

Kaeksamun 객사문

This gateway at the back of the main post office and close to the telephone and telegraph office, has been declared a national treasure. The gate is all that remains of an official government inn which was first built in 936 during the reign of King Taejo of the Koryŏ dynasty. Known as Imyonggwan, the inn was eventually converted into an ele-

---

Sacred Mountains

All of Korea's mountains are sacred in some sense – each has its own *sanshin* (mountain god). Of course, some mountains are more sacred than others. The mountains with major temples are more sacred to the Buddhists, but those change according to history. To get some idea of which mountains are most sacred to Buddhists, look on a good map for mountains with many temples on them. Good examples would be Namsan of Kyŏngju or Palgongsan north of Taegu.

For the Shamanists, Paekdusan in North Korea is now No 1, due to the large volcanic crater-lake and the legend of Tan'gun (see Paekdusan section in the North Korea chapter) and also because of the reunification issue. Hallasan, on Cheju, is considered by some as an opposite-end counterpart to Paekdusan, because it's also an old volcano with a (small) lake, and Cheju has a rich tradition of Shamanism.

T'aebaeksan in south-east Kangwŏn-do Province is very holy for Shamanists; it's the temporary home for many of them and an alternative Tan'gun-legend site.

Other mountains famous for Shamanism, magical events and powerful sanshins are: Myohyangsan and Kŭmgangsan in North Korea, Chirisan at the intersection of three southern provinces, Kyeryongsan west of Taejon City, Moaksan in Chŏllabuk-do Province, Mudŭngsan outside Kwangju City, Inwangsan in west-central Seoul, Puk'ansan to the north of Seoul, and Manisan on Kanghwa Island (the third major Tan'gun-worship site). All those are important to Buddhists too, except Hallasan, Mudŭngsan, Inwangsan and Manisan. ∎

mentary school in 1929 and later demolished by the Japanese occupation authorities. The gateway is a fine example of Koryŏ architecture with tapered wooden columns and an unusual gabled roof instead of the normal hipped roof. It's also one of the few such structures from that period which was never painted.

Kyŏngp'o Provincial Park 경포도립공원

This is another beachside park, but it's very developed, commercialised and touristy. It's six km north of Kangnŭng and can be reached by city bus.

Places to Stay

The majority of yŏgwan and yŏinsuk are in the streets opposite the two bus terminals. Right next to the express bus terminal are four yŏgwan: the *Chongno-jang*, *Kŭraendŭjang*, *Pando-jang* and *Uri-jang*. Opposite the inter-city bus terminal on the other side of Kyodongno is the *Hwanghae Yŏgwan*. Expect to pay at least W16,000 in all of these places.

Places to Eat

There are plenty of restaurants of various kinds around the bus stations and particularly in the street opposite the inter-city bus terminal, but seafood usually costs the earth so check prices before you order.

Getting There & Away

Bus The express bus terminal and inter-city bus terminal are blessedly adjacent to one another. One has to wonder why it can't always be like that. Buses which depart from the express bus terminal include the following:

Seoul: buses depart every 10 to 20 minutes between 6 am and 7.40 pm. The fare is W9400 (1st class) or W6200 (2nd class) and the journey takes 3¾ hours.

Tong-Seoul: buses depart every 45 minutes between 6.30 am and 7.40 pm. The fare is W9400 (1st class) or W6200 (2nd class) and the journey takes 3½ hours.

Wonju: buses depart every 1¼ hour from 6.30 am to 6.20 pm. The fare is W5000 (1st class) or W3300 (2nd class) and the journey takes 2¼ hours.

Taejŏn: buses depart 10 times daily between 8 am and 6.40 pm. The fare is W11,000 (1st class) or W7300 (2nd class) and the journey takes four hours.

Buses depart from the inter-city bus terminal to the following destinations:

Ch'unch'ŏn: buses depart every 30 minutes from 6.30 am to 6 pm. The fare is W7000 and the jorney takes four hours.

Odaesan: (buses terminate at Wolchŏngsa) every hour between 6.10 am and 6.45 pm. The fare is W1500 and the journey takes 1½ hours.

Seoul: express buses depart every 30 minutes from 8.45 am to 5.30 pm. The fare is W8400 and the journey takes four hours. There are also regular inter-city buses every hour from 6 am to 5.40 pm and these cost W6200.

Sokch'o: buses depart every 10 minutes from 5.40 am to 9.30 pm. The fare is W2900 and the jouney takes 1½ hours.

Pusan: nonstop express buses depart every hour from 8.10 am to 4 pm. The fare is W13,800 and the journey takes six hours. There are also slightly slower inter-city buses on this route stopping at east coast towns such as Uljin, P'ohang and Kyŏngju. These buses leave every hour from 6.20 am to 2.58 pm. The fare is the same as the express buses to Pusan but they take 7½ hours.

T'aebaek: buses depart every hour between 6 am and 2.50 pm. The fare is W4600 and the journey takes four hours.

Wonju: buses depart every 30 minutes between 6.20 am and 7.10 pm. The fare is W3300 and the journey takes 2½ hours.

Train T'ong-il class trains depart Seoul's Ch'ŏngnyangni station twice daily at 10 am and 11 pm. The fare is W8100 and the journey takes seven hours.

TONGHAE 동해

This is a fairly ugly east coast town with little to recommend it. Most travellers will come here to catch a boat to Ullŭngdo, but the nearby Murŭng Valley is worth visiting.

Orientation

Tonghae is a city of very poor design, and

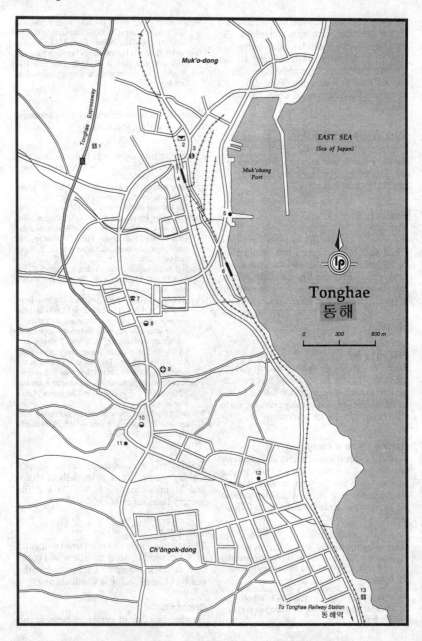

Muk'o-dong

EAST SEA
(Sea of Japan)

Tonghae Expressway

Muk'ohang
Port

Tonghae
동해

0   300   600 m

Ch'ŏngok-dong

To Tonghae Railway Station
동해역

1	Taewonsa Temple 대원사
2	Muk'o Post Office 묵호 우체국
3	Hanil Bank 한일은행
4	Muk'o Railway Station 묵호역
5	Muk'o Ferry Terminal 묵호여객선터미널
6	Muk'ohang Railway Station 묵호항역
7	Telephone Office 전화국
8	Express Bus Terminal 고속버스터미널
9	Tonghae Hospital 동해병원
10	Tonghae Complex Bus Terminal 동해종합버스터미널
11	New Tonghae Tourist Hotel 뉴동해관광호텔
12	City Hall 시청
13	Kamch'usa Temple 감추사

one wonders if the town planners weren't hitting the soju bottle when they drew up the street blueprints. The town is divided into two sections: Tonghae to the south, the Muk'o port district to the north. The two bus terminals are one km from each other, but neither is conveniently located near anything else.

Murŭng Valley 무릉계곡

This beautiful, forested valley has quiet temples and hidden hermitages around it. Kwanŭmsa, at the entrance to the valley, is the largest temple and features a seated golden Buddha outside the main hall.

A hiking path leads to Samhwasa, although if you take this route it's an up and back trip. Yongch'u Waterfall is one of the parks notable features.

The Murŭng Valley can get quite packed out on weekends when residents of Tonghae head for the hills to escape their dull city. The only way to escape the hoards of hikers is to visit on a weekday.

Cooking is permitted only in designated campsites. There are no hotels in the valley, but nearby Tonghae can accommodate you.

Getting There & Away

Bus Tonghae sits on the main east coast highway, so bus connections are fairly good. Places you can get to by bus from Tonghae include:

Kangnŭng: buses depart every 10 minutes from 6.15 am to 10.20 pm. The fare is W1400 and the journey takes 40 minutes.

Pusan: buses run 15 times daily between 7 am and 3.44 pm. The fare is W12,400 and the journey takes 6½ hours.

Samch'ŏk: buses depart every 10 minutes between 6 am and 10.20 pm. The fare is W600 and the journey takes 20 minutes.

Seoul: buses depart 13 times daily between 8.29 am and 5.52 pm. The fare is W9500 and the journey takes about five hours.

Sokch'o: buses depart 12 times daily between 8.10 am and 7.40 pm. The fare is W4500 and the journey takes 2½ hours.

T'aebaek: buses depart seven times daily between 7.55 am and 7.10 pm. The fare is W2900 and the journey takes 3½ hours.

Taegu: buses run 28 times daily between 6 am and 4.50 pm. The fare is W12,100 and the journey takes 6½ hours.

Ulsan: buses depart only twice daily at 11.52 am and 2.08 pm. The fare is W11,800 and the journey takes 3⅓ hours.

Wonju: buses depart three times daily between 7.57 am and 10.56 am. The fare is W5700 and the journey takes 3½ hours.

Train Aside from the two sprawling sections of Tonghae already mentioned, there is even a third section several km further to the south of everything else. Tonghae station is in this area, so far away from town that no one uses it. Muk'o has a railway station, and that's where you should get off if you arrive by train. Trains from Seoul run according to the schedule outlined in the boxed table.

Boat The whole point of visiting Tonghae is to catch the Ullŭngdo ferry. For information on this boat, see the Ullŭngdo section in the Kyŏngsangbuk-do chapter.

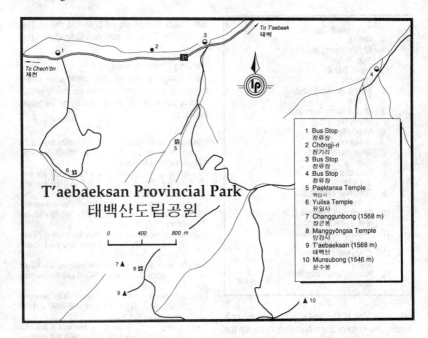

T'aebaeksan Provincial Park
태백산도립공원

0   400   800 m

1	Bus Stop 정류장
2	Chŏngji-ri 정기리
3	Bus Stop 정류장
4	Bus Stop 정류장
5	Paektansa Temple 백담사
6	Yuilsa Temple 유일사
7	Changgunbong (1568 m) 장군봉
8	Manggyŏngsa Temple 망경사
9	T'aebaeksan (1568 m) 태백산
10	Munsubong (1546 m) 문수봉

T'AEBAEKSAN PROVINCIAL PARK
태백산도립공원

T'aebaeksan (big white mountain) is the sixth highest mountain in South Korea. The mountain actually consists of two twin peaks, Changgunbong (1568 metres) and Munsubong (1546 metres).

T'aebaeksan is also considered by Shamanists to be one of Korea's three most sacred mountains. On the summit is the Ch'onjedan Altar where religious ceremonies are occasionally held.

Not surprisingly, the park has a number of temples, including Manggyŏngsa, Paektansa, Yuilsa and Mandoksa.

Tanggol Valley is another spot which attracts pilgrims. There is a shrine here called Tan'gunsong, dedicated to Tan'gun the mythical progenitor of the Korean race.

Getting There & Away
Bus The town of T'aebaek is a small city just north of the park. From T'aebaek, it's

another 20 minutes to the park on a city bus. These run every 10 minutes between 6.20 am and 11 pm. Many of these buses are marked 'Sododanggol' which is the entrance to the park.

T'aebaek is well-connected to the outside world with bus service to many places including:

Andong: buses depart three times daily between 10.40 am and 4 pm. The fare is W6200 and the journey takes 2¾ hours.

Ch'unch'ŏn: buses depart four times daily between 6.20 am and 2.30 pm. The fare is W10,500 and the journey takes 5¾ hours.

Kangnŭng: buses depart 21 times daily between 5.40 am and 7.30 pm. The fare is W4200 and the journey takes 2½ hours.

P'ohang: buses depart three times daily between 9.55 am and 11.55 am. The fare is W9000 and the journey takes five hours.

Pusan: buses depart three times daily between 6.30 am and 1.25 pm. The fare is W14,200 and the journey takes seven hours.

Seoul: buses depart 20 times daily between 6 am and

Wonju
원주

0   300   600 m

To Seoul
서울

PLACES TO STAY

3   Yŏngch'ŏnsa
    영천사
12 Wonju Hotel
    원주호텔
14 Won'gyŏngsa
    원경사
15 Ch'ŏnwangsa
    천왕사
18 Taehŭng-jang Yŏgwan
    대흥장여관
19 Songdo-jang Yŏgwan
    송도장여관
20 K'ŭraun-jang Yŏgwan
    크라운장여관

OTHER

1   Express Bus Terminal
    고속버스터미널
2   Inter-City Bus Terminal
    시외버스터미널
4   Railway Station
    원주역
5   Ilgwangsa
    일광사
6   Solimsa
    소림사
7   City Hall
    시청
8   Telephone Office
    전화국
9   Pomunsa
    보문사
10 Wonju Christian Hospital
    원주기독병원
11 Central Market
    중앙시장
13 Wonju University
    원주대학교
16 Post Office
    우체국
17 Police
    경찰서
21 Kangwon Bank
    강원은행

5.20 pm. The fare is W10,700 and the journey takes 5½ hours.

Sokch'o: buses depart eight times daily between 7.40 am and 4.40 pm. The fare is W7100 and the journey takes 4¼ hours.

Taegu: buses depart 23 times daily between 7.30 am and 6.55 pm. The fare is W10,300 and the journey takes 5½ hours.

Yŏngju: buses depart 18 times daily between 6.50 am and 5.10 pm. The fare is W5000 and the journey takes 2¾ hours.

Train Trains depart from Seoul's Ch'ŏngnyangni railway station according to the schedule in the boxed table.

WONJU 원주
This large, nondescript town is mainly of interest to travellers wanting to visit nearby Ch'iaksan National Park.

Getting There & Away
Buses departing Wonju go to a number of destinations including the following:

Seoul: buses depart around twice hourly between 6.20 am and 9.10 pm. The fare is W3700 and the journey takes 1¾ hours.

Kangnŭng: buses depart 29 times daily between 6 am and 7.30 pm. The fare is W3300 and the journey takes 2¾ hours.

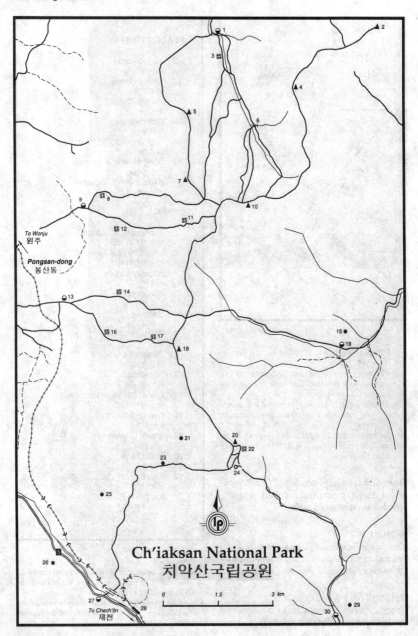

To Wonju
원주

Pongsan-dong
봉산동

To Chech'ŏn
제천

Ch'iaksan National Park
치악산국립공원

0   1.5   3 km

PLACES TO STAY

26 Kŭmdae-ri Resort
금대리

OTHER

1 Bus Stop
정류장
2 Maehwasan
(1084 m)
매화산
3 Kuryongsa Temple
구룡사
4 Ch'ŏnjibong
(1086 m)
천지봉
5 T'oggibong (887 m)
토끼봉
6 Seryŏm Waterfall
세렴폭포
7 Sambong (1072 m)
삼봉
8 Pŏmmunsa Temple
범문사
9 Bus Stop
정류장
10 Pirobong (1288 m)
비로봉
11 Ipsŏksa Temple
입석사
12 Sŏkgyŏngsa Temple
석경사
13 Bus Stop
정류장

14 Kwanŭmsa Temple
관음사
15 Pugok-ri
부곡리
16 Kukhyangsa Temple
국향사
17 Pomunsa Temple
보문사
18 Hyangnobong (1042 m)
향로봉
19 Bus Stop
정류장
20 Namdaebong (1181 m)
남대봉
21 Yŏngwonsansŏng Fortress
영원산성
22 Sangwonsa Temple
상원사
23 Yŏngwonsa
영원사
24 Spring
쌍룡수
25 Haemisansŏng (Old Fortress)
해미산성
27 Bus Stop
정류장
28 Ch'iak Railway Station
치악역
29 Sŏngnam-ri
성남리
30 Bus Stop
정류장

Taegu: buses depart eight times daily between 9.10 am and 7.10 pm. The fare is W9200 and the journey takes 3½ hours.

Taejŏn: buses depart every 30 minutes from 9.50 am to 6.30 pm. The fare is W5300 and the journey takes three hours.

Pusan: buses depart six times daily between 9.40 am and 5.10 pm. The fare is W13,000 and the journey takes five hours.

Sokch'o: buses depart four times daily between 5.40 am and 4.27 pm. The fare is W7600 and the journey takes four hours.

Andong: buses depart seven times daily between 8.28 am and 6 pm. The fare is W6900 and the journey takes 3¼ hours.

Yŏngju: buses depart eight times daily between 7.20 am and 7.30 pm. The fare is W5100 and the journey takes three hours.

Ch'ŏngju: buses depart 33 times daily between 6.45 am and 7.30 pm. The fare is W4400 and the journey takes 3¼ hours.

Ch'unch'ŏn: buses depart 84 times daily between 6 am and 9.10 pm. The fare is W3500 and the journey takes 2¼ hours (or 1½ hours for the express).

T'aebaek: buses depart 25 times daily between 7 am and 8.20 pm. the fare is W7100 and the journey takes four hours.

Train Trains to Wonju depart from Seoul's Ch'ŏngnyangni railway station according to the schedule in the following boxed table.

CH'IAKSAN NATIONAL PARK
치악산국립공원

This national park is just east of Wonju. The highest peak is Pirobong (1288 metres), but there are a number of other high peaks (over 1000 metres) which are lined up along a north-south axis. This includes Unbong,

Maehwabong, Namdaebong and Hyangno-bong. Ch'iaksan is close enough to Seoul to attract the usual horde of technical rock climbers who come to challenge the peculiar rock formations in this park.

The northern part of Ch'iaksan National Park harbours a fairly large temple, Kuryongsa. Another notable temple here is Sangwonsa.

There is a touristy resort area at the south-ern end of the park called Kŭmdae which you might either enjoy or wish to avoid.

Getting There & Away

Bus From yŏinsuk, you can catch a city bus to Kuryongsa inside the park. These buses run every 25 minutes between 6 am and 9 pm. The cost is W670 and the journey takes 45 minutes.

Trains from Seoul to Ch'unch'ŏn

Class	Time	Frequency	Travel Time	Fare
Mugunghwa	8.30 am-9 pm	6 daily	1½ hrs	W2800
T'ongil	6.45 am-8 pm	8 daily	1 hr 50 min	W2000
Pidulgi	6.10 am-7.05 pm	2 daily	2 hr 10 min	W1000

Trains from Seoul to Tonghae

Class	Time	Frequency	Travel Time	Fare
Saemaul	5 pm	1 daily	5½ hrs	W15,300
Mugunghwa	2 pm	1 daily	5½ hrs	W9100
T'ongil	10 am, 11 pm	2 daily	6 hrs	W6200

Trains from Seoul to T'aebaek

Class	Time	Frequency	Travel Time	Fare
Saemaul	5 pm	1 daily	4 hrs	W12,200
Mugunhwa	2 pm	1 daily	4¼ hrs	W7200
T'ongil	10 am, noon	2 daily	5 hrs	W4900

Trains from Seoul to Wonju

Class	Time	Frequency	Travel Time	Fare
Saemaul	9 am, 5 pm	2 daily	1 hr 30 min	W5300
Mugunghwa	11 am-6 pm	3 daily	1 hr 40 min	W3100
T'ong-il	10 am-11 pm	7 daily	1 hr 50 min	W2100
Pidulgi	6.30 am-7 pm	4 daily	2 hr 30 min	W1200

Kyŏngsangbuk-do 경상북도

TAEGU 대구

As the country's third largest city, Taegu is of significant economic importance as an industrial and commercial centre. The city is pleasant enough, but it offers little in the way of outstanding scenic attractions. However, it's a useful staging point for reaching one of the country's most famous temple-monastery complexes, Haeinsa, in Kayasan National Park .

Herbal Medicine Market 약령시장

In the central area, about one km south of Taegu station, is the Herbal Medicine Market (yakryŏng shijang). This is one of the largest medicine markets in Korea, and if you've missed the one in Seoul then you should come here for a look. Stock up on everything from lizard's tails to magic mushrooms.

Turyu Park 두류공원

In the south-west part of the city is Turyu Park. The prime feature here is Taegu Tower, an attempt (not too successful) to compete with Seoul Tower. Other amenities in the park include a swimming pool, roller skating rink, the Culture & Arts Hall, a soccer pitch, baseball field and Songding Lake.

Apsan Park 앞산공원

At the far southern end of Taegu is Apsan Park which, at 17 square km, is Taegu's largest. The most notable attraction here is the cable car running 800 metres to the summit of Apsan, but you can walk up by following a four-km trail. Near the base of the cable car ride is the Memorial Museum of Victory in Naktonggang, which celebrates a victorious (for the South) battle near the Naktong River during the Korean War.

An archery range, a horse riding ground and swimming pool are all nice touches. Taesŏngsa and Taedŏksa are two temples built to remind you that this is indeed Korea.

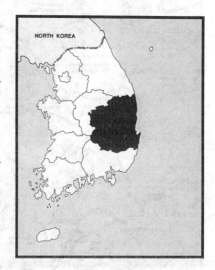

Places to Stay – bottom end

The Taeyŏng-jang Yŏgwan is one of several relatively cheap (around W18,000) places near the centre. However, most travellers overnighting in Taegu will probably prefer to stay near one of the bus terminals.

There are plenty of yŏgwan around the express bus terminal and the Tongdaegu railway station. The north side of this railway station has the thickest concentration of yŏgwan, examples being the Shinra-jang Yŏgwan, Tongdaegu-jang Yŏgwan, Hyŏndae-jang Yŏgwan and Pyŏl-jang Yŏgwan. Prices for doubles start around W16,000.

Over at the east inter-city bus terminal there are only three yŏgwan. The line-up includes Tonggŭng-jang Yŏgwan, Tongshin Yŏgwan and Taesŏng-jang Yŏgwan. A room with private bath can be had for W16,000.

Places to Stay – middle

The Crown Tourist Hotel (☎ 755-3001; fax

Kyŏngsangbuk-do
경상북도

755-3367) is just behind the express bus terminal in the eastern part of town. There are a few single rooms for W15,465, but most rooms are doubles costing W42,149, plus 20% tax and surcharge.

Next door is the *Tongdaegu Hotel* (☎ 757-6141; fax 756-6623). Doubles/twins cost W50,000/55,000, plus 20% tax and surcharge.

The following mid-range places all add 20% tax and surcharge to the tariff:

Arirang Hotel: 474-5, Turyu 3-dong, Talso-gu. Doubles/twins cost W29,200/49,587 (☎ 624-4000; fax 624-4240).

Emerald Hotel: 459-7, Pokhyon-dong, Puk-gu. Singles/doubles cost W24,200/25,200 (☎ 951-3031; fax 951-3035).

Hilltop Hotel: 3048-35, Taemyong-dong, Nam-gu. Doubles/twins cost W32,975/37,313 (☎ 651-2001; fax 651-2006).

Hotel Ariana: 200-1, Tusan-dong, Susong-gu. Doubles/twins cost W42,000/48,000 (☎ 765-7776; fax 765-7157).

Hwangkum Hotel: 847-1, Hwanggum-dong, Susong-gu. Singles/doubles cost W30,000/40,000 (☎ 765-6006; fax 766-8004).

Hwangshil Hotel: 45-1, Shinch'on 3-dong, Tong-gu (near express bus terminal). Doubles/twins cost W40,000/42,000 (☎ 751-2301; fax 751-2305).

New Jongro Hotel: 23, Chongno 2-ga, Chung-gu. Doubles/twins cost W25,410/27,830 (☎ 252-4101; fax 252-4568).

New Yŏngnam Hotel: 177-7, Pomo-dong, Susong-gu. Twins cost W40,000 to W50,000, suites are W55,000 (☎ 752-1001; fax 755-0086).

Riverside Hotel: 1006-34, Ipsok-dong, Tong-gu. Doubles/twins cost 32,670/48,400, while suites are 60,500 (☎ 982-8877; fax 982-7311)

Tongin Hotel: 5-2, Samdok-dong 1-ga, Chung-gu (500 metres from Taegu station). Doubles cost W39,929 to W56,350 (☎ 426-5211; fax 423-7400).

Tongsan Hotel: 360, Tongsan-dong, Chung-gu. Doubles cost W26,620 (☎ 253-7711; fax 253-7717).

Places to Stay – top end

As usual, there is a 20% tax and surcharge at the following top-end places:

Grand Hotel: 563-1, Pomo-dong, Susŏng-gu. Doubles/twins cost W66,000/69,000 (☎ 742-0001; fax 756-7164) .

Hotel Kŭmho: 28, Haso-dong, Chung-gu. Doubles/twins cost W66,000/69,000 (☎ 252-6001; fax 253-4121).

Soosung Hotel: 888-2, Tusan-dong, Susong-gu. Twins/suites cost W50,600/95,455(☎ 763-7311; fax 764-0620).

Entertainment

If you stay in Taegu overnight the centre of town (around the Taebo Department Store) is quite lively in the evenings with bars, restaurants, karaoke parlours, nightclubs and the like.

Things to Buy

Aside from the herbal medicine market, Taegu's other unique shopping area is opposite the front gate of Camp Walker. The large military contingent stationed here makes this a sort of mini-It'aewon.

There are a couple of interesting underground arcades in the centre. Easiest to find is the Taegu station arcade. A bit to the south is Central Arcade, Taegu's largest.

Getting There & Away

Air Both Asiana and Korea Air do frequent flights between Taegu and Seoul, and between Taegu and Cheju. Korean Air offers a Sokch'o-Taegu flight, although this is in fact via Seoul.

Bus There are six bus terminals in Taegu: express bus terminal (kosok t'ŏminŏl); east inter-city bus terminal (tongbu shi'oe t'ŏminŏl); west inter-city bus terminal (sŏbu shi'oe t'ŏminŏl); west express bus terminal (sŏ kosok t'ŏminŏl); south inter-city bus terminal (nambu shi'oe t'ŏminŏl); north inter-city bus terminal (pukbu shi'oe t'ŏminŏl).

Local buses which connect the east inter-city bus terminal with Tongdaegu railway station and the west inter-city bus terminal include bus Nos 1, 12, 22, 126 and 127. Two other buses which you can use between the east and west inter-city bus terminals (but which don't go past the railway station) are bus Nos 33 and 120. In addition, bus No 76 connects Tongdaegu station with Taegu station and the west inter-city bus terminal. Should you be anywhere else in the city and want to get to the west inter-city bus terminal then bus Nos 1, 12, 31, 32, 35, 71, 75, 88, 89 and 101 will get you there.

Buses from the express bus terminal depart to the following destinations:

Seoul: buses depart every five to 10 minutes from 6 am to 8 pm. The fare is W11,200 (1st class) or W7500 (2nd class) and the journey takes 3¾ hours.

Kyŏngju: buses depart every 15 to 30 minutes from 6.50 am to 9.10 pm. The fare is W2600 (1st class) or W1700 (2nd class) and the journey takes under one hour.

Pusan: buses depart every 15 minutes from 5.40 am to 9 pm. The fare is W5300 (1st class) or W3500 (2nd class) and the journey takes 1¾ hours.

Kwangju: buses depart every 30 minutes from 6.30 am to 6.30 pm. The fare is W8400 (1st class) or W5600 (2nd class) and the journey takes 3¾ hours.

Buses from the east inter-city bus terminal go to the following cities:

Kangnŭng: buses depart every 40 minutes from 5 am to 2.50 pm. The fare is W13,400 and the journey takes 7½ hours.

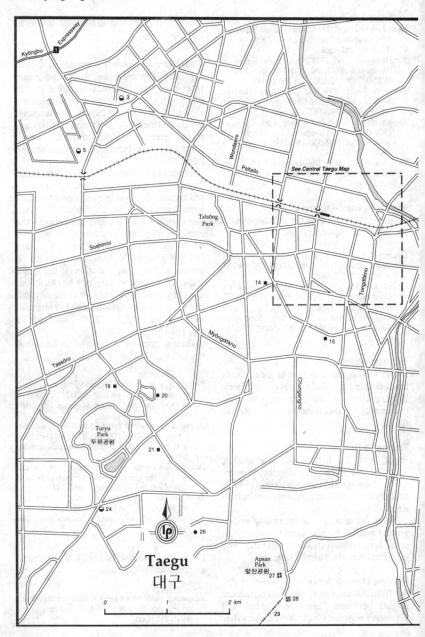

Taegu
대구

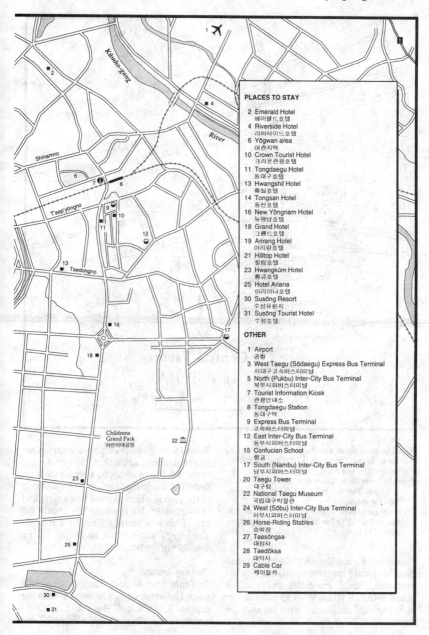

PLACES TO STAY

2 Emerald Hotel
  애머랄드호텔
4 Riverside Hotel
  리버사이드호텔
6 Yŏgwan area
  여관지역
10 Crown Tourist Hotel
  크라운관광호텔
11 Tongdaegu Hotel
  동대구호텔
13 Hwangshil Hotel
  황실호텔
14 Tongsan Hotel
  동산호텔
16 New Yŏngnam Hotel
  뉴영남호텔
18 Grand Hotel
  그랜드호텔
19 Arirang Hotel
  아리랑호텔
21 Hilltop Hotel
  힐탑호텔
23 Hwangkŭm Hotel
  황금호텔
25 Hotel Ariana
  아리아나호텔
30 Susŏng Resort
  수성유원지
31 Susŏng Tourist Hotel
  수성호텔

OTHER

1 Airport
  공항
3 West Taegu (Sŏdaegu) Express Bus Terminal
  서대구고속버스터미널
5 North (Pukbu) Inter-City Bus Terminal
  북부시외버스터미널
7 Tourist Information Kiosk
  관광안내소
8 Tongdaegu Station
  동대구역
9 Express Bus Terminal
  고속버스터미널
12 East Inter-City Bus Terminal
  동부시외버스터미널
15 Confucian School
  향교
17 South (Nambu) Inter-City Bus Terminal
  남부시외버스터미널
20 Taegu Tower
  대구탑
22 National Taegu Museum
  국립대구박물관
24 West (Sŏbu) Inter-City Bus Terminal
  서부시외버스터미널
26 Horse-Riding Stables
  승마장
27 Taesŏngsa
  대성사
28 Taedŏksa
  대덕사
29 Cable Car
  케이블카

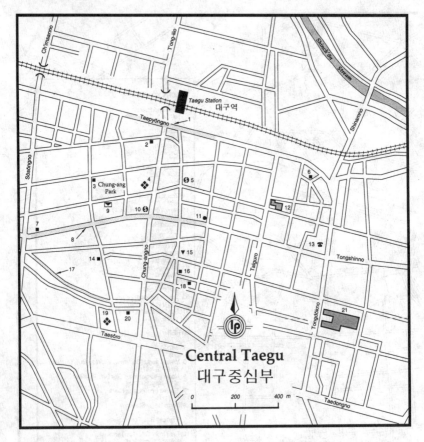

Central Taegu
대구중심부

Chimsanno

Tong-ilo

Shinch'ŏn Stream

Taegu Station
대구역

Taepyŏngno — 1

Sŏobŏngno

3 Chung-ang
Park

Chung-angno

Tongshinno

Taeguro

Tongdŏkno

21

Taesŏro

Taesŏngno

Taedongno

0   200   400 m

Kyŏngju: buses depart every eight minutes from 4.30
am to 10 pm. The fare is W1700 and the journey
takes under one hour.
Sokch'o: buses depart every 40 minutes from 7 am to
2.20 pm. The fare is W16,300 and the journey
takes seven hours.
P'ohang: buses depart every five minutes from 6.30
am to 9 pm. The fare is W3300 and the journey
takes 1½ hours.

Buses to Kimch'ŏn (for Chikchisa and
Sudosan) leave from the north inter-city bus
terminal. There are buses every seven
minutes from 6.10 am to 10.30 pm. The fare
is W2400 and the journey takes just over one
hour.

Train Taegu station, in the town centre, is for
local trains only, and unless you want to stay
in the downtown area, don't get off the train
here! The Tongdaegu station, on the east side
of the city, is where express trains stop, and
in most cases this is where you should get
off. Trains departing Seoul station for
Tongdaegu station run according to the
schedule in the boxed table.

Getting Around
To/From the Airport Taegu's airport is
north-east of the city about two km from the
express bus terminal. Bus No 31 (W300)
wends a circuitous route to the airport. There

PLACES TO STAY

2 New Taegu Hotel
뉴대구호텔

3 Savoy Hotel
사보이호텔

6 Taeyŏng-jang Yŏgwan
대영장여관

7 Hotel Kŭmho
호텔금호

14 New Chongno Tourist Hotel
뉴종로관광호텔

16 Kukje Hotel
국제호텔

18 Tongin Hotel
동인호텔

20 YMCA
—

PLACES TO EAT

15 Maxim's Restaurant
맥심

OTHER

1 Taegu Station Underground Arcade
대구역 지하상가

4 Taebo Department Store
대보 백화점

5 Korea First Bank
제일은행

8 Central Underground Arcade
중앙 지하상가

9 Taegu Post Office
대구 우체국

10 Korea Exchange Bank
외환은행

11 Korean Air
대한항공

12 City Hall
시청

13 East Taegu Telephone Office
동대구 전화국

17 Herbal Medicine Market
약령시장

19 Tonga Shopping Centre
동아쇼핑센타

21 Kyŏngbuk Hospital
경북대병원

are also seat buses from the centre costing W600. A taxi from the airport to the centre will cost around W4000 and takes about 20 minutes.

Subway Taegu is currently building a subway and it might be in operation by the time you read this. No maps of the subway system were available at the time of writing.

Car If you feel the urge and have the cash, cars can be rented at Yongil Rent-A-Car (☎ 952-1001).

P'ALGONGSAN PROVINCIAL PARK
팔공산도립공원

Just 20 km north of Taegu's urban sprawl is P'algongsan Provincial Park. Pirobong (1192 metres) is the highest point in the park, and is connected by ridges to Tongbong (East Peak, 1155 metres) and Sobong (West Peak, 1041 metres). However, this is not a wilderness park, and the splendid scenery is somewhat marred by an 18-hole golf course, numerous luxury hotels and a large gondola.

A major feature of the park is Tonghwasa, a large temple with a history stretching back over 1000 years. Even more conspicuous is the nearby Grand Stone Buddhist Image for Unification Desire. This is the largest statue of Buddha in Korea.

Getting There & Away
City bus Nos 76 (standing) or 376 (seat bus) from Tongdaegu (east railway station area) can take you to P'algongsan. These buses run at least once every 30 minutes from 5 am until 10 pm and take 50 minutes for the journey.

KAYASAN NATIONAL PARK
가야산국립공원

This national park straddles the border between two provinces: Kyŏngsangbuk-do and Kyŏngsangnam-do.

Hikers will no doubt want to challenge Kayasan, a pretty peak 1430 metres. It is even possible to walk from here along a 22 km trail to Sudosan (see Sudosan section in this chapter).

The most famous attraction in the park is Haeinsa, on the Kyŏngsangnam-do side of

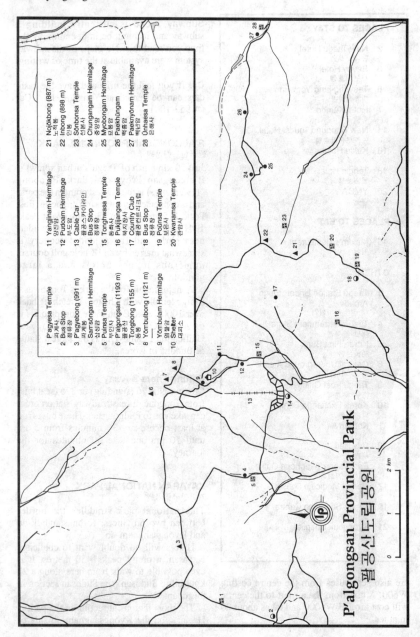

1 Pagyesa Temple 파계사	11 Yangjinam Hermitage 양진암
2 Bus Stop 정류장	12 Pudoam Hermitage 부도암
3 Pagyebong (991 m) 파계봉	13 Cable Car 팔공스카이라인
4 Sansŏngam Hermitage 삼성암	14 Bus Stop 정류장
5 Puinsa Temple 부인사	15 Tonghwasa Temple 동화사
6 P'algongsan (1193 m) 팔공산	16 Pukjijangsa Temple 북지장사
7 Tongbong (1155 m) 동봉	17 Country Club 팔공컨트리클럽
8 Yŏrŏbulbong (1121 m) 염불봉	18 Bus Stop 정류장
9 Shelter 대피소	19 Poŭnsa Temple 보은사
10 Shelter 대피소	20 Kwanamsa Temple 관암사
	21 Nojŏkbong (887 m) 노적봉
	22 Inbong (898 m) 인봉
	23 Sonbonsa Temple 선본사
	24 Chungangam Hermitage 중암암
	25 Myobongam Hermitage 묘봉암
	26 Paekhŭngam 백흥암
	27 Paeknyŏnam Hermitage 백련암
	28 Ŭnhaesa Temple 은해사

P'algongsan Provincial Park
팔공산도립공원

1 Kayasan (1430 m)
가야산
2 Shelter
대피소
3 Pibongsan (858 m)
비봉산
4 Wondangam Hermitage
원당암
5 Hŭngjeam Hermitage
흥제암
6 Yongt'apsŏnwon Hermitage
용탑선원
7 Haeinsa Temple
해인사
8 Chisokam Hermitage
지족암
9 Paekryŏnam Hermitage
백련암
10 Yongmun Waterfall
용문폭포
11 Kŭmsŏnam Hermitage
금선암

12 Ch'iin-ri
치인리
13 Samsŏnam Hermitage
삼선암
14 Pohyŏnam Hermitage
보현암
15 Yaksuam Hermitage
약수암
16 Kukilam Hermitage
국일암
17 Bus Stop
정류장
18 Observatory
관광전망대
19 Kilsangam Hermitage
길상암
20 Resthouse
농신정
21 Ticket Booth
매표소

Kayasan National Park
가야산국립공원

0   0.5   1 km

To Taegu

the border. This is the repository of the Tripitaka Koreana – more than 80,000 carved wood blocks on which are the complete Buddhist scriptures as well as many illustrations remarkably similar to those you're likely to encounter in Nepal. The blocks are housed in two enormous buildings complete with a simple but effective ventilation system to prevent their deterioration.

The buildings are normally locked, and although it's possible to see the blocks through the slatted windows, one of the friendly monks may open them up for you if you show an interest. Even if you don't manage to get into the library there's plenty of interest in the other buildings of the complex.

The wood blocks which you see today are actually the second set and they were carved during the 14th century when the Koryŏ dynasty king, Kojong, was forced to take refuge on Kanghwa Island during the Mongol invasion of the mainland. The first set, completed in 1251 after 20 years work, was destroyed by these invaders. The Tripitaka was moved from Kanghwa Island to Haeinsa in the early years of the Yi dynasty.

Haeinsa itself has origins going back to

the beginning of the 9th century when it was founded by two monks, Sunung and Ijong, following many years of study in China. It was not until the early days of the Koryŏ dynasty in the mid-10th century that it attained its present size.

The main hall, Taejkwangjon, was burnt down during the Japanese invasion of 1592 and again (accidentally) in 1817, although miraculously, the Tripitaka escaped destruction. The hall was reconstructed again in 1971. Other reconstruction has been undertaken since then, principally on the monks' quarters, and all of it, naturally, along traditional lines.

Haeinsa is one of the most beautiful temples in Korea but part of its beauty lies in its natural setting of mixed deciduous and coniferous forest. It's a romantic's paradise in wet weather when wisps of cloud drift at various levels through the forest.

Entry to the temple costs W600 plus, and you have to pay W400 entry to the national park. The temple is about 20 minutes walk from where the bus drops you.

Places to Stay

Most people visit as a day trip from Taegu, but it is pleasant and worthwhile to spend the night. Accommodation is available in the tourist village below the temple, and ranges from minbak to yŏgwan. You won't have to look hard – ajimahs meet arriving buses with offers of places to stay. Expect room prices to be higher here than elsewhere, but in the off-season you can easily do some productive bargaining.

Getting There & Away

The best way to go is from Taegu. Buses to the national park and Haeinsa run from Taegu's west inter-city bus terminal once every 20 minutes from 6.30 am until 7.50 pm. The fare is W2100 and the ride takes 1⅓ hour.

The west inter-city bus terminal in Pusan has only one bus daily departing at 9.50 am for Haeinsa. The bus departs Haeinsa at 4 pm to return to Pusan. The fare is W6000 and the journey takes 2½ hours.

Buses from Chinju to Haeinsa run once hourly between 7 am and 5.50 pm. These cost W4200 and it takes two hours to make the journey.

The obscure town of Kŏch'ang has buses to Taegu which stop at Haeinsa en route. These depart Kŏch'ang every 40 minutes from 6.30 am to 8.50 pm.

Masan is a small city outside of Pusan. Departures from Masan to Haeinsa are twice daily at 8 am and 3 pm. The ride takes 2½ hours and costs W4500.

KIMCH'ŎN 김천

Kimch'ŏn is a useful staging point to visit the nearby Chikchisa Temple and Sudosan (a mountain). There's little of cultural interest in Kimch'ŏn since it was completely destroyed during the Korean War and is totally modern, but it's pleasant enough for spending the night.

Places to Stay – bottom end

On the north side of the railway station is a collection of yŏgwan and yŏinsuk. One place is the Ch'onil Yŏinsuk which charges W8000 for a dinky box of a room with no window. Better accommodation, but at twice the price, is found in front of the railway station at the Chung'ang Yŏgwan and Myongbo Yŏgwan. Other places of relatively upmarket value include the Tong'il-jang Yŏgwan and Ŭhwa-jang Yŏgwan.

Places to Stay – middle

There are at least two places in town which qualify as mid-range accommodation. One is the Kimch'on Tourist Hotel (☎ 32-9911), on the east side of Chasan Park, near the river. On the west side of town is the equally salubrious Grand Tourist Hotel. Both places have doubles starting at W30,000 plus 20% tax and surcharge.

Getting There & Away

Bus Kimch'ŏn has both an express bus terminal and a more popular inter-city bus terminal. The railway station is sandwiched between the two bus terminals, and all three places are within walking distance of each

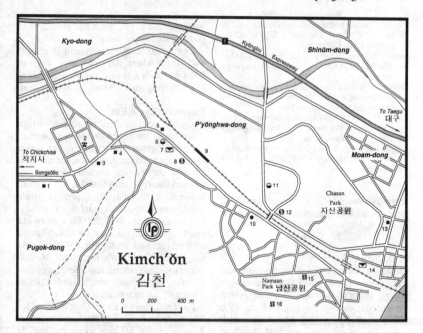

Kyo-dong

Kyŏngbu Expressway

Shinŭm-dong

P'yŏnghwa-dong

To Taegu
대구

To Chickchisa
직지사

Songsŏllo

Moam-dong

Chasan
Park
자산공원

Kimch'ŏn
김천

Pugok-dong

Namsan
Park 남산공원

0   200   400 m

PLACES TO STAY

1　Grand Tourist Hotel
　그랜드관광호텔
3　Tong'il-jang
　Yŏgwan
　동일장여관
4　YMCA
　–
5　Ŭhwa-jang Yŏgwan
　으화장여관
13　Kimch'ŏn Tourist
　Hotel
　김천관광호텔

OTHER

2　Telephone Office
　전화국
6　Express Bus
　Terminal
　고속버스터미널
7　Post Office
　우체국
8　Bank
　은행
9　Railway Station
　김천역
10　City Hall
　시청

11　Inter-City Bus
　Terminal
　시외버스터미널
12　Bank
　은행
14　Central Post Office
　김천우체국
15　Kwanŭmsa
　관음사
16　Kaeunsa
　개운사

other. Buses from the inter-city bus terminal go to the following destinations:

Andong: buses depart every 40 minutes from 6.20 am to 7 pm. The fare is W5000 and the journey takes three hours.

Kŏch'ang: (for Haeinsa & Kayasan National Park)

buses depart every 30 minutes from 6.10 am to 9 pm. The fare is W3000 and the journey takes 1¼ hours.

Kumi: buses depart every 10 minutes from 6 am to 10.30 pm. The fare is W1000 and the journey takes 30 minutes.

Kyŏngju: buses depart every 30 minutes from 6.10 am to 9 pm. The fare is W3000 and the journey takes 1⅓ hours.

P'ohang: buses depart seven times daily between 7.22 am and 4.52 pm. The fare is W5500 and the journey takes 3½ hours.

Songnisan: buses depart just once daily at 1.30 pm. The fare is W3300 and the journey takes two hours.

Taegu: buses depart every seven minutes between 6.30 am and 9.50 pm. The fare is W2400 and the journey takes just over one hour.

Taejŏn: buses depart 12 times daily between 7.20 am and 7.30 pm. The fare is W2800 and the journey takes just over one hour.

Yŏngju: buses depart every 20 minutes from 6.35 am to 7.15 pm. The fare is W5100 and the journey takes three hours.

Train For trains on the Seoul-Kimch'ŏn route see the schedule outlined in the boxed table.

CHIKCHISA 직지사

Chikchisa is one of Korea's largest and most famous temples. Situated in the foothills of Hwang'aksan west of Kimch'ŏn, it was first constructed during the reign of the 19th Shilla king, Nul-ji (417-458 AD), which makes it one of the very first Buddhist temples built in Korea. It was rebuilt in 645 AD by priest Chajang who had spent many years studying in China and brought back to Korea the first complete set of the Tripitaka Buddhist scriptures. Further reconstruction was done in the 10th century but the temple was completely destroyed during the Japanese invasion of 1592. Although there were originally over 40 buildings at Chikchisa, only some 20 or so remain, the oldest of which date from the reconstruction of 1602.

Chikchisa's most famous son is priest Sa-myong or Son'gun, a militant monk, who spent many years in Kŭmgangsan (the Diamond Mountains in North Korea). He organised troops to fight against the Japanese in 1592 and later became the chief Korean delegate to the Japanese court when a peace treaty was negotiated in 1604. Following the completion of the treaty, Sa-myong returned to Korea with over 3000 released prisoners of war.

Entry to the temple costs W1000. It's a very popular temple to visit, especially at weekends, so if you don't like crowds then go there during the week.

The actual temple compound is quite a walk from where the buses stop – about 1½ km – so in summertime it's a good idea to get an early start to avoid the midday heat.

Places to Stay & Eat

There's a well-established tourist village down where the buses stop with a range of minbak, yŏgwan and restaurants, so if you don't want to stay in Kimch'ŏn you can stay close to the temple. As with most of the tourist villages next to temples, the yŏgwan here tend to be relatively expensive so it's worth enquiring about minbak. Typically, you'll pay around W15,000 for a room but don't expect a private bath for that. Yŏgwan with private bath cost around W20,000. At the bottom end, both the *Seoul Minbak* (signposted as such) and the *Kyongnam Shikdang*, a restaurant which also doubles as a minbak, are recommended.

For food, there's a small but good selection of restaurants with the usual range of Korean dishes but the speciality here is 'mountain vegetarian food' *(sanchai na'mul)* which, if you haven't already tried it, is worth a spin. Most of these places also offer a range of home-brewed country wines and liqueurs which are definitely worth investigating even if you don't have a particular yen for genuine mountain food.

Getting There & Away

There are local buses from Kimch'ŏn to Chikchisa every 10 minutes from 6.20 am to 10.40 pm which cost W330 and take about 20 minutes. If you arrive in Kimch'ŏn by train, walk out of the train station, turn right and head up the main road for a further 25 metres or so. You'll find the bus stop there. These buses also pass by the express and inter-city bus terminals, so you can pick them up from there.

SUDOSAN 수도산

Due south of Kimch'ŏn is Sudosan (1317 metres). The mountain is also known as Pulyongsan and the summit is called

Shinsondae. When the weather is clear, you can even see the peaks in nearby Kayasan National Park.

Enchanting mountain scenery like this would not be complete without a temple, and Sudosan pitches in with Ch'ong'amsa at the base of the mountain. The temple is at the mouth of Sudo Valley, from where you can hike up to Sudoam Hermitage near the summit.

Near the temple is *Ch'ong'am Yŏgwan* (☎ 39-0194) where you can find comfortable double rooms for W16,000. Otherwise, stay in Kimch'ŏn.

Buses between Kimch'ŏn and Sudosan (Ch'ong'amsa) run eight times daily between 7.30 am and 6.50 pm. The fare is W1570 and the ride takes 1½ hours.

ANDONG 안동

Andong is a small town north of Taegu and Kyŏngju. The whole area surrounding Andong is notable for having preserved much of its traditional character. Though Andong itself is not a particularly interesting town, there are numerous interesting places to visit in the vicinity.

Most of Andong's sights are outside the city – some of them a considerable distance away – and getting to them requires a series of bus rides. However, there are a few interesting spots right on the edge of town.

Andong Folk Village 안동민속촌
Almost within walking distance of Andong is the Andong Folk Village. It's nowhere near as large as its cousin outside of Suwon, south of Seoul, but it serves a different purpose. Andong Folk Village was built to house all the cultural assets which were moved to prevent them from being flooded by the reservoir when Andong Dam was built in 1976.

There is a series of relocated and partially reconstructed traditional-style buildings ranging from simple thatched peasants' farmhouses to the more elaborate mansions of government officials and the like with their multiple courtyards.

Where this village differs from the one at Suwon is that many of the houses are also

restaurants, and for atmosphere and quality of food it cannot be beaten. Koreans have already discovered this and it's a very popular place to go for lunch or dinner. You'll find both the people who run the restaurants and their guests to be very friendly indeed. It has to be *the* place to meet people in Andong. Not only that, but the prices of meals here are very reasonable with the two simpler restaurants near the top of the hill being the cheapest.

The village is situated about three km to the east of Andong, close to the dam wall on the opposite side of the river from the road which runs alongside the railway track. A concrete bridge connects the two sides at this point. Note that this is not the first bridge across the river at the smaller dam on the outskirts of Andong but the one beyond it. Local bus No 3 from the city centre will get you here.

Chebiwon (Amitaba Buddha) 제비원
Andong is also famous for the huge rock-carved Amitaba Buddha known as Chebiwon, some five km north of Andong on the road to Yŏngju. The body and robes of this Buddha are carved on a boulder over 12 metres high on top of which is the head and hair carved from two separate pieces of rock. There's also a very small temple nearby, close to the highway, which is attended by a nun. Entry is free.

To get there take bus No 54 from the main street in Andong. Buses are very frequent (usually every five minutes) and take about 10 minutes to get there. Local buses to Yŏngju can also drop you off by Chebiwon.

Places to Stay
There is a good selection of yŏgwan and yŏinsuk close to the express and inter-city bus terminals on Hwarangno. Two of the cheapest are the *Yonga Yŏinsuk* and the *Pŏsong Yŏinsuk*. Both cost W10,000 per room without bath.

More expensive yŏgwan face the inter-city bus terminal. The top-notch place in town is the Park Tourist Hotel (☎ 27101)

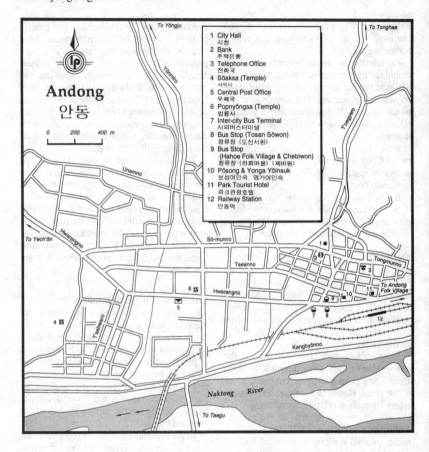

Andong
안동

0   200   400 m

To Yŏngju
To Tonghae
To Yech'ŏn
To Andong Folk Village
To Taegu

Yonnimo
T'aegyegno
Unamno
Hwarangno
Sŏ-munno
Taeanno
Hwarangno
Kangbyŏnno
T'aehwaro

Naktong   River

1 City Hall
  시청
2 Bank
  주택은행
3 Telephone Office
  전화국
4 Sŏaksa (Temple)
  서악사
5 Central Post Office
  우체국
6 Popnyŏngsa (Temple)
  법룡사
7 Inter-city Bus Terminal
  시외버스터미널
8 Bus Stop (Tosan Sŏwon)
  정류장 (도산서원)
9 Bus Stop
  (Hahoe Folk Village & Chebiwon)
  정류장 (하회마을) (제비원)
10 Pŏsong & Yonga Yŏinsuk
  보성여인숙, 영가여인숙
11 Park Tourist Hotel
  파크관광호텔
12 Railway Station
  안동역

where twins/suites cost W40,000/44,000, plus 20% tax and surcharge.

Getting There & Away

Air Although there is no airport in Andong, there is one at the nearby obscure town of Yech'on. Asiana Airlines runs two flights daily between Seoul and Yech'on.

By bus between the airport and Andong, takes 30 minutes and costs W2000.

Bus The inter-city bus terminal serves both express and regular buses. Some of the buses

to Seoul also stop at Tanyang, a useful destination for exploring central Korea. From Andong, there are buses to the following destinations:

P'ohang: buses depart nine times daily between 6.19 am and 5.54 pm. The fare is W4260 and the journey takes 2½ hours.

Pusan: buses depart 23 times daily from 6.19 am to 5.22 pm. The fare is W5790 and the journey takes 4½ hours.

Seoul: buses depart 32 times daily between 7 am and 6.45 pm. The fare is W7730 and the journey takes over four hours.

Taegu: buses depart every seven minutes from 6.40 am to 9.10 pm. The fare is W2980 and the journey takes 1¾ hours.

Taejŏn: buses depart once every 1¼ hours from 7.25 am to 3.50 pm. The fare is W5880 and the journey takes 4½ hours.

Yŏngju: buses depart 20 times daily between 7.30 am and 11.35 pm. The fare is W1300 and the journey takes one hour.

Train Trains run from Seoul's Ch'ŏngnyangni railway station to Andong. See the schedule outlined in the boxed table.

AROUND ANDONG
Hahoe Folk Village 하회마을

For a memorable journey off the beaten track, back into 16th-century Korea, it's definitely worth making the effort to visit the village of Hahoe, some 24 km west of Andong. This village has to be one of Korea's most picturesque destinations. Apart from the refrigerators, TVs and various other electrical appliances in the houses, precious little has changed for centuries. Not only do the residents want to keep it that way but the government actually funds the costs of preservation and restoration. As a result, you'll be hard pressed to find anything quite as earthy and traditional as Hahoe which is a genuine village with roots going back some 600 years – unlike the Folk Village at Suwon which is basically a tourist production. At present, there are about 130 traditional houses here.

Hahoe is a favoured location for shooting the sets of historical films and it has been discovered by the tour bus companies, so during the summer holidays it can be overrun with day-trippers. The only way to partially avoid the hordes is to stay overnight and try not to visit on a weekend. Outside of the holiday season there are no drawbacks of this nature.

There's no entry fee to the village or to the various houses which are open to the public, but remember to respect people's privacy if you step beyond the entrance gates. These are their homes, after all. The most important of the houses usually have a sign outside describing their history.

Places to Stay & Eat There are a number of minbak available in Hahoe – most of them around where the buses stop – which cost W10,000 per room on average. Some have signs (and there's even one in English saying 'Welcome Foreign Visitors'!) but if you're not sure then ask around. Dinner can usually be provided on request.

Camping is permitted. There are no regular yŏgwan or yŏinsuk.

There's a restaurant of sorts down by the river. It's a family house and there's no sign but everyone knows where it is. If you can't find it, ask at the fairly large general store by the river. It's about 60 metres from there. They have quite an extensive menu, the food is good and the people who run it are friendly. Meals cost from W2000 per dish and there's a choice of Korean and Chinese food. No English is spoken.

The general store at the bus stop also does a brisk trade in snacks and cold drinks but they don't offer full meals.

Getting There & Away From central Andong, there are only five buses daily to Hahoe. The fare is W720 and the journey takes 50 minutes. A taxi costs W8000 one way.

If you have your own transport then you have to keep your wits about you as there are no signs for Hahoe on the main roads and it's easy to get lost. Take route No 34 out of Andong towards Yech'on and turn off left along the 916 just past Pungsan. From there you drive a further five to six km and again turn off left.

Tosan Sŏwon Confucian Institute
도산서원

This is some 28 km to the north of Andong on the road to T'aebaek and Tonghae. It was founded in 1557 AD by Yi Toegye, Korea's foremost Confucian scholar (whose portrait appears on the W1000 banknote), during the reign of King Sonjo. During the middle years of the Yi dynasty it functioned for several centuries as the most prestigious school for those who aspired to high office in the civil service, and it was here that the qualifying examinations took place. Confucianism is no longer taught at the Institute and the buildings and grounds have been converted into a museum which is open to the public every day. It's a particularly beautiful spot that is often used by Korean film directors for making historical documentaries and the like.

A brochure (partially in English) is available but perhaps only worth buying for the photographs. Entry costs W280 (less for students and those under 24 years old).

Getting There & Away Catch a city bus from the main street in front of the inter-city bus terminal in Andong. There are 20 buses daily, but don't take the first one because the institute doesn't open until 9 am. The fare is W780 and the journey takes about 40 minutes. These buses take you direct to the village. You can also take local bus No 66 (W300) but it will drop you two km before the village and from there you'll have to walk or take a taxi.

Ch'ŏngnyangsan Provincial Park
청량산도립공원

Just north of Tosan Sŏwon is Ch'ŏngnyangsan Provincial Park. The most notable feature in the park is Ch'ŏngnyangsan (870 metres), the summit of which is called Kumt'apbong. There are 11 other scenic peaks, eight caves and Kwanjang Waterfall. The largest temple in the park is Ch'ongnyangsa, and there are a number of small hermitages.

There are no hotels in the park and most visitors stay in Andong. However, there is a restaurant and store.

Getting There & Away The park can be approached by bus from either Andong or the obscure town of Ponghwa. From Andong, there are five buses daily between 5.50 am and 5.10 pm and the ride takes 1½ hour. From Ponghwa, there are five departures daily between 7.50 am and 6.20 pm and the ride takes just over one hour.

Pusŏksa 부석사

Another out-of-the-way place that's worth visiting is Pusŏksa, a temple about 60 km north of Andong between Yŏngju and T'aebaek. This temple was established in 676 AD by monk Uisang after he had returned to Korea from China, bringing with him the teachings of Hwaom Buddhism. Though burnt to the ground in the early 14th century by invaders, it was reconstructed in 1358 and escaped destruction during the Japanese invasions under Hideyoshi at the end of the 16th century.

This stroke of good fortune has resulted in the preservation of the beautiful main hall (Muryangsu-jon) to this day, making it the oldest wooden structure in Korea. It also has what are considered to be the oldest Buddhist wall paintings in the country as well as a unique gilded-clay sitting Buddha.

Getting There & Away Transport to Pusŏksa is from Yŏngju or P'unggi, in either case taking about one hour. From Yŏngju, there are buses every 50 minutes between 6.40 am and 7.20 pm costing W1010. From P'unggi, buses are hourly between 7 am and 7.40 pm.

Chuwangsan National Park
주왕산국립공원

To the east of Andong and almost by the coast is Chuwangsan National Park. In the past, Chuwangsan was known as Sokpyongsan which means 'stone screen mountain'. As the name suggests, it's a rocky peak with some vertical faces. Like most of Korea's national parks, it boasts the requisite temples, hermitages, valleys, forests and waterfalls. The park gets its share of holidaymakers trying to get away from it all in a summer stampede.

There are a number of yŏgwan in the park including the *Jinbo-jang* (☎ 72-9595), *Kukil* (☎ 873-2218), *Munhwajang* (☎ 72-9900) and *Sambojang* (☎ 874-2088). All of these places charge around W16,000 for a double.

The most upmarket hotel in the park is the *Chuwangsan Hotel* (☎ 72-6801) which has rooms costing from W30,000 to W50,000.

In order to give the environment a chance

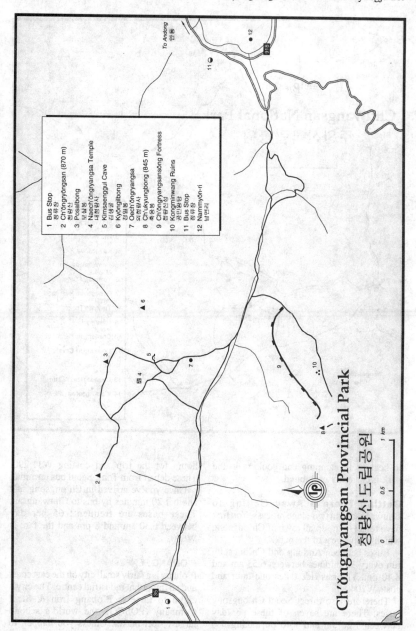

Ch'ŏngnyangsan Provincial Park
청량산도립공원

1	Bus Stop	정류장
2	Ch'ŏngnyŏngsan (870 m)	청량산
3	Posalbong	보살봉
4	Naech'ŏngnyangsa Temple	내청량사
5	Kimsaenggul Cave	김생굴
6	Kyŏnilbong	경일봉
7	Oech'ŏngnyangsa	외청량사
8	Chukyungbong (845 m)	축융봉
9	Ch'ŏngnyangsansŏng Fortress	청량산성
10	Kongminwang Ruins	공민왕유적
11	Bus Stop	정류장
12	Nammyŏn-ri	남면리

To Andong 안동

Chuwangsan National Park
주왕산국립공원

0   400   800 m

1 Kŭmŭngwangi (812 m)
  금은꽝이
2 3rd Waterfall
  제삼폭포
3 2nd Waterfall
  제이폭포
4 Kwangamsa
  꽝암사
5 1st Waterfall
  제일폭포
6 Yonhwagul Cave
  연화굴
7 Paekryŏnam Hermitage
  백련암
8 Taejŏnsa Temple
  대전사
9 Mujanggul
  무장굴
10 Chuwangam Hermitage
  주왕암
11 Chuwanggul Cave
  주왕굴
12 Bus Stop
  정류장
13 Chuwangsan (720 m)
  주왕산
14 K'aldŭnggogae (732 m)
  칼등고개

To Ch'ŏngsong
청송

Sangŭi-dong
상의동

to heal itself, camping and cooking in the park is currently prohibited.

Getting There & Away Getting to Chuwangsan is a two-stage process. You first have to get to the small town of Ch'ŏngsong which is due west of the park.

Buses between Andong and Ch'ŏngsong run every 30 minutes between 6.55 am and 8.40 pm. The bus ride takes one hour and costs W2040.

There are also direct Seoul-Ch'ŏngsong buses. There are seven of these per day between 7.20 am and 1.40 pm taking 5½ hours for the trip and costing W11,290. These depart from Tong-Seoul bus terminal.

Once you've arrived in Ch'ŏngsong, it's another 20 minutes by bus to Chuwangsan. These buses are frequent; 65 per day between 6.30 am and 8 pm and the fare is W650.

P'OHANG 포항
P'ohang is a fairly small city on the east coast and an important industrial centre. The city's claim to fame is P'ohang Iron & Steel Company (POSCO), the world's second largest steel maker. Unless you happen to

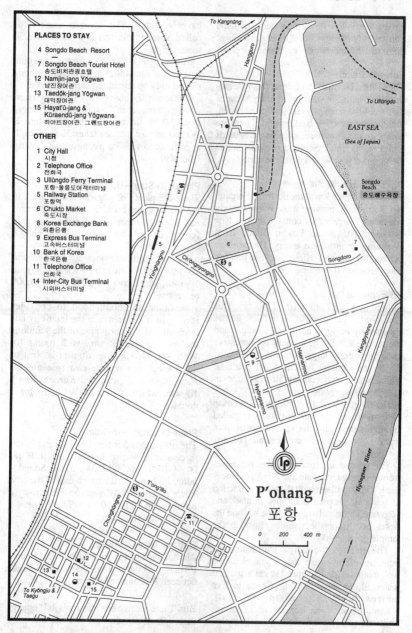

PLACES TO STAY

4 Songdo Beach Resort
—
7 Songdo Beach Tourist Hotel
송도비치관광호텔
12 Namjin-jang Yŏgwan
남진장여관
13 Taedŏk-jang Yŏgwan
대덕장여관
15 Hayat'ŭ-jang &
Kŭraendŭ-jang Yŏgwans
하이트장여관, 그랜드장여관

OTHER

1 City Hall
시청
2 Telephone Office
전화국
3 Ullŭngdo Ferry Terminal
포항-울릉도여객터미널
5 Railway Station
포항역
6 Chukto Market
죽도시장
8 Korea Exchange Bank
외환은행
9 Express Bus Terminal
고속버스터미널
10 Bank of Korea
한국은행
11 Telephone Office
전화국
14 Inter-City Bus Terminal
시외버스터미널

To Kangnŭng

Hangguro

To Ullŭngdo

EAST SEA
(Sea of Japan)

Songdo
Beach
송도해수욕장

Songdoro

Ch'ŏngnyongno

Yonghangno

Kangp'ohano

Haeranno

Hyŏngsanno

Hyŏngsan River

T'ong'ilro

Chungangno

P'ohang
포항

0   200   400 m

To Kyŏngju &
Taegu

have a particular interest in steel smelters, you are only likely to use P'ohang as a transit point to Ullŭngdo or Po'gyŏngsa.

Songdo Beach 송도해수욕장
The closest beach to the centre, this is something of a local summer resort area. A row of pine trees has been planted next to the beach, making an attractive background. There are complete facilities here, including lifeguards and a resort hotel. Seafood restaurants can dish up raw fish which costs the earth.

Pukbu Beach 북부해수욕장
This beach, three km to the north of P'ohang, is 1.7 km long, making it the longest sandy beach on Korea's east coast. City bus Nos 101 and 105 go to Pukbu Beach from P'ohang about once every 10 minutes between 6 am and 10.30 pm; the journey takes around 20 minutes.

Po'gyŏngsa 보경사
Po'gyŏngsa is 30 km north of the city. This area boasts 12 splendid waterfalls, gorges spanned by bridges, hermitages, stupas and the temple itself. The scenery is impressive enough to draw large numbers of Koreans during the summer holidays, and you'd be well advised to visit during off-peak times to escape these crowds.

Hikers may wish to challenge Naeyonsan (930 metres). The summit itself is called Hyangnobong, and the return trip by foot from Po'gyŏngsa is 20 km (around six hours by foot).

The temple is close to where the buses from P'ohang terminate and there's the inevitable tourist village with the usual collection of souvenir shops, restaurants, minbak and yŏgwan. There's also a camp site beyond the ticket booth for the temple. Entry to the temple costs W900.

The trail to the gorge and waterfalls branches off from the tourist village and is well maintained. It's about 1½ km to the first waterfall, Ssangsaengp'ok, which is five metres high. The sixth waterfall, Kwanump'ok, is an impressive 72 metres high and has two columns of water with a

cave behind it. The seventh waterfall is called Yonsanp'ok, and is a respectable 30 metres high.

As you head further up the trails, the going gets difficult and the ascent of Hyangnobong should only be attempted early in the day.

There are six buses daily from the intercity bus terminal in P'ohang to Po'gyŏngsa from 10.40 am to 5.10 pm. The fare is W1260 and the journey takes 30 minutes. It is possible to visit Po'gyŏngsa as a day trip from Kyŏngju.

Places to Stay – bottom end
There are plenty of yŏgwan and yŏinsuk in the streets going back from the ferry terminal. Most of them cater for the overnight ferry trade and there's not a lot to choose between them.

Two of the better ones are the *Saehanil Yŏgwan* and nearby *Kwanglim-jang Yŏgwan*, which cost W16,000 and W18,000 respectively.

Another neighbourhood to consider staying in is the area near the inter-city bus terminal. On the north side of the station is the *Namjin-jang Yŏgwan* with rooms for W16,000. *Taedŏk-jang Yŏgwan* is west of the station, and on the east side are the *Hayat'ŭ-jang Yŏgwan* and *Kŭraendŭ-jang Yŏgwan* which both cost W17,000 for a double.

Places to Stay – middle
The only upmarket hotel in P'ohang is the three-star *P'ohang Beach Tourist Hotel* (☎ 41-1401; fax 42-7534), 311-2 Songdo-dong, P'ohang, on the beach east of the city. There's a choice of Korean or Western-style rooms from W30,250 to W73,205, plus a 20% tax and surcharge.

Getting There & Away
Air Asiana and Korean Air both fly Seoul-P'ohang. Asiana also operates a flight between P'ohang and Cheju.

Bus There are two bus terminals in P'ohang: the express bus terminal and the inter-city bus terminal. Buses from the express bus terminal go to the following destinations:

Kwangju: buses depart every 2½ hours from 8 am to 6 pm. The fare is W12,100 (1st class) or W8000 (2nd class) and the journey takes 2¾ hours.
Seoul: buses depart every 20 minutes from 6.30 am to 6 pm. The fare is W14,800 (1st class) or W7200 (2nd class) and the journey takes five hours.
Taejŏn: buses depart every 2¼ hours from 7 am to 6.10 pm. The fare is W9500 (1st class) or W6400 (2nd class) and the journey takes 3¼ hours.

All other buses go from the inter-city bus terminal. This includes the following destinations:

Andong: buses depart 15 times daily between 8.10 am and 6.30 pm. The fare is W5130 and the journey takes 2½ hours.
Kangnŭng: buses depart every 25 minutes from 4.40 am to 5.39 pm. The fare is W8730 and the journey takes four hours by express or 5½ hours on the non-express bus.
Pusan: buses depart every 10 minutes from 6.45 am to 8.30 pm. The fare is W3130 and the journey takes 1½ hours.
Sokch'o: buses depart 19 times daily between 8.36 am and 5.17 pm. The fare is W11,260 and the journey takes 7¾ hours.
Taegu: buses depart every five minutes from 5.30 am to 10 pm. The fare is W2820 and the journey takes 1½ hours.

All buses going to Pusan, Taegu and Seoul go via Kyŏngju so you can take any of these to get to Kyŏngju as long as they're not express buses. The journey takes 40 minutes.

Train There are a few trains from Pusan, although buses are certainly more convenient. Seoul-P'ohang saemaul-class trains cost W20,800 and run twice daily, taking 4¾ hours to make the journey.

Boat For details of the ferries to Ullŭngdo, refer to the Ullŭngdo section.

Getting Around
To/From the Airport The airport bus costs W700 and takes 25 minutes. A taxi covers the distance in less than 20 minutes and costs W6000.

ULLŬNGDO 울릉도
Isolated in the storm-lashed Sea of Japan (which the Koreans call the East Sea), this rugged island is one of Korea's most unusual hidden treasures.

It was captured from pirates as the result of an order from King Yeji, the 22nd king of the Shilla dynasty, in order to secure the east coast of the peninsula. From then until 1884, this small volcanic island remained essentially a military outpost, but from that year on, migration to the island for settlement was sanctioned by the government. From the large number of small churches you might well be forgiven for thinking that a large part of the population are not only Christian but came to the island for some religious purpose.

Due to the rugged forested mountains and spectacular cliffs which rise steeply out of the sea, the island is only sparsely populated and the farms are small. Out of a population of 20,000, 10,000 live in Todong and another 5000 in Chŏdong. Most of the people live in small villages along the coast and make their living harvesting fish and (more recently) summer tourists. Everywhere you look there are racks of drying squid, seaweed and octopus. There are virtually no roads and transportation, except for two buses, is limited to fishing boats and walking.

Information
There are no banks on Ullŭngdo, so take enough local currency with you (including enough to see you through a typhoon). Good maps of Ullŭngdo can be bought at the ferry piers in Ullŭngdo and P'ohang, and sometimes on the boat itself.

Todong 도동
Todong is the island's administrative centre and largest town. Like a pirate outpost it is almost hidden away in a narrow valley between two craggy, forested mountains with a very narrow harbour front making it visible only when approached directly.

It's hardly what you might call a traditional Korean town since it was only settled in the late 19th century (there are few tile-roofed houses for instance) but its plain concrete facades are offset by its interesting position sprawling up the steep valley behind the harbour. Nevertheless, what it might lack aesthetically it makes up for with friendliness.

Boat Trips

One of the things you must do is take a boat trip around the island (about 56 km in all). The coast line is absolutely spectacular and it's easy to imagine that this must be the very end of the earth. Vast craggy cliffs plunge precipitously into the sea, battered by the powerful waves of the northern ocean. Offshore, enormous sea-stacks rise vertically out of the depths and reach for the clouds.

Kong'am (Elephant Rock) is perhaps the most famous of these stacks. Its name is derived from the peculiar weathered appearance of the rock structure which is not unlike the skin of an elephant. On a calm day you may be lucky enough to sail through its natural arch.

Further inland the cliffs are backed by mist-covered, deep-green mountains which support gnarled forests of ancient juniper. Tiny hamlets cling precariously to their sides.

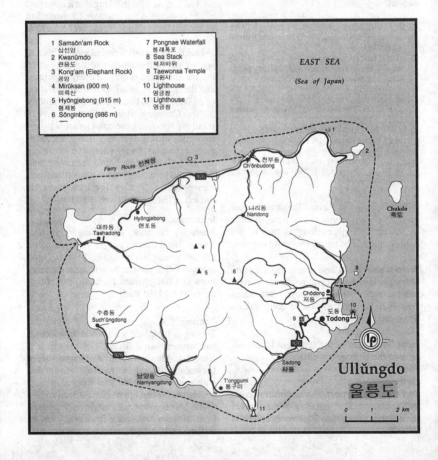

There's also the offshore islet of Chukdo (Bamboo Island), famous for its sweet watermelon. There are three families here who bravely continue to wrest a living from the plateau but who find that every time they have to replace a cow they have to literally carry it on their backs up the stone steps which is the only access up the vertical cliff walls!

There are two boats available for this exotic trip. The one which most tourists find themselves on is operated by the government out of Todong. It leaves daily from the ferry wharf at 9 am, costs W3500 and takes about 3½ hours. It has room for about 130 passengers. The only drawback to this boat (apart from being with 130 other people) is that it doesn't call at Chukdo and is too large to sail through the natural arch at Kong'am.

If you prefer something more personal then take a bus to Chŏdong and ask around for the other boat. Everyone knows about it and, if you're staying overnight in Chŏdong, you'll be asked if you want to go on a trip. This boat isn't officially licensed (neither are penguins in Antarctica) but it's been going for years. It costs a little more at W5000 but it only takes about 25 passengers and it's a better trip because it gives you the opportunity to (briefly) explore Chukdo and it's small enough to sail through the natural arches when the weather is calm.

Waterfalls & Caves

As Ullŭngdo gets more than its fair share of rain, it naturally has a number of waterfalls and caves. Pongnae Waterfall is the easiest to reach, about five km from Todong or just 1½ km from Chŏdong along a gravel and stone walkway. The track is obvious so you cannot get lost.

Unfortunately for those who like bathing in waterfalls, swimming is not allowed here as some of the water is used to supply Chŏdong. Nevertheless, it's a pleasant walk and close to the falls is the natural rock 'refrigerator' which is mentioned in all the tourist literature. Fed by a current of cold air from far underground, drinks can be kept

very cool without gas or electricity. The cafe which surrounds it also offers snacks such as *pindatok* and other vegetarian food.

T'onggumi 통구미

The small fishing village of T'onggumi, west of Todong, is also worth visiting. The road from Todong follows a tortuous path along the coastal cliffs the whole way. This could raise the hair on your head but there's no denying that it's spectacular. You'll find the villagers extremely friendly – tourists simply don't get this far. There are beautiful views from the hill at the back of the village.

Hiking

Sŏnginbong This is the highest peak (986 metres) on the island and the tip of a now dormant volcano. Various pathways lead to the summit. One suggested route is to take the road to Sadong (where there's a military barracks), turn right and just keep going up through the houses and fields. You'll eventually find a trail at the end of the fields. There are occasional signs where you can get your bearings. Even if you get lost, which is unlikely, it doesn't matter since the island is so small. From the summit there are awesome views over the whole island.

Another route is to follow the main street uphill in Todong until you reach the stream. Follow the stream course for 100 metres past the last house where you will see a trail branch off to the right. Follow this straight up. The path to the summit is marked at regular intervals. After about an hour's climb you reach an area with wooden benches and tables that serve as a teahouse during the peak season. It's a 1½-hour climb from here to the summit.

Instead of descending the mountain along the same path, you can take a different track which will eventually bring you to Chŏdong via the Pongnae Waterfall. This track starts from the teahouse/rest area which you pass on the way up the mountain. Half an hour down this track you will reach the first barn.

Continue around it (avoiding the path forking off to the right) and down to the second barn and then follow the steep path down to the stream where you will find the small cafe with the natural cooler. From here it's a short walk down to Chŏdong.

If you have the stamina and the time, instead of returning to either Chŏdong or Todong from the summit, you can head north to the small fishing village of Ch'ŏnbudong, although you may well have to stay overnight in the village if you do this. Head towards the second crater which is tilled and complete with a small church and several farm houses. There are hot springs in the area too. From here, a steep descent will take you to Ch'ŏnbudong. If you're lucky, a fishing-boat taxi may be available to take you back to Chŏdong or Todong. If not, find a camping spot along the beach or ask around for a minbak. There are a number of small restaurants where you can buy a seafood meal or you can ask the family to cook for you if you are staying in a minbak. To get back to Chŏdong or Todong overland follow the island ring road to the east. It's an enjoyable three to four-hour walk above the cliffs.

There is a small Buddhist temple called Taewonsa off the trail that leads to Sŏnginbong just outside of Todong – it's signposted. It's nothing special but the bell is finely crafted and the setting is very mellow.

Island Ring Road The ring road is approximately 40 km long. Rather than take this road the whole way (which would demand two to three days) it's more enjoyable to catch a fishing boat taxi in the morning from Todong Harbour to Ch'ŏnbudong, and then walk either westward or eastward back to Todong. Negotiation for the boat is necessary, otherwise you'll pay at least twice what the locals do.

Places to Stay

Yŏgwan prices in Ullŭngdo rise steeply in the summer peak season (20 July to 20 August) when the island is thronged with Korean vacationers.

If you travelled 2nd class on the ferry, you may already have been offered accommodation with a family which lives on the island. Every ferry is met by ajimahs extolling the virtues of their yŏgwan and minbak. By all means, go and have a look at what's on offer but don't settle for anything you're not satisfied with – there's plenty of choice and good choices at that.

The cheapest places to stay are minbak. The usual price is W8000 per room. Recommended is the one above the Taerim Honda motorbike shop, on the main street up the hill, which has rooms upstairs. It's very clean and has a private bath and toilet facilities for guests.

For campers with their own tents, there's a landscaped site just below the mineral springs which costs W2000 per tent. A shower and toilet block are on site.

There's a good selection of yŏgwan available but during the summer months package tours from the mainland fill up the most popular ones and the guests tend to party into the small hours and make a lot of noise with the karaoke sound systems. It's great if you're drunk and want to join in; not much fun if you want to sleep! The *Song'in Yŏgwan* (☎ 791-2078) is one such place. It's clean but has no hot water and costs W9000 a double without bathroom plus W2000 per extra person. Much quieter is the *Yong'il Yŏgwan* (☎ 791-2663) which is very clean and costs W8000 a double without bathroom.

Some of the better-appointed yŏgwan (all with private bath) include the following:

Cheil-jang:	26 rooms	W18,000	(☎ 791-2637)
Kyongil-jang:	11 rooms	W18,000	(☎ 791-2616)
Seun-jang:	20 rooms	W18,000	(☎ 791-2171)
Taedong-jang:	26 rooms	W18,000	(☎ 791-3372)
Tonghae:	14 rooms	W15,000	(☎ 791-3307)
Yaksu-jang:	8 rooms	W18,000	(☎ 791-2728)

For a little more money, there is the *Ullŭng Hotel* (☎ 791-6611) which boasts 36 double rooms at W25,000. For the same price you can also stay at the 30-room *Beach Hotel* (☎ 791-3132).

At the top end of the market is the *Ullŭng*

FERRIES TO ULLŬNGDO

P'ohang-Ullŭngdo

Period	P'ohang	Ullŭngdo	Frequency	Travel Time	Ship's Name
6 Aug-15 Jul	noon	10 am	every 2 days	7½ hours	Daea Express
22 Jul-16 Aug	noon	11.30 pm	daily	7½ hours	Daea Express
16 Aug-25 Jul	10 am	3 pm	daily	½ hour	Sea Flower
26 Jul-15 Aug	10 am	4.30 am	daily	3½ hours	Sea Flower

Hup'o-Ullŭngdo

Period	Hup'o	Ullŭngdo	Frequency	Travel Time	Ship's Name
1 Jun-19 Jul	noon	4 pm	daily	2½ hours	Ocean Flower
21 Aug-30 Oct	noon	4 pm	daily	2½ hours	Ocean Flower
21 Jul-20 Aug	10 am, 6 pm	5 am, 2 pm	2 daily	2½ hours	Ocean Flower
24 Jul-10 Aug	7 pm	3 pm	daily	2½ hours	Sea Flower

Sokch'o-Ullŭngdo

Period	Sokch'o	Ullŭngdo	Frequency	Travel Time
1 Mar-20 Jul	2 pm	9 am	daily	4 hours
21 Jul-20 Aug	9 am	4 am	daily	4 hours
21 Aug-31 Oct	2 pm	9 am	daily	4 hours

Tonghae (Muk'o)-Ullŭngdo

Period	Tonghae	Ullŭngdo	Frequency	Travel Time
16 Jul-20 Aug	9.30 am, 5 pm	5.30 am, 1 pm	2 daily	2½ hours
21 Mar-15 Jul	1 pm	8.30 am	daily	2½ hours
21 Aug-31 Oct	1 pm	8.30 am	daily	2½ hours
1 Nov-20 Mar	1 pm	10.30 am	Tu & Fri	2½ hours

Fares to Ullŭngdo

Route	Ship's Name	berth	deluxe	1st class	2nd class
Hup'o	Ocean Flower	–	–	–	W25,250
P'ohang	Daea Express	W33,470	–	W22,310	–
P'ohang	Sea Flower	–	W36,000	W32,800	–
Sokch'o	Taewon Catamaran	–	–	W32,500	–
Tonghae	Taewon Catamaran	–	–	W21,800	–

Marina Hotel (☎ 791-0020). There are 30 rooms and doubles cost W46,000.

If you've been hiking around the island, it is worth paying a visit to the *mok yok tang* (bathhouse) in Todong, even if you are staying in a room with a bath/shower. For W2000 you'll be given soap, shampoo, body lotion, a towel and a body scrubber and your introduction to a room full of 'madly splashing bodies' all intent on the same hedonistic pursuits. The bathhouse is on the main street a few doors up from the harbour on the left-hand side.

At Chŏdong there are a number of yŏgwan around the bus station, but one place which can be recommended is the unsignposted yŏgwan by the big tree on the way to the Pongnae Waterfall. A double room with TV, private bath and boiling hot water costs W15,000.

Entertainment

For a cold beer, try the *Son'il Haegwan* which is a bar and 'nightclub'. Sometimes, a live band performs in the evenings. The ajimah who runs it is very friendly and according to one traveller, 'won't bat an eyelid at the spectacle of foreigners going through beer by the case'. Of course, be prepared to suffer karaoke that sounds like a sonic representation of the island's chief product – squid.

Getting There & Away

Boat You can get to Ullŭngdo by ferry from P'ohang, Hup'o, Sokch'o and Tonghae. Although boats from P'ohang are the slowest, they run reliably all year round because P'ohang is the major seaport conducting trade with Ullŭngdo. Tourists generally prefer the boats from Sokch'o, Tonghae or Hup'o because they are faster, but they may be cancelled during winter. The boat from Sokch'o is a very new service (starting in late summer of 1994) and there is still some question about its reliability – conceivably, the service could be cancelled if it doesn't make money.

Ferries are also frequently cancelled whenever the weather is rough, even during the summer peak season. If you happen to be on Ullŭngdo when the weather turns foul, you may have to spend more time on the island than you had originally planned.

Booking in advance may be necessary during July and August but otherwise you can buy your ticket at the boat terminal. Advance bookings and news about cancelled ferries can be obtained in Seoul by ringing Seoul Daea Express (☎ (02) 514-6226, 514-6766). You can also ring up the passenger terminals at the various ports: P'ohang (☎ (0562) 42-5111/2); Hup'o (☎ (0565) 787-2811/2); Tonghae (☎ (0394) 31-5891/2); Ullŭngdo (☎ (0566) 791-4811/3). At the time of writing, there was still no contact phone number for the pier in Sokch'o.

Some travel agents also make reservations and get tickets, although you might have to book a tour through them. Departure times are outlined in the boxed table.

Getting Around

There are paths and dirt tracks which connect all the habitable places around the island and a surfaced ring-road circumnavigating the island.

Three public bus routes are currently available and if you use them you'll end up getting to know both the drivers and the people who use the buses quite well. It's a tightly-knit community! Buses between Todong and Chŏdong leave every half an hour from 6.15 am to 8.40 pm, cost W170 and take about five minutes. Between Todong and T'onggumi they leave every 40 minutes from 6 am to 7.40 pm, cost W300 and take about half an hour.

In addition to the public buses there are a number of minibuses available between the same towns. The fares are the same. There are also several taxis available at the standard price (minimum of W1000 for the car plus the distance charge).

Kyŏngju 경주

For almost 1000 years, Kyŏngju was the capital of the Shilla dynasty and for nearly 300 years of that period, following Shilla's conquest of the neighbouring kingdoms of Koguryo and Paekche, the capital of the whole peninsula. It had its origins way back in 57 BC at a time when Julius Caesar was laying the foundations of the Roman Empire, and survived until the 10th century AD when it fell victim to internal division and invasion. A time span like that is rare for any dynasty anywhere in the world.

Following its conquest by Koryŏ in 918 when the capital of Korea was moved far to the north, Kyŏngju fell into a prolonged period of obscurity during which time it was pillaged and ransacked by the Mongols in the early 13th century and by the Japanese in the late 16th century. Yet, despite these ravages and the neglect of centuries, the city survived to experience a cultural revival which began early in this century and continues today. A great deal of restoration work has been accomplished, all of it to original specifications, and almost every year archaeologists uncover yet another treasure trove of precious relics which help throw more light on what life was like during Shilla times.

Today, Kyŏngju is an expanding but still relatively small provincial town with friendly, easy-going people, but its major draw is that it's literally an open-air museum. In whatever direction you care to walk you will come across tombs, temples, shrines, the remains of palaces, pleasure gardens, castles, Buddhist statuary and even an observatory. It's an incredible place but these examples of Shilla artistry at the bottom of the valley are only the most conspicuous and accessible of the sights which Kyŏngju has to offer. In the forested mountains which surround the city are thousands of Buddhist shrines, temples, inscriptions, rock carvings, pagodas and statues. Enthusiasts can and do spend weeks wandering around these places and never grow tired of it.

There is an entry fee to most of the sites (which goes towards maintenance, reconstruction and archaeological research) and if you pay separately at each site it will burn a hole in your pocket. You can avoid some of this by buying a combination ticket at the entrance to Tumuli Park for just W2000 (W1000 for students) which gets you into the park itself and a number of other sites including Taenung, Anapji Pond, King Muyol Tomb, P'osŏkjongi, Kim Yu-shin Tomb, Onŭng and Chomsongdae. It's worth buying but it's not an all-inclusive ticket– you'll still have to pay separately at many of the sites outside the central area.

Orientation

Central Kyŏngju is a fairly compact city sandwiched between the railway station and two bus stations. About five km to the east is Pomun Lake, a resort area with a country club, golf course, luxury hotels, condominiums and posh restaurants with all the trimmings.

From the centre, a 16-km drive to the south-east brings you to Pulguksa, one of Korea's most famous temples and a major tourist drawcard. Next to the temple is the resort village of Pulguk-dong.

Surrounding Kyŏngju is Kyŏngju

National Park. It's not one contiguous park, but rather numerous separate districts. To the east of the city is the T'ohamsan District which is the largest. Another significant piece of the park is the Namsan District, south of downtown Kyŏngju. To the west are the Hwarang and Sŏak districts, and to the north-east is the Sokŭmgang District. Other pieces of the park can be found further afield on the coast near Taebon.

Information

There is a tourist information kiosk (☎ 772-9289) outside the Kyŏngju express bus terminal with English-speaking staff. This place also dishes out decent maps of the area. There is a similar tourist information kiosk (☎ 772-3843) in front of the railway station.

If you're going to spend a lot of time exploring Kyŏngju and the surrounding area and are interested in the legends, the detailed history and current archaeological debate of the Shilla remains, then it's worth getting hold of a copy of *Korea's Golden Age* by Edward B Adams (Seoul International Publishing House). This is a beautifully illustrated guide to all known Shilla sites written by a man who was born in Korea and who has spent most of his life there. The book is difficult or impossible to buy in Kyŏngju, so pick up a copy at one of the large bookshops in Seoul.

Central Area

Tumuli Park 대릉원 In the heart of Kyŏngju City is a huge walled area containing 20 tombs of the Shilla monarchs and members of their families. Many of them have been excavated in recent years to yield fabulous treasures which are on display at the National Museum. One of the tombs, the Ch'ŏnmach'ong (Heavenly Horse Tomb

Tumuli Park is open daily from 8.30 am to 6.30 pm (1 April to 31 October) and 8.30 am to 5 pm (1 November to 31 March). Entry costs W700 (W350 for students).

Tombs in Nosŏ-dong 노소동릉 Across the other side of the main road and closer to the city centre is the Nosŏ-dong District where

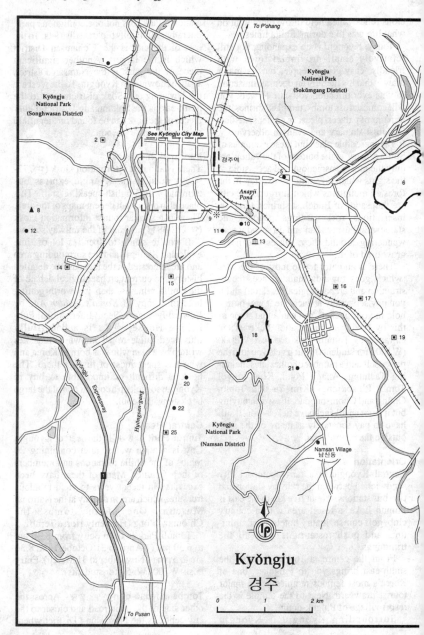

To P'ohang

Kyŏngju
National Park
(Sokŭmgang District)

Kyŏngju
National Park
(Songhwasan District)

See Kyŏngju City Map

경주역

Anapji
Pond

Kyŏngju Expressway

Hyŏngsan-gang

Kyŏngju
National Park
(Namsan District)

Namsan Village
남산동

To Pusan

Kyŏngju

경주

0   1   2 km

To Pusan

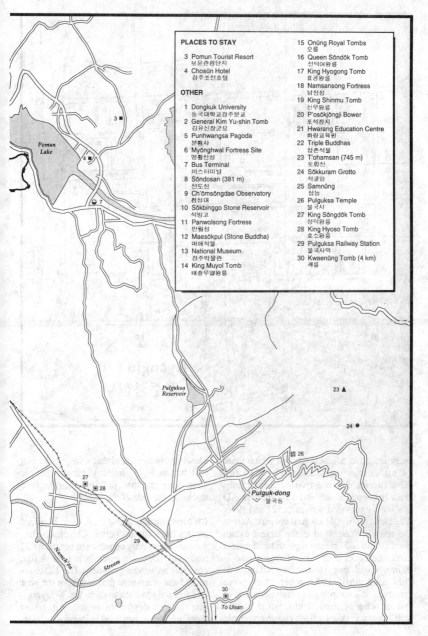

PLACES TO STAY

3 Pomun Tourist Resort
보문관광단지
4 Chosŭn Hotel
경주조선호텔

OTHER

1 Dongguk University
동국대학교경주분교
2 General Kim Yu-shin Tomb
김유신장군묘
5 Punhwangsa Pagoda
분황사
6 Myŏnghwal Fortress Site
명활산성
7 Bus Terminal
버스터미널
8 Sŏndosan (381 m)
선도산
9 Ch'ŏmsŏngdae Observatory
첨성대
10 Sŏkbinggo Stone Reservoir
석빙고
11 Panwolsong Fortress
반월성
12 Maesŏkpul (Stone Buddha)
마애석불
13 National Museum
경주박물관
14 King Muyol Tomb
태종무열왕릉

15 Onŭng Royal Tombs
오릉
16 Queen Sŏndŏk Tomb
선덕여왕릉
17 King Hyogong Tomb
효공왕릉
18 Namsansong Fortress
남산성
19 King Shinmu Tomb
신무왕릉
20 P'osŏkjŏngji Bower
포석정지
21 Hwarang Education Centre
화랑교육원
22 Triple Buddhas
삼존석불
23 T'ohamsan (745 m)
토함산
24 Sŏkkuram Grotto
석굴암
25 Samnŭng
삼능
26 Pulguksa Temple
불국사
27 King Sŏngdŏk Tomb
성덕왕릉
28 King Hyoso Tomb
효소왕릉
29 Pulguksa Railway Station
불국사역
30 Kwaenŭng Tomb (4 km)
괘릉

Pomun Lake

Pulguksa Reservoir

Pulguk-dong
불국동

Namch'ŏn Stream

To Ulsan

Kyŏngju City
경주중심부

there are other Shilla tombs for which there is no entry fee. Sŏbongch'ong and Kŭmgwanch'ong are two adjacent tombs built between the 4th and 5th centuries AD and were excavated between 1921 and 1946. The finds included two gold crowns. Across the road is Ponghwadae, the largest extant Shilla tomb at 22 metres high and 250 metres circumference. Adjoining Ponghwadae is Kŭmnyongch'ong. Houses covered much of this area until 1984 when they were removed. It's tempting to climb to the top of one or other of these tombs, but if you do you'll have park guardians chasing you and

blowing whistles! And that's despite the fact that hundreds of similarly minded people have done just that, judging from the bare tracks up the side of the tombs.

Ch'ŏmsŏngdae 첨성대 A few hundred metres from Tumuli Park is Ch'ŏmsŏngdae, a stone observatory constructed between 632 and 646 AD. Its apparently simple design conceals an amazing subtlety. The 12 stones of its base symbolise the months of the year and from top to bottom there are 30 layers – one for each day of the month. Altogether there are 366 stones used in its construction,

PLACES TO STAY

4　Buhojang Hotel
　부호장여관
6　Hotel Kirin
　기린장여관
7　Hotel Seorimjang
　서림장여관
8　Oksan-jang Yŏgwan
　옥산장여관
9　Hanjin-Jang Yŏgwan
　한진장여관
12　Taesong Shikdang
　대성식당
14　Hyŏpsŏng Tourist Hotel
　협성관광호텔
21　Cheil Yŏinsuk
　제일여인숙
23　Myŏngji Yŏgwan
　명지여관
24　Sŏnin-jang Yŏgwan
　선인장여관
34　Tonghae Yŏinsuk
　동해여인숙
36　Ch'onil Hotel
　천일호텔

PLACES TO EAT

11　Sŏrabŏl Panjŏm Chinese
　Restaurant
　서라벌 (중국집)
13　Grand Restaurant
　그랜드식당
17　Americana Hamburger
　아메리카나
26　Shiga Restaurant & Bar
　시가식당
30　Sarangch'ae Restaurant
　사랑채식당

OTHER

1　Inter-City Bus Terminal
　시외버스터미널
2　Tourist Information Kiosk
　관광안내소
3　Express Bus Terminal
　고속버스터미널
5　Korean Air
　대한항공
10　Bus Stop for Pulguksa
　정류장 (불국사)
15　Chung'ang Market
　중앙시장
16　Fruit & Vegetable Market
　청과물시장
18　Telephone Office
　전화국
19　Railway Station
　경주역
20　Tourist Information Kiosk
　관광안내소
22　Post Office
　우체국
25　Yurim Teahouse
　유림
27　City Hall
　시청
28　Bicycle Rental
　자전거대여
29　Pŏpchangsa Temple
　법장사
31　Kŭmnyongch'ong Tomb
　금령총
32　Kŭmgwanch'ong Tomb
　금관총
33　Sŏbongch'ong Tomb
　서봉총
35　Ponghwadae Tomb
　봉화대
37　Korea Exchange Bank
　외환은행

roughly one for each day of the year. There are numerous other technical details relating to the tower's position, angles and the direction of its corners in relation to certain stars. Entry costs W150 unless you have a combination ticket.

Panwolsong 반월성 A little further on from Ch'ŏmsŏngdae, on the right-hand side at the junction with the main road, is Panwolsong (Castle of the Crescent Moon). Panwolsong was once the royal castle and the site of a fabled palace which dominated the whole area. There's hardly anything left of this fortress today except Sŏkbinggo or 'Stone Ice House' which was once used as a food store. There's no entry charge.

Anapji Pond 안압지 Across the other side of the road (on the left-hand side) is Anapji Pond, constructed by King Munmu in 674 AD as a pleasure garden to commemorate the unification of Shilla. Only remnants of the palace which once stood here remain, but when the pond was drained for repair in 1975 thousands of relics were dredged up, including a perfectly preserved royal barge now displayed in the National Museum. Entry to Anapji Pond costs W550 (W270 for students) unless you have a combination ticket.

National Museum 경주박물관 Continuing a little further up along the main road you come to the National Museum. This beautiful new building, whose design is based on classical Korean architecture, houses the best collection of historical artefacts of any museum in Korea, including the National Museum in Seoul.

Outside the main building, in its own pavilion, hangs the Emille Bell, one of the largest and most beautifully resonant bells ever made in Asia. It's said that its ringing can be heard over a three-km radius when struck only lightly with the fist. Unfortunately, you won't be allowed to test this claim! The museum has the same opening hours as Tumuli Park. Entry costs W200 (W110 for students).

Punhwangsa Pagoda 분황사 Completing this circuit is the Punhwangsa Pagoda. It was built in the mid 600s AD during the reign of Queen Sondok and is the oldest datable pagoda in Korea. It originally had nine storeys but only three are left today. The magnificently carved Buddhist guardians and stone lions are a major feature of the pagoda.

To get there, follow the willow-lined road across from the National Museum until you reach the first intersection. Turn right at the intersection and then take the first lane on the right. The walk will take about 20 to 25 minutes in all. Entry costs W600 (W300 for students).

South Area

Onŭng Tombs 오릉 Travelling south from the city over the first river bridge you will come to the Onŭng Tombs, five of the most ancient tombs in the area, including the

2000-year-old tomb of the kingdom's founder. Entry costs W200 (W100 for students) unless you have a combination ticket.

P'osŏkjŏngji 포석정지 Further down the road (quite a walk) is P'osŏkjŏngji Bower, a banquet garden set in a glade of shade trees (not the originals) where there remains a fascinating reminder of Shilla elegance. This is a curious granite waterway (bower) carved in the shape of an abalone through which a stream once flowed. The stream is still there but its course is now too low to feed the granite waterway.

Entry costs W300 (W150 for students) unless you have a combination ticket.

P'osŏkjŏngji Bower
Legend has it that the king, in the company of concubines and courtiers, would sit beside the waterway while dancers performed in the centre. One of the favourite games played here was for the king to recite a line of poetry and command one of his guests to respond with a matching line, at the same time placing a cup of wine on the water. If the guest couldn't come up with a matching line by the time the cup reached him, he was required to drain it to the last drop. Although there are records of similar entertainment in imperial China, P'osŏkjŏngji is the only banquet garden left in the world. ■

Triple Buddhas 삼존석불 Less than one km down the road from P'osŏkjŏngji, on the left-hand side, are three mysterious statues known as the Triple Buddhas. Discovered only in 1923, it's not known how they came to arrive here since they are not of Shilla origin but display the massive boldness characteristic of the Koguryo style.

Samnŭng 삼능 Last on this circuit, just a few minutes' walk past the Triple Buddhas, are a group of four tombs known as Samnŭng. The tomb separate from the rest is the burial place of King Kyongae who was killed when a band of robbers raided P'osŏkjŏngji during an elaborate banquet. Nearly 1000 years separates these tombs from those in the Onŭng compound.

Local bus No 23 will get you to any of these sites.

West Area

King Muyol Tomb 태종무열왕릉 The main tomb of the Muyol group is that of King Muyol who, in the mid-7th century, paved the way for the unification of Korea by conquering the rival Paekche kingdom. Just as you enter the tomb compound, there is an interesting monument to his exploits in the form of a tortoise carrying a capstone finely carved with intertwined dragons symbolising the power of his position. Entry to the tombs costs W300 (W150 for students) unless you have a combination ticket.

General Kim Yu-shin Tomb 김유신장군묘
Back towards town and along a branch road which initially follows the river is the tomb of General Kim Yu-shin. He was one of Korea's greatest military heroes who led the armies of both Muyol and his successor, Munmu, in the 7th-century campaigns which resulted in the unification of the country. Though smaller in scale than the tomb of King Muyol, the tomb of General Kim is much more elaborate and surrounded by finely carved figures of the zodiac. The tomb stands on a wooded bluff overlooking the city. Entry costs W300 (W150 for students) unless you have a combination ticket.

South-East Area

Pulguksa 불국사 Built on a series of stone terraces about 16 km south-east of Kyŏngju, Pulguksa is the crowning glory of Shilla temple architecture. It really is magnificent. Korea has never gone in for huge, monolithic (though magnificent) temples like the Potala Palace in Lhasa; instead it concentrates on the excellence of its carpentry, the incredible skill of its painters and the subtlety of its landscapes.

Originally built in 528 AD during the reign of King Pob-hung and enlarged in 751,

it survived intact until destroyed by the Japanese in 1593. From then until recently it languished in ruin and although a few structures were rebuilt it never regained its former glory until 1970, when the late President Park Chung-hee ordered its reconstruction along the original lines. Work was completed in 1972.

Standing on the highest level and looking down you are presented with a rolling sea of tiles formed by one sloping roof after the next. The painting of the internal woodwork and of the eaves of the roofs should be one of the Seven Wonders of the World. Down in the courtyard of the first set of buildings are two pagodas which survived the Japanese vandalism and which stand in complete contrast to each other. The first, Tabotap Pagoda, is of plain design and typical of Shilla artistry while the other, Sokkatap Pagoda, is much more ornate and typical of those constructed in the neighbouring Paekche kingdom. Copies of these two pagodas stand outside the main building of the Kyŏngju National Museum. Entry to the temple costs W1500 (W750 for students).

To get to Pulguksa from the city take bus Nos 11, 12, 101 or 102. Bus Nos 12 and 102 go via Pomun Lake on the way out and via Namsan Village on the way back. Bus Nos 11 and 101 do the opposite. The fare on bus Nos 11 and 12 is W120. On bus Nos 101 and 102 it is W300 since these are express buses. The buses drop you at Pulguk-dong (Pulguk Village) just below the temple.

Sŏkkuram Grotto 석굴암 High up in the mountains above Pulguksa, reached by a long, winding sealed road, is the famous Sŏkkuram Grotto, where a seated image of the Sakyamuni Buddha looks out over the spectacular landscape towards the distant East Sea. Constructed in the mid-8th century out of huge blocks of granite – quarried far to the north at a time when the only access was a narrow mountain path – it bears striking resemblance to similar figures found in China and India (especially those at Badami, north of Mysore). As a result of its simplicity and perfection, it is regarded by scholars as one of the greatest works of Buddhist art in the whole of North-East Asia.

It's certainly very impressive, yet when the Koryŏ dynasty was overthrown and Buddhism suppressed during the Yi dynasty, the Sŏkkuram fell into disrepair and was forgotten until accidentally rediscovered in 1909. This was the time of the Japanese occupation and, had the regional governor had his way, it might very well have ended up in a Japanese museum. Luckily the local Korean authorities refused to cooperate in its removal. In 1913, a two-year restoration was undertaken but incompetence unfortunately resulted in the destruction of much of the superstructure. In 1961 another, more thorough, restoration under the auspices of UNESCO began. It was completed three years later.

The one disappointing thing about Sŏkkuram Grotto is that the Buddha is encased in a shiny, reflective glass case and photographs are not permitted. Entry to the grotto costs W1500 (W740 for students).

Both Pulguksa and Sŏkkuram Grotto literally crawl with tourists every day of the week during the summer months and the place can take on the air of a mass picnic, so don't expect a wilderness experience.

To get to the grotto from Pulguksa, take one of the frequent minibuses which leave from the tourist information pavilion (☎ 746-4747) in the car park below the temple. The return fare is W950. The minibuses terminate at a car park and from there it's a 400-metre walk along a shaded gravel track to the grotto. You get about one hour to visit the grotto before the buses return. Alternatively, there's a well-marked hiking trail from Pulguksa to the grotto (about 3½ km long) which you may prefer to take.

Kwaenŭng Tomb 괘릉 Several km further off to the south-east along the main road is Kwaenŭng Tomb. It is worth visiting for its unusual carved figures which line the approach to the tomb – military guards, civil officials, lions and monkeys. The military figures are quite unlike any others in the Kyŏngju area with their wavy hair, heavy beards and prominent noses. It's said they may represent the Persian mercenaries who are known to have served the court of Shilla. The tomb itself is decorated with carved reliefs of the 12 animals of the zodiac. This tomb compound is rarely visited. Entry costs W200 (W100 for students).

To reach Kwaenŭng Tomb from Pulguksa, take bus No 12 which will take you to the junction with the main road where the Pulguk railway station is. Change here for a bus going along the main road and tell the driver where you are heading. It's usually four or five stops from here depending on who wants to get off or on. The fare is W300. Get off when you see a billboard at the side of the road with an illustration of Kwaenŭng Tomb on it. Take the sealed road on the left-hand side and follow it for about one km. It takes you directly to the tomb.

There are frequent buses back into Kyŏngju from the main road which go via the National Museum and the railway station – bus No 15 and 35 are two which cover this route. Simply flag them down. The fare is W300.

Buddah at Sokkurum Grotto, Kyŏngju

Places to Stay – bottom end

The *Hanjin-jang Yŏgwan* (☎ 771-4097; fax 772-9679 is two blocks north-east of the bus terminal and easily identified by a large English sign on the roof. The owner, Mr Kwon Young-joung, speaks good English, hands out free maps and is very knowledgeable about local sights. This place has become a sort of backpackers' unofficial travel and information centre for Kyŏngju. Prices for singles/doubles start at W14,000/18,000 to W20,000. For a third person it costs 30% more. Guests have free use of a washing machine and refrigerator.

There are heaps of other yŏgwan near the bus terminal, all charging similar or higher prices. Closest to the railway station is the *Buhojang Hotel* which charges W18,000 for a double. Nearby, *Hotel Kirin* has the same rates. *Hotel Seorimjang* asks W20,000 and *Oksan-jang Yŏgwan* costs W23,000.

The *Tonghe Yŏinsuk*, just opposite the Sŏbongch'ong (a tomb) in the Nosŏ-dong District, has rooms for W8000. The ajimah is friendly but doesn't speak English. Also, this small place tends to fill up, but it's worth checking out if you need the cheapest room available.

Other bottom-end places are near the railway station. The cheapest amongst these is no doubt the *Cheil Yŏinsuk* but it's almost always full with long-term boarders. You can try the nearby *Sŏnin-jang Yŏgwan* and *Myŏngji Yŏgwan*.

Places to Stay – middle

There are two mid-range hotels in Kyŏngju itself, all charging approximately W35,000 for a double. Closest to the bus terminal is the *Hyŏpsŏng Tourist Hotel*. In the centre of town is the *Ch'ŏnil Hotel*.

The tourist village of Pulguk-dong, near Pulguksa, has a large number of upmarket yŏgwan charging mid-range prices. The plushest of the mid-range places in Pulguk-dong is the *Pulguksa Tourist Hotel* (☎ 746-1911; fax 746-6604). Doubles/twins/suites cost W31,000/ 39,000/100,000, plus 20% tax and surcharge.

Places to Stay – top end

Kyŏngju's top hotels are all outside the city either along the shores of Lake Pomun or at Pulguk-dong (close to Pulguksa). All of these places stick on an extra 20% tax and surcharge.

Pulguk-dong 불국동 The most expensive in this neighbourhood is the five-star *Kolon Hotel* (☎ 746-9001; fax 746-6331). This place boasts Kyŏngju's only casino. Twin rooms cost from W80,000 to W92,000 and suites are W120,000 to W800,000.

Pomun Lake Area 보문호 The other top-range hotels are on the shore of Pomun Lake. This includes the following:

Chosŭn Hotel: San 410, Shinp'yong-dong, has 302 rooms and five-star facilities. Room rates are singles W74,000, twins W86,000 to W100,000, suites W120,000 to W1,000,000 (☎ 745-7701; fax 40-8349).

Hilton Hotel: 370, Shinp'yong-dong. Room rates are twins W110,000 to W118,000, suites W135,000 to W1,600,000 (☎ 745-7788; fax 745-7799).

Hotel Concorde: 410, Shinp'yong-dong. Singles/twins/suites cost W86,000/110,000/ 130,000 to W550,000 (☎ 745-7000; fax 745-7010).

Hotel Hyundae: 477-2, Shinp'yong-dong. Twins cost W95,000 to W100,000, suites cost W200,000 to W2,000,000 (☎ 748-2233; fax 748-8234).

Korea Resort Condominium: 601-8, Shinp'yong-dong. Rooms start at W73,500 (☎ 745-1500; fax 745-1509).

Places to Eat

There's an excellent choice of restaurants in Kyŏngju including Korean, Chinese, Japanese, Western and seafood. The seafood restaurants, as elsewhere in Korea, tend to be very expensive. Many are marked on the street map handed out by the Hanjin-jang Yŏgwan.

If you'd like a break from Korean food then the *Shiga Restaurant & Bar* on Tongsongno is a good place to go. It offers a range of Western-style food including such things as spaghetti with meat sauce. This restaurant is easy to miss as it's on the 1st floor and there's no sign in English although it does say in English underneath the han'gŭl, 'Western Restaurant'.

The fast food isn't really all that fast at *Americana Hamburger*, but it isn't bad either. The fried chicken is especially recommended.

Going up somewhat in price, the *Grand Restaurant* enjoys a well-deserved reputation for its pulgogi, although they also serve a good range of other dishes. The menu is in both English and Korean.

Taesong Shikdang, on Sosongno, is a popular restaurant doing Korean dishes. The food is good and the prices reasonable but avoid their ginseng chicken which is somewhat bland and watery. Pulgogi served here is excellent.

Just a couple of doors to the south on Sosongno is *Sŏrabŏl Panjŏm Chinese Restaurant*. The food here is reasonably priced and good.

Sarangch'ae Restaurant is an upmarket traditional Korean restaurant with all the trimmings. It's just to the west of Pŏpchangsa (a small temple) and City Hall.

Entertainment

Soju tents set up in the evening along the riverbank to the north of town. This is a good place to enjoy snacks and alcoholic drinks at reasonable prices.

If you'd prefer something non-alcoholic, Yurim Teahouse is off the eastern end of Taejŏngno in a small alley.

Things to Buy

The price tags in many shops are geared to the Japanese tourist market – you can often get a 30% discount simply by pointing to the price tag and saying, 'I'm not Japanese'.

Getting There & Away

Air There is no airport at Kyŏngju itself, but the busy airports at Pusan and Taegu are readily accessible. Indeed, there is direct bus service between Kyŏngju and Kimhae Airport in Pusan (W6000), so flying is a reasonable proposition if your time is limited.

Tickets for both Korean Air and Asiana Airlines can be booked at one of the two agencies in town. The first of these is at the back of the express bus terminal and has a large Korean Air sign prominently displayed. The other is the Han Jin Tourist Agency on Hwarangno (no connection with the Hanjin-jang Yŏgwan).

Bus Kyŏngju has an express bus terminal and inter-city bus terminal, conveniently adjacent to each other. Buses depart from the express bus terminal to the following destinations:

Kwangju: buses depart twice daily at 6.30 am and 6.30 pm. The fare is W8400 (1st class) or W5600 (2nd class) and the journey takes 3¾ hours.

Pusan: buses depart every 30 minutes from 7 am to 7.30 pm. The fare is W3100 (1st class) or W2000 (2nd class) and the journey takes one hour. This bus does *not* stop at T'ongdosa (a temple) halfway between Kyŏngju and Pusan; you need the regular inter-city bus for this.

Seoul: buses depart every 35 minutes from 7 am to 6.10 pm. The fare is either W13,500 (1st class) (2nd class) or W9000 and the journey takes 4¼ hours.

Taegu: buses depart every 20 minutes from 6.50 am to 9.10 pm. The fare is W2600 (1st class) (2nd class) or W1700 and the journey takes 50 minutes.

Taejŏn: buses depart every three hours between 8.20 am and 6 pm. The fare is W8300 (1st class) or W5500 (2nd class) and the journey takes 2¾ hours.

Buses depart from the inter-city bus terminal to the following destinations:

Andong: buses depart 12 times daily from 7.10 am to 5.15 pm. The fare is W7100 and the journey takes 3½ hours.

Kangnŭng: buses depart every 30 minutes from 5.50 am to 4.30 pm. The fare is W11,300 and the journey takes 6½ hours.

Kimch'ŏn: (for Chikchisa) buses depart five times daily between 9.25 am and 5.20 pm. The fare is W4400 and the journey takes 2¼ hours.

P'ohang: buses depart every 10 minutes from 5.30 am to 10.50 pm. The fare is W1200 and the journey takes about 40 minutes.

Pusan: buses depart every 10 minutes from 6.10 am to 9.40 pm. The fare is W2100 and the journey takes one hour. This is the bus to take if you intend to visit T'ongdosa, a temple halfway between Kyŏngju and Pusan.

Sokch'o: buses depart eight times daily between 9 am and 2.20 pm. The fare is W14,200 and the journey takes eight hours.

Taegu: buses depart every 10 minutes from 6.10 am to 9 pm. The fare is W1700 and the journey takes one hour.

Train Trains connecting Seoul to Kyŏngju are infrequent and you'll probably do better travelling by bus. Departures are from Seoul station except for the T'ongil train which departs from Ch'ŏngnyangni station. There are also trains between Pusan and Kyŏngju, but again, buses are more frequent. Refer to the boxed table on p 237 for the Seoul-Kyŏngju train schedule.

Getting Around

Bus Many local buses terminate outside the inter-city bus terminal alongside the river but these are mostly relatively long-distance local buses. For the shorter routes (eg to Pulguksa), buses can be picked up along Sosongno and Taejŏngno.

Four of the most important buses as far as travellers go are Nos 11, 12, 101 and 102. These are the buses you need for Pomun Lake, Pulguksa and Namsan Village. Bus Nos 12 and 102 go to Kyŏngju, Pomun Lake, Pulguksa, Namsan Village, Kyŏngju. Bus Nos 11 and 101 go to Kyŏngju, Namsan Village, Pulguksa, Pomun Lake, Kyŏngju. Bus Nos 11 and 12 are standing buses and the fare is W300. Bus Nos 101 and 102 are seat buses and the fare is W600. All four buses pass the National Museum on their way out and on their way back. One of these buses comes along about once every five minutes.

Bicycle Hiring a bicycle for a day or two is an excellent way of getting around the sites in the immediate vicinity of Kyŏngju. There are two places that bicycles can be rented from but the most convenient is probably the one along Taejŏngno. None of these bicycles has gears so going uphill can be hard work.

Around Kyŏngju

SOUTH OF KYŎNGJU

There are literally thousands of other relics from the Shilla kingdom scattered over the mountains all the way from Kyŏngju to P'ohang on the eastern seaboard, to Taegu in the west and to Pusan in the south. There are also many other places of interest dating from the Chosŏn period as well as places of spectacular geographical beauty.

Namsan 남산

One of the most rewarding areas to explore within easy reach of Kyŏngju is Namsan, a mountain south of the city. Not only is it worth hiking around this area purely for its scenic beauty but the mountain is strewn with royal tombs, pagodas, rock-cut figures, pavilions and the remains of fortresses, temples and palaces. There are hundreds of paths which you can follow alongside the streams which come tumbling down the mountain as well as the 'Namsan Skyway' which is a winding gravel road which starts out close to P'osŏkjŏngji Bower, skirts the ridges of Namsan and ends up at Namsan Village near T'ongiljŏn (Unification Hall). The paths and tracks are all well-trodden and you cannot get lost, although at times you will need to scout around for relics which are not immediately visible since few of them are signposted. Whichever point you decide to take-off from, you're in for an exhilarating experience.

If your time is limited then two suggested day-long trips are:

Trip No 1 Take local bus No 23 from the inter-city bus terminal and get off at P'osŏkjŏngji Bower on the west side of Namsan (or at the Samnŭng tombs if you've already visited P'osŏkjŏngji). From P'osŏkjŏngji walk to the Samnŭng tombs

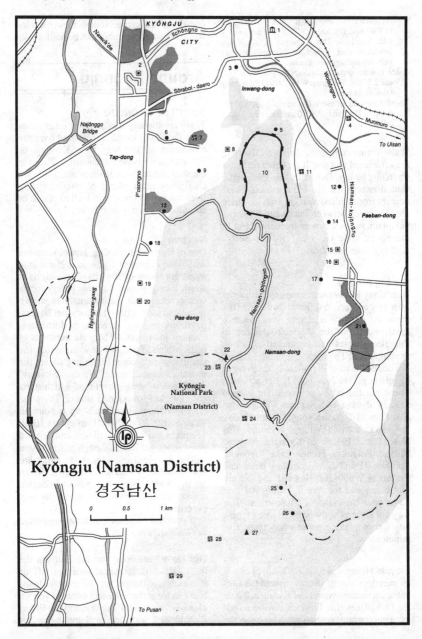

Kyŏngju (Namsan District)

경주남산

Kyŏngju National Park

(Namsan District)

1	National Museum
	경주박물관
2	Onŭng (Royal Tombs)
	오릉
3	Sangsŏjang
	상서장
4	Mangdŏksaji (Old Temple Site)
	망덕사지당간지주
5	Maaejosanggun (Carved Figures)
	마애조상군
6	Najŏng Well
	나정
7	Namgansaji (Temple Site)
	남간사지
8	King Ilsŏng Tomb
	일성왕릉
9	Ch'angnimsaji Pagoda
	창림사지삼층석탑
10	Namsansŏngji (Castle Site)
	남산성지
11	Porisa Temple
	보리사
12	Kyŏngbuk Forest Research Institute
	경북임업시험장
13	P'osŏkchŏngji Bower
	포석정지
14	Hwarang Education Centre
	화랑교육원
15	King Hŏngang Tomb
	헌강왕릉
16	King Chŏnggang Tomb
	정강왕릉
17	T'ongiljŏn (Unification Hall)
	통일전
18	Triple Buddhas
	삼체석불
19	Samnŭng Tombs
	삼릉
20	King Kyŏng'ae Tomb
	경애왕릉
21	Namsanni Pagoda
	남산사지석탑
22	Namsan (466 m)
	남산
23	Sŏkkasaji (Temple Site)
	—
24	Yongjangsaji (Temple Site)
	용장사지
25	Stone Buddha
	신선암마애보살반가상
26	Stone Carved Buddhist Images
	칠불암마애석상
27	Kŭmosan (495 m)
	금오산
28	Ch'ŏngsa Temple
	천용사
29	Waryongsa Temple
	왈용사

(about one km) via the Sambulsa triangle. From the Samnŭng tombs take the track which follows the stream up the side of Namsan to the crest of the mountain. On the way up there you will pass many freestanding and rock-cut images and a small hermitage near the summit where an old bearded monk lives. Follow the trail along the saddle until it joins the Namsan Skyway – the views from the saddle might inspire you to become a monk up here.

Carry on south along the Skyway towards Namsan Village for about half a km until the road makes a sharp turn to the left. A detour straight on from this point will bring you to two pagodas. Neither of these are visible from the road and the trail leading to them is somewhat indistinct. Also, the pagoda furthest from the road is not visible until you are just past the first, so it's easy to miss. From here, backtrack to the Skyway and continue on down to Namsan Village, where you should visit the twin pagodas and Sochulji (a pavilion and adjoining pond). The latter is an idyllic little spot described in legends going back to the early days of Shilla. If you've had enough for one day at this point you can catch local bus Nos 12 or 102 back to Kyŏngju from Unification Hall. If not, you could carry on south past Namsan Village to the seven Buddha reliefs of Chilbul'am. From there you would have to return to Namsan Village and take a bus back to Kyŏngju.

Trip No 2 Take local bus No 11 and get off as soon as the bus crosses the river, about 2½ km past the National Museum. From here you can visit Porisa in the Miruk Valley – a beautifully reconstructed nunnery set amidst old conifer trees with a number of ancient freestanding images. It is possible to make your way over the hill at the back of this temple to Pagoda Valley but it's a rough climb. If you don't have the right footwear it's perhaps easier to backtrack down to the bridge over the river and turn left there. Take the track along the west side of the river for several hundred metres until you come to a small village. Turn left here and head up

Pagoda Valley. The first temple you come to is Okryongsa. Just beyond it you will find the greatest collection of relief carvings anywhere in Korea, as well as a pagoda.

Returning to the river bridge and looking across to the main road to Ulsan you will see two stone pillars standing in a thicket of trees in the middle of paddy fields. These pillars are all that remain standing of what was once a huge temple complex during Shilla times. If you like fossicking for ancient reliefs then this is the spot to do it. If that doesn't particularly interest you then head off down to Namsan Village and take any of the trails which lead up into the mountains.

EAST OF KYŎNGJU
There are a number of interesting places to visit along or not far off the road between Kyŏngju and Taebon on the east coast, and the road which takes you there passes through a beautiful and thickly forested section of Kyŏngju National Park.

Kirimsa 기림사
This is the first place of interest once you've descended from the pass which takes you through Kyŏngju National Park. The temple was one of the largest complexes near the Shilla capital and its size (14 buildings in all) compares with that of Pulguksa, yet it is rarely visited by foreigners. You can enjoy this temple in peace and quiet as you will certainly never come across the picnic multitudes common at Pulguksa.

The temple has its origins back in early Shilla times when a monk named Kwangyu arrived from India and acquired a following of some 500 devotees. Known originally as Imjongsa, its name was changed to the present one in 643 AD when the temple was enlarged. The present buildings date from 1786 when Kirimsa was rebuilt. It's a very interesting temple with a number of impressive statues including a large Pirochana Buddha with attendants in the main hall, a Yaksa Yorae (Buddha of Medicine) in the adjacent hall and a gold-lacquered Bodhisattva of Mercy in the hall behind. The latter is said to date from 1501. The walls and beams of the various halls are superbly painted.

Perhaps the most amazing feature of this temple is the very unusual gold Buddha with eight main arms and hundreds of smaller arms radiating from the body plus a number of smaller heads in the hair of the main statue. The arms hold all manner of symbolic objects including a Tibetan-style *dorjes*, a Shiva trident and a bunch of grapes among other things. There's no other Buddha image vaguely similar to it anywhere else in Korea except at Naejangsa (see the Chŏllabuk-do chapter) and it has a decidedly Hindu feel about it. Entry to the temple costs W700 (less for those under 24 years old). The best time to visit is at 11 am when the chanting begins in every hall.

There are the beginnings of a small tourist village at the entrance to the temple and minbak rooms are available if you want to stay for the night.

If you have the time, check out the rock-cut image of the Buddha at Kolgul'am, off to the west along a footpath (two km) closer to the turn-off from the main road. It will take you about 25 minutes to get to the image.

Getting There & Away Getting to Kirimsa requires a degree of perseverance since there are no direct buses from Kyŏngju. What you have to do is take a bus from the inter-city bus terminal in Kyŏngju to Taebon and ask the driver to drop you off at Andong-ni where the turn-off to the temple goes off on the left-hand side. From here to the temple it's about six km along a paved road. There are local buses from Andong-ni to the temple but they only go four times daily at 6.20, 10.10 am, 1.10 and 6 pm. These buses originate in Kamp'o about eight km up the coast from Taebon. For the rest of the day you'll either have to walk, hitch a ride or take a taxi.

Kamunsa 가문사
About one km back from Taebon Beach, along the main road to Kyŏngju, stand the remains of what was once a large temple in Shilla times. All that is left are two three-storeyed pagodas – among the largest in

Korea – and a few foundation stones. The pagodas are prototypes of those constructed following the unification of Shilla. A huge bell, some four times larger than the Emille bell in the National Museum at Kyŏngju, once hung in Kamunsa but was stolen by the Japanese during their 1592 invasion, when they tried to take it back to their homeland. They didn't get far and the bell was lost in the ocean close to Taebon. A search was made for the bell several years ago by a team from Kyŏngju National Museum but it was unsuccessful. There are plans to try again.

Entry to the site is free.

Munmu Sea Tomb 문무왕해중릉

The small, rocky islet off the coast at Taebon is the site of the famous underwater tomb of the Shilla king, Munmu (661-681 AD). It's perhaps the only underwater tomb in the world and at low tide it can be seen through the clear water of the pool in the centre of the islet.

Munmu had made it known that on his death, he wished his body to be burned and the ashes buried at sea close to a temple, Kamunsa. The idea behind these unusual funeral rites was that his spirit would become a dragon and protect the eastern shores of the Shilla kingdom from Japanese pirates. His wishes were carried out by his son, Shinmu, who became the next Shilla king.

The tomb was not rediscovered until 1967. There is speculation that the rock visible in the centre pool is actually a stone coffin but most experts dismiss this as a flight of fantasy although no investigations have been carried out.

It used to be possible to hire boats at the beach to take you out to the islet but access is now restricted and you need special permission from the police. Even if you're successful, it's questionable whether it's worth paying W5000 just to see a stone slab in the middle of a rock pool.

North of Taebon is Taebon Beach, and to the south is Ponggil Beach. Both are popular with Koreans especially during the summer holiday period but there's nothing special about this stretch of coastline. Like the rest

of the east coast, too, the inevitable barbed wire fence lines the beach.

Places to Stay Camping along the beach is prohibited but you can set up your tent along the banks of the river, back from the town where the bridge crosses it. Taebon itself has a number of minbak where you can stay for the night.

There are a number of restaurants along the beaches at Taebon which specialise in seafood but they're ridiculously expensive at W30,000 for a meal! Ask the price of seafood first, or else suffer indigestion when you get the bill.

Getting There & Away To get to Taebon from Kyŏngju you need to take a bus going to Kamp'o. These leave from the inter-city bus terminal (bay No 2). There are buses every 30 minutes from 8.20 am to 8.30 pm daily, the first at 6.50 am and the last at 7.50 pm. The fare is W1500 and the journey takes about one hour.

NORTH OF KYŎNGJU 양동

The places of interest north of Kyŏngju are perhaps best seen as two separate day trips, although it's just possible to see them all in a single day so long as you make an early start.

Yangdong Folk Village

Having steeped yourself in Shilla history, it's now time to immerse yourself in a different period of Korea's past which has escaped the ravages of modernisation. Yangdong fits the bill perfectly. Here is a beautiful and peaceful Yi dynasty village full of superb traditional wooden houses and mansions. It's been designated as a preservation area, like Hahoe outside of Andong and Sŏng-ŭp on Chejudo, so it's an excellent opportunity to soak up the atmosphere of what life was like in most Korean villages before the advent of concrete and corrugated iron.

The village was established in the 15th and 16th centuries and consists of around 150 large and small houses typical of the *yangbang* class – a largely hereditary class based on scholarship and official position as opposed to wealth. It was the birthplace of Son-so (1433-84), a scholar-official who was one of the key figures involved in quashing the revolt against King Sejo in 1467. It was also the birthplace of Son Chung-ton (1463-1529), otherwise known as Ujae, and of Yi On-jok (1491-1553), a famous Confucian scholar during the early years of the Yi era but more widely known by his pen name Hoejae.

Most of the houses are still lived in so you need to observe the usual courtesies when looking around, but the larger mansions stand empty and are open to the public. There's a plaque outside the more important structures on which you'll find the name of the building and an account of who built it and in what year. Most of these mansions are left open but there may be one or two which are locked. If that's the case, ask for the key at the nearest house. There are no entry fees to any of the buildings.

Of the larger buildings, make sure you see the Yi Hui-tae House, Shimsujong and Hyangdam House. There's a booklet for sale with a map and coloured photographs (entirely in Korean) at the general store at the entrance to the village. It's worth picking up even if you can't read Korean as it gives you a good idea of the lay-out of the village. A half-hour's walk from the village stands Korea's second largest Confucian study hall which was built in honour of Yi On-jok and completed in 1575.

You're very unlikely to come across any other tourists in this village as it rarely features in any of the tourist literature. Possibly as a result of that, the people who live here are very friendly and it's easy to strike up a conversation and be invited to take tea and snacks. You should plan on spending several hours here.

There are no restaurants in Yangdong but there are two general stores where you can buy snacks, cold drinks and the like.

Getting There & Away From Kyŏngju, bus Nos 1, 2, 18, 55, 57 and 88 will get you to within 1½ km of Yangdong. These local buses go down the Kyŏngju-P'ohang main road and then turn around after they've crossed the large river bridge. They then turn off to the right just before the bridge and head for Angang. A little way down this road is another fork to the right and this is where the buses will drop you. From here it's 1½ km to Yangdong, initially following the railway line and then going under it. You can't get lost as there's only the one road into the village.

There are no local buses which go directly into Yangdong from Kyŏngju but bus No 1 from Angang (not the same as the No 1 from Kyŏngju) goes there three times daily. This bus returns to Angang from Yangdong at around 11 am, 5 and 7.50 pm.

To get back to Kyŏngju from Yangdong, simply walk back to the turn-off where the bus originally dropped you. There are plenty of buses from there back to Kyŏngju. Alternatively, if it's early enough in the day, take a bus to Angang from the turn-off and another bus from there to Oksan Sŏwon, west of Angang.

Oksan Sŏwon 옥산서원
Oksan Sŏwon was once one of the two most important Confucian schools in Korea and like its counterpart, Tosan Sŏwon, outside of Andong, one of the few such scholarly institutes to escape the destruction wrought on them by the father of King Kojong in the 1860s. It was established in 1572 in honour of Yi On-jok (1491-1553) by another famous Confucian scholar, Yi Toegye, and enlarged in 1772. A fire accidentally destroyed some of the buildings early this century so that only 14 structures remain today.

When first established in the 1500s, these *sŏwon* quickly became the centres of learning as well as of political intrigue and their alumni were numbered in the thousands. Indeed, they rapidly became so powerful that the Yi kings lost their supremacy over the Confucian scholars who thenceforth effectively controlled the entire country's economy and its political direction. Were a scholar to commit a crime, he was tried not by the state but by the Confucian college.

The Korean kings were not to regain their supremacy until several centuries later.

These days, although they no longer function, the sŏwon are regarded as an important part of the country's cultural heritage since it was at these schools that most of the calligraphy and paintings of the Yi dynasty's last three centuries were produced.

Oksan Sŏwon has a sublime setting surrounded by shade trees and overlooking a stream with a waterfall and rock pools – an ideal place for contemplation and study. The main gate is usually unlocked so you can wander at will through the walled compound. Only one building is presently occupied by the family which looks after the place. There's no entry fee.

During the summer holiday period, the banks of the stream are a popular camping spot and swimming is possible in the rock pools below the waterfall.

Tongnaktang A 10-minute walk beyond Oksan Sŏwon along the main road up the valley will bring you to Tongnaktang which was built in 1516 as the residence of Yi On-jok after he left the government service. Like the sŏwon, it has a timeless and relaxing atmosphere to it, as well as a beautiful pavilion which overlooks the stream. The walled compound is partly occupied by a family which looks after the place but you can wander at will through the rest of it. The main entrance gate is usually unlocked and there's no entry fee.

Chonghyesa Beyond Tongnaktang, and off to the left surrounded by rice fields, is the unusual 13-storied stone pagoda of Chonghyesa. It's a huge structure and the only one of its type in Korea. It's origins are somewhat obscure but it's generally agreed that it dates from the unified Shilla period. The temple, of which the pagoda once formed part, was destroyed during the Japanese invasion of 1592.

Todŏksa About 2¼ km beyond the pagoda of Chonghyesa, high up in the forested mountains near the end of the valley, is the small temple of Todŏksa. It's a beautiful little place perched on a rock outcrop from which two springs emerge, and the views are magnificent. There are five buildings in all, including a tiny hermitage above the temple itself but complete with its own ondol heating system. It's a steep walk up from the main road along a well-worn path but definitely worth the effort. It's about as far as you can get from the madding crowd and hardly anyone ever comes up here except the monks and the family who look after the cooking and cleaning. If male travellers were to bring their own food and drink, the monks would undoubtedly offer them somewhere to sleep.

To get to Todŏksa, take the main sealed road up the valley past Tongnaktang, ignoring the gravel road which forks off to the right just after you cross the first bridge. Several hundred metres beyond this you come to a second bridge where the tarmac ends. A little further on from here you'll see a rusty sign on the left-hand side with a painting of a temple on it and a zigzag path leading up to it. This is where you turn off and head up the mountain. It's about 900 metres from here to the temple. Don't be put off by the steepness of the path as it gets gentler further up. You'll know you're on the right track when you come across a rock in the middle of the track saying (in Korean), 'Todŏksa 700 metres'. There's a similar sign at the 500-metre point. For most of the way the path is shaded by trees so you can come up here even on a hot day. It's possible to hitch a ride with trucks along the main sealed road as there's a rock quarry near the end of the valley – you may hear the occasional explosion when blasting is in progress.

Places to Stay & Eat You can camp alongside the stream either at Oksan Sŏwon or at Tongnaktang, plus there's a signposted camp site adjacent to Tongnaktang with basic facilities.

On the opposite side of the stream from Oksan Sŏwon, there's a tiny tourist complex consisting of restaurants and shops offering souvenirs and cold drinks.

Getting There & Away The most convenient way of getting to Oksan Sŏwon from Kyŏngju is to take the bus to Angang, which also stops at Oksan Sŏwon. The bus leaves Kyŏngju every 30 minutes between 7.25 am and 10.30 pm and the journey take about 30 minutes.

There are also local buses between Angang and Oksan Sŏwon other than the one from Kyŏngju. The stop for these buses in Angang is close to the post office and opposite a supermarket on the road to Yŏngch'ŏn. It's about seven km from Angang to Oksan Sŏwon. A taxi from Angang to Oksan Sŏwon will cost about W5000.

WEST OF KYŎNGJU

A number of interesting day trips are possible to the west of Kyŏngju and include Buddhist temples, hermitages, the headquarters of a unique Korean religion known as Chundo'kyo, the remains of fortresses and a special vegetarian village.

Yongdamjŏng 용담정

Along a minor road in the heart of the countryside stands Yongdamjŏng, the temple complex of the Chundo'kyo (Heavenly Way) religion. This unique Korean religion was founded by Choe Che-woo in 1860. The religion incorporates aspects of Confucianism, Buddhism and Taoism. Choe was regarded by the Yi dynasty authorities as a troublesome subversive at a time when Korea was attempting to shut out foreign influences and he was martyred in Taegu in 1864. At the same time, the original buildings of this temple were burned to the ground. His followers were a determined bunch, however, and, despite further repression, rebuilt the temple only to have it burned yet again. The most recent reconstruction was in 1960, this time with government assistance after the area had been made part of the Kyŏngju National Park. It's a beautiful, tranquil area of wooded mountains and terraced rice fields, where farmers continue to cultivate the land in the traditional manner.

Getting There & Away To get there, take bus No 5 from the inter-city bus terminal in Kyŏngju and ask the driver to drop you at the turn-off for the temple. It's a short walk from where the bus drops you.

Pokdu'am 북두암

This is another interesting day trip, not far from Kŏnch'ŏn, which involves a steep walk to the top of a thickly forested mountainside. Close to the top is Pokdu'am, a hermitage where you will find a huge rock-face out of which 19 niches have been carved. The three central niches hold a figure of the historical Buddha flanked by two bodhisattvas (Munsu and Pohyon) while the remainder house the 16 arhat. The carving is of recent age and, although there's an unoccupied house up here, the actual hermitage which used to stand here was burned down in 1988 when an electrical fault started a blaze. There's also a recently erected statue of Kwanseum, the Goddess of Mercy, just beyond the rock face.

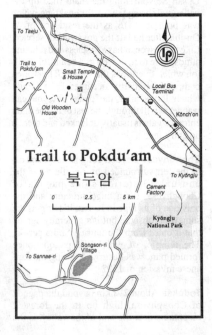

Trail to Pokdu'am

북두암

Trains from Seoul to Tongdaegu

Class	Time	Frequency	Travel Time	Fare
Saemaul	8 am-11.20 pm	16 daily	3 hrs	W15,600
Mugunghwa	6.10 am-11.55 pm	28 daily	3¾ hrs	W9300
T'ong-il	6.10 am-10.30 pm	14 daily	4 hrs	W5600

Trains from Seoul to Kimch'ŏn

Class	Time	Frequency	Travel Time	Fare
Saemaul	9 am, 5.30 pm	2 daily	2½ hrs	W12,300
Mugunghwa	7.30 am-11.55 pm	28 daily	2¾ hrs	W6300
T'ongil	6.10 am-10.30 pm	14 daily	3¼ hrs	W4300

Trains from Seoul to Andong

Class	Time	Frequency	Travel Time	Fare
Saemaul	9 am	1 daily	4 hours	W12,400
Mugunghwa	11 am, 6 pm	2 daily	4¼ hours	W6300
T'ongil	1 pm-9 pm	3 daily	4¾ hours	W4300

Trains from Seoul to Kyŏngju

Class	Time	Frequency	Travel Time	Fare
Saemaul	9 am-6.30 pm	4/day	4 hr 10 min	W19,500
Mugunghwa	9 pm	once/day	5 hr 25 min	W10,000
T'ongil	9 pm	once/day	7 hr 20 min	W7,600

The old couple who used to live here and maintain the hermitage have moved down to the small temple to the right at the start of the trail.

While unique to Korea, the rock-face niches of Pokdu'am are only part of the reason why it's worth coming out here. The climb itself would be ample justification since there are spectacular views over the surrounding countryside from various points along the trail. The trail is well maintained and easy to follow but bring your own liquid refreshments as there are no springs along the way. The walk there will take around 1½ hours, less coming back down.

Getting There & Away Bus No 28 from Kyŏngju will take you direct to the village of Songson-ni which is where the trail begins. There are buses at 9.15, 10 and 11.27 am and the buses will have Sannae-ri in the front window.

If you can't find one of these buses, then take any bus along the old highway to Taegu and get off at the bus station in Kŏnch'ŏn. These buses are very frequent and the fare to Kŏnch'ŏn is W600. From the bus station in Kŏnch'ŏn, take one of the frequent local buses to Songson-ni Village (about 2½ km, W300).

Where the bus drops you, you'll see a blue and white sign saying 'Songson-ni' and a pedestrian crossing painted across the road. A few metres up from these, a river comes down the valley to your right. Take the gravel road on the far side of this river and continue on until you get to the point at which it crosses the river by a concrete causeway (less than one km). Take the left-hand fork before the causeway and after a few metres you'll see a small temple off to the right. The trail to Pokdu'am bears off to the left at this point and is well marked with Korean characters painted onto rocks. It's impossible to get lost.

Chusa'am 주사암

This hermitage is on the opposite side of the

valley from Pokdu'am and is the oldest in the area. It was founded by monk Uisang some 1300 years ago and has provided a home for several famous monks.

To get to this hermitage, use the same buses to get to Songson-ni as you would for Pokdu'am and take the same gravel road up into the valley, but instead of turning off at the concrete causeway, continue on over it and up the other side of the valley. About halfway between the causeway and Chusa'am, some 200 metres off the main gravel road, is Mankyo'am, the area's third hermitage.

Ura Village 우라마을

Also west of Kyŏngju is the special vegetarian village of Ura. The inhabitants of this village consist of some 30 unmarried women and two or three old men, all of them Christians who eat only raw vegetarian foods such as pine needles, wild herbs, weeds and roots. In summer, they drink a juice made from mountain grasses and in winter, from pine needles. It's possible to visit this village and to sample a meal here if you make prior arrangements. The Hanjin-jang Yŏgwan in Kyŏngju can make arrangements if you get a small group together.

Kyŏngsangnam-do 경상남도

PUSAN 부산

Pusan is the second largest city and principal port of South Korea. Its population stands at around 3½ million and is rising steadily. It was the only major city to escape capture by the Communists during the Korean War, although at the time its population was swelled by an incredible four million refugees.

Pusan has a superb location nestled in between several mountain ridges and peaks, but on the other hand this also makes for a very spread-out city and, away from the subway line, it takes a lot of time to get from one place to another.

Many travellers regard Pusan as a concrete jungle to be got through quickly, or merely as a place from which to take the ferries to Yŏsu, Cheju-do or Shimonoseki (Japan) or for domestic and international flights from Kimhae International Airport. This is a great pity since it has a cosmopolitan ambience all of its own which is quite distinct from Seoul, even though it doesn't have old temples and palaces surrounded by areas of wooded tranquillity right in the heart of the city. It's a city which can grow on you if you're prepared to spend the time exploring it, and if it's wooded tranquillity that you're looking for then there are endless possibilities in the mountains which separate the various parts of the city.

Its distinct ambience is a result of the number of foreign sailors passing through. Unlike other ports, it's a relatively safe place to explore, even at night, and you're in little danger of being robbed. However, the recent establishment of diplomatic relations between South Korea and Russia has brought in a large number of Russian sailors – their reputation for drunkenness and the aggression this sometimes inspires, is well deserved.

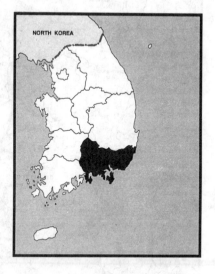

Orientation

The central part of the city is squeezed into a narrow strip of land between a series of mountain peaks and steep slopes and the harbour. The ferry terminals, central business district, CPO, Pusan railway station, and a whole collection of hotels, yŏgwan and yŏinsuk are at the southern end of this strip. Through the centre of this is Pusan's main road, Chung'angno, a broad six to eight-lane boulevard which gets incredibly busy during rush hours. The subway follows this road for much of its course.

The bus terminals, of which there are three in total, are all a long way from this area. The main two of interest to travellers – the express bus terminal and the east inter-city bus terminal – are about 11 km to the north but within easy reach of the subway. The east inter-city bus terminal is right outside Myŏngnyun-dong subway station and the express bus terminal is a 12-minute walk from Tongnae subway station.

Information

Tourist Office Pusan City Tourist Informa-

Kyŏngsangnam-do
경상남도

tion Centre (☎ 462-9734) is in the City Hall. KNTC (☎ 973-1100) has a tourist information kiosk at Kimhae Airport, and the airport has another information centre (☎ 973-2800) run by the city government. There is also an information kiosk outside Pusan railway station (☎ 463-4938) and at the Kukje ferry terminal (☎ 460-3331 ext 5450) where you catch the international Pukwan ferry to Japan.

Foreign Consulates Foreign embassies which are represented in Pusan include:

Japan
    1147-11 Ch'oryang-dong, Tong-gu (☎ 465-5101/5)
Russia
    10th Floor, Korea Exchange Bank, 89-1 Chung'ang-dong 4-ga, Chung-gu (☎ 441-9904)
USA
    American Consulate Bldg, 24 Taech'ŏng-dong 2-ga, Chung-gu (☎ 246-7791)

Airline Offices The main airline offices of interest – Korean Air and JAL – are along Chung'angno between City Hall and Pusan railway station. Asiana Airlines main office is between the two on the road which con-

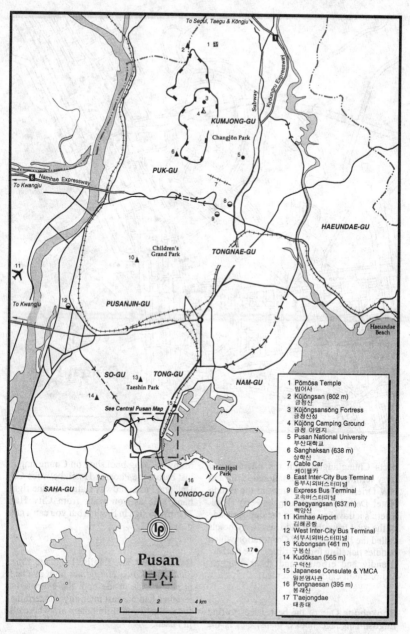

To Seoul, Taegu & Kŏngju

Kyŏngju Expressway

Subway

KUMJONG-GU

Changjŏn Park

PUK-GU

Namhae Expressway
To Kwangju

HAEUNDAE-GU

Children's
Grand Park

TONGNAE-GU

To Kwangju

PUSANJIN-GU

Haeundae
Beach

SO-GU
Taeshin Park

TONG-GU

NAM-GU

See Central Pusan Map

SAHA-GU

Hamjigol
Park

YONGDO-GU

Pusan
부산

0   2   4 km

1	Pŏmŏsa Temple
	범어사
2	Kŭjŏngsan (802 m)
	금정산
3	Kŭjŏngsansŏng Fortress
	금정산성
4	Kŭjŏng Camping Ground
	금정 야영지
5	Pusan National University
	부산대학교
6	Sanghaksan (638 m)
	상학산
7	Cable Car
	케이블카
8	East Inter-City Bus Terminal
	동부시외버스터미널
9	Express Bus Terminal
	고속버스터미널
10	Paegyangsan (637 m)
	백양산
11	Kimhae Airport
	김해공항
12	West Inter-City Bus Terminal
	서부시외버스터미널
13	Kubongsan (461 m)
	구봉산
14	Kudŏksan (565 m)
	구덕산
15	Japanese Consulate & YMCA
	일본영사관
16	Pongnaesan (395 m)
	봉래산
17	T'aejongdae
	태종대

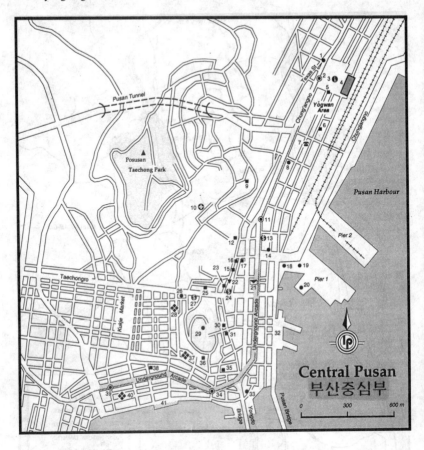

Central Pusan
부산중심부

0   300   600 m

nects Chung'angno with the international ferry terminal. Thai International, SAS and NW Orient have their offices in the Bando Hotel. Delta has its office in the Ferry Hotel. There's a travel agency on the opposite side of the road from the Bando and Ferry hotels called the Jinsung Travel Corporation which handles ticketing for all airlines. The staff are friendly and efficient and speak English. Major credit cards are accepted.

Bookshops One of the best places to find English-language books, maps, etc, is the Munwoo Dang bookshop on Chung'angno, just before the Phoenix Hotel, between City Hall and Pusan railway station, on the right-hand side as you walk from City Hall. There's no sign in English but you can't miss it.

Newspapers The English-language *Korea Times* and *Korea Herald* are both available at newsstands inside both the express bus terminal and the east inter-city bus terminal. It's unlikely you'll find them anywhere else in Pusan.

PLACES TO STAY

5 Arirang Hotel
아리랑호텔

6 Plaza Hotel
프라자호텔

9 Commodore Hotel
코모도호텔

12 Kŭmhwa Yŏgwan
금화여관

15 Ch'ŏnch'o-jang Yŏgwan
천초장여관

16 Ferry Hotel
훼리호텔

17 Bando Hotel
반도호텔

23 Hyundae Yŏinsuk
현대여인숙

25 Sorabol Hotel
서라벌호텔

30 Tower Hotel
타워호텔

31 Pusan Hotel
부산호텔

35 Tongyang Tourist Hotel
동양관광호텔

36 Royal Hotel
로얄호텔

38 Phoenix Hotel
피닉스호텔

PLACES TO EAT

22 Roast Chicken & Duck Restaurant
부로이라

OTHER

1 Foreigners' Arcade
외인전용상가

2 Pusan Subway Station
부산역

3 Tourist Information Kiosk
관광안내소

4 Pusan Railway Station
부산역

7 Telephone Office
전화국

8 Korean Air
대한항공

10 Maryknoll Hospital
메리놀병원

11 Chung'ang-dong Station
중앙동

13 Korea Exchange Bank
외환은행

14 Asiana Airlines
아시아나항공

18 Customs Office
부산세관

19 Immigration Office
출입국관리사무소

20 Kukje Ferry Terminal
연안여객선터미널

21 Central Post Office (CPO)
중앙우체국

24 Korea First Bank
제일은행

26 USIS
미국문화원

27 Bank of Korea
한국은행

28 Yuna Department Store
유나백화점

29 Pusan Tower
부산타위

32 Ferry Terminal
부관훼리터미널

33 City Hall & Tourist Information
시청

34 Namp'o-dong Station
남포동

37 Mihwadang Department Store
미화당백화점

39 Chagalch'i Station
지갈치

40 Shinch'ŏnji Department Store
신천지백화점

41 Chagalch'i Fish Market
자갈치시장

Pusan Tower 부산타위

Finding things to do in Pusan other than going shopping or nightclubbing usually involves stretching your legs and getting a bit out of town, but in the centre it's certainly worth taking the lift to the top of Pusan Tower for the fine views over the city. The return fare in the lift is W1000. Coffee and soft drinks are available at the top but there's no restaurant.

Chagalch'i Fish Market 자갈치시장

Pusan's huge fish market is worth a visit for those who enjoy watching catches unloaded from the boats and the haggling which goes on between the fishermen and the buyers. It's on the harbour front south of the central business district. Get there *early* though! Things quieten down by the time office workers are on their way to work.

Haeundae Beach 해운대해수욕장

Some 14 km north-east of the city centre are Pusan's beach resorts, the main one being Haeundae. Beaches there certainly are, and they're undoubtedly a welcome sight for those who live and work in Pusan, but they get incredibly crowded in summer. Haeundae is regarded as the most popular beach in all of Korea. So popular, in fact, that you'll have to slither through a mass of squirming bodies greased with suntan oil (could be fun) to reach the water. Haeundae Beach is 1.2 km long and is open from late June to early September. All the usual facilities from changing rooms to hot dog vendors are much in evidence.

Buses go direct from Pusan station to Haeundae every 10 minutes. The journey takes 50 minutes and costs W550.

T'aejongdae 태종대

If the Korean Riviera doesn't appeal, try a day out at T'aejongdae on Yongdo just across the bridge from City Hall. Once past the suburbs, it's a very pleasant place with beautiful views out to sea. It's not a national park so there are no entry fees. To get there, take bus No 30 from the city centre which takes about 20 minutes. Avoid taking a taxi because they go through the gate and that will cost you W2000 on top of the taxi fare.

Taeshin Park 대신공원

This park, high up above the city on Kubongsan (north-west of Pusan railway station), offers a complete contrast to the frenetic commercial and industrial activity below. And the views are superb! The park is densely wooded with huge conifers and there are medicinal springs as well. The simplest way to get there is to take a local bus to Dong-A University's Taeshin campus and walk from there. Alternatively, take the subway to Sŏdaeshin-dong subway station and walk from there.

Kŭjŏngsansŏng 금정산성

Pusan's answer to the mountain-top fortresses of Seoul is north-west of the northern suburb of Tongnae, high on the ridges of Kŭmjŏngsan (790 metres) and Sanghaksan mountains. To see it properly, you really need to put aside a whole day though you could combine it with a visit to the Buddhist temple of Pŏmŏsa, a little beyond the northern extremity of the fortress. This impressive walled fortress with four imposing gates in traditional style is the largest in Korea and covers an area of over eight sq km. Construction of the fortress began in 1703 and was not completed until 1807. It's a popular place for weekend picnics and, weather permitting, the views from various points are terrific.

The best way to start a trek around this mountain fortress is to take the subway to Myŏngnyun-dong subway station and either walk to the park entrance from there (about 20 minutes) or take a taxi. As you leave the subway station, if you look straight ahead and a little to your right, you can see the cable car installations on the mountain side ahead. This is where you're heading for. Whether you're taking a taxi or walking, first cross the pedestrian bridge to the other side of the road and stay to the right-hand side of the east inter-city bus terminal. Walkers should then follow this road down to the first junction, bear right and continue on past a large concrete and brick church (on the left hand side) and then take the next left. At the end of this road, turn right in front of a (signposted) three-storey stone pagoda and then take the next left up a fairly steep hill. This road veers to the right and you'll find yourself outside the park entrance gate. Entry to the park costs W250.

At the park entrance there's a Buddhist temple, pavilions, an aquarium, zoo, botanical gardens, folk art exhibition hall, restaurants, a children's playground and the cable car station. Take the cable car to the top. It operates daily every 20 to 30 minutes (depending on demand) from 9 am to 7 pm and costs W1200 (one way) and W1800 (return). For children, the prices are W900 and W1100 respectively. This is an exciting ride with fantastic views which takes you up 540 metres over a total distance of 1260 metres. Once at the top you start walking but if you want a drink or a meal beforehand then there are two restaurants up there. It's also possible to walk here from the bottom but it's a steep climb.

Pŏmŏsa 범어사

This Buddhist temple was founded in 678 by priest Uisang during the reign of King Munmu, one of the greatest of the Shilla rulers. Uisang is revered as one of the greatest of the early Buddhist scholars and spent some 10 years of his life studying in China following his entry into the priesthood. Despite its proximity to Pusan, Pŏmŏsa is a world away from the concrete jungle down at sea level. Surrounded by peaceful, deciduous forest, it is one of the largest temples in Korea – and one of the most beautiful. The Chogyemun Gate, Belfry and Main Hall, in particular, are all sublime examples of Korean Buddhist art and architecture. A visit here on Buddha's birthday is an absolute must!

Much of the original temple was destroyed during the Japanese invasion of 1592 to 1593 but not before priest Sosan had defeated a Japanese army at this very same spot. Nevertheless, quite a few things remain from the Shilla period including pagodas, stone lanterns and pillars. The rest of the temple was reconstructed in 1602 and there were other renovations in 1613 and 1713. Don't miss this place. It is simply incredible.

Getting there is simplicity itself. Take the subway and get off at Pŏmŏsa subway station. From there it's about 2½ km – you can take bus No 90 or a taxi to the temple.

Organised Tours

The Tourist Development Corporation operates a number of bus tours to places of interest around the city and further afield. They're useful if your time is limited. Most of the tours depart from Pusan railway station. They include:

Historical Sites Tour
Buses leave Pusan station daily at 10 am and 2 pm. This is a four-hour trip and costs W2000. It visits Chungyolsa Shrine and the temple of Pŏmŏsa.

Hot Spring Tour
Buses leave Pusan station on weekdays at 10 am and on holidays at 9 am. This is an eight-hour trip and you visit the Pugok Hot Springs. The fare is W8400.

Holiday Tour
Buses leave Pusan station only on holidays between 9 am and noon and visit two temples, T'ongdosa and Naewonsa, north of Pusan.

Places to Stay – bottom end

Accommodation around the two major bus terminals is almost exclusively yŏgwan. Yŏinsuk only seem to be available around the railway station.

There are no yŏinsuk around the bus terminals, but heaps of yŏgwan costing around W16,000 to W18,000. Staying by the east inter-city bus terminal is reasonably convenient because it's near a subway station. Some yŏgwan in this neighbourhood include: *Taedŏk-jang Yŏgwan*, *Misŭng-jang Yŏgwan* (☎ 554-9558), *Arŭm-jang Yŏgwan*, *Ch'owon-jang Yŏgwan*, *Pusan-jang Yŏgwan* (☎ 556-0674) and *Tongon-jang Yŏgwan* (☎ 554-8781).

By the express bus terminal you can find the following yŏgwan: *Samu-jang Yŏgwan*, *Poksŏng-jang Yŏgwan*, *P'yŏnghwa-jang Yŏgwan*, *Kosok-jang Yŏgwan* and *Nakwon-jang Yŏgwan*.

Places to Stay – middle

If you're looking for something with a more Western flavour then there's a good choice of mid-range hotels in the downtown area.

On the south side of Pusan station are the *Arirang Hotel* and *Plaza Hotel*. To the west of City Hall is the *Tongyang Tourist Hotel*. All three of these places offer two-star accommodation with rooms starting at W35,000. Other mid-range places in the centre include:

Bando Hotel: 36 Chung'ang-dong 4-ga, Chung-gu.
Room rates for doubles/twins are W38,962/39,000 (☎ 469-0561; fax 464-0553).

Ferry Hotel: 37-16 Chung'ang-dong 4-ga, Chung-gu.
Three-star accommodation with rooms from
W40,000 (☎ 463-0881).

Tower Hotel: 20 Tonggwang-dong 3-ga, Chung-gu.
Two-star accommodation with doubles from
W30,000 to W34,240, twins W35,200, suites
W60,500 (☎ 241-5151; fax 243-1005).

Places to Stay – top end

Pusan's top hotels are to be found in three
clusters, one around the city centre (Chung-
gu) and another around Chasongdae Park
(Tong-gu) near the Pŏmil-dong subway
station. The third cluster is a long way from
town at Haeundae beach resort. Assume that
most of the hotels mentioned in this section
will accept all major credit cards, that the
staff speak English and Japanese and that all
the usual creature comforts are available.
Also figure on paying an extra 20% tax and
surcharge in these stratified surroundings. In
alphabetical order the top end includes:

Commodore Hotel: 743-80 Yŏngju-dong, Chung-gu.
Five-star accommodation with doubles/twins for
W61,300/70,500 and suites for W113,300 to
W350,000 (☎ 466-9101; fax 462-9101).

Crown Hotel: 830-30 Pŏmil-dong, Tong-gu. Four-star
accommodation with doubles/twins for
W50,600/51,700 and suites for W120,000 to
W200,000 (☎ 635-1241; fax 642-1626).

Phoenix Hotel: 8-1, Namp'o-dong 5-ga, Chung-gu.
Four-star accommodation with twins/suites for
W42,893/100,000 (☎ 245-8061; fax 241-1523).

Pusan Hotel: 12-2, Tonggwang-dong 2-ga, Chung-
gu. Four-star accommodation with
singles/doubles/twins for W33,057/50,710/
52,000 and suites for W77,107 to W181,818
(☎ 241-4301; fax 244-1153).

Royal Hotel: 2-72, Kwangbok-dong 2-ga, Chung-gu.
Four-star accommodation with twins/suites for
W55,00/99,000 (☎ 241-1051; fax 241-1161).

Sorabol Hotel: 37-1 Taech'ŏng-dong 1-ga, Chung-
gu. Five-star accommodation with
singles/doubles/twins for W36,860/63,360/
74,381 and suites for W107,439 to W330,579
(☎ 463-3511; fax 463-3510).

Places to Eat

There are several streets full of restaurants of
various kinds off Chung'angno between the
CPO and the Bando and Ferry hotels. Take
your pick but if you're looking for seafood
make sure you know the price of a meal

before you order. Seafood – particularly if
it's raw – can be very expensive.

At Pusan Tower, try the small fish restaurant on the south side of the tower, halfway
up the steps from the street below. (These
steps take a tortuous route over the roofs of
the buildings which cling to the side of the
hill and they go past a billiard hall).

Travellers in need of a break from endless
plates of kimch'i should head for 'Texas St'
where there are a number of Western-style
fast-food outlets.

If you're looking for a meal at the express
bus terminal, there are cafes inside where
you can eat for W1000 per dish. The east
inter-city bus terminal boasts the largest
McDonald's this side of Seoul.

Entertainment

Most of the bars and cocktail lounges around
the Royal Hotel on the bottom side of the
Pusan Tower cater for Korean businessmen
and are relatively expensive. In many of
them you are obliged to buy a snack (anju)
with your first drink and that can cost you
anything from W5000 to W10,000. For
something more down to earth, head for
Texas St which runs more or less parallel to
Chung'angno from opposite Pusan station.
This is Pusan's answer to Seoul's It'aewon –
an area of music clubs, bars and pick-up
joints that attracts American GIs, Russian
sailors and the odd foreign traveller. It hasn't
got the same range as It'aewon but at least a
few beers won't burn a large hole in your
pocket.

The heavily made-up mini-skirted girls
who hang around outside the clubs might, on
first impressions, suggest the raucous beer-
swilling fleshpots of Thailand or the
Philippines. Once inside, however, such
impressions rapidly evaporate. By comparison with Pattaya and Angeles City, these
clubs are like a vicarage tea party. The music
might be loud but the clients certainly aren't
and the hostesses even less so. And there are
no floor shows. You could bring an evange-
list here without inviting a lecture on hellfire
and damnation and the evils of the flesh!

You'll see very few Koreans in the clubs

of 'Texas St'. They go elsewhere for the pleasures of the flesh and it's a mind-boggling experience to take a look at where they go. Westerners know the area as 'Green St' (and taxi drivers understand that) but Koreans know it as Wanwol-dong. There's perhaps no other more bizarre experience for Westerners in Korea than to visit this area. There are three parallel streets literally lined with brothels. But these are no ordinary brothels. Each has a huge plate-glass window where as many as two dozen women, in traditional Korean costume, sit under intense pink lighting, waiting for a client to choose them. These are not strictly *kisaeng* (the Korean equivalent of the Japanese *geisha*) since real kisaeng would be horrified by such indiscretion. Nevertheless, this is no bawdy Texas St. Everyone is on their best behaviour (after all, they are Koreans) and there's not a Westerner in sight.

Things to Buy

The Foreigners' Arcade at Texas St caters to the non-Korean although. Russian sailors are most enthralled by the place, and you can watch them hauling away everything from fake Reeboks to Mitsubishi refrigerators.

The enormous and rapidly expanding underground arcade between the Chung'ang-dong and Chagalch'i subway stations is like one big fashion parade – row after row of clothing stores.

The Kukje market is Pusan's answer to Namdaemun in Seoul. It's definitely worth a stroll.

Pusan has the usual collection of department stores (with requisite restaurants and superalthoughs in the basements). Some you might want to check out include Mihwadang, Yuna and Shinch'ŏnji.

Getting There & Away

Air Pusan has one of South Korea's three international airports (the other two being in Seoul and Cheju). However, the only two international flights are to Fukuoka and Sendai in Japan.

Despite the dearth of international flights, many foreign airlines have offices in Pusan.

These seem to be clustered on the Bando Hotel. Here you will find representatives for Delta Airlines, Air France, JAL, KLM, THAI Airways and Singapore Airlines.

As for domestic flights, the Seoul-Pusan route is one of Korea's busiest. There are also frequent flights between Pusan and Cheju. A little-used domestic route is the Kwangju-Pusan flight offered by Asiana Airlines.

Bus The express bus terminal (kosok t'ŏminŏl) and the east inter-city bus terminal (tongbu shi'oe t'ŏminŏl) are a long way from the city centre in Tongnae suburb. The east inter-city bus terminal is more convenient, being next to Myŏngnyun-dong subway station. The express bus terminal is about one km from the Tongnae subway station. Tongnae is the first subway station which is above ground going north so you can't miss it, and Myŏngnyun-dong is the next station going north.

If you can find one, local bus No 57 connects the express bus terminal with Tongnae subway station, but you'll probably wind up walking or taking a taxi.

There is one other bus terminal and that is the west inter-city bus terminal (sŏbu shi'oe t'ŏminŏl) in the Puk suburb in the western part of the city, about halfway to Kimhae International Airport. The only time you'd be likely to use this station is if you want to go to small towns and cities to the west of Pusan. Local bus No 15 connects this terminal with the city centre.

It's easy to find the bus you want at the express bus terminal since all the signs are in both Korean and English. This is not the case at the other two terminals, where all the signs are in Korean.

From the express bus terminal, there are buses to the following destinations:

Ch'ŏngju buses depart every 1⅓ hour from 7 am to 6 pm. The fare is W12,000 (1st class) or W8000 (2nd class) and the journey takes 4½ hours.

Chinju: buses depart every 15 minutes from 6 am to 9 pm. The fare is W4400 (1st class) or W3000 (2nd class) and the journey takes 2¼ hours.

Inch'ŏn: buses depart six times daily from 7 am to 5 pm. The fare is W18,500 (1st class) or W12,300 (2nd class) and the journey takes 6½ hours.

Kwangju: buses depart every 20 minutes from 6 am to 6.20 pm. The fare is W10,200 (1st class) or W6800 (2nd class) and the journey takes 4¼ hours.

Kyŏngju: buses depart every 30 minutes from 7 am to 7.30 pm. The fare is W3100 (1st class) or W2000 (2nd class) and the journey takes one hour.

Seoul: buses depart every five to 10 minutes from 6 am to 6.40 pm. The fare is W15,800 (1st class) or W10,600 (2nd class) and the journey takes 5¼ hours.

Sunch'ŏn: buses depart every 40 minutes from 7 am to 7 pm. The fare is W7500 (1st class) or W5000 (2nd class) and the journey takes three hours.

Taegu: buses depart every 15 minutes from 5.40 am to 9 pm. The fare is W5300 (1st class) W3500 (2nd class) and the journey takes 1¾ hours.

Taejŏn: buses depart every 50 minutes from 6 am to 6.30 pm. The fare is W10,700 (1st class) or W7100 (2nd class) and the journey takes 3½ hours.

Yŏsu: buses depart every 50 minutes from 6 am to 6.10 pm. The fare is W8700 (1st class) or W5800 (2nd class) and the journey takes 3½ hours.

Some useful buses departing from the east inter-city bus terminal include the following:

Andong: buses depart eight times daily between 8.30 am and 3.50 pm. The fare is W7700 and the journey takes four hours.

Chinhae: buses depart 15 times daily between 7.24 am and 8.15 pm. The fare is W2500 and the journey takes 1¾ hours.

Chinju: buses depart every 30 minutes between 6.55 am and 8.40 pm. the journey takes two hours.

Ch'unch'ŏn: buses depart every 1¾ hour between 7.40 am and 4 pm. The fare is W16,500 and the journey takes eight hours.

Kangnŭng: buses depart 16 times daily between 7 am and 3.20 pm. The fare is W13,800 and the journey takes six hours.

Kimhae: buses depart every 50 minutes from 6.20 am to 6.20 pm. The fare is W900 and the journey takes 45 minutes.

Kyŏngju: buses depart every 10 minutes between 5.30 am and 9 pm. The fare is W2100 and the journey takes one hour.

Masan: buses depart every nine minutes from 6.20 am to 9.50 pm. The fare is W1800 and the journey takes 50 minutes.

P'ohang: buses depart every 10 minutes between 5.30 am and 9 pm. The fare is W3600 and the journey takes 1¾ hours.

Sokch'o: buses depart eight times daily between 7 am and 2 pm. The fare is W16,700 and the journey takes 7½ hours.

T'aebaek: buses depart once daily at 9.50 am. The fare is W14,200.

Taegu, 11 times daily between 8.10 am and 7 pm. The fare is W3800 and the journey takes 1¾ hours.

Yŏsu: buses depart six times daily between 7 am and 5.35 pm. The fare is W7700 and the journey takes four hours.

Some buses from the west inter-city bus terminal depart for the following destinations:

Chinhae: buses depart every 15 minutes between 6 am and 9.30 pm. The fare is W1900 and the journey takes one hour.

Haeinsa: buses depart once daily at 9.50 am. The journey takes 2½ hours and costs W6000.

Hwaŏmsa: (Chirisan National Park) buses depart once every hour between 6.40 am and 5 pm. The fare is W6800 and the journey takes 3¼ hours.

Masan: buses depart every four minutes between 5.40 am and 10.30 pm. The fare is W1700 and the journey takes 45 minutes.

Ssanggyesa: (Chirisan National Park) buses depart four times daily between 10.35 am and 6.10 pm. The fare is W6100 and the journey takes 2¾ hours.

Train The Seoul-Pusan line is one of Korea's busiest. Departures from Seoul station are outlined in the train timetable at the end of this chapter.

Boat Details of the international ferries from Pusan to Shimonoseki and Pusan to Osaka can be found in the Getting There chapter. Details of ferries between Pusan and Cheju are in the Cheju-do chapter.

Student discounts are available on domestic ferries but the notice to this effect is only in Korean so you have to enquire about this.

The journey between Pusan and Yŏsu via the Hallyŏ Haesang National Park on the *Angel* hydrofoil is a popular trip, but the ferries are completely enclosed by glass windows. There are no open decks and you must occupy a seat, which may face backwards. There's usually no need to book in advance but if you want to be certain then give the company a ring – English is spoken.

There are four offices that you can telephone (☎ (02) 416-8611 Seoul ; ☎ (051) 469-3851 Pusan ; ☎ (0557) 645-3121 Ch'ungmu; ☎ (0662) 63-2191 Yŏsu). The summer-season schedule is outlined in the boxed table.

Getting Around
To/From the Airport There are two airport terminal shuttle buses which connect Kimhae Airport with the city. Bus No 201 runs from the airport terminal to Chung-gu (the city centre) via Kupo, Sasang, Somyon, Pusan station and City Hall. Bus No 307 runs from the airport terminal to Haeundae Beach via Kupo, Mandok, the express bus terminal, Tongnae Hot Springs, Allak Rotary and the Yachting Centre. The fare on either is W600. Both buses leave every 10 minutes from 5 am to midnight. The journey time from the city centre is one hour, but it's only 40 minutes from the express bus terminal. There are also buses directly from the airport to Kyŏngju.

A taxi from the airport to the city centre will cost around W8000. Outside the airport terminal is a large sign indicating (in English) what the current taxi fares are to various points in the city.

Bus Buses which run down Chung'angno as far as City Hall include Nos 26, 34, 42, 55, 127 and 139. The fare is W130 or W120 if you buy a token beforehand.
Buses which run down Chung'angno as far as City Hall include Nos 26, 34, 42, 55, 127 and 139. The fare is W130 or W120 if you buy a token beforehand.

Subway The subway is an excellent way of getting around Pusan although there is only one line which basically follows the main north-south road through the city. It runs from near Kudok Stadium, around the central shopping district of Chung-gu, past Chagalch'i Fish Market and onto Chung'angno. From there it continues on past Pusan railway station, east inter-city bus

---

Ferries Departing From Pusan

Pusan	Sŏngp'o	Ch'ungmu	Saryangdo	Samch'ŏnp'o	Namhae	Yŏsu
7 am	8.20 am	8.40 am	9.10 am	9.35 am	10.10 am	10.40 am
9.10 am	10.30 am	–	–	–	–	–
11.15 am	12.35 am	12.55 am	1.25 pm	1.50 pm	2.15 pm	2.45 pm
1.10 pm	2.30 pm	–	–	–	–	–
3.10 pm	4.30 pm	4.50 pm	5.20 pm	5.45 pm	6.20 pm	6.50 pm
5.10 pm	6.30 pm	–	–	–	–	–

Yŏsu	Namhae	Samch'ŏnp'o	Saryangdo	Ch'ungmu	Sŏngp'o	Pusan
–	–	–	–	7 am	7.20 am	8.40 am
7 am	7.45 am	8.20 am	8.45 am	9.15 am	9.35 am	10.55 am
–	–	–	–	11.05 am	11.25 am	12.45 pm
11.15 am	11.50 am	12.15 pm	12.40 pm	1.10 pm	1.30 pm	2.50 pm
–	–	–	–	3.20 pm	3.40 pm	5 pm
3.10 pm	3.55 pm	4.30 pm	4.55 pm	5.25 pm	5.45 pm	7.05 pm

Ferry Fares

Pusan						
W6720	Sŏngp'o					
W8690	W2020	Ch'ungmu				
W10,580	W4160	W2490	Saryangdo			
W12,310	W6320	W4750	W2290	Samch'ŏnp'o		
W14,500	W8290	W6720	W4350	W2080	Namhae	
W17,120	W11,530	W9950	W7420	W5090	W4220	Yŏsu

Pusan Subway
부산지하철

Nop'o-dong 노포동
Pŏmŏsa 범어사
Namsan-dong 남산동
Tushil 두실
Kusŏ-dong 구서동
Changjŏn-dong 장전동
Pusan University 부산대학교
Onch'ŏnjang 온천장
East Inter-City Bus Terminal — Myŏngnyun-dong 명륜동
Express Bus Terminal — Tongnae 동래
Teachers' College 교육대학
Yŏnsan-dong 연산동
Yŏnje 연제
Yangjŏng 양정
Pujŏn 부전
Sŏmyŏn 서면
Pŏmnaegol 범내골
Pŏmil-dong 범일동
Chwach'ŏn-dong 좌천동
Pusanjin 부산진
Ch'oryang 초량
Pusan Station 부산역
Ferry Terminals & Central — Chung'ang-dong 중앙동
Namp'o-dong 남포동
Fish Market — Chagalch'i 자갈치
T'osŏng-dong 토성동
Tongdaeshin-dong 동대신동
Sŏdaeshin-dong 서대신동

terminal, Pusan National University and ends up in the northern suburb of Kŭmjŏng.

It's a cheap and very convenient way of getting around. All signs are in both Korean and English. Fares depend on the distance travelled – W350 for one sector or W400 for two sectors. There are automatic ticket vending machines at the stations as well as staffed ticket windows.

Car Car enthusiasts can hire vehicles at one of the following agencies in Pusan: Hankuk (☎ 205-3240); Pusan (☎ 469-1100); and Youngnam (☎ 469-5000).

AROUND PUSAN

T'ongdosa 통도사

This Buddhist temple was founded in 646 AD during the reign of Queen Sondok of the Shilla dynasty and is the largest and one of the most famous temples in Korea. Like many other Buddhist temples in Korea such as Pŏpchusa, Kapsa, Pulguksa and Haeinsa, it's situated in beautiful surroundings amid forested mountains and crystal-clear streams. There are some 65 buildings in all, including 13 hermitages scattered over the mountains behind the main temple complex.

The temple's founder, priest Chajang, studied Buddhism for many years in China before returning to Korea and making T'ongdosa the country's foremost temple. He also brought back with him from China what were reputed to be part of the Buddha's ashes. They were enshrined in the elaborate tomb known as the Sokka Sari-tap which is the focal point of T'ongdosa.

There are some exceptionally beautiful buildings here and it's well worth making the effort to stop off here between Pusan and Kyŏngju or vice versa. There are usually some 200 monks in residence here, so it's more than likely that a ceremony or chanting will be going on when you arrive. The temple is traditionally a Zen temple. Entry costs W300.

Getting There & Away There are two ways to get to T'ongdosa. The first way is to take the Pusan-Taegu inter-city (not express) bus from either Pusan or Kyŏngju. Tell the ticket office where you want to go and they'll make sure you get on the right bus, which makes a number of stops at places just off the freeway between Pusan and Kyŏngju including T'ongdo. From where the bus drops you, it's less than one km into T'ongdo Village. You'll probably have to walk this stretch. At the village you have the choice of taking a taxi or walking to the temple. It's about 1½ km from the village and taxis. If you have the time, it's worth walking as the road follows a beautiful mountain stream with many rock carvings along the way.

There's also a direct bus to T'ongdo Village from the east inter-city bus terminal in Pusan. This way means you won't have to walk from the freeway to T'ongdo Village. There are regular buses from the village to both Pusan and Ulsan. If you don't want to carry your pack to the temple you can leave it at the bus terminal.

Naewonsa 내원사
South-east of T'ongdosa on the opposite side of the freeway is Naewonsa, another temple complex. There is a nunnery here with some 50 Buddhist nuns and one priest. You can get to Naewon by bus from T'ongdo Village, followed by a walk along a very picturesque mountain stream. Swimming is possible in the stream in summertime.

Getting There & Away There are direct buses from the east inter-city bus terminal in Pusan to Naewonsa every hour from 7 am to 7 pm. The journey takes about one hour.

KAJISAN PROVINCIAL PARK
가지산도립공원
Residents of Pusan and Kyŏngju looking for a change of pace often head up to this park which is known for it's rocky terrain. Kajisan itself is a respectable 1240 metres in elevation and presents a moderately challenging hike.

Soknamsa is the park's main temple and the point where the bus drops you off is where most hikers start from. A good 20-km walk (around 12 hours) would be from Soknamsa to Kajisan, returning via Oksan, Taebisa (another temple) and Unmunsan.

Admission to the park costs W600.

Getting There & Away
From Pusan's east inter-city bus terminal, there is just one bus daily to Soknamsa. It departs at 3.15 pm and takes just over one hour.

Buses are much more frequent from Ulsan. These depart seven times daily between 9 am and 4.30 pm. Tickets cost W1170 and the journey takes just over one hour.

CHINJU 진주
Chinju is a relatively small city on the Namhae Expressway and is one possible base from which to explore the eastern side of Chirisan National Park. Kurye, however, is a more convenient base for the western side which is where the famous temples are sited (see the Chŏllanam-do chapter).

Chinju spans both sides of the large Nam River, which is dammed upstream at the confluence with the Dokchon River. It's a pleasant city with a history going back to the time of the Three Kingdoms period. There's quite a large, partially forested hillock overlooking the river where most of the historical relics and sites of the city are to be found.

Information
The Chinju Culture & Tourism Centre (☎ 42-6456) is at the entrance of the pavilion at Ch'oksŏknu.

Chinju Fortress 진주성
The most interesting part of Chinju is the hillock which is actually the remains of Chinju Fortress. This was once a walled fortress, built during the Koryŏ dynasty, but it was partially destroyed during the Japanese invasion of 1592 to 1593. One of the major Korean-Japanese battles was fought here in which some 70,000 Korean soldiers and civilians lost their lives. The wall was rebuilt in 1605 by the provincial commander in chief, Lee Su-ill, and it's the remains of this which you see today.

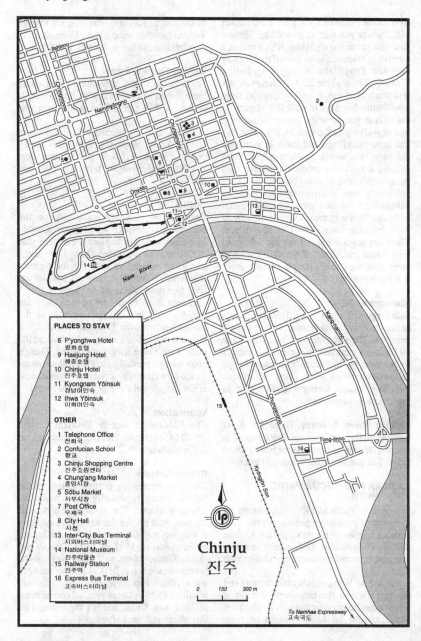

PLACES TO STAY

6 P'yonghwa Hotel
평화호텔
9 Haejung Hotel
해중호텔
10 Chinju Hotel
진주호텔
11 Kyongnam Yŏinsuk
경남여인숙
12 Ihwa Yŏinsuk
이화여인숙

OTHER

1 Telephone Office
전화국
2 Confucian School
향교
3 Chinju Shopping Centre
진주쇼핑센타
4 Chung'ang Market
중앙시장
5 Sŏbu Market
서부시장
6 Post Office
우체국
8 City Hall
시청
13 Inter-City Bus Terminal
시외버스터미널
14 National Museum
진주박물관
15 Railway Station
진주역
16 Express Bus Terminal
고속버스터미널

Nammyŏngno

Ch'ŏngamno

Chungangno

Ilshinno

Ünyŏllo

Nam River

Kaengnamno

Chungangno

Kyŏngŏn Sŏn

Tong-jinno

Chinju
진주

0   150   300 m

To Namhae Expressway
고속국도

Inside the walls are several places of interest as well as a number of traditional gateways and shrines.

Ch'oksŏngnu 촉석루

Overlooking the river is Ch'oksŏngnu, a large pavilion which was first built in 1368 during the Koryŏ dynasty and used as an exhibition hall for the poems of famous scholars and civil officials. Despite having survived the turbulent years of the Japanese invasion, it was finally burnt down during the Korean War. Various efforts were made to repair it after that event but it has now been completely rebuilt in the original style.

Also worth noting are the impressive gates to the fortress including Sojangdae, Pukchangdae and Yongsam Pojongsa. The latter served as the front gate for the Kyŏngnam provincial government during the days of the Yi dynasty when its headquarters were inside the fortress.

National Museum 진주박물관

Also inside the fortress is the Chinju National Museum, a modern structure in traditional style. The museum specialises in artefacts from the Kaya period although it also has many objects dating from the time of the Japanese invasion in 1592. It's open every day except Monday. Entry costs W110.

Confucian School 향교

Just outside the city on the hillside to the east is the Confucian School. This was founded in 987 during the reign of the Koryŏ king, Songjong, as a local school. Scholars of the Chinese classics and medicine lectured there. The school is open to the public.

Chinyangho 진양호

About five km west of Chinju is the huge Namgang Dam which was constructed from 1962 to 1969. The dam wall is 21-metres high and one km long.

On the northern side of the dam there is a recreational and resort area known as Chinyangho (Chinyang Lake). There are lookout platforms, hotels, coffee shops and restaurants. You can hire motor boats and launches.

To get there from Chinju, take local bus No 16 from the centre (Unyolno). The fare is W300.

Places to Stay

One of the cheapest places to stay, and excellent value, is the *Kyongnam Yŏinsuk*. The building is new and very clean. Both single and double rooms cost W4000 and there are cold-water showers. Similar is the *Ee-hwa Yŏinsuk* which has rooms for W4000 single or double, and triples for W5000. It's also very clean and the rooms have fans but there's no hot water.

If you'd prefer your own bathroom then try the *Songjukjang Yŏgwan*, which costs W9000 for a single or double.

Getting There & Away

Air Small as it is, Chinju boasts an airport. There are flights to Chinju from Seoul on both Asiana Airlines and Korean Air. There is also a Cheju-Chinju flight with Korean Air.

Bus Both the railway station and the express bus terminal are in the section of the city south of the Nam River, about 1½ km from the centre. Take local bus No 15 if you don't want to walk.

Buses depart from the express bus terminal to the following destinations:

Kwangju: buses depart every two hours from 7 am to 7 pm. The fare is W6400 (1st class) or W4300 (2nd class) and the journey takes 2¾ hours.
Pusan: buses depart every 15 minutes from 6 am to 9 pm. The fare is W4400 (1st class) or W3000 (2nd class) and the journey takes 1¾ hours.
Seoul: buses depart every 30 minutes from 6.30 am to 6 pm. The fare is W15,400 (1st class) or W10,300 (2nd class) and the journey takes five hours.
Taegu: buses depart every 40 minutes from 6.40 am to 7 pm. The fare is W5600 (1st class) or W3700 (2nd class) and the journey takes 2¼ hours.

The inter-city bus terminal is close to the centre on the northern side of the river. Buses depart from this terminal to the following destinations:

Haeinsa: buses depart every hour from 6.40 am to 5.30 pm. The fare is W3630 and the journey takes 2½ hours.

Kwangju: buses depart five times daily from 9 am and 6.30 pm. The fare is W3740 and the journey takes 2¾ hours.

Okch'ŏnsa: (Yŏnhwasan Provincial Park) buses depart once hourly between 7.40 am and 8.40 pm. The fare is W1070 and the journey takes 1½ hours.

Pusan: buses depart every 10 minutes from 5.50 am to 9.10 pm. The fare is W2590 and the journey takes 1½ hours.

Seoul: buses depart only twice daily at 8 am and 8.40 am. The fare is W9000.

Songnisan: buses depart twice daily at 9.10 am and 10.48 am.

Ssanggyesa: buses depart once hourly from 7.31 am and 4.15 pm. The fare is W2710 and the journey takes 2½ hours.

Taegu: buses depart every 30 minutes from 6.30 am and 7.40 pm. The fare is W3240 and the journey takes two hours.

Taejŏn: buses depart 10 times daily between 7.40 am and 5.40 pm. The fare is W7130 and the journey takes 4½ hours.

Taewonsa: buses depart every 40 minutes from 7.15 am to 9 pm. The fare is W1600 and the journey takes 1¼ hours.

Yŏsu: buses depart twice daily at 7 am and 1.50 pm. The fare is W3760 and the journey takes 2½ hours.

Train A railway snakes its way between Kwangju and Pusan, and another line offers a more direct route to Seoul. Direct trains from Seoul to Chinju run according to the schedule in the train timetable section at the end of this chapter.

Getting Around
To/From the Airport Local buses to the airport cost W540 and take 40 minutes to make the journey. Faster seat buses cost W800 and take only 20 minutes. A taxi costs W8000.

YŎNHWASAN PROVINCIAL PARK
연화산도립공원

This small park, south-east of Chinju, offers pleasant scenery and is home to one moderate-sized temple, Okch'ŏnsa. There are also

three hermitages, Paeknyon'am, Ch'ongnyon'am and Yondae'am.

There are two hiking courses which can take you to the summit of Yŏnhwasan (477 metres). One course starts from Yesong-ni, goes to Okch'onsa, Songgogae Pass and Odoro. This route is 4.2 km and requires about two hours of walking.

A variation on the theme is to start from Yesong-ni, then to the hermitage at Paeknyon'am, Okch'ŏnsa and finally the summit of Yŏnhwasan. This walk is 4.7 km and takes about 2½ hours.

Admission to Yŏnhwasan Provincial Park costs W200.

Access to the park is by inter-city bus from Chinju. Buses depart Chinju inter-city bus terminal for Okch'ŏnsa once hourly between 7.40 am and 8.40 pm. The journey takes 1½ hours and costs W1070.

CHIRISAN NATIONAL PARK
지리산국립공원

Straddling the border of three provinces is Chirisan National Park, which offers some of Korea's best hiking opportunities. The park is also noted for the variety of flora and fauna .

Mountaineers are delighted with the place. Chirisan is honeycombed with well-maintained trails which take you up to the ridge, forming the backbone of the park. There are many peaks over 1500 metres high including South Korea's second highest mountain – Ch'onwangbong at 1915 metres.

There are seven shelters with dormitory accommodation along the saddle of the mountain ridge which forms the backbone of the park. You need to bring your own bedding, food and tea/coffee although there is a limited range of canned and packaged foods for sale at inflated prices. All the shelters have access to spring water.

If you're going to do some trekking in this park, get hold of a copy of the National Parks Authority's leaflet, *Chirisan National Park (KSN)*, which has a map of the area indicating the road-heads, trails, camp sites, shelters, temples and other points of interest. It's sufficiently accurate for most people's purposes; if you intend to get off the marked trails you'll need one or more of the topographical maps produced by the national cartography service. These are available from Chung'ang Atlas Map Service in Seoul.

There are three principal areas of the park, each with its own temple. Two of the three temples lie in Kyŏngsangnam-do, Ssanggyesa and Taewonsa. Another temple, Hwaŏmsa, is approachable from Kurye in Chŏllanam-do Province (see the Chŏllanam-do chapter for details).

Taewonsa 대원사

At the extreme eastern end of Chirisan National Park is Taewonsa, which is the most accessible part of the park from Chinju.

The Taewonsa entrance to the park offers the most direct route for the assault on Ch'onwangbong, Chirisan's highest peak. The lower part of the route follows a stream decorated with boulders, pools and small waterfalls, the largest of which is Mujaech'igi.

Entry to Taewonsa costs W600 for adults.

Places to Stay Camping offers the cheapest option. Second cheapest are minbak, and one place in this league is *Sakkun Minbak* (☎ 72-1212) where rooms start at W10,000.

Yonhwa Yŏgwan (☎ 72-9054) offers rooms for W13,000. Nearby is the plusher *Kwonhu-jang Yŏgwan* (☎ 72-9036), where doubles cost W16,000.

Getting There & Away Buses from Chinju to Taewonsa run every 40 minutes between 7.15 am and 9 pm. The journey takes 1¼ hours and cost W1600.

Ssanggyesa 쌍계사

In the south-eastern part of the park is Ssanggyesa, one of the principal temples of the Chogye Order of Korean Buddhism. The temple was originally built in 722 AD to enshrine a portrait of monk Yukcho which two Shilla monks brought back with them from China. The temple was originally named Okch'ŏnsa but received its present name from Chonggang-wang around 886

AD in tribute to the Zen monk, Chingam-sonsa, who enlarged the temple in 840 AD after he returned from studying in China. Chingam-sonsa was also responsible for establishing the tea plantations on the slopes of Chirisan using seeds which he brought back from China. The temple has been renovated several times by a number of prominent monks and there are several national treasures listed here.

This temple has a sublime setting amid steep forested hillsides and is entered by a series of massive gateways housing the various guardians of the temple. A crystal-clear rocky stream, spanned by a bridge divides the compound into two halves, and if you follow the path which crosses this stream further up into the mountain it will take you to the waterfall of Pulil-pokpo. It's about two km from Ssanggyesa to the falls.

Entry to the temple costs W1200 (less for those under 24 years old).

Places to Stay & Eat Buses to Ssanggyesa terminate in a small village on the opposite side of the main river from the temple, so to get to the temple you first have to cross the river bridge. There are restaurants, souvenir shops and minbak both in the village where the buses stop and alongside the sealed road which leads to the temple beyond the ticket office, plus one yŏgwan. Expect to pay around W10,000 for a room at a minbak. You can camp either in the village where the buses stop (thus avoiding repeated entry fees) or alongside the stream below the temple compound.

Getting There & Away There are buses from Chinju to Ssanggyesa once hourly between 7.31 am and 4.15 pm. The fare is W2710 and the journey takes 2½ hours.

From Yŏsu, there are direct buses to Ssanggyesa four times daily between 7.30 am and 2.25 pm. The fare is W3900 and the journey takes 2¼ hours.

From Pusan's west inter-city bus terminal, there are buses to Ssanggyesa four times daily between 10.35 am and 6.10 pm. The fare is W6100 and the journey takes 2¾ hours.

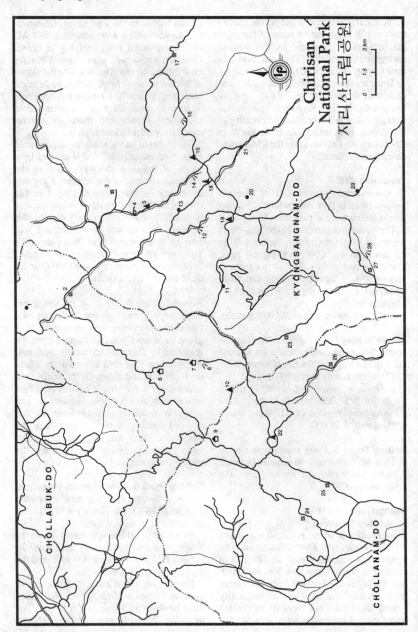

Chirisan
National Park
지리산국립공원

0   1.5   3 km

CHŎLLABUK-DO

CHŎLLANAM-DO

KYŎNGSANGNAM-DO

1	Paekjam'am Hermitage 백장암	16	Mujaech'igi Waterfall 무재치기 폭포
2	Shilsangsa Temple 실상사	17	Taewonsa Temple 대원사
3	Pyŏksongsa Temple 벽송사	18	Chesŏktan Shrine 제석단
4	Ch'ilsŏn Spring 칠선약수	19	Yŏngshinbong (1651 m) 영신봉
5	Sŏnnyŏt'ang Hill 선녀탕	20	Sesŏkp'yongjŏn Field 세석평전
6	T'akyongso Shelter 탁용소	21	K'albawi Boulder 칼바위
7	Pyŏngp'ungso Shelter 병풍소	22	Nogodan Shrine 노고단
8	Tanshim Waterfall 단심 폭포	23	Ch'ilbulsa Temple 칠불사
9	Yongso Shelter 용소	24	Ch'ŏnŭnsa Temple 천은사
10	Panyabong (1751 m) 반야봉	25	Hwaŏmsa Temple 화엄사
11	Pyŏksoryŏng Crag 벽소령	26	Yŏngoksa Temple 연곡사
12	Kanaeso Waterfall 가내소 폭포	27	Ssanggyesa Temple 쌍계사
13	Hadongpawi Boulder 하동바위	28	Pulil-pokpo Waterfall 불일 폭포
14	Tŭngsŏn Waterfall 등선 폭포	29	Ch'ŏnghakdong (Old Village) 청학동 도인촌
15	Ch'onwangbong (1915 m) 천왕봉		

There are buses direct from Kurye (in Chŏllanam-do Province) to Ssanggyesa approximately nine times daily from 8.15 am to 6.10 pm. The fare is W730 and the journey takes 35 minutes. There are similar local buses direct to Ssanggyesa from Hadong to the south-east.

Trains from Seoul to Pusan

Class	Time	Frequency	Travel Time	Fare
Saemaul	8 am-11.20 pm	14 daily	4¼ hours	W21,500
Mugunghwa	7.30 am-11.55 pm	25 daily	5 hours	W11,000
T'ongil	6.10 am-10.30 pm	11 daily	5¼ hours	W7600

Trains from Seoul to Chinju

Class	Time	Frequency	Travel Time	Fare
Mugunghwa	8.45 am, 10 pm	2 daily	6 hr 15 min	W12,300
T'ongil	12.30 pm, 11.50 am	2 daily	6 hr 40 min	W8400

Chŏllanam-do 전라남도

KURYE 구례

Kurye is probably the best gateway to Chirisan National Park – at least for the southern part of the park. It's a small town, south of the western end of the park, and connected to Kwangju, Yŏsu and Chinju by frequent buses. There's also a railway station with connections from Chŏnju and Sunch'ŏn but the railway station is some seven km south of the town. In Kurye, there's a good selection of yŏinsuk, yŏgwan, restaurants and shops where supplies can be obtained.

Getting There & Away

Not surprisingly, Kurye has only one bus terminal. Buses depart from Kurye to the following places:

Hwaŏmsa: (Chirisan National Park) buses depart every 20 minutes from 8 am to 8 pm. The fare is W310 and the ride takes about 15 minutes.

Kwangju: buses depart every 20 minutes from 6.30 am to 8.10 pm. The fare is W2500 and the journey takes 1½ hours.

Pusan: buses depart every 30 minutes from 7 am to 6.40 pm. The fare is W5630 and the journey takes 3½ hours.

Seoul: buses depart twice daily at 10 am and 4.10 pm. The fare is W9250 and the journey takes four hours.

Sanggyesa: (Chirisan National Park) buses depart nine times daily between 6.15 am and 6.10 pm. The fare is W730 and the ride takes 35 minutes.

Yŏsu: buses depart 30 times daily between 5.40 am and 8 pm. The fare is W2640 and the journey takes two hours.

HWAŎMSA 화엄사

One of the three famous temples in Chirisan National Park and certainly one of the oldest, Hwaŏmsa was founded by priest Yongi in 544 AD after his return from China and is dedicated to the Virochana Buddha. The temple has suffered five major devastations including the Japanese invasion of 1592 but, luckily, not everything was destroyed in those various cataclysms. It was last rebuilt in 1636.

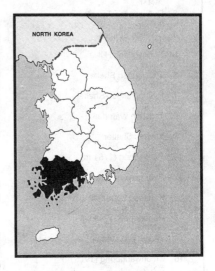

The most famous structure surviving from the old days is a unique three-storey pagoda supported by four stone lions as well as Korea's oldest and largest stone lantern. The huge two-storey Kakwang-jon Hall, whose wooden pillars tower nearly 49 metres, was once surrounded by stone tablets of the Tripitaka Sutra (made during the Shilla era) but these were destroyed during the Japanese invasion. Many of the pieces have since been collected and are preserved at the museum.

Entry to Hwaŏmsa costs W950 (less for students and those under 24 years old).

The tourist village below the temple has the usual collection of souvenir shops, restaurants, minbak and yŏgwan plus you can camp if you have your own tent.

Getting There & Away

Most likely, you will get to Hwaŏmsa from Kurye. However, there are also direct buses from Sunch'ŏn to Hwaŏmsa three times daily between 10.35 am and 4.25 pm. From

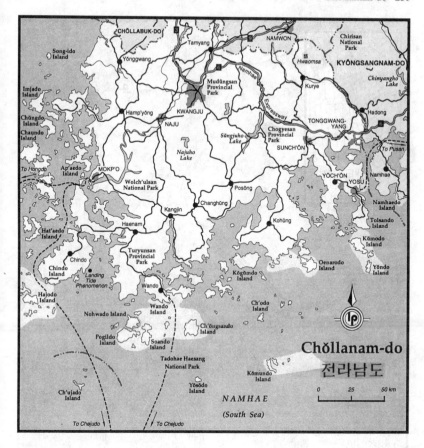

Chŏllanam-do
전라남도

NAMHAE
(South Sea)

Pusan's west inter-city bus terminal, there are buses to Hwaŏmsa once hourly between 6.40 am and 5 pm.

YŎSU 여수

Yŏsu lies about halfway along the mountainous and deeply indented southern coastline of Korea. It's a spectacularly beautiful area peppered with islands and peninsulas. A large part of the area between Yŏsu and Pusan now makes up the Hallyŏ Haesang National Park. One of the most popular trips in this part of the country is to take the hydrofoil from Yŏsu to Pusan (or vice versa) via Namhae, Samch'ŏnp'o, Ch'ungmun and Sŏngp'o.

Orientation

Due to the mountainous terrain of the peninsula where Yŏsu is located, the city is divided into a number of distinct parts, although the centre essentially consists of the area between the railway station and the passenger ship terminal. The bus terminal is a long way from the centre (about 3½ km) along the road to Sunch'ŏn so you'll need to take a local bus or taxi between the two. The airport is even further out but a shuttle bus

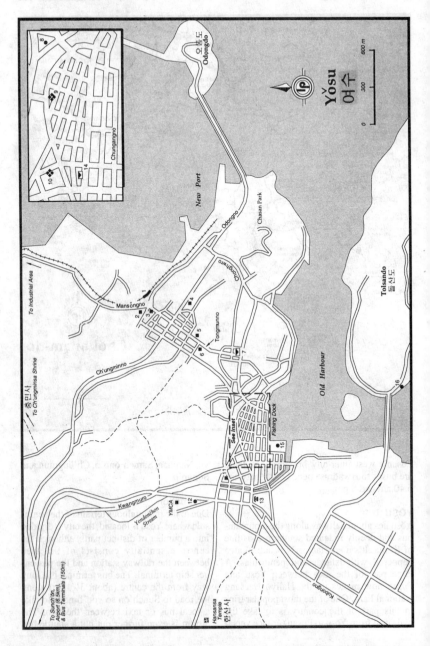

오동도
Odongdo

New Port

Chasan Park

Yŏsu 여수

Odongno

Chŏngho

Tolsando
돌산도

Mansŏngno

Ch'ungminno

Tongmunno

Old Harbour

흥민사
To Ch'ungminsa Shrine

See Inset

Fishing Dock

Kwangmuro

YMCA

Yŏndŏnch'ŏn
Stream

Hansansa
Temple
한산사

Kŭbongno

To Sunch'ŏn,
Airport (6.5km)
& Bus Terminals (150m)

Chungangno

PLACES TO STAY

2 Osŏng & Taedong Yŏinsuks
오성여인숙. 대동여인숙

3 Kungsil-jang &
Kwangsŏng-jang Yŏgwans
궁실장여관. 광성장여관

4 Yŏsu Hotel
여수호텔

5 Sejong Hotel
세종관광호텔

6 Yŏsu Park Hotel
여수파크호텔

11 Yŏsu Beach Hotel
여수비치호텔

OTHER

1 Railway Station
여수역

7 Yŏsu Post Office
여수우체국

8 Chinnamgwan Pavilion
지남관

9 Samoa Department Store
사모아백화점

10 Citizens Department Store
시민백화점

12 Korean Air
대한항공 매표소

13 Telephone Company
전화국

14 Kyodong Post Office
교동우체국

15 Ferry Terminal
여객선터미널

16 Turtle Ship
거북선

operates into the centre whenever there are flights. The fare is W600.

The Korean Air office is about halfway between the city centre and the bus station.

There are *no* lockers available at either the bus terminal or the railway station. This is a real drag if you just want to stop off at Yŏsu for a few hours and explore.

Chinnamgwan 지남관
In the centre of town stands the huge Chinnamgwan, one of the longest pavilions in Korea. It's a beautiful old building with massive poles and beams, which was originally constructed for receiving officials and holding ceremonies and later used as military quarters.

In the summer months it's used a lot by the old men of the town as a place to gather and talk and perhaps throw down a bottle of soju. They're a friendly bunch and will probably draw you into conversation since very few Westerners ever visit Yŏsu.

Entry to the pavilion costs W200.

Ch'ungminsa 충민사
High up on the hill which overlooks the area between City Hall and the railway station is the Ch'ungminsa Shrine dedicated to Admiral Yi. It was built in 1601 by another naval commander, Yi Si-ŏn, although it has been renovated since then. There are excellent views over Yŏsu and the harbour area but it's a steep climb.

Odongdo 오동도
Another popular spot in Yŏsu is Odongdo, an island which is linked to the mainland by a 730-metre-long causeway. It's a craggy, tree-and-bamboo-covered island with a lighthouse and picnic spots and is crisscrossed with walking trails. The best time to see the island is in spring when it's covered with camellia blossoms. Entry costs W400 – Odongdo is actually part of the Hallyŏ Haesang National Park. Local bus Nos 1 and 2 will take you here from the centre of town. The fare is W250.

A restaurant complex has been built on the island and the speciality is seafood but you can forget about eating here as meals are outrageously priced at W30,000!

One of the most enjoyable things to do here is to take the tourist launch around the island. The launches are berthed halfway along the causeway and drop you off next to the restaurant complex. The trip costs W1000 and the launches leave any time there are sufficient passengers.

Admiral Yi's Turtle Ship 거북선
Yŏsu's historical claim to fame is in connection with Admiral Yi, who routed the Japanese navy on several occasions during the 16th century. On display in Yŏsu is a

full-size recreation of one of the admiral's famous iron-clad war vessels, known as turtle ships (kŏbuksŏn).

The ship can be found on the island of Tolsando, which is south of town and connected to the mainland by an enormous suspension bridge. From the bridge you can see dozens of souvenir stalls, or maybe even the ship itself – it's moored in the water and you can go inside.

Hansansa 한산사

If you're up to a more substantial trek there is the Hansansa, a temple high up on the wooded mountain slopes to the west of Yŏsu. The temple was built in 1194 by a high priest named Bojo during the reign of the Koryŏ king, Myŏngjong.

The trail up to the temple is well marked and the views are superb. The best view of all is not from the temple itself, however, but from a point five-minutes walk away.

To get there, take the trail through the woods to the right of the temple as you face it and descend onto a small platform where the local people do their washing. Then turn left up through an area dotted surrealistically with gym equipment and posters telling you how to do push-ups, and on to the highest point – a grassy cliff-top. The views are practically 180°. At the laundry trough you may be lucky enough to come across a shamanistic performance.

Mansŏng-ni Beach 만성리해수욕장

Mansŏng-ni Beach is almost unique in Korea because of its black sand. The black sand soaks up the sun's summer rays and gets quite hot, and Koreans are fond of burying themselves up to the neck and letting themselves cook – this is supposed to relieve all those aches and pains. Whether or not you wish to bake yourself in a sand cast, the beach is about 300 metres long and fine for swimming. Mansŏng-ni is three km north of Yŏsu and can be reached by frequent city buses which run between 5.40 am and 8.30 pm and cost W250.

Places to Stay – bottom end

The majority of yŏgwan and yŏinsuk are clustered along the road which connects the harbour front to the railway station. The cheapest places near the railway station are the *Osŏng Yŏinsuk* and *Taedong Yŏinsuk*. Also near the railway station, but decidedly higher priced, are the *Kungsil-jang Yŏgwan* and *Kwangsŏng-jang Yŏgwan*.

There are three relatively upmarket yŏgwan near the bus station are the *Ŭnsu-jang Yŏgwan*, *Po'ŭn-jang Yŏgwan* and *Tŏkwon-jang Yŏgwan*.

Places to Stay – middle

The places in this price category charge 20% tax and surcharge additional to the room rate.

Yŏsu Beach Hotel (☎ 63-2011; fax 63-1625) is on the west side of town and not on the beach at all. Nonetheless, it's still a nice place to stay. Doubles/twins/suites cost W41,818/46,281/84,298.

The *Sejong Hotel* (☎ 62-6111; fax 62-1929) is a somewhat older place about ½ km south-west of the railway station. Doubles/twins/suites cost W37,190/ 44,630/79,340.

Almost directly opposite the Sejong Hotel is the *Yŏsu Park Hotel* (☎ 63-2334; fax 63-2338). Doubles/twins/suites cost W22,700/ 26,400/56,300.

The *Yŏsu Hotel* (☎ 62-3131; fax 62-3491) is another two-star hotel near the railway station. Room prices for twins are W30,000 to W48,000 and suites cost W60,000.

Places to Eat

There's a good range of restaurants of various categories in the central business district with the cheaper ones being closest to the old fishing dock. If you're looking for seafood, there are three restaurants on the right-hand side between the traffic roundabout and the dock front, but only one of them offers meals at a reasonable price – W3000 to W4000 for fried fish and the usual trimmings. The other two quote ridiculous prices, although they do specialise in raw seafood.

Getting There & Away

Air There are direct flights between Yŏsu and Seoul, and also Yŏsu and Cheju.

Bus The express and inter-city bus terminals are next to each other on the western side of the city on the road out to Sunch'ŏn and the airport.

The only buses departing from the express bus terminal go to Seoul. These depart once hourly from 6.40 am to 5.40 pm and take almost six hours. The fare is W16,200 (1st class) or W10,800 (2nd class).

Buses departing from the inter-city bus terminal include the following:

Chinju: buses depart three times daily between 8.10 am and 6.50 pm. The fare is W4400 and the journey takes 2¼ hours.

Chŏnju: buses depart six times daily between 7 am and 6.15 pm. The fare is W6900 and the journey takes 3¾ hours.

Hwaŏmsa: buses depart five times daily between 7.25 am and 3.07 pm. The fare is W3300 and the journey takes 2/1¼ hours.

Kwangju: buses depart 25 times daily between 6.10 am and 8.40 pm. The fare is W4500 and the journey takes about two hours.

Mokp'o: buses depart 16 times daily between 5.50 am and 6.10 pm. The fare is W7200 and the journey takes 3¾ hours.

Pusan: buses depart 18 times daily between 6 am and 10.40 pm. The fare is W16,200 (1st class) or W5700 (2nd class) and the journey takes 3½ hours.

Seoul: buses depart 20 times daily between 5.40 am and 7 pm. The fare is W10,800 (1st class) or W8700 (2nd class) and the journey takes 5½ hours.

Ssanggyesa: (Chirisan National Park) buses depart four times daily between 7.30 am and 2.25 pm. The fare is W3900 and the journey takes 2¼ hours.

Taegu: buses depart six times daily between 7.25 am and 5.25 pm. The fare is W7900 and the journey takes five hours.

Taejŏn: buses depart twice daily at 8.20 am and 1.55 pm. The fare is W9400 and the journey takes five hours.

Train You can get to Yŏsu by train from Kwangju, Pusan or Seoul. Departures from Seoul station to Yŏsu are nine times daily. Refer to the schedule in the train timetable section at the end of this chapter.

Boat All boats into and out of Yŏsu dock at the large passenger ship terminal at the western end of the old fishing dock. You can get boats here to many of the islands off the south coast and to the east of Yŏsu. There are no ferries to Chejudo from here.

The main ferry of interest to travellers is the *Angel* hydrofoil to Pusan via Namhae, Samch'ŏnp'o, Saryangdo, Ch'ungmu and Sŏngp'o. It isn't necessary to book in advance, except during the holiday season (July and August). The schedule for the hydrofoil is in the Pusan section.

Getting Around

To/From the Airport If you arrive by air, the airport is about seven km north of town on the way to Sunch'ŏn. The airport is served by local buses and there's no need to take a taxi – simply walk the few metres from the terminal buildings to the road and wait for a bus which will have the destination in the front window. The fare is W300 on a standing bus (W600 on a seat bus) and the journey to the express bus terminal takes about 40 minutes.

A taxi between the airport and Yŏsu will cost around W10,000.

Bus The express and inter-city bus terminals are far to the north of town. City bus Nos 3, 5, 6, 7, 8, 9, 10, 11, 13 and 17 go past the two bus terminals but probably the most useful is bus No 11 which connects the bus terminals with the railway station via the centre of town.

SUNCH'ŎN 순천

Sunch'ŏn is a pleasant city to the north of Yŏju, but for travellers it's mainly a base for exploring Chogyesan Provincial Park.

Chuktobong Park 죽도봉공원

On the east side of the Tongch'on River is Chuktobong Park. As in Chinju, Sunch'ŏn has its cherry blossom festival sometime in April when the trees cooperate, and if you happen to be here at that time then check out Chuktobong Park. The park has the requisite observation tower, although

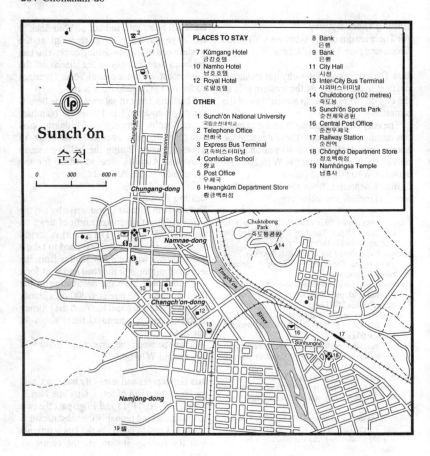

Sunch'ŏn
순천

0   300   600 m

Chungang-dong

Namnae-dong

Chuktobong
Park
죽도봉공원

Changch'on-dong

Tongch'on
River

Sunhungno

Namjŏng-dong

PLACES TO STAY

7	Kŭmgang Hotel 금강호텔
10	Namho Hotel 남호호텔
12	Royal Hotel 로얄호텔

OTHER

1	Sunch'ŏn National University 국립순천대학교
2	Telephone Office 전화국
3	Express Bus Terminal 고속버스터미널
4	Confucian School 향교
5	Post Office 우체국
6	Hwangkŭm Department Store 황금백화점
8	Bank 은행
9	Bank 은행
11	City Hall 시청
13	Inter-City Bus Terminal 시외버스터미널
14	Chuktobong (102 metres) 죽도봉
15	Sunch'ŏn Sports Park 순천체육공원
16	Central Post Office 순천우체국
17	Railway Station 순천역
18	Chŏngho Department Store 정호백화점
19	Namhŭngsa Temple 남흥사

it isn't likely to provide serious competition to Seoul Tower or Pusan Tower. The archery range looks like it would be fun, but it's for members only.

Confucian School 향교

On the west side of town is the Confucian School. The school was founded in 1407, but moved several times before reopening at its present location in 1801. As elsewhere in Korea, Sunch'ŏn's Confucian School became a shrine after the government examination system was abolished in 1894.

Places to Stay

Yŏinsuks around the railway station are reasonably plush – some rooms for W10,000 even come with private bath. There are not nearly so many yŏinsuks near the bus terminal. Most inter-city buses make a stop near the railway station, so it might be wise to get off there if you want to look for cheap accommodation. Otherwise, you'll have to take a city bus or taxi to commute between the inter-city bus terminal and the railway station.

More upmarket accommodation can be found at the *Kŭmgang Hotel* (☎ (0661) 52-

8301; fax 52-9193). Doubles here cost W52,030, twins W56,870 to W60,500 and suites W75,020, plus 20% for tax and surcharges.

The other fancy place in town is the *Royal Hotel* (☎ 741-7000; fax 741-7180) with twins for W42,975 to W47,934 and suites for W61,983 to W231,405, plus 20%.

Getting There & Away

Air Sunch'ŏn shares an airport with neighbouring Yŏsu. There are direct flights between Sunch'ŏn-Yŏsu and Seoul, and also Sunch'ŏn-Yŏsu and Cheju.

Bus There are two bus stations in town, and express bus terminal and inter-city bus terminal. Buses departing from the express bus terminal go to the following cities:

Pusan: buses depart every 30 minutes from 7.20 am to 7.10 pm. The fare is W7500 (1st class) or W5000 (2nd class) and the journey takes three hours.
Seoul: buses depart every 45 minutes from 6.30 am to 6 pm. The fare is W15,000 (1st class) or W10,000 (2nd class) and the journey takes 5¼ hours.
Taegu: buses depart seven times daily between 7.30 am and 6 pm. The fare is W8400 (1st class) or W5600 (2nd class) and the journey takes 3½ hours.

Some useful buses departing from the inter-city bus terminal go to the following destinations:

Chindo: buses depart six times daily between 10.42 am and 3.42 pm. The fare is W6700 and the journey takes 3¾ hours.
Chinju: buses depart every 30 minutes from 7 am to 7.40 pm. The fare is W2800 and the journey takes 1½ hours.
Chŏnju: buses depart once hourly from 7.45 am to 7 pm. The fare is W5400 and the journey takes three hours.
Hwaŏmsa: (Chirisan National Park) buses depart three times daily between 10.35 am and 4.25 pm. The fare is W1800 and the journey takes 1½ hours.
Kurye: (Chirisan National Park) buses depart once hourly from 6.05 am to 8.10 pm. The fare is W1600 and the journey takes one hour.

Kwangju: buses depart every 15 minutes from 6.30 am to 9.40 pm. The fare is W3200 and the journey takes 1½ hours.
Mokp'o: buses depart every 1⅓ hours from 6.40 am to 7.05 pm. The fare is W5700 and the journey takes 2¾ hours.
Pusan: buses depart every 20 minutes from 9.30 am to 7 pm. The fare is W5000 and the journey takes three hours.
Songgwangsa: (Chogyesan Provincial Park) buses depart every 40 minutes from 6.50 am to 6.35 pm. The fare is W1600 and the journey takes 1¼ hours.
Sŏnamsa: (Chogyesan National Park) buses depart three times daily between 9.35 am and 4.45 pm. The fare is W1100 and the journey takes 30 minutes.
Ssanggyesa: (Chirisan National Park) buses depart six times daily between 7.25 am and 3.10 pm. The fare is W2400 and the journey takes two hours.
Taegu: buses depart 15 times daily between 7 am and 7.10 pm. The fare is W6400 and the journey takes four hours.
Taejŏn: buses depart three times daily between 9.15 am and 2.45 pm. The fare is W7900 and the journey takes 4½ hours.
Wando: buses depart nine times daily between 7.34 am and 6.35 pm. The fare is W6000 and the journey takes 3½ hours.
Yŏsu: buses depart every 10 minutes from 6.30 am to 10.30 pm. The fare is W1500 and the journey takes 50 minutes.

Train Trains to Sunch'ŏn depart from Seoul station according to the schedule in the train timetable section at the end of this chapter.

CHOGYESAN PROVINCIAL PARK
조계산도립공원

This provincial park is somewhat special. The largest faction by far of Korean Buddhists is the Chogye sect. Songgwangsa, located in this park, is the main temple of the Chogye faction, and it's one of the top five temples in Korea. On the other side of the mountain is another temple, Sŏnamsa. There is a spectacular hike over Chogyesan (884 metres), the peak which separates the two temples. The walk takes six hours if you go over the peak, or four hours if you go around it. Either route is fantastic.

There is an entry fee of W800 for Songgwangsa, or W700 for Sŏnamsa.

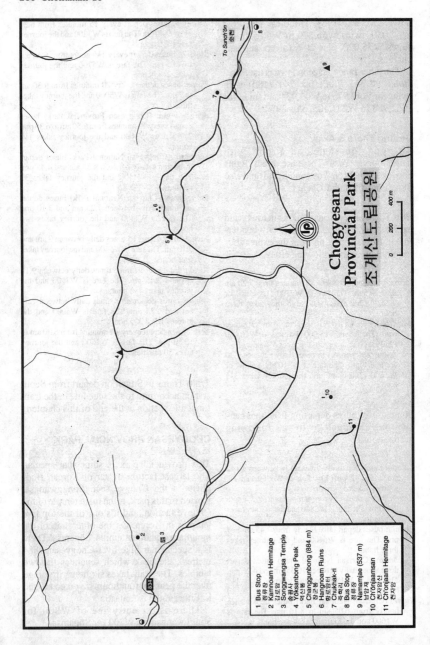

Chogyesan
Provincial Park
조계산도립공원

To Sunch'ŏn 순천

0   200   400 m

1   Bus Stop
    정류장
2   Kamnoam Hermitage
    감로암
3   Songgwangsa Temple
    송광사
4   Yoksŏnbong Peak
    역선봉
5   Changgunbong (884 m)
    장군봉
6   Hangnoam Ruins
    학노암터
7   Chukhak-ri
    죽학리
8   Bus Stop
    정류장
9   Namamjae (537 m)
    남암재
10 Ch'ŏnjaamsan
    천자암산
11 Ch'ŏnjaam Hermitage
    천자암

Places to Stay

Yŏgwan at Songgwangsa charge a fairly standard price of W16,000 for doubles. Some of the yŏgwan available here include the *Chogyesan-jang* (☎ 53-2130), *Kŭmgang* (☎ 53-2063) and *Songgwang* (☎ 53-2122).

At Sŏnamsa, the going rate for doubles is W15,000. Some good yŏgwan here are the *Chowon-jang* (☎ 54-5811), *Hyondaesan-jang* (☎ 54-9102), *Kwankwang-jang* (☎ 54-6350), *Namilgak* (☎ 54-6188), *New Chogyesan-jang* (☎ 51-9121) and *Sonamgak* (☎ 54-6029).

Getting There & Away

From Kwangju there are buses to Songgwangsa nine times daily between 8.45 am and 9 pm taking 1½ hours for the journey. From Kwangju there are also buses to Sŏnamsa once daily at 7.50 am.

From Sunch'ŏn there are buses to Songgwangsa every 40 minutes from 6.50 am to 6.35 pm, taking 1¼ hours for the journey. From Sunch'ŏn there are also buses to Sŏnamsa three times daily between 9.35 am and 4.45 pm, taking 30 minutes for the journey.

KWANGJU 광주

Though Kwangju has been the provincial capital of Chŏllanam-do for centuries and is the fifth largest city in Korea, there is precious little left of its traditional heritage. This is a sprawling all-modern concrete and glass city with few redeeming features, so it's not surprising that most travellers give it a miss or, at the most, spend a night en route to somewhere else.

In recent times it has acquired a reputation for its student and industrial worker radicalism. All this has its roots in the 'Kwangju massacre' of 1980. A series of events in that year (described in the History section in the Facts about the Country chapter) led to large scale student protests against the government.

On 18 May 1980, the military moved into Kwangju – the soldiers had no bullets, but they used bayonets to murder dozens of protesters. Outraged local residents broke into armories and police stations, and used the seized weapons and ammunition to drive the military forces out of the city. The city of Kwangju enjoyed nine days of complete freedom before the brutal military response came. On 27 May, soldiers armed with loaded M16 rifles retook the city, and most leaders of the protests were summarily shot. The total civilian death toll has been estimated at around 200, with over 1000 injured and thousands more arrested.

Democracy has now arrived in South Korea and there have been demands (mostly from students) to put those military figures responsible for the massacre on trial. This seems unlikely to happen since the chief culprit was former President Chun Doo-Hwan who ruled South Korea more or less as a dictator for about eight years. Chun voluntarily relinquished power in 1988, but part of the package deal to get him out of office was a promise not to prosecute him for past misdeeds. Thus, the students have a permanent hopeless cause over which to protest.

Hopeless or not, neither the protesters nor the soldiers show any lack of enthusiasm. Kwangju-massacre commemorative riots are held annually in the central area of the city on 18 May, and these often continue for two or three days. In order to avoid a repeat of the massacre, the soldiers are no longer permitted to carry guns or bayonets, but there are plenty of clubs, riot shields and tear gas. The students do their bit with steel bars, rocks, bottles and firebombs. The protests tend to be near the railway station, and by sheer coincidence one of our Lonely Planet writers arrived in time to walk right into it! He describes the tear gas as 'worse than kimch'i' – if you plan to visit Kwangju, 18 May is probably not the best time to do it.

Information

The Kwangju Tourist Association (☎ 224-3702) has a branch in Kwangju Airport.

Kwangju National Museum
국립광주박물관

Just about the only sight worth (just barely) seeing is the National Museum. It was built

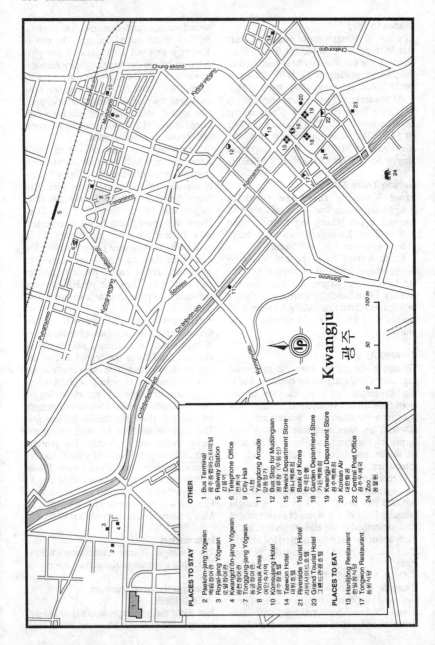

Chung-akono

Chebongno

Kyŏng-yangno

Mudŭngno

Tongnimno

Kŭmnamno

Sŏmuno

Sorimno

Chŏngbyŏn-uro

Punruuno

Kyŏng-yangno

Taebongno

Chŏnbyŏnchŏngno

Kyŏngsangno

Kwangju
광주

0   50   100 m

PLACES TO STAY

2 Paekkim-jang Yŏgwan
  백림장여관
3 Royal-jang Yŏgwan
  로얄장여관
4 Kwangch'ŏn-jang Yŏgwan
  광천장여관
7 Tonggung-jang Yŏgwan
  동궁장여관
8 Yŏinsuk Area
  여인숙지역
10 Kŭmsujang Hotel
  금수장호텔
14 Taere Hotel
  대레호텔
21 Riverside Tourist Hotel
  리버사이드호텔
23 Grand Tourist Hotel
  그랜드관광호텔

PLACES TO EAT

13 Hanijŏng Restaurant
  한일정식당
17 Tongwon Restaurant
  동원식당

OTHER

1 Bus Terminal
  광주종합버스터미널
5 Railway Station
  강불역
6 Telephone Office
  전화국
9 City Hall
  시청
11 Yangdong Arcade
  양동 상가
12 Bus Stop for Mudŭngsan
  무등산 버스정류장
15 Hwani Department Store
  하나백화점
16 Bank of Korea
  한국은행
19 Garden Department Store
  가든백화점
20 Kwangju Department Store
  광주백화점
22 Central Post Office
  광주우체국
24 Zoo
  동물원

mainly to house the contents of a Chinese Yuan dynasty junk which sank off the coast some 600 years ago and was only rediscovered in 1976. Exhibits include celadon vases, cups and apothecaries' mortars and pestles, almost all of them in perfect condition. The rest of the museum is taken up by 11th to 14th-century Buddhist relics, scroll paintings from the Yi dynasty and white porcelain.

The museum is open daily, except Mondays, from 9 am to 5 pm (winter) and 9 am to 6 pm (summer).

The museum is to the far north of the city centre, and north of the Honam Expressway. City buses (W250) run from the railway station to the museum every 10 minutes, taking about 15 minutes for the journey. The other alternative is to go by taxi (if you can get one) which would cost around W2500. Entry to the museum costs W200.

Mudŭngsan Provincial Park
무등산도립공원

Overlooking Kwangju is Mudŭngsan Provincial Park, the summit of which reaches 1187 metres. At the base of the mountains is a resort area and, further up the slopes is Chungshimsa, a Buddhist temple surrounded by a tea plantation. This plantation, established initially by a famous Yi dynasty artist at the end of the 19th century, is famous for its green tea and there are two nearby processing factories. Another temple in the park is Wonhyosa and there is also Yaksa'am, a small Buddhist hermitage.

Although it's not one of Korea's spectacular parks, Mudŭngsan's thick forests offer a splendid display of colours during autumn. There are plenty of streams through the forest and it's popular hiking country.

There is a cafe about one km into the park from the entrance which sells soft drinks and snacks. This is your last chance to stock up on rations before you head for the upper slopes.

To get to the entrance of the park, take local bus No 18 from the inter-city bus terminal (or from the bus stop on Chebongno).

The bus costs W300 and takes about 40 minutes.

Tamyang Bamboo Crafts Museum
담양대나무박물관

North of Kwangju is the obscure town of Tamyang, otherwise unremarkable except for its Bamboo Crafts Museum. The Koreans claim that this is the first museum dedicated solely to the art of bamboo craftwork. Including the basement, the museum contains three floors and also harbours the requisite souvenir shop.

The Bamboo Crafts Museum (☎ 757-0086) is open from 9 am to 6 pm.

Buses to Tamyang run from Kwangju every 10 minutes between 5.30 am and 10.45 pm. The journey takes 30 minutes and tickets cost W770.

Places to Stay – bottom end

The bus terminal recently moved way out to the west of town, which is inconvenient in terms of finding yŏgwan. Currently there are three yŏgwan to the north-east of the bus terminal.

The cheapest in this neighbourhood is the *Paekrim-jang Yŏgwan* (☎ 363-0356) which costs W17,000. The two others are the *Royal-jang Yŏgwan* (☎ 369-9600) and *Kwangch'ŏn-jang Yŏgwan* (☎ 362-2350) which both charge W20,000. No doubt more yŏgwan will be built in this area in the near future.

The alleys opposite the railway station have cheap yŏinsuk plus a number of yŏgwan. In this area you can find the relatively plush *Tonggung-jang Yŏgwan* (☎ 524-7314) which costs W18,000.

Places to Stay – middle & top-end

As always, figure on an additional 20% tax and surcharge at mid-range and top-end places. The *Taewon Hotel* in the centre has rooms starting at W35,000. Other places in the central area include:

Grand Hotel: 121 Pullo-dong, Tong-gu. Doubles/twins/suites cost W41,040/50,661/89,000 to W250,000 (☎ 224-6111; fax 224-8933).

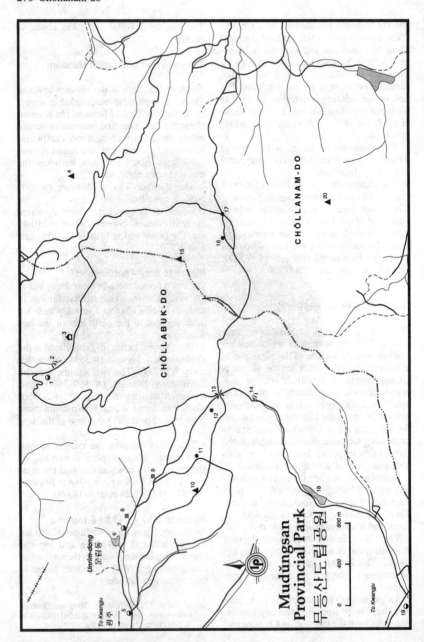

CHŎLLANAM-DO

CHŎLLABUK-DO

Unrim-dong
운림동

To Kwangju
광주

To Kwangju

Mudŭngsan
Provincial Park
무등산도립공원

0   400   800 m

1	Bus Stop	정류장
2	Seshim Waterfall	세심폭포
3	Mudŭng Hut	무등산장
4	Puksan	북산
5	Bus Stop	정류장
6	No 1 Reservoir	제1저수지
7	Bus Stop	정류장
8	Munbinjŏngsa Temple	문빈정사
9	Chungshimsa Temple	중심사
10	Saeinbong Peak	새인봉
11	Yaksaam Hermitage	약사암
12	Shelter	대피소
13	Chungmŏrijae Pass	중머리재
14	Yongch'u Waterfall	용추폭포
15	Chŏnwangbong (1187 m)	천왕봉
16	Sŏkbulam Hermitage	석불암
17	Kyubongam Hermitage	규봉암
18	No 2 Reservoir	제2저수지
19	Bus Stop	정류장
20	Anyangsan (853 m)	안양산

Koreana Tourist Hotel: 120-9, Shinan-dong (one block from the railway station). Doubles/twins/suites cost W63,500/73,000/120,000 (☎ 526-8600; fax 526-8666).

Palace Hotel: 11-4, Hwanggum-dong, Tong-gu. Doubles/twins/suites cost W49,421/51,240/100,000 to W124,000(☎ 222-2525; fax 224-9723).

Riverside Tourist Hotel: 72-1, Honam-dong, Tong-gu. Doubles/twins cost W36,860/43,800 to W63,640 and suites cost W107,440 (☎ 223-9111; fax 223-9112).

On the eastern outskirts of Kwangju and about halfway up Mudŭngsan is the city's best hotel, the *Shinyang Park Hotel* (☎ 228-8000; fax 232-3731), 40, Chisan-dong, Tong-gu. This is a four-star hotel with doubles/twins/suites for W49,590/63,640/115,700.

Places to Eat

Here again, Kwangju disappoints. While fine food undoubtedly exists, the railway station and bus station areas (where most travellers will be staying) are nearly devoid of decent places to eat. For a Korean city, this is odd indeed.

In the central area, some better places to eat include the *Haniljŏng Restaurant* and *Tongwon Restaurant*.

Getting There & Away

Air There are Kwangju-Seoul and Kwangju-Cheju flights on both Asiana Airlines and Korean Air. Asiana Airlines also operates a flight between Kwangju and Pusan.

Bus Kwangju is unique amongst large Korean cities in that it has only one bus terminal. The terminal is out in the west end of town, and city bus Nos 7, 9, 13, 17, 36 and 101 connect the bus terminal with the railway station area. The bus station has an information window with staff who can do marvellous things like book air tickets!

Unfortunately, you are likely to need a lot of help from the folks at the information window when you try to buy a ticket. Kwangju may well be the first place where you encounter the extremely annoying ticket machines. Rather than buying tickets from people, you've got to first feed W1000 notes into a machine and then press buttons (which are all in Korean) for your destination. You'll first need to determine the price of your ticket, make sure you have sufficient W1000 notes (which you get from another window), only to find that half the notes are rejected because maybe they have a few creases or dirt on them. The whole procedure is complicated, time-consuming and error-prone, and most foreigners cannot deal with it unless a local Korean provides assistance. Considering all the rioting Kwangju has experienced over past political issues, it's a wonder these ticket machines haven't inspired a full-scale insurrection.

Assuming you can deal with the ticket machines (no mean feat), you can get a bus from Kwangju to the following places:

Ch'ŏngju: express buses depart eight times daily between 6 am and 7 pm. The fare is W7900 (1st class) or W5300 (2nd class) and the journey takes 2¾ hours.

Chindo: buses depart every 40 minutes from 5.10 am to 7.45 pm. The fare is W6000 and the journey takes three hours.

Chinju: express buses depart every two hours from 7 am to 7 pm. The fare is W6400 (1st class) or W4300 (2nd class) and the journey takes 2½ hours.

Chŏngju: buses depart every 15 minutes from 5.55 am to 9.30 pm. The fare is W1900 and the journey takes one hour.

Chŏnju: express buses depart every 20 minutes from 6.30 am and 8.30 pm. The fare is W4100 (1st class) or W2700 (2nd class) and the journey takes 1½ hours.

Haenam: (for Turyunsan Provincial Park) buses depart every 20 minutes from 5 am to 9.30 pm, taking 1¾ hours for the journey and costing W3900.

Kurye: (transfer point for Hwaŏmsa & Chirisan National Park) buses depart every 20 minutes from 6.15 am to 8.10 pm. The fare is W2900 and the ride takes 1½ hours.

Kyŏngju: express buses depart only twice daily at 9.40 am and 3.40 pm. The fare is W10,800 (1st class) or W7200 (2nd class) and the journey takes 5¼ hours.

Mokp'o: buses depart every 10 minutes between 5.20 am and 10 pm. The fare is W3000 and the journey takes 1¾ hours.

Paegyangsa: (Naejangsan National Park) buses depart every 50 minutes from 6.15 am to 7.50 pm. The fare is W1700 and the journey takes one hour.

Pusan: express buses depart every 20 minutes from 6 am to 6.20 pm. The fare is W10,200 (1st class) or W6800 (2nd class) and the journey takes 4¼ hours.

Seoul: express buses depart every five to 10 minutes from 6.30 am to 6 pm. The fare is W12,000 (1st class) or W8000 (2nd class) and the journey takes about four hours.

Songgwangsa: (Chogyesan Provincial Park) buses depart nine times daily between 8.45 am and 9 pm. The fare is W2650 and the journey takes 1½ hours.

Ssanggyesa: (Chirisan National Park) buses depart twice daily at 6.50 am and 2.10 pm. The fare is W3800 and the journey takes two hours.

Taegu: express buses depart every 30 minutes from 6.30 am to 6.30 pm. The fare is W8400 (1st class) or W5600 (2nd class) and the journey takes 3¾ hours.

Taejŏn: express buses depart every 20 to 30 minutes from 6 am to 8 pm. The fare is W7200 (1st class) or W4800 (2nd class) and the journey takes 2¾ hours.

Tamyang: (Bamboo Museum) buses depart every 10 minutes between 5.30 am and 10.45 pm. The fare is W900 and the ride takes 30 minutes.

Tong-Seoul: express buses depart every 30 minutes from 6 am to 7.30 pm. The fare is W12,400 (1st class) or W8300 (2nd class) and the journey takes about four hours.

Wando: buses depart every 30 minutes from 4.50 am to 7.45 pm. The fare is W5600 and the journey takes 2¾ hours.

Yŏsu: buses depart every 15 minutes between 5.30 am and 9 pm. The fare is W4500 and the journey takes 2½ hours.

Train Trains depart Seoul station for Kwangju according to the schedule in the train timetable section at the end of this chapter.

Getting Around
To/From the Airport Local buses from the railway station area and bus terminal cost W300 and take 40 minutes to reach the airport. Seat buses cost W600 and take 30 minutes. A taxi between the airport and the centre cost around W5500.

Car Cars can be hired from Kumkang Rent-A-Car (☎ 371-4400).

MOKP'O 목포
The fishing port of Mokp'o is at the end of the railway line near the south-western tip of mainland Korea. Mokp'o is the departure point for some of the cheapest ferries to Chejudo (the other place being Wando further south) and for the ferries to the islands west of Mokp'o, the most interesting of which is Hongdo.

The town is of little interest and most travellers only stay overnight. If you have some time to spare it's worth wandering

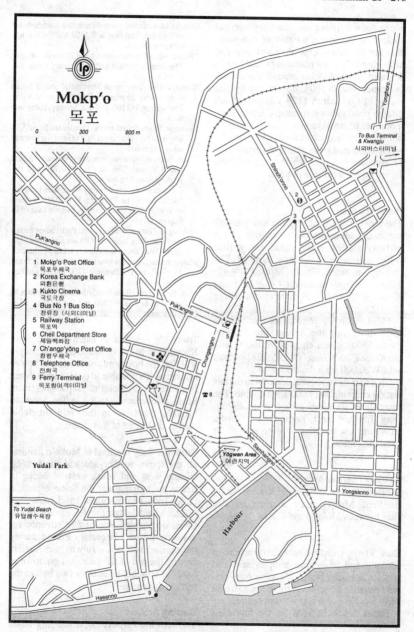

Mokp'o
목포

0   300   600 m

*To Bus Terminal
& Kwangju*
시외버스터미널

1 Mokp'o Post Office
  목포우체국
2 Korea Exchange Bank
  외환은행
3 Kukto Cinema
  국도극장
4 Bus No 1 Bus Stop
  정류장 (시외디미널)
5 Railway Station
  목포역
6 Cheil Department Store
  제일백화점
7 Ch'angp'yŏng Post Office
  창평우체국
8 Telephone Office
  전화국
9 Ferry Terminal
  목포항어객터미널

Puk'angno

Puk'angno

Shinch'ŏnno

Chungangno

Yonghŏro

Yŏgwan Area
여관지역

Samhangno

Yongsanno

Yudal Park

To Yudal Beach
유달해수욕장

Harbour

Haeanno

along the waterfront near the ferry terminal to see the incredible number of octopuses that are for sale – kept alive writhing and slithering in aerated plastic tubs and bowls. It's also worth walking around Yudal Park (entrance fee W500), dominated by the rocky hill Yudalsan (229 metres) which affords good views and sunsets. Up here are a number of small temples, pavilions and a botanical garden, all of them connected by well-maintained trails. Along the south side of Yudalsan is a road which leads to Yudal Beach on the west side of town.

Places to Stay

The most convenient yŏgwan and yŏinsuk are in the streets on the south side of the railway station since these are within walking distance of the ferry terminal. The line-up includes *Wando Yŏinsuk* (☎ 42-8105), *Oddugi Yŏinsuk* (☎ 44-9411) and *Kwangju Yŏinsuk* – all three places charge W10,000.

More expensive yŏgwan are also ubiquitous including the *Sŏhae-jang Yŏgwan* (☎ 43-5300) which charges W18,000, and the *Kukje P'ak'ŭ Hotel* (☎ 245-2281) which asks W20,000 for a double.

There are three yŏgwan adjacent to the bus station charging W17,000 for a double. The three places are *Kŏbuk-jang Yŏgwan*, *Porim-jang Yŏgwan* and *Yurim-jang Yŏgwan*. However, few travellers wish to stay so far from the centre.

Getting There & Away

Air Both Asiana Airlines and Korean Air fly the Seoul-Mokp'o route. Korean Air also flies between Mokp'o and Cheju.

Bus There's only one bus terminal in Mokp'o and it services both express and regular inter-city buses. It's some considerable distance from the centre of town so take local bus No 1 or a taxi into the centre.

Buses depart Mokp'o for the following places:

Chindo: buses depart every 40 minutes from 6.40 am to 7.10 pm. The fare is W4300 and the journey takes two hours.

Chŏnju: buses depart hourly from 8.10 am to 5.45 pm. The fare is W5900 and the journey takes 3½ hours.

Haenam: (for Turyunsan Provincial Park) buses depart every 20 minutes from 6.40 am to 8 pm. The fare is W2100 and the journey takes one hour.

Kwangju: buses depart every 15 minutes from 5.15 am to 10 pm. The fare is W3000 and the journey takes 1½ hours.

Pusan: buses depart nine times daily between 7.50 am and 3.30 pm. The fare is W10,700 and the journey takes 6½ hours.

Seoul: express buses depart every 30 minutes between 6 am and 6.30 pm. The fare is W14,200 (1st class) or W9500 (2nd class) and the journey takes 5¼ hours.

Taehŭngsa: (Turyunsan Provincial Park) buses depart six times daily between 8.40 am and 4 pm. The fare is W2500 and the journey takes 1½ hours.

Wando: buses depart six times daily between 7.55 am and 5.40 pm. The fare is W4200 and the journey takes 2¼ hours.

Yŏsu: buses depart once hourly from 6.15 am to 6.50 pm. The fare is W7200 and the journey takes 3½ hours.

Train It's possible to catch a train from Kwangju to Mokp'o, although most people will find the bus more convenient. If you're in a hurry, it's possible to catch a train direct from Seoul to Mokp'o. Departures from Seoul station are detailed in the Seoul to Mokp'o timetable in the train timetable section at the end of this chapter.

Boat The ferry terminal at Mokp'o handles all the ferries to Chejudo and the smaller islands west and south-west of Mokp'o. Inside the terminal are the ticket offices, a coffee shop, pharmacy and snack bars.

The schedule for the ferries are in the Cheju-do chapter. Booking in advance for these ferries isn't necessary except during the summer holidays – July to mid-August. During the rest of the year, just go down to the boat terminal an hour or two before the ferry is due to sail.

Getting Around

To/From the Airport Local standing buses

to the airport cost W780 and take nearly an hour. Much better are the airport buses for W1000. A taxi costs around W12,000 and takes 20 minutes.

TADOHAE HAESANG NATIONAL PARK
다도해해상국립공원

Consisting of more than 1700 islands and islets, Tadohae Haesang (archipelago marine) National Park occupies the southwest corner of the Korean peninsula. Of course, many of the islets are little more than rocks which appear above the surf occasionally, but others are large enough to support small communities of people who earn their living from fishing and catering to summer tourists.

There are scores of local ferries from Mokp'o to the larger of these small islands. The most popular islands with Korean tourists are Hongdo and Hŭksando. Indeed, Hongdo is so popular with holidaymakers during July and August that it's often difficult to get on a ferry and equally difficult finding accommodation if you want to stay on the island overnight. During July your only option to get a night's sleep might be camping.

These are not the only islands you can visit, of course, but if you're planning a trip around the less well known of them then you really need a copy of the national bus, boat, rail and flight timetables booklet (*Shigakp'yo*) already mentioned in the Getting Around chapter. Armed with this booklet (and the coloured maps which it contains detailing boat connections) it's possible to work out a route and an approximate schedule although you'll need help with translation as the timetables are entirely in a mixture of Korean and Chinese (though mostly Korean). There are a series of maps in the booklet detailing the boat connections. There's no better way of getting off the main tourist circuits than by visiting some of these islands.

Hongdo 홍도

This is the most popular and beautiful of the islands west of Mokp'o. It's comparable with Ullŭngdo, off the east coast, in that it rises precipitously from the sea and is bounded by sheer cliffs, bizarre rock formations, and wooded hillsides cut by steep ravines. There are also many islets which surround the main island, and sunsets are spectacular on clear days. Where it differs from Ullŭngdo is that it is much smaller, being only some six km long, and the main land mass rises to only a third of the height of its eastern cousin. That doesn't make it any the less interesting but the only way you can see the island properly is by boat as there are no shoreline roads or paths. The island is designated as a nature reserve and there is an admission fee of W1100.

Ferries to Hongdo land at Il-gu, the larger and more southerly of the island's two villages which is where the minbak, yŏgwan and telephone office are situated. It's also the only village where electricity is available, thanks to a small generator. Like I-gu, its smaller neighbour to the north, there's a tiny cove which provides shelter to fishing boats. The two villages are connected by a footpath which follows the high ground and walking between the two places will take you about one hour.

Places to Stay There's a good choice of minbak, yŏinsuk and yŏgwan in Il-gu at the usual prices (except during the summer holiday period when prices can double). One simply calls itself the *Hongdo Island Minbak* (☎ 74-3761), and charges begin at W10,000 in the summer season. You can expect to pay W15,000 to W20,000 for a double in a yŏgwan during summer, but sometimes more.

Getting There & Away Hongdo is 115 km west of Mokp'o, and there are two ferries making the Mokp'o-Hongdo run during summer. To find out the current departure times, you can phone the ferry company in Mokp'o (☎ 44-9915).

The fast boat is the *Namhae Star*, which takes 3½ hours to make the one-way journey. In the summer months there are three departures daily between the hours of 7.50 am and 2 pm. The fare is W16,850.

The slow ferry takes 5½ hours to make the journey. It runs just once daily, departing Mokp'o at 9 am. The fare is W5450.

Expect the schedule to be cut back somewhat in the winter season.

Hŭksando 흑산도

Hŭksando is a small group of islands to the east of Hongdo, the largest of which is called Taehŭksando (great Hŭksando). It's larger and more populated than Hongdo, and is reminiscent of Chejudo in that numerous stones litter the island. These have been used to create fields enclosed with dry-stone walls. Attached to rope, these stones are also used to hold down thatch roofs in windy weather.

There are several villages on Hŭksando and, since the island doesn't rise anywhere near as steeply from the sea as Hongdo, farming is possible on the coastal fringes. The villages are connected by trails and you can walk around the island in a day, assuming you make an early start.

The largest village, Ye-ri, has an excellent harbour and was formerly a whaling centre. It's also where the ferries from the mainland land and where most of the island's accommodation is to be found. There's a sizeable fishing fleet which moors here. The other village is Chin-ni.

Places to Stay & Eat Unlike on Hongdo, you shouldn't have any problems finding accommodation on this island even during the summer holiday period. Ye-ri has a good selection of minbak for around W10,000. One is run by the *Fisheries Cooperative* (☎ 75-9253). You can also try the *Taedo Yŏinsuk* and the *Yusong Yŏinsuk* which are close to each other opposite the train (there's no railway on the island but an engine, coal tender and passenger car have been set up here as a kind of children's playground).

In Chin-ni there are at least two minbak: the *Chin-ni 1-gu* (☎ 75-9229) and *Chin-ni 2-gu* (☎ 75-9414).

With a substantial fishing fleet, you might

expect that cheap seafood is available on Hŭksando but, as elsewhere in Korea, this isn't necessarily the case. Be sure to ask the price of a meal before you order because it can be very expensive.

Getting There & Away All the ferries from Mokp'o to Hongdo call at Hŭksando so you can use any of them to get to this island. The fast ferry from Mokp'o takes 2½ hours and costs W13,450.

WOLCH'ULSAN NATIONAL PARK
월출산국립공원

This national park is small enough to hike from east to west in a day (start early though). The ascent is steep and strenuous, but you'll be rewarded with great views for your efforts.

Wolch'ulsan National Park is reminiscent of Taedunsan Provincial Park near Taejŏn (see the Ch'ungch'ŏngnam-do chapter). There are crags and spires, steel stairways on the trail and, at one point, a steel bridge crossing a huge gap between rocks.

The park's highest peak, Ch'ŏnwangbong, reaches a modest 809 metres above sea level. Nonetheless, the area does boast beautiful and rugged rock formations.

The park's three principal temples are Ch'onhwangsa (north-east area), Togapsa (west area) and Muwisa (south area). While the temples are not spectacular, they do add a nice touch to this scenic area.

Admission to Wolch'ulsan National Park costs W700.

Places to Stay

There is a designated camping area, but you are not permitted to camp elsewhere. Near Togapsa is the *Injong Minbak* (☎ 72-0432) which costs W10,000. Near Ch'onhwangsa are the *Pausan-jang Minbak* (☎ 73-3784) and *Sanjang Minbak* (☎ 73-4900) .

Getting There & Away

The small community of Yŏng-am has buses directly to Ch'onhwangsa inside the park. These buses run only three times daily between 6.20 am and 4.30 pm, taking 10

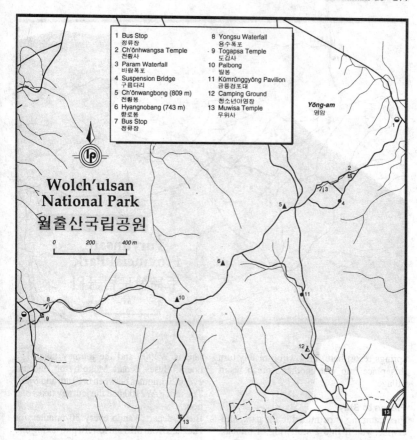

1 Bus Stop
정류장
2 Ch'ŏnhwangsa Temple
천황사
3 Param Waterfall
바람폭포
4 Suspension Bridge
구름다리
5 Ch'ŏnwangbong (809 m)
천황봉
6 Hyangnobang (743 m)
향로봉
7 Bus Stop
정류장
8 Yongsu Waterfall
용수폭포
9 Togapsa Temple
도갑사
10 Palbong
발봉
11 Kŭmrŭnggyŏng Pavilion
금릉경포대
12 Camping Ground
청소년야영장
13 Muwisa Temple
무위사

Yŏng-am
영암

Wolch'ulsan
National Park
월출산국립공원

0   200   400 m

minutes for the journey and costing W310. If you miss the bus, you should be able to catch a taxi.

Kurim-ni is the entrance to the park for Togapsa, but it's four km from the temple. Buses from Yŏng-am to Kurim-ni run every 20 minutes between 6.20 am and 4.30 pm, taking 15 minutes for the ride.

Buses run from Kwangju to Yŏng-am every 10 minutes between 5 am and 10 pm, taking one hour for the journey which costs W1930.

There are buses from Wando to Yŏng-am departing every 20 minutes from 6.03 am to 7.38 pm. The fare is W2920 and the journey takes 1½ hours.

TURYUNSAN PROVINCIAL PARK
두륜산도립공원

The highest peak in this park, Turyunbong (703 metres), is the most south-western peak on the Korean peninsula. Here you'll find Taehŭngsa, a major Zen meditation temple. There are dramatic views from the temple – you can see all the way to the ocean.

Turyunsan is a great place and not to be missed, but you should probably see it soon because there are nasty plans to develop a hot

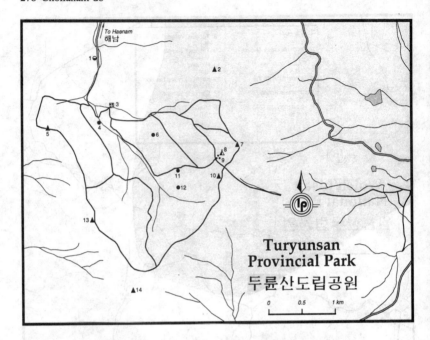

**Turyunsan
Provincial Park**
두륜산도립공원

0   0.5   1 km

springs resort here. That will probably turn this place into just another Korean resort village.

Places to Stay

Free camping is permitted in the park. Otherwise, you'll find a scattering of minbak. Some people prefer to stay in Haenam where there are three yŏinsuks right around the corner from the bus terminal.

Getting There & Away

Access to the park is from the nearby town of Haenam. The bus will unload passengers at the newly built tourist village at the entrance to the valley – there is a shuttle bus from there to the old entrance about two km up the road (or you can walk in about 30 minutes). From the old entrance to Taehŭngsa takes about another 15 minutes on foot.

Buses from Kwangju to Haenam depart every 20 minutes from 5 am to 9.30 pm. The fare is W3900 and the journey takes 1¾ hours. Buses depart Mokp'o for Haenam every 20 minutes between 6.40 am and 8 pm. The fare is W2100 and the journey takes one hour.

Buses depart Wando every 30 minutes for Haenam from 6.15 am to 7.10 pm, taking one hour to make the journey.

Local buses depart Haenam for Taehŭngsa every 30 minutes between 6 am and 7.30 pm. The fare is W310 and the journey takes 20 minutes.

WANDO 완도

The island of Wando is off the south-western tip of the mainland and is famous throughout Korea for the quality of its seaweed (kim). At certain times of the year you'll see this seaweed drying in racks around the island in much the same way as squid are dried on Ullŭngdo and along the north-east coast.

The town of Wando has a quiet, rural

1	Bus Stop	정류장
2	Kogyebong (638 m)	고계봉
3	Taehŭngsa Temple	대흥사
4	Ch'ŏngshinam Hermitage	청신암
5	Hyŏlmangbong (379 m)	혈망봉
6	Iljiam Hermitage	일지암
7	Karyŏnbong (703 m)	가련봉
8	Camping Ground	야영지
9	Manilam (Ruins)	만일암터
10	Tŭryunbong (630 m)	두륜봉
11	Chinbulam Hermitage	진불암
12	Sangwonam Hermitage	상원암
13	Yŏnhwabong (613 m)	연화봉
14	Taedunsan (671 m)	대둔산

atmosphere and a look of benign neglect about it. Unfortunately most of the old tiled-roofed traditional buildings have disappeared but the narrow streets are still there. In fact they are so narrow that the somewhat decrepit local buses only go down one street. It's a very small town so you can't get lost.

There are both sandy and pebble beaches on the island. These days, the island is connected to the mainland by bridge and there is a ferry service to Chejudo.

Ch'ŏngdo-ri 정도리

Ch'ŏngdo-ri is the main pebble beach on the island and it is a very attractive sight. To get there from the town of Wando, take a local bus from the centre close to the ferry terminal and get off at Sajong-ni. From there it's a one-km walk to the beach. There's a small cafe on the beach which offers beer and soft drinks but no food.

Myŏngsashim-ni 명사심리

Myŏngsashim-ni (otherwise known as Myongsajang) is the main sandy beach and very beautiful. At certain times of the year it's a little harder to get to than Ch'ŏngdo-ri since it involves a trip by local ferry, and they'll only sail if there's sufficient demand.

The ferries leave from the local ferry terminal which is about one km from the main terminal serving the Chejudo ferries. The fare is W300 and the trip takes about half an hour. There are three to four ferries per day when there are sufficient passengers. Buses wait for the ferries at the far end and take you from there to the beach.

Places to Stay

There's a good choice of yŏinsuk in Wando and they all charge more or less the same. The *Tongmyon Yŏinsuk* in front of the post office is good value at W10,000 a double. Next door is the *Sujong Yŏinsuk* which is similar and charges the same price. At the back of the post office is the *Kwangju Yŏinsuk*.

More upmarket yŏgwan charge from W15,000 to W20,000 for a double. Yŏgwans in this cetegory include the *Tongrim-jang* (☎ 54-4040), *Ch'onji-jang* (☎ 54-2569) and *Yurim-jang* (☎ 52-3360).

The deluxe accommodation in town is the *Wando Garden Hotel* (☎ 52-5001) which cost W25,000 to W30,000 for a double room.

Getting There & Away

Bus You can catch a bus from Wando to the following locations:

Haenam: (Turyunsan Provincial Park) buses depart every 30 minutes from 6.15 am to 7.10 pm. The fare is W1860 and the journey takes one hour.
Kwangju: buses depart about every 20 minutes from 5.44 am to 7 pm. The fare is W4850 and the journey takes 2½ hours.
Mokp'o: buses depart every 50 minutes from 8 am to 6.40 pm. The fare is W3600 and the journey takes 1¾ hours.
Pusan: buses depart once hourly from 7.25 am to 3.10 pm. The fare is W10,210 and the journey takes almost seven hours.

Seoul: buses depart four times daily between 8.10 am and 2.15 pm. The fare is W11,000 and the journey takes 6½ hours.

Yŏsu: buses depart twice daily at 11.17 am and 4.20 pm. The fare is W6470 and the journey takes three hours.

Yŏng-am: (Wolch'ulsan National Park) buses depart every 20 minutes from 6.03 am to 7.38 pm. The fare is W2920 and the journey takes 1½ hours.

Boat Wando is connected to Chejudo by ferry. The schedule for these ferries is in the Cheju-do chapter.

If you want to explore some of the nearby islands there are ferries from Wando to Ch'ŏngsando, Noktongdo, Nohwado, Chodo and Sokhwapo.

To Ch'ŏngsando there is a slow boat (1½ hours) and a fast boat (30 minutes). Similarly, to Noktongdo there is a slow boat (3½ hours) and a fast boat (2¼ hours). To Chodo by one of these boats takes 3¾ hours and to Sokhwapo it is one hour.

If you're heading for Mokp'o from Wando and would prefer to go by sea rather than by

bus, there is a daily ferry which leaves Wando at 8 am and takes seven hours. The ferry calls at many places en route.

Getting Around
The bus terminal is a long way from the centre of town (about 1½ km). If the walk doesn't appeal to you there are local buses and taxis into the centre.

POGILDO 보길도
An island further to the south of Wando, Pogildo boasts three fine beaches. The sandy spot where everyone heads for is Chungni Beach, also known as Pogildo Beach. Yesong-ni Beach, at the southern end of the island, is a pebbly beach, but is dramatic for its evergreen forest. The island boasts several thick groves of pine trees, and there is also a temple called Namunsa. The other beach is called Soanp'o Beach.

Pogildo is the old home of Yun Son-do, a famed poet during the Chosŏn dynasty. The

Trains from Seoul to Yŏsu

Class	Time	Frequency	Travel Time	Fare
Saemaul	9.40 am, 6.05 pm	2 daily	5½ hours	W21,700
Mugunghwa	8.05 am-10.45 pm	5 daily	6 hours	W12,800
T'ong-il	10.08 am-9.45 pm	2 daily	6¾ hours	W 8800

Trains from Seoul to Sunch'on

Class	Time	Frequency	Travel Time	Fare
Saemaul	9.40 am, 6.05 pm	2 daily	4¾ hours	W19,800
Mugunghwa	8.05 am-10.45 pm	5 daily	5¼ hours	W11,700
T'ong-il	8.20 am-11.50 pm	5 daily	5¾ hours	W8000

Trains from Seoul to Kwangju

Class	Time	Frequency	Travel Time	Fare
Saemaul	9.05 am, 5.10 pm	2 daily	3¾ hours	W17,400
Mugunghwa	11.05 am-11.30 pm	4 daily	4¼ hours	W10,200
T'ong-il	8.20 am, 7.45 pm	2 daily	4½ hours	W7000

Trains from Seoul to Mokp'o

Class	Time	Frequency	Travel Time	Fare
Saemaul	10.05 am, 4.05 pm	2 daily	4¾ hours	W20,200
Mugunghwa	7.20 am-8.50 pm	4 daily	5½ hours	W11,900
T'ong-il	11.20 am-11.05 pm	4 daily	6 hours	W8200

story goes that Yun Son-do took temporary shelter from a typhoon here while on his way to Chejudo. He was so impressed by the beauty of the island that he decided to stay for the next 10 years. During that time, he is said to have built 25 buildings on the island, and also penned some of his best poems such as *Fisherman's Prose*.

Pogildo is very much a summer resort, which means it can get a bit packed out at such times. On the other hand, visiting during the winter wouldn't be much fun, and most hotels will close then anyway. You might try to hit it in June or September, which will just miss the tourist crunch season.

The festival of Admiral Chang Po-ko is held here on the 15th day of the first moon, although you aren't likely to visit at that time unless you're a member of the Polar Bear Club.

Getting There & Away

There are ferries five times daily between Wando and Pogildo, starting at 8 am and ending at 5.30 pm. The journey takes 1½ hours and costs W3000. Between 15 July and 20 August, the schedule is increased to eight times daily.

CHINDO 진도

This is another large island south of Mokp'o and is connected to the mainland by a bridge. The most remarkable thing to see here is the dramatic rise and fall of the tides, which experience some of the largest tide changes in the world. There is an island far off the south-east coast of Chindo which, in early March of every year, can be reached on foot

during the low tide by crossing a spit of tidal land 2.8 km in length and 40 metres wide.

The experience is officially known as the Landing Tide Phenomenon *(kanjuyuk kyedo)*. This phenomenon was witnessed in 1975 by the French ambassador to Korea, who later described it in a French newspaper as 'Moses' Miracle.' The name easily stuck as South Korea has a very large population of Christians, and some view this parting of the seas as akin to the great biblical miracle that allowed the Jews to escape from ancient Egypt. Not surprisingly, large numbers of people come to view this event, and what you often get to see is a line of people stretching for 2.8 km – seemingly walking on water!

As you will no doubt be told by locals, Chindo is home to a unique breed of dog simply known as the 'Chindo dog' *(Chindo kae)*.

Getting There & Away

Bus Buses depart Chindo for the following places:

Kwangju: buses depart every 30 minutes from 6.05 am to 7.35 pm. The fare is W5210 and the journey takes 2½ to three hours.

Mokp'o: buses depart 12 times daily from 6.34 am to 7 pm. The fare is W3670 and the journey takes 2¼ hours.

Pusan: buses depart twice daily at 6.15 am and 12.45 pm. The fare is W10,210 and the journey takes 6¾ hours.

Seoul: buses depart four times daily between 8.10 am and 11.30 am. The fare is W12,000.

Yŏsu: buses depart twice daily at 11.25 am and 3 pm. The fare is W7090 and the journey takes four hours.

Cheju-do 제주도

Eighty-five km off the southernmost tip of the peninsula lies Korea's windswept island of myth and magic. Isolated for many centuries from mainland developments, it acquired its own history, cultural traditions, dress, architecture and even language. The latter, for instance, although classified only as a dialect, was the result of the island's occupation between 1276 and 1375 by the Mongols and is as different from Korean as Provençal is from French. Mainlanders can experience difficulty understanding what is being said on this island.

There is also the enigma of the *harubang*, or grandfather stones, carved from lava rock, whose purpose is still debated by anthropologists. Certainly parallels are easily drawn between these and the mysterious statues found on such places as Easter Island and Okinawa, yet debates about whether they once represented the legendary guardians of the gates to Chejudo's ancient towns seem largely irrelevant as you stand next to them in the gathering twilight at Sŏng-ŭp, Chejudo's ancient provincial capital. But what can be said for sure is that no other symbol personifies Cheju-do so completely as the harubang. They're even painted on the sides of the local buses. Not surprisingly, the production of imitation harubang for sale to tourists has been a lucrative growth industry. Indeed, so many harubang are being carted home by Japanese and foreign tourists that future generations of archaeologists may well wonder if harubang were not part of some worldwide religious movement.

This is not to suggest that Cheju-do doesn't share in the Korean cultural tradition since it clearly has done for millennia, but the differences are sufficiently evocative to draw people from all over Korea in search of legend. Cheju-do was, for instance, the last redoubt of a faction of the Koryŏ army which was determined to resist the Mongol armies even after the king had made peace with the invaders and returned to his capital at

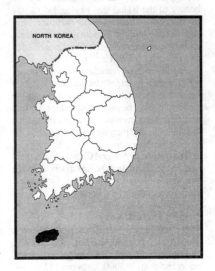

Kaesong. They were later slaughtered to the last man, west of what is today Cheju City in 1273.

Later, during Yi dynasty times, Cheju-do was the island on which the Dutch merchant vessel, *Sparrowhawk*, was wrecked on its way to Japan in 1653. Those who survived the wreck were taken to Seoul by order of the king and forced to remain there for the next 13 years until they were finally able to escape to Japan in a small fishing vessel. An account of those years, written by Hendrick Hamel, one of the survivors, became a best seller in Europe at the time and was the first accurate description of the so-called Hermit Kingdom that Europe received.

A remote provincial outpost it may have been until recently, but over the last two decades Cheju-do has changed radically. The catalyst was tourism. It began as the favoured honeymoon destination for Korean couples drawn here by the lure of the warm south and the difficulties of obtaining a pass-

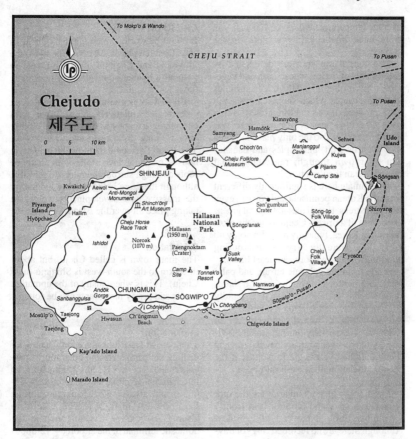

port which would have allowed them to go further afield. The honeymooners still arrive in droves, although more and more prefer to take their romantic interlude in Guam (which is cheaper).

Adding to the tourist boom are Japanese who arrive by the plane-load direct from Japan into Cheju-do's flashy international airport. Indeed, Cheju is rapidly becoming Korea's second busiest airport, and a whole new suburb (Shinjeju) consisting of four and five-star hotels, restaurants and associated services, has been built next to the airport just to milk the tourist market.

Chejudo is touted in the tourist literature as Korea's Hawaii, and indeed it offers some Hawaiian-style geographical features. In particular, there is the almost 2000-metre-high extinct volcano of Hallasan, the highest mountain in South Korea, with its own crater lake and several well-marked hiking trails. Then there are the beaches dotted around the island; the impressive Chŏngbang and Ch'ŏnjiyŏn waterfalls at Sŏgwip'o on the south coast; the famous volcanic cone at Sŏngsan which rises steeply from the ocean on the eastern tip of the island; and the lava-tube cave of Manjanggul, whose 9°C average temperature will make you wish you were back in the balmy warmth on the surface.

The coastal lowlands are dominated by small fields of barley, wheat, corn and vegetables, but further inland there are enormous grazing pastures which support horses and cattle. Indeed, it was the Mongols who first used Chejudo's pastures on which to rear their horses. It's also the only place in Korea where citrus fruit, pineapples and bananas can be grown though, regrettably, that doesn't mean they're cheap!

The climate here is significantly different from the Korean peninsula and you can even find palm trees. But all the subtropical greenery comes at a price – Chejudo has the most rainfall in Korea, typically recording only 60 clear days annually. Try to visit during autumn, when downpours are least likely.

Aside from the volcanic terrain and palm trees, another feature which Chejudo shares with Hawaii is that the island is rapidly becoming commercialised. While the place has not yet been 'ruined', it's certainly no wilderness. Especially during summer holidays, you trip over so many newlyweds and rental cars that you begin to wonder if the entire population of Seoul hasn't been relocated here.

Another possible annoyance are the bird hunters who descend on the island from 1 November through the end of February. Although there are no recorded cases of travellers getting blown away by bird hunters, the sound of shotguns blasting can detract from your enjoyment of the backcountry. It's probably no coincidence that the bird hunting season comes during the winter when visitors to Chejudo are fewest.

In spite of these minor negative points, you shouldn't miss Chejudo when you come to Korea. This place has a very different flavour from the mainland and is definitely worth exploring. There are also a number of sporting activities to keep you amused on this island. Some possibilities include: hiking, golf, snorkelling, scuba diving, windsurfing, sailing, fishing, hang gliding and horseback riding.

CHEJU CITY 제주

It might be worth explaining that 'Cheju' is actually three places. There is Cheju-do (the province) and Chejudo (the island, spelled without a hyphen), and finally Cheju City, the island's capital.

Cheju City is a relaxing place as Korean cities go. It's a relatively compact town, with everything except the bus terminal within easy walking distance of everywhere else. You'll still find some traditional Cheju-style houses made of lava stone with thatched roofs and high surrounding dry-stone walls, although these are being quickly hidden by the massive new developments which are taking place all over the island.

Orientation

The main town is called Cheju, but about three km to the south-west is Shinjeju (new Cheju). This is where many of the upmarket hotels and pricey restaurants can be found.

Information

There are at least four places in Cheju City dishing out pamphlets and other tourist paraphernalia. The KNTC has a branch in the international terminal of the airport (☎ 42-0032) and also in the Changmun Tourist Complex (☎ 38-0326). The Cheju-do Tourist Association has a branch in the domestic terminal of the airport (☎ 42-8866) and at the Cheju port passenger terminal (☎ 22-7181).

Kwandŏkjŏng 관덕정

This 15th-century pavilion is one of Cheju's most interesting buildings, complete with harubang. It's the oldest building of its type on the island and draws a steady flow of domestic tourists out to get the perfect photo of themselves standing in front of something.

In the morning, an interesting and extensive daily market sets up nearby which sells everything from clothes to apples which are grown on Hallasan's southern slopes.

Folkcraft & Natural History Museum
민속자연사박물관

The Folkcraft & Natural History Museum, on the hill at the back of town and close to the KAL Hotel, is excellent. There is a recreation of a traditional thatched house in the local style, local crafts, folklore and marine displays. There's also a film about the island (in Korean) which is shown five times daily for no extra charge. Entry costs W550 and the museum is open daily, except for Monday, from 9 am to 5 pm.

Samsŏnghyŏl 삼성혈

Nearby is Samsŏnghyŏl, a Confucian-style mausoleum which has now become a shrine. Essentially it's just an empty house like many other such shrines on the mainland, and it's touch and go whether or not you think it's worth the W400 admission fee.

Yongdu'am 용두암

The Yongdu'am (dragon's head rock) on the seashore to the west of town, which you'll find eulogised in all the tourist literature, might be worth a visit if you have nothing to do for a couple or hours but you can place it at the bottom of your priority list. On the other hand, no Korean honeymoon is complete without a photograph of the newlyweds taken at this spot.

Moksŏgwon 목석원

About six km outside of Cheju City on the cross-island Highway No 1 is Moksŏgwon, a natural sculpture garden of stone and wood. If you've ever found yourself taking home interesting-looking pieces of wood and stone which have been carved by the elements, you'll love this place.

It was put together over many years by a local resident. It comprises objects found all over the island, many of them originating from the roots of the jorok tree which is found only on Cheju-do. The wood of this tree is very dense – it sinks in water – and it was formerly used for making combs and tobacco boxes. Along with the natural objects, there are many old grinding stones

and even harubang. The collection is now maintained by the government.

Entry costs W300 (W100 for students). To get there, take a bus from the local bus station.

Organised Tours

Even if you consider yourself a dyed-in-the-wool budget traveller, you just might want to consider taking a tour of Chejudo. Some of these tours are not expensive and can save you considerable hassle since the island's sights are so spread out.

Probably the cheapest and most readily available tours for foreigners are those which can be booked in Cheju Airport at the information counter. There are tours departing daily from the airport at 9 am and finishing around 6 pm. Most tours are in fact two days – west Chejudo is explored the first day and the east part of the island is covered on the second day. These two-day tours cost W37,000. A one-day tour covers west Chejudo and costs W21,000.

Places to Stay – bottom end

Since Cheju-do is such a popular place for honeymooners and young people on holiday, there is an excellent choice of cheap places for most of the year. You may have to do a little bit of legwork from mid-July to mid-August, however, when it gets quite crowded and prices tend to rise. Most of the cheapies are on or off Sanjiro Rd, and between this road, Kwandongno and the sea front.

If you arrive by boat you'll probably be met by people from the various yŏgwan and yŏinsuk offering you a room. If you think what you're being offered sounds like a good deal then go and have a look. Most yŏinsuk cost around W7000.

The *Yangsando Yŏinsuk* (☎ 22-9989), only a stone's throw from the boat terminal on Sanjiro Rd, has been a popular place to stay for years. It's very clean and has hot water in the communal bathroom. The owners are very friendly and helpful. Ask for a room on the top floor which has an open flat roof, good views and is quiet.

Also good value is the *Hanil Yŏinsuk*. All

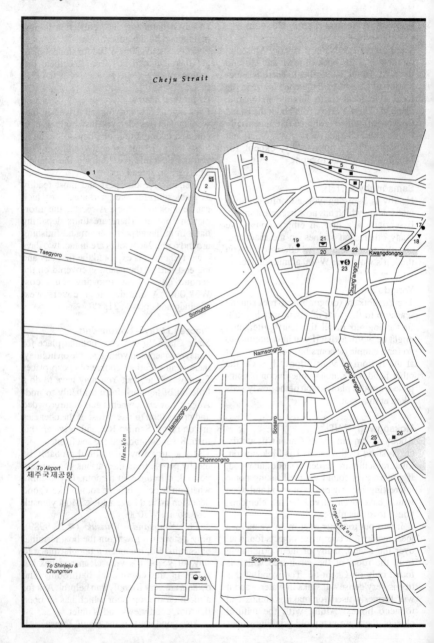

Cheju Strait

Taegyoro

Somunno

Namsongno

Hanchŏn

Namgyoro

Kwangdongno

Chung'angno

Chung'angno

Sosaro

Chonnongno

Sŏrŭngch'ŏn

To Airport
제주국제공항

To Shinjeju &
Chungmun

Sogwangno

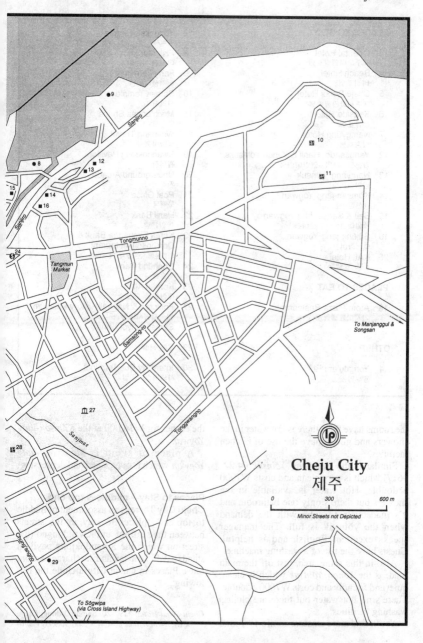

Cheju City
제주

0   300   600 m

Minor Streets not Depicted

To Manjanggul &
Songsan

To Sŏgwipo
(via Cross Island Highway)

PLACES TO STAY

3 Oriental Hotel
제주오리엔탈호텔
4 Beach Hotel
비치호텔
5 Cheju Seoul Hotel
제주서울관광호텔
6 Seaside Hotel
해상호텔
7 Namgyŏng Hotel
남경호텔
12 Yangsando, Hanil & Yonan Yŏinsuks
양산도, 한일, 연안여인숙
13 Namyang Yŏinsuk
남양여인숙
14 Kŭmsan-jang Yŏgwan
금산장여관
15 Seil & Sansu-jang Yŏgwan
세일여관, 산수장여관
16 Sujŏng-jang Yŏgwan
수정장여관
26 KAL Hotel
KAL 호텔

PLACES TO EAT

18 Atom Plaza Restaurant
가자아톰플라자

OTHER

1 Yongdu'am Rock
용두암

2 Yongaksa Temple
용악사
8 Fish Market
어시장
9 Ferry Terminal
여객선터미널
10 Sarasa Temple
사라사
11 Moch'ungsa Shrine
모충사
17 Waybang Travel
외방여행사
19 Kwandŏkjong Pavilion
관덕정
20 Underground Arcade
지하상가
21 Post Office
우체국
22 Hanil Bank
한일은행
23 Korea Exchange Bank &
Don Jose Restaurant
외환은행, 돈 호세 레스토랑
24 Chohŭng Bank
조흥은냉
25 Korean Air
대한항공 매표소
27 Folkcraft & Natural History Museum
민속자연사박물관
28 Samsŏnghyŏl Shrine
삼성혈
29 City Hall
시청
30 Inter-City Bus Terminal
시외버스터미널

the rooms have fans, there is hot water in the showers and guests have the use of kitchen facilities.

Similar is the *Namyang Yŏinsuk* (☎ 22-9617) which is very clean and costs W7000 a double. Hot water is available in the showers but there's only one bathroom and it's inadequate to cope with the demand when the yŏinsuk is full. The manager speaks excellent English and is helpful. Guests have the use of a washing machine.

Also in this same area, just off the main road, is the *Yonan Yŏinsuk* which is clean, quiet and friendly and costs W7000 a double. There's no hot water but there are clothes washing facilities.

You'll find more creature comforts around

the corner for W16,000 at the *Kŭmsan-jang Yŏgwan*.

A place to avoid is *Mankyŏng-jang Yŏgwan* which is overpriced and depressing.

Places to Stay – middle & top end
Cheju City There is an assortment of middle to top-end places to stay in the streets between the seafront and Kwandongno (the street on which the Kwandŏkjŏng pavilion stands). Add 20% tax and surcharge to room rates. Places in Cheju City include the following:

Cheju Seoul Hotel: 1192-20, Samdo 2-dong, Cheju City. Twins/suites cost W59,500/90,991. Facili-

Top: Bridge at Chungmun Beach, Chejudo Island (CHP)
Left: The beach at Wando Island (CHP)
Right: Rock-carved Buddah, Namsan mountain, outside Kyŏngju (GC)

Left: Sŏraksan National Park (CHP)
Right: The last haul, Taedunsan, south of Taejon (CHP)
Bottom: Sŏraksan National Park (RS)

ties include a nightclub, beauty salon and cocktail lounge (☎ 52-2211; fax 51-1701).

Honey Hotel: 1315, Ido 1-dong, Cheju City. Doubles/twins cost W59,500/100,000. The hotel is near the beach (☎ 58-4200; fax 58-4303).

Hotel Lagonda: 159-1, Yongdam 1-dong, Cheju City. Doubles/twins cost W70,000/100,000. Facilities include a cocktail lounge, banquet hall, sauna and shopping arcade (☎ 58-2500; fax 55-0027).

KAL Hotel: 1691-9, Ido 1-dong, Cheju City. Singles/doubles/deluxe twins/suites cost W45,000/82,000/120,000/150,000 to W500,000. Facilities include restaurants, sauna, health club, indoor swimming pool, casino and nightclub (☎ 53-6151; fax 52-4187) .

Oriental Hotel: 1197, Samdo 2-dong, Cheju City. Twins cost W70,000. Facilities include banquet hall, casino, bowling alley, sauna, shopping arcade and game room (☎ 52-8222; fax 52-9777).

Palace Hotel: 1192-18, Samdo 2-dong, Cheju City. Singles/twins/suites cost W38,000/59,500/110,000. Facilities include a sauna and game room (☎ 53-8811; fax 53-8820).

Seaside Hotel: 1192-21, Samdo 2-dong, Cheju City. Singles/doubles/suites cost W31,000/41,500/58,000. Facilities include a karaoke lounge (☎ 52-0091; fax 52-5002).

VIP Park Hotel: 917-2, Nohyong-dong, Cheju City. Singles/doubles/suites cost W31,000/49,000/123,967 (☎ 43-5530; fax 43-5531) .

Shinjeju The other major area for flashy hotels is in Shinjeju, a few km south-west of the centre Add 20% tax and surcharge to room rates.

Cheju Nam Seoul Hotel: 291-30, Yon-dong, Shinjeju. Twins/suites cost W110,000/160,000 to W1,000,000. Facilities include a casino, health club, indoor swimming pool and sauna (☎ 42-4111; fax 46-4111).

Continental Hotel: 268, Yon-dong, Shinjeju. Twins cost W49,000. Facilities include restaurant, bar and beauty shop (☎ 47-3390; fax 46-8847).

Grace Hotel: 261-23, Yon-dong, Shinjeju. Twins/suites W49,000/107,438 (☎ 42-0066; fax 43-7111).

Grand Hotel: 263-15, Yon-dong, Shinjeju. Standard/superior/deluxe rooms cost W86,000/130,000/154,000. Facilities include a casino, health club, swimming pool, nightclub and sauna (☎ 47-5000; fax 47-0278).

Green Hotel: 274-37, Yon-dong, Shinjeju. Singles/twins cost W34,000/59,500. Facilities include banquet hall, nightclub, health club and sauna (☎ 42-0071; fax 42-0082).

Hawaii Hotel: 278-2, Yon-dong, Shinjeju. Twins cost W59,500. Facilities include a cocktail lounge, coffee shop, restaurants and banquet hall (☎ 42-0061; fax 42-0064).

Hotel Cheju Royal: 272-34, Yon-dong, Shinjeju. Twins/suites cost W59,000/118,000 to W219,000. Facilities include restaurants, bar, nightclub and sauna (☎ 43-2222; fax 42-0424).

Island Hotel: 263-12, Yon-dong, Shinjeju. Twins cost W59,500. Facilities include a cocktail lounge, coffee shop, restaurants, sauna, game room, karaoke bar, beauty salon, and shops (☎ 43-0300; fax 42-2222).

Marina Hotel: 300-8, Yon-dong, Shinjeju. Twins/suites cost W49,000/100,000 (☎ 46-6161; fax 46-6170).

Milano Hotel: 273-49, Yon-dong, Shinjeju. Singles/twins/suites cost W31,000/49,000/100,000 (☎ 42-0088; fax 42-7705).

Mosu Hotel: 274-13, Yon-dong, Shinjeju. Twins/suites cost W59,509/90,991. Facilities include a sauna, barbershop, beauty salon, game room, nightclub and bowling alley (☎ 42-1001; fax 42-7466).

Pearl Hotel: 277-2, Yon-dong, Shinjeju. Twins/suites cost W59,500/120,000 (☎ 42-8871; fax 42-1221).

Raja Hotel: 268-10, Yon-dong, Shinjeju. Twin/suites W49,000/107,438 (☎ 47-4030; fax 46-9731).

Simong Hotel: 260-9, Yon-dong, Shinjeju. Twin/suites cost W49,000/107,000 (☎ 42-7775; fax 46-7111).

Tamra Hotel: 272-29, Yon-dong, Shinjeju. Singles/twins cost W31,000/49,000. Facilities include restaurant and bar (☎ 42-0058; fax 42-4551).

Places to Eat

As elsewhere in Korea, the biggest problem with finding a place to eat is knowing where to start.

Just along Sanjiro Rd alone (the road leading from the ferry terminal to the first junction) there are Korean, seafood, Chinese, Japanese, Western-style and fried chicken restaurants. Many of them offer cheap food but check the prices before you eat.

Atom Plaza (☎ 53-7271) on Sanjiro Rd is a good place to splurge on fried chicken, hamburgers, pizza and kimbap.

A variation on this theme is offered by the *Don José Restaurant*. It's at the junction between Kwangdongno and Chungangno next to the Korea Exchange Bank and has a

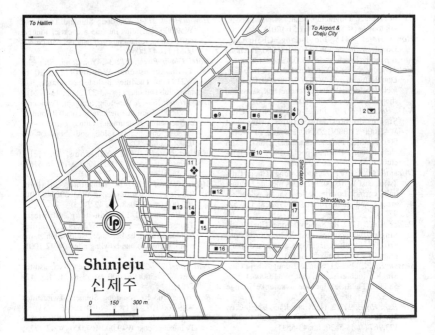

To Hallim

To Airport &
Cheju City

Shindaero

Shindökno

Shinjeju
신제주

0   150   300 m

sign in English. It's essentially a Western-style restaurant with an extensive menu including generous servings of pizza and superb salads. It's top food at a reasonable price.

There are a couple of odd places to eat in the Underground Arcade which runs under Kwangdongno.

Entertainment

Cheju abounds with nightclubs which lay on live bands, although most of them are to be found in the large hotels and cater to people with money to burn. Ditto for casino gambling, which sucks in money from (mostly Japanese) foreign tourists like a vacuum cleaner.

There are several clubs in the alleys between Kwangdongno and the seafront which don't have cover charges and you simply pay for what you eat and drink. Some of these places give the impression from their entrances that they're striptease joints, but

even if that's what they aspire to be, you can be sure the entertainment will be quite tame. Like the nightclubs in the large hotels, there will be live music – usually modern Korean ballads done by a singer, electric guitarist and keyboard player with bass and drum synthesiser. Thanks to the karaoke syndrome, members of the audience frequently front-up to the microphone to wail and croak their way through a song.

Getting There & Away

Air Both Korean Air and Asiana Airlines operate domestic flights to Cheju-do – see the Getting Around chapter for routes and airfares.

There are international flights to Fukuoka and Sendai in Japan.

The main Korean Air office is opposite the KAL Hotel on Chungangno. The main Asiana Airlines office is in Shinjeju. However, it's very easy to book tickets from numerous travel agents around town. A good

PLACES TO STAY

5 Country Tourist Hotel
컨트리관광호텔

6 Cheju Nam Seoul Hotel
제주남서울호텔

8 Sŏwon Hotel
서원호텔

10 Hotel Cheju Royal
제주로얄호텔

12 Milano Hotel
미라노호텔

13 Grand Hotel
그랜드호텔

15 Mosu Hotel
모수관광호텔

16 Hawaii Hotel
하와이관광호텔

17 Cosmos Hotel
코스모스호텔

OTHER

1 Marina Hotel
마리나호텔

2 Post Office
우체국

3 Korea First Bank
제일은행

4 Asiana Airlines
아시아나항공 매표소

7 Sammu Park
삼무공원

9 Cheju Rent-A-Car
제주렌트카

11 Kagopa Department Store
가고파백화점

14 Halla Rent-A-Car
한라렌트카

one is Waybang Travel on Sanjiro Rd which is right in the centre and not far from the cheap yŏinsuk.

Boat There are ferries from Cheju City to Mokp'o, Wando, and Pusan. On the southern coast there are ferries from Sŏgwip'o to Pusan. There are student discounts available on all of the ferries but you have to ask for them. The seas in the straits between Cheju-do and the mainland are often quite rough – if you're not a good sailor it might be worth your while taking one of the faster ferries or even flying.

Schedules vary from one season to another. Not surprisingly, boats are most frequent during summer and the following schedules all assume you are travelling during peak times. If travelling during the off-peak season, it's a good idea to ring up first or check the schedule immediately upon arrival in Pusan, Mokp'o or Wando.

Pusan-Cheju There is a choice of four ferries to Cheju-do from Pusan – two to Cheju City and two to Sŏgwip'o via Sŏngsan (on the eastern tip of the island). All these ferries depart from the domestic ferry terminal in Pusan. The timetables at the terminal are in both Korean and English.

From Pusan to Cheju City, you can take the car ferry *Queen*. It sails from Pusan on Tuesday, Thursday and Sunday at 7 pm and from Cheju City on Monday, Wednesday and Saturday at 7.30 pm. The journey takes about 12 hours and the fares are from W12,580 to W88,300. You can ring for the latest ferry schedules (☎ (02) 312-2585 Seoul; ☎ (051) 464-6601/3 Pusan; ☎ (064) 56-4511/2) Cheju.

Tongyang Car Ferry No 5 or No 6 sails Pusan-Cheju daily except Sunday. Departures from Pusan or Cheju are at 7.30 pm and the journey takes 12 hours. Fares are from W12,580 to W88,300. You can telephone for information (☎ (02) 730-7788 Seoul; ☎ (051) 463-0605 Pusan; ☎ (064) 51-1901/5) Cheju.

The Cheju Car Ferry No 1 and No 3 to Sŏgwip'o alternate with each other. The ferry departs from Pusan daily except Saturday at 6.30 pm. From Sŏgwip'o there's a daily departure except Saturday at 5 pm. The journey takes 13 hours. The one-way fares range from W12,730 to W38,060. For information ring ☎ (051) 465-6131/5 (Pusan) or ☎ (064) 62-3768 (Sŏgwip'o).

Mokp'o-Cheju Tongyang Car Ferry No 2 departs Mokp'o daily except Sunday at 4 pm. Departures from Cheju are daily except Monday at 5 pm. The journey takes 5½ hours and costs from W8380 to W23,190. For the latest information, ring up (☎ Seoul

(02) 730-7788, Pusan (051) 463-0605, Cheju (064) 51-1901/5), Mokp'o (0631) 43-2111).

Wando-Cheju Hanil Car Ferry No 1 sails from Wando daily except the first and third Thursday of each month at 7.20 am. In the opposite direction it departs Cheju at 4 pm daily except the second and fourth Friday.

Hanil Car Ferry No 2 departs Wando at 9.20 am daily except on the second and fourth Thursday of every month. It departs Cheju at 5 pm daily except the second and fourth Friday.

The journey takes three hours and fares range from W8020 to W10,310. The schedule is cut back in the winter. Call for the latest information (☎ (02) 535-2101 Seoul; ☎ (064) 22-4170 Cheju; ☎ (0633) 54-3294) Wando.

Getting Around
To/From the Airport The airport is about two km west of the city. There's a frequent local bus service (bus No 100, W400) which takes 20 minutes between the airport and the ferry terminal via the local bus station and Shinjeju. A taxi will cost W1500.

There is also a frequent airport limousine (really a bus) which runs from the airport to Sŏgwip'o (W2700) via Ch'ungmun (W1800). Bus No 600 also does this run but is considerably slower.

Bus Arriving by boat, there's no need to take a taxi or bus since most of the cheap yŏgwan and yŏinsuk are only a few minutes' walk from the ferry terminal. You probably won't have to use Cheju city buses at all except to get to the airport or the local bus terminal (about two km).

Buses to the local bus terminal are a little more tricky since most of them are not numbered. You can find them at the bottom of the hill in the centre of town on Chungangno – keep asking the conductors and the other people waiting at the stop. The alternative is to take bus No 3 to the big junction past the KAL Hotel and then take another bus along Sogwangno where the terminal is. You'll

also need to use the city buses if you need to go to Shinjeju.

There are plenty of buses to most places of interest around the island. Provided you have your destination written down in Korean characters along with the route you want to take, it's very unlikely you'll be sold the wrong ticket or ever board the wrong bus. The people here are very helpful. But before heading out on an exploration of the island by bus, consider the virtues of taking a tour (see the Organised Tours section earlier in this chapter). A rough guide to the bus routes is as follows:

P'yosŏn: via San'gumburi and Sŏng-ŭp. Buses terminate at Cheju Folk Village near P'yosŏn.
Sŏngsan: via the eastern coast road.
Hallasan and Sŏgwip'o: via cross-island Highway No 1.
Hallasan and Ch'ungmun: via cross-island Highway No 2.
Taejŏng and Hwasun: via inland routes.
Ch'ungmun and Sŏgwip'o: via inland routes.
Sŏgwip'o: via Hallim, Taejŏng, Hwasun and Ch'ungmun following the western coast road.
Hallim and Sŏgwip'o partially via western coast road and partially via inland routes.

To see the main points of interest on the island use the following routes:

Soehaeson Route: This coast road heading west will give you the best selection of beaches on the island, including Iho, Kwakchi, Hyŏpchae and, on the southern coast, Ch'ungmun. All buses along this road stop at the Hyŏpchaegul Lava Caves and Sanbanggulsa Grotto.
Tonghaeson Route: The coast road going east from Cheju City will take you to Hamdok and Kimnyŏng beaches, the turn-off for the Kimnyŏng and Mangjanggul caves and the volcanic cone of Song San Po.
Cross-Island Highway No 1: skirts the eastern side of Hallasan, passing three points at which you can start the trek to the summit of Hallasan, and ends at Sŏgwip'o.
Cross-Island Highway No 2: passes two points at which you can start the trek up Hallasan and ends at Ch'ungmun. Buses taking this route will have 'No 2' in the window.
Tongbusan Route: is a minor route connecting Cheju City with P'yosŏn. It branches off from cross-island Highway No 1 on the lower northern slopes of Hallasan and goes past San'gumburi

and Sŏng-ŭp to end at Cheju Folk Village (near P'yosŏn).

A few examples of schedules and fares include:

Cheju City-Sŏgwip'o (via cross-island Highway No 1) There are buses every 12 minutes from 6 am to 9.15 pm which cost W1800 and take about one hour. Fares and journey times are proportionately less if you're getting off at the start of the Hallasan trekking trails.

Cheju City-Ch'ungmun (via cross-island Highway No 2) There are buses every 20 minutes from 6.20 am to 8 pm which take about one hour and cost W1900. Fares and journey times are proportionately less if you're getting off at the start of the Hallasan trekking trails.

Cheju City-Sŏng-ŭp-P'yosŏn (via the Tongbusan route) There are buses every 30 minutes from 6 am to 9 pm which cost W1550 to Sŏng-ŭp and W950 to P'yosŏn. The journey to Sŏng-ŭp takes about one hour.

Cheju City-Sŏngsan (via the eastern coast road) There are buses every 20 minutes from 5.30 am to 9.40 pm which cost W1500 and take about one hour. These buses will drop you at the turn-off for the Mangjanggul Caves.

Car Given the rural nature of the island (though decidedly less so, year by year), renting a car almost makes sense. There are numerous car rental companies on Cheju-do, as follows:

Asia (☎ 48-2290); Donga (☎ 43-1515); Green (☎ 43-2000); Hanra (☎ 55-5000); Hansung (☎ 47-2100); Jaeil (☎ 46-3230); Jeju (☎ 42-3301); Pomhan (☎ 48-4002); Sŏkkwan (☎ 48-2800); Woori (☎ 52-9661)

Most upmarket hotels also have a car-rental desk in the lobby.

Helicopter For a mere W27,500, you can fly for 25 minutes from Cheju Airport to Sŏgwip'o. Bargain hunters may want to fly from Cheju Airport to Ch'uja-dong, which takes 20 minutes and costs W16,780.

SŎGWIP'O 서귀포
On the southern coast of Cheju-do, Sŏgwip'o is the island's second largest town after Cheju City and is connected to the mainland by ferries from Pusan. It isn't a particularly attractive town in itself but its

setting at the foot of Hallasan, whose lower slopes are covered with citrus groves, is quite spectacular. Its main attractions are the Ch'ŏnjiyŏn and Chŏngbang waterfalls. It's also the nearest place to Ch'ungmun Beach that you can find accommodation other than scarce minbak at Ch'ungmun Village.

Chŏngbang Waterfall 정방폭포
This waterfall is 23 metres high and it's claimed in the tourist literature that it is the only waterfall in Asia which falls directly into the sea. This isn't quite correct since the Toroki Falls on the south coast of Yakushima in Japan also do this and are even larger than Ch'ŏnjiyŏn. All the same, these falls are a very impressive sight and are only a 10 to 15-minute walk from the centre of town. Off the coast you can see several small, partially forested and very rocky islands. Entry costs W500.

Ch'ŏnjiyŏn Waterfall 천지연폭포
This waterfall is on the other side of town at the end of a beautifully forested and steep gorge through which a path and bridge have been constructed. Like the Chŏngbang Waterfall, Ch'ŏnjiyŏn is a 10 to 15-minute walk from the centre of town by the fishing harbour. Entry costs W500.

Places to Stay – bottom end
There are quite a few yŏgwan in the small streets around the centre of town. Some reasonable places include the *Manbu Yŏgwan* and nearby *Namyang-jang Yŏgwan* where rooms cost W16,000.

Places to Stay – middle & top end
In the last few years, Sŏgwip'o has become a resort town and there are a number of top-end hotels. Add 20% tax and surcharge to the room rates. The line-up includes:

Country Tourist Hotel: 291-41, Yon-dong, Shinjeju. Twins/suites cost W59,500/170,000. Facilities include a sauna, game room and beauty salon (☎ 47-4900; fax 47-4915).

KAL Hotel: 486-3, T'op'yong-dong, Sŏgwip'o City. Twins/suites cost W70,000/100,000 to W350,000. Facilities include a casino, indoor &

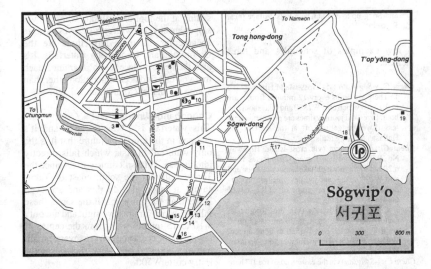

Sǒgwip'o
서귀포

0   300   600 m

outdoor swimming pools, tennis courts, nightclub, sauna, shopping arcade and golf course (☎ 32 9851; fax 32-3190).

Lions Hotel: 803, Sogwi-dong, Sǒgwip'o. Singles/twins/suites cost W31,000/41,500/80,500. Facilities include a nightclub and bar (☎ 33-5651; fax 33-3617).

New Kyungnam Tourist Hotel: 314-1, Sogwi-dong, Sǒgwip'o. Doubles/twins cost W59,500/90,000. Facilities include restaurant, bar, shops, beauty salon, sauna and game room (☎ 33-2121; fax 33-2129).

Paradise Hotel: 511, T'op'yong-dong, Sǒgwip'o. Doubles W59,500 to W130,000, twins W140,000. Facilities include health club, outdoor swimming pool, sauna and karaoke bar (☎ 63-2100; fax 32-9355).

Park Hotel: 674-1, Sogwi-dong, Sǒgwip'o. Twins/suites cost W41,500/70,000. Facilities include nightclub, sauna and indoor swimming pool (☎ 62-2161; fax 33-2882).

Prince Hotel: 731-3, Sohong-dong, Sǒgwip'o. Twins cost W70,000 to W110,000 (☎ 32-9911; fax 32-9900).

Sun Beach Hotel: 820-1, Sogwi-dong, Sǒgwip'o. Twins cost W59,500. Facilities include banquet hall and game room (☎ 63-3600; fax 63-3609).

CH'UNGMUN BEACH 중문해수욕장

This is rated in the tourist literature as the best and longest beach on the island which it conceivably is, but as beaches go around the world it would hardly rate a mention. Certainly it lacks the sharp volcanic rock outcrops which can make swimming hazardous on some of the island's other beaches, such as Kwakchi, but it would still disappoint travellers who have experienced well-known beaches in the Philippines, Thailand, Indonesia etc.

None of this has prevented the developers from moving in, and in a big way. Ch'ungmun is now Cheju's largest beach resort with a number of five-star hotels, condominiums, restaurants and a marine park. It also gets very crowded indeed during the summer holiday season. Other than the attractions of the beach, it's worth visiting the Chonjeyon Waterfall (not to be confused with the Ch'ŏnjiyŏn Waterfall in Sǒgwip'o) which is a 20-minute walk from the beach up to the bridge on the coastal highway. Entry costs W700.

Overlooking the beach is the Royal Marine Park which contains a dolphinarium, aquarium and restaurant complex. If you're interested in seeing performing dolphins after all the research that's been done into the effects of captivity on these animals there are shows at 11 am, 1.30, 2.40 and 4.30 pm daily.

PLACES TO STAY

2 New Kyungnam Tourist Hotel
신경남관광호텔

3 Lion's Hotel
라이온스호텔

10 Kŭmwu Hotel
금우호텔

12 Manbu Yŏgwan
만부여관

13 Namyang-jang Yŏgwan
남양장여관

15 Park Hotel
파크호텔

18 Paradise Hotel
파라다이스호텔

19 KAL Hotel
KAL호텔

OTHER

1 Ch'ŏnjiyŏn Waterfall
천지연폭포

4 Inter-City Bus Terminal
시외버스터미널

5 Telephone Company
전화국

6 Mokhwa Department Store
목화백화점

7 Post Office
우체국

8 Tongmyŏng Department Store
동명백화점

9 Bank
국민은행

11 City Hall
시청

14 Airport Bus Stop
정류장 (공항)

16 Ferry Terminal
서귀항터미널

17 Chŏngbang Waterfall
정방폭포

If you're not interested in seeing this sort of thing then the aquarium itself isn't worth the entry fee. Entry to the park costs W3000 (W2300 for those under 24 years old).

Places to Stay

There's nowhere cheap to stay at the beach itself as this is the territory of those with money to burn. The only place you can find cheap accommodation is in Ch'ungmun Village itself which is quite a walk from the beach and along the highway. Here there's a limited number of yŏgwan to choose from at the usual rates with an additional 20% tax and surcharge. The more upmarket places include:

Hyatt Regency Cheju: 3039-1, Saektal-dong, Sŏgwip'o (Ch'ungmun). Singles/twins cost W82,000/124,000 to W142,000. The five-star facilities includes a casino (☎ 33-1234; fax 32-2039).

Jungmun Hotel Sea Village: 2563-1, Ch'ungmun-dong, Sŏgwip'o (Ch'ungmun). Doubles/suites cost W63,000/140,000. Facilities includes restaurants and karaoke bar (☎ 38-5511; fax 38-1260).

Korea Resort Condominium: 2822-5, Saektal-dong, Sŏgwip'o (Ch'ungmun). Twins cost W70,000. Facilities include a disco, outdoor swimming pool and video rental shop (☎ 38-4000; fax 32-3493).

Shilla Hotel: 3039-3, Saektal-dong, Sŏgwip'o City (Ch'ungmun). Twins cost W140,000 to W220,000. The facilities are five-star and includes a casino (☎ 38-4466; fax 38-3982).

Places to Eat

There's a reasonably good restaurant next to the Royal Marine Park but it's fairly expensive so if you're short on funds, you'll have to eat either in Ch'ungmun Village, where there are a few simple restaurants, or in Sŏgwip'o.

SŎNG-ŬP FOLK VILLAGE 성읍민속촌

A short bus ride north of P'yosŏn lies Cheju-do's former provincial capital which was founded in Koryŏ times in the 13th century. It became the provincial headquarters in 1423 during the reign of King Sejong and remained as such until 1914 when the administrative unit was abolished. Today it's designated as a folk village and its traditional architecture and character have been preserved with government assistance or, at least, most of it has. Many of the traditional houses have actually been abandoned to the tourists and, if you look closely, you'll find that concrete and asbestos are edging their way into the occupied houses. Purists baulk at this, of course, but is it feasible to expect the residents to continue living in 19th-century conditions just so that tourists can come and peek at what they'd call 'genuine' or 'rustic'?

These modern incursions aside, Sŏng-ŭp is definitely worth a visit, since this is what all Chejudo's villages and towns used to look like before concrete, corrugated iron and modern plumbing made their appearance and transformed the Korean landscape. There's also a good collection of original harubang here, although they have been removed from the village entrance and resited in a small park. To be sure, there are much more recent harubang on display in the nearby souvenir shops. The only other significant alteration which has been made to the village is the provision of a parking lot for coaches and cars and a number of tourist restaurants.

There's a large sign in English and Korean in the centre of the village where the buses stop, describing the main features of the village and the history of the principal sites, so take time to have a look at it. Otherwise, take off down the narrow lanes and discover the place for yourself. Remember that most of the houses are still occupied so observe the usual courtesies regarding privacy. There are no entry fees to any of the buildings and you will not be hassled to buy tourist trash.

Places to Stay & Eat
There's a reasonable selection of restaurants ranging from simple to more elaborate along the main street of Sŏng-ŭp but no yŏgwan as such. If you'd like to stay here for the night then you'll have to ask around for a minbak.

Getting There & Away
The schedule for the buses from Cheju City to P'yosŏn via San'gumburi and Sŏng-ŭp can be found in the Cheju City section. In Sŏng-ŭp, the bus timetable board indicates there are buses from Cheju City to Sŏng-ŭp and P'yosŏn every half-hour from 6 am to 10 pm and from P'yosŏn to Sŏng-ŭp and Cheju City every half-hour from 6.30 am to 10 pm. Local people dispute the existence of the later buses and say they don't always arrive. What they do agree on is that there are buses

from Sŏng-ŭp to Cheju City every half-hour from 7 am to 8 pm so it's best to assume that the last bus back to Cheju City is at 8 pm.

These are the same buses which run past San'gumburi.

CHEJU FOLK VILLAGE 제주민속촌
In addition to Sŏng-ŭp, there is also a specially built folk village just outside of P'yosŏn and close to the town's fine beach. It portrays 19th-century Cheju and contains three habitat zones – coastal, plain and mountain – plus there's a shamanistic area as well as official buildings to house magistrates, government officials and records. Though essentially a modern creation, all the construction here is authentically traditional and some of the cottages were brought intact from other areas and so are 200 to 300 years old. There's also a performance yard where folk songs and legends are enacted.

Like other such folk villages, there are a number of restaurants offering traditional food as well as makkoli, beer and soft drinks.

The Cheju Folk Village is open daily from 9 am to 6 pm and entry costs W2300 – there are special concessions for children and students.

SAN'GUMBURI CRATER
산굼부리 분화구
By the side of the road, on the way from Sŏng-ŭp to Cheju City, lies the huge San'gumburi volcanic crater. Larger than the one at Sŏngsan, this crater is some 350 metres in diameter and around 100 metres deep. The floor of the crater is covered with grass but the steep sides are densely forested with evergreen oak and other broad-leaved trees as well as a few pine trees. Craggy rocks line the rim. The crater is home to deer, badgers, reptiles and many species of bird. There's a walking trail which follows the rim, but you're not allowed down in the crater itself.

Buses from Cheju City to Sŏng-ŭp and P'yosŏn pass by the gate and will stop if you want to get off. You can't miss this place as it's fronted by a huge parking lot and a tourist village by the entrance gate.

Entry to the crater costs W500 (W270 for those under 24 years old).

MANJANGGUL 만장굴

East of Cheju and about 2½ km off the coast road from Kimnyŏng Beach are the caves of Manjanggul. The main section of the caves is almost seven km long (!!) with a height and width varying from three to 20 metres, making it the longest known lava tube in the world. If you've never seen one of these before then make sure you visit this place.

Take a sweater with you and a reasonable pair of shoes. It's damp down there (87% to 100% humidity) and the temperature rarely rises above a chilly 9°C. The cave is well-lit as far as a huge lava pillar (about one km from the entrance) which is as far as you're allowed to go without special permission. The caves are open every day from 9 am to 6 pm and entry costs W1000.

Much closer to the turn-off from the main highway, but alongside the same road which leads to the Manjanggul Caves, are another series of lava tubes known as the Kimnyŏngsagul Caves. They're not as long as the Manjanggul Caves – 700 metres divided into four parts – but they're almost as spectacular, and there are actually two tubes, one on top of the other, at this site. Unfortunately, without a powerful flashlight, you won't be able to investigate the legend of the snake since there are no electric lights in these caves and the steps leading down to them are semi-derelict. Things are unlikely to remain this way for long, however, given the popularity of the Manjanggul Caves and

the revenue potential for opening up the Kimnyŏngsagul Caves but, for the present, there's no entry charge.

Getting There & Away

To get to the Manjanggul and Kimnyŏngsagul caves, take a bus from Cheju City going to Sŏngsan and get off at the Kimnyŏng turn-off (signposted for the caves). From here there are local buses to the Manjanggul Caves every 30 to 60 minutes between 7.50 am and 6.30 pm which cost W170. There's a full schedule for the buses posted in the window of the ticket office at the Manjanggul Caves. Alternatively, you can hitch a ride or walk to the caves.

SŎNGSAN 성산

Sŏngsan is the town at the extreme eastern tip of Chejudo nestled at the foot of the spectacular volcanic cone known as Sunrise Peak (Sŏngsan-ilch'ubong); its sides plunge vertically into the surf. If the conditions are favourable you can watch Chejudo's famous *haenyo* (diving women) searching for seaweed, shellfish and sea urchins. Unlike Hallasan, there's no longer any crater lake on the summit and the area below the jagged outer edges of the peak is continuously harvested for cattle fodder (it supports luxurious grass). It is definitely one of Cheju-do's most beautiful areas. If you want to catch the sunrise, you'll have to spend the night here in a local yŏgwan. Entry to Sunrise Peak costs W500.

Apart from walking around the crater, there are boats available to sail you around

Lava Tubes

These lava tubes are associated with an ancient legend regarding a huge snake which supposedly lived in them. In order to placate this snake and prevent harm befalling the nearby farms and villages, a 15 or 16-year-old virgin girl was annually sacrificed by being thrown into the cave. This horrific practice was stopped in 1514 by a magistrate newly appointed to the area. He persuaded the reluctant villagers to perform the usual ritual but to omit the sacrifice whereupon, as the story goes, the angry snake emerged, was killed by the villagers and burnt to ashes. For his pains, the magistrate inexplicably fell ill and died soon afterwards but there was no reappearance of the snake. ■

but they only go when demand is sufficient and the sea is calm. The price is W4000.

Places to Stay

Facing the road which leads to the tourist complex and entrance gate to Sunrise Peak is the *Suji Yŏgwan* where you can get a room with bath and hot water for W16,000. Round the corner from the Suji Yŏgwan is the *Sŏngsan Yŏinsuk* which is also a pleasant place to stay.

Going up in price, there is the *Chaesong-jang Yŏgwan*, opposite the post office, on the bottom road which has rooms for W18,000.

Getting There & Away

There are frequent buses to Sŏngsan from Cheju City which take about 1½ hours. Make sure that the bus you get on is going right into Sŏngsan and not just to Tongnam, the town on the main coast road where you have to turn off for Sŏngsan. If you get dropped here, it's a 2½-km walk into Sŏngsan.

UDO 우도

North-east of Sŏngsan, off the coast, is the attractive island of Udo which is still very rural and where there are no vehicles other than a few tractors and a single minibus. It's about as far as you can get from civilisation in this part of the world, plus there are superb views to Sunrise Peak (Sŏngsan-ilch'ubong), two sandy beaches completely free of rubbish, and a community of haenyo, who work in the cove below the lighthouse.

Places to Stay & Eat

One place to stay on the island is the *Tungdae Yŏinsuk*, close to the ferry pier, where you can get a room for W7000. Since there are no restaurants in this village, you should arrange to have your meals at the yŏinsuk. Minbak are also available but there are no signs so you'll have to ask around.

Getting There & Away

There are ferries from the port at Sŏngsan to Udo. The ticket office and ferry pier are quite a walk from the centre of Sŏngsan so leave yourself enough time to walk (about 15 minutes). From March to June and during October, ferries depart Sŏngsan at 10 am, noon, 3 and 6 pm and from Udo at 8 and 11 am, 2 and 5 pm. From July to September they depart Sŏngsan at 8.50 and 10.30 am, 2, 4 and 7 pm, and from Udo at 7.30 and 9.30 am, 1, 3 and 6 pm. From November to February the ferries leave Sŏngsan at 10 am, noon, 2 and 5 pm, and from Udo at 8 and 11 am, 1 and 4 pm.

HYŎPCHAEGUL 협재굴

About 2½ km south of Hallim, on the north-western side of the island, are a group of lava tube caves, the most famous of which is Hyŏpchaegul which was only discovered in the 1950s. Hyŏpchaegul is actually a system of several interconnected lava tubes. Although much shorter than Mangjanggul Cave, it is one of the few lava tubes in the world which has stalagmites and stalactites. Usually, these are only found in limestone caves. In Hyŏpchaegul, the stalactites and stalagmites are due to the presence of large quantities of pulverised shells in the soil above the cave, which have been blown up from the sea shore over thousands of years. Entry to the caves costs W960 (W480 for those under 24 years old). It's advisable to hire an umbrella in wet weather otherwise you'll be soaked to the skin. They're available at the cave entrance.

There's an extensive tourist complex and a mini-folk village around the entrance and the paths into and out of the cave are tediously designed to force you to pass through as many souvenir shops as possible.

Also part of the complex is a Botanical Gardens, although entry to this costs a further W500.

The other caves in this area are not commercialised and include Ssangynonggul, Hwanggumgul, Sŏch'ongul and Chogitgul. The largest and most spectacular of these is Sŏch'ongul which is some three km long. Its two entrances resemble a huge subterranean botanical gardens.

Getting There & Away

To get there, take a bus going along the west

coast road. You can't miss the caves as the entrance is by the side of the road and all the buses stop here.

SANBANGGULSA 산방굴사

About seven km east of Taejŏng rises the massive volcanic cone of Sanbangsan, and halfway up its southern slope overlooking the ocean is a natural cave which was turned into a temple by a Buddhist monk during Koryŏ times. It's quite a steep walk up, and although the grotto itself is only of marginal interest, the views are worth the effort. Water dripping from the roof of the cave is said to be the tears of Sanbang-gok, the patron goddess of the mountain. Lower down, near the entrance, are two recently built temples where there always seems to be something going on. There's a cafe about halfway up to the grotto which is a great place to sit and have a cold drink.

Entry to the site costs W500 (W250 for those under 24 years old).

Across the other side of the road is a rocky promontory where a plaque has been erected by both the Korean and Dutch governments to commemorate the shipwreck of the Dutch merchant vessel, *Sparrowhawk*, in 1653. It's known as the Hamil Monument after Hendrick Hamel.

The entrance to the grotto is beside the coast road so you can't miss it. Buses plying between Taejŏng and Sŏgwip'o will get you there.

KAP'ADO & MARADO
가파도. 마라도

South of Taejŏng (or Mosŭlpo as the nearby beach is called) lie Kap'ado and Marado, the most southerly points of Korea. Both are inhabited. Kap'ado, the nearest and largest of the islands, is flat and almost without trees, and crops have to be cultivated behind stone walls to protect them from the high winds which sweep the island. Many of the inhabitants earn their living by fishing.

Unlike Kap'ado, Marado rises steeply from the sea and its grassy top supports cattle grazing, although it is only half the size of Kap'ado and there are only about 20 families living there.

Getting There & Away

There are two daily ferries from Taejŏng to Kap'ado at 8.30 am and 2.30 pm which take about half an hour and cost W360 (half price for children). To Marado, there is one ferry daily from Taejŏng at 10 am which takes about 50 minutes and costs W510 (half-price for children). Neither of these ferries sail during rough weather.

The ferry terminal in Taejŏng is by the fishing harbour and is about one km from the centre of town which is where the buses drop you. There are yŏinsuk, yŏgwan and restaurants in Taejŏng if you prefer to stay overnight in order to catch the morning ferry. It's possible to miss this ferry if you attempt to get to Taejŏng from Cheju City by early morning bus.

HALLASAN NATIONAL PARK
한라산국립공원

Walking to the top of Hallasan is one of the highlights of a visit to Chejudo, but make sure you get off to an early start. No matter how clear the skies may look in the morning, the summit is often obscured by cloud in the early afternoon which is when you should be on the way down. Anyone can do this trek. No experience is necessary and no special equipment required. Just make sure you have a decent pair of jogging shoes or hiking boots and something warm (it gets chilly up there at nearly 2000 metres). Rain gear is also advisable as the weather is very changeable on the mountain.

There are five well-marked trails: Yongshil (from the south-west side), Orimok (north-west side), Kwanŭmsa (north side), Tonnaek'o (south side) and Sŏngpan'ak (east side). The trails all connect with one or other of the two cross-island highways. Entry to the national park costs W1600 unless you arrive very early (before the ticket sellers come to work). Detailed trail maps are available free of charge at all the ticket offices which are at the beginning of the trails.

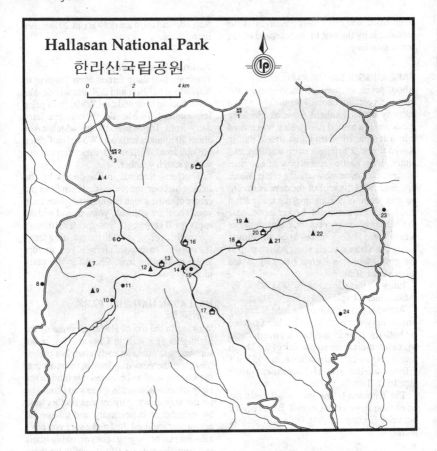

Hallasan National Park
한라산국립공원

The two shortest trails (Yongshil and Orimok) are the ones coming in from the west side – the Yongshil trail is slightly shorter. It takes about 2½ hours to climb to the summit along either of these and about two hours to get back down again. Coming from the north or east side you should plan about four or five hours to the summit. The Tonnaek'o from the south is the most difficult trail of all and should be avoided unless you're fit and experienced at climbing. If you have camping equipment, there are several sites where you can pitch a tent. Close to all the ticket offices are places

where you can buy soft drinks, snacks and even soju.

Rock slides frequently close trails. You'll have to make local enquiries to find out which ones are currently open.

There's quite a large and active Buddhist monastery – Kwanumsa – close to the trail of the same name.

Places to Eat

There are a number of restaurants at the start of some of the trails. The one at the start of the Sŏngkwanak Trail is open year round as is the one at the '1100 Meter Rest Area' about

1	Kwanŭmsa Temple 관음사	13	Witsaeorŭm Shelter 윗새오름 대피소
2	Ch'ŏnwangsa Temple 천왕사	14	Hallasan (1950 m) 한라산
3	Sŏnnyŏ Waterfall 선녀폭포	15	Paengnoktam Crater 백록담
4	Ŏsŭngsaengorŭm (1169 m) 어승생오름	16	Yongchingak Shelter 용진각 대피소
5	T'amna Gorge Shelter 탐라계곡 대피소	17	P'yŏngjigwe Shelter 평지궤 대피소
6	Spring 샘터	18	Chindallae Shelter 진달래밭 대피소
7	Ŏsŭllŏngorŭm (1335 m) 어슬렁오름	19	Hukpulgŭnorŭm (1391 m) 흙붉은오름
8	Sŏngnŏl Rest Area (1100 m) 1100고지휴게소	20	Sara Shelter 사라 대피소
9	Pollaeorŭm (1362 m) 불래오름	21	Saraorŭm (1338 m) 사라오름
10	Rest Area 휴게소	22	Sŏngnŏlorŭm (1215 m) 성닐오름
11	Yŏngshil Rocks 영실기암	23	Sŏngp'anak Rest Area 성판악휴게소
12	Witsaeorŭm (1714 m) 윗새오름	24	Suak Gorge 수악계곡

halfway between the trail entry points on the western side of the mountain (on cross-island Highway No 2).

Getting There & Away

To get there from Cheju City, simply decide which trail you want to start off on and then take the appropriate bus along either of cross-island highways. Tell the driver or conductor which trail you want to go on and they'll make sure you're put down at the right spot.

Chŏllabuk-do 전라북도

CHŎNJU 전주

Chŏnju is the provincial capital of Chŏllabuk-do. Other than its value as a major transit point, the town isn't likely to hold your interest for long.

The most interesting sights are on the southern end of town. This would include the city's museum, P'ungnammun (a large gate) and the old Confucian School. At the southernmost extreme of town is Wansan Park, home to a few notable temples such as Anhaengsa and Ch'ilsŏngsa.

Places to Stay

There is a good collection of yŏgwan sandwiched between the express bus terminal and the inter-city bus terminal. Just opposite the latter is the *Tongkwang-jang Yŏgwan* where rooms start at W16,000. Close to the railway station are numerous other yŏgwan in the same price range, such as the *Haekŭm-jang Yŏgwan*, *Wŏlgung-jang Yŏgwan* and *Riberi-jang Yŏgwan*.

The *Chŏnju Hotel* (☎ 83-2811; fax 83-4478) offers rooms at the following rates: singles/doubles/twins/suites W22,000/35,000/40,000/70,000, plus 20% tax and surcharge.

The *Koa Hotel* (☎ 85-1100; fax 85-5707) is also known as Core Hotel, and it's the most upmarket place in town. Twins cost W72,500 and suites are W100,000 to W450,000, plus 20% tax and surcharge.

Getting There & Away

Bus From the express bus terminal, there are buses to the following places:

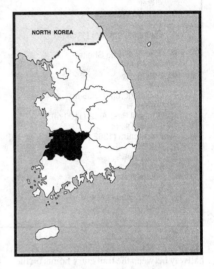

Seoul: buses depart every five to 15 minutes from 6 am to 8.30 pm. The fare is W8900 (1st class) or W5900 (2nd class) and the journey takes 3¾ hours.

Taegu: buses depart every 1⅓ hours from 7 am to 6.40 pm. The fare is W8400 (1st class) or W5600 (2nd class) and the journey takes 3¾ hours.

Taejŏn: buses depart every 30 minutes from 6.30 am to 8.30 pm. The fare is W3800 (1st class) or W2500 (2nd class) and the journey takes 1¼ hours.

Tong-Seoul: buses depart every 40 minutes from 6 am to 8.20 pm. The fare is W9400 (1st class) or W6200 (2nd class) and the journey takes 3¾ hours.

Kwangju: buses depart every 20 minutes from 6.30 am to 8.30 pm. The fare is W4100 (1st class) or W2700 (2nd class) and the journey takes 1¾ hours.

Pusan: buses depart 10 times daily between 7 am and 5.30 pm. The fare is W12,100 (1st class) or W8100 (2nd class) and the journey takes 5¼ hours.

From the inter-city bus terminal you can get to a number of destinations including:

Ch'ŏngju: buses depart every 30 minutes from 7.30 am to 6.35 pm. The fare is W4200 and the journey takes two hours.

Chinan: (Maisan National Park) buses depart every 10 minutes from 6.30 am to 9.30 pm. The fare is W1500 and the journey takes 50 minutes.

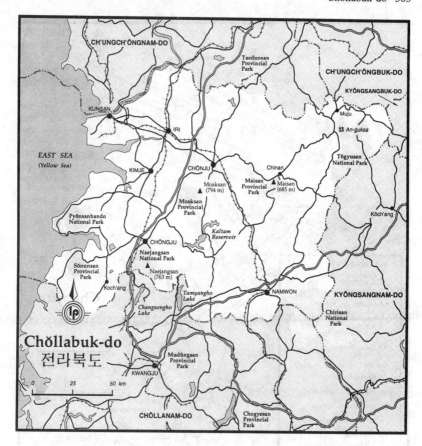

Chŏllabuk-do
전라북도

Chinju: buses depart every 20 minutes from 6.34 am
to 5.48 pm. The fare is W6600 and the journey
takes 3½ hours.

Chŏngju: buses depart every 10 minutes from 6.20 am
to 10 pm. The fare is W1500 and the journey
takes one hour.

Hwaŏmsa: (Chirisan National Park) buses depart
every 20 minutes from 7 am to 6.10 pm. The fare
is W3800 and the journey takes 3½ hours.

Koch'ang: (Sŏnunsan Provincial Park) buses depart
every 30 minutes from 6.10 am to 8.30 pm. The
fare is W2400 and the journey takes 1½ hours.

Kurye: (Chirisan National Park) buses depart 25 times
daily between 6.10 am and 6.10 pm. The fare is
W3600 and the journey takes two hours.

Kwangju: buses depart six times daily from 10.10 am

to 6.20 pm. The fare is W2700 and the journey
takes 1½ hours.

Mokp'o: buses depart every 1¼ hours from 6.10 am
to 4.10 pm. The fare is W5900 and the journey
takes four hours.

Muju: (Tŏgyusan National Park) buses depart every
40 minutes from 6.20 am to 8.30 pm. The fare is
W3800 and the journey takes 2½ hours.

Puan: (Pyŏnsanbando National Park) buses depart
every 28 minutes from 6.15 am to 9 pm. The
fare is W1800 and the journey takes 55
minutes.

Pusan: buses depart 14 times daily between 6.44 am
and 4.20 pm. The fare is W9300 and the journey
takes six hours.

Seoul: buses depart four times daily between 7.58 am

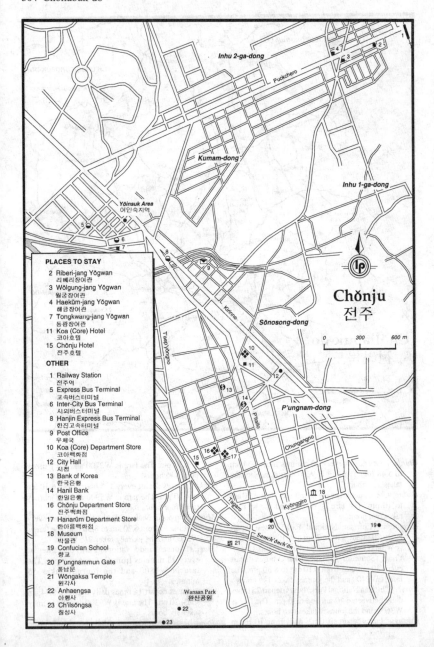

Inhu 2-ga-dong

Puckchero

Kumam-dong

Inhu 1-ga-dong

Yŏinsuk Area
여인숙지역

Chŏnju
전주

Kirinno

Sŏnosong-dong

0   300   600 m

Taep'yongno

P'ario

P'ungnam-dong

Chungangno

PLACES TO STAY

2 Riberi-jang Yŏgwan
   리베리장여관
3 Wŏlgung-jang Yŏgwan
   월궁장여관
4 Haekŭm-jang Yŏgwan
   해금장여관
7 Tongkwang-jang Yŏgwan
   동광장여관
11 Koa (Core) Hotel
   코아호텔
15 Chŏnju Hotel
   전주호텔

OTHER

1 Railway Station
   전주역
5 Express Bus Terminal
   고속버스터미널
6 Inter-City Bus Terminal
   시외버스터미널
8 Hanjin Express Bus Terminal
   한진고속터미널
9 Post Office
   우체국
10 Koa (Core) Department Store
   코아백화점
12 City Hall
   시청
13 Bank of Korea
   한국은행
14 Hanil Bank
   한일은행
16 Chŏnju Department Store
   전주백화점
17 Hanarŭm Department Store
   한아름백화점
18 Museum
   박물관
19 Confucian School
   향교
20 P'ungnammun Gate
   풍남문
21 Wŏngaksa Temple
   원각사
22 Anhaengsa
   안행사
23 Ch'ilsŏngsa
   칠성사

Taguro

Kyŏnggiro

Samch'ŏnch'ŏn

Wansan Park
완산공원

and 4.29 pm. The fare is W5900 and the journey takes 6½ hours.

Yŏsu: buses depart 11 times daily between 6.18 am and 6.10 pm. The fare is W6900 and the journey takes four hours.

Train The railway station is inconveniently situated a long way from the centre and not as useful as the bus terminals. There are 11 direct trains daily from Seoul station to Chŏnju. Refer to the schedule in the train teimetable section at the end of this chapter.

Getting Around
Bus No 79-1 goes from the bus terminal area to Moaksan Provincial Park, but it also goes to the centre so is useful for getting around town. Taxis are of course readily available.

MAISAN PROVINCIAL PARK
마이산도립공원

Maisan means 'horse ears mountain', which roughly describes the shape of the two rocky outcrops which make up the twin peaks (Maibong). The east peak (Sutmaisan) is considered male and reaches a height of 678 metres. The west peak (Ammaisan) is regarded as female and is slightly taller at 685 metres.

T'apsa (Pagoda Temple) is stuck between the two 'horse ears'. It's a temple of unique design, decorated by hundreds of stone formations created by stacking rocks on top of one another.

For the best views, climb up the small path to the summit of Ammaisan which is to the left of the souvenir stands when coming down from the main temple.

There are two other temples on the mountain called Ŭnsusa and Kŭmdangsa. There is a camping ground just opposite Ŭnsusa.

Admission to Maisan Provincial Park costs W650.

Getting There & Away
Bus transport is via the tiny town of Chinan at the park's entrance. First take a bus from Chŏnju (every 10 minutes from 6.30 am until 9.30 pm) to Chinan – the journey takes 50 minutes. From Chinan, buses to the temple

1 Bus Stop
   정류장
2 Car Park
   주차장
3 Sutmaisan (678 m)
   숫마이산
4 Ammaisan (685 m)
   암마이산
5 Ŭnsusa Temple
   은수사
6 T'apsa Temple
   탑사
7 Nadosan
   나도산

To Chinan
진안

To Kŭmdangsa
& Imshil
금당사 · 임실

Maisan Provincial Park
마이산도립공원

0   250   500 m

go every 30 minutes between 8 am and 6.20 pm and the ride takes 10 minutes.

TŎGYUSAN NATIONAL PARK
덕유산국립공원

The park's most significant geological feature is Tŏgyusan (1614 metres), the fourth tallest peak in South Korea. Kuch'on-dong is the main tourist village, located at the southern (upper) end of a 30-km-long valley. From Kuch'on-dong you can walk six km to the south (uphill) along the valley to Paengnyonsa, a small temple from where you begin the ascent of Tŏgyusan.

The two main temples in this park are Anguksa and Songgyesa, which are not in Kuch'on-dong and are usually approached by a different route. However, you can hike from Kuch'on-dong to Anguksa (18 km, seven hours) over a beautiful footpath, but there is no back-country trail to Songgyesa. A nice feature of these two temples is that they are not quite as famous in Korea as other

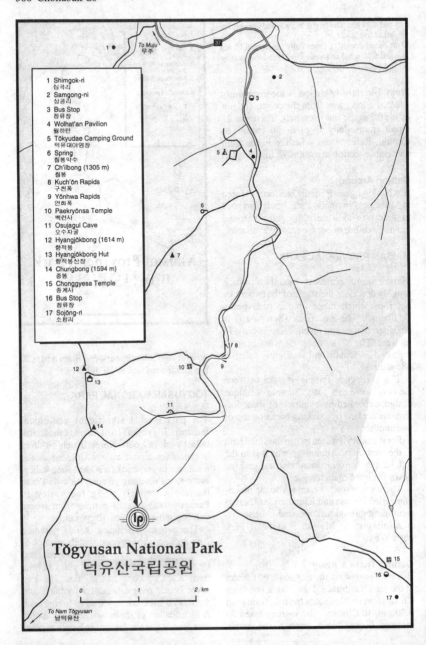

1 Shimgok-ri
   심곡리
2 Samgong-ni
   삼공리
3 Bus Stop
   정류장
4 Wolhat'an Pavilion
   월하탄
5 Tŏkyudae Camping Ground
   덕유대야영장
6 Spring
   철봉약수
7 Ch'ilbong (1305 m)
   철봉
8 Kuch'ŏn Rapids
   구천폭
9 Yŏnhwa Rapids
   연화폭
10 Paekryŏnsa Temple
   백련사
11 Osujagul Cave
   오수자굴
12 Hyangjŏkbong (1614 m)
   향적봉
13 Hyangjŏkbong Hut
   향적봉산장
14 Chungbong (1594 m)
   중봉
15 Chonggyesa Temple
   충계사
16 Bus Stop
   정류장
17 Sojŏng-ri
   소정리

To Muju
무주

To Nam Tŏgyusan
남덕유산

Tŏgyusan National Park
덕유산국립공원

0   1   2 km

large temples, so they tend to be less packed out.

Tŏgyusan is also home to the Muju Resort, which becomes a popular ski area, during winter.

Admission to the national park costs W700.

Places to Stay

There are two designated camping areas in the park: one at Samgong-ni (near Kuch'on-dong) and a larger one at Tŏgyu at the eastern edge of the park near Songgyesa. Back-country camping and cooking are prohibited.

Samgong-ni is one km north of Kuch'on-dong and there are three yŏgwan here costing around W10,000. This includes *Kumsan Yŏgwan* (☎ 322-3081), *Yongnam Yŏgwan* (☎ 322-3257) and *Kunsan Yŏgwan* (☎ 322-3079).

More expensive yŏgwan are in Kuch'on-dong, which puts them close to the bus stop and tourist shops. In these places you can expect to pay from W15,000 to W25,000. Some of the many choices include the *Tŏgyu Yŏgwan* (☎ 322-3074) and *Korea House* (☎ 322-0911).

Staying in a minbak is a possibility, and chances are good that you'll be greeted at the stop by various ajimah offering you a place to stay for around W10,000.

Upmarket accommodation is offered at the *Muju Resort* (☎ 324-9000) where rooms cost a mere W145,200. The resort is four km from Kuch'on-dong and accessible by bus.

Getting There & Away

Bus Muju is the main gateway to the park, although you can also get there from Yŏngdong in Ch'ungch'ŏngnam-do Province. Buses depart Muju for Kuch'on-dong 27 times daily between 7.10 am and 8.25 pm. The fare is W1240 and the journey takes 50 minutes. You can do this same trip by taxi for around W16,000.

Buses depart Yŏngdong for Kuch'on-dong 17 times daily between 7.05 am and 9.40 pm. The fare is W2200 and the journey takes 1½ hours.

You can approach Muju from Taejŏn (see

Ch'ungch'ŏngnam-do chapter). Take a bus from Taejŏn's east inter-city bus terminal to Muju. Buses leave Taejŏn every 30 minutes from 6.20 am to 6.20 pm. The fare is W2140 and the journey takes about 2¼ hours.

Buses from Chŏnju to Muju depart every 40 minutes between 6.20 am and 8.30 pm. The fare is W3800 and the ride takes 2½ hours.

There are five direct buses daily from Seoul to Muju, departing the Seoul express bus terminal between 8.30 am and 2.35 pm. The ride takes three hours and costs W6410.

You can also go direct from Seoul to Yŏngdong. Buses depart Seoul express bus terminal every 1⅔ hours between 7.10 am and 6.40 pm, taking 2¾ hours for the trip which costs W4670. There are also three departures daily from Tong-Seoul (east Seoul) express bus terminal to Yŏngdong between 7 am and 4.50 pm.

Train You can't get a train to the park, but trains run from Seoul to Yŏngdong according to the following schedule:

MOAKSAN PROVINCIAL PARK
모악산도립공원

The area has nice views from (794 metres), but the big attraction here is the temple of Kŭmsansa. The temple was built in 599 AD. There are a number of buildings on the temple grounds, including the unusually-shaped pagoda in front of the main hall. The main hall itself is home to two huge golden Buddhas. Also unique and interesting is the row of black Buddhas in the second main hall.

Admission to Moaksan Provincial Park costs W1000.

Places to Stay

There is a camping ground close to Kŭmsansa, near the Maningyo Bridge. Minbak are readily available for around W10,000. Yŏgwan are also easy to find – try the *Moaksan-jang* (☎ 43-4411) which has rooms from W15,000.

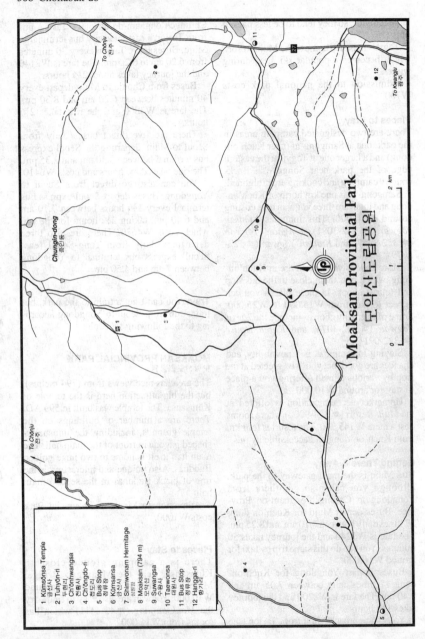

Moaksan Provincial Park
모악산도립공원

1 Kŭmsŏnsa Temple
  금산사
2 Tuhyŏn-ri
  두현리
3 Ch'ŏnhwangsa
  천황사
4 Ch'ŏngdo-ri
  청도리
5 Bus Stop
  정류장
6 Kŭmsansa
  금산사
7 Shimwŏnam Hermitage
  심원암
8 Moaksan (794 m)
  모악산
9 Suwangsa
  수왕사
10 Taewonsa
  대원사
11 Bus Stop
  정류장
12 Hangga-ri
  항가리

To Chŏnju
전주

To Kwangju
광주

Chungin-dong
중인동

Getting There & Away

Transport is most convenient from the city of Chŏnju, where you can catch bus No 79-1 to Kŭmsansa – this runs every 30 minutes between 6.20 am and 8.45 pm. The fare is W600 and the ride takes 25 minutes.

PYŎNSANBANDO NATIONAL PARK
변산반도국립공원

The park occupies a peninsula in the extreme western part of Chŏllabuk-do. It's dotted with temples such as Naesosa (the largest) and Kaeamsa. The park's highest peak is Sabyŏnsan (492 metres).

On the north side of the park is Pyŏnsan Beach, one of the cleanest sandy beaches on the west coast. It's absolutely amazing to see the change of tides here – at low tide you can almost walk to distant offshore islands.

As the west end of the park is Ch'aesŏkkang, and the main sight here is a cliff dropping straight into the sea. It really isn't all that impressive, but it attracts large numbers of Korean tourists.

Admission to Pyŏnsanbando National Park costs W700.

There are camping grounds, but back-country camping and cooking is prohibited in the park. Yŏgwan cost from W15,000 to W20,000 for a double. There are yŏgwan near Naesosa and also at Pyŏnsan Beach.

Getting There & Away

From Chŏngju there are buses to either Naesosa or Ch'aesŏkkang, and the latter take longer since they go by way of Shint'aein and Puan (although the scenery is fine). Puan is a major transit point. The buses going by way of Puan stop at Pyŏnsan Beach and then terminate at Ch'aesŏkkang. At Ch'aesŏkkang, you can change to a bus heading for Naesosa. Buses from Puan to Ch'aesŏkkang depart every 10 minutes from 7.15 am to 8.35 pm. The fare is W930 and the journey takes 40 minutes.

You can get to Puan from Chŏnju, Chŏngju or Kimje. From Chŏnju, buses depart for Puan every 28 minutes from 6.15 am to 9 pm and take 55 minutes. From Chŏngju, buses go to Puan every 30 minutes

between 7.30 am and 7.40 pm and take 40 minutes. From Kimje, buses depart for Puan every five minutes from 5.40 am to 9.50 pm and takes 30 minutes.

CHŎNGJU 정주

It's certainly easy to confuse this town with Chŏnju, the provincial capital. It's even easier to confuse Chŏngju with Ch'ŏngju, the provincial capital of Ch'ungch'ŏngbuk-do – the only difference in spelling between the two places is the addition of an apostrophe in the latter! Exercise care when buying bus tickets to get to any of these places.

The only reason why you'd want to go to Chŏngju is to get to neighbouring Naejangsan National Park, or to Sŏnunsan Provincial Park which is slightly further afield.

Getting There & Away

Bus Chŏngju's express bus terminal and inter-city bus terminal are next to each other – basically opposite sides of the same complex. Nevertheless, the buses from each terminal go to different destinations. From the express bus terminal there are departures as follows:

Seoul: buses depart every 20 to 30 minutes between 6 am and 8 pm. The fare is W10,100 (1st class) or W6700 (2nd class) and the journey takes 3¼ hours.

Tong-Seoul: buses depart every 1½ hours from 6.30 am to 6.40 pm. The fare is W10,600 (1st class) or W7000 (2nd class) and the journey takes 3¼ hours.

The inter-city bus terminal has departures for the following destinations:

Chŏnju: buses depart every 20 minutes from 6.40 am to 8.20 pm. The fare is W1500 and the journey takes 1¼ hours.

Kimje: (Pyŏnsanbando National Park) buses depart once hourly from 7.40 am to 7.30 pm. The fare is W1500 and the journey takes one hour.

Koch'ang: (Sŏnunsan Provincial Park) buses depart every 10 minutes from 6.15 am to 9 pm. The fare is W1100 and the journey takes 40 minutes.

Kwangju: buses depart every 10 minutes from 6.40 am to 9.50 pm. The fare is W1900 and the journey takes 1¼ hours.

Mokp'o: buses depart five times daily between 8.05

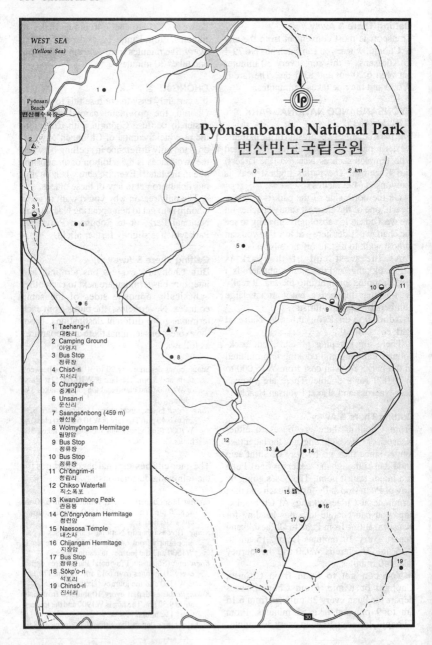

WEST SEA
(Yellow Sea)

Pyŏnsan
Beach
변산해수욕장

Pyŏnsanbando National Park
변산반도국립공원

0   1   2 km

1 Taehang-ri
  대항리
2 Camping Ground
  야영지
3 Bus Stop
  정류장
4 Chisŏ-ri
  지서리
5 Chunggye-ri
  중계리
6 Unsan-ri
  운산리
7 Ssangsŏnbong (459 m)
  쌍선봉
8 Wolmyŏngam Hermitage
  월명암
9 Bus Stop
  정류장
10 Bus Stop
   정류장
11 Ch'ŏngrim-ri
   청림리
12 Chikso Waterfall
   직소폭포
13 Kwanŭmbong Peak
   관음봉
14 Ch'ŏngryŏnam Hermitage
   청련암
15 Naesosa Temple
   내소사
16 Chijangam Hermitage
   지장암
17 Bus Stop
   정류장
18 Sŏkp'o-ri
   석포리
19 Chinsŏ-ri
   진서리

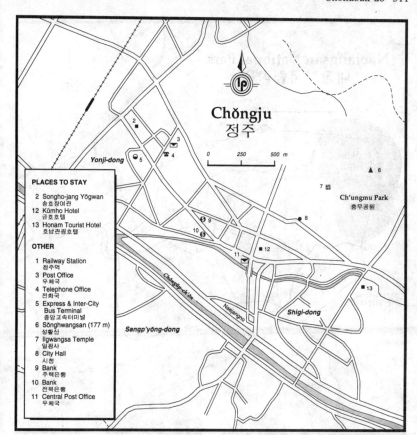

Chŏngju
정주

PLACES TO STAY

2 Songho-jang Yŏgwan
송호장여관
12 Kŭmho Hotel
금호호텔
13 Honam Tourist Hotel
호남관광호텔

OTHER

1 Railway Station
정주역
3 Post Office
우체국
4 Telephone Office
전화국
5 Express & Inter-City
Bus Terminal
중앙고속터미널
6 Sŏnghwangsan (177 m)
성황산
7 Ilgwangsa Temple
일광사
8 City Hall
시청
9 Bank
주택은행
10 Bank
전북은행
11 Central Post Office
우체국

Yonji-dong

Ch'ungmu Park
충무공원

Sangp'yŏng-dong

Chŏngŭp-ch'ŏn

Naejangno

Shigi-dong

0   250   500 m

---

am and 5.15 pm. The fare is W4500 and the journey takes 3½ hours.

Naejangsa: (Naejangsan National Park) buses depart once hourly from 6.20 am to 7.20 pm. The fare is W500 and the journey takes 25 minutes.

Puan: (Pyŏnsanbando National Park) buses depart every 30 minutes from 7.30 am to 7.40 pm. The fare is W1400 and the journey takes 40 minutes.

Pusan: buses depart five times daily between 8.40 am and 4.20 pm. The fare is W9500 and the journey takes 4½ hours.

Seoul: buses depart four times daily between 9.40 am and 4.40 pm. The fare is W6700 and the journey takes 3½ hours.

Taegu: buses depart twice daily at 9.20 am and 3 pm. The fare is W7800 and the journey takes five hours.

Taejŏn: buses depart 11 times daily between 8.30 am and 7 pm. The fare is W3500 and the journey takes 1¾ hours.

Train You can get trains directly from Seoul to Chŏngju. Departures from Seoul station are outlined in the schedule in the train time-table section at the end of this chapter.

NAEJANGSAN NATIONAL PARK
내장산국립공원

Yet another beautiful national park, the landscape is arranged like an amphitheatre. Once you've climbed to the rim, you can walk all

Naejangsan National Park
내장산국립공원

To Chŏngju
정주

To Paekamsan
백암산

---

the way to the other side, although it's strenuous. There are ladders to help hikers master the cliffs, and the views are just amazing all around. It takes at least three hours to walk the circuit, but try to allow more.

Temples in the park include Naejangsa and Paegyangsa. Other sights spread out all over this large park include Todogam Hermitage, the Kumson and Wonjok valleys, Todok Waterfall and Yonggul Cave.

Getting There & Away

You get to Naejangsan from Chŏngju (not to be confused with Chŏnju which is further north). The bus drops you off in a tourist village, from where you have a 30-minute walk to Naejangsa and the start of the climb.

SŎNUNSAN PROVINCIAL PARK
선운산도립공원

Sŏnunsan is a gorgeous place with a temple called Sŏnunsa, and small sub-temples perched all around a gorge near the sea. One enthusiastic traveller wrote 'this place is possibly the most beautiful spot in all Korea, if not the world'. Perhaps this is an

PLACES TO STAY

10 Naejangsan Hotel
내장산관광호텔

OTHER

1 Manghaebong (650 m)
망해봉
2 Pulch'ulbong (610 m)
불출봉
3 Sŏraebong (622 m)
서래봉
4 Yŏnjibong (670 m)
연지봉
5 Spring
산삼약수
6 Wonjŏkam
원적암
7 Paekryŏnam Ruins
백련암터
8 Spring
백년수
9 Bus Stop
정류장

11 Shuttle Bus Stop
서틀버스정류장
12 Todŏk Waterfall
도덕폭포
13 Cable Car
케이블카
14 Naejangsa Temple
내장사
15 Yonggul Cave
용굴
16 Kŭmsŏn Waterfall
금선폭포
17 Kkach'ibong (717 m)
까치봉
18 Munp'ilbong (675 m)
문필봉
19 Shinsŏnbong (763 m)
신선봉
20 Yŏnjabong (673 m)
연자봉
21 Changgunbong (696 m)
장군봉

exaggeration, but you'd have a hard time not enjoying this park.

Follow the path past Sŏnunsa and turn right when you see a little shop across the creek (to your left), then take a left at the next intersection and you'll come to a her-mitage. There you will find a large image of Buddha engraved into the side of a cliff. To your right will be a stairway, which you can climb to reach a small image above the Buddha image. This Buddha image was made during the Paekche

Trains from Seoul to Chŏnju

Class	Time	Frequency	Travel Time	Fare
Saemaul	9.40 am, 6.05 pm	2 daily	3 hours	W13,300
Mugunghwa	8.05 am-10.45 pm	5 daily	3¼ hours	W7900
T'ong-il	10.08 am-11.50 pm	4 daily	3½ hours	W5400

Trains from Seoul to Yŏngdong

Class	Time	Frequency	Travel Time	Fare
Mugunghwa	7.30 am-11.55 pm	21 daily	2¼ hours	W6100
T'ong-il	6.10 am-10.28 pm	9 daily	2½ hours	W4200

Trains from Seoul to Chŏngju

Class	Time	Frequency	Travel Time	Fare
Saemaul	9.05 am-5.10 pm	4 daily	3 hours	W14,200
Mugunghwa	7.20 am-11.30 pm	8 daily	3½ hours	W8400
T'ong-il	8.20 am-11.05 pm	6 daily	3 hr 55 min	W5700

period by the Chinese – the artists of this masterpiece built a precarious scaffolding of sticks and branches in order to perform this artistic feat.

Places to Stay

There are several minbak and yŏgwan in the park near Sŏnunsa, although some people stay in nearby Koch'ang (why bother?). Some of the places in the park include the *Tongbaek Yŏgwan* (☎ 62-1560), *Sonun-jang Yŏgwan* (☎ 61-2035) and *Sansaedo Yŏgwan* (☎ 61-0204). Expect to pay between W15,000 and W20,000 for a double room. Minbak can be had for W10,000.

Getting There & Away

There are only five buses daily Chŏngju to the park. Failing that, get the bus from Chŏngju to Koch'ang – these run every 10 minutes from 6.15 am until 9 pm and the ride takes 40 minutes. From Koch'ang there are buses to Sŏnunsa once every 45 minutes from 7 am until 8.20 pm. Do not confuse Koch'ang with Kŏch'ang – the latter is in Kyŏngsangnam-do Province halfway between Kwangju and Taegu.

Ch'ungch'ŏngnam-do 충청남도

TAEJŎN 대전

This is Korea's sixth largest city with a population close to one million. You aren't likely to come here for the city itself, but Taejŏn is a very useful transit point for many interesting places in this part of Korea.

Information

There is a tourist information kiosk (☎ 632-1338) in the Taejŏn express bus terminal. There is also a tourist information booth (☎ 273-8698) in the forecourt of Taejŏn railway station.

Pomunsan 보문산

While Taejŏn isn't known for stunning scenery, the southern side of town boasts Pomunsan. This is a small mountain park dotted with temples and hermitages, and there is a short cable-car ride to reach a scenic lookout. Some of the temples on the mountain's slopes include Wongaksa, Tŏksu'am, Songhaksa, Porimsa and Pokkŭn'am.

Taejŏn Expo Science Park
대전엑스포 과학공원

Taejŏn's claim to fame was Expo '93. Although 1993 has come and gone, most of the exhibits have been preserved in one form or another. It might be worth a visit if you have time to spare in Taejŏn. Even if science parks are not your cup of tea, there is an outstanding roller coaster.

The Expo site is at the far northern end of town, and there is even a separate Expo railway station (eksŭpo yok). However, the Expo site is still about two km west of this station and you'll probably need a taxi to get there.

Yusŏng Hot Springs 유성온천

On the west side of Taejŏn, near the Honam Expressway, is the hot springs resort of Yusŏng. There really isn't much here for budget travellers. Essentially, it's a collec-

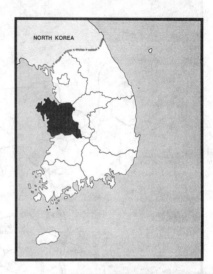

tion of large, fancy and expensive hotels where the mostly Korean and Japanese clientele go for a soak at the indoor tubs. If you want to travel in five-star style, then it's a great place to stay. Otherwise, give it a miss. You can reach Yusŏng by taking a taxi – it's about a 15-minute ride from the centre.

Places to Stay – bottom end

Since the main reason for coming here is to get to someplace else, you'll do best to stay near the bus terminal you plan to depart from. There are several bus stations, but the ones most used by travellers are the express bus terminal and the east inter-city bus terminal. These two terminals are next to one another, a rare convenience in Korea. Yŏgwan in this area are not the cheapest – figure on paying around W18,000 for a double. Some options include *Yaksu-jang P'ak'ŭ Yŏgwan* (☎ 625-0240), *Pugok P'akŭ Yŏgwan* (☎ 627-7980) and *Honey Park Hotel*.

Places to stay in the centre are marginally

Ch'ungch'ŏngnam-do
충청남도

cheaper but only practical if you're arriving or departing by train. A cheap place to stay in this area is the *Yŏng'il Yŏinsuk*, which has rooms for W10,000.

Directly opposite is the *Yŏngsŏng Yŏgwan* (☎ 282-9060), which is good value at W12,000 a single. Rooms are clean, well-furnished and have private bath. The best rooms are on the 2nd floor at the back. Both floors of the yŏgwan have rooms in the centre of the building which have no windows so make sure you get a side room – they cost the same.

More expensive but a fine place to stay is the *Sŏrin-jang Yŏgwan* (☎ 283-6221) in the block next to the Yongsong Yŏgwan. Rooms cost W18,000. There's a choice of Korean or Western-style rooms and a cocktail bar in the basement.

If you'd like a room overlooking the river try either the *Ilshin-jang Yŏgwan* or *P'yŏnghwa-jang Yŏgwan*. They're situated next to each other and have rooms for W18,000.

Places to Stay – middle
The only mid-range hotel in Taejŏn – in the centre of the city – is the *Taejŏn Tourist Hotel*

PLACES TO STAY

4 Pugok P'ak'ŭ &
 Yaksu-jang P'ak'ŭ Yŏgwans
 부곡파크여관, 약수장파크여관
5 Honey Park Hotel
 하니파크여관

OTHER

1 Taejŏn Expo Science Park
 대전엑스포 과학공원
2 Expo Railway Station
 엑스포역
3 Taejŏn Tower
 대전탑
6 Express Bus Terminal
 고속버스터미널
7 East Inter-City Bus Terminal
 동부시외버스터미널
8 Taejŏn Railway Station
 대전역
9 Sŏdaejŏn Railway Station
 서대전역
10 West Inter-City Bus Terminal
 서부시외버스터미널
11 Taejŏn Stadium
 대전공설운동장
12 Wongaksa Temple
 원각사
13 Tŏksuam Hermitage
 덕수암
14 Pomunsan Scenic Lookout
 보문산전망대
15 Purimsa Temple
 보림사
16 Pokkŭn'am Hermitage
 복근암
17 Songhaksa Temple
 송학사

Taejŏn
대전

0   0.5   1 km

See Central Taejŏn Map

Pomunsan
Park
보문산공원

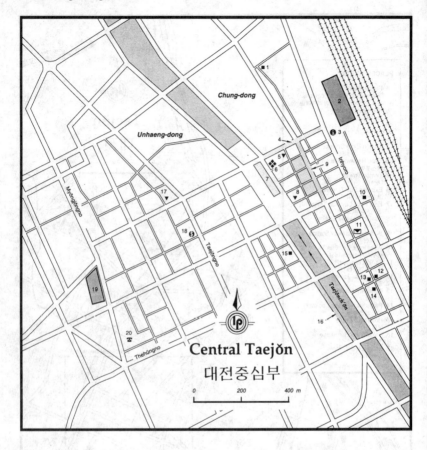

Central Taejŏn
대전중심부

0   200   400 m

(☎ 273-8131; fax 273-0131) 20-16, Won-dong, Tong-gu. Singles/twins/suites cost W29,960/33,200/47,000, plus 20% tax and surcharge. The hotel has Western and Korean restaurants, a coffee shop and nightclub.

Places to Stay – top end

All of Taejŏn's top-end places are far to the west of the city centre at the hot springs resort of Yusŏng. Staying out here could be convenient if you have your own car since Yusŏng is adjacent to the Honam Express-way, but for most travellers this just isn't a viable option. Without your own wheels you'll probably have to take a taxi (about 15 minutes from the centre).

There are several hotels with middle and top-end rooms:

Adria Hotel:442-5, Pongmyong-dong, Yusŏng-gu. Doubles/twins/suites cost W63,000/73,000/220,000 (☎ 824-0210; fax 823-5805).

Hongin Tourist Hotel: 536-8, Pongmyong-dong, Yusŏng-gu. Doubles/twins cost W46,000/47,000 (☎ 822-2000; fax 822-9410).

Mugunghwa Hotel: 549-1, Pongmyong-dong, Yusŏng-gu. Doubles/twins/suites cost W39,200/47,100/77,100 (☎ 822-1234; fax 822-1237).

PLACES TO STAY

1	YMCA
	–
10	Taejŏn Tourist Hotel
	대전관광호텔
12	Yŏng'il Yŏinsuk
	영일여인숙
13	Yŏngsŏng Yŏgwan
	영성여관
14	Sŏrin-jang Yŏgwan
	서린장여관
15	Ilshin-jang & P'yŏnghwa-jang Yŏgwans
	일신장여관. 평화장여관

PLACES TO EAT

5	Uncle Joe's Hamburgers
	조아저씨
8	Taejŏn Department Store
	대전백화점
17	Tongyang Department Store
	동양백화점

OTHER

2	Taejŏn Railway Station
	대전역
3	Tourist Information Kiosk
	관광안내소
4	Underground Arcade
	지하상가
6	Chung'ang Department Store
	중앙백화점
7	Hongmyŏng Arcade
	홍명상가
9	Central Market
	중앙시장
11	Central Post Office
	대전 우체국
16	Night-time Soju Tents
	대폿집
18	Korea Exchange Bank
	외환은행
19	City Hall
	시청
20	Telephone Office
	대전 전화국

Onch'on Hotel: 549-15, Pongmyong-dong, Yusŏng-gu. Singles/twins/suites cost W20,000/30,000/50,000 (☎ 820-8888; fax 820-8270).

Princess Hotel: 536-3, Pongmyong-dong, Yusŏng-gu. Twins/suites cost W40,000/60,000 (☎ 822-9200; fax 823-9909).

Riviera Yusŏng Hotel: 444-5, Pongmyong-dong,
Yusŏng-gu. Doubles/twins/suites cost W84,000/94,500/240,000 to W700,000 (☎ 823-2111; fax 822-0071).

Royal Tourist Hotel: 202-5, Pongmyong-dong, Yusŏng-gu. Room cost W30,000 to W52,000 (☎ 822-0720; fax 823-4019).

Yusŏng Hotel: 480, Pongmyong-dong, Yusŏng-gu. Doubles/twins/suites cost W71,000/75,000/120,000 to W550,000 (☎ 822-0811; fax 822-0041).

All these hotels tack on an extra 20% for tax and service charge. You can also be sure that the more expensive places accept major credit cards, offer a choice of Korean and Western-style rooms, have Korean, Japanese and Western-style restaurants, coffee shop, bar, karaoke nightclub and laundry/dry-cleaning services.

Places to Eat

Halfway between the river and Inhyoro (the street on which the post office and the railway station are situated) is the *Central Market*. All around here are many different restaurants and street stalls where you can eat well and cheaply.

It's a very colourful neighbourhood and worth a stroll even if you aren't hungry. People flock to this market every day of the week from all over the city and outlying areas but as the day starts early (usually by 6 am) many places close around 9.30 pm.

Those less adventurous could do worse than eat at the restaurants in the basements of one or other of the department stores. One of the cheapest of these is the one in the basement of the *Tongyang Department Store*, at the corner of Taejŏngno and Chung'angno Rds. It's a popular place with students, in part because dishes are so cheap (starting at around W1000).

More expensive, but with a much greater range of dishes, is the *Taejŏn Department Store*. They offer Korean, Japanese and Western cuisine with plastic models of the food displayed at the entrance to the restaurant. There's a good variety of dishes available for between W2500 and W4500, all the way up to a huge 'doormat' steak for W10,000.

Uncle Joe's Hamburgers is related to the chain in Seoul with the same name. Besides the hamburgers, check out the ice cream – probably the best in Korea.

Entertainment

Like all Korean cities, the centre of Taejŏn is peppered with beer bars and cocktail bars but most of them are a poor choice for meeting local people as they're broken up into a series of curtained partitions to give couples or small groups of friends a degree of privacy.

Far better is to spend the evening joining the makkoli and soju hordes on the benches in the sea of tents around the Hongmyŏng Arcade, by the river and opposite the Taejŏn Department Store. This is an extremely popular spot (even in the depths of winter!) and by the time you leave you'll have met half of Taejŏn. These places stay open until around midnight.

There is an upmarket nightclub on the top floor of the Tongyang Department Store which frequently plays Korean chartbusters. You need to be part of a fairly substantial group if you're on a budget since the group entry price is about W30,000. Another place in this bracket is the Casablanca nightclub, on the 9th floor of the Taejŏn Tourist Hotel, which runs from 7.30 pm to 3 am. Group entry rates here are W30,000 which buys you three large bottles of beer with snacks. There's a live band on every night plus frequent Korean singers. There's also a similar nightclub at the Joong Ang Tourist Hotel, where the group cover charge is W32,000.

Getting There & Away

Bus There are three bus terminals in Taejŏn: the west inter-city bus terminal (sŏbu shi'oe t'ŏminŏl), the east inter-city bus terminal (tongbu shi'oe t'ŏminŏl) and the express bus terminal (kosok t'ŏminŏl): The latter two are located side by side on the eastern outskirts of town and are the most used by travellers.

Some useful buses from the express bus terminal go to the following destinations:

Chŏnju: buses depart every 20 to 30 minutes from 6.30 am to 8.30 pm. The fare is W3800 (1st class) or W2800 (2nd class) and the journey takes 1¼ hours.

Kangnŭng: buses depart 10 times daily between 8 am and 6.40 pm. The fare is W11,000 (1st class) or W7300 (2nd class) and the journey takes four hours.

Kwangju: buses depart every 40 minutes from 6.40 am to 7.10 pm. The fare is W7200 (1st class) or W4200 (2nd class) and the journey takes almost three hours.

Kyŏngju: buses depart every three hours from 7.50 am and 5.30 pm. The fare is W8300 (1st class) or W5500 (2nd class) and the journey takes 2¾ hours.

P'ohang: buses depart every two hours between 7 am and 7 pm. The fare is W9500 (1st class) or W6400 (2nd class) and the journey takes 3¼ hours.

Pusan: buses depart every two hours from 6 am to 6.30 pm. The fare is W10,700 (1st class) or W7100 (2nd class) and the journey takes 3¾ hours.

Seoul: buses depart every five to 10 minutes from 6 am to 9.40 pm. The fare is W5900 (1st class) or W4000 (2nd class) and the journey takes 1¾ hours.

Taegu: buses depart every 20 minutes from 6.30 am to 8.30 pm. The fare is W5800 (1st class) W3800 (2nd class) and the journey takes two hours.

Tong-Seoul: buses depart every 30 minutes between 6 am and 8.30 pm. The fare is W6500 (1st class) or W4300 (2nd class) and the journey takes 1¾ hours.

The east inter-city bus terminal offers a side selection of buses, including those going to the following destinations:

Andong: buses depart every 1½ hours between 6.25 am and 5.05 pm. The fare is W8000 and the journey takes 4½ hours.

Ch'ŏngju: buses depart every six minutes from 6.30 am to 9.40 pm. The fare is W1400 and the journey takes 45 minutes.

Chinju: buses depart 12 times daily between 7.40 am and 6.20 pm. The fare is W8300 and the journey takes four hours.

Hongsŏng: (Tŏksan Provincial Park) buses depart every 14 minutes from 7 am to 7 pm (these buses terminate in Sosan, not Hongsŏng). The fare is W4800 and the journey takes 2¼ hours.

Kŭmsan: (International Ginseng Market) buses depart every seven minutes from 5.45 am to 10 pm. The fare is W1500 and the journey takes 40 minutes.

Songnisan National Park: buses depart 36 times daily between 6.22 am and 8.10 pm. The fare is W2700 and the journey takes 1¾ hours.

A   Old City gate at night, Chŏnju (MM)
B   T'apsa Pagoda Temple, Maisan (MM)
C   Black Buddhas at Kŭmsansa Temple, Chŏnju (MM)
D   Sochul-ji and pond, Namsan Village, Kyŏngju (GC)

Top: Mass transit, P'yŏngyang, North Korea (RS)
Middle: P'yŏngyang subway (RS)
Bottom: Back streets of Kaesong, North Korea (RS)

Sudŏksa: (Tŏksan Provincial Park) buses depart only once daily at 4.37 pm. The fare is W5000 and the journey takes 2½ hours.

T'aean: (T'aean Haean National Park) buses depart every 14 minutes from 7 am to 6.47 pm. The fare is W7100 and the journey takes four hours.

T'aebaek: (T'aebaeksan Provincial Park) buses depart three times daily between 7.10 am and 1.43 pm. The fare is W12,300 and the journey takes five hours.

Taedunsan Provincial Park: buses depart 10 times daily between 7.20 am and 5.30 pm. The fare is W1500 and the journey takes one hour.

Wonju: buses depart every 30 minutes from 8.01 am to 5.10 pm. The fare is W5300 and the journey takes 2½ hours.

Buses from the west inter-city bus terminal go to the following destinations:

Ch'ŏnan: (Independence Hall) buses depart every 10 minutes from 6.30 am to 8.25 pm. The fare is W1900 and the journey takes 1¾ hours.

Ch'ŏngyang: (Ch'ilgapsan Provincial Park) buses depart 30 times daily between 6.30 am and 7.50 pm. The fare is W3100 and the journey takes two hours.

Chŏngju: buses depart every 40 minutes from 8.30 am to 7 pm. The fare is W3500 and the journey takes 1¾ hours.

Chŏnju: buses depart every 20 minutes from 6.45 am to 6.11 pm. The fare is W2500 and the journey takes two hours.

Kapsa: (Kyeryongsan National Park) buses depart seven times daily between 7.29 am and 5.50 pm. The fare is W2100 and the journey takes one hour.

Kimje: buses depart 20 times daily between 6.55 am and 7.20 pm. The fare is W3300 and the journey takes 1½ hours.

Kongju: buses depart every five minutes from 6.29 am to 10.30 pm. The fare is W1600 and the journey takes one hour.

Nonsan: (Kwanch'oksa) buses depart every five minutes from 6 am to 10 pm. The fare is W1600 and the journey takes 50 minutes.

Puyŏ: buses depart every five minutes from 6 am to 9.35 pm. The fare is W2400 and the journey takes 1¼ hours.

T'aean: (T'aean Haean National Park) buses depart five times daily between 8.35 am and 4.31 pm. The fare is W7000 and the journey takes 3¾ hours.

Taedunsan Provincial Park: buses depart 12 times daily between 7.30 am and 6.20 pm. The fare is W1200 and the journey takes 50 minutes.

Yesan: (Tŏksan Provincial Park) buses depart 39 times daily between 6.51 am and 7.03 pm. The fare is W3800 and the journey takes two hours.

Yŏsu: buses depart twice daily at 9.30 am and 3.15 pm. The fare is W9400 and the journey takes five hours.

Train There are two railway stations in Taejŏn. Taejŏn railway station, in the centre of the city, serves the main line between Seoul and Pusan and all trains en route to either of those cities stop here. The other station on the west of town is Sŏdaejŏn railway station. This station serves the line to Mokp'o via Iri, Kimje and Chŏngju; if you're heading for Kwangju you must change at Yŏngsanpo.

Trains departing Seoul station for Taejŏn run according to the schedule in the train timetable section at the end of this chapter.

Getting Around

Bus The most important local bus as far as travellers are concerned is the No 841 which connects the east inter-city/express bus terminals with the west inter-city bus terminal via Taejŏn railway station and the city centre. Bus No 851 also connects Taejŏn railway station with the east inter-city/express bus terminals and bus No 714 connects Taejŏn railway station with the west inter-city bus terminal. The fare is W300 on all city buses.

Car Car rental agencies include the following:

Ch'ungnam (☎ 625-6564); Daesung (☎ 631-2670); Hyundai (☎ 533-4565)

KŬMSAN 금산

In the south-east corner of Ch'ungch'ŏngnam-do is the obscure market town of Kŭmsan. This town wouldn't rate a mention in a guidebook to Korea if it were not for the fact that 80% of the nation's ginseng is collected and marketed here.

Overseas buyers who purchase in bulk come to Kŭmsan for one-stop shopping. Individual travellers with a particular interest in ginseng might want to come take a look, but all the retail ginseng products found in Kŭmsan are also available in other parts of Korea. The town's main ginseng markets include the Kŭmsan Ginseng International Market, Kŭmsan Undried Ginseng Centre, Kŭmsan Ginseng Shopping Centre and Kŭmsan Medicinal Herb Market.

From 21 to 23 September, Kŭmsan is host to Korea's Ginseng Festival.

Not surprisingly, ginseng-based foods are a local speciality in Kŭmsan's restaurants. Ginseng chicken soup *(samgye t'ang)* is the most famous and perhaps healthiest of these dishes, but also look in the stores for tasty ginseng candy.

Getting There & Away

The easiest access is from Taejŏn's east inter-city bus terminal. From Taejŏn, buses to Kŭmsan cost W1500 and depart once every seven minutes between 5.45 am and 10 pm, taking 40 minutes for the journey.

TAEDUNSAN PROVINCIAL PARK
대둔산도립공원

Being a very mountainous country, Korea boasts many provincial parks offering craggy peaks with spectacular views over the surrounding countryside, but this park ranks among the best.

Aside from the views, the climb to the summit of Taedunsan (878 metres) along steep, stony tracks is an adventure in itself. Calm nerves are required here since the ascent involves crossing a hair-raising steel rope bridge stretched precariously between two rock pinnacles followed by an incredibly steep and long steel stairway. Those in search of a thrill have struck gold. Vertigo sufferers should go somewhere else for the day. It's very popular on weekends with local people as well as others from further afield huffing and puffing their way to the summit loaded with goodies for the inevitable picnic. On these precarious slopes you'll even meet amazing old grandfathers *(haroboji)* and grandmothers *(halmoni)* ascending the heights so rapidly that it makes the younger folks lose face *(ch'emyŏni ansŏkda)*.

The ascent will take between two and 2½ hours for any reasonably fit person and about one hour for the descent. There are soft drink stalls at various places on the climb but prices tend to be double what you would pay in urban areas – not that that's going to deter you from digging deep if you go up there in the summer. For the determined budget traveller, fresh water is available free at certain points. Entry to the park costs W600.

Places to Stay

There are a number of minbak available at the entrance to the park where the buses drop off passengers. Most of these are souvenir shops with one or two rooms to let, and you can figure on starting the bidding at W10,000.

Getting There & Away

Access to Taedunsan is from Taejŏn. From Taejŏn's east inter-city bus terminal there are departures 10 times daily between 7.20 am to 5.30 pm. The fare is W1500 for the one-hour trip. From Taejŏn's west inter-city bus terminal, departures are 12 times daily between 7.30 am and 6.20 pm.

KWANCH'OKSA 관촉사

This old Buddhist temple outside Nonsan is famous throughout Korea for possessing the second largest Buddha in the country. It has some features which are unique in Korea, and is well worth a visit. The Unjin Miruk statue was built in 968 AD during the Koryŏ dynasty and stands 18 metres high. It's made out of three massive pieces of granite – one piece for the head and body and two pieces for the arms – and must have presented some interesting construction problems. The courtyard in which it stands is surrounded by typical Korean temple buildings as well as a five-storey pagoda, and stone lanterns. If you're lucky, you may come across a small festival going on here. Admission costs W600 (W500 for students and those under 24 years old).

Places to Stay

There's a small yŏgwan just below the temple entrance, although most people visit

1 Surak-ri
   수락리
2 Bus Stop
   정류장
3 T'aegosa Temple
   태고사
4 Nakjodae Summit
   낙조대
5 Taedunsan (878 m)
   대둔산
6 Suspension Bridge
   구름다리
7 Bus Stop
   정류장
8 Sŏkch'ŏnam Hermitage
   석천암
9 Hwarang Waterfall
   화랑폭포
10 Kŭmgang Waterfall
   금강폭포
11 Anshimsa Temple
   안심사

To Taejŏn
대전

Taedunsan Provincial Park
대둔산도립공원

0   400   800 m

To Chŏntv
전주

as a day trip. You might want to stay in nearby Nonsan rather than bustling Taejŏn.

Getting There & Away

Buses for Nonsan depart from Taejŏn's west inter-city bus terminal every five minutes from 6 am to 10 pm. The fare is W1600 for the 50-minute ride. When you arrive in Nonsan you will find yourself at the inter-city bus terminal. Walk out of the bus terminal onto the main street and turn right. Continue up the street for about 500 metres and then take the road which forks to the right. A little way down this road you'll see a signposted bus stop for Kwanch'oksa. Wait here for the local bus which take you direct to the temple. The buses also have Kwanch'oksa on the front and they run every 15 to 20 minutes. The fare is W300 and the journey takes about eight minutes. You'll also find other buses to Kwanch'oksa circling around the downtown area.

PUYŎ 부여

South of the wooded hill Pusosan, around which the Paengma River makes a wide sweep, Puyŏ is the site of the last capital of the Paekche kingdom. The capital was

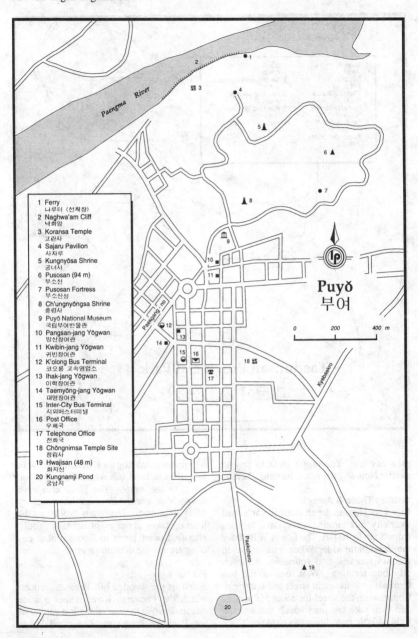

1 Ferry
  나루터 (선착장)
2 Naghwa'am Cliff
  낙화암
3 Koransa Temple
  고란사
4 Sajaru Pavilion
  사자루
5 Kungnyŏsa Shrine
  궁녀사
6 Pusosan (94 m)
  부소산
7 Pusosan Fortress
  부소산성
8 Ch'ungnyŏngsa Shrine
  충령사
9 Puyŏ National Museum
  국립부여박물관
10 Pangsan-jang Yŏgwan
  방산장여관
11 Kwibin-jang Yŏgwan
  커빈장여관
12 K'olong Bus Terminal
  코오롱 고속영업소
13 Ihak-jang Yŏgwan
  이학장여관
14 Taemyŏng-jang Yŏgwan
  대명장여관
15 Inter-City Bus Terminal
  시외버스터미널
16 Post Office
  우체국
17 Telephone Office
  전화국
18 Chŏngnimsa Temple Site
  정림사
19 Hwajisan (48 m)
  화지산
20 Kungnamji Pond
  궁남지

Puyŏ
부여

0   200   400 m

moved here from Kongju in 538 AD and flourished until destroyed by the combined forces of Shilla and the Tang dynasty of China in 660 AD.

Today it's a quiet provincial town surrounded by wooded hills and paddy fields. The people who live here are friendly and very traditionally minded. Of the Paekche ruins, not a great deal remains save for the kings' burial mounds a little way out of town, a few foundation stones of the army's arsenal, a food store on Pusosan and a five-storey stone pagoda – one of only three surviving from the Three Kingdoms period.

The main point of interest is the museum, opened in 1971, which has one of the best collections of artefacts from the Paekche kingdom you will find in Korea as well as other exhibits from later periods in the country's history.

Information

There is a tourist information kiosk (☎ 30-2585) at the entrance to Pusosan.

Puyŏ National Museum 국립부여박물관

The museum houses bronze spearheads, daggers, pottery and musical instruments from the 5th to 4th centuries BC, Paekche dynasty jars, Buddha images and examples of roof tiles embossed with various designs, as well as a collection of celadon vases, funeral urns and bronze bells dating from the 6th to 14th centuries. There is also a number of interesting stone objects – baths, lanterns, Buddha images etc – in the gardens in front of the museum. Unfortunately, there's very little explanation of the various objects in the museum so it's of limited interest to those without a knowledge of Korean archaeology.

Recently moved into the grounds of the museum are three Puyŏ county government offices dating from the late Chosŏn period. They include the county magistrate's office, his residence and a guest house for government officials.

The museum is open daily, except Mondays, from 9 am to 6 pm in summer and 9 am to 5 pm in winter. Entry costs W200.

Pusosan 부소산

Rising up behind the museum is the pine-forested hill of Pusosan which is where the royal palace and fortress of the Paekche kings once stood. It's now a popular park criss-crossed with paths and roads and it contains a number of very attractive temples and pavilions with some excellent views over the surrounding countryside. Also on this hill are the ruins of the Paekche army's food store where it's said that it is still possible to find carbonised rice, beans and barley.

Pusosan is associated with the legend of the 3000 court ladies who threw themselves onto the rocks from a high cliff – known as Naghwa'am – above the Paengma River, preferring death to capture by the invading Chinese and Shilla armies when the Paekche kingdom finally came to an end. People come from all over Korea to see this spot. A stroll around this peaceful hillside, combined with a visit to the museum, is a pleasant and relaxing way to spend a morning or afternoon.

The park is open every day and costs W1000 entry (W500 for students and those under 24 years old). There is a detailed map at the entrance, although all the points of interest are marked in Chinese characters.

Chongnimsa 정림사

This small temple site, near the centre of town contains a five-storey pagoda dating from the Paekche period and a weatherbeaten, seated stone Buddha from the Koryŏ dynasty. The Buddha is one of the strangest you're ever likely to see and bears an uncanny resemblance to the Easter Island statues.

Kungnamji Pond & Pavilion 궁남지

About one km past Chongnimsa, and surrounded by paddy fields, stands a pavilion which was originally constructed by King Mu of the Paekche kingdom as a pleasure garden for the court ladies. Until a few years ago it stood in virtual ruins but restoration was then undertaken and the bridge which takes you across the pond to the pavilion is now in good repair. It's a beautiful place to sit and relax and watch the activity in the surrounding paddy fields.

Royal Paekche Tombs 왕릉

About two km from Puyŏ, along the road to Nonsan, stands an extensive collection of Paekche royal tombs dating from 538 to 660 AD which are similar to those at Kongju. Most of them have been excavated and are open for viewing; however they're of limited interest because the contents have been removed and the wall painting in the 'painted tomb' is actually a reconstruction. What is worth seeing here is the museum, which has been designed to resemble a tomb. Inside is a number of scaled-down reproductions of the various tombs showing their manner of construction as well as a burial urn.

The area around the tombs has been landscaped and is a popular picnic spot.

The tombs are open daily and entry costs W350. To get there, take a local Puyŏ-Nonsan bus or hire a taxi (W2000). You can't miss the site as it's right next to the road on the left-hand side.

Places to Stay

Close to the Puyŏ National Museum is the *Pangsan-jang Yŏgwan*. The ordinary rooms cost W16,000, rooms with air-con cost W18,000 and there's one room with a water bed for W25,000.

In the same neighbourhood is the *Kwibin-jang Yŏgwan* which has rooms for W18,000.

To the north of the bus terminal is the *Ihak-jang Yŏgwan* (☎ 835-4521) and the neighbouring *Taemyŏng-jang Yŏgwan* (☎ 835-3877). Both places offer ondol-style rooms starting at W16,000.

Getting There & Away

There are two bus terminals in Puyŏ, both close to one another. The K'olong bus terminal is, in fact, just a patch of dirt for K'olong Express Bus Company buses. The only time you'll use it is if you want an express bus to Seoul. All other buses use the inter-city bus terminal opposite the post office.

Buses depart from the inter-city bus terminal according to the following timetable:

Ch'ŏngju: buses depart every 30 minutes from 6.40 am to 7.10 pm. The fare is W2880 and the journey takes two hours.

Chŏnju: buses depart once hourly from 8.23 am to 5.55 pm. The fare is W2330 and the journey takes 1¾ hours.

Seoul: buses depart every 20 minutes from 6.50 am to 6.30 pm. The fare is W4820 and the journey takes three hours.

Taejŏn: (via Nonsan, thus Kwanch'oksa) buses depart every eight minutes from 6.28 am to 9.40 pm. The fare is W2090 and the journey takes 1¼ hours.

Yesan: (for Tŏksan Provincial Park) buses depart every 50 minutes from 7.30 am to 8 pm. The fare is W2280 and the journey takes two hours.

KONGJU 공주

Kongju was the second capital of the Paekche kingdom established in 475 AD after its first capital, south of the Han River near Seoul, was abandoned. Nothing remains of the first capital today except for a few artefacts preserved in the National Museum at Seoul. At Kongju, however, there are far more tangible remains in the form of a whole collection of tombs of the Paekche kings.

The tombs are clustered together on a wooded hillside outside of Kongju. Inevitably, most of them were looted of their treasures over the centuries and nothing was done to preserve what remained until the Japanese carried out excavations in 1907 and 1933. Even these excavations were marred by the looting which went on once the tombs were opened up. In 1971, while work was in progress to repair some of the known tombs, archaeologists came across the undisturbed tomb of King Munyŏng (501-523 AD), one of the last monarchs to reign here. The find was one of 20th century Korea's greatest archaeological discoveries, and hundreds of priceless artefacts, which form the basis of the collection at the National Museum in Kongju, were unearthed.

Kongju is today a fairly small provincial market town and educational centre but its Paekche origins are celebrated with an annual festival held in mid-October which lasts for three to four days. It includes a large parade down the main street, fireworks, traditional dancing on the sands of the

Kŭmgang River, traditional games and sports and various other events at local sites. If you're around at that time, go to the Kongju Cultural Centre for full details.

Information

There is a tourist information kiosk (☎ 856-7700) at the entrance to the west gate of Kongsan fortress.

Kongju National Museum
국립공주박물관

The museum, opened in 1972, was built to resemble the inside of King Munyŏng's tomb. It houses the finest collection of Paekche artefacts in Korea including two golden crowns, part of a coffin, gold, jade and silver ornaments, bronze mirrors and

Stone Figure

utensils as well as Bronze Age daggers, arrowheads and axes, an Iron Age bell and a number of Buddhist images. Outside the museum is an interesting collection of stone images. The museum is open daily, except Mondays, from 9 am to 6 pm during the summer and 9 am to 5 pm in the winter. Admission is W110 (W50 for students and those under 24 years old).

King Muryŏng Tomb 백제무령왕릉

The Paekche tombs are clustered together on Sangsan-ni hill, a 20-minute walk from the centre of town. By the entrance to the site is the Muryŏng Tomb Model Hall. The star attraction is King Munyŏng's tomb, but only three of the burial chambers are open for viewing at present. Previously it was possible to go into the chambers themselves but it was found that moist warm air entering from the outside was causing deterioration of the patterned bricks and tiles inside so they're now all protected by hermetically sealed glass windows.

Entry to the tombs costs W330 (W110 for students and those under 24 years old). They're open daily from 9 am to 6 pm.

Kongsansŏng 공산성

This mountain fortress was once the site of the Paekche Royal Palace, but now it's a park with pavilions and a temple. The castle walls, although they had their origin in Paekche times, are the remains of a 17th-century reconstruction.

Places to Stay

Because the two bus terminals recently moved to the other side of the river, there is so far only one yŏgwan in the neighbourhood, the *Kŭmgangpak'ŭ Yŏgwan*. Undoubtedly more will be built as time goes on. The bus terminal itself is a good place to eat, with a cheap Chinese restaurant upstairs.

Across the river in the town are many other reasonable places to stay. The selection includes the *Samwon Yŏinsuk* (☎ 55-2496), which is very clean and run by friendly

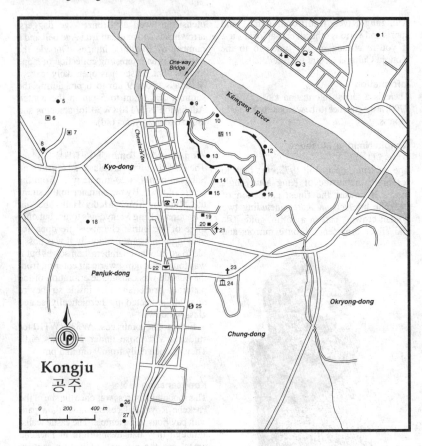

One-way Bridge

Kŭmgang River

Chemindch'ŏn

Kyo-dong

Panjuk-dong

Okryong-dong

Chung-dong

Kongju
공주

0   200   400 m

people. It costs W8,000. There's a shady courtyard but no hot water.

Going up in price, the *Kŭmho-jang Yŏgwan* (☎ 55-5305) has been a popular place to stay for years. They offer rooms for W10,000 (W9000 if you haggle) plus W3000 extra for a third person. All the rooms have a bath, hot water, TV and fan.

Those looking for a mid-range hotel should try the *Kongju Tourist Hotel* (☎ 55-4023; fax 55-4028) where twins/suites cost W33,000/55,000, plus 20% for tax & service charge.

Getting There & Away

Both the express bus terminal and inter-city bus terminal are on the north side of the river, opposite the town. You'll have to take a bus or taxi, or else walk about 1½ km to commute between the terminal and the town. Bus No 8 goes from the bus terminal to the centre, but you must return on bus No 1! Taxis charge around W1500.

Buses depart the express bus terminal for Seoul every 40 minutes from 7 am to 7 pm. The fare is W5900 (1st class) or W3900 (2nd class) and the journey takes 2¼ hours.

PLACES TO STAY

4 Kŭmgangpak'ŭ Yŏgwan
금강파크여관

14 Kongwan-jang Yŏgwan
공원장여관

15 Kongju Tourist Hotel
공주관광호텔

19 Samwon Yŏinsuk
삼원여인숙

20 Kŭmho-jang Yŏgwan
금호장여관

OTHER

1 Kongju University
공주대학교

2 Express Bus Terminal
고속버스터미널

3 Inter-City Bus Terminal
시외버스터미널

5 Songsan-ri Ancient Gravesite
송산리고분군

6 King Muryŏng Tomb
백제무령왕릉

7 Muryŏng Tomb Model Hall
무령왕릉모형관

8 Kongju Historical Site Office
공주 사적관리사무소

9 Observation Platform
전망대

10 Kongbungnu (pavilion)
공북루

11 Yŏngŭnsa (temple)
영은사

12 Lotus Pond
연지

13 Ssangsujŏng Pavilion
쌍수정

16 Kwangbongnu (pavilion)
광복루

17 Telephone Office
전화국

18 Confucian School
향교

21 Baptist Church
침례교회

22 Post Office
우체국

23 Catholic Church
천주교교회

24 Kongju National Museum
국립공주박물관

25 Korea First Bank
제일은행

26 City Hall
시청

27 Kongju Teachers' College
공주교육대학

Buses depart the inter-city bus terminal for the following destinations:

Ch'ŏngju: buses depart 45 times daily between 6.10 am and 9 pm. The fare is W1600 and the journey takes 1¼ hours.

Ch'ŏngyang: (Ch'ilgapsan Provincial Park) buses depart 51 times daily between 7.14 am and 8.04 pm. The fare is W1340 and the journey takes one hour.

Kapsa: (Kyeryongsan National Park) buses depart nine times daily between 6.40 am and 4 pm. The fare is W660 and the journey takes 25 minutes. You'll probably do better to take city bus No 2 which is more frequent.

Puyŏ: buses depart 65 times daily between 6.30 am and 9.45 pm. The fare is W1280 and the journey takes 45 minutes.

Seoul: buses depart 91 times daily between 6.50 am and 7.30 pm. The fare is W3440 and the journey takes 2¼ hours.

Taejŏn: buses depart every few minutes from 6.40 am to 10 pm. The fare is W1370 and the journey takes one hour. Many stop at Nonsan; the stop for the temple of Kwanch'oksa (ask first).

Yesan: (Tŏksan Provincial Park) buses depart 42 times daily between 6.25 am and 8.15 pm. The fare is W1950 and the journey takes 1¼ hours.

KYERYONGSAN NATIONAL PARK
계룡산국립공원

This park's unusual name means 'rooster dragon mountain', apparently because some locals thought the mountain resembled a dragon with a rooster's head. Regardless of what it's called, Kyeryongsan (845 metres) is a worthwhile peak to climb. This area of forested mountains and crystal clear streams between Kongju and Taejŏn is a popular hiking spot and also contains within its boundaries two of Korea's most famous temples, Kapsa and Tonghaksa.

The best way to see the two temples is to set off early in the day and walk from one to the other. This takes about four hours at a comfortable pace. The trails are well marked and signposted but, other than a number of hermitages scattered over the mountain and the tourist villages at the temples themselves, there are no facilities, so bring food and drink with you.

Entry to the national park costs W1300

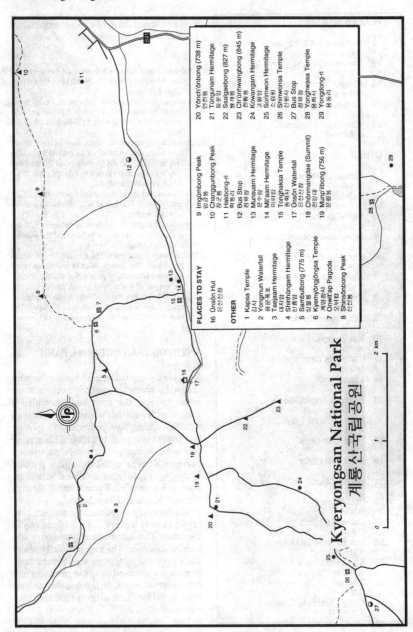

Kyeryongsan National Park 계룡산국립공원

PLACES TO STAY

16 Ŭnsŏn Hut
은선산장

OTHER

1 Kapsa Temple
갑사
2 Yongmun Waterfall
용문폭포
3 Taejaam Hermitage
대자암
4 Shinhŭngam Hermitage
신흥암
5 Sambulbong (775 m)
삼불봉
6 Kyemyŏngjŏngsa Temple
계명정사
7 Onwit'ap Pagoda
오뷔탑
8 Shinsŏnbong Peak
신선봉

9 Imgŭmbong Peak
임금봉
10 Changgunbong Peak
장군봉
11 Hakbong-ri
학봉리
12 Bus Stop
청유장
13 Munsuam Hermitage
문수암
14 Mit'aam Hermitage
미태암
15 Tonghaksa Temple
동학사
17 Ŭnsŏn Waterfall
은선산장
18 Chŏnmangdae (Summit)
천황대
19 Munp'ilbong (756 m)
문필봉

20 Yŏnch'ŏnbong (738 m)
연천봉
21 Tŭngunam Hermitage
등운암
22 Ssalgaebong (827 m)
쌀개봉
23 Ch'ŏnhwangbong (845 m)
천황봉
24 Kowangam Hermitage
고왕암
25 Sorimwon Hermitage
소림원
26 Shinwonsa Temple
신원사
27 Bus Stop
청유장
28 Yonghwasa Temple
용화사
29 Yongdong-ri
용동리

2 km
0   1   2 km

(less for students and those under 24 years old).

Kapsa 갑사

At the western end of the park stands Kapsa, one of the oldest Buddhist temples in Korea, dating back to the Unified Shilla period (8th to 10th centuries AD). Unlike many of the temples in Korea which have been either restored or completely rebuilt, some of the buildings here are original. Times are obviously changing, however, as there's now even a souvenir stall in the temple compound itself – usually these things are found only in the tourist villages. The monks at this temple are not keen on people photographing the Buddhas in the main hall even when no one is praying, so ask first if that's what you want to do.

Tonghaksa 동학사

This temple stands at the eastern end of the park and although the buildings here are nowhere near as old as those at Kapsa, the complex is a large one and the setting is stunning. As at Kapsa, there's a small tourist village down the road from the temple with the usual facilities.

Places to Stay

There are small camping grounds at both Kapsa and Tonghaksa, but back-country cooking and camping are prohibited. Both temples have the requisite tourist villages with some pricey yŏgwans (W20,000 to W30,000). If you want to conserve funds, you can expect to pay W15,000 for a minbak.

Getting There & Away

Bus From Kongju, there are 13 buses daily to Kapsa between 6.40 am and 6 pm, taking 25 minutes for the ride. From Kongju, you can also take city bus No 2. From Taejŏn's west inter-city bus terminal, there are seven buses daily to Kapsa between 7.30 am and 5.50 pm. The buses terminate at the tourist village which is about one km below the actual temple.

Tonghaksa is best approached by city bus from Taejŏn. From Taejŏn, there are seat buses every eight minutes between 6.30 am and 11 pm, taking 40 minutes for the ride and costing W550. Less expensive (W250) city buses go from Taejŏn every 30 minutes. There are only four buses daily from Kongju to Tonghaksa.

Taxi If you take a taxi to either of these temples the drivers will demand that you pay around 1½ to double what the meter would indicate. The reason for this is that they can't be sure of getting a return fare. On the other hand, if you're coming back from either of the temples then you can often get a taxi for much less than the normal meter fare for the same reason, so it's worth considering if you can fill the taxi.

MAGOKSA 마곡사

Another fairly remote and beautiful temple north-west of Kongju off the main road to Onyang, is Magoksa. It was first constructed by the Zen Master Chajangyulsa during the reign of the first Shilla queen, Son-dok (632-647 AD), a major patron of Buddhism who introduced Chinese Tang culture into Korea. The temple was reconstructed during the middle years of the Koryŏ dynasty but since then, apart from additional structures erected during the middle of the Yi dynasty, precious little has changed so you're in for a real treat of genuine Koryŏ religious art.

Magoksa's Chonbul-jon Hall, with its three huge golden Buddhas is simply incredible both in size and execution. That beams of this size were lifted into place in the days before cranes is almost beyond belief. Another gem at this temple is the Yongsan-jon Hall with its three golden Buddhas flanked by four smaller Boddhisatvas and backed by a thousand pint-sized white-painted devotees – all of them slightly different from each other. Entry to the temple costs W800.

There's a small tourist village alongside the river before the temple entrance gate but not many places to stay as such. Most of the structures are souvenir shops and restaurants but, of the latter, some are attractively placed overlooking the river. You can eat well and

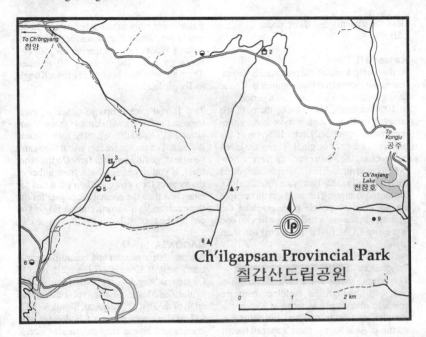

Ch'ilgapsan Provincial Park
칠갑산도립공원

0   1   2 km

PLACES TO STAY

2   Ch'ilgap Hut
    칠갑산장
4   Changgok Hut
    장곡산장

OTHER

1   Bus Stop
    정류장
3   Changgoksa Temple
    장곡사
5   Bus Stop
    정류장
6   Bus Stop
    정류장
7   Ch'ilgapsan (561 m)
    칠갑산
8   Samhyŏngjebong Peak
    삼형제봉
9   Ch'ŏnjang-ri
    천장리

fairly cheaply at these or sit and relax with a cold beer. If you want to stay overnight, then the best place is the minbak on the other side of the river from the restaurants and reached by a footbridge. Make arrangements early in the day as it only has a few rooms.

Getting There & Away

Kongju has city buses which go directly to Magoksa every 30 minutes between the hours of 6 am and 8 pm. The fare is W800 for the 37 km-journey which takes 40 minutes. A taxi from Kongju to the temple would cost around W10,000.

CH'ILGAPSAN PROVINCIAL PARK
칠갑산도립공원

The summit of Ch'ilgapsan reaches a modest 561 metres above sea level, but it's a pleasant area with hiking trails and forests. The main temple here is Changgoksa, and there is a smaller temple called Chonghyesa.

Getting There & Away

The small city of Ch'ŏngyang is the gateway to the park. From Ch'ŏngyang, there are city buses to Changgoksa eight times daily between 8 am and 8.10 pm, taking 20 minutes for the ride which costs W520.

Buses depart Taejŏn's west inter-city bus terminal for Ch'ŏngyang 30 times daily between 6.30 am and 7.50 pm and takes two hours for the journey. From Kongju there are 51 departures daily for Ch'ŏngyang between 7.14 am and 8.05 pm, taking one hour for the trip.

CH'ŎNAN 천안

Probably the only reason you would come to Ch'ŏnan is to visit the Independence Hall of Korea, about 10 km south-east of the city, and the temple of Kagwonsa, to the north-east where the largest copper statue of the Buddha in Asia stands. The city itself is of no special interest.

Information

There is a tourist information office (☎ 550-2438) outside the Ch'ŏnan railway station.

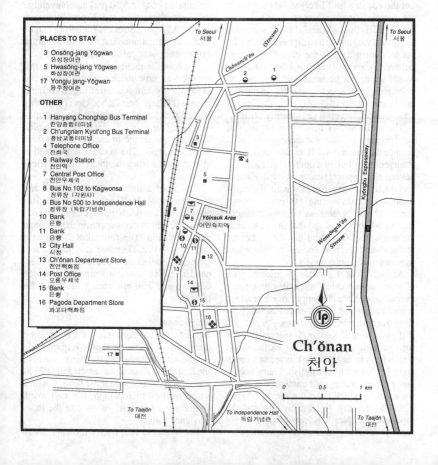

PLACES TO STAY

3 Onsŏng-jang Yŏgwan
온성장여관
5 Hwasŏng-jang Yŏgwan
화성장여관
17 Yongju jang-Yŏgwan
용주장여관

OTHER

1 Hanyang Chonghap Bus Terminal
한양종합터미널
2 Ch'ungnam Kyot'ong Bus Terminal
충남교통터미널
4 Telephone Office
전화국
6 Railway Station
천안역
7 Central Post Office
천안우체국
8 Bus No 102 to Kagwonsa
정류장 (각원사)
9 Bus No 500 to Independence Hall
정류장 (독립기념관)
10 Bank
은행
11 Bank
은행
12 City Hall
시청
13 Ch'ŏnan Department Store
천안백화점
14 Post Office
오룡우체국
15 Bank
은행
16 Pagoda Department Store
파고다백화점

To Seoul 서울

Ch'ŏnanch'ŏn (Stream)

Yŏinsuk Area 여인숙지역

Kyŏngbu Expressway

Wonsŏngch'ŏn Stream

Ch'ŏnan 천안

0   0.5   1 km

To Taejŏn 대전

To Independence Hall 독립기념관

To Taejŏn 대전

The Independence Hall of Korea
독립기념관

Most former colonies have celebrated independence by simply taking over the bricks and mortar of the colonial authorities, renaming streets in the capital, and constructing stadiums where an extravaganza is staged on the anniversary of their independence. Some, it is true, have embarked on new mega-dollar capitals carved out of the bush, but very few of these have been successful and some have been the ruination of the national economy.

South Korea has avoided these pitfalls, but the country isn't likely to be outdone in the nationalism department. The Independence Hall is South Korea's bid in the contest to create a vast modern edifice eulogising the nation's integrity and the uniqueness of its culture. When you see this place (and it *is* worth seeing), it becomes apparent that all stops were pulled out to make this an uncompromising yet superb display of South Korea's artistic talent and civil engineering skills.

The main hall of this totem to national sovereignty is like something out of a science fiction movie. It is also enormous. Built entirely out of concrete and tiles, it nevertheless epitomises traditional Korean architecture. North Korea's Kim Il-sung – famous for constructing egotistical monuments to his 'greatness' – was insanely jealous when he realised that South Korean architects handily outdid his 'Great Leader statues' and carbon-copies of European monuments and memorials.

At the back of this hall is a whole complex of seven air-con exhibition halls cataloguing the course of Korean history from the earliest recorded times up until the present. It's possibly the best museum in Korea – or rather it is if you can read Korean. Unfortunately for foreign visitors, most of the explanations which accompany the exhibits are in Korean and there's very little English. There's obviously a high propaganda content to much of the exhibits which chart the course of late-19th/20th-century Korean history, and the Japanese and North Koreans come in for some particularly virulent condemnation.

Although Japanese travellers might be nonplussed by how they're portrayed, travellers of other nationalities generally find this place very enjoyable. There's also the Circle Vision Theatre which presents a 15-minute film on Korea's scenic beauty, its traditions, customs and development using the latest audio-visual techniques and equipment.

Entry to the Independence Hall costs W1500 (W1000 for students and W700 for children). Entry to the Circle Vision Theatre is an extra W1500. The Hall is open daily from March to October from 9 am to 6.30 pm (admission ends at 5.30 pm) and November to February from 9 am to 5.30 pm (admission ends at 4.30 pm). Strollers for babies can be rented at the entrance but the lack of ramps makes them only partially useful.

The complex includes several restaurants, a bookshop, post office, souvenir shops and even a bank where you can change travellers' cheques. A large-format booklet is available (in English) with coloured photographs describing the many features of the complex including the theme of each of the various exhibition halls. The booklet is free and is also available from the main tourist offices in Seoul.

City buses shuttle between Ch'ŏnan and Independence Hall every few minutes between 6 am and 8.50 pm. A convenient bus is No 500 which stops opposite the Ch'ŏnan railway station. The ride takes 20 minutes and costs W500. There are also buses direct from the Seoul express bus terminal to Independence Hall every 40 minutes between 6.30 am and 7.20 pm, taking 1¾ hours for the journey.

Kagwonsa 각원사

Some seven km north-east of Ch'ŏnan, on the slopes of Taejosan stands Kagwonsa, a temple which has the largest bronze statue of the Buddha in Asia. It was erected in 1977 as a kind of plea for the reunification of Korea and is over 14 metres high. It's well worth combining a trip here with one to the Independence Hall.

Local bus No 102, from Ch'ŏnan railway

station area, will take you to Kagwonsa, or look for bus No 46. Both are rather infrequent. From where the bus drops you it's a steep walk up over 200 steps to the temple precincts.

Getting There & Away
Bus Buses depart Ch'ŏnan for the following destinations:

Ch'ŏngju: buses depart every 20 minutes from 7 am to 9.20 pm. The fare is W1600 and the journey takes 50 minutes.

Chŏnju: buses depart four times daily between 8.28 am and 3.31 pm. The fare is W5500 and the journey takes 3½ hours.

Ch'unch'ŏn: buses depart four times daily between 10.20 am and 6.20 pm. The fare is W6000 and the journey takes 2½ hours.

Hongsŏng: (for Tŏksan Provincial Park) buses depart every 30 minutes from 6.55 am to 8.05 pm. The fare is W2600 and the journey takes 1¾ hours.

Kongju: buses depart every 10 minutes from 6.55 am to 9 pm. The fare is W1900 and the journey takes one hour.

Puyŏ: buses depart every 20 minutes from 8 am to 8.30 pm. The fare is W3400 and the journey takes two hours.

Seoul: buses depart every five to 10 minutes from 8.20 am to 8.40 pm. The fare is W2200 and the journey takes 1¼ hours.

Sudŏksa: (Tŏksan Provincial Park) buses depart only once daily at 6.38 pm, and the ride lasts 1¾ hours. It's usually better to take a bus to Yesan where you can change buses for Sudŏksa.

Suwon: buses depart every 10 minutes from 6.40 am to 9.10 pm. The fare is W2100 and the journey takes one hour.

T'aean: (T'aean Haean National Park) buses depart every 30 minutes from 7.21 am to 7.01 pm. The fare is W4500 and the journey takes 2½ hours.

Taejŏn buses depart every 20 minutes from 6.40 am to 9 pm. The fare is W1900 and the journey takes one hour.

Wonju (for Ch'iaksan National Park) buses depart eight times daily between 7.30 am and 7.10 pm. The fare is W5200 and the journey takes 2¼ hours.

Yesan (for Tŏksan Provincial Park) buses depart every 30 minutes from 6.55 am to 8.45 pm. The fare is W1700 and the journey takes 1¼ hour.

Train Ch'ŏnan straddles one of the most heavily travelled railway lines in the country, and it is often difficult to get even a standing-room ticket on weekends. Trains depart

Seoul station for Ch'ŏnan according to the schedule in the train timetable at th end of this chapter.

HONGSŎNG 홍성
This is the main staging post for a visit to Sudŏksa and Tŏksan Provincial Park. The town is not a major attraction, but it's pleasant enough and you might even want to spend the night. Hongsŏng is an old fortress town with parts of its city wall and one beautiful gate still remaining.

Places to Stay
There is the usual collection of yŏgwan spread out around the town. Yŏinsuks are harder to find – there is one near the city gate and also across the river from the bus terminal. Expect to pay W8000 at a yŏinsuk and double that for a yŏgwan.

Getting There & Away
Bus There is only one bus terminal in town handling both express and inter-city buses. Local city buses with the word 'Sudŏksa' (in Korean) written on the windshield can get you to Tŏksan Provincial Park. Some useful buses leave for Hongsŏng to the following places:

Ch'ŏnan: buses depart every 10 minutes from 6.35 am to 9.32 pm. The fare is W2600 and the journey takes 1½ hours.

Ch'ŏngju: buses depart nine times daily between 7.43 am and 6.30 pm. The fare is W4100 and the journey takes 2¾ hours.

Seoul: buses depart every 40 minutes from 7.35 am to 7.15 pm. The fare is W5100 and the journey takes 2¼ hours.

Sŏsan: (T'aean Haean National Park) buses depart every 10 minutes from 6.40 am to 10.10 pm. The fare is W1500 and the journey takes 50 minutes.

Sudŏksa: (Tŏksan Provincial Park) buses depart every 30 minutes from 7.45 am to 8.30 pm. The journey takes 40 minutes.

Taejŏn: buses depart every 30 minutes from 6.30 am to 7 pm. The fare is W4800 and the journey takes 2¼ hours.

Train The railway station is about a 15-minute walk east of the bus terminal. There are a few trains to Ch'ŏnan and Seoul, but in general you'll get around more quickly by bus.

TŎKSAN PROVINCIAL PARK
덕산도립공원

This park has incredible scenery and should not be missed it you're in the area. Attractions include pretty valleys, pine forests, large boulders, rocks and waterfalls. There is also the peak of Tŏksungsan which reaches a modest 495 metres elevation. The park is nicknamed 'little Kŭmgangsan' – Kŭmgangsan is in North Korea and is considered the country's most spectacular mountain range.

On the southern slope of Tŏksungsan is Sudŏksa, a Buddhist temple known for its large contingent of resident nuns. The other main temple in the park is called Chonghyesa.

Admission to Tŏksan Provincial Park costs W800.

Getting There & Away
Access is either from Hongsŏng or Yesan (Hongsŏng is somewhat better). Buses depart Yesan for Sudŏksa 12 times daily between 8.20 am and 7.05 pm. The fare is W800 and the ride takes 50 minutes.

You can easily get to Yesan from Taejŏn's west inter-city bus terminal. You can also get to Yesan from Ch'ŏnan and Kongju.

From Seoul's Nambu bus terminal, there are two buses daily to Sodŏksa departing at 7.20 am and 1.45 pm.

T'AEAN HAEAN NATIONAL PARK
태안해안국립공원

T'aean Haean (seashore) National Park offers some dramatic coastal scenery, four large sandy beaches and about 130 islands and islets. The largest island by far is Anmyŏndo, which is reached by bridge. From north to south, the four main beaches are Ch'ŏllip'o, Mallip'o, Yŏnpo and Mongsanp'o. Mallip'o seems to be the most popular.

This is the nearest national park to Seoul offering beachside scenery. Not surprisingly, July and August are the peak months and the beaches can be wall-to-wall with bodies and beach umbrellas. Visiting slightly off-season (June or September) is recommended.

Admission to the park costs W700.

Places to Stay
There are plenty of minbak and yŏgwan, many against the beach with no thought given to aesthetics. These places can fill up during the July-August peak season, and you can forget it on weekends and holidays.

Getting There & Away
Access is from the town of T'aean, which is still about 16 km from the beach at Mallip'o. Local city buses run from T'aean to the beaches.

You can most easily get to T'aean from Taejŏn's east inter-city bus terminal or from Ch'ŏnan. You can also catch a train from Seoul to the small town of Hongsŏng and from there get a bus to T'aean.

Trains from Seoul to Taejŏn

Class	Time	Frequency	Travel Time	Fare
Saemaul	8 am-11.20 pm	18 daily	1½ hours	W8100
Mugunghwa	7.30 am-11.55 pm	28 daily	1¾ hours	W4800
T'ong-il	6.10 am-10.30 pm	4 daily	1¾ hours	W3300

Trains from Seoul to Ch'ŏnan

Class	Time	Frequency	Travel Time	Fare
Saemaul	9.30 am-11.20 pm	3 daily	1 hour	W5300
Mugunghwa	7.20 am-11.55 pm	45 daily	1 hour	W2800
T'ong-il	6.10 am-11.50 pm	33 daily	1¼ hours	W2000

1 Illaksan (521 m)
   일락산
2 Illaksa Temple
   일락사
3 Sŏkmunbong (653 m)
   석문봉
4 Oknyŏ Waterfall
   옥녀폭포
5 Namyŏn Tomb
   남연군묘
6 Bus Stop
   정류장
7 Sŏwonsan (472 m)
   서원산
8 Podŏksa Temple
   보덕사
9 Kayasan (677 m)
   가야산
10 Bus Stop
   정류장
11 Tŏksan Hot Springs
   덕산온천
12 Tŏksungsan (495 m)
   덕숭산
13 Chonghyesa Temple
   정혜사
14 Kyŏnsŏngam Hermitage
   견성암
15 Sudŏksa Temple
   수덕사
16 Bus Stop
   정류장
17 Suamsan (260 m)
   수암산

Tŏksan Provincial Park
덕산도립공원

0   1   2 km

To Ch'ŏnan
천안

45

622

Yongbongjŏ
Reservoir
용봉저수지

To Yongbongsan
용봉산

Ch'ungch'ŏngbuk-do 충청북도

CH'ŎNGJU 청주

Another small provincial capital in central Korea, Ch'ŏngju is a useful launching pad for nearby Songnisan National Park. The town has a few minor sights, but nothing to hold your interest for long.

Sangdangsansŏng 상당산성

This huge fortress is to the north-east of Ch'ŏngju on the slopes of Uamsan. There are four gates still standing and also the wall is in good nick, thanks to a recent renovation. It takes about 40 minutes to walk the length of the wall.

The history of the fortress is unclear. One legend claims that it was built in the Shilla dynasty by the father of Kim Yu-shin who was the leader of a military contingent called the Hwarang. Another story says it was built by Kosŏng of the Paekche kingdom. Whoever first built it, the fortress was falling apart until it was renovated in 1716. These days it's past its prime as a fortress, but remains a weekend getaway for Ch'ŏngju residents along with nearby Samil Park.

Sangdangsansŏng is not a major tourist attraction, but is one of the few quick journeys you can do out of town if you're spending the night in Ch'ŏngju. The fortress is 30 minutes by city bus from downtown – enquire at the bus terminal.

Places to Stay

The best collection of yŏgwan is in an alley on the east side of the inter-city bus terminal (see map). There are fewer places near the express bus terminal.

Close to the express bus terminal is the upmarket *Ch'ongju Royal Tourist Hotel* (☎ 221-1300; fax 221-1319), 227-22, Somun-dong. Singles/doubles/twins/suites cost W37,439/38,000/64,100/80,000, plus 20% tax and service.

The plushest hotel is the *Ch'ongju Tourist Hotel* (☎ 64-2181; fax 66-8215) which is way out in the west end of town. Doubles

cost W38,200, twins W41,700 to 57,500 and suites W83,200 to W153,600, plus 20% tax and service.

Getting There & Away

There is an express bus terminal and inter-city bus terminal in Ch'ŏngju. Departures from the express bus terminal are as follows:

Kwangju: buses depart every 1½ hours from 6 am to 7 pm. The fare is W7900 (1st class) or W5300 (2nd class) and the journey takes 2¾ hours.

Pusan: buses depart every 1⅓ hour from 7 am to 6 pm. The fare is W12,000 (1st class) or W8000 (2nd class) and the journey takes 4½ hours.

Seoul: buses depart every five to 10 minutes from 5.50 am to 10 pm. The fare is W5000 (1st class) or W3300 (2nd class) and the journey takes 1¾ hours.

Taegu: buses depart every hour from 1½ hour from 7.30 am to 7.10 pm. The fare is W7700 (1st class) or W5100 (2nd class) and the journey takes 2¾ hours.

Ch'ungch'ŏngbuk-do
충청북도

Tong-Seoul: buses depart 30 minutes from 6 am to 9 pm. The fare is W5300 (1st class) or W3500 (2nd class) and the journey takes 1¾ hours.

Departures from the inter-city bus terminal are as follows:

Ch'ŏnan: buses depart every 20 minutes from 6.50 am to 9.10 pm. The fare is W1360 and the journey takes 50 minutes.

Ch'ungju: buses depart every 10 minutes from 6.15 am to 9 pm. The fare is W2410 and the journey takes 1¾ hours.

Chech'ŏn: buses depart every 10 minutes from 6.20 am to 8.15 pm. The fare is W1040 and the journey takes 50 minutes.

Chŏnju: buses depart 20 times daily between 7.20 am and 6.35 pm. The fare is W3580 and the journey takes two hours.

Ch'unch'ŏn: buses depart 12 times daily between 8.55 am and 5.55 pm. The fare is W6760 and the journey takes 3¾ hours.

Hongsŏng: (Tŏksan Provincial Park) buses depart nine times daily between 7.43 am and 6.30 pm. The fare is W4100 and the journey takes 2¾ hours.

Muju: (Tŏgyusan National Park) buses depart five times daily between 7 am and 2.50 pm. The fare is W3540 and the journey takes 2½ hours.

Puyŏ: buses depart every 40 minutes from 6.25 am to

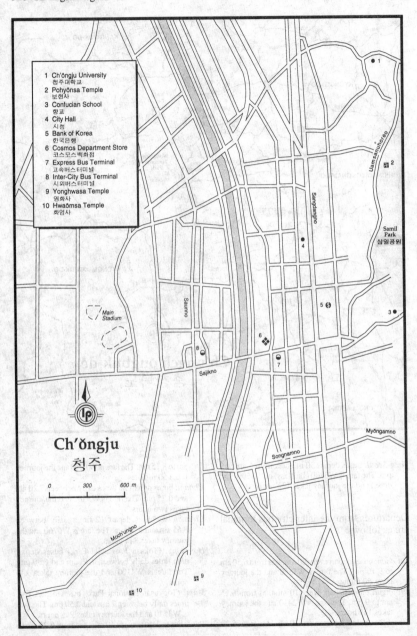

1 Ch'ŏngju University
청주대학교
2 Pohyŏnsa Temple
보현사
3 Confucian School
향교
4 City Hall
시청
5 Bank of Korea
한국은행
6 Cosmos Department Store
코스모스백화점
7 Express Bus Terminal
고속버스터미널
8 Inter-City Bus Terminal
시외버스터미널
9 Yonghwasa Temple
영화사
10 Hwaŏmsa Temple
화엄사

Uamsamuhoreo

Sangdangno

Samil
Park
삼일공원

Saunno

Main
Stadium

Sajikno

Ch'ŏngju
청주

0   300   600 m

Myŏngamno

Songnamno

Mochungno

7.30 pm. The fare is W2880 and the journey takes two hours.

Seoul: buses depart every 20 minutes from 6.30 am to 8.40 pm. The fare is W2900 and the journey takes 1¾ hours.

Songnisan National Park: buses depart every 10 minutes from 6.30 am to 8.35 pm. The fare is W2430 and the journey takes 1½ hours.

Suwon: buses depart every 15 minutes from 6.40 am to 8.40 pm. The fare is W2990 and the journey takes 1½ hours.

Taejŏn: buses depart every four minutes from 6.30 am to 9.40 pm. The fare is W1260 and the journey takes 35 minutes.

Wonju: buses depart every 25 minutes from 7.30 am to 6.05 pm. The fare is W3770 and the journey takes 3¾ hours.

SONGNISAN NATIONAL PARK
속리산국립공원

Songnisan National Park is one of the finest scenic areas in central Korea. Not surprisingly, there are numerous excellent walks. A favourite hike leads to the summit of Ch'unhwangbongsee Songnisan National Park, *see also* trekking (CCB) (1058 metres), the park's highest summit.

Although the area's great scenic beauty is a major attraction, Songnisan National Park is really distinguished by Pŏpchusa, one of the largest and most magnificent temple sites in Korea.

Construction of the temple was begun as early as 553 AD during the Shilla dynasty, which was when the Taeongbojŏn Hall with its enormous golden Buddhas and the five-roofed Palsangjŏn Hall were constructed. At the time it was one of the largest sanctuaries in Korea. Repairs were undertaken in 776 AD but in 1592 it was burned to the ground during the Japanese invasion. Reconstruction began in 1624 and it's from this time that the present Palsang-jŏn Hall dates, making it one of the few wooden structures at Pŏpchusa to survive since the 17th century. Most of the others were constructed or reconstructed towards the end of the Yi dynasty.

Pŏpchusa is, however, famous for yet another reason. Until 1986, it had the largest Buddha statue in Korea – possibly in the whole of North-East Asia – and the 27-metre-high, concrete statue of the Maitraya

Buddha dominated the temple compound. It took 30 years to build and was completed only in 1968. It featured prominently in all the tourist literature of this area. Unfortunately, by the 1980s, the statue had begun to crack so, in late 1986, it was demolished. In its place has risen a new statue (33 metres high), this time made out of 160 tons of brass which sits on top of a massive white stone base containing a ground-level shrine. This gigantic project, which cost about US$4 million, was completed in late 1989.

There are many other interesting features at Pŏpchusa including stone lanterns, a rock-cut seated Buddha, a huge bell and an enormous iron cauldron cast in 720 AD which was used to cook rice for the 3000 monks who lived here during its heyday.

As though the magnificence of the temple buildings themselves were not enough, Pŏpchusa is surrounded by the luxuriously forested mountains of Songnisan National Park which, although at its best in the autumn, is beautiful at any time of the year. There are scenic well-marked hiking trails in the mountains above the temple and several hermitages where you may be able to stay for the night.

Admission fees are W1600 for adults; W900 for students and W600 for children.

Information
The national park headquarters is near the park entrance. You might be able to get a map here, but don't count on it. Perhaps the most useful service this place offers is the left-luggage room (signposted in English).

Places to Stay
Like all important temple complexes in Korea, Pŏpchusa has its own tourist village (called Songni-dong) before the entrance to the national park except it's more like a small town. Songni-dong has expanded by leaps and bounds over the last 10 years and there's a wide choice of places to stay. Prices here are pushed upwards by the fact that this is a resort area. Minbak with shared bath go for W15,000 while yŏgwan with private bath start at W20,000. However, we were able to

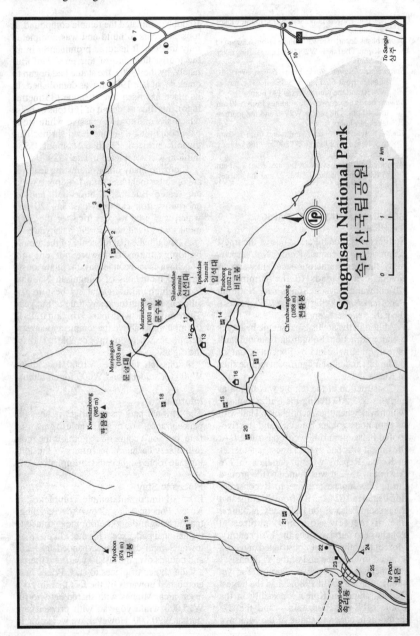

Songnisan National Park
속리산국립공원

To Sangju
상주

0   1   2 km

Kwanŭmbong
(985 m)
관음봉 ▲

Myobon
(874 m)
묘봉 ▲

Munjangdae
(1033 m)
문장대

Munsubong
(1031 m)
문수봉

Shinsŏndae
Summit
신선대

Ipŏkdae
Summit
입석대

Pirobong
(1032 m)
비로봉

Ch'unhwangbong
(1058 m)
천황봉

Songni-dong
속리동

To Poŭn
보은

1 Sŏngbulsa Temple
성불사

2 Osong Waterfall
오송폭포

3 Park Office
공원관리사무소

4 Camping Ground
야영지

5 Changam-ri
장암리

6 Bus Stop
정류장

7 Yongyu-ri
용유리

8 Bus Stop
정류장

9 Bus Stop
정류장

10 Changgak Waterfall
장각폭포

11 Kyŏngopdae Rock
경업대

12 Spring
장수약수

13 Kŭmgang Shelter
금강대피소

14 Sanggoam Hermitage
상고암

15 Pokch'ŏnam
복천암

16 Piro Hut
비로산장

17 Sanghwanam Hermitage
상환암

18 Chungsajaam Hermitage
중사자암

19 Yŏjŏkam Hermitage
여적암

20 T'algolam Hermitage
탈골암

21 Pŏpchusa
법주사

22 Park Office
공원관리사무소

23 Songnisan Tourist Hotel
속리산관광호텔

24 Camping Ground
야영지

25 Bus Stop
정류장

yŏgwan hang out by the bus terminal and solicit business.

If you're looking for an upmarket place, Songni-dong can accommodate you. The best in town is the *Hotel Songnisan* (☎ 42-5281) where doubles go for a cool W50,000. Next to the best is the *Poŭn Hotel* (☎ 43-1818), with doubles for W31,000.

There's a free camp site (signposted 'Camping Ground' in English) on the opposite side of the river from the village, which usually isn't crowded. Facilities are good and include clean toilets and wash basins.

Places to Eat
As with places to stay, there are any number of restaurants in Songni-dong, most of them along the main road to the park entrance. You can get virtually any Korean dish at one or other of these restaurants (except fresh seafood) and a few of them specialise in 'mountain food'. Since this is a resort area, expect to pay more for a meal at any of these restaurants than you normally would elsewhere.

Getting There & Away
The most useful direct buses go from Songnisan to Ch'ŏngju, Taejŏn and Seoul, but a few other destinations are also on the timetable. Buses leave from Songnisan for the following places:

Ch'ŏngju: buses depart every 10 minutes from 6.10 am to 7.50 pm. The fare is W2430 and the journey takes 1½ hours.

Seoul: buses depart once hourly from 6.10 am to 6.35 pm. The fare is W5330 and the journey takes three hours.

Suwon: buses depart seven times daily from 7.30 am to 5.50 pm. The fare is W5770 and the journey takes three hours.

Taegu: buses depart five times daily between 9.33 am and 6.26 pm. The fare is W5930 and the journey takes 3½ hours.

Taejŏn: buses depart every 10 minutes from 6.30 am to 7.56 pm. The fare is W2340 and the journey takes 1¾ hours.

bargain a 10% discount on a weekday at the *Chongshim-jang Yŏgwan* (☎ 43-3910), and you might even negotiate something cheaper during winter. The owners of minbak and

CH'UNGJU 충주
Ch'ungju is an unremarkable town on the north slope of the Sobaek mountain range. If

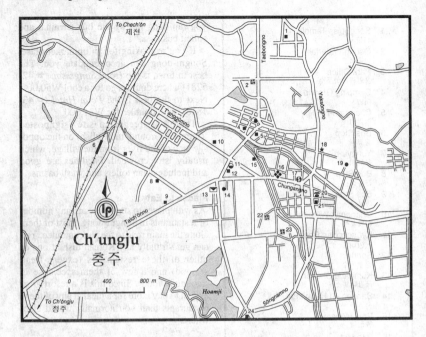

Ch'ungju
충주

you're exploring Ch'ungch'ŏngbuk-do Province, it's very likely you'll at least pass through Ch'ungju but unlikely that you will need to spend the night. However, the town is the main jumping off point for Suanbo Hot Springs, Woraksan National Park, Ch'ungjuho (lake) and some ski resorts.

Getting There & Away

Bus Ch'ungju has only one bus terminal, conveniently located in the centre of town. There are also local city buses which can be caught across the street from the terminal, and these travel to some useful destinations such as Suanbo Hot Springs, Ch'ungjuho and Woraksan National Park.

From the bus terminal itself, there are departures to the following destinations:

Andong: buses depart six times daily between 10.30 am and 6.05 pm. The fare is W6100 and the journey takes three hours.

Ch'ŏngju: buses depart every seven minutes from 6.15 am to 7 pm. The fare is W2800 and the journey takes 1¾ hours.

Chech'ŏn: buses depart every 20 minutes from 7 am to 8.35 pm. The fare is W2000 and the journey takes 1¼ hours.

Ch'unch'ŏn: buses depart every 1½ hours from 9.25 am to 7 pm. The fare is W5900 and the journey takes 3½ hours.

Seoul: buses depart every 15 minutes from 5.40 am to 8.35 pm. The fare is W3700 and the journey takes two hours.

T'aebaek: buses depart only once daily at 9.05 am. The fare is W7400 and the journey takes four hours.

Taegu: buses depart every 35 minutes from 6 am to 6.15 pm. The fare is W8200 and the journey takes 4¼ hours.

Taejŏn: buses depart every 20 minutes from 7 am to 6.40 pm. The fare is W4200 and the journey takes two hours.

Wonju: buses depart every 15 minutes from 6.40 am to 8.15 pm. The fare is W2400 and the journey takes 1¼ hours.

Train There is one train daily from Seoul to Ch'ungju. It departs Seoul station at 6.40 pm, costs W4100 and takes 2¾ hours to reach Ch'ungju.

SUANBO HOT SPRINGS 수안보온천

The town of Suanbo is a resort village at the base of the Sobaek mountains, 21 km from Ch'ungju. Apart from being one of South Korea's premier hot springs resorts, Suanbo is also known for its golf courses and skiing facilities.

Not surprisingly, Suanbo's amenities are no secret, and the area can be overrun with tourists at any time of year. Needless to say, on holidays it seems like half of Seoul has migrated here in pursuit of pleasure and you'd be wise to schedule your visit when most of the Korean populace is at work.

For those who can afford the ticket, Waikiki Hotel can furnish the latest in recreation facilities (golf, skiing and others you hadn't thought of). This place also does boat tours on nearby Ch'ungjuho.

Places to Stay – bottom end

There are two youth hostels in Suanbo, although one is all but inaccessible. The one where you have a chance of getting in is the *Namju Youth Hostel* (☎ 846-0397; fax 846-0396), which is 1½ km from Suanbo Hot Springs towards the skiing grounds at Suanbo Aurora Valley. There are 300 beds and the cost is W6600 per person. Reservations can be made at the Korean Youth Hostel Association (☎ (02) 725-3031) in Seoul.

The other place is the *Hanal Youth Hostel* (☎ 846-3151) which is one km from Suanbo. Despite the huge size of this hostel (724 beds) it seems to be *always* full. You can try calling their office in Seoul (☎ (02) 752-0803) to see, if by some mistake, there is a vacancy, but the general consensus of opinion is that it's almost hopeless.

Of course, you don't need to stay in a youth hostel unless your budget is rock bottom. For around W18,000 you can get a decent double room in a yŏgwan, although prices can go higher on weekends and holidays when demand is high. There are far too many yŏgwan to list, but a small sample could include:

Chayon Onch'on-jang (☎ 846-3366) 30 rooms; *Hanil Onch'on-jang* (☎ 846-3411) 64 rooms; *Hayan-jang* (☎ 846-4345) 30 rooms; *Ihwa-jang* (☎ 846-2381) 37 rooms; *New Chongsu-jang* (☎ 846-5577) 24 rooms;

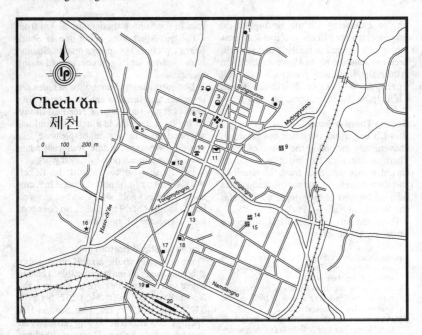

Chech'ŏn
제천

0   100   200 m

Nulbom-jang (☎ 846-6651) 26 rooms; Okch'on-jang
(☎ 846-3611) 44 rooms; Onch'on-jang (☎ 846-3161)
38 rooms; Seoul-jang (☎ 846-2711) 60 rooms;
Shinhung-jang Onch'on (☎ 846-3711) 34 rooms;
Taewon-jang) (☎ 846-7373) 30 rooms

Places to Stay – top end
Suanbo is hardly backpacker haven – pricey
hotels are available to all who can afford it.
Add 20% for tax and service.

If you're flush with cash, consider the
following:

Suanbo Hotel: 50 rooms with doubles/suites for
    W39,800/165,000 (☎ 846-2311; fax 846-2315)
Suanbo Park Hotel: 113 rooms with doubles/
    twins/suites for W47,400/50,000/85,700 (☎ 846-
    2331; fax 846-3705)
Suanbo Sangnok Hotel: 101 rooms with twins/suites
    for W50,800/90,000 to W280,000 (☎ 845-3500)
Waikiki Suanbo Hotel: 102 rooms with doubles/
    twins/suites for W47,400/50,200/72,000 (☎ 846-
    3333; fax 846-0500)

Getting There & Away
There is a city bus from Ch'ungju going to
Suanbo every 1¼ hour from 5.40 am to 8
pm. The fare is W840 and the ride takes 40
minutes. Long-distance inter-city buses
depart Suanbo according to the following
schedule:

Andong: buses depart every 1½ hours. The fare is
    W4730 and the journey takes 2½ hours.
Ch'ŏngju: buses depart every 40 minutes from 7.05
    am to 7 pm. The fare is W2820 and the journey
    takes 1¾ hours.
Seoul: buses depart every 20 minutes from 7.40 am to
    7.40 pm. The fare is W4590 and the journey takes
    2¼ hours.
Taegu: buses depart every 35 minutes from 6.30 am
    to 6.45 pm. The fare is W6310 and the journey
    takes 3¼ hours
Taejŏn: buses depart four times daily between 8.45
    am and 3 pm. The fare is W4080 and the journey
    takes 2¾ hours.

CHECH'ŎN 제천
Chech'ŏn is another useful transit point in

PLACES TO STAY

5 Paeut'ang Yŏgwan
배우탕여관

6 Tongshin-jang Yŏgwan
동신장여관

7 P'unggi-jang Yŏgwan
풍기장여관

12 Haengun Tourist Hotel
행운관광호텔

13 Sŏrin-jang Yŏgwan
서린장여관

17 Kadŭn-jang Yŏgwan
가든장여관

18 Rotde-jang Yŏgwan
롯데장여관

19 Kŭrin-jang Yŏgwan
그린장여관

OTHER

1 City Hall
시청

2 Tongbu Express Bus Terminal
동부고속버스터미널

3 Inter-City Bus Terminal
시외버스터미널

4 Won'gaksa Confucian School
원가사향교

8 Central Supermarket
중앙쇼핑

9 Pokch'ŏnsa Temple
복천사

10 Telephone Office
전화국

11 Post Office
우체국

14 Won'gaksa Temple
원각사

15 Hansansa Temple
한산사

16 Police
경찰서

20 Railway Station
제천역

the northern part of Ch'ungch'ŏngbuk-do, but you aren't likely to come here just to enjoy the town.

Ŭirimji Pond 의림지

The nearest sight is Ŭirimji Pond to the north-west of town. The 'pond' is in fact a small reservoir, two km in circumference. It's part of the oldest irrigation system in Korea and has been designated an historic monument.

History aside, the pond is picturesque, surrounded by pines and willows. The scenery is dressed up by two pavilions, Kyonghoru and Yonghojong.

Local city buses run from Chech'ŏn to Ŭirimji Pond every 10 minutes from early morning until late in the evening. The fare is W250.

Places to Stay

With luck, you will not need to spend the night in Chech'ŏn, but there are plenty of yŏgwan to accommodate you if the occasion should arise. Prices are typically W18,000 for a double. Typical of this genre is the *Sŏrin-jang Yŏgwan* (☎ 42-3663), about 500 metres north of the railway station.

Getting There & Away

Bus Chech'ŏn has two bus stations, the Tongbu express bus terminal and the inter-city bus terminal. From the Tongbu express bus terminal there are buses to Seoul every 40 minutes between 6.30 am and 7.10 pm. The fare is W7500 (1st class) or W5400 (2nd class) and the journey takes 2¾ hours.

From the inter-city bus terminal there are buses to the following places:

Andong: buses depart 17 times daily between 8.13 am and 7.05 pm. The fare is W5200 and the journey takes three hours.

Ch'ŏngju: buses depart 15 times daily between 6.15 am and 7.40 pm. The fare is W4800 and the journey takes three hours.

Ch'unch'ŏn: buses depart seven times daily between 9.52 am and 7.30 pm. The fare is W5200 and the journey takes three hours.

Ch'ungju: buses depart every 10 minutes from 6.15 am to 8.10 pm. The fare is W2000 and the journey takes 1¼ hours.

Kangnŭng: buses depart every 50 minutes from 6.20 am to 5 pm. The fare is W6000 and the journey takes four hours.

Kuinsa: buses depart 13 times daily between 7.10 am and 7.40 pm. The fare is W2000 and the journey takes 1¾ hours.

Seoul: buses depart every 30 minutes from 6.40 am to 8 pm. The fare is W5400 and the journey takes three hours.

T'aebaek: buses depart every 40 minutes from 9.10 am to 9.25 pm. The fare is W5400 and the journey takes 2¾ hours.

Taegu: buses depart 11 times daily between 8.13 am and 7.05 pm. The fare is W930 and the journey takes five hours.

Taejŏn: buses depart 24 times daily between 6.15 am and 5.40 pm. The fare is W6200 and the journey takes 3¾ hours.

Tanyang: buses depart every 15 minutes from 6.50 am to 9.10 pm. The fare is W1200 and the journey takes 50 minutes.

Wonju: buses depart every 10 minutes from 6.55 am to 9.30 pm. The fare is W1700 and the journey takes one hour.

Yŏngju: buses depart 32 times daily between 8.13 am and 8.40 pm. The fare is W3400 and the journey takes two hours.

Train Trains to Chech'ŏn depart from Seoul's Ch'ŏngnyangni station at the terminus of subway line No 1. The schedule from Seoul is outlined in the train timetable section at the end of this chapter.

WORAKSAN NATIONAL PARK
월악산국립공원

This park gets relatively few visitors (by Korean standards), but still offers fine hiking

Woraksan National Park
월악산국립공원

Ch'ungjuho Lake 충주호

Songgye-ri 송계리

Mt Woraksan (1093 m) 월악산

Mt Mansubong (983 m) 만수봉

To Suanbo 수안보

Miruk-ri 미륵리

To Mirŭksa 미륵사

1 Podŏkam Hermitage 보덕암
2 Bus Stop 정류장
3 Bus Stop 정류장
4 East Gate 동문
5 Tŏkchusa Temple 덕주사
6 Tŏkjusa Buddha Statue 덕주사지마애불
7 Shinruksa Temple 신륵사
8 Bus Stop 정류장
9 Tojŏn-ri 도존리
10 Bus Stop 정류장

through picturesque forests. On the north slope of the park is Songgye, a valley six km in length which forms the main entrance to the Woraksan area. At the northern end of the valley is Songgye-ri, the tourist village which offers basic facilities. Further south in Songgye Valley is Tokchu Valley, which branches east, and Tokchusa temple.

At the southern (upstream) end of Songgye Valley is a collection of ruins which at one time was the temple of Mirŭksa. It's believed that Mirŭksa was built in the late Shilla or early Koryŏ period. A five-storey and three-storey stone pagoda are preserved here, as well as a standing stone Buddha. There is a charge of W400 for visiting the site.

Major peaks worth climbing include Chuhulsan (1106 metres), Munsubong (1162 metres) and Hasolsan (1028 metres).

A circuit of the major sights could be: Songgye-ri – Songgye Valley – main ridge – Woraksan summit (1093 metres) – information board – 960 Peak – Tokchusa – entrance to Tokchu Valley. Total distance is 9.6 km and hiking time about 4½ hours.

The east end of Woraksan is approached from Tanyang on an entirely different road. Here you will find the much ballyhooed Tanyang P'algyong (Eight Scenic Wonders). Essentially, these wonders are rock formations with names like 'Middle Fairy Rock, Upper Fairy Rock' etc. These wonders are accessible by highway and therefore more visited by windshield tourists, but you'll get a better look at the park on foot.

Admission to Woraksan National Park costs W700 for adults, W450 for students and W200 for children.

Places to Stay & Eat

There are four tiny villages in the park which offer minbak. Rooms cost around W15,000 to W20,000 depending on what the market will bear. The four villages are Worak-ri, Songgye-ri, Miruk-ri and T'anji-ri. The villages have a small assortment of restaurants and grocery stores. Back-country camping and cooking are prohibited.

Getting There & Away

Local buses from Ch'ungju ply the route to Songgye every 1¼ hours between 6.25 am and 5.45 pm. The journey takes 1¼ hours and costs W1260.

There are also four buses daily from Chech'ŏn to Songgye between 7 am and 5.50 pm. The fare is W1720 and the journey takes two hours.

TANYANG 단양

Tanyang is an up-and-coming resort town nestled between the mountains halfway across the peninsula, close to the eastern end of an artificial lake, south of Wŏnju and north of Songnisan National Park. It's a very relaxing place to spend a few days and there are plenty of interesting things to see and do in the area.

The town itself is a recent creation and completely modern, since the old town of the same name was partially flooded by the waters of the dam. Indeed, Tanyang is in reality called Shin Tanyang (New Tanyang) while the original place (which still partially exists) is called Ku Tanyang (Old Tanyang).

The lake stretches almost all the way to Ch'ungju further west. Like Lake Soyang, east of Ch'unch'ŏn, there are boats along the lake. There's also a very attractive bridge which connects the town to the eastern shore of the lake and Kosu Donggul, one of Korea's most famous limestone caves. From here, the very scenic Highway No 595 branches off to Yŏngwol and the east coast.

Information

There's a tourist information kiosk (☎ 22-1146) on the eastern side of the bridge into town (on the way to Kosu Donggul), on which quite a lot of money has obviously been spent but they have precious little information other than a booklet (in Korean) containing photographs of places of tourist interest in the area.

The ferry terminal for boats to Ch'ungju is on the lake shore in the centre of town. It deals only with boats going to the dam wall (near Ch'ungju). You cannot pick up sight-

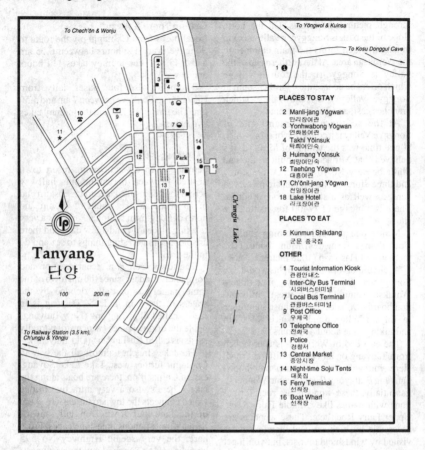

PLACES TO STAY

2 Manli-jang Yŏgwan
만리장여관
3 Yonhwabong Yŏgwan
연화봉여관
4 Takhi Yŏinsuk
탁희여인숙
8 Huimang Yŏinsuk
희망여인숙
12 Taehŭng Yŏgwan
대흥여관
17 Ch'ŏnil-jang Yŏgwan
천일장여관
18 Lake Hotel
라크장여관

PLACES TO EAT

5 Kunmun Shikdang
군문 중국집

OTHER

1 Tourist Information Kiosk
관광안내소
6 Inter-City Bus Terminal
시외버스터미널
7 Local Bus Terminal
관광버스터미널
9 Post Office
우체국
10 Telephone Office
전화국
11 Police
경찰서
13 Central Market
중앙시장
14 Night-time Soju Tents
대폿집
15 Ferry Terminal
선착장
16 Boat Wharf
선착장

Map labels: To Chech'ŏn & Wonju; To Yŏngwol & Kuinsa; To Kosu Donggul Cave; Ch'ungju Lake; Tanyang 단양; To Railway Station (3.5 km), Ch'ungju & Yŏngju; 0 100 200 m

seeing boats here. These only leave from Todam Sambong, a few km north of Tanyang.

The railway station is on the opposite side of the lake, over the road bridge, about four km west of Tanyang (this is a different bridge from the one in the centre of town) where the old town used to stand. Local buses run to the station from Tanyang at 8.05, 9, 10.15 am, noon, 2.15, 3.45, 4.30, 5.20 and 8.30 pm.

Kosu Donggul   고수동굴
Across the bridge from the centre of Tanyang is one of Korea's most famous limestone

caves. Koreans flock here by the thousands during the summer holiday period. At that time of year you literally cannot move for people and it will take you an excruciating hour or more to walk round the system.

Kosu Donggul are certainly spectacular and extensive caves – or rather they must have been before the catwalks and miasmic spiral steel staircases were installed up the main vertical galleries, but these do aid access.

A considerable amount of vandalism is also apparent on the tips of stalactites and stalagmites within reach of eager souvenir hunters. Nevertheless, it's perhaps worth visiting the caves if the crowds are not too great.

You should allow about one hour to get through the caves which are about 1300 metres long. Just outside the caves is an extensive tourist complex with yŏgwan, restaurants and souvenir shops which completely obscure the entrance to the caves. Prices of everything are well above average.

Ch'ŏngdong Donggul 청동동굴
About four km beyond Kosu Donggul, keeping left at the only road junction, is the smaller cave of Ch'ŏngdong Donggul which is some 300 metres long and was discovered only in 1977. Unlike its larger cousin which has both vertical and horizontal galleries, this cave is essentially just a vertical drop. Entry costs W990 (less for those under 24 years old).

There's the inevitable tourist village below the caves with yŏgwan, restaurants and a camp site.

There are local buses from Tanyang to Ch'ŏngdong Donggul at 7.05, 8.30, 10.30, and 11.40 am, and at 12.30, 1, 1.50, 3, 3.50, 4.40, 5.40, 7 and 8 pm.

Nodong Donggul 노동동굴
If, instead of keeping to the left at the road junction, you turned right across the concrete bridge, continued on up the hill and then down the other side, you would arrive at the third set of caves. Nodong Donggul was the most recently discovered cave and is every bit as spectacular as Kosu Donggul with a length of around one km. There are the usual steel staircases and catwalks to make access possible but nowhere near the same number of people visit this cave so you don't get that feeling of claustrophobia that is possible in Kosu Donggul.

There are local buses from Tanyang to Nodong Donggul at 6.40, 8.50, 11 am, 1.40, 3.40, 5.45 and 8 pm.

Ch'ungjuho 충주호
When the water level is high (late summer), Ch'ungjuho (Ch'ungju Lake) is an impressive body of water. It's considerably less impressive in spring when the water level drops, leaving an ugly 'bathtub ring' around the shoreline. Nevertheless, the cruises are pleasant and well worthwhile if the weather cooperates.

All the pleasure craft are moored at Todam Sambong, about three km north of Tanyang via the lakeside road. You cannot board them at Tanyang despite what the signs outside the ferry terminal suggest. There are local buses to Todam Sambong from Tanyang at 7.50, 10 am, 12.10, 1.30, 2.30, 5.10 and 7.40 pm. The buses will have Todam Sambong (in Korean) in the window and the journey takes about 10 minutes.

There are two varieties of boat which you can hire: speed boats taking up to six passengers; and slower open-decked boats which take many passengers.

The speed boats are good fun and the drivers really take them through their paces but it doesn't give you much time to take in the sights. They go when full and operate between 9.30 am and 5.10 pm. There are two options available: the first is a short eight-minute trip essentially just to the natural arch (Songmun) and around the island of Todam Sambong; the second is an 18-minute trip which goes down the lake as far as Tanyang and then returns.

The slow boats are perhaps preferable as they are more mellow and you see far more of the sights along the lake. In theory these go once an hour and operate between 9 am and 5 pm. There are two options available. The first is an 18-km round trip taking nearly an hour. The second is a 40-km round trip taking 2½ hours.

The ticket office for the slow boats is on the top side of the car park and down at the jetty for the speed boats. It's important to realise that when the water level is down (which is often the case in spring), there will be no boats at all in Tanyang. However, you may be able to pick them up further downstream.

There are a number of lakeside restaurants here, two of them with large PA systems so you can expect live music or disco in the evenings. If you stay until late, however, you'll have to take a taxi back to Tanyang.

Places to Stay

Expect to pay around W15,000 for a yŏgwan and W10,000 for a yŏinsuk. Just north and west of the bus terminal are a couple of narrow lanes chock-a-block with yŏgwan. The bottom-end place to say here is *Takhi Yŏinsuk* (☎ 423-0181). Nearby are the *Yonhwabong Yŏgwan* (☎ 22-3557) and *Manli-jang Yŏgwan* (☎ 22-2402).

Another relative cheapie is the *Huimang Yŏinsuk* on the top side of the main street near the junction with the road which crosses the bridge.

There are also scores of yŏgwan along the main street all the way down towards the bridge which leads to the railway station, but the most convenient places to stay are the yŏgwan between the main street and the lakeside in the centre of town. Some of these places have rooms overlooking the lake; a good example being the *Ch'ŏnil-jang Yŏgwan*.

Places to Eat

As is typical in Korean resorts, you'll be tripping over restaurants every couple of meters. *Sambong Shikdang* does a mean pulgogi, or you can score excellent Chinese food at the *Kunmun Shikdang* opposite the inter-city bus terminal.

An excellent alternative to the restaurants in the evenings are the soju tents on the lakeside road close to the ferry terminal. There's a variety of cheap snacks available at any of these or you can simply sit there and enjoy a cold beer or soju at the usual price.

For those who prefer to put their own food together, there's a market area with the usual range of foodstuffs.

Getting There & Around

Bus The inter-city bus terminal is well-organised and even has a printed schedule of local buses. If you can read Korean and are planning on spending some time here then it's worth asking for a copy of this. Some buses which depart from the inter-city bus terminal go to the following destinations:

Andong: buses depart 15 times daily between 7.05 am to 7.53 pm. The fare is W1700 and the journey takes 2½ hours.

Samch'ŏk: buses depart only twice daily at 11.45 am and 1.45 pm. The fare is W4320 and the journey takes six hours. This ride is particularly scenic.

Seoul: buses depart four times an hour between 7.10 am to 7.15 pm. The fare is W3030 and the journey takes nearly four hours. These buses also stop in Wŏnju and Chech'ŏn.

Taegu: buses depart eight times daily between 7 am to 3.30 pm. The fare is W2620 and the journey takes four hours. These buses also stop in Andong.

Train Trains from Seoul to Tanyang depart from Seoul's Ch'ŏngnyangni station at the terminus of subway line No 1. Trains depart Seoul according to the train timetable at the end of this chapter.

Boat Ferries connect Tanyang with Ch'ungju at the western end of the lake (the dam wall is actually outside Ch'ungju but local buses connect the ferry pier to the centre of town).

The boats run between 8.30 am and 4.30 pm in summer (9.30 am to 3.30 pm in winter) and cost W6120 per person. The journey takes slightly over two hours. When the water level is down, you can catch the boats further downstream at Changhwa. For more information about the boats, have a Korean speaker ring up the Tanyang Boat Company (☎ 22-3355) in Tanyang, or the Ch'ungju Lake Cruise Company (☎ 851-5771) in Ch'ungju. There's a notice warning passengers (in English and Korean) that, 'Drinking, dancing, disturbances and demoralisation are not allowed on board'. Meals and drinks are available on these boats.

SOBAEKSAN NATIONAL PARK
소백산국립공원

Sobaeksan (little white mountain) National Park is one of Korea's largest, on a par with the more well-known Sŏraksan National Park. But unlike Sŏraksan, Sobaeksan lacks the dramatic cliffs and rock formations.

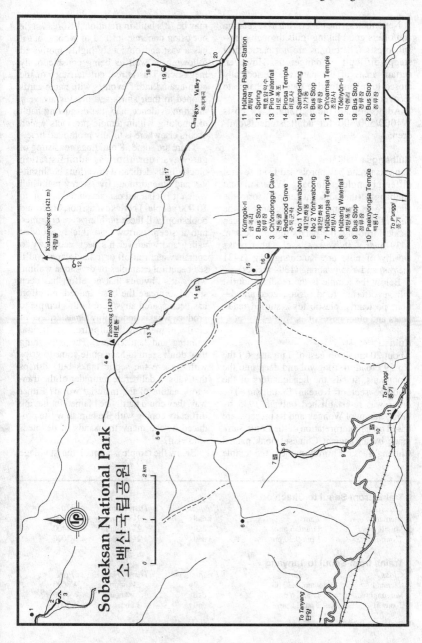

Sobaeksan National Park 소백산국립공원

1	Kŭmgok-ri	금곡리
2	Bus Stop	정류장
3	Ch'ŏndonggul Cave	천동굴
4	Redwood Grove	주목군락지
5	No 1 Yŏnhwabong	제1연화봉
6	No 2 Yŏnhwabong	제2연화봉
7	Hŭibangsa Temple	희방사
8	Hŭibang Waterfall	희방폭포
9	Bus Stop	정류장
10	Paektyŏngsa Temple	백룡사

11	Hŭibang Railway Station	희방역
12	Spring	백초암약수
13	Piro Waterfall	비로폭포
14	Pirosa Temple	비로사
15	Samga-dong	삼가동
16	Bus Stop	정류장
17	Ch'oamsa Temple	초암사
18	Tŏkhyŏn-ri	덕현리
19	Bus Stop	정류장
20	Bus Stop	정류장

Kukmangbong (1421 m)

Pirobong (1439 m)

Chukgye Valley

To P'unggi 풍기

To Tanyang 단양

0 1 2 km

Nevertheless, the park is rich in vegetation and offers good hiking trails through pleasant forests. The climbs are *not* particularly steep, difficult or dangerous. However, certain areas of the park are periodically closed to hikers to give nature a chance to recover from human impact.

Admission to the national park costs W1000/500/300 for adults/students/children.

Hŭibangsa 희방사

Sobaeksan can be approached from several different angles. Hŭibang Waterfall and Hŭibangsa (the adjacent temple) form the entrance to the main climbing area of the park. This is the area from where you can tackle Pirobong, the park's highest peak at 1439 metres above sea level. Other peaks worthy of note are Kukmangbong (1421 metres) and Yonhwabong (1394 metres).

Below the temple is the requisite tourist village offering food, drink, accommodation, postcards, plastic toys, stuffed teddy bears and other necessities.

Kuinsa 구인사

About 20 km north-east of Tanyang, off the No 595 road to Yŏngwol and deep into the mountains, stands the headquarters of the Chontae sect of Korean Buddhism. The order was re-established only in 1945 by monk Sangwol Wongak and its precepts are based on an interpretation of the Lotus Sutra made by an ancient Chinese monk named Chijang Taesa. Entirely modern the temple

may be (it's built in traditional Korean style but using concrete instead of wood), but it has a vast and obviously highly motivated following as well as being conspicuously mega-rich. This is real cult territory of the born-again kind. Devotees with name cards clipped to their shirts and dresses are very much in evidence, and that disgusting habit of smoking within temple precincts which occurs elsewhere is totally prohibited here.

There are some 38 buildings consisting of gateways, dormitories, administration blocks, halls dedicated to various bodhisattvas and an enormous five-storey main hall which it is claimed can accommodate up to 10,000 people. There's even a post office and bookshop! All these buildings are crammed into a steep, narrow and thickly wooded valley and wherever it's been necessary to contain water run-off or to landscape, you'll see beautiful examples of dry-stone walling where it's obvious that no effort has been spared to create the best. Indeed, no effort has been spared anywhere in this temple to produce what is undeniably a masterpiece of civil engineering, sculpture, traditional painting and landscaping. The only thing they don't seem to have quite come to grips with yet are the septic tanks but perhaps that's just a deliberate reminder of the transitory nature of the material world? Either way, they could hardly be blamed for having difficulty coping with the human waste produced by the many thousands of devotees who visit.

Below the temple is a small tourist village

Trains from Seoul to Chech'ŏn

Class	Time	Frequency	Travel Time	Fare
Saemaul	9 am	1 daily	2¼ hours	W7500
Mugunghwa	11 am, 6 pm	2 daily	2¼ hours	W4400
T'ong-il	1 pm-9.30 pm	3 daily	2½ hours	W3000

Trains from Seoul to Tanyang

Class	Time	Frequency	Travel Time	Fare
Saemaul	9 am, 4.30 pm	2 daily	2¼ hours	W8600
Mugunghwa	11 am, 6 pm	2 daily	2 ¾ hours	W4400
T'ong-il	1 pm-11 pm	5 daily	3 hours	W3000

with a number of souvenir shops (mostly religious paraphernalia), restaurants, a couple of yŏinsuk and a public toilet which you won't want to use.

Getting There & Away

There are seven nonstop buses daily from Tanyang to Hŭibangsa between 9.40 am and 7 pm, taking 40 minutes for the journey. Local buses also run from P'unggi (in Kyŏngsangbuk-do Province) to Hŭibangsa every 30 minutes between 6.30 am and 7.10 pm, taking 30 minutes for the ride. And there are also 21 local buses daily from Yŏngju (also in Kyŏngsangbuk-do Province) to Hŭibangsa between 6.30 am and 7.10 pm, taking 30 minutes for the journey.

Kuinsa is approached over a totally different road. There are four express buses plus 14 local buses from Tanyang to Kuinsa which leave 18 times daily between 5.40 am and 8.30 pm, and the journey takes 40 minutes. There are also 13 buses daily from Chech'ŏn to Kuinsa running between the hours of 7.10 am and 5.40 pm.

North Korea 북한

Workers' paradise or totalitarian dictatorship – your image of North Korea or the Democratic People's Republic of Korea (DPRK) may depend on your ideology. While other formerly hardline Communist countries are opening up to Western-style capitalism, North Korea remains devoutly Marxist. No other country maintains such a rigid Stalinist system.

This may not sound like a travellers' paradise. Indeed, it is entirely possible that North Korea hosts fewer foreign tourists than any other country on earth. And those who do manage a visit are restricted to seeing certain places and must be accompanied by a guide the whole time. Visitors also find that they are subjected to nonstop propaganda – the 'US imperialist aggressors' and 'South Korean puppet stooges' are the favourite themes. And finally, all this costs plenty – North Korea is one of the most expensive countries in the world to visit.

So why go?

Simply put, North Korea is fascinating. Tourists are drawn to this country out of pure curiosity. Furthermore, it's an education you aren't likely to forget – many tourists have commented that their visit to North Korea was easily their most memorable journey. Some think of it as a Stalinist theme park, a dictatorship *par excellence* – almost too surreal to be believable. Regardless of the weird politics, there is no denying that North Korea is a beautiful country that has hardly been touched by commercialised tourism.

Some travellers come away from North Korea impressed by the cleanliness and orderliness of the society. Many come away horrified. But the big question is whether or not you'll be able to go at all.

North Korea periodically opens and closes its doors to foreign tourists, and at the time of this writing it was slammed shut once again. Yet that could all change tomorrow – the only thing predictable about North Korea is that it's unpredictable. The country is in desperate financial condition and badly needs every dollar of hard currency that tour-

ists could bring. But at the same time, North Korea is the world's most xenophobic country. All foreign tourists are regarded as potential spies and saboteurs. The government is especially paranoid that tourists will 'pollute' the people's minds with foreign ideas like free enterprise and democracy.

One might have thought the opening up of eastern Europe and the former Soviet Union would have encouraged some sort of reform efforts in North Korea. However, the opposite has happened. The former USSR established diplomatic relations with South Korea in 1990, and China followed suit in 1992. While North Korea reacted angrily to these moves, there were nevertheless hopeful signs that the regime would begin a process of economic and political cooperation with its neighbours.

But it was not to be. Since 1993 North Korea's already frosty relations with the rest of the world have declined sharply, with revelations about a secret nuclear weapons programme. The disintegration of the Com-

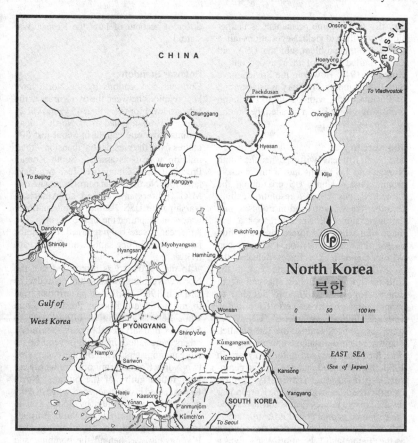

North Korea
북한

EAST SEA
(Sea of Japan)

Gulf of
West Korea

munist bloc has left North Korea with few friends. Increasingly isolated, armed to the teeth and led by a regime that is intractably hostile, the 'hermit kingdom' is withdrawing ever further into its shell. Tourists hoping to get a glimpse of this unique country might be in for a long wait.

Facts about the Country

HISTORY
See the South Korean History section in the Facts about the Country chapter for Korean history prior to 1945.

North Korea's history as a separate political entity began from the end of WW II. The USA, the UK and the USSR had made a deal at the Yalta Conference in the closing days of the war – the USSR was temporarily to occupy Korea north of the 38th parallel to accept the Japanese surrender, while the USA would occupy the south. This 'temporary' partitioning was also imposed in Germany, with the same tragic result. In 1948, the uncompromising Kim Il-sung became head of North Korea and the temporary division became permanent as neither side was willing to yield. Negotiations failed to resolve the problem, but the USA and USSR pulled most of their troops out of Korea by 1949. However, the Soviets gave Kim Il-sung massive military assistance, and on 25 June 1950, with US aid to the South on its way, North Korea invaded the South.

The Korean War

The North Koreans swiftly pushed the South Korean and US troops into a tiny enclave around Pusan. Under US prompting, the United Nations passed a resolution calling for other countries to send in troops to halt the aggression. The war effort took a dramatic turn when UN forces landed behind enemy lines at Inch'ŏn on 15 September. Within a month, UN forces defeated the North Koreans, pushing them back to the Chinese border. Fortunes changed again when China's Mao Zedong decided to support the North Korean effort and sent in 180,000 Chinese 'volunteers'. UN forces were pushed back again to the 38th parallel. The war reached a stalemate while negotiations for a truce dragged on for two years. In 1953, the war ended with the Korean peninsula split at the ironically named Demilitarised Zone (DMZ). The Korean War resulted in two million deaths and devastated the country's economy and infrastructure.

North Korea, which refers to this conflict as the 'Fatherland Liberation War', gives a different account of how the Korean War started.

Postwar Standoff

Constant provocations by the North have kept relations between the two Koreas at the subzero level for more than 45 years. On 21 January 1968, a squad of 31 North Korean commandos were caught in Seoul just 500 metres from the presidential mansion – their mission was to assassinate South Korean President Park Chung-hee. Just two days later, four North Korean patrol boats and two MIG fighters intercepted an American warship, the USS *Pueblo*, in international waters and captured the crew of 83 men. The Americans were only returned 11 months later, except for one sailor who died in captivity.

In the 1970s it was discovered that the North was drilling invasion tunnels under the DMZ. In 1983, North Korean terrorists tried to murder South Korean President Chun while he was making an official visit to Burma. Chun survived the bomb blast but 21 others were killed, including several South Korean ministers. The Burmese captured two North Korean army officers who were later found guilty of the outrage. North Korea denied involvement and suggested the whole thing was a stunt by South Korean agents trying to discredit the North. Burma's leaders needed no convincing that P'yŏngyang was behind the bombing and

---

Fatherland Liberation War
One propaganda pamphlet, *An Earthly Paradise for the People*, has this to say about the war:

The US imperialists, who had boasted of being the strongest in the world, frantically pounced upon the Korean people in league with the south Korean puppet army plus the troops of 15 satellite countries.

However, the American imperialists who were assured of a glorious victory in this grim war were covered all over with wounds and surrendered to the heroic Korean people. As a result, the Korean people and their young People's Army held a military parade in honour of their victory in the presence of President Kim Il-sung, the ever-victorious and iron-willed brilliant commander.

This was a great victory and natural outcome attained under the wise leadership of the great President Kim Il-sung. ■

promptly broke off diplomatic relations with North Korea.

In 1987, two North Koreans posing as Japanese tourists boarded a South Korean civilian airliner and planted a bomb, causing 115 deaths. Both terrorists tried to commit suicide with cyanide but one, Kim Hyun-hui, survived. She later revealed to South Korean authorities that she learned Japanese from Yaeko Taguchi, a former bar hostess who was abducted from Japan in 1978 by North Korean kidnappers. (North Korea's refusal to answer questions about Miss Taguchi's whereabouts caused normalization talks with Japan to break down.)

As in previous terrorist attacks, North Korea professed innocence and claimed the whole thing was a trick by the South Korean 'puppet clique' trying to discredit the North. Miss Kim was eventually freed and is said to be living in Seoul, although the relatives of those who died in the explosion have vigorously protested her release.

North Korea's position regarding the USA and the present South Korean government is well summed up in the following quote from *Women of Korea* (1991, volume 2), a magazine published in P'yŏngyang:

The US imperialists have stationed more than 40,000 troops and more than 1000 nuclear weapons in South Korea, and they, with the nearly one million puppet troops, are preparing an invasion against North Korea...Their aim is to create 'two Koreas', to divide Korea permanently and to continuously occupy South Korea as their colony and, using south Korea as a bridgehead, to make an invasion of North Korea and the other countries of Asia.

Japan

If the USA is North Korea's No 1 enemy, then Japan is certainly No 2. In November 1990, Kim Il-sung surprised everyone by telling a visiting Japanese politician that his country was ready to establish diplomatic relations with Japan. However, the first round of talks with Japan did not go well – North Korea demanded billions of US dollars as war reparations from Japan, and

---

Japan
The North Korean book entitled *Kim Il-sung on the Five-Point Policy for National Reunification* has this to say:

The Japanese militarists, dancing to the tune of the US imperialists, have also hampered the North-South dialogue and taken many actions against the reunification of our country. The US imperialists and the Japanese militarists aim, in the final analysis, at keeping our country divided indefinitely, and making south Korea their permanent colony and commodity market. ■

---

billions more for the 45 years of 'cold war' following WW II.

An issue which continues to anger Japan is that of the 'Japanese spouses'. In the 1950s, about 100,000 Koreans who had been living in Japan were repatriated to North Korea (by their own will, not forcibly). They took with them nearly 3000 Japanese wives. Then the door was slammed shut and no-one was allowed to leave. So for the past 35 years or so, these women have been unable to visit their families. Pleas on their behalf from Japan have been ignored. However, P'yŏngyang has turned them into a considerable source of revenue, having made it clear to their families in Japan that the way these women are treated depends on how much cash the family contributes to North Korea. Recent talks with Japan on this issue produced this official statement from the North Koreans:

That the Japanese have failed to visit their native towns freely is due to the abnormal relations between the two countries; the Japanese spouses are leading a stable life in our country; and when the relations between the two countries have been normalised, their free travel will be possible.

Translated, this means that Japan must pay billions of US dollars so that relations with North Korea can be 'normalised', and only then will the women be free to leave.

In spite of electric fences and heavy patrols, some North Koreans have successfully escaped to Japan in makeshift boats. North Korea responded in 1983 by kidnapping two Japanese sailors on the high seas; this was known as the Fujisanmaru incident. The Koreans said they would only return the sailors if Japan handed over all the North Korean escapees. Japan refused and the sailors were held until 1991, when North Korea finally released them in an attempt to woo the Japanese into establishing diplomatic relations.

Cold War Continues

Apparently, this was not enough. Normalisation talks between Japan and North Korea ground to a halt when US military experts rolled out satellite photos showing that North Korea appears to be developing nuclear weapons at its reprocessing centre near Yŏngbyŏn, north of P'yŏngyang. Japan now says it will not establish diplomatic relations with North Korea unless international inspections of the Yŏngbyŏn site are permitted. P'yŏngyang turned the argument around and said it would only open Yŏngbyŏn to international inspection if the USA also opened its military bases in the South to inspection for nuclear materials. The North claims that the USA has over 1000 nuclear warheads based in the South.

In 1991, the USA surprised North Korea by offering to withdraw all nuclear weapons from the Korean peninsula. Western military sources also say North Korea possesses huge quantities of chemical and biological weapons which could kill millions if launched against the South. Many assume that the USA would respond to a nerve gas attack on Seoul with an equally devastating nuclear attack against P'yŏngyang. But all this is speculation unless it actually happens, which no sane person wants to see.

In spite of this ultra-tense atmosphere, 1991 saw other signs of a thaw in the icy relations between the two Koreas. Officials from P'yŏngyang visited Seoul for talks and, to the great surprise of the rest of the world, emerged with a non-aggression accord at the end of the year. The agreement sidestepped the difficult issue of nuclear weapons but the South Korean prime minister offered to open his country's facilities to inspection by officials from the North – indicating that the USA had probably removed its weapons already. Talk of establishing a free trade zone open to foreign investors was another hopeful sign that the relations between the two Koreas were finally improving. Optimists began to talk of the possibility of peaceful reunification of the country.

In the end it was the pessimists who proved correct. An inspection team from the International Atomic Energy Agency (IAEA) was denied access to North Korean nuclear facilities in January 1993. Further pressure from IAEA caused P'yŏngyang to announce in March that it would withdraw from the Nuclear Non-Proliferation Treaty. Negotiations accomplished nothing, with P'yŏngyang demanding the total withdrawal of US military forces from the Korean peninsula as the price of cooperation on the nuclear issue. P'yŏngyang insists that its nuclear reactors are for peaceful purposes only, and points to South Korea's considerable nuclear power programme as justification for its actions. However, South Korea cooperates with IAEA while North Korea doesn't.

North Korea's nuclear ambitions brought harsh condemnation from the rest of the world. P'yŏngyang countered with shrill threats, which resulted in a statement from US President Bill Clinton that a military strike from the North would result in 'the end of North Korea as they know it'. Even relations with China, North Korea's one remaining friend, deteriorated. A watered-down statement was issued by the United Nations in 1994 with Chinese cooperation, calling on North Korea to comply with IAEA's nuclear safeguards. P'yŏngyang rejected the statement. Satellite photos showed that North Korea was moving most of its army (the world's fifth largest) to the DMZ, and many wondered if the two Koreas were sliding towards another inevitable war.

One peculiar irony of North Korea's nuclear programme is that some in the South support it. An unholy alliance of extreme leftists and rightists wants the North to develop nuclear weapons because the united Korea which they dream about should indeed be a nuclear power 'to counter the Japanese threat'.

And Now What?

On 29 June 1994, Kim Il-sung surprised everyone with an announcement that he would freeze North Korea's nuclear programme and would meet with South Korean President Kim Young-sam for talks. The talks never occurred because Kim Il-sung died of a heart attack on 8 July.

Kim Il-sung (the 'Great Leader') had long planned that power should be passed to his son, Kim Jong-il (the 'Dear Leader'). Dynastic succession runs counter to Marxist theory, and this is the first such case in a communist society. But if one is to believe the North Korean news media, Kim Junior has indeed smoothly assumed power with no opposition whatsoever from other possible contenders to the throne. However, outsiders have no way of knowing what might really be happening in North Korea.

Little is actually known about Kim Jong-il, but all accounts from the few who have met him indicate that he lacks the charisma of his father. Kim is never seen publicly, not even for official functions held in his honour. He showed up for his father's funeral but kept silent, looked dazed and feeble and made no speeches. There is speculation that he is in poor health, and Western intelligence reports indicate that he is heavily introverted and devotes much of his time to watching foreign videos.

Then there is the question of palace intrigue. Other possible contenders to the throne include Kim Song-ae (Kim Il-sung's widow); Kim Pyong-il, the North Korean ambassador to Finland (Kim Jong-il's step-brother); and Vice President Kim Yung-ju (Kim Jong-il's uncle). Most outsiders speculate that Kim Jong-il will ruthlessly purge all potential political opponents, but whoever can control the military will no doubt have the final say. Kim Jong-il will obviously do his best to stay on top – the world can only watch and wait as the Korean drama unfolds.

GEOGRAPHY

North Korea occupies 55% of the land area on the Korean peninsula. The northern and eastern regions are mostly rugged mountains and not well suited for agriculture.

A trip to North Korea makes an interesting comparison to the South. While South Korea suffers from some serious environmental problems, there is almost no pollution in the North, whether it be industrial waste or just pure trash. The one thing which strikes most visitors to North Korea is its squeaky-clean appearance. This is a result not just of the lack of consumer goods and their packaging but of determined policies which keep it that way. The streets of P'yŏngyang are washed down twice a week and before dawn each day street cleaners are out sweeping up any litter or leaves they can find. You'd be hard pressed to find a single piece of paper on the streets despite the absence of litter bins. Even in the countryside, women are assigned a particular stretch of the main road to sweep and keep clean – each and every day.

The apparent lack of people is also one of the most striking features of the countryside (or at least of that part which you're allowed to see) and you may get to wondering where all those 21 million people actually live and work. Even in P'yŏngyang, only on Sunday do you see substantial numbers of people out on the streets.

The other major contrast is the lack of traffic on the highways. Most of what you'll see will be army vehicles. There are very few passenger cars. North Korea has no automobile manufacturing plants and must import cars from abroad. As a result, there's nothing remotely like the traffic congestion and vehicle exhaust pollution which characterises many South Korean cities.

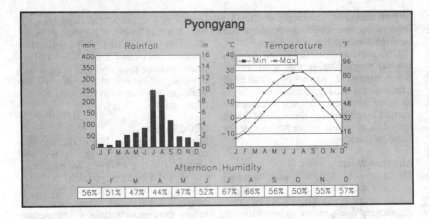

Pyongyang

Rainfall (mm / in)

J F M A M J J A S O N D

Temperature (°C / °F) — Min — Max

J F M A M J J A S O N D

Afternoon Humidity

J	F	M	A	M	J	J	A	S	O	N	D
56%	51%	47%	44%	47%	52%	67%	66%	56%	50%	55%	57%

CLIMATE

The weather is similar to South Korea but colder and drier in winter. Autumn is the best time for a visit, with crisp, dry weather and a chance to see the leaves changing colour. Over 60% of the annual rainfall occurs from June to September. Average monthly temperatures and precipitation for P'yŏngyang are as follows:

GOVERNMENT

Kim Il-sung totally dominated the politics of North Korea from 1948 until his death in 1994. If there was anyone who outdid Stalin or Mao Zedong in the cult of personality then it was Kim Il-sung. Not only was his word God's will, but huge statues and portraits of him litter the North Korean countryside and the cities. He was referred to as 'His Excellency' and 'the Greatest Genius the World has ever Known'.

His death has created a vacuum. Kim Il-sung ruled supremely and Kim Jong-il was expected to inherit the country. To the extent that any outsider can understand North Korea's political system, the government of North Korea is a family affair, consisting of Kim Jong-il, various aunts, uncles, cousins, stepbrothers and so on. The US military speculates that probably fewer than 10 people actually control the country, but the

Korean Workers' Party provides a sort of 'window-dressing'. There is also a Politburo consisting mainly of geriatric generals who have been locked into office since the last Party Congress in 1980.

You'll see political slogans (in Korean) mounted on every hillside and you need never be in doubt as to whether someone is a North Korean or not. Everybody, young or old, at home or abroad, wears a small metal badge with the face of the 'Great Leader' on it. No one yet knows if these will be replaced with 'Dear Leader' badges.

This sort of cult following and passionate belief in every gem of wisdom which fell from the Great Leader's lips is a cornerstone of the education system and nobody escapes it. It even has its attraction for some university students in South Korea, who espouse Kim's totalitarian strictures on the evils of South Korea's political, economic and social policies and his passionate anti-Western rhetoric. When Kim Il-sung died, a small but hardline faction of students in South Korea held mourning ceremonies for him despite a strict ban on such activities. The irony of all this is that, although many things are far from perfect in the South, few of the most leftist South Korean students would prefer life in Kim's utopia.

Within North Korea, opposition to the regime is brutally suppressed. You may take with a pinch of salt claims by North Koreans that prisons don't exist, although they do admit to maintaining 're-education centres'. Photos taken by Western spy satellites confirm the existence of these and Amnesty International estimates that there are over 100,000 political prisoners in North Korea. From the handful of defectors who have made it to the West, imprisonment, torture and execution are the routine penalties for opposing the North Korean regime. Punishing the families of successful defectors is also said to be a common practice.

It may seem incredible to Western liberals accustomed to multiparty democracy that such totalitarianism could exist in the late 20th century, but it does. If any society comes close to the nightmare depicted in George Orwell's book *1984*, North Korea is it.

ECONOMY

Capitalism does not exist here, not even to allow street vendors. The Marxist economy has been augmented with Kim Il-sung's ideology of *juche* (self reliance) which has resulted in the country spurning overseas aid and trade, especially with the West. The country has poured its resources into the military, heavy industries, and monuments and statues of the Great Leader, all at the expense of agriculture and consumer goods.

North Korea is widely believed to be in a period of steep economic decline as subsidies from the former USSR ended in 1990. However as the government's statistics are pure fantasy, outsiders can only make educated guesses about the North Korean economy. The latest statistics from the North Korean government indicate an annual growth rate of about 2.5%. Outside sources claim the economy is now shrinking at around 2% to 5% per year, although it is hard to see how the economy can decline much further since it is already close to subsistence level.

North Korea owes more than US$800 million in defaulted loans to Western banks – the country borrowed the money, then simply refused to repay. As a result, North Korea has a zero credit rating and cannot borrow additional funds for development projects, nor will most countries sell anything to North Korea on other than a cash or barter basis. As for exports, North Korea has little to sell, except weapons and ammunition which have found a ready market in Africa and the Middle East.

In late 1992 and early 1993, there was a brief period of optimism when North Korea passed a number of encouraging foreign investment laws. The much-ballyhooed Foreign Enterprise Act made it legal for wholly-owned foreign companies to set up operations in free-trade zones. To that end, a free-trade zone was established in north-east Korea along the Tumen River bordering Russia and China. Not surprisingly, the whole exercise came to nothing due to the rapidly escalating political crisis over North Korea's nuclear ambitions.

Most recently, North Korea has been earning hard currency by exporting labour – workers are shipped off to logging and mining camps in Siberia. This is only possible because Siberia, unlike the rest of Russia, is still controlled by hardline Communist Party bosses who have little regard for human rights. However, despite stringent security at the camps, many North Koreans have escaped and made their way to Moscow, where they can apply to the South Korean embassy for political asylum. The policy of the Russian government is to permit North Korean defectors to leave the country as they wish. Those North Koreans who escape to China are not so lucky – the Chinese government 'repatriates' them to what is no doubt a horrific fate.

POPULATION & PEOPLE

The population is approximately 22 million – about half the population of the South. The government has encouraged population growth which is estimated at 2.1% annually.

You won't be seeing any minority groups; Korea is ethnically almost totally homogeneous.

ARTS

One thing you must say for Kim Il-sung – he did indeed promote traditional Korean arts and culture. His motives for doing so are a subject of debate. Kim was a fierce nationalist, relentlessly emphasising the superiority of Korean culture. North Koreans are told that they are culturally superior, their country is the best in the world, and Kim Il-sung was the greatest man in the world. The focus on Korea's cultural superiority reinforces Kim's position as the greatest leader of all time and also helps divert attention from North Korea's serious problems.

Whatever ulterior motives the regime might have, tourists with an interest in traditional arts can benefit – visits to Korean song-and-dance performances can easily be arranged. Some even argue that in terms of traditional culture, the North is the 'real Korea'.

RELIGION

As far as Buddhist temples go, they do exist, and in some cases have been renovated, but they no longer function, as the religion is regarded as an expression of a so-called bourgeois mentality and is therefore proscribed. Confucianism has been similarly suppressed. The traditional arts associated with such temples and shrines, on the other hand, have been harnessed to serve the greater glory of Kim Il-sung's 'vision'. Christians and showcase Christian churches do exist, although they're few in number and any belief in the holy trinity is likely to be expressed in the form of the Great Leader (Kim Il-sung), the Dear Leader (Kim Jong-il), and the holy spirit of Juche – the national ideology of self-reliance.

LANGUAGE

This is essentially the same as that of South Korea, but the North has developed a somewhat different accent and vocabulary. Very few people speak English or any other foreign language.

Facts for the Visitor

VISAS & EMBASSIES

North Korea was opened up to Western group tourism in 1986 and to individual Western travellers in 1989. In a typical year, North Korea only permits about 200 Westerners to visit, although Asians are given more slack. Unfortunately, at the moment tourist visas are frozen while North Korea decides how to deal with its nuclear crisis and the rise to power of Kim Jong-il. However, business visas are still possible – plutonium vendors take note.

Your best bet is to first approach the North Korean visa office in Macau. They are in the business of selling tours and will normally respond much more favourably to travellers than the North Korean embassy in Beijing. They offer several standard tours of varying lengths, or you may put together a specialised itinerary of your own. You fill out a visa application which they fax off to P'yŏngyang straight away. They can usually give you an approval or rejection within 10 minutes. The first question will be 'Are you a journalist?' If you really want to go to North Korea, you'd better say 'No'. They normally issue your visa as soon as you pay the full charge. Three photographs are required and there is a US$15 visa fee. If you're with a group of over 16 people, the 16th person visits free of charge.

The fee you pay only covers your tour within North Korea. You still must book your transport to and from P'yŏngyang. The normal starting point is Beijing, and you book at China International Travel Service (CITS) in the Beijing International Hotel. You must then inform the North Korean visa office in Macau. They will call ahead to make sure that your guide is there to meet you, that your hotels are booked and that transport within Korea is arranged. You'd better also call or fax the visa office in Macau – the North Korean embassy in Beijing has often proved to be unreliable.

Trying to book your tour directly with the North Korean embassy in Beijing is much less certain. Some travellers have received a warm welcome at the embassy, while others have been told 'the person you need to see won't be back for two months'. Assuming they respond favourably, you may be issued the visa in anything between 10 minutes and three weeks. As in Macau, you must pay for the entire trip in advance in hard currency before your visa is issued, and then arrange your own transport to/from North Korea.

There are no little tricks like entering on a transit visa and then extending after arrival. Don't even think about sneaking in to North Korea. This is one country where you dare not thumb your nose at the authorities.

Getting your visa extended is easy as long as you pay. Just how much your extended stay will cost is subject to negotiation, but include in your calculations your hotel bill, meals and a service charge for your guide. If you want a visa extension and can come up with the cash, your guide will make all the arrangements.

Even citizens of the USA have been allowed to visit, despite North Korea's vehemently anti-US stand. The same goes for Japanese nationals.

The visa is not stamped into your passport (which might prejudice future visits to the USA or South Korea) but onto a separate sheet of paper which will be retained by the immigration authorities when you leave North Korea.

If your time is limited and you want to arrange everything before arriving in Macau or China, there are a few travel agents (very few!) who deal with tours to North Korea. See the Tours section for details.

Most likely, you'll be entering and returning through China. This means you should get a dual or multiple-entry visa for China. Otherwise, you can arrange a return visa at the Chinese embassy in P'yŏngyang, but this will consume some of your scarce time and North Korea is an expensive place to hang around.

Booking a tour through a travel agent usually requires a minimum wait of six weeks, two weeks of which are needed to process your visa application – you must part with your passport for these two weeks. In the UK, try Regent Holidays Ltd (☎ (0117) 21-1711), 13 Small St, Bristol BS1 1DE. In Australia, try Passport/Red Bear Travel (☎ (03) 824-7183; fax 822-3956), 320 Glenferrie Rd, Malvern

3144; or Orbitours (☎ (02) 221-7322), 7th Floor, Dymocks Bldg, 428 George St, Sydney 2000. In Hong Kong, the agent specialising in these trips is Wallem Travel (☎ 528-6514), 46th Floor, Hopewell Centre, 183 Queen's Rd East, Wanchai.

The China International Travel Service (CITS) office in Shenyang, Liaoning Province, has been known to book tours to North Korea. The Beijing CITS does not book these tours or help you obtain a visa, but they do arrange transport.

North Korean Embassies

Visas can be obtained at the following places:

China
  Embassy of the Democratic People's Republic of Korea, Ritan Beilu, Jianguomenwai, Chaoyang District, Beijing (☎ 532-1186)
Macau
  DPR Korea-Macau International Tourism Company, 23rd Floor, Nam Van Commercial Centre, 57-9 Rua da Praia Grande (☎ 33-3355; fax 33-3939)
Russia
  Embassy of the Democratic People's Republic of Korea, PO Box ulitsa Mosfilmovskaya 72 (☎ 578-7580) (telex 413272 ZINGG SU)

Red Tape & Restrictions

If you feel burdened by all the red tape and restrictions, then spare a thought for the North Korean people. Even within the country, special permission is required for a change of location. Those who are allowed to go overseas for study invariably have to choose a Communist country as their destination: most go to Chinese universities. At all those universities where there's a Korean contingent, they form an exclusive bloc and never, at any time, socialise with non-Koreans, even at a departmental level. In addition, there's always a political cadre to keep watch over them and report any misdemeanours. Likewise, all North Korean businesspeople are required to attend special political education classes once a week to keep them doctrinally pure. ∎

Foreign Embassies in North Korea

There are about 25 embassies, but the only ones of significant size are the Chinese and Russian embassies. The rest are small offices staffed by one or two people representing mostly Third World countries in Africa and the Middle East. The only Western country with a full-time representative is Sweden.

CUSTOMS

North Korean Customs are surprisingly easy – we were not hassled at all. Apart from the usual prohibitions against guns and narcotics, the government lists several other things which you may not bring in:

* Telescopes and magnifiers with over six magnification
* Wireless apparatus and their parts
* Publications, video tapes, recording tapes, films, photos and other materials which are hostile to our socialist system or harmful to our political, economic and cultural development and disturb the maintenance of social order
* Seeds of tobacco, leaf tobacco and other seeds

MONEY
Currency

The unit of currency is the won = 100 jon. There are bank notes for W1, W5, W10, W50 and W100, and coins for W1 and jon 1, 5, 10 and 50.

In addition, there are three types of North Korean currency. The first is coloured green (for won) or blue (for jon) if you're converting hard currency. The second is coloured red if you're exchanging 'non-convertible' currency (basically Communist bloc and Third World currency). The last is local currency for use by Koreans only.

Local currency comes in both banknotes and coins whereas green/blue and red currency comes only in banknotes. As a foreigner, you must pay for hotels, restaurants and goods bought in stores in either green/blue or red banknotes and change will only be given in matching notes.

Red currency is North Korea's way of saying it doesn't particularly want roubles or the like. There are certain limits on consumer goods that can be bought with red currency.

There are also two sets of prices for certain goods – a green price and a red price. The red price is often up to 10 times greater than the green price.

The only time you're likely to need local currency is if you use the Subway in P'yŏngyang since the escalator takes only coins. You'll also need coins if you want to make a call from a public pay phone.

Exchange Rates

The only convertible currencies you are able to exchange easily are the Deutschmark, French franc, British pounds, US dollars and Japanese yen. Exchange rates are as follows:

Germany	DM1	=	W1.32
France	FFr1	=	W0.38
Britain	UK£1	=	W3.30
USA	US$1	=	W2.22
Japan	¥100	=	W2.22

There is also a highly punitive 'external exchange rate' of US$1 = W0.97. Usually, you will not have to worry about this, but some travellers have run into it when trying to buy air tickets from outside North Korea (see the Getting There & Away section in this chapter).

Changing Money

Foreigners must exchange money at hotels. You are much better off changing cash rather than travellers' cheques since the hotels have a W3 service charge for cashing cheques.

There's no black market but you can, with some people, swap green for red or local currency. Most Koreans would love to have the green currency since it can be used to buy rare imported goods.

Currency declaration forms are usually issued when you get your visa, or at the border/airport on entry and you must fill in an exit currency form when you leave. It's probably best to make sure you get a currency form to avoid hassles on leaving, but if you don't, your guides can generally sort things out without too much trouble.

Costs

All in all, it's going to be an expensive trip, even more so than Japan. You're looking at between US$70 and US$190 per day all-inclusive (not including transport to/from North Korea). You can save up to US$25 per day by choosing 'standard' accommodation rather than 'deluxe'. There are also four price levels depending on the number of persons in your group: one person, two to five persons, six to nine persons or 10 to 15 persons. A 16th person can go for free.

Prices quoted by the DPRK travel office in Macau for a single traveller are as follows: four days all-inclusive tour in deluxe/standard accommodation, US$646/544; five days, US$840/717; eight days, US$1487/1272; and 11 days, US$2130/ 1821.

Transport to/from P'yŏngyang costs extra. See the Getting There & Away section for details.

If it's any consolation, they do give very good service for the money.

WHAT TO BRING

There is a shortage of basic consumer items, so bring everything you think you'll need. Korean men smoke like chimneys and foreign cigarettes make good gifts – you can buy a carton of Dunhills at the hard currency shops for US$14, but if you have a cheaper source bring them. Marlboro reds are especially valued since they are not available in North Korea.

Postage stamps seem to be glueless, so a glue stick will prove valuable.

TOURIST OFFICES
Local Tourist Offices

Ryohaengsa (☎ (8502) 81-7201), the government tourist agency, is also known as the Korea International Tourist Bureau. You can reach them by telex (5998 RHS KP) or fax (8502) 81-7607). The mailing address is: Ryohaengsa, Central District, P'yŏngyang, Democratic People's Republic of Korea.

Overseas Reps

DPRK-Macau International Tourism Company (☎ 33-3355; fax 33-3939) is on the 23rd Floor, Nam Van Commercial Centre, 57-9 Rua da Praia Grande, Macau. This is currently the easiest place to arrange a visa.

BUSINESS HOURS & HOLIDAYS

Official working hours are Monday to Saturday from 9 am to 6 pm. Public holidays include: New Year's Day, 1 January; Kim Jong-il's birthday, 16 February; Kim Il-sung's birthday, 15 April; Armed Forces Day, 25 April; May Day, 1 May; National Foundation Day, 9 September; Korean Workers' Party Foundation Day, 10 October.

CULTURAL EVENTS

By all means try to be in P'yŏngyang during Kim Jong-il's birthday (16 February) or Kim Il-sung's birthday (15 April). Both events are huge extravaganzas with military-style parades and portraits of the Great and Dear Leaders being carried through the streets.

Of course, now that Kim Il-sung has died, there is the possibility that this event will be cancelled and a holiday will be made on 8 July, to commemorate the day of his death.

An interesting thing about the Dear Leader's birthday is that it's been changed: he was born in 1942 but this was recently changed to 1941 and all previous North Korean history books have had to be altered to reflect the new 'reality'. Just why Kim Jong-il was made one year older is subject to speculation, but the currently accepted theory is that the Great Leader liked even numbers and wanted his son to be exactly 30 years younger than he was.

POST & TELECOMMUNICATIONS
Postal Rates

A postcard to Australia costs W1.30. To the USA it's W1.50.

Sending Mail

You needn't bother trying to track down the post office, since most major hotels offer postal service.

You're best off sending postcards since these give the authorities a chance to read what you've said without having to tear open your letters. Saying a few nice things about how clean and beautiful North Korea is will increase the chances of your mail getting through.

Receiving Mail

You can forget about the central post office and poste restante. Given the short time you're likely to be spending in North Korea, it's hardly worth bothering trying to receive any letters. However, if you want to try, the most likely place to receive your mail is at the P'yŏngyang Koryŏ Hotel, Tonghung-dong, Central District, P'yŏngyang; or care of Ryohaengsa, Central District, P'yŏngyang. There is a better than average chance that your letters will be opened and read.

Telephone

It's easy to book an overseas call from major hotels, and some even offer international direct dialling (IDD) right from your room. Phone calls usually go through without much trouble.

Public pay phones require 10 jon coins, which means you'll need some local money if you want to use them. Coin-operated phones are not very common even in P'yŏngyang, but you probably won't find too many people to call anyway.

If you are dialling direct to North Korea from abroad, the country code is 850. A number of Western countries do not have phone connections with North Korea, but making an IDD call from Beijing to P'yŏngyang is very easy.

Fax, Telex & Telegraph

Fax and telex services are readily available from major hotels like the Koryŏ in P'yŏngyang. Telegraph (cable) service does not seem to be available.

TIME

The time in Korea is Greenwich Mean Time plus nine hours. When it is noon in Korea it is 2 pm in Sydney or Melbourne, 3 am in London, 10 pm the previous day in New York and 7 pm the previous day in Los Angeles or San Francisco.

ELECTRICITY

Electric power is 220 V, 60 Hz, although luxury hotels often have an outlet for 110 V. If so, this will be clearly labelled. All outlets are of the US type with two flat prongs, but no ground (earth) wire.

BOOKS

Literature about North Korea is rare, and tourist literature is even rarer. The easiest place to get travel brochures is from the DPR Korea-Macau International Tourism Company in Macau. These are printed in several languages – English, German, French, Japanese, Chinese etc, and give all the major sites open to foreign tourists, the hotels, an airline schedule and a breakdown of suggested itineraries ranging from three to 16 days.

The North Korean embassy in Beijing has these brochures but does not give them to Westerners, although ethnic Koreans seem to be able to obtain them without difficulty. If you get into the North Korean embassy, immediately to your right is a waiting room. If you manage to get in there, they have free copies of various glossy-colour magazines such as *Women of Korea* and *Democratic People's Republic of Korea*. You may take these with you.

Another source of information is the book *Korean Review* by Pang Hwan Ju (Foreign Languages Publishing House, P'yŏngyang, 1987), which gives information on North Korea's flora & fauna, minerals, history, economy, politics and sightseeing.

Within North Korea, there are numerous propaganda books and pamphlets. Though these have scant useful information, they are rare gems for collectors.

Maps of P'yŏngyang and Korea can be purchased at major tourist hotels.

As for getting a general feel for the place, what could be more relevant than George Orwell's *1984* or *Animal Farm*? Read these before or after you arrive, as it would not be wise to carry them through North Korean Customs.

Perhaps more to the point is a report on human rights in North Korea published jointly by Asia Watch (Washington DC, USA) and the Minnesota Lawyers International Human Rights Committee. A brief summary of this report appeared in the *Far Eastern Economic Review* (19 January 1989), which should be available from libraries in Hong Kong and elsewhere. North Korea has harshly denounced this report.

MEDIA

Information about the rest of the world is hard to come by in North Korea. The press is rigidly controlled and prints only what the government tells it to print, which is mostly stories about happy workers, loyal soldiers, US imperialist aggressors, South Korean puppets, the superhuman feats of Kim Il-sung and 'new discoveries' about Kim Jong-il's mythological childhood.

Likewise, TV programmes are all designed to reinforce the reigning ideology. North Koreans cannot receive foreign news broadcasts because all radios and TVs are designed to pick up only the government broadcasting frequencies.

Newspapers & Magazines

There are no foreign publications available, so if you want to read *Time* or *Newsweek*, you'll have to bring your own copies.

As for local publications in English, the selection is severely limited. There are free magazines everywhere in a variety of languages, especially the colourful *Democratic People's Republic of Korea* magazine. This is filled with the usual tirade against US imperialists and South Korean puppets, plus articles about the Great Leader and Dear Leader. You'll also learn that the Juche idea is a shining beacon of hope which has swept the world by storm.

At the tourist hotels you can pick up a free weekly English-language newspaper, the *P'yŏngyang Times*, but every issue is practically the same. The *P'yŏngyang Times* reported that our 500-room hotel with 20 guests in residence was 'always full'.

Radio & TV

There are two AM radio stations and two

regular TV stations. It is said that there is a third TV station which broadcasts cultural events on holidays only, but we haven't seen it. The two TV stations broadcast approximately from 6 pm to 11 pm. Like the rest of the mass media, the content is thoroughly politicised.

It's interesting to note that approximately one hour per week of North Korean TV is now shown in South Korea. When this was first permitted, the South Koreans were fascinated, but quickly grew bored with it. You can rest assured that no South Korean TV shows are shown in the North except for news clips of student protests and riots.

FILM & PHOTOGRAPHY

You can buy colour print film at reasonable prices from the hard currency gift shops, but everything else is expensive so bring what you need. There are photoprocessing facilities on the second floor at the Koryŏ Hotel, but you'd probably be better off waiting until you return to China, Hong Kong or elsewhere. This same place can do visa photos in case you need some.

If you visit the International Friendship Exhibition (IFE) centre at Myohyangsan, you'd be wise to bring a tripod and cable release for time exposures because an electronic flash is not permitted. Since many of the exhibits are behind glass, a polarising filter would also come in handy.

You are surprisingly free to photograph what you like, but ask first before taking pictures of soldiers. In many cases, permission *will* be given. The only time we had a problem was when we tried to photograph a long queue of people trying to buy ice-cream cones. A man jumped out of the crowd and put his hand over the lens.

HEALTH

There seems to be no problem with food and most Koreans drink their water unboiled. You won't have to worry about eating from dirty street stalls either, because there aren't any.

That having been said, North Korea does not seem like a good place to get sick since there are shortages of basic Western medicines. On the other hand, you could try traditional Korean medicine which is similar to the Chinese variety.

WOMEN TRAVELLERS

We saw a few foreign women travelling in North Korea, but they were always part of a group that included men. This isn't to say that a single woman or group of women couldn't travel without male companions in North Korea, but it seems to be a very rare occurrence. Also, we never saw a female guide leading any of these tour groups, although Ryohaengsa claims that female guides are available. It's the opposite situation in South Korea, where most tour guides are women.

One thing we can say for sure – North Korea is a very male-dominated society. In spite of the regime's constant attempts to show complete equality between the sexes, there are no women holding any positions of importance (except possibly Kim Song-ae, Kim Il-sung's widow). This is not mere speculation on our part – we talked to numerous embassy people who had spent years in North Korea, and all assured us that of the hundreds of high government officials they met, not a single one was female. However, there are two North Korean women who are revered: the Great Leader's mother, Kang Ban-sok, sometimes referred to as the 'Mother of Korea', and Kim Jong-suk, mother of the Dear Leader.

DANGERS & ANNOYANCES

As far as we can tell, crime is not a problem. The North Korean penal system is an enigma, but we'd be willing to guess that thieves are dealt with harshly – possibly with torture or the death penalty. This doesn't mean you should be careless with your valuables, but the chance of theft is probably lower than in most countries.

The one thing which will get you into serious trouble is to insult the Great Leader or the Dear Leader. We know of one Austrian visitor who put out his cigarette butt on a newspaper, right on the face of a photo of Kim Il-sung. The maid found it in his hotel room and informed the police. This resulted in a frightening confrontation, with threats, shouting, pushing and shoving. The Austrian was quickly booted out of the country, and can probably count himself lucky that he wasn't arrested.

Climbing up into the lap of a Great Leader statue for a photo is just not on (standing in front of it is OK). You needn't be overly paranoid, but assume that your actions are being watched and offensive activities will be reported. Also assume that your hotel room has hidden microphones, and keep your political opinions to yourself. The last thing you need in North Korea is to be accused of 'espionage'.

Male travellers should not even think about touching a North Korean woman regardless of how friendly, charming and receptive she might seem to be. Even something fairly innocent like shaking hands could be construed as an 'immoral act' and could result in serious punishment for both parties to this 'crime'. As for relations between North Korean men and foreign women, it's a big unknown. Most North Korean men would probably not dare touch a foreign woman, but given the fact that Korea is a bastion of male chauvinism, it would probably be viewed less seriously than contact between a foreign man and a Korean woman.

Besides thinking about dangers to yourself, give some thought to the Koreans you meet. Giving them gifts like foreign coins or photos of yourself could have unpredictable consequences for them. What might seem like an innocent act for you might result in them spending time in a concentration camp.

The US Treasury Department has a list of regulations (available from US embassies) governing the economic conduct of US citizens abroad. One little-known rule is that US citizens may not use a credit card in North Korea – not for the purchase of goods or even to pay living expenses! Breaking this rule is a crime and the violator may be prosecuted.

WORK

Aside from business opportunities in weapons sales, work opportunities are scarce in North Korea. A handful of foreigners have actually gotten English teaching jobs in North Korea, but such opportunities are rare and pay is zilch. On the other hand, the teachers have reported that they were treated well.

ACCOMMODATION

You will have to stay at certain designated hotels everywhere you go. These are modern, multi-star hotels which have been built specifically for foreign tourists and, as you might expect, they're expensive, although there are several grades of them. Local yŏgwan probably exist (at least government-owned), although not anywhere near in the same numbers as in South Korea and you're not allowed to stay at them. And since you must stay in the large tourist hotels, this also limits where you can go.

FOOD

Despite continuous reports of food shortages, foreigners with US dollars eat very well. Your guide orders your food, so if you have any special requests, make your wishes known early. The food is heavily based on meat, fish and poultry – vegetarians are liable to have a difficult time. There is a tendency to order Western food for Westerners, so if you want Korean food, ask for it.

DRINKS

Korean beer is not bad, but most hard liquor is imported. As for nonalcoholic beverages, North Korea produces mineral water and some pleasant-tasting carbonated fruit drinks. There are plenty of imported drinks available in the hotels and hard currency shops, including Coca-Cola.

Getting There & Away

AIR

There are flights between Beijing and P'yŏngyang by either the Chinese national airline, Air China, once weekly, or the North Korean airline, Koryŏ Air (also known as Chosŏnminhang), twice weekly. The flight takes less than two hours. We found the staff at the Air China office in P'yŏngyang to be very friendly – although they were much preoccupied with raising fish in the bathtub and vegetables on the terrace because they couldn't buy these things without hard currency.

The airfares are insane. The one-way Beijing-P'yŏngyang ticket costs US$120, but a one-way P'yŏngyang-Beijing flight is US$274 if the ticket is bought in China! If bought in P'yŏngyang, it's only US$120! This is because Air China calculates the fare using the absurd 'external exchange rate' of US$1 = W0.97. To make it more absurd, a round-trip Beijing-P'yŏngyang-Beijing air ticket, bought in China, costs US$230, or US$44 less than a one-way ticket.

There are flights between the Russian city of Khabarovsk and P'yŏngyang in either direction by either Aeroflot or Koryŏ Air and between Moscow and P'yŏngyang. There are a few odd flights to Bangkok.

You're advised to book as far in advance as possible, although most aircraft fly nearly empty. Occasionally, delegations of diplomats descend on P'yŏngyang for some special event and seats suddenly become scarce. Apparently, there never was a problem of getting bounced by the Great Leader – he was afraid of flying and all his journeys abroad were made overland.

Sunan International Airport is 30 km west of P'yŏngyang, about 20 minutes by car.

TRAIN

There are four trains per week in either direction between Beijing and P'yŏngyang via Tianjin, Tangshan, Jinxi, Dandong and Shinŭiju. The Chinese trains leave on Monday and Thursday and the North Korean trains leave on Wednesday and Saturday. All these trains leave Beijing at 4.48 pm and arrive at P'yŏngyang the next day at 3.55 pm (about 23 hours). Going the other way, trains depart P'yŏngyang at noon on Monday, Wednesday, Thursday and Saturday. The one-way fare is US$101 in hard sleeper (economy class) or US$115 in soft sleeper (first class).

Chinese trains are more comfortable than the North Korean ones. North Korean trains don't have air-conditioning even in the soft sleeper section, and the windows are locked so ventilation is nonexistent.

The North Korean train is actually two carriages attached to the main Beijing-Dandong train, which are detached in Dandong (Chinese side) and then taken across the Yalu River bridge to Shinŭiju (Korean side), where more carriages are added for local people. Non-Koreans remain in their original carriages.

Customs and Immigration on both sides of the border are relatively casual and your passport will be taken away for stamping. The trains spend about four hours at the border for Customs and Immigration – two hours at Dandong and two hours at Shinŭiju. You are permitted to wander around the stations but you should not attempt to go beyond the entrance gate.

Shinŭiju station will be your first introduction to North Korea and the contrasts with China will be quite marked. Everything is squeaky-clean and there are no vendors plying their goods. A portrait of the Great Leader looks down from the top of this station, and at all other railway stations in North Korea. You may wander around the station and take photos. One of the buildings is a rest area for foreign passengers, and here you will encounter the first of many billboards with photos and captions in English: 'The US Aggression Troops Transferring Missiles'; 'South Korean Puppet Police'; 'US Imperialists & South Korean Stooges' etc.

Soon after departing Shinŭiju, you will be presented with a menu (complete with colour photographs) of what's for dinner. The food is excellent and the service is fine. It's all very civilised. Make sure you have some small denomination US dollar bills to pay for the meal, as this is not included as part of the package deal you paid for in advance. There are no facilities for changing money at Shinŭiju or on the train. The dining car is for the use of non-Koreans only.

Your guide will meet you on arrival at P'yŏngyang railway station and accompany you to your hotel. Likewise, when you leave North Korea, your guide will bid you farewell at P'yŏngyang railway station or the airport and you travel to China unaccompanied.

When leaving North Korea, you can link up with the Trans-Siberian train at Shinŭiju/Dandong in China. To make this connection you need to take the noon train from P'yŏngyang on Saturday which arrives in Moscow the following Friday. There's also the possibility of crossing directly from North Korea into Russia in the north-east via Hasan and then taking the Trans-Siberian to Moscow. The P'yŏngyang-Moscow journey takes seven days and costs US$432 in a soft-sleeper carriage, or you could go hard sleeper to Vladivostok in 30 hours for US$121.

BOAT

A passenger ship, the *Sam Jiyon*, plies between Wonsan on the east coast of North Korea and Nagasaki (Japan) once a month. It's a North Korean ship and is primarily intended to enable Koreans living in Japan to visit their homeland – most of the Koreans living in Japan originally came from North Korea. It's popular with youth groups from Japan, who get VIP treatment on arrival in the North, and is a possible port of entry if you already have a visa for North Korea.

If you have limited time at your disposal, you'll need to know the departure dates of this ship. North Korean embassies *may* know the details but don't be surprised if they don't or won't tell you. Don't just think you can hop on this ship even if you have a North Korean visa – you'd better clear it with the North Korean embassy first, and in any event, a guide must be informed that you're coming so you will be met on arrival.

You can get information about the ship by contacting the General Association of Korean Residents in Japan (SOREN). SOREN is P'yŏngyang's mouthpiece in Japan, with branches all over the country, and heavily-guarded headquarters in Tokyo. Members of SOREN run many of Japan's *pachinko* (slot machine) parlours, and a sizeable chunk of their cash goes to subsidise the North Korean economy.

LEAVING NORTH KOREA

You should make your reservations for departure before you arrive in North Korea. The North Korean government tourist agency, Ryohaengsa, can easily do this for you as long as you inform them in advance.

If departing by air, your guide will accompany you to the airline office so you can buy your ticket, or to reconfirm your outbound flight if you've already bought one. You must pay an airport departure tax of W13 at the time you reconfirm, rather than at the airport.

Moneychanging facilities are available at the airport but not at the railway station.

Getting Around

Public transport isn't anywhere near as well developed in North Korea as it is in the South. However, you will have only a few opportunities to use it, usually accompanied by your guide.

One thing you'll notice is the distinct lack of traffic in the countryside. Most of the vehicles you'll see will be military transports.

AIR

There are no regularly scheduled domestic flights. There are occasional charters to Paekdusan for W2000 return, but these only fly if there are sufficient passengers, which is seldom the case.

BUS

There are hardly any public buses in the countryside or between major cities, a reflection of the fact that North Koreans are not allowed to move freely around their own country without permission. Most of the time you'll be travelling by car accompanied by your driver and guide. If you're with a larger group, you'll ride in a specially arranged tourist bus. Naturally, this will limit your chances of meeting local people. On the other hand, if you can't speak Korean then this is probably an advantage of sorts, although it does mean you'll stand out a mile as a foreigner.

Being conspicuous is no great disadvantage in itself since Confucianism still rules, although under a different guise. Children will wave at you as you pass by, while adults will smile and maybe even chat (in Korean) if you happen to stop and get out on the streets. They've been encouraged to give visiting foreigners a warm welcome.

TRAIN

You'll probably take the railway to visit some of the major sights such as Kaesŏng and Myohyangsan. You'll be accompanied by your guide during these trips, and you'll ride in ornate 1950s sleeper cars rather than the dilapidated hard-seat carriages used by the masses. Indeed, the North Koreans often put on separate trains just for foreigners.

BICYCLE

A major contrast with China is the distinct lack of bicycles. There are almost none in P'yŏngyang and very few elsewhere. Outside of P'yŏngyang, most people walk. Presumably, the absence of bicycles in P'yŏngyang indicates a ban on their use. Occasionally, you'll come across a few in a department store in P'yŏngyang, usually with no price tags on them. Certainly you cannot rent bikes anywhere.

Finally, even if you did have your own bike, you'd be hard-pressed to find your way around either in the cities or in the countryside because there are no street signs in the cities or direction signs in the countryside and road maps are almost impossible to find. The only street map you'll find available is for P'yŏngyang.

ORGANISED TOURS

You must be accompanied at all times by a guide whose fees you will already have paid. In a few places you are allowed to walk around alone – basically P'yŏngyang and a few of the beauty spots – although this is only reluctantly conceded. Guides are available who can speak English, French, German, Chinese, Japanese and Russian as well as a number of other languages.

Tours booked through a private travel agent are more expensive than booking directly with Ryohaengsa, but only slightly. Presumably, the travel agents are shielding you from all the hassles of dealing with the North Korean bureaucracy and CITS in Beijing. For a five-day trip, Wallum Travel in Hong Kong charges US$880 for one person; US$683 each for two to five persons; US$502 each for six to nine persons; US$485 for 10 to 15 persons; a 16th person can go for free. If booked in conjunction with a Trans-Siberian tour, these charges are reduced by US$153 per person.

There are a number of special-interest tours. One is the 'Tour for Traditional Korean Medical Treatment'. This involves acupuncture, moxibustion (suction using vacuum flasks) manipulative (chiropractic) treatment and physical therapy. Cure rates of 90% are claimed for most illnesses. The costs for these treatments vary, but don't expect it to be cheap.

One of the more unusual manifestations of North Korea's cultural policy is the invention of 'alphabetical dance notation'. This is a method of writing down dance movements much the same way music is recorded on paper using special notation. Tourists are invited to study this system by taking a dance tour. The cost per person runs from US$435 to US$750 for an eight-day course, depending on the number of people in the class. The cost for a fifteen-day course is US$860 to US$1500. The price includes accommodation, meals, transport and some sightseeing as well as the course. Ryohaengsa can supply you with more details.

P'yŏngyang 평양

P'yŏngyang is a superb example of the regime's determination to project its own image of progress, discipline and the wellbeing of its citizens. You won't find here the hustle and bustle, the noise and smells of other cities in Asia.

North Korea's version of the model Communist capital city excludes people with disabilities (except the Great Leader, who had a large visible bulge on the back of his head from a benign brain tumour). Also excluded are the very old, bicycles, animals and street vendors. Even pregnant women were banned for a while. All this has attracted the critical attention of the foreign press, and possibly because of such criticism, there is now one token disabled man who is often seen riding a modified bicycle near the Koryŏ Hotel (even though bikes are banned in the city). A few elderly people have also recently appeared around the Koryŏ Hotel (where most foreigners stay), but their numbers are exceedingly low.

It's said that only those with proven records of unswerving loyalty to the country's leaders are allowed to live in P'yŏngyang.

P'yŏngyang is the showpiece of North Korea and is peppered with distinctive landmarks and monuments, many of them in honour of the Great Leader. A notable one is the 170-metre high Tower of the Juche Idea, crowned with a beacon which flickers at night. There's also the extraordinary 13-lane boulevard which connects the city centre with the outer suburb of Kwangbok over three km away – a ridiculous extravagance given the scarcity of traffic, although no more of a profligate waste than many of the other grandiose monuments. Not surprisingly, a few things are named after the Great Leader: Kim Il-sung Square, Kim Il-sung Stadium, Kim Il-sung University and Kim Il-sung Higher Party School.

Fascinating indicators of the mentality of the regime are the stores with big glass display windows, well stocked with goods for all to see. The problem is that the doors are always locked and no-one is inside.

Orientation

Like Seoul, the city is built on the banks of

a major river, in this case the Taedong. Like the Han, it often freezes over in winter. One of the major sights are the two mid-river fountains which rise to a height of 150 metres. Your guide will proudly tell you they're the highest in the world, and this is probably true (Canberra's single jet reaches only 140 metres and the one in Geneva only 122 metres).

If walking around the city, beware of jay-walking even if there's not a car in sight! There are underground walkways or pedestrian crossings at all major intersections and *everyone*, without exception, uses them. There are also traffic police at all such points standing on wooden plinths. If you attempt to jay-walk, the nearest one will give a sharp blast of her whistle (they're mostly women) and a smart remonstration will quickly bring you back in line.

Things to See

Since P'yŏngyang is one of the few places where you'll be allowed to walk around unaccompanied (with a little gentle but persistent persuasion), it's a good idea to take this opportunity either before or after you've been chauffeured around the main sights. If you request it, you can, for instance, be dropped on the far side of the city at Liberation Tower and walk back from here to the centre calling in at department stores along the way if you want.

Your first day out in P'yŏngyang will undoubtedly be a guided tour of the monuments by car. How many of them you will see depends on the time available and what preferences you express. It's a good idea to make your preferences known as early as possible after arrival in North Korea or even beforehand if you want to be sure of being taken to the ones of your choice.

One of the principal monuments is the **Tower of the Juche Idea**, a 170-metre phallic symbol which you can get to the top of by express lift for an unencumbered view of the city. The ride costs W5. In an alcove at the bottom are commemorative messages from various parts of the world hewn in stone and brick extolling the concept of Juche. As

the plaques indicate, the Juche idea is also referred to as Kim Il-sungism.

Other monuments include the **Arch of Triumph**, which marks the spot where Kim Il-sung made his rallying speech following the departure of the Japanese, and which is a full three metres higher than its counterpart in Paris, and the **Chollima Statue**, a bronze Petasus representing the high-speed progress of the socialist reconstruction of North Korea. On Munsu Hill, overlooking the Taedong River, is the **Grand Monument** itself. As you might expect, this is where an enormous and highly polished bronze statue of the Great Leader stands, flanked by carvings of oppressed but ultimately victorious ' workers.

Of a more traditional nature are the **Chilsong** and **Taedong Gates**, two of the old city's gates, the latter with a two-tiered roof similar to its counterpart in Seoul.

For an exposition of North Korea's version of the country's history there is the **Korean Central History Museum**. The counterpart to the South's Independence Hall outside Ch'ŏnan, the museum houses exhibits, artefacts and drawings tracing Korean history from prehistoric times right up to the revolution. Your guide will provide a running commentary.

Arch of Triumph

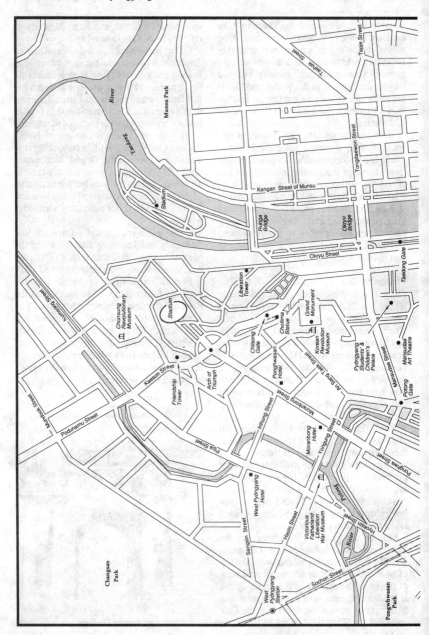

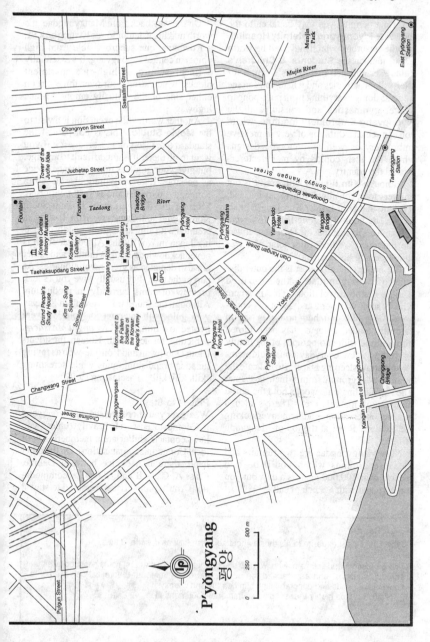

If time permits, you may be taken to the showcase **P'yŏngyang Maternity Hospital**.

Other institutes which may well be worth a visit include the **Students' & Children's Palace**, established in 1963 as a centre for after-school activities and where you can see students doing everything from ping-pong to dance, gymnastics and music, and the **P'yŏngyang Embroidery Institute**, where you can see an exhibition of very impressive embroidery as well as prototype designs which are then copied by manufacturers around the country.

Although **Kim Il-sung University** is not on every tour, you might want to pay it a visit. It is here that Dear Leader Kim Jong-il graduated. The book *Kim Jong-il In His Young Days* makes it clear that the Dear Leader was the university's foremost scholar and was soon teaching his teachers.

The major site of interest is the outer district of **Mangyongdae** – the so-called 'Cradle of the Revolution'. This is where Kim Il-sung was born and spent his childhood. His old thatched house is set in carefully tended gardens, has been turned into a shrine with photographs of his family as well as a few everyday household items (Kim's straw sleeping mat etc) to indicate the humble background from which he came. The surrounding pine woods hold the burial mounds of his relatives. There's also a marble observation platform overlooking the Taedong River at the top of Mangyong Hill.

Near Mangyongdae are two funfairs and pleasure grounds which you'll be told receive over 100,000 visitors a day, but you can take that with a pinch of salt.

On the way back from Mangyongdae, it's worth making a detour to see **Kwangbok St**, a Kowloonesque suburb visible from high points in central P'yŏngyang. It's essentially a linear suburb of high-rise apartment blocks, which stretch for over three km on either side of the virtually empty 13-lane highway.

Another worthwhile excursion is a visit to the **Movie Studio**. This is not part of the standard tours, so you must request it if you want to go there. It is not difficult to arrange, but give your guide as much advance notice as possible. Like everything else in North Korea, the movie studio is very politicised. Most of the films are anti-US, anti-South Korean and anti-Japanese. Kim Il-sung is credited with almost single-handedly defeating Japan in WW II (the Allied war effort is never acknowledged). His mother and father are also depicted as great revolutionaries. As part of the tour, they usually give you a sneak preview of films currently in production. Although the sound tracks are all in Korean, your guide will interpret for you. We were treated to a film, called *Kwangju Massacre*, depicting former South Korean presidents Chun Doo-hwan and Roh Tae-woo as raving lunatics brandishing guns while screaming 'kill, kill, kill!'. Fascinating stuff.

Places to Stay

Wherever you choose to stay in P'yŏngyang it's going to cost you heavily (unless you have contacts and/or are a member of your local Communist organisation). On the other hand, there is a choice between Deluxe, Class A, Class B and Class C accommodation. You'll probably be pressured to stay at

---

Kim Jong-il
When the Dear Leader read his thesis about socialism, it was described thus:

The professors and scholars, who were so strict about scientific matters, could not suppress their surging emotions, and approached the author who made immortal theoretical achievements, shaking his hands and congratulating him heartily and warmly.
His thesis was highly assessed as an immortal document. ■

the deluxe *P'yŏngyang Koryŏ Hotel* (☎ 38-106), a 45-storey tower with a revolving restaurant on top. It's a five-minute walk from the railway station and it's where most foreigners stay. The hotel has 500 rooms, and given the small number of tourists, it's unlikely you'll have to worry about getting a reservation.

There are some other deluxe hotels, but most are inconveniently located. There's the *Tourist Hotel*, about seven km from the city centre; the *Angol Hotel*, at a similar distance from the centre; and the *Yanggakdo Hotel*, about four km from the centre.

The skyline of P'yŏngyang is dominated by the incredible *Ryugyong Hotel*, a 105-storey pyramid with 3000 rooms and five revolving restaurants. Originally conceived as the world's largest luxury hotel, the pyramid was erected in 1989 but the North Koreans apparently ran out of money before they could complete it. The building now sits as an empty shell and it's unlikely further work will be done unless there is a dramatic increase in tourism. Tourist pamphlets produced in North Korea often show the building photographed at night with lights on inside. The photos are a sham: the building is not even wired for electricity. It's about four km from the centre.

Further down the scale, in class B, are the *Potonggang Hotel* (☎ 48301), a fairly modest hotel about four km from the centre with 161 rooms; the *Sosan Hotel*, about four km from the railway station; the *Ryanggang Hotel* with 330 rooms, also four km from the centre; and the *Youth Hotel*, about 10 km from the centre with 465 rooms.

The most popular C class hotel is the *Changgwangsan Hotel* (☎ 48366), with 326 rooms, less than two km from the railway station. In the heart of the city is the *P'yŏngyang Hotel* (☎ 38161), with 170 rooms. The *Taedonggang Hotel* (☎ 38346), with 60 rooms, is also in the centre of the city.

Places to Eat

You'll usually eat at your hotel but eating elsewhere can be arranged. Many foreigners hang out in the coffee shop of the *Changgwangsan Hotel* but prices are high. As for the 'local restaurants', these in fact cater to foreigners or privileged Koreans with access to hard currency. Don't think you'll be able to eat along with the working class. Just where the locals eat is a mystery – either they bring food from home or they're fed at the workplace, but there are certainly no pavement restaurants or food stalls like you find all over South Korea. If you want to eat outside your hotel, you should make this clear to your guide.

Entertainment

The streets are deserted at night. For North Koreans, the evening is presumably spent sitting by the radio or TV listening to testimonials by happy workers and profound speeches by the Great Leader.

There are a few discos for decadent foreigners (no Koreans allowed). Don't get your hopes up though – the largest disco managed to attract 20 customers (19 males and one female) when we visited on a Saturday night during the peak summer season. The most popular disco is on the top floor of building No 2 in the Changgwangsan Hotel (☎ 48366). It's open from 9.30 pm until midnight and costs W2.

The Koryŏ Hotel has a dance hall, but the cover charge is W25 so it's usually empty except for a few Japanese karaoke enthusiasts. The second floor of the same hotel has a billiards room which is a good place to socialise with embassy staff, journalists and whoever else happens to be in town.

Things to Buy

While there are scarcely any consumer goods on the shelves, North Korea offers plenty of unique souvenirs which make fantastic conversation pieces.

To the south of the P'yŏngyang Koryŏ Hotel on Changgwang St is a place selling postage stamps (sign in English) and it's well worth your time to stop in here. One postage stamp shows a crowd of angry Koreans beating a US soldier to death while someone sticks a knife through his throat. Another shows two soldiers, one Korean and one Chinese, standing shoulder to shoulder while brandishing AK-47s. You might enjoy the stamps depicting North Korea's version of the space shuttle, but even more bizarre are the stamps proudly displaying the British royal family. Just why Charles and Diana are so popular in North Korea is one of those great mysteries. And finally, one guess whose picture is displayed on the largest stamps.

Many tourists have expressed an interest in purchasing the metal badge which every North Korean wears, with the Great Leader's picture printed on it. However, these are not for sale.

Ginseng is for sale in hotels, but prices are ridiculously high. You can buy it much more cheaply in the South. However, if you're an aspiring acupuncturist, you can find acupuncture needles in the medicine shops at rock-bottom prices.

Getting Around

All public transport in P'yŏngyang costs 10 jon. They want it in coins, so you'll need local money. As a general rule, foreigners are discouraged from using the public transport system except for the subway (underground) which is something of a showcase.

Bus It's unlikely you'll ever use the urban bus network as the queues are phenomenally long and the buses crammed to bursting point, but if you do they run until 10 pm each day. Women with children form separate queues and have priority in boarding buses.

Tram P'yŏngyang's tram began service in 1991. It's not a bad way of getting around, but it's often extremely crowded.

Taxi You won't find taxis plying the streets as in most major capital cities, but you can book a taxi from a tourist hotel. The word 'taxi' is not written on the car, nor will you see a meter, but the fare is based on distance. The fare is approximately W2 per km, depending on the type of vehicle (Mercedes are most expensive). The price also rises

slightly late at night. In the rare event that you don't find a taxi waiting outside your hotel, you can call one (☎ 10507).

Subway You should definitely visit a subway station if only to see the extravagance with which the stations have been constructed. Each station is designed differently, with varying bronze sculptures, murals, mosaics and chandeliers, and all the pillars, steps, corridors and platforms are fashioned in marble. Stations have names which translate as Liberation, Reunification, Reconstruction, and so on. The trains themselves are nowhere near as impressive as the stations, being dim and dingy, but each car contains a picture of His Excellency.

There are 17 stations in all, served by two lines covering a total length of 24 km; the present system was completed in 1978. There are grand plans to extend it to Mangyongdae (P'yŏngyang's western district) and eventually to Chinnamp'o (P'yŏngyang's seaport). Each station has a map of the system indicating where you are. The cost of a ride on this system is a standard 10 jon and it's a very convenient way of quickly visiting different parts of the city.

Around the Country

What you get to see outside of P'yŏngyang depends on what sort of itinerary you request and how much time you have. It will also be limited to the places where tourist hotels are located. The following is a selection of places but isn't meant to be exhaustive. If you wish to go elsewhere, then it's worth attempting to get permission. Few such requests, it seems, are refused, although they may initially cause raised eyebrows. On the other hand, if you do succeed in getting permission to visit places which aren't on the suggested tourist circuits, you must be prepared to accept last-minute cancellations. This even happens to group tours occasionally.

MYOHYANGSAN 묘향산

A visit here from P'yŏngyang can be adequately covered in a day trip using the train as your means of transport. It's 160 km from the capital.

The train leaves P'yŏngyang daily at 6 am and arrives at Myohyangsan at 9 am. On the return journey, the train leaves Myohyangsan at 7 pm and arrives P'yŏngyang at 10.20 pm. Breakfast is taken on the train in the foreigners-only dining car.

The main centre of interest in Myohyangsan is the International Friendship Exhibition (IFE) centre, about three to four km from the railway station. It's another of those monuments to the greater glory of the Great Leader and, to a lesser extent, of the Dear Leader. It's a six-storey building in traditional Korean style which houses gifts given to Kim Il-sung and Kim Jong-il from all over the world and is magnificently set amongst densely wooded hills.

You need to be on your best behaviour here, as the building is maintained as a hallowed shrine. You must take off your hat if you have one, and shoe covers must be worn when walking around. You may be permitted to open the golden doors to the shrine, but you must first put on a pair of gloves before touching the sacred handle. During your tour, you'll be escorted the whole time by a woman in traditional Korean costume. The building has been lavishly endowed with marble stairways, huge bronze doors and thick carpets. There are no windows and each room is thermostatically temperature-controlled. It's quite cold inside, so bring a jacket even in summer.

The list of donors reads like a roster of the dead and discredited: Stalin, Mao, Castro, Ceausescu, Honecker, Gaddafi etc. Nevertheless, the gifts are quite fascinating: a bullet-proof Zil limousine from Stalin, a luxurious train carriage from Mao Zedong, a stuffed alligator from the Sandinistas, carvings, pottery and paintings, many of which are exquisitely executed. The gifts are arranged by country with a note, in English, of who sent them and when. There are 120 rooms in total and it's not possible to see them all in one day.

When you've seen the exhibition, hike three km up the Sangwon Valley, via a clearly defined pathway, stone steps and a suspension footbridge to three sets of waterfalls (Kŭmgang, Taeha and Sanju). Nearby, there's an observation platform from which you can view the surrounding countryside. A short hike above the falls is a Buddhist temple – Sangwonsa – which is in good order though no longer used.

There's also the Buddhist temple Pohyonsa, just a short walk from the IFE at the start of the hike up Sangwon Valley, which consists of several small pagodas and a large hall housing images of the Buddha, as well as a museum which sports a collection of wood-block Buddhist scriptures. You'll be told that these wooden buildings are 950 years old and have never been rebuilt – amazing since they look very new and sit on a concrete foundation.

The village of Myohyangsan itself consists of just one main street lined by traditional Korean houses. The main tourist hotel in this vicinity is the *Hyangsan Hotel*, about halfway between the station and the IFE, rated as class A. There is also the class C *Chongbyong Hotel*, and the class D *Chongchon Hotel* about one km from the railway station.

KAESŎNG 개성

Kaesŏng (population 200,000) is one of the few North Korean towns where burial sites of the former kings and queens of Korea can be seen. You can see the burial mounds along with associated statuary of King Kongmin (the 31st Koryŏ king who reigned between 1330 and 1374) and his queen, about 13 km from the centre of the city. It's a very secluded site and there are splendid views over the surrounding tree-covered hills from a number of vantage points. You'll need a car to get there.

In the city are a number of obligatory tourist sights. Included among them are the **Sonjuk Bridge**, a tiny clapper bridge built in 1216 and, opposite, the **Pyochung Stele**, similar to those at the shrines outside of Kyŏngju and elsewhere in South Korea. A short drive from town is the **Songgyungwan Confucian College** which was originally built in 992 and rebuilt after fire in the 17th century. Today it's a museum of vases and other relics. The buildings surround a wide courtyard dotted with ancient trees.

Kaesŏng is a modern city with wide streets and is of scant interest, although it does have an interesting old part consisting of traditional tile-roofed houses sandwiched between the river and the main street. There's also Nammun (South Gate) at the beginning of the main street which dates from the 14th century. From the main street, a wide driveway sweeps up to the summit of Chanamsan, on top of which there's a massive bronze statue of – guess who?

If you stay in Kaesŏng, you'll be based at either the *Channamsan Hotel* or *Kaesŏng Minsok Hotel*. If you have a choice, definitely choose the latter, which is built in the traditional Korean yŏgwan style. Both hotels are class C.

To get to Kaesŏng you can either take the train or a car, although a car is preferable if you want to see the towns en route. Driving time between P'yŏngyang and Kaesŏng is about 3¼ hours with a tea stop at a tourist halt built on a rocky outcrop overlooking the Sohung River along the way.

P'ANMUNJŎM 판문점

This is one of the most morbidly fascinating sights in Korea. Even if you've visited this 'Truce Village' from the South, the trip from the northern side is well worth the effort.

To get there, you drive out of Kaesŏng on the 'Reunification Highway', a six-lane freeway devoid of traffic with military checkpoints every 20 km. The freeway is supposed to connect P'yŏngyang to Seoul, and the last exit before the DMZ has a large sign saying 'Seoul 70 km'. You drive up to a sentry box at the entrance to the DMZ where a military officer gives you a brief rundown of the history of P'anmunjŏm aided by a large model of the 'Truce Village'. After that you'll be escorted to the Joint Security Zone by military officers in a car. From the car park, you enter a large building that faces the row of huts which straddle the demarcation line and then exchange glances with burly US marines, South Korean soldiers and the tourists on the other side in their pagoda viewing tower. Unless meetings are in progress, you'll be permitted to visit the very room where the endless peace negotiations go on. After that, it's back to the main building for an exposition of the North Korean view of things.

The whole setting looks very serene, with well-tended gardens, trees, rice fields and chirping birds. Hard to imagine that all around you the countryside is bristling with camouflaged tanks, nuclear warheads, nerve gas canisters, biological weapons and land mines. If war were to break out during your visit, you'd be incinerated in a minute. Imagine that.

On the way out of the DMZ, you are given a chance to visit the gift shop. There are some real collectors' items here, including a classic hate-mongering book called *P'anmunjŏm* published in a variety of languages:

The US imperialist aggressors drew the Military Demarcation Line to divide Korea and her people by artificial means. P'anmunjŏm is a place through which the line runs and a court which exposes and vehemently denounces the US imperialist criminal aggression in Korea to the whole world. The US imperialists started a war of aggression (1950-53) in order to swallow up the whole of Korea. But here at P'anmunjŏm they went down on their knees before the Korean people and signed the Armistice Agreement.

The next stop on the agenda is the 'Wall'. According to the North, the Americans and South Koreans have built a concrete wall all the way across the peninsula (248 km) along the southern side of the DMZ.

The wall is in fact an anti-tank barrier which has been there for many years and attracted no attention whatsoever from the North until around 1990 when the Berlin Wall was torn down. Suddenly, the North realised the propaganda potential, and the 'Korean Wall' was added as one of the compulsory stops for foreign tour groups. You'll be able to view the wall through telescopes from four km away. You'll then be taken into a

The Wall

As the *P'anmunjŏm* puts it:

The South Korean puppets have hindered North-South dialogues against the burning desire of the Korean people for national reunification and their great expectations for the talks. They committed another ineffaceable crime against the nation. They built a reinforced concrete wall along the Military Demarcation Line to divide the country and cut the national ties forever at the dictates of the US imperialists. ■

room and be shown a video and given a lecture on the burning desire of the Korean people for reunification. All very gripping stuff.

One of the things you probably won't be shown is the triple electric fence on the north side of the DMZ. The fence carries 3300 volts and is set on a concrete base to prevent tunneling under it. Supposedly designed to keep invaders out, it's hard to imagine that this flimsy fence couldn't be blown away instantly by South Korean artillery. Like the Berlin Wall, its chief purpose seems to be keeping people in, not out.

KŬMGANGSAN 금강산

South of Wonsan, on the east coast, Kŭmgangsan (the Diamond Mountains) are the North Korean equivalent of the South's Sŏraksan and Odaesan mountains – an area of outstanding natural beauty. It's also one place where North Korea is believed to maintain large concentration camps for political prisoners, but don't expect to be shown these as part of your tour.

The usual route to Kŭmgangsan is by car from P'yŏngyang to Onjong-ni via Wonsan along the new highway (around 315 km or four hours in all). The first part of the journey to Wonsan can also be done by train, although it's not so interesting doing it this way.

Going by car, you stop off at a teahouse at Sinp'yŏng Lake – a very attractive area and a centre of honey production. The new road is quite spectacular and involves passing through 18 tunnels between Sinp'yŏng and Wonsan, the longest of which is some 4½ km long. The port city of Wonsan was shelled to rubble in the Korean War, so it's an entirely modern town with a seven-lane boulevard leading down to the waterfront. Tourists are taken to the class C *Songdowon Hotel* and the adjoining *Kŭmgang Restaurant*.

'Sticker Shock'

You would be hard-pressed to find anybody in Korea who does not support reunification of their divided country. Indeed, if there is anything that both North and South Korea can agree on, it is the 'burning desire of the Korean people for reunification'. Furthermore, every Korean agrees that the sooner the country can reunify, the better.

Or do they? Having witnessed the great financial burden that the former West Germany has incurred trying to absorb the East, many South Koreans have started to ask just how much it might cost them. This question has sent economists scurrying for their computers, and the price sticker they've come up with has raised more than a few eyebrows.

All figures are rough estimates, but it is thought that the cost of absorbing North Korea into the South Korean economy would require up to US$250 billion in direct government handouts, plus perhaps US$1 trillion in private investment. The high figures have much to do with the fact that North Korea is in far worse financial shape than the former East Germany ever was. And this is to say nothing of the potential social problems as millions of northern economic refugees pour into the South to search for better-paying jobs.

While you won't find any South Koreans opposing reunification, many seem to be having second thoughts. Even if North Korea collapses, maybe that electric fence on the DMZ ought to be kept in place just a little bit longer. Southern politicians have been indicating that perhaps reunification is 'too expensive' for now and should be postponed until some unspecified time in the future. ■

From Wonsan, the road more or less follows the coastline, and you'll get glimpses of the double electric fence which runs the entire length of the east coast. South Korea has a similar coastal fence, although in the South it isn't electrified. They'll be an obligatory stop for tea at Shijung Lake. Your final destination is the village of Onjong-ni and the *Kŭmgangsan Hotel*, rated class B. The hotel is quite a rambling affair consisting of a main building and several outer buildings which include chalets, a shop, dance hall and bathhouse (fed by a hot spring). The village, 15 minutes' walk from the hotel, is worthy of a guide-less visit and consists of a cluster of traditional Korean houses and small garden plots crammed with vegetables.

Much like Sŏraksan in the South, Kŭmgangsan is divided into Inner, Outer and Sea Kŭmgang, and the main activities here are hiking, mountaineering, boating and sightseeing. The area is peppered with former Buddhist temples and hermitages, waterfalls, mineral springs Samil Lake and a museum. It's up to you how long you spend here and what you do, but maps of the area are provided to help you decide where you want to go.

Two of the most popular excursions are to **Kuryong Falls** and **Samil Lake**. The waterfalls are a 15-minute drive from the hotel via Onjong-ni along an unsurfaced road through conifer forest to the Mongran Restaurant. The restaurant is hemmed in by steep rock faces and its balcony overlooks the river below the waterfalls. It's a pleasant place to eat lunch. From the restaurant it's a 4½ km walk along footpaths, over rocks and across suspension bridges to the falls. Your guide will regale you with legends about the area and the stories behind the rocks which are supposed to resemble such things as elephants, frogs, turtles, fried dumplings etc. At the falls, which are some 70 metres high, there's a viewing platform. It's a very attractive area and popular with artists. (Many of the paintings you see in Korea were inspired by the views in the area.)

Samil Lake is located in an area of conifer forests and was once connected to the sea, and although you can see the ocean from here you're not permitted to go to the seashore at this point. Boats are available for hire at the lake, and for meals there's the Danpung Restaurant on the lakeside.

PAEKDUSAN 백두산

The highest mountain in the whole of Korea at 2744 metres, Paekdusan (Mt Paekdu) sits astride the Korean/Chinese border in the far north. It's a sacred spot to both South and North Koreans – according to Korean mythology, this is where the Korean race began. The story goes that in the year 2333 BC, Hwanung (son of the lord of heaven) descended from heaven and met a bear and a tiger. He offered them a chance to become human, but first they had to pass a test – they had to stay in a cave all winter and eat only garlic. The tiger failed the test, but the bear succeeded and emerged from the cave as a beautiful woman. She mated with Hwanung and produced Tan'gun, the progenitor and first king of the Korean race.

It should be no mystery then why North Korea claims that Kim Jong-il was born here, even though all sources outside North Korea maintain that Kim was born in the Russian city of Khabarovsk. New North Korean mythology even claims that flying white horses were seen by witnesses after baby Kim entered the world.

Revolutionary Trees
A North Korean pamphlet explains:

Slogan-bearing trees, relics and remains in the period of the anti-Japanese revolutionary struggle organised and led by the great leader Comrade Kim Il-sung are recently being discovered in various parts of the country...During the anti-Japanese revolutionary struggle the great leader Comrade Kim Il-sung set up more than ten districts of secret camps in the primitive forests of Mt Paekdu and led to victory the Korean revolution as a whole, centred on the anti-Japanese armed struggle. ■

North Korea's current history books also claim that Kim Il-sung established his headquarters at Paekdusan, from where he defeated the Japanese. To prove this, you'll be shown revolutionary slogans which the Great Leader and his comrades carved on the trees. You'll be told that more and more of these carvings are being discovered every year, and some are so well-preserved you'd almost think they'd been carved yesterday if you didn't know better.

Outside of North Korea, no history books claim that this mountain was ever a battlefield during WW II. Nevertheless, the North Korean book *Kim Jong-il In His Young Days* describes the Dear Leader's difficult childhood during the nonexistent battles at Paekdusan (see the fact box opposite).

History continues to evolve in North Korea, with new discoveries being made every year. The North Koreans 'discovered' the tomb of Tan'gun (the progenitor of the entire Korean race) in 1993. Tan'gun was also the first king of the Korean people, and he founded the first capital of Kochosŏn (ancient Korea) at the legendary city of Asadal. Korean scholars have always said that Asadal was in Manchuria (north-east China). But North Korean scholars now insist that this is incorrect and in fact Asadal was built on the site of what is now P'yŏngyang.

On top of the now-extinct volcano is a crater lake (Lake Chon) which is some 14 km in circumference and reaches a maximum depth of 380 metres. This makes it one of the deepest alpine lakes in the world.

The Dear Leader's Young Days
His childhood was replete with ordeals.

The secret camp of the Korean People's Revolutionary Army in the primeval forest was his home, and ammunition belts and magazines were his playthings. The raging blizzards and ceaseless gunshots were the first sounds to which he became accustomed.

Day in and day out fierce battles went on and, during the breaks, there were military and political trainings. On the battlefield, there was no quilt to warmly wrap the newborn child. So women guerrillas gallantly tore cotton out of their own uniforms and each contributed pieces of cloth to make a patchwork quilt for the infant. ∎

Places to Stay
Hotels to stay at in this area include the *Hyesan Hotel*, in the town of the same name, the *Samjiyon Sin Hotel*, some 67 km from Hyesan, and the *Onsupyong Hotel*. The first two are class B hotels whilst the latter is a class C hotel.

Getting There & Away
Paekdusan is only accessible from around late June to mid-September. Access to the mountain is by air or train followed by car.

You can also visit the mountain and crater lake from the Chinese side – a trip that's now popular with South Korean tourists. Paekdusan is called Changbaishan in Chinese and the crater lake is named Tianchi (Lake of Heaven).

Lake of Heaven
Many legends have grown up around the Lake of Heaven. Dragons, and other things that go bump in the night, were believed to have sprung from the alpine waters. In fact, they're still believed to do so. There have been intermittent sightings of unidentified swimming objects – Asia's own Loch Ness beasties or aquatic yetis or what have you. Since the lake is frozen over in winter and temperatures are well below zero, it would take a pretty hardy monster to survive (even plankton can't). Sightings from the Chinese and North Korean sides point to a black bear, fond of swimming, and oblivious to the paperwork necessary for crossing these tight borders. On a more profound note, Chinese and Korean couples throw coins into the water, pledging that their love will remain as deep as the lake, and as long-lived. ∎

Glossary

ajimah – a married or older woman; a term of respect for a woman who runs a hotel, restaurant or other business

am – hermitage

bawi – large rock

bong – peak

ch'a – tea

chaebol – huge corporate conglomerate

chihach'ŏl yŏk – subway station

dae – great, large

-do – province

do – island

donggul or **gul** – cave

-ga – section of a long street

gak, nu or **ru** – pavilion

gil – street

gung or **kung** – palace

-gu – urban district

gun – county

hae – sea

hagwon – private language school often employing foreign teachers

han'gŭl – Korean phonetic alphabet

hanja – Chinese-style writing system

harubang – 'grandfather stones' found on Chejudo

hesuyokjang – beach

ho – lake

insam – ginseng

jŏng – hall of a temple

kimch'i – spicy fermented cabbage, the national dish

kŏbuksŏn – 'turtle ship', the iron-clad warships made famous by Admiral Yi

konghang – airport

kongwon – park

maekju – beer

makkŏli – white rice wine

minbak – guesthouse, a private home with rooms for rent

mok yok t'ang – bathhouse

mun – gate

myŏn – township

myo or **tae** – shrine

nam – south

no or **ro** – large street, boulevard

nŭng or **rŭng** – tomb

nyŏng or **ryŏng** – mountain pass

ondol – underfloor heating

p'okp'o – waterfall

p'yŏng – a unit of measure, one p'yŏng equals 3.3 square metres

paduk – Korean chess, same as the Japanese game *go*

puk – north

pulgogi – barbecued beef & vegetables grilled at the table, the most popular dish with foreigners

ri or **ni** – village

sanjang – mountain hut

sansŏng – fortress built on a mountaintop

san – mountain

sa – temple

shich'ŏng – city hall

shi – city

soju – potato 'vodka'

sŏ – west

sŏwon – former Confucian academies which are now preserved as national treasures

ssirum – Korean wrestling, similar to Japanese sumo wrestling

t'aekkyŏn – the original form of t'aekwondo

t'aekwondo – Korean martial arts

t'ap – pagoda

t'ongil – unification

tabang – tearoom

taepiso – mountain shelter

tong – east

ŭp – town

wonch'ŏn – hot spring

yak – medicine

yŏgwan – small family-run hotel, usually with private bath

yŏinsuk – small family-run hotel with closet-sized rooms and shared bath

Index

TEXT

Update – June 1996

NORTH KOREA

A reader reports on a tour of North Korea:

I arranged the trip and visa through an Australian agent although I ended up travelling with two people from Classic Oriental Tours in Sydney (☎ (02) 9261 3988), who look like getting exclusive rights to run tours from Australia. As pre-arranged, I picked up my visa in Beijing and had no problems at all – in fact was in and out in 10 minutes, which is a great deal better than most of my other visa experiences!

I flew in and got the train out, as that proved easier to arrange. It worked out really well. Flying in I met a few other foreigners – UN experts etc, who were interesting to talk to, while by catching the train (which leaves at noon) I effectively got an extra morning in P'yongyang, while the plane people were shipped off at about 8 am. I was able to walk around in this time and get more of a feel for the place than was possible with a guide.

Customs coming in was surprisingly easy. This might be another advantage of flying in. Going out on the train there was quite a perfunctory baggage search. The only thing they got excited about was the less than US$1 worth of North Korean currency I had, which was confiscated, although not angrily.

I'd recommend taking any decent newspapers, magazines etc, you happen to acquire with you, for the benefit of the resident foreign community, which is starved for news, and which will welcome such offerings with open arms.

I always travel on my own, but this time with the tour I was very glad to end up with a couple of other people. I think just you and a guide for five days would get more than a little claustrophobic!

The exhortations to the locals to smile and be friendly to tourists you mention seem to have worn off, or perhaps been countermanded. I found it almost impossible to get anyone to meet my eye or smile (even children) and I felt as though I was surrounded by a 'cone of invisibility'. It was also very hard to take photos of people except the guards in the DMZ who we were told to photograph at will!

In winter it seemed as though the only place it was possible to stay in P'yongyang was the Koryo Hotel which was quite OK. The hotel shop has most things you would need in the way of toiletries, etc, so there is no need to panic about forgetting something, although prices are high.

Natalie Bennet

SOUTH KOREA

Politically, South Korea has been having a rather tumultuous time lately, with two ex-

Dear traveller

Prices go up, good places go bad, bad places go bankrupt...and every guidebook is inevitably outdated in places. Fortunately, many travellers write to us about their experiences, telling us when things have changed. If we reprint a book between editions, we try to include the best of this information in an Update section. We also make travellers' tips immediately available on our award-winning World Wide Web Internet site (http://www.lonelyplanet.com) and in a free quarterly newsletter, *Planet Talk*.

Although much of this information has not been verified by our own first-hand research, we believe it can be very useful. We cannot vouch for its accuracy, however, so bear in mind it could be wrong.

We really enjoy hearing from people out on the road, and apart from guaranteeing that others will benefit from your good and bad experiences, we're prepared to bribe you with the offer of a free book for sending us substantial useful information.

I hope you do find this book useful – and that you let us know when it isn't. Thank you to everyone who has written.

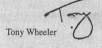

Tony Wheeler

presidents being prosecuted for corruption and treason. Several tragic building collapses, probably caused by corrupt and sloppy construction methods, have also undermined people's faith in the country's business community.

Government members and bureaucrats have been discouraged from playing golf. Their fellow golfers tend to be rich businesspeople, and golf courses offer plenty of privacy for cooking up deals and conspiracies.

Money

The exchange rate in June 1996 was approximately W100 = US$0.13.

Getting There & Away

The international air departure tax is now W9000.

There are some new sea routes from China, including Dalian-Inch'on, Tianjin-

Inch'on, Yantai-Pusan, Weihai-Inch'on and Qingdao-Inch'on.

Getting Around
Bus fares have risen but the prices are still low.

Places to Stay
Youth hostels have opened in Kyongju, Kumi, Namhae, Tongdosa, Tanyang, Yusong, Kyerongsan, Puyo, Hwayang Valley and several other places in Kyongi-do. Unfortunately they are often full. More hostels are under construction (including one on Cheju-do).

Communications
Apparently some people worked out how to make free IDD calls from public phones, so the authorities have removed IDD facilities to several countries, such as the Philippines. This only applies to public phones.

Seoul
The US embassy phone number (page 112) should be ☎ 397 4114.

The Kyongbokkung Palace now has a cheaper entry fee for visitors under 24 (W300) and Changtokkung uses the system too (W1100).

Entertainment Bars in major hotels are allowed to stay open until 2 am.

It's the Korean Traditional Performing Arts Centre (next to the Seoul Arts Centre) that has the Saturday afternoon performances (see page 112). It's a good idea to book in advance. The best way to get there is to go to Nanku Subway terminal, walk past the bus terminal to the main highway and turn right. It's about a 15-minute walk. The Cargo Truck Terminal is a lot farther away.

Cy Wert

Getting Around Ordinary taxis will take more than one fare at a time if somebody is going in the general direction of the person already in the car. The trick is to shout a destination in a slowing taxi's window as it passes. This doesn't mean you get to share the fare; both passengers have to pay the full amount.

Kangnung
The bus stations have been moved to a very remote location near the No 4 expressway.

Kyongju
The combination ticket which used to allow entry to the Tumuli Park and other sites is no longer available. If you want to walk the trails without the hordes accompanying you, don't come on a Wednesday, and plan an early departure on any day.

Naksan
Watching the sunrise from Naksan Provincial Park might no longer be possible, as one entrance is blocked by a gate and the main entrance above the youth hostel doesn't open until the guards arrive.

TRAVELLERS' TIPS & COMMENTS
Chinju is another of Korea's cities that sticks in the memory for both the historic beauty spots and the friendly nature of the people. It is well worth staying three or four days and wandering around the main shopping drag at night again is a must. Not only are some of the finest street vendors selling delicious nibbles, but the area has a permanent party atmosphere.

Be prepared to speak to every school kid you meet, they are all interested in where you come from and many will actually offer to act as guides. It can become overbearing when hundreds of people are all talking constantly at you and wearing a walkman is sometimes the only way you can have any peace.
Richard Watson

ACKNOWLEDGMENTS
The information in this Update was compiled from various sources, and from reports by the following travellers: Robert Langridge, Konrad M, Kampbell Salehi, Richard Watson and Cy Wert.

PLANET TALK

Lonely Planet's FREE quarterly newsletter

We love hearing from you and think you'd like to hear from us.

*When...*is the right time to see reindeer in Finland?
*Where...*can you hear the best palm-wine music in Ghana?
*How...*do you get from Asunción to Areguá by steam train?
*What...*is the best way to see India?

For the answer to these and many other questions read PLANET TALK.

Every issue is packed with up-to-date travel news and advice including:

- a letter from Lonely Planet co-founders Tony and Maureen Wheeler
- go behind the scenes on the road with a Lonely Planet author
- feature article on an important and topical travel issue
- a selection of recent letters from travellers
- details on forthcoming Lonely Planet promotions
- complete list of Lonely Planet products

To join our mailing list contact any Lonely Planet office.

Also available: Lonely Planet T-shirts. 100% heavyweight cotton.

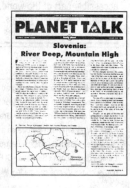

LONELY PLANET ONLINE

Get the latest travel information before you leave or while you're on the road

Whether you've just begun planning your next trip, or you're chasing down specific info on currency regulations or visa requirements, check out the Lonely Planet World Wide Web site for up-to-the-minute travel information.

As well as travel profiles of your favourite destinations (including interactive maps and full-colour photos), you'll find current reports from our army of researchers and other travellers, updates on health and visas, travel advisories, and the ecological and political issues you need to be aware of as you travel.

There's an online travellers' forum (the Thorn Tree) where you can share your experiences of life on the road, meet travel companions and ask other travellers for their recommendations and advice. We also have plenty of links to other Web sites useful to independent travellers.

With tens of thousands of visitors a month, the Lonely Planet Web site is one of the most popular on the Internet and has won a number of awards including GNN's Best of the Net travel award.

http://www.lonelyplanet.com

LONELY PLANET PRODUCTS

Lonely Planet is known worldwide for publishing practical, reliable and no-nonsense travel information in our guides and on our web site. The Lonely Planet list covers just about every accessible part of the world. Currently there are eight series: *travel guides, shoestring guides, walking guides, city guides, phrasebooks, audio packs, travel atlases* and *Journeys* – a unique collection of travellers' tales.

EUROPE

Austria • Baltic States & Kaliningrad • Baltic States phrasebook • Britain • Central Europe on a shoestring • Central Europe phrasebook • Czech & Slovak Republics • Denmark • Dublin city guide • Eastern Europe on a shoestring • Eastern Europe phrasebook • Finland • France • Greece • Greek phrasebook • Hungary • Iceland, Greenland & the Faroe Islands • Ireland • Italy • Mediterranean Europe on a shoestring • Mediterranean Europe phrasebook • Paris city guide • Poland • Prague city guide • Russia, Ukraine & Belarus • Russian phrasebook • Scandinavian & Baltic Europe on a shoestring • Scandinavian Europe phrasebook • Slovenia • St Petersburg city guide • Switzerland • Trekking in Greece • Trekking in Spain • Ukranian phrasebook • Vienna city guide • Walking in Switzerland • Western Europe on a shoestring • Western Europe phrasebook

NORTH AMERICA

Alaska • Backpacking in Alaska • Baja California• California & Nevada • Canada • Hawaii • Honolulu city guide • Los Angeles city guide • Mexico • New England • Pacific Northwest USA • Rocky Mountain States • San Francisco city guide • Southwest USA • USA phrasebook

CENTRAL AMERICA & THE CARIBBEAN

Central America on a shoestring • Costa Rica • Eastern Caribbean • Guatemala, Belize & Yucatán: La Ruta Maya • Jamaica

SOUTH AMERICA

Argentina, Uruguay & Paraguay • Bolivia • Brazil • Brazilian phrasebook • Buenos Aires city guide • Chile & Easter Island • Colombia • Ecuador & the Galápagos Islands • Latin American Spanish phrasebook • Peru • Quechua phrasebook • Rio de Janeiro city guide • South America on a shoestring • Trekking in the Patagonian Andes • Venezuela

AFRICA

Arabic (Moroccan) phrasebook • Africa on a shoestring • Cape Town city guide • Central Africa • East Africa • Egypt & the Sudan • Ethiopian (Amharic) phrasebook • Kenya • Morocco • North Africa • South Africa, Lesotho & Swaziland • Swahili phrasebook • Trekking in East Africa • West Africa • Zimbabwe, Botswana & Namibia • Zimbabwe, Botswana & Namibia travel atlas

ALSO AVAILABLE:

Travel with Children • Traveller's Tales

MAIL ORDER

Lonely Planet products are distributed worldwide. They are also available by mail order from Lonely Planet, so if you have difficulty finding a title please write to us. North American and South American residents should write to Embarcadero West, 155 Filbert St, Suite 251, Oakland CA 94607, USA; European and African residents should write to 10 Barley Mow Passage, Chiswick, London W4 4PH; and residents of other countries to PO Box 617, Hawthorn, Victoria 3122, Australia.

NORTH-EAST ASIA

Beijing city guide • Cantonese phrasebook • China • Hong Kong, Macau & Canton • Hong Kong city guide • Japan • Japanese phrasebook • Japanese audio pack • Korea • Korean phrasebook • Mandarin phrasebook • Mongolia • Mongolian phrasebook • North-East Asia on a shoestring • Seoul city guide • Taiwan • Tibet • Tibet phrasebook • Tokyo city guide

INDIAN SUBCONTINENT

Bengali phrasebook • Bangladesh • Delhi city guide • Hindi/Urdu phrasebook • India • India & Bangladesh travel atlas• Indian Himalaya• Karakoram Highway • Nepal • Nepali phrasebook • Pakistan • Sri Lanka • Sri Lanka phrasebook • Trekking in the Indian Himalaya • Trekking in the Nepal Himalaya

SOUTH-EAST ASIA

Bali & Lombok • Bangkok city guide • Burmese phrasebook • Cambodia • Ho Chi Minh city guide • Indonesia • Indonesian phrasebook • Indonesian audio pack • Jakarta city guide • Java • Laos • Lao phrasebook • Malaysia, Singapore & Brunei • Myanmar (Burma) • Philippines • Pilipino phrasebook • Singapore city guide • South-East Asia on a shoestring • Thailand • Thailand travel atlas • Thai phrasebook • Thai audio pack • Thai Hill Tribes phrasebook • Vietnam • Vietnamese phrasebook • Vietnam travel atlas

MIDDLE EAST & CENTRAL ASIA

Arab Gulf States • Arabic (Egyptian) phrasebook • Central Asia • Iran • Israel • Jordan & Syria • Middle East • Turkey • Turkish phrasebook • Trekking in Turkey • Yemen

Travel Literature: The Gates of Damascus

ISLANDS OF THE INDIAN OCEAN

Madagascar & Comoros • Maldives & Islands of the East Indian Ocean • Mauritius, Réunion & Seychelles

AUSTRALIA & THE PACIFIC

Australia • Australian phrasebook • Bushwalking in Australia • Bushwalking in Papua New Guinea • Fiji • Fijian phrasebook • Islands of Australia's Great Barrier Reef • Melbourne city guide • Micronesia • New Caledonia • New South Wales & the ACT • New Zealand • Northern Territory • Outback Australia • Papua New Guinea • Papua New Guinea phrasebook • Queensland • Rarotonga & the Cook Islands • Samoa • Solomon Islands • South Australia • Sydney city guide • Tahiti & French Polynesia • Tasmania • Tonga • Tramping in New Zealand • Vanuatu • Victoria • Western Australia

Travel Literature: Islands in the Clouds • Sean & David's Long Drive

THE LONELY PLANET STORY

Lonely Planet published its first book in 1973 in response to the numerous 'How did you do it?' questions Maureen and Tony Wheeler were asked after driving, bussing, hitching, sailing and railing their way from England to Australia.

Written at a kitchen table and hand collated, trimmed and stapled, *Across Asia on the Cheap* became an instant local bestseller, inspiring thoughts of another book.

Eighteen months in South-East Asia resulted in their second guide, *South-East Asia on a shoestring*, which they put together in a backstreet Chinese hotel in Singapore in 1975. The 'yellow bible', as it quickly became known to backpackers around the world, soon became *the* guide to the region. It has sold well over half a million copies and is now in its 8th edition, still retaining its familiar yellow cover.

Today there are over 180 titles, including travel guides, walking guides, language kits & phrasebooks, travel atlases and travel literature. The company is one of the largest travel publishers in the world. Although Lonely Planet initially specialised in guides to Asia, we now cover most regions of the world, including the Pacific, North America, South America, Africa, the Middle East and Europe.

The emphasis continues to be on travel for independent travellers. Tony and Maureen still travel for several months of each year and play an active part in the writing, updating and quality control of Lonely Planet's guides.

They have been joined by over 70 authors and 170 staff at our offices in Melbourne (Australia), Oakland (USA), London (UK) and Paris (France). Travellers themselves also make a valuable contribution to the guides through the feedback we receive in thousands of letters each year.

The people at Lonely Planet strongly believe that travellers can make a positive contribution to the countries they visit, both through their appreciation of the countries' culture, wildlife and natural features, and through the money they spend. In addition, the company makes a direct contribution to the countries and regions it covers. Since 1986 a percentage of the income from each book has been donated to ventures such as famine relief in Africa; aid projects in India; agricultural projects in Central America; Greenpeace's efforts to halt French nuclear testing in the Pacific; and Amnesty International.

'I hope we send the people out with the right attitude about travel. You realise when you travel that there are so many different perspectives about the world, so we hope these books will make people more interested in what they see. These are guidebooks, but you can't really guide people. All you can do is point them in the right direction.'
– Tony Wheeler

LONELY PLANET PUBLICATIONS

Australia
PO Box 617, Hawthorn 3122, Victoria
tel: (03) 9819 1877 fax: (03) 9819 6459
e-mail: talk2us@lonelyplanet.com.au

USA
Embarcadero West, 155 Filbert St, Suite 251,
Oakland, CA 94607
tel: (510) 893 8555 TOLL FREE: 800 275-8555
fax: (510) 893 8563
e-mail: info@lonelyplanet.com

UK
10 Barley Mow Passage, Chiswick,
London W4 4PH
tel: (0181) 742 3161 fax: (0181) 742 2772
e-mail: 100413.3551@compuserve.com

France:
71 bis rue du Cardinal Lemoine, 75005 Paris
tel: 1 44 32 06 20 fax: 1 46 34 72 55
e-mail: 100560.415@compuserve.com

World Wide Web: http://www.lonelyplanet.com